James Osmond / Alamy

PHILIP'S ROAD ATLAS

2017 COMPLETE BRITAIN & IRELAND

www.philips-maps.co.uk

First published in 2009 by Philip's
a division of Octopus Publishing Group Ltd
www.octopusbooks.co.uk
Carmelite House, 50 Victoria Embankment
London EC4Y 0DZ
An Hachette UK Company
www.hachette.co.uk

Eighth edition 2016
First impression 2016

ISBN 978-1-84907-412-4 (spiral)
ISBN 978-1-84907-413-1 (hardback)

Cartography by Philip's
Copyright © 2016 Philip's

Map data

This product includes mapping data licensed from Ordnance Survey®, with the permission of the Controller of Her Majesty's Stationery Office. © Crown copyright 2016. All rights reserved. Licence number 100011710.

ORDNANCE SURVEY® OF NORTHERN IRELAND

The map of Ireland on pages XVIII–XIX is based upon the Crown Copyright and is reproduced with the permission of Land & Property Services under delegated authority from the Controller of Her Majesty's Stationery Office, © Crown Copyright and database right 2016, PMLPA number 100503, and on Ordnance Survey Ireland by permission of the Government © Ordnance Survey Ireland / Government of Ireland Permit number 9040.

No part of this publication may be reproduced, stored in a retrieval system or transmitted in any form or by any means, electronic, mechanical, photocopying, recording or otherwise, without the permission of the Publishers and the copyright owner.

While every reasonable effort has been made to ensure that the information compiled in this atlas is accurate, complete and up-to-date at the time of publication, some of this information is subject to change and the Publisher cannot guarantee its correctness or completeness.

The information in this atlas is provided without any representation or warranty, express or implied and the Publisher cannot be held liable for any loss or damage due to any use or reliance on the information in this atlas, nor for any errors, omissions or subsequent changes in such information.

The representation in this atlas of any road, drive or track is no evidence of the existence of a right of way.

Information for National Parks, Areas of Outstanding Natural Beauty, National Trails and Country Parks in Wales supplied by the Countryside Council for Wales.

Information for National Parks, Areas of Outstanding Natural Beauty, National Trails and Country Parks in England supplied by Natural England. Data for Regional Parks, Long Distance Footpaths and Country Parks in Scotland provided by Scottish Natural Heritage.

Gaelic name forms used in the Western Isles provided by Comhairle nan Eilean.

Data for the National Nature Reserves in England provided by Natural England. Data for the National Nature Reserves in Wales provided by Countryside Council for Wales. Darparwyd data'n ymwneud â Gwarchodfeydd Natur Cenedlaethol Cymru gan Gyngor Cefn Gwlad Cymru.

Information on the location of National Nature Reserves in Scotland was provided by Scottish Natural Heritage.

Data for National Scenic Areas in Scotland provided by the Scottish Executive Office. Crown copyright material is reproduced with the permission of the Controller of HMSO and the Queen's Printer for Scotland. Licence number C02W0003960.

Printed in China

*Data from Nielsen Total Consumer Market 2015, Weeks 1–48

Inside back cover: **County and unitary authority boundaries**

Road map symbols

M6	Motorway, toll motorway
4 · 5	Motorway junction – full, restricted access
S · S	Motorway service area – full, restricted access
	Motorway under construction
A453	Primary route – dual, single carriageway
S · S	Service area, roundabout, multi-level junction
4 · 5	Numbered junction – full, restricted access
	Primary route under construction
	Narrow primary route
Derby	Primary destination
A34	A road – dual, single carriageway
	A road under construction, narrow A road
B2135	B road – dual, single carriageway
	B road under construction, narrow B road
	Minor road – over 4 metres, under 4 metres wide
	Minor road with restricted access
2	Distance in miles
	Scenic route
TOLL	Toll, steep gradient – arrow points downhill
	Tunnel
	National trail – England and Wales
	Long distance footpath – Scotland
	Railway with station
	Level crossing, tunnel
	Preserved railway with station
	National boundary
	County / unitary authority boundary
	Car ferry, catamaran
	Passenger ferry, catamaran
	Hovercraft
CALAIS *Ferry*	Ferry destination
	Car ferry – river crossing
	Principal airport, other airport
	National park
	Area of Outstanding Natural Beauty – England and Wales **National Scenic Area** – Scotland **forest park / regional park / national forest**
	Woodland
	Beach
	Linear antiquity
	Roman road
·⊡· · ⚔ 1066	Hillfort, battlefield – with date
☀ · 🍁 · ▲795	Viewpoint, nature reserve, spot height – in metres
⚑ · ▲ · ◎	Golf course, youth hostel, sporting venue
⋏ · 🚐 · ⋏🚐	Camp site, caravan site, camping and caravan site
🛒 · **P&R**	Shopping village, park and ride
29	Adjoining page number – road maps

Approach map symbols

M6	Motorway
	Toll motorway
6 · 5	Motorway junction – full, restricted access
S	Service area
	Under construction
A6	Primary route – dual, single carriageway
S	Service area
○	Multi-level junction
⊙	roundabout
	Under construction
A195	A road – dual, single carriageway
B1288	B road – dual, single carriageway
	Minor road – dual, single carriageway
	Ring road
3	Distance in miles
	Congestion charge area
COSELEY ●	Railway with station
LOXDALE ⊙	Tramway with station
M ⊖ ⊖	Underground or metro station

Town plan symbols

	Motorway
	Primary route – dual, single carriageway
	A road – dual, single carriageway
	B road – dual, single carriageway
	Minor through road
→	One-way street
	Pedestrian roads
	Shopping streets
	Railway with station
City Hall	Tramway with station
🏛	Bus or railway station building
	Shopping precinct or retail park
	Park
🏛	Building of public interest
🎭 🎥	Theatre, cinema
P ♿	Parking, shopmobility
Bank ⊖	Underground station
West St ●	Metro station
H ≋	Hospital, Police station
PO	Post office

Tourist information

✝ Abbey, cathedral or priory	🐎 Farm park	🏛 Roman antiquity
🏛 Ancient monument	✿ Garden	⋎ Safari park
🐬 Aquarium	⚓ Historic ship	🎋 Theme park
🖼 Art gallery	🏛 House	Tourist information centre
🐦 Bird collection or aviary	🏛 House and garden	i open all year i open seasonally
🏰 Castle	▦ Motor racing circuit	
🏛 Church	🏛 Museum	🐘 Zoo
Country park 🎪 England and Wales Scotland	⊙ Picnic area	✦ Other place of interest
	🚂 Preserved railway	
	🏇 Race course	

Relief

Feet	metres
3000	914
2600	792
2200	671
1800	549
1400	427
1000	305
0	0

Road map scales

3·15 miles to 1 inch • 1 : 200 000

0 1 2 3 4 5 6 miles
0 1 2 3 4 5 6 7 8 9 10 km

Parts of Scotland

4.18 miles to 1 inch • 1 : 265 000

0 1 2 3 4 5 6 miles
0 2 4 6 8 10 km

Scottish Highlands and Islands

5.24 miles to 1 inch • 1 : 332 000

0 1 2 3 4 5 6 7 8 miles
0 2 4 6 8 10 12 km

Orkney and Shetland Islands 1 : 400 000, 6.31 miles to 1 inch

Motorway service areas

Restricted motorway junctions

M1 Junction 34

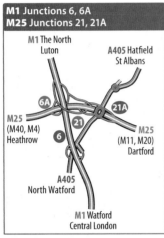

M1 Junctions 6, 6A
M25 Junctions 21, 21A

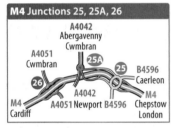

M4 Junctions 25, 25A, 26

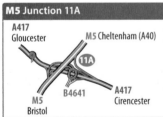

M5 Junction 11A

M8 Junctions 8, 9 · M73 Junctions 1, 2
M74 Junctions 2A, 3, 3A, 4

M1	Northbound	Southbound
2	No exit	No access
4	No exit	No access
6A	No exit. Access from M25 only	No access. Exit to M25 only
7	No exit. Access from A414 only	No access. Exit to A414 only
17	No access. Exit to M45 only	No exit. Access from M45 only
19	No exit to A14	No access from A14
21A	No access	No exit
23A		Exit to A42 only
24A	No exit	No access
35A	No access	No exit
43	No access. Exit to M621 only	No exit. Access from M621 only
48	No exit to A1(M) southbound	

M3	Eastbound	Westbound
8	No exit	No access
10	No access	No exit
13	No access to M27 eastbound	
14	No exit	No access

M4	Eastbound	Westbound
1	Exit to A4 eastbound only	Access from A4 westbound only
2	Access from A4 eastbound only	Access to A4 westbound only
21	No exit	No access
23	No access	No exit
25	No exit	No access
25A	No exit	No access
29	No exit	No access
38		No access
39	No exit or access	No exit
41	No access	No exit
41A	No exit	No access
42	Access from A483 only	Exit to A483 only

M5	Northbound	Southbound
10	No exit	No access
11A	No access from A417 eastbound	No exit to A417 westbound

M6	Northbound	Southbound
3A	No access. Exit to M42 northbound only	No exit. Access from M6 eastbound only
4A	No exit. Access from M42 southbound only	No access. Exit to M42 only
5	No access	No exit
10A	No access. Exit to M54 only	No exit. Access from M54 only
11A	No exit. Access from M6 Toll only	No access. Exit to M6 Toll only
20	No exit to M56 eastbound	No access from M56 westbound
24	No exit	No access
25	No access	No exit
30	No exit. Access from M61 northbound only	No access. Exit to M61 southbound only
31A	No access	No exit
45	No access	No exit

M6 Toll	Northbound	Southbound
T1		No exit
T2	No exit, no access	No access
T5	No exit	No access
T7	No access	No exit
T8	No access	No exit

M8	Eastbound	Westbound
8	No exit to M73 northbound	No access from M73 southbound
9	No access	No exit
13	No exit southbound	Access from M73 southbound only
14	No access	No exit
16	No exit	No access
17	No exit	No access
18		No exit
19	No exit to A814 eastbound	No access from A814 westbound
20	No exit	No access
21	No access from M74	No exit
22	No exit. Access from M77 only	No access. Exit to M77 only
23	No exit	No access
25	Exit to A739 northbound only. Access from A739 southbound only	Access from A739 southbound only
25A	No exit	No access
28	No exit	No access
28A	No exit	No access

M9	Eastbound	Westbound
1A	No exit	No access
2	No access	No exit
3	No exit	No access
6	No access	No exit
8	No exit	No access

M11	Northbound	Southbound
4	No exit. Access from A406 only	No access. Exit to A406 only
5	No access	No exit
9	No access	No exit
13	No access	No exit
14	No exit to A428 westbound	No exit. Access from A14 westbound only

M20	Eastbound	Westbound
2	No access	No exit
3	No exit Access from M26 eastbound only	No access Exit to M26 westbound only
11A	No access	No exit

M23	Northbound	Southbound
7	No exit to A23 southbound	No access from A23 northbound
10A	No access	No access

M25	Clockwise	Anticlockwise
5	No exit to M26 eastbound	No access from M26 westbound
19	No access	No exit
21	No exit to M1 southbound. Access from M1 southbound only	No exit to M1 southbound. Access from M1. southbound only
31	No exit	No access

M27	Eastbound	Westbound
10	No exit	No access
12	No access	No exit

M40	Eastbound	Westbound
3	No exit	No access
7	No exit	No access
8	No exit	No access
13	No exit	No access
14	No access	No exit
16	No access	No exit

M42	Northbound	Southbound
1	No exit	No access
7	No access Exit to M6 northbound only	No exit Access from M6 northbound only
7A	No access. Exit to M6 southbound only	No exit
8	No exit. Access from M6 southbound only	Exit to M6 northbound only. Access from M6 southbound only

M45		Eastbound	Westbound
M1 J17		Access to M1 southbound only	No access from M1 southbound
With A45		No access	No exit

M48	Eastbound	Westbound
M4 J21	No exit to M4 westbound	No access from M4 eastbound
M4 J23	No access from M4 westbound	No exit to M4 eastbound

M49	Southbound	Northbound
18A	No exit to M5 northbound	No access from M5 southbound

M53	Northbound	Southbound
11	Exit to M56 eastbound only. Access from M56 westbound only	Exit to M56 eastbnd only. Access from M56 westbound only

M56	Eastbound	Westbound
2	No exit	No access
3	No access	No exit
4	No exit	No access
7		No access
8	No exit or access	No exit
9	No access from M6 northbound	No access to M6 southbound
15	No exit to M53	No access from M53 northbound

M57	Northbound	Southbound
3	No exit	No access
5	No exit	No access

M58	Eastbound	Westbound
1	No exit	No access

M60	Clockwise	Anticlockwise
2	No exit	No access
3	No exit to A34 northbound	No exit to A34 northbound
4	No access from M56	No exit to M56
5	No exit to A5103 southbound	No exit to A5103 northbound
14	No exit	No access
16	No exit	No access
20	No access	No exit
22		No access
25	No access	
26		No exit or access
27	No exit	No access

M61	Northbound	Southbound
2	No access from A580 eastbound	No exit to A580 westbound
3	No access from A580 eastbound. No access from A666 southbound	No exit to A580 westbound
M6 J30	No exit to M6 southbound	No access from M6 northbound

M62	Eastbound	Westbound
23	No access	No exit

M65	Eastbound	Westbound
9	No access	No exit
11	No exit	No access

M66	Northbound	Southbound
1	No access	No exit

M67	Eastbound	Westbound
1A	No access	No exit
2	No exit	No access

M69	Northbound	Southbound
2	No exit	No access

M73	Northbound	Southbound
2	No access from M8 or A89 eastbound. No exit to A89	No exit to M8 or A89 westbound. No access from A89

M74	Northbound	Southbound
3	No access	No exit
3A	No exit	No access
7	No exit	No access
9	No exit or access	No access
10		No exit
11	No exit	No access
12	No access	No exit

M77	Northbound	Southbound
4	No exit	No access
6	No exit	No access
7	No exit or access	
8	No access	No access

M80	Northbound	Southbound
4A	No access	No exit
6A	No exit	
8	Exit to M876 northbound only. No access	Access from M876 southbound only. No exit

M90	Northbound	Southbound
2A	No access	No exit
7	No exit	No access
8	No access	No exit
10	No access from A912	No exit to A912

M180	Eastbound	Westbound
1	No access	No exit

M621	Eastbound	Westbound
2A	No exit	No access
4	No exit	
5	No exit	No access
6	No access	No exit

M876	Northbound	Southbound
2	No access	No exit

A1(M)	Northbound	Southbound
2	No access	No exit
3		No access
5	No access	No access
14	No exit	No access
40	No access	No access
43	No exit. Access from M1 only	No access. Exit to M1 only
57	No access	No exit
65	No access	No exit

A3(M)	Northbound	Southbound
1	No exit	No access
4	No access	No access

A38(M)	Northbound	Southbound
With Victoria Rd, (Park Circus) Birmingham	No exit	No access

A48(M)	Northbound	Southbound
M4 Junc 29	Exit to M4 eastbound only	Access from M4 westbound only
29A	Access from A48 eastbound only	Exit to A48 westbound only

A57(M)	Eastbound	Westbound
With A5103	No access	No access
With A34	No access	No access

A58(M)		Southbound
With Park Lane and Westgate, Leeds		No access

A64(M)	Eastbound	Westbound
With A58 Clay Pit Lane, Leeds	No access	No exit
With Regent Street, Leeds	No access	No access

A74(M)	Northbound	Southbound
18	No access	No exit
22		No exit

A194(M)	Northbound	Southbound
A1(M) J65 Gateshead Western Bypass	Access from A1(M) northbound only	Exit to A1(M) southbound only

M3 Junctions 13, 14 · M27 Junction 4

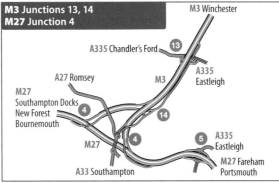

M6 Junctions 3A, 4A · M42 Junctions 7, 7A, 8, 9 · M6 Toll Junctions T1, T2

M6 Junction 20 · M56 Junction 4

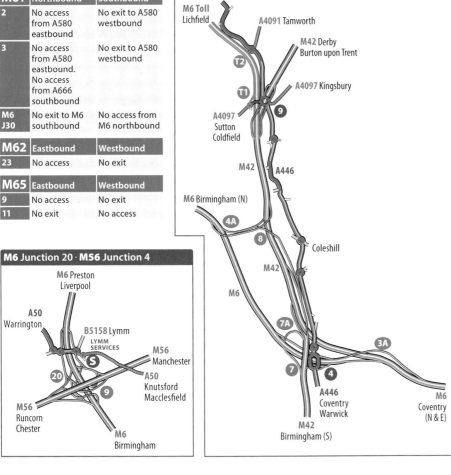

M62 Junctions 32A, 33 · A1(M) Junctions 40, 41

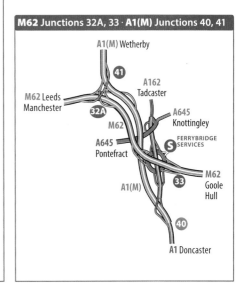

Mobile Layby Cafés – gourmet or gruesome?

Do you drive on by?

Stephen Mesquita,
Philip's On the Road Correspondent

▲ A roadside snack van sign in Herefordshire *Jeff Morgan / Alamy*

Have you ever done this? You're driving along on one of Britain's A-Roads. It's sometime between 6am and 2pm. You're feeling a bit peckish. You see a layby coming up. There's a notice by the road. Something about hot food. There's a van flying a Union Jack. There are a couple of truck drivers there, queueing up. You might even catch a tempting whiff of something frying.

And you drive straight past. Not really for you? You've never eaten in a layby so you'll wait for a place you know and recognise. Or buy a sandwich at the next petrol station.

Well, that's what I've always done. Up until yesterday. That's when I set out, with my trusty accomplice (and Philip's Sales Supremo) Stuart, to see if my lifelong prejudices were justified.

Butty Vans

A quick word about terminology first. We're going to drop the 'Mobile Layby Cafés' and go with 'Butty Vans'. Stuart and I were out to beat The Breakfast Buns from Butty Vans in One Morning Record.

And so it was with some trepidation that we set off from Northampton and headed for our first Butty Van. Here's confession number one: as soon as we'd photographed the bacon roll that we'd ordered, we polished it off.

This was a good start – and in stark contrast to our Motorway Service Area research, where the fare was so unappetising that we tried only a tiny portion of each item and left the rest.

And as the day started, so it went on. Of the eight buns, only one really disappointed. The other seven were tasty, hot, great value and came with friendly chat. Stuart and I polished almost all of them off – and two especially good ones were down the gullets of Philip's intrepid breakfast critics before you could say 'another bacon roll please'.

▲ The first bacon butty of the day in a layby alongside the A43

Eight in a Day

Would I recommend eight in a day? As a gastronomic experience, no. It's too much salt intake (my car was littered with empty bottles of water by the end of the day). And I did long for a freshly made flat white by the end of the day.

But a Butty Van breakfast or snack every now and again? Absolutely. Now I've done it once, I'll be very happy to do it again. In fact, I'm rather ashamed I hadn't managed to overcome my prejudices before now.

So to answer my question. Gourmet: no. Gruesome: certainly not. A tasty roadside snack, piping hot, cooked to order and served with a smile – definitely. I'll have one of those.

Butty Vans – what you need to know

● **Layby cafes are licensed by the local authority**, normally annually, to do business in a particular layby.

● **Food Hygiene is an important part of their credibility** – most of them display their certificates prominently.

● **You can't go there for dinner.** Most open early (often around 6am) and shut up around 2pm (sometimes 3pm).

● **They aren't just found in laybys on A Roads.** Some are on industrial estates and business parks.

● **The good ones are there come rain or shine** (bad weather can be good for business) most days of the year.

● **Most of them have a name:** we sampled the fare at Dom's Doorsteps, Taste Buds Snacks, Sizzlers, Delicias and Smell the Bacon.

▼ Roadside snack van, Perthshire *Mar Photographics / Alamy*

Butty Vans vs. Motorway Service Areas– how they compare

If you're expecting Butty Vans to serve up the fare you get at your local deli, you probably don't need to read on. The buns are not made of artisanal sourdough ciabatta. The butter isn't Danish unsalted. The bacon didn't cost £15 a kilo. The eggs probably aren't fresh from the farm that morning. Butty Vans aren't posh.

But the point is this – all the Butty Vans we ate at were owned by people who took great pride in what they did. We met one real foody proprietor who told us he'd been to a burger fair the weekend before and always offered specials ('Codfinger'; 'Blue Burger Special'). All of them were aware that, to compete against the big brands, they had to offer good food at good prices.

The ingredients were perfectly decent. The bacon was almost universally of a better quality than we tasted last year in our Full English Breakfast campaign in Motorway Service Areas. And it was all cooked to order in front of you, which gave it one spectacular advantage over the Motorway Service Areas. It was hot.

And it was a fraction of the price.

The only disappointment was the tea and coffee. But at £0.70–£0.80 a cup, you should know what you're getting and you get what you pay for – although at one Butty Van, the teabags were Yorkshire Tea.

You can compare further in our
Butty Van vs. Motorway Service Area checklist:

	Butty Vans	Motorway Services
Good Value for Money	✔	✗
Proud of what they do	✔	✗
Cooked to Order	✔	rarely
Meal Hot	✔	✗
Quality of ingredients	See above	See above
Quality of hot drinks	✗	✗
Friendly Service	✔	✗
Parking	✔	✔
Easy to find	✗	✔

● **It's a competitive business** – and their regulars (mostly truck drivers and white van men on A Roads) are discerning customers who expect tasty food at reasonable prices. We heard one van driver say he draws the line at paying £1 for a cup of tea.

● **We were made very welcome**, even though it was obvious we weren't their usual clientele.

Our thanks to all the proprietors who answered our questions about their businesses so openly.

Eight Meals in a Bun between 9am and 2pm – how was it for me?

Meal in a Bun One

Location	A43 West of Northampton
Meal	Bacon roll plus tea
Price	£2.50 plus £0.60

Verdict Generous helping of tasty bacon, cooked in front of us and piping hot. The tea was wet and warm.

Meal in a Bun Two

Location	A43 Brackley
Meal	Sausage and Bacon roll plus tea
Price	£3.20 plus £0.50

Verdict A breakfast on its own served with a smile and lots of chat. The ingredients were nothing special but all tasty.

Meal in a Bun Three

Location	A422 between Buckingham and Milton Keynes
Meal	Bacon and Egg roll plus coffee
Price	£3.00 plus £0.80

Verdict Another very decent breakfast in a bun, with the egg cooked to order. Yorkshire Tea teabags spurned for instant coffee. Should have had the tea.

Meal in a Bun Four

Location	Harding Road, Milton Keynes
Meal:	Sausage and Egg roll plus tea
Price:	£2.25 plus £0.50

Verdict Sausage and egg: not expensive ingredients but properly cooked, nice and hot and at a nugatory price.

Meal in a Bun Five

Location	Yardley Road Industrial Estate, Olney
Meal	Double egg roll
Price	£2.50

Verdict I was stupid. I had a double egg sandwich (which was tasty) but I was rightly berated by Mr Sizzler for not being more adventurous and having one of his speciality burgers or chicken dishes. The things I sacrifice to make these surveys fair.

Meal in a Bun Six

Location	A505 West of Royston
Meal	Bacon Roll
Price	£2.00

Verdict The best bread (slightly toasted) and loads of decent bacon for £2.00. I rest my case. I should have added: cooked by Italians. They know how to cook, the Italians. Even good old English Bacon butties. Buonissimo!

Meal in a Bun Seven

Location	A505 West of Royston
Meal	Bacon Roll
Price	£2.50

Verdict A bit disappointing. Bread tough, bacon tough. Our only below par experience of the day.

Meal in a Bun Eight

Location:	A505 East of Royston
Meal:	Sausage roll
Price:	£3.00

Verdict This café was called *Smell the Bacon* but the sausages were from *Musks* of Newmarket. They were delicious! They seemed to disappear remarkably quickly, Stuart.

How to find Butty Vans

Most Butty Vans are either an 'impulse buy' (you see them as you pass by) or have their regular customers who know where they are. But say you are planning a journey and you want to know for sure there's a Butty Van at a point on your route. Then you need the free app from Butty Van Finder (go to buttyvan.com). We don't even need to describe it: these screen grabs say it all.

Enter the Butty Van Competition

Send us your personal recommendations for *Breakfast On the Move* **(Butty Vans or anywhere else) by email, with pictures if possible, and tell us why you recommend them – or any amusing stories you have.**

Send them by 31st December 2017.

The 25 best entries in our opinion will each receive a free copy of the *Philip's Royal Geographical Society Essential World Atlas* (worth £25).

Email your entries to buttyvan@octopusbooks.co.uk

For terms and conditions, visit www.octopusbooks.co.uk/assets/OctopusPublishingGroup/Downloads/PhilipsNavigatorCompetitionTandCs.pdf

Matt Botwood / Alamy

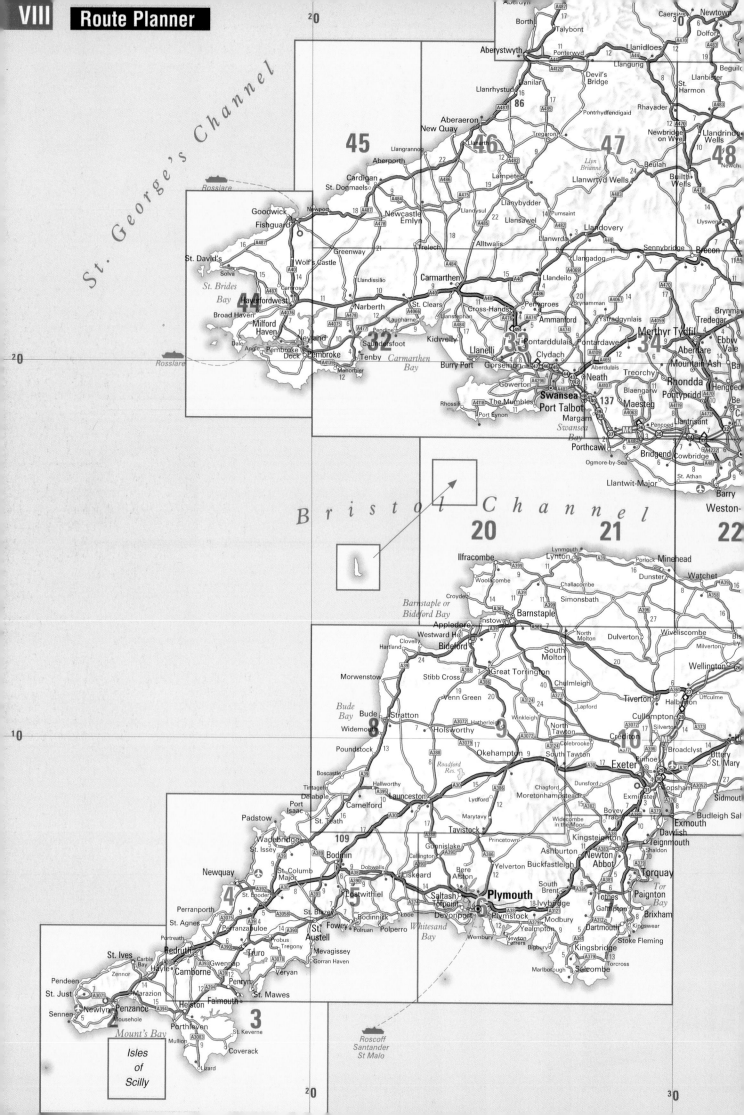

Scale

1:1000000   1cm = 10km   1 inch = 15.78 miles

Motorway	Primary route	**Distances** - in miles
M6	A519	120 major
junctions - full, restricted	single/dual carriageway	12 minor
Toll motorway	A519 A Road	Railway
Services	B Road	National boundary
	Ferry route	Airport

Dieppe

Scale bar: 0 5 10 15 20 25 30 35 40 45 50 miles

0 10 20 30 40 50 60 70 80 km

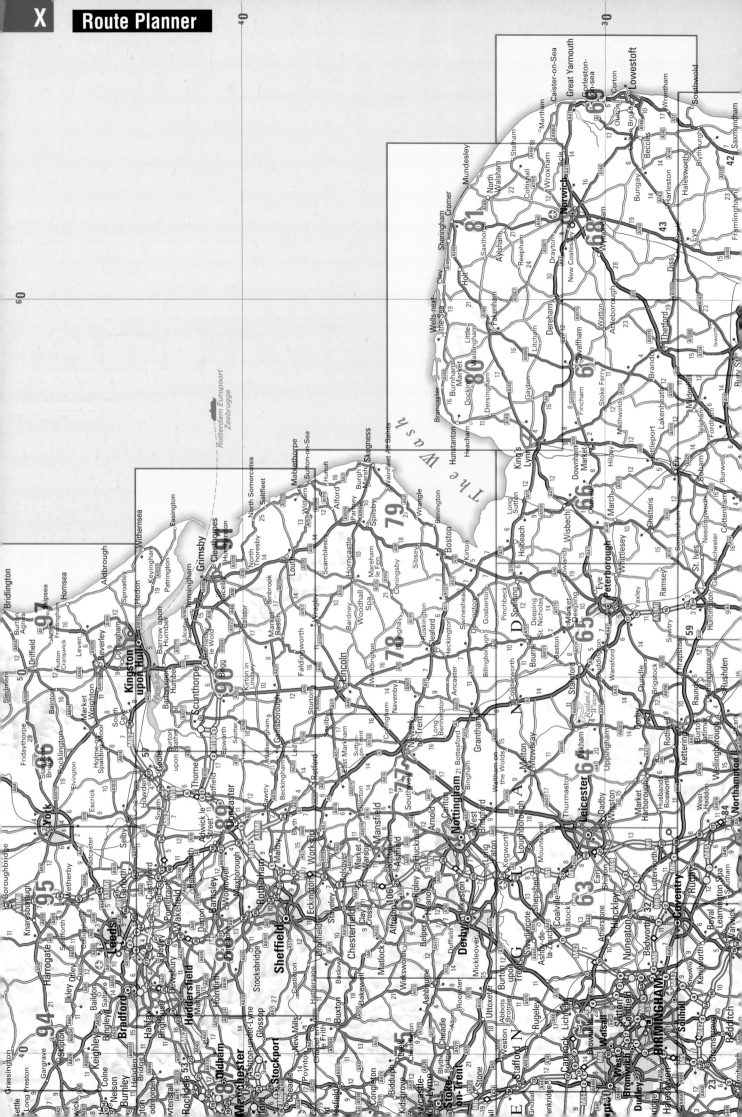

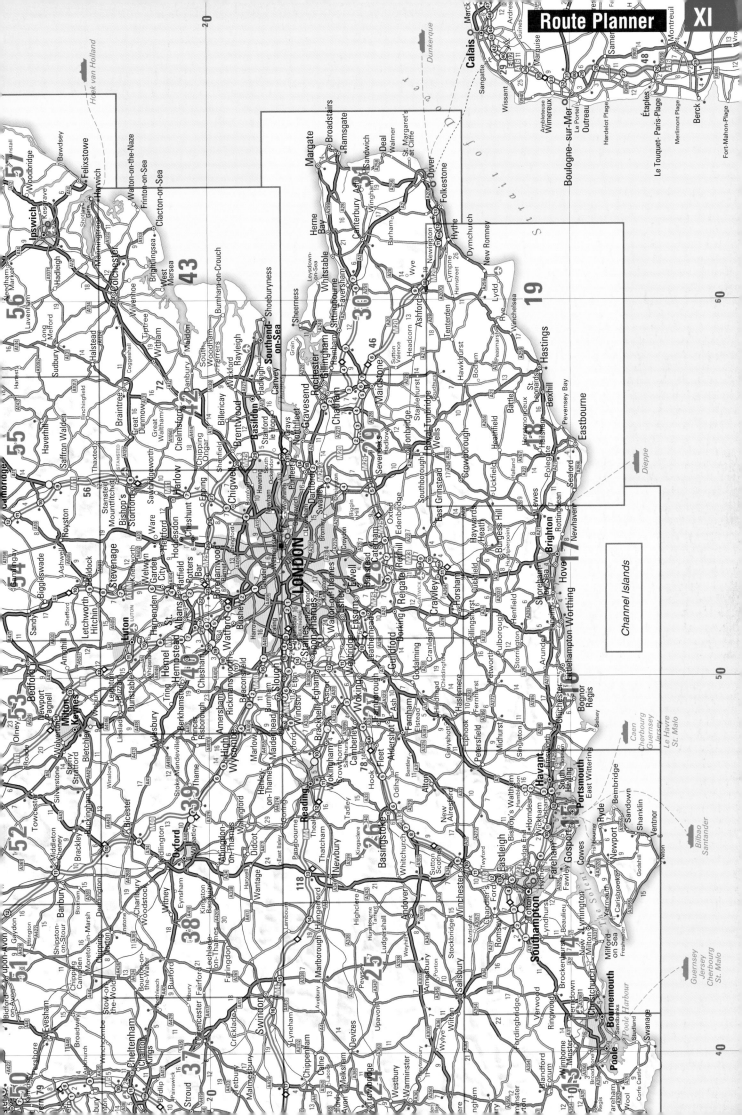

NORTH

SEA

Amsterdam

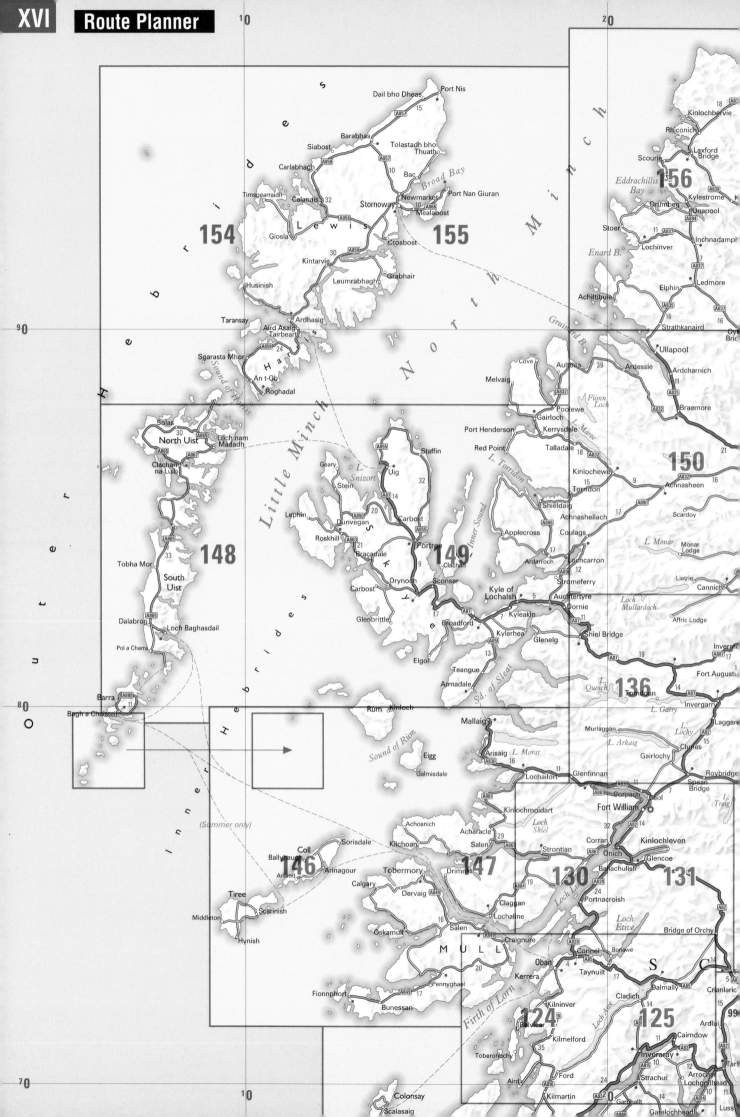

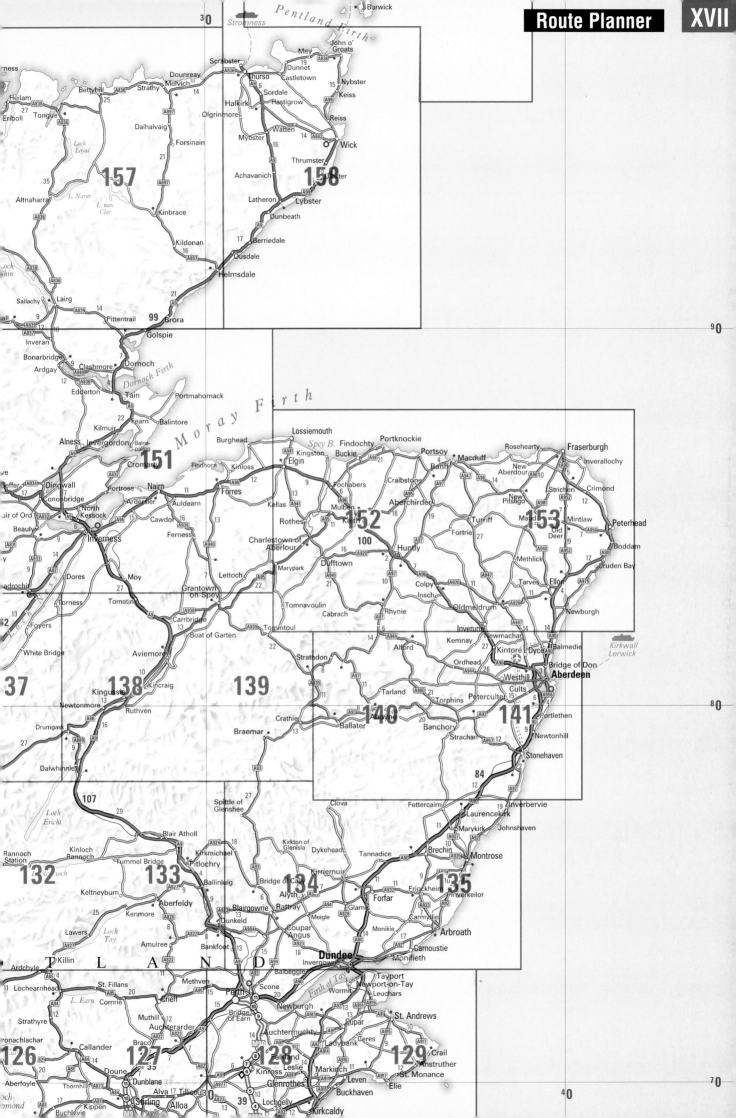

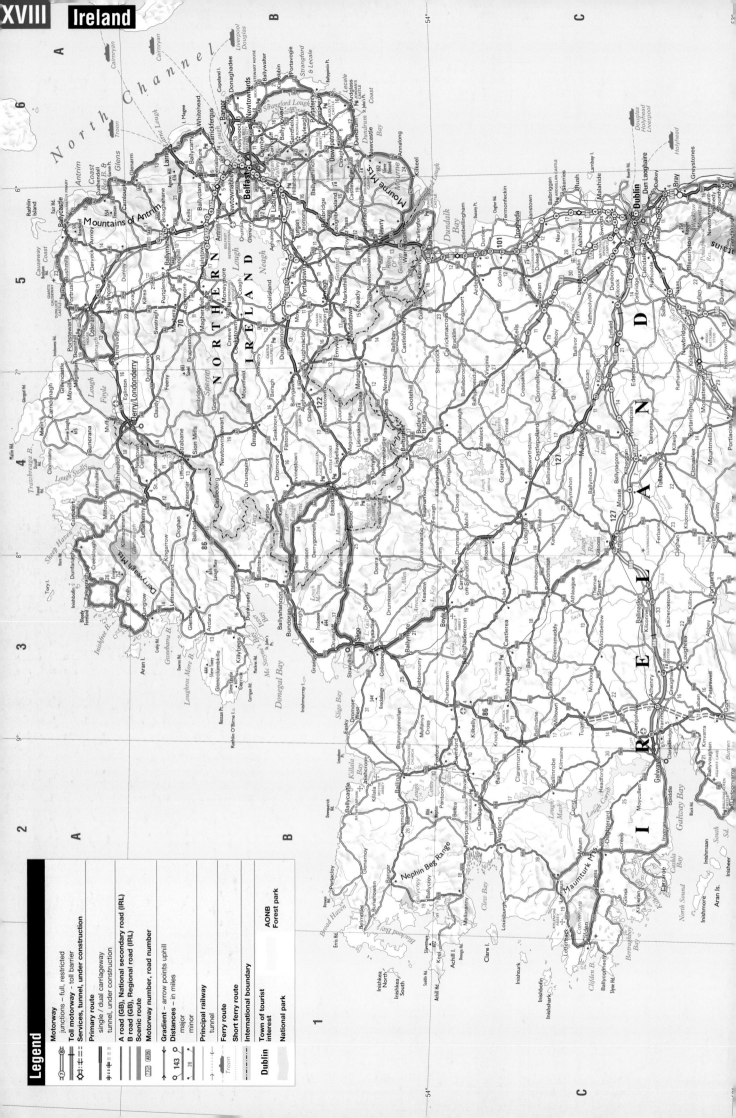

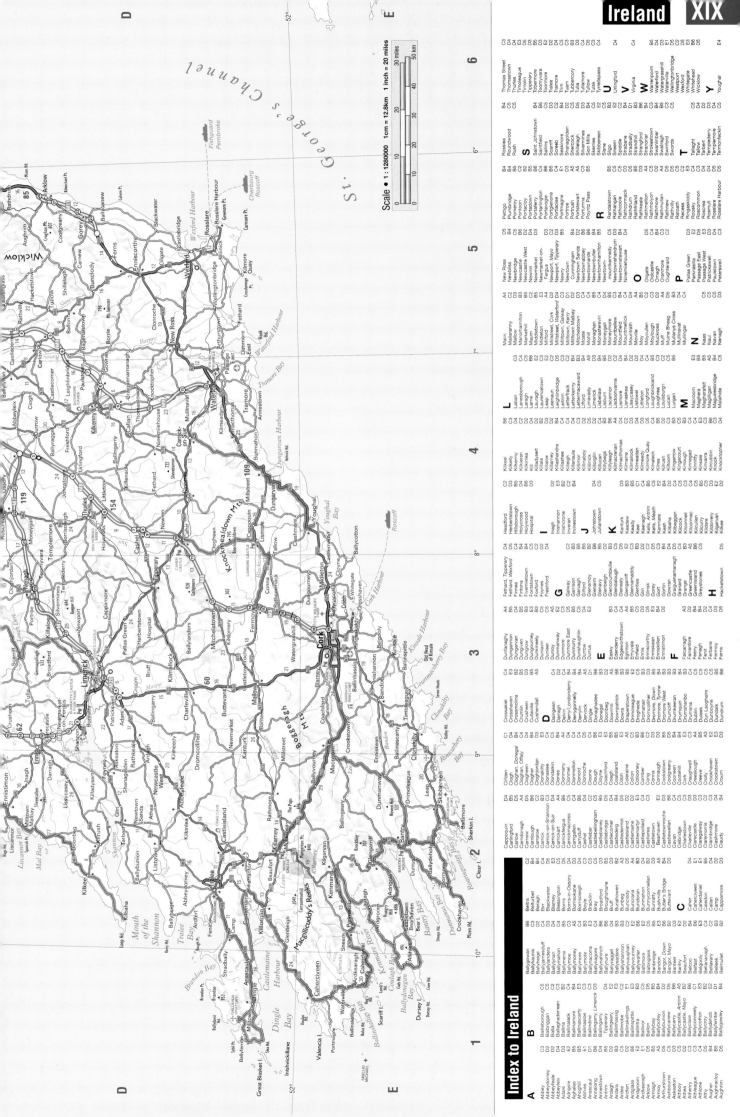

Ireland XIX

Scale 1 : 1 280 000 • 1cm = 12.8km 1 inch = 20 miles

St. George's Channel

Index to Ireland

Distance table

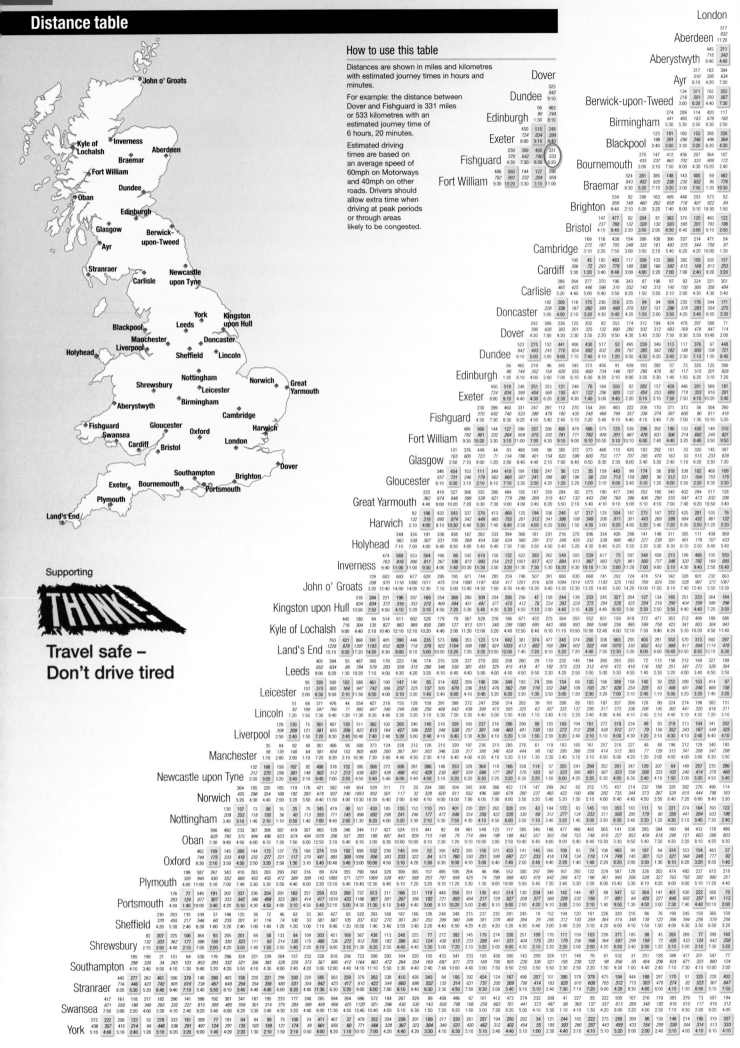

How to use this table

Distances are shown in miles and kilometres with estimated journey times in hours and minutes.

For example: the distance between Dover and Fishguard is 331 miles or 533 kilometres with an estimated journey time of 6 hours, 20 minutes.

Estimated driving times are based on an average speed of 60mph on Motorways and 40mph on other roads. Drivers should allow extra time when driving at peak periods or through areas likely to be congested.

Supporting

THINK!

Travel safe –
Don't drive tired

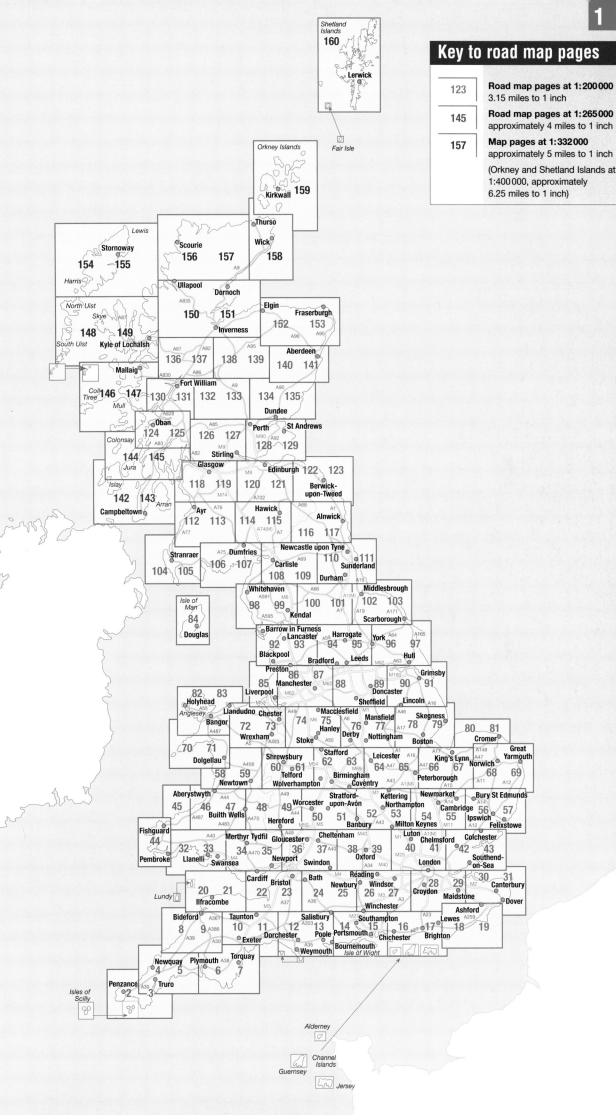

Key to road map pages

123	**Road map pages at 1:200 000** 3.15 miles to 1 inch
145	**Road map pages at 1:265 000** approximately 4 miles to 1 inch
157	**Map pages at 1:332 000** approximately 5 miles to 1 inch (Orkney and Shetland Islands at 1:400 000, approximately 6.25 miles to 1 inch)

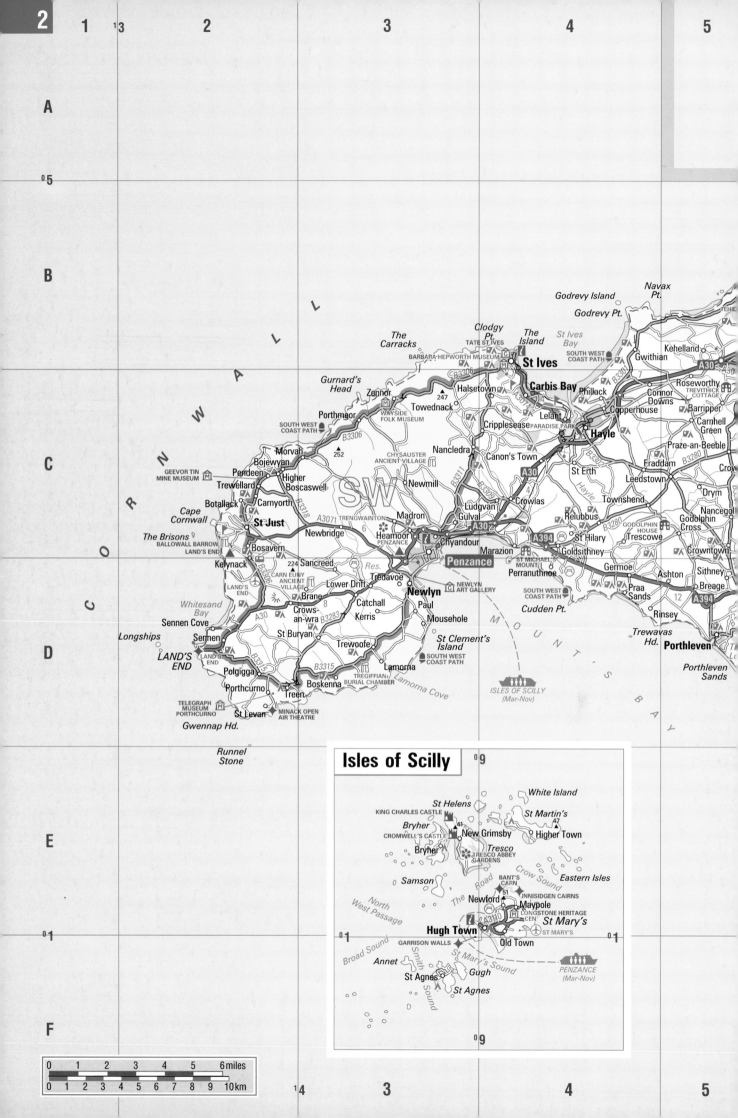

1   13   2   3   4   5

A

05

B

Godrevy Island
Navax Pt.
Godrevy Pt.
TEHIL

Clodgy Pt.
The Carracks
TATE ST IVES
The Island
St Ives Bay
St Ives
SOUTH WEST COAST PATH
Gwithian
A30
Kehelland
Roseworthy
TREVITHICK COTTAGE
Connor Downs
Barripper
Carnhell Green

Gurnard's Head
Zennor
BARBARA HEPWORTH MUSEUM
B3306
Carbis Bay
Phillack
Copperhouse
Praze-an-Beeble

Porthmeor
247
Towednack
Halestown
Lelant
PARADISE PARK
Hayle
Fraddam
B3280
Crow

WAYSIDE FOLK MUSEUM
Cripplesease
St Erth
Leedstown
Drym

Morvah
252
CHYSAUSTER ANCIENT VILLAGE
Nancledra
Canon's Town
St Erth
Townshend
Nancegol
Godolphin Cross

C

Bojewyan
Pendeen
SW
Newmill
B3311
A30
Crowlas
Relubbus
GODOLPHIN HOUSE
Trescowe
Crowntown

GEEVOR TIN MINE MUSEUM
Higher Boscaswell
Madron
Ludgvan
Gulval
St Hilary
Goldsithney
Germoe
Ashton
Sithney
Breage

Trewellard
Carnyorth
Botallack
TRENGWAINTON
Heamoor
PENZANCE
Chyandour
Marazion
A394
ST MICHAEL'S MOUNT
Perranuthnoe
Praa Sands
A394

Cape Cornwall
St Just
A3071
Penzance
SOUTH WEST COAST PATH
Cudden Pt.
Rinsey

The Brisons
BALLOWALL BARROW
LAND'S END
Bosavern
224
Sancreed
Tredavoe
NEWLYN ART GALLERY
Newlyn

Kelynack
CARN EUNY ANCIENT VILLAGE
Lower Drift
Catchall
Paul
Trewavas Hd.
Porthleven

LAND'S END
Brane
8
Kerris
Mousehole
MOUNT'S BAY
Porthleven Sands

Whitesand Bay
Crows-an-wra
B3283
St Clement's Island

Sennen Cove
A30
St Buryan
SOUTH WEST COAST PATH

Longships
Sennen
Trewoofe
ISLES OF SCILLY (Mar-Nov)

D

LAND'S END
LAND'S END
B3315
Lamorna

Polgigga
Boskenna
TREGIFFIAN BURIAL CHAMBER
Lamorna Cove

Porthcurno
Treen

TELEGRAPH MUSEUM PORTHCURNO
St Levan
MINACK OPEN AIR THEATRE

Gwennap Hd.

Runnel Stone

Isles of Scilly

09

St Helens
White Island

KING CHARLES CASTLE
St Martin's
47

Bryher
41
Higher Town

CROMWELL'S CASTLE
New Grimsby

Bryher
Tresco
TRESCO ABBEY GARDENS

E

Samson
Crow Sound
Eastern Isles

North West Passage
BANT'S CARN
INNISIDGEN CAIRNS

The Road
51
Maypole
LONGSTONE HERITAGE CEN.

Newford
St Mary's

Hugh Town
A3110
ST MARY'S
Old Town

01
01
01

GARRISON WALLS

Broad Sound
St Mary's Sound
PENZANCE (Mar-Nov)

Annet
Gugh
Smith Sound

St Agnes
St Agnes

09

F

0 1 2 3 4 5 6 miles
0 1 2 3 4 5 6 7 8 9 10km

14   3   4   5

Alderney
3½ miles to 1 inch

Guernsey
3½ miles to 1 inch

A

B

TURNER CONTEMPORARY
THE SHELL GROTTO
Foreness Pt.
Margate
Cliftonville
Kingsgate
NORTH
FORELAND
MARGATE
Westgate on Sea
DREAMLAND
Northdown
St Peter's
LIGHTHOUSE
RECULVER
RECULVER TOWERS
AND ROMAN FORT
Minnis Bay
BROADSTAIRS
BLEAK HOUSE
HERNE
BAY
Reculver
Hillborough
Birchington
QUEX HOUSE
Isle of Thanet
SPITFIRE AND
HURRICANE MEM.
Northwood
DICKENS HOUSE MUSEUM
Beltinge
A299
Greenhill
Broomfield
Herne
St Nicholas
at Wade
A28
Acol
Manston
Newington
Dumpton
Calcott
Boyden
Gate
A299
WINDMILL
B2190
Ramsgate
Hoath
Sarre
A253
Way
MARITIME MUSEUM
Chislet
Monkton
15
Minster
Cliffsend
Upstreet
West Stourmouth
Pegwell
Hersden
A28
Grove
STODMARSH
East Stourmouth
Westmarsh
SANDWICH &
PEGWELL BAY
Pegwell
Bay
oadoak
Westbere
Preston
Ware
RICHBOROUGH
CASTLE
Stodmarsh
Elmstone
Hoaden
ST AUGUSTINE'S
CROSS
A256
Sturry
Fordwich
WINGHAM
WILDLIFE
PARK
Great Stonar
Canterbury
Wickhambreux
Ickham
A257
Sandwich
Sandwich
Bay
ST AUGUSTINE'S ABBEY
Littlebourne
Wingham
Guilton
Ash
TOLL
Royal St George's
P&R
A257
HOWLETTS WILD
ANIMAL PARK
Marshborough
Stone Cross
TR
A2
Bramling
Staple
Woodnesborough
Worth
Bekesbourne
Goodnestone
Gore
Ham
Patrixbourne
GOODNESTONE PARK
Eastry
Finglesham
Adisham
Knowlton
MARITIME AND
LOCAL HISTORY MUSEUM
Bridge
Chillenden
Betteshanger
Sholden
Bishopsbourne
Aylesham
Easole Street
Northbourne
DEAL
THE
DOWNS
Kingston
Nonington
Snowdown
Great
Mongeham
DEAL CASTLE
pper Hardres
ardres
Barham
Tilmanstone
Elvington
Walmer
Womenswold
Ripple
WALMER CASTLE
AND GARDENS
Derringstone
Barfrestone
East
Studdal
Sutton
ssingham
EAST KENT
RLY
Ringwould
Kingsdown
Woolage
Green
Eythorne
West
Langdon
Martin
Denton
Coxhill
Shepherdswell
Martin Mill
A256
Wingmore
LYDDEN
Coldred
East
Langdon
Whitfield
Guston
St Margaret's at Cliffe
Wootton
Lydden
LYDDEN
TEMPLE EWELL
West
Cliffe
THE BAY MUSEUM
minge
orest
Selsted
Ewell
Minnis
ST JOHN'S
COMMANDERY
Temple
Ewell
THE PINES
GARDEN
St Margaret's Bay
Elham
BUTTERFLY
CENTRE
CRABBLE
CORN MILL
SOUTH
FORELAND
Swingfield
Minnis
Buckland
ROMAN PAINTED
HOUSE
WHITE
CLIFFS
Ottinge
Swingfield
Street
Densole
Drellingore
Alkham
Maxton
CASTLE & HELLFIRE CORNER
CALAIS
DUNKERQUE
Lyminge
West
Hougham
Farthingloe
DOVER
KENT BATTLE OF
BRITAIN MUSEUM
hodes
innis
Paddlesworth
Hawkinge
Capel le
Ferne
Aycliff
A20
DE BRADELEI
WHARF
chinghill
CHANNEL
TUNNEL
EAST CLIFF &
WARREN
SAMPHIRE
HOE
Newington
East Wear
Bay
ELHAMVALLEY
RLY MUS
Cheriton
Folkestone
Saltwood
ROTUNDA
CLIFF LIFT
Sandgate
Hythe
19

C

D

E

F

G

5   6   7   8   5 9

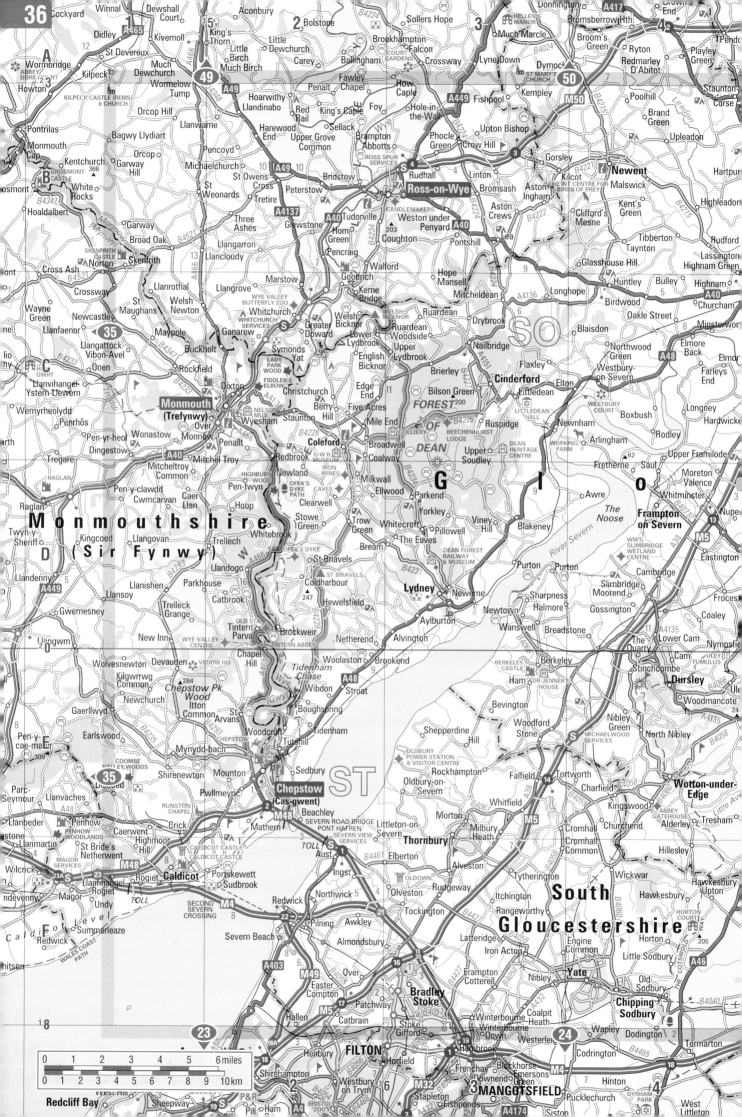

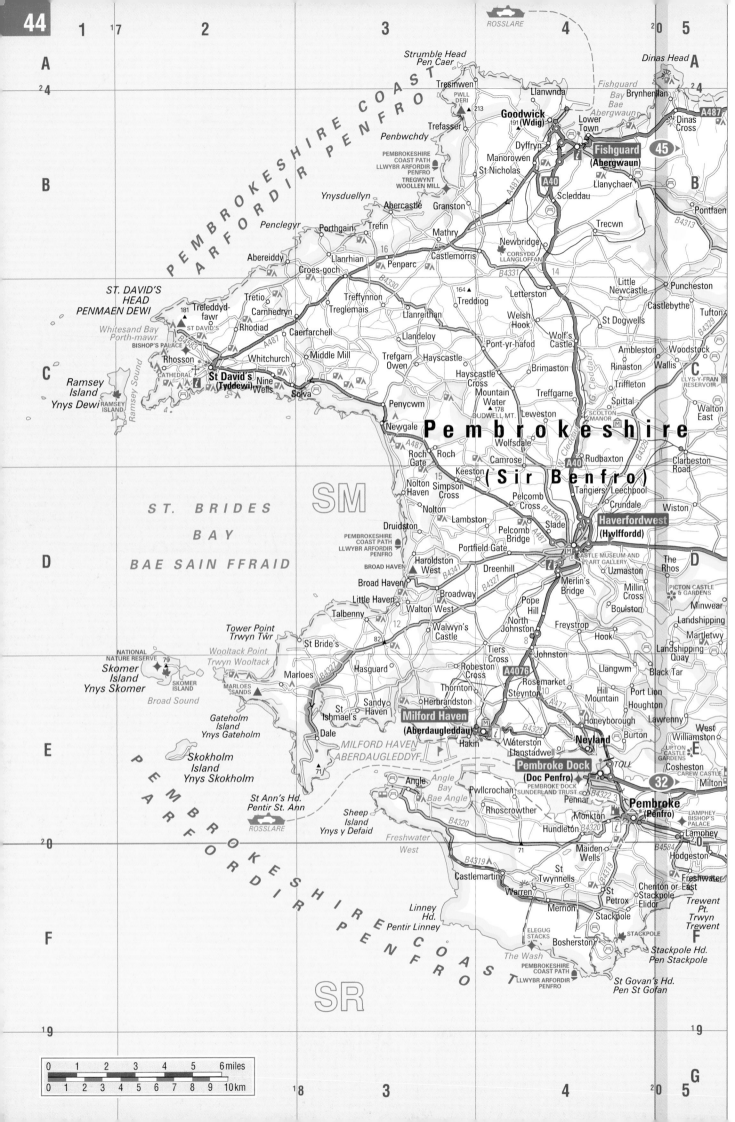

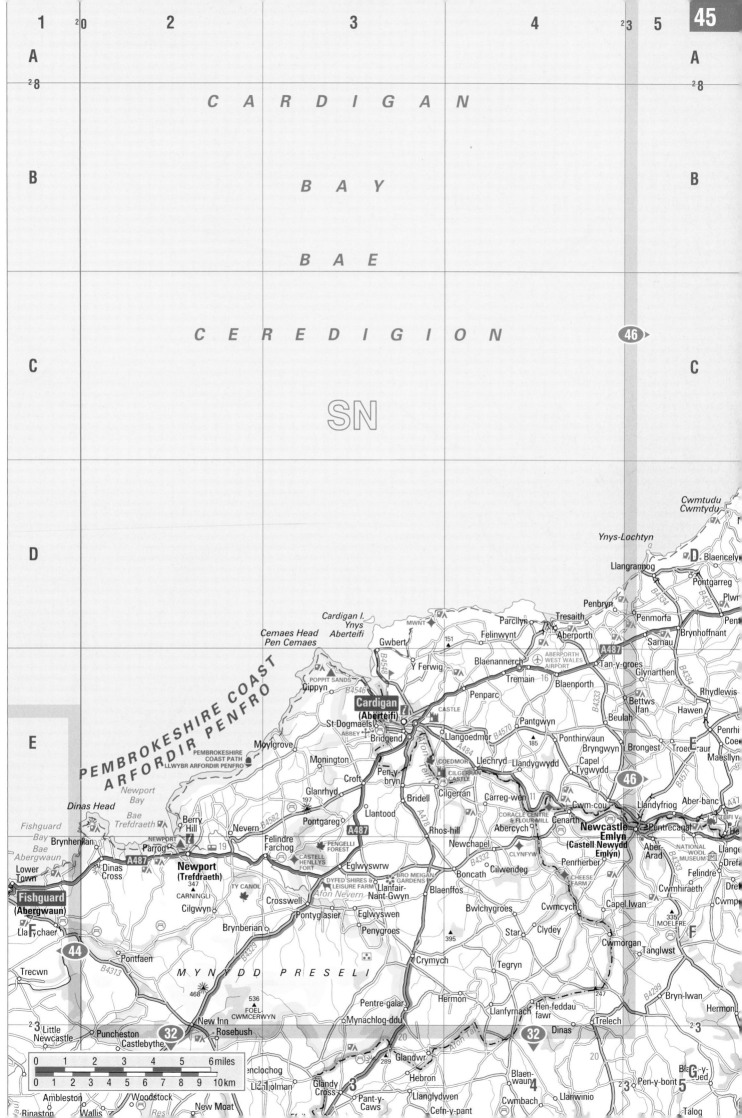

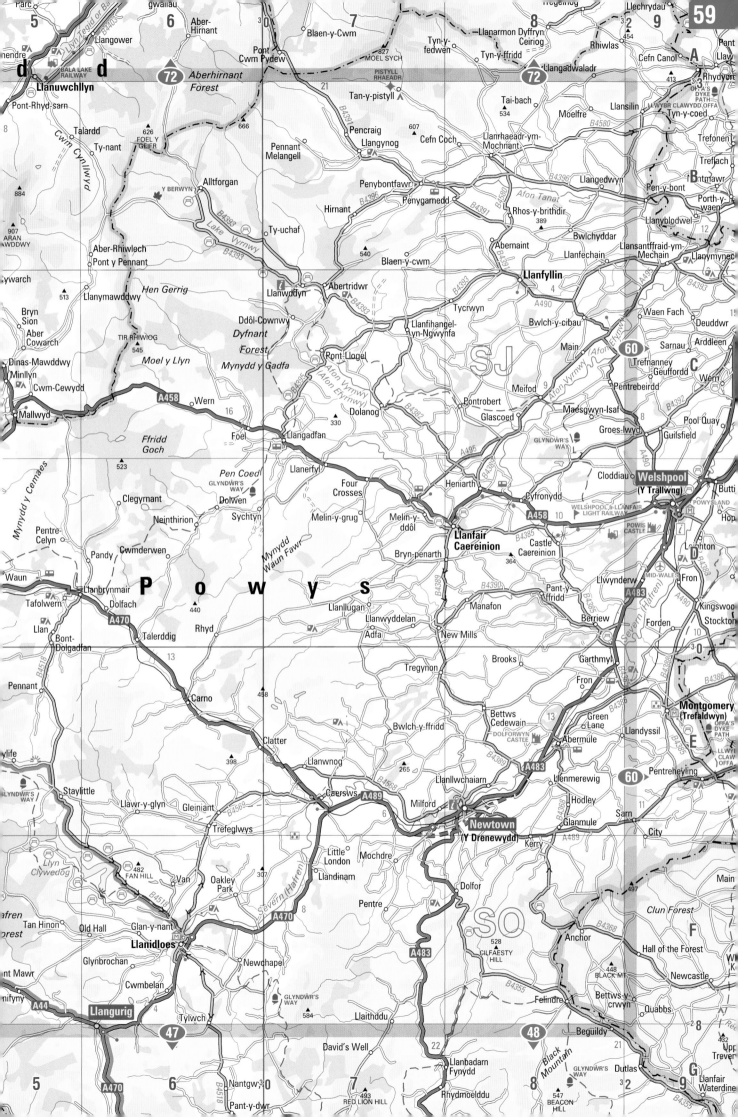

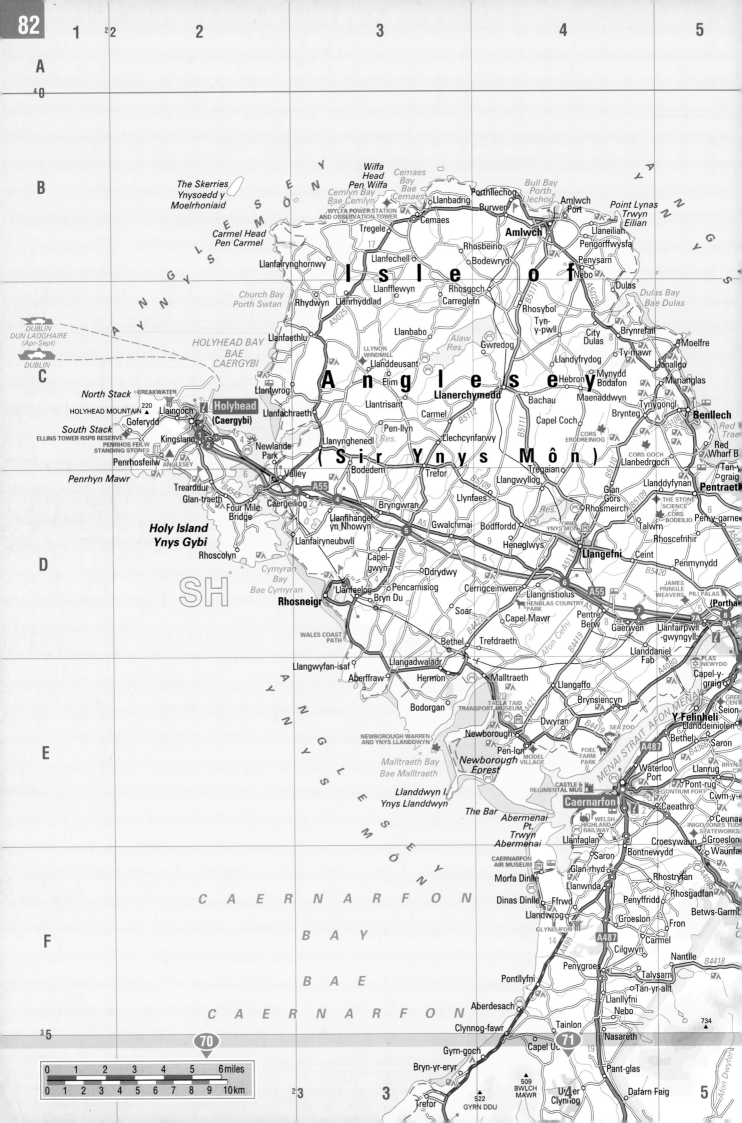

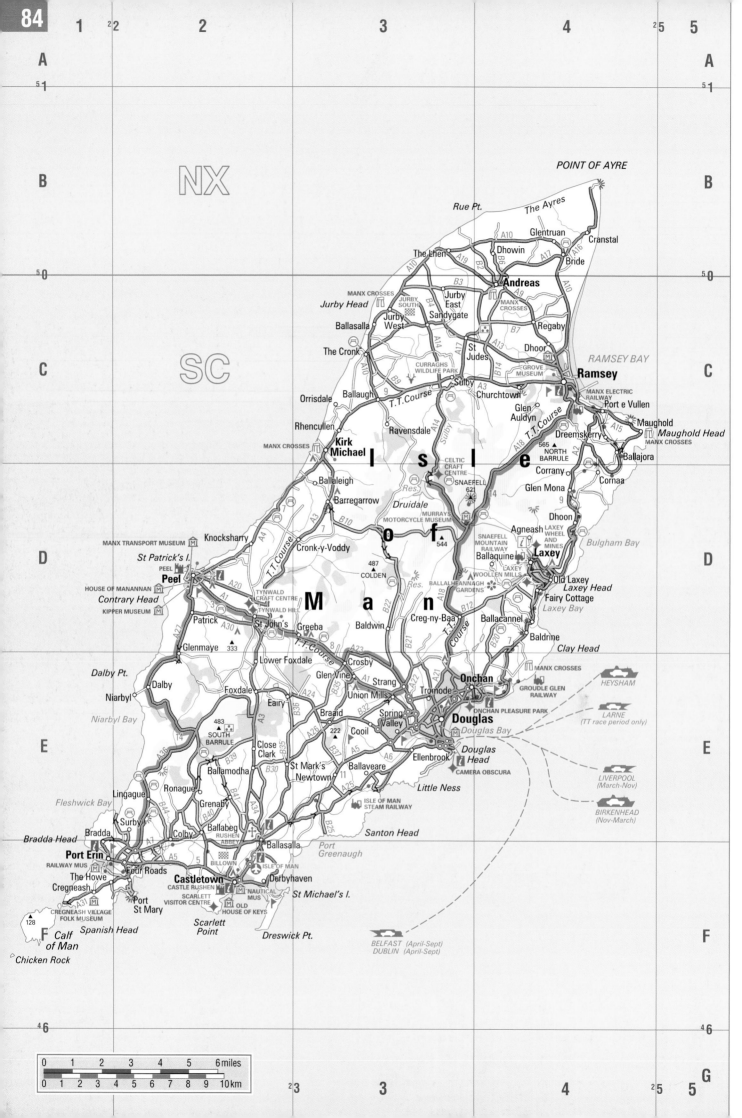

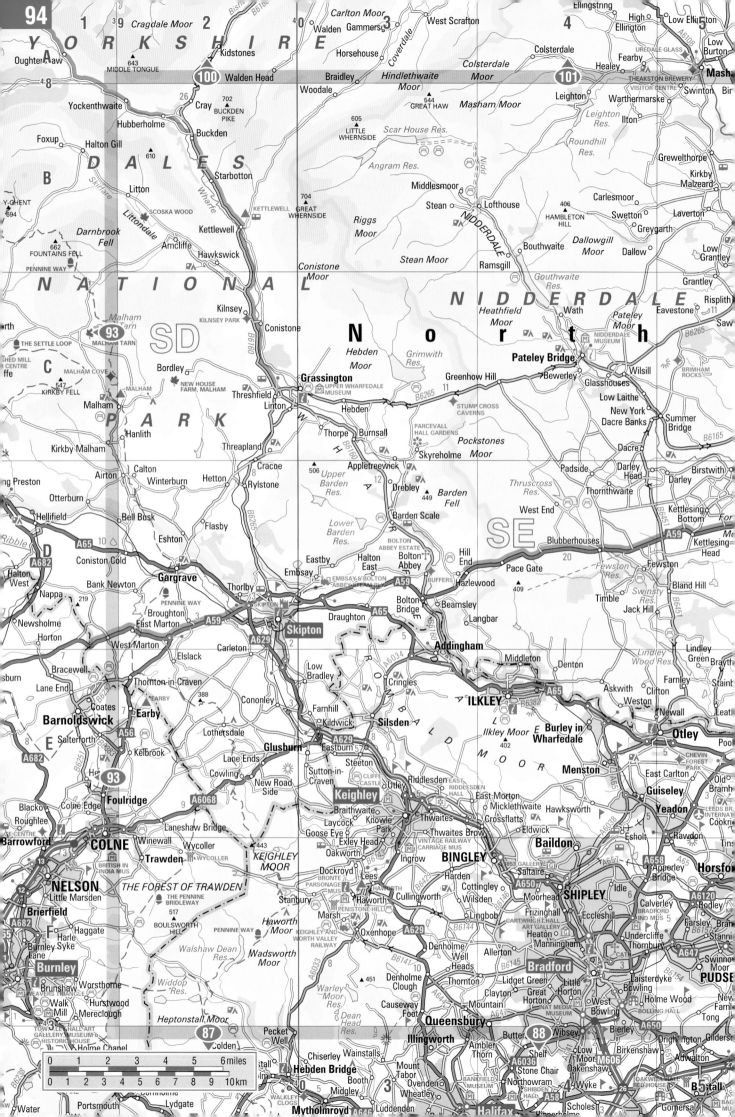

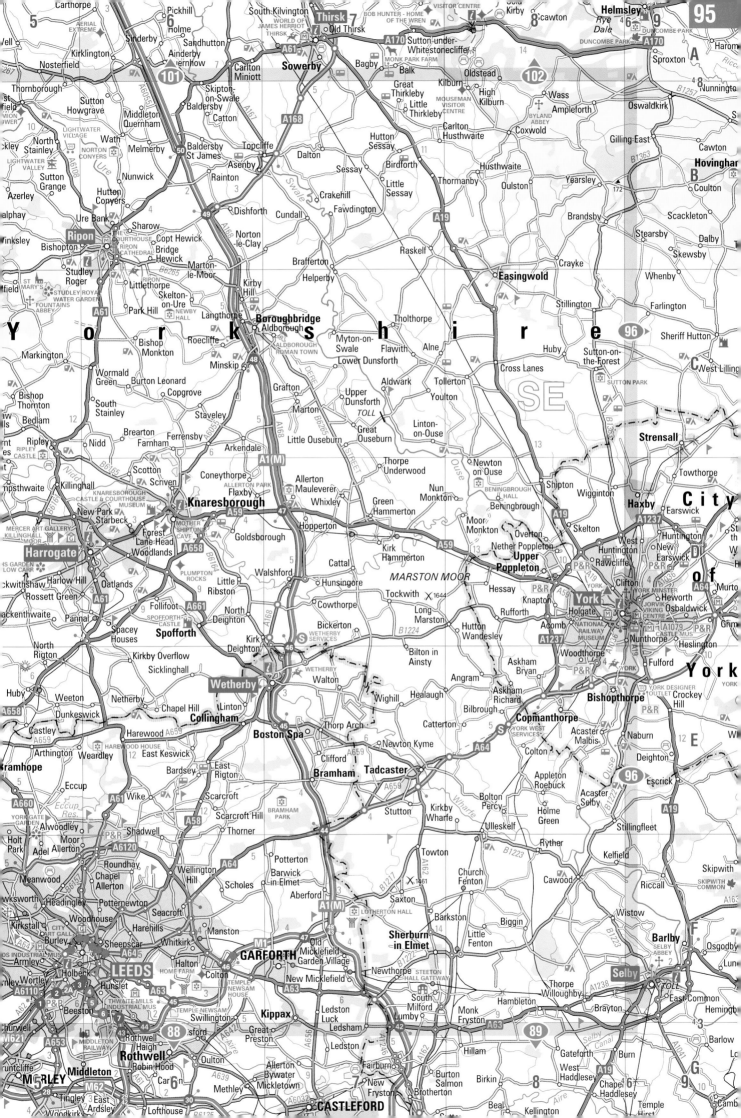

1   ¹8   2   3   ²0   4

A

⁵8

LARNE

BELFAST

B

Milleur Pt.

Corsewall Pt.

Barnhills

North Cairn

South Cairn

Dounan Bay

Mains of Airies

C

Slouchnawen Bay

NW

Portencalzie

B738
Loch
Connell

Corsewall

Kirkcolm

Ervie

B798

Low
Salchrie

Knocknain

B738

Leswalt

B7043

Craigencross

The Wig

LOCH RYAN

Bennane Hd.

112

Colmone

CARLETON
STLE
5

B734 265

Knockdoli

Heronsford

Ballantrae Bay

Glen Ti

Ballantrae

Balkisso

Downan Pt.

Auchencrosh

439
BENERAIF

A77

Mark

17

Glen App

257

Cairnryan

*Penwhirn
Res.*

Braid Fell

A77

Innermessan

Main Water

Glenstockadale

A718

A751

Black Loch
CASTLE KENNED
GARDENS

Broadsea Bay

T   H   E   E   R

Stranraer

CASTLE OF
ST JOHN
VISITOR
CENTRE

Aird

White Loch

Castle Kennedy

H

Black Hd.

Knockglass

B738

STRANRAER
MUSEUM

*Soulseat
Loch*

A75

Mark

Lochans

B7077

182

A77

Torrs

D

Dunskey Ho.

LITTLE
WHEELS

Portpatrick

5

Awhirk

8

Stoneykirk

A716

B7084

6

Luce S

Port of Spittal Bay

B7042

Cairngarroch

KIRKMADRINE
STONES

Sandhead

Cairngarroch Bay

Sandhead Bay

Money Hd.

Clachanmore

Hole Stone Bay

ARDWELL GDNS

Ardwell

E

Ardwell Pt.

Ardwell
Mains

*Chapel Rossa
Bay*

Logan
Mains

10

LOGAN
BOTANIC
GARDEN

Balgowa
Pt.

Mull of Logan

LOGAN FISH POND
MARINE LIFE CENTRE

⁵4

Port Nessock or Port Logan Bay

Port Logan

Cairnywellan Hd.

B7065

A716

Clanyard Bay

Low Clanyard

Kirkmaide

Laggantalluch Hd.

Drummore

F

164

Damnaglaur

B7041

Crammag Hd.

Cairngaan

Port Kemin

| 0 | 1 | 2 | 3 | 4 | 5 | 6 miles |
| 0 | 1 | 2 | 3 | 4 | 5 | 6 | 7 | 8 | 9 | 10km |

¹9   3   ²0   4   5

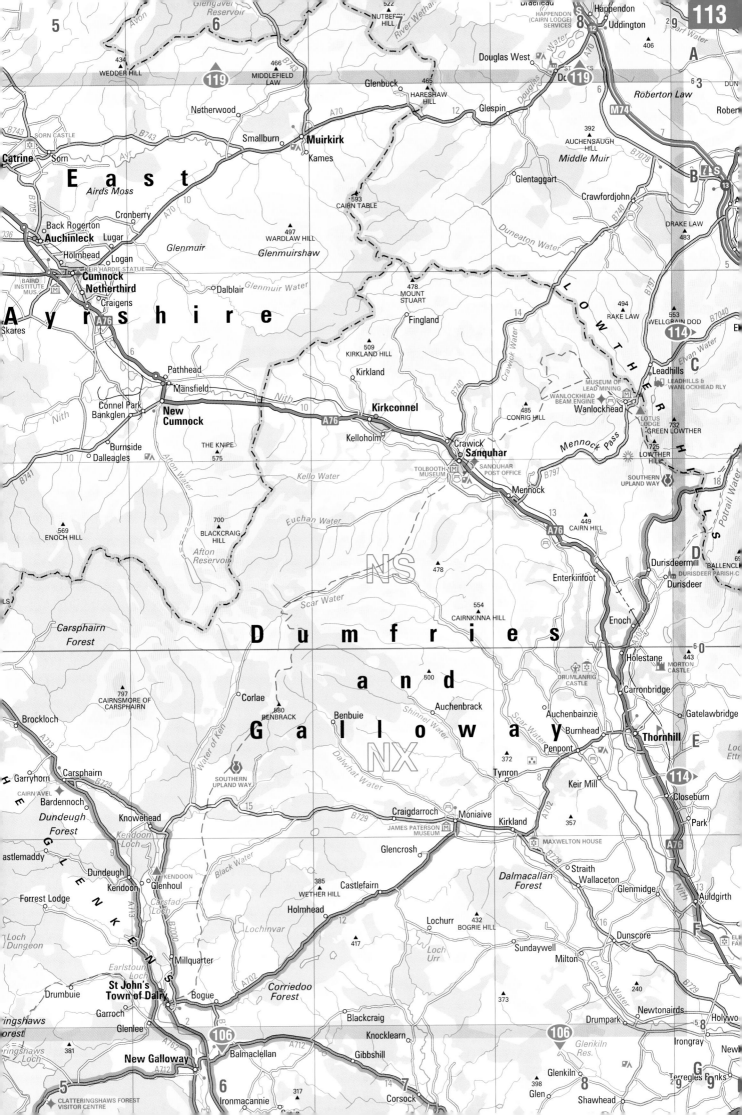

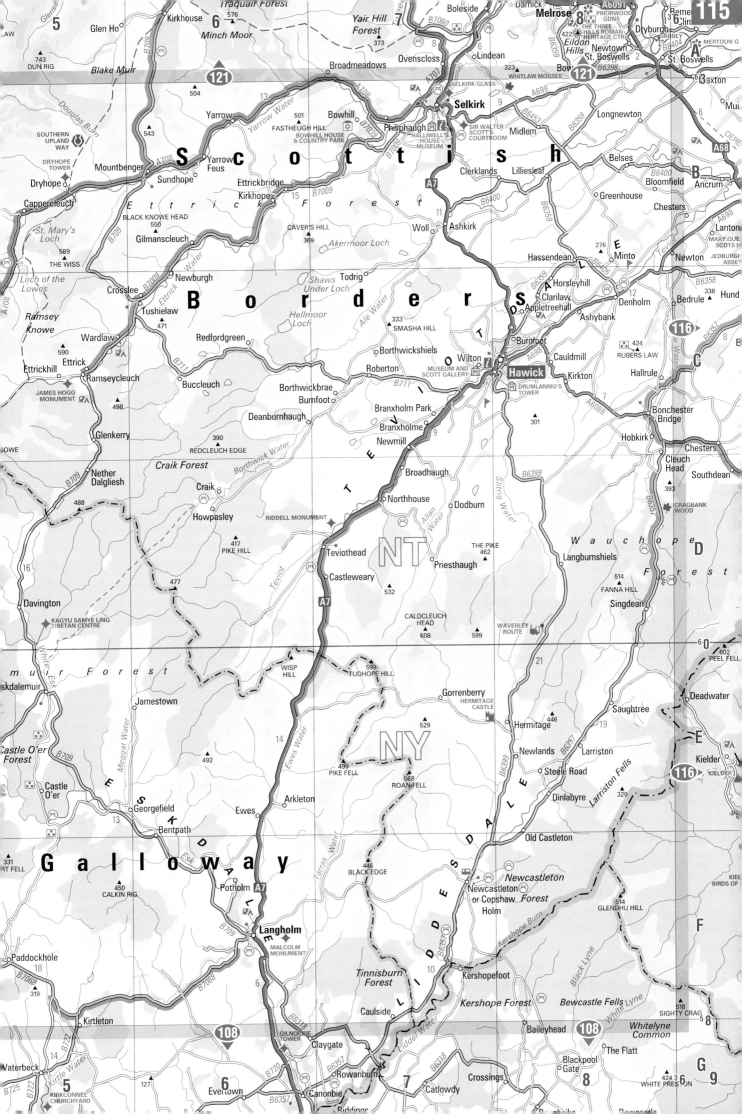

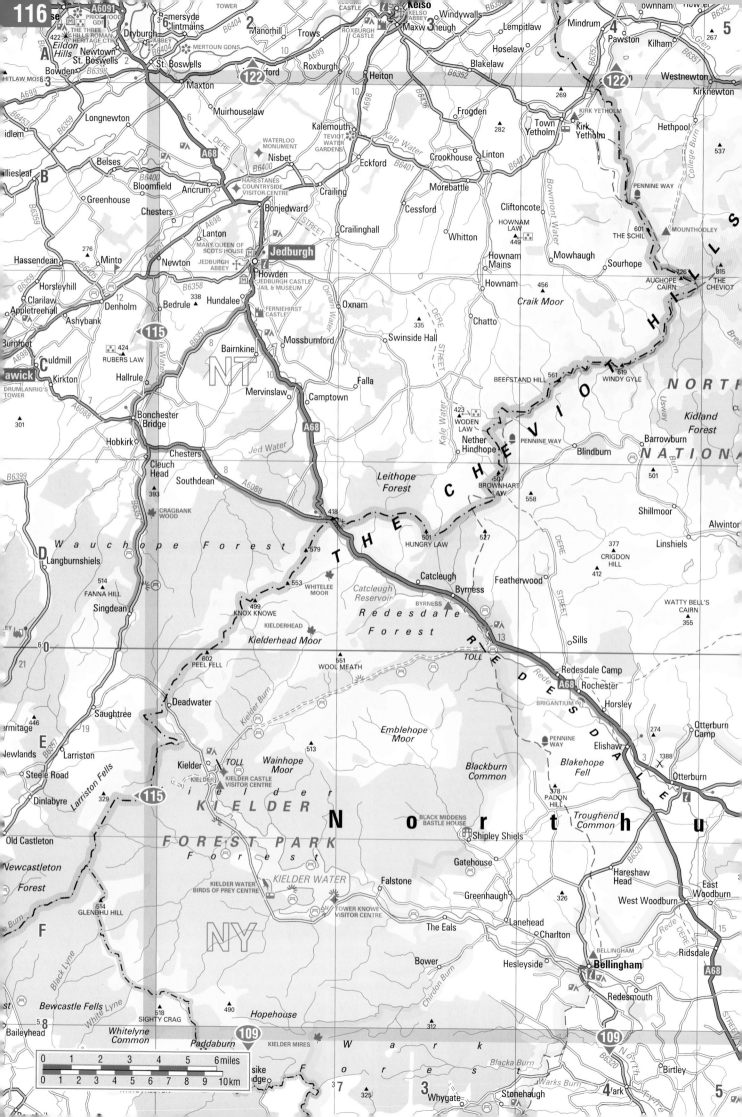

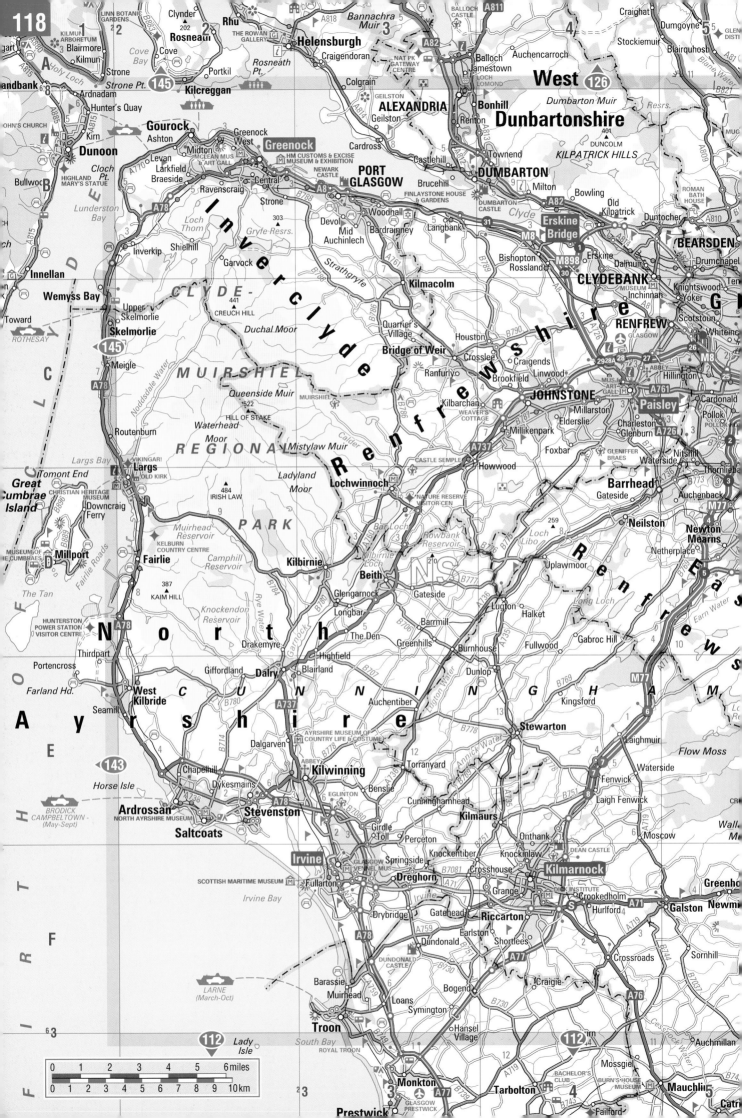

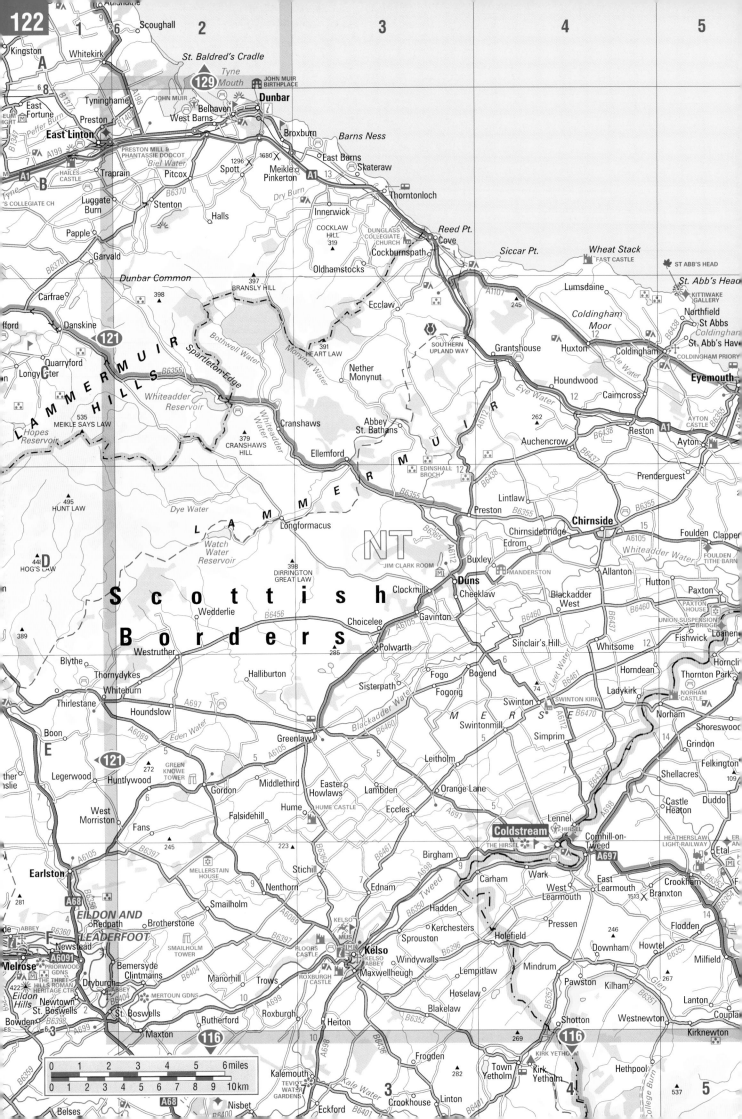

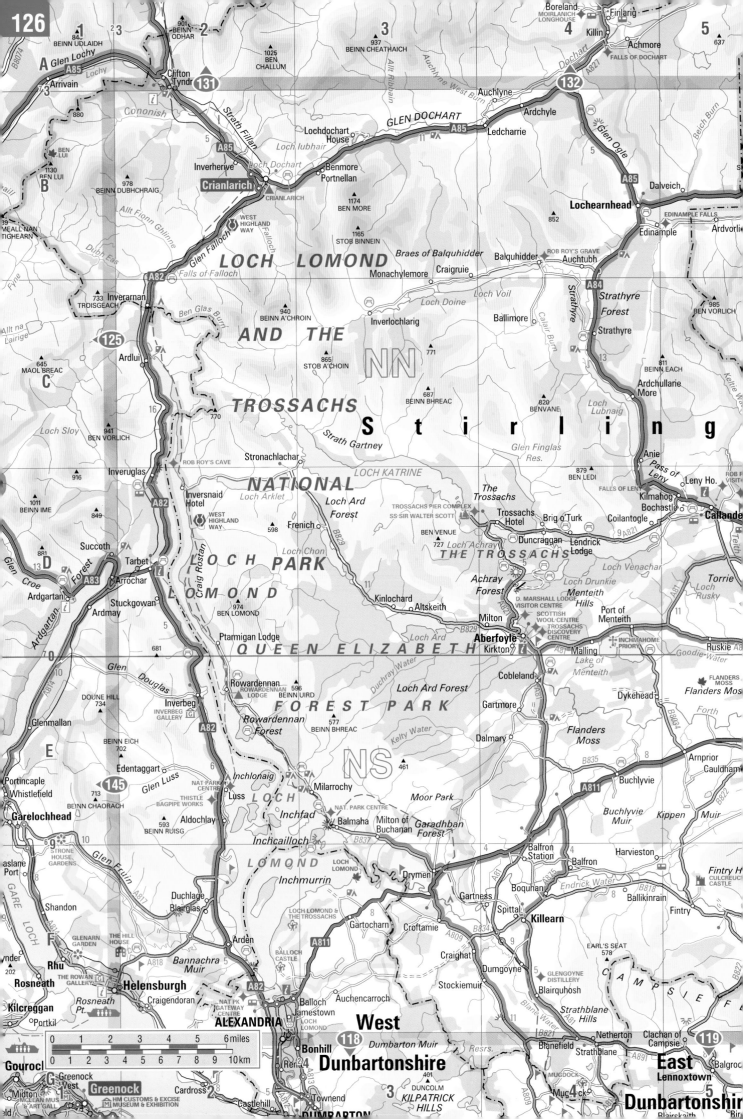

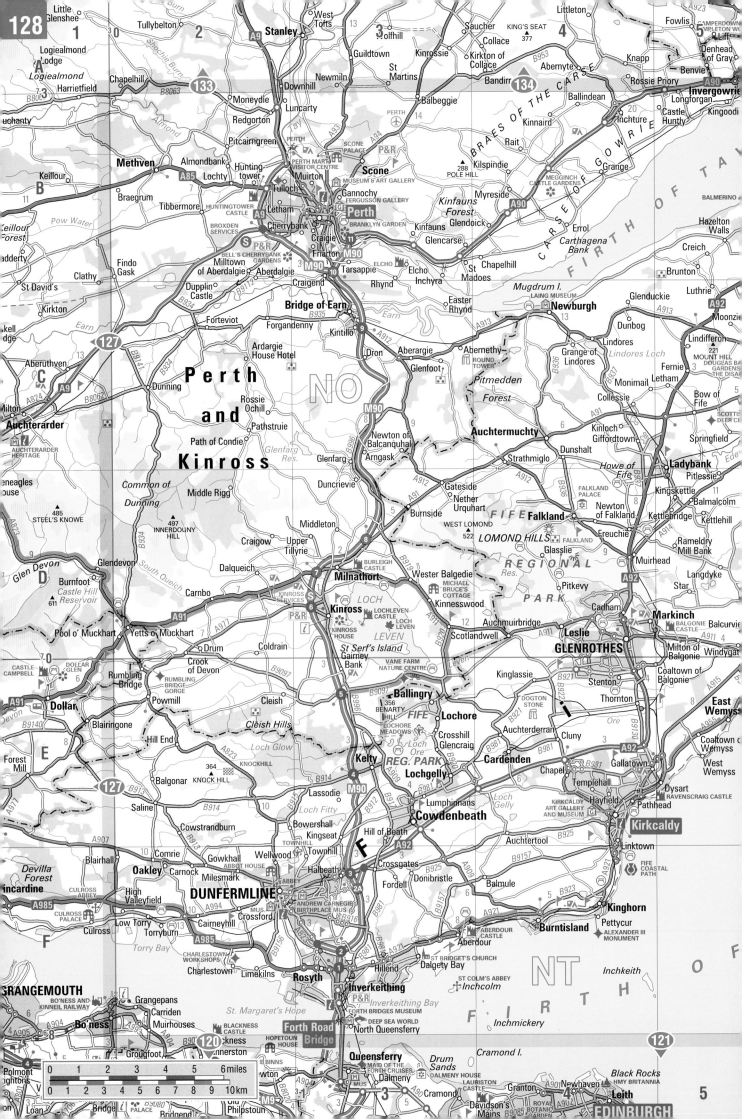

Dundee

5   Downfield   Fintry
Douglas &   6   Baldovie
Angus   A92   Mains of   7   **Carnoustie**
Ardestie   CARNOUST   8   3 7   9   A

DANT WORKS   Craigie   Craigie   West   Barry Links
Lochee   MUS AND   Ferry
MILLS   ART GALL   Stannergate   Broud   Barnhill   Monifieth
CONSERVATORY   Dundee   FRIGATE UNICORN   134   BROUGHTY CASTLE   Buddon Ness   135   7 3   A
University   DISCOVERY   MUSEUM
BOTANIC   DUNDEE   Tay Bridge   POINT   Tayport   Tentsmuir   Buddon Ness
GARDENS   A85   Newport-on-Tay   A92   Scotscraig   TENTSMUIR

Kirkton   Woodhaven   B946   Tay Rail   Wormit   Pickletillem   Tentsmuir   B
Bottomcraig   Bridge   A914   Forest
Balmerino   12   Gauldry   Rhynd
Kilmany   Lucklawhill   Carrick   13
Rathillet   Balmullo   13   A914   **Leuchars**   Eden Mouth
Logie   LEUCHARS NORMAN CHURCH

Kilmaron   Dairsie or   Guardbridge   C
Castle   Osnaburgh   A91   Kincaple   EDEN ESTUARY CENTRE   ST ANDREWS BAY
Cupar   A91   Strathkinness   Newpark   ST ANDREWS   **St Andrews**   St Andrews Aquarium
B939   BRITISH GOLF MUS   CATH & ST RULE'S TOWER
Kemback   Balone   Brownhills   Buddo Ness   C
Blebocraigs   CRAIGTOUN   ST ANDREWS   Boarhills   Babbet Ness
B940   Pitscottie   Denhead   BOTANIC GARDEN
Hill of Tarvit   Baldinnie   217   Prior   B9131   Kingsbarns   Cambo Ness   Carr Brigs
Mansionhouse   Bridgend   Muir   Stravithie   CAMBO GARDENS   Tullybothy Craigs
Ceres   Cameron   Dunino   Balcomie   Craighead   Fife Ness
COTSTARVIT   Craigrothie   FIFE FOLK   Res.   Cameron   Burn   B940   Crail Tolbooth
TOWER   MUSEUM   Peat Inn   Kingsmuir   Craighead
B939   Radernie   Lochty   SCOTLAND'S   Crail   D
Woodside   Lathones   SECRET BUNKER   Crail   CRAIL MUSEUM AND
New Gilston   B940   Pitcorthie   HERITAGE CENTRE
Montrave   11   Largoward   Carnbee   Pitkierie   West Ness
Wester   KELLIE CASTLE   B9171   FIFE COASTAL
Bonnybank   Newburn   AND GARDEN   Kilrenny   PATH   NO
Kennoway   Lundin   A915   Arncroach   B9171   Anstruther Easter
Scoonie   Links   Drumeldrie   Colinsburgh   B9131   SCOTTISH FISHERIES MUSEUM
ROBINSON   B942   Abercrombie   Anstruther Wester   D
SILVERBURN   CRUSOE STATUE   Lower   Kilconquhar   Pittenweem
LETHAM GLEN   ESTATE   Largo   Balchrystie   ST FILLAN'S CAVE
Leven   Largo Bay   A917   Ardross   St Monans   ST MONAN'S WINDMILL
Innerleven   Ruddons Pt.   Elie   ST MONAN'S
Methil   MUSEUM   Earlsferry   Sauchar Pt.   CHURCH   Isle of May
Buckhaven   Chapel   ISLE OF MAY
FIFE COASTAL   Ness   Isle of May   7 0
PATH   E

F O R T H   Fidra   Craigleith   Bass Rock   F
Eyebroughy   SCOTTISH SEABIRD CENTRE
North   MUSEUM   NT
DIRLETON CASTLE   Berwick   TANTALLON CASTLE
Gullane Bay   & GARDENS   Auldhame
Gullane   Muirfield   Dirleton   187   Scoughall   F
West   A198   Kingston   Whitekirk   St. Baldred's Cradle
Aberlady Bay   Fenton   B1345   Fenton   Tyne Mouth   JOHN MUIR
Aberlady   Barns   MYRETON   Drem   BIRTHPLACE
121   MOTOR MUSEUM   B1377   Tyninghame   122   JOHN MUIR   Dunbar
Craigielaw   GOSFORD   THE CHESTERS   East   Preston   West Barns   Belhaven
Gosford Bay   HOUSE   FORT   MUSEUM   Fortune   A198   Barns
Spittal   Ballencrieff   OF FLIGHT   B1347   East Linton   PRESTON MILL &   Broxburn   Ness
SETON   Athelstaneford   Peffer Burn   PHANTASSIE DOOCOT   6 8
COLLEGIATE   HOPETOUN MON   181   HAILES   A199   1296   1650   East Barns   G
5   CHURCH   6   JANE WELSH   7   Biel Water   8   Spott   9
Cockenzie   B1377   Longniddry   CARLYLE MUSEUM   A1   Tranrain   Pitcox   Meikle   A1   Skateraw
and Port Seton

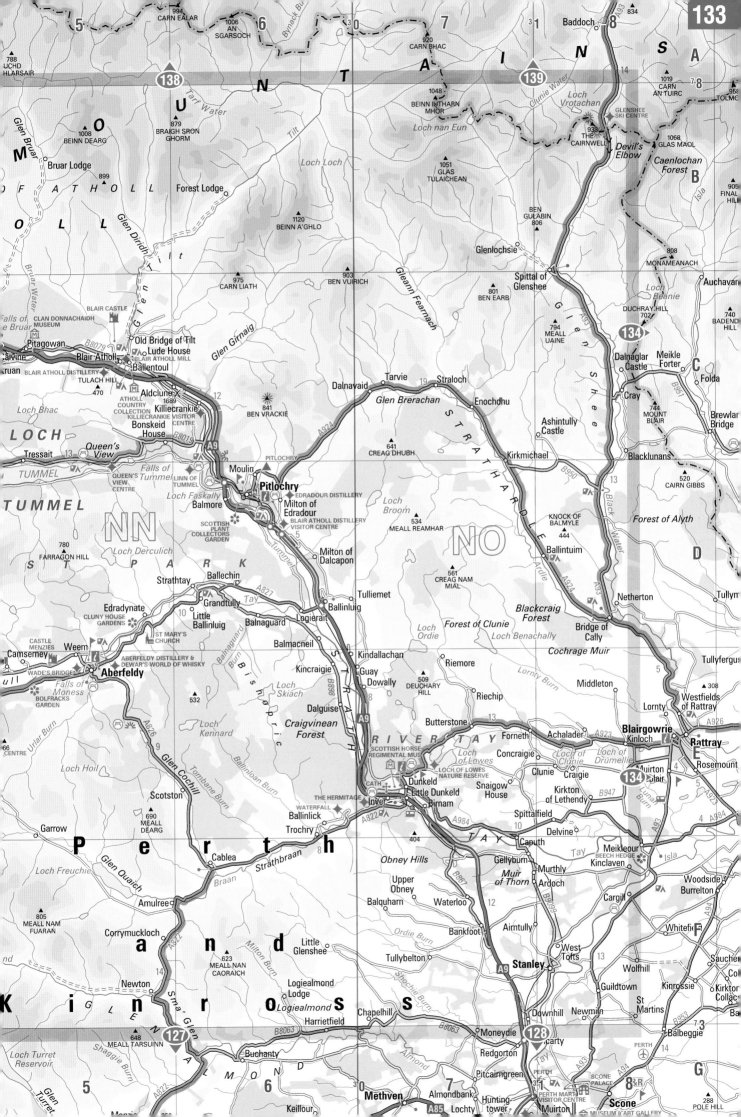

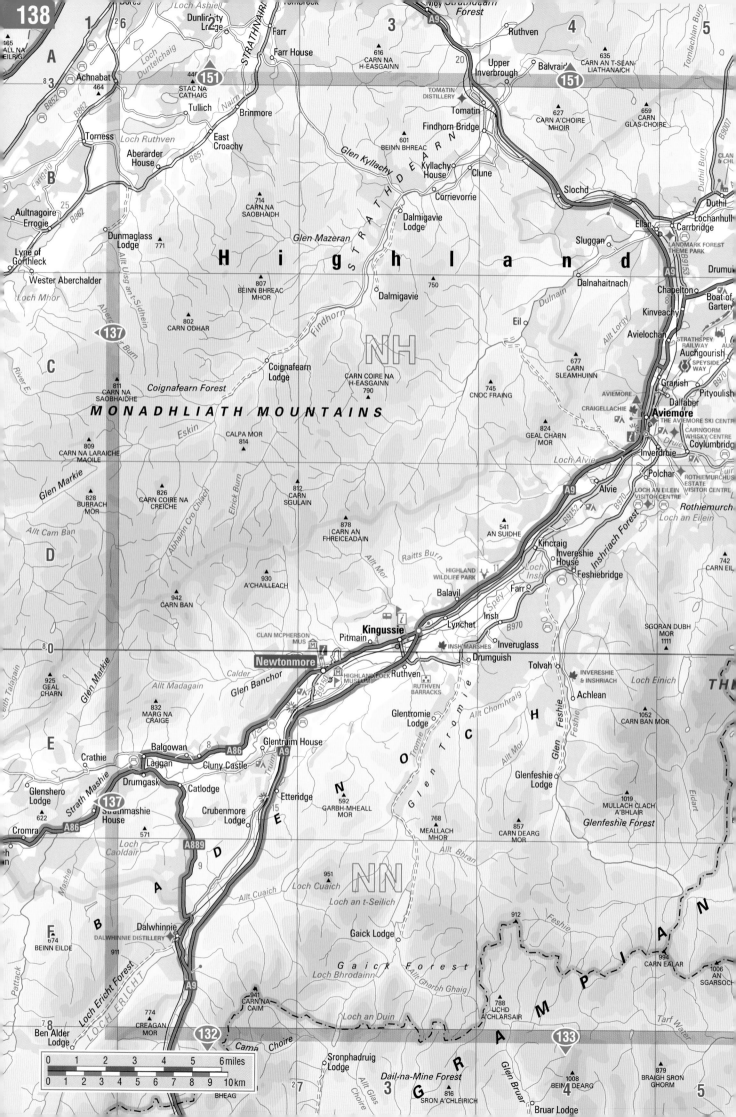

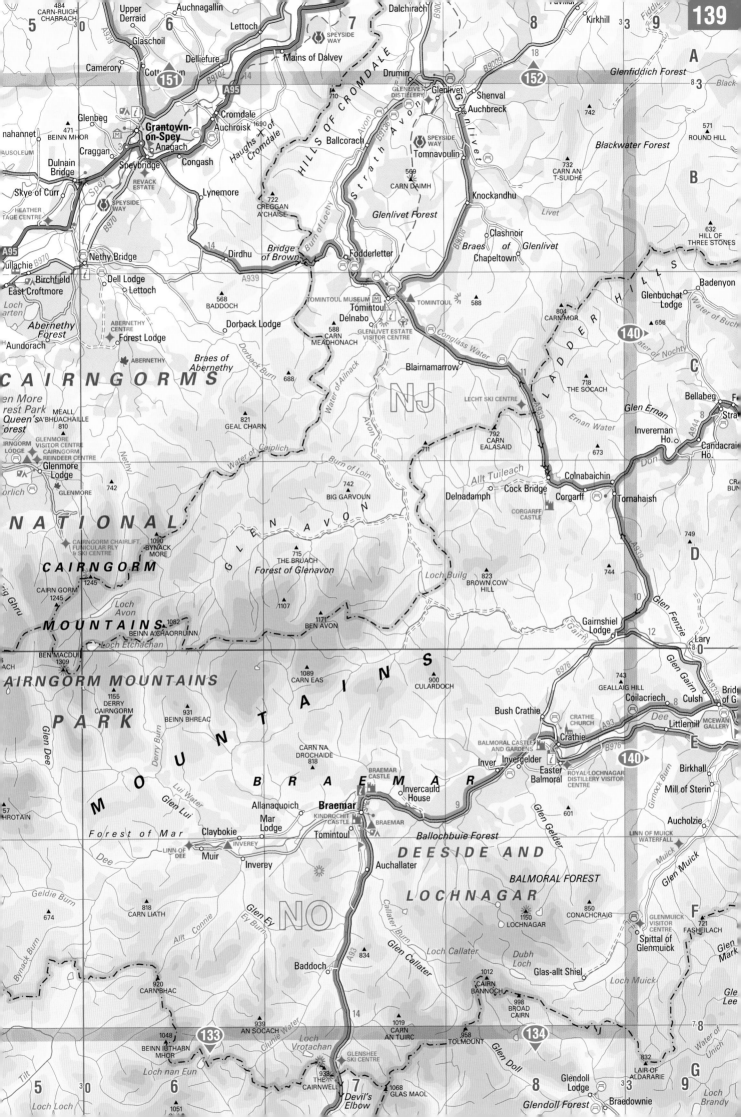

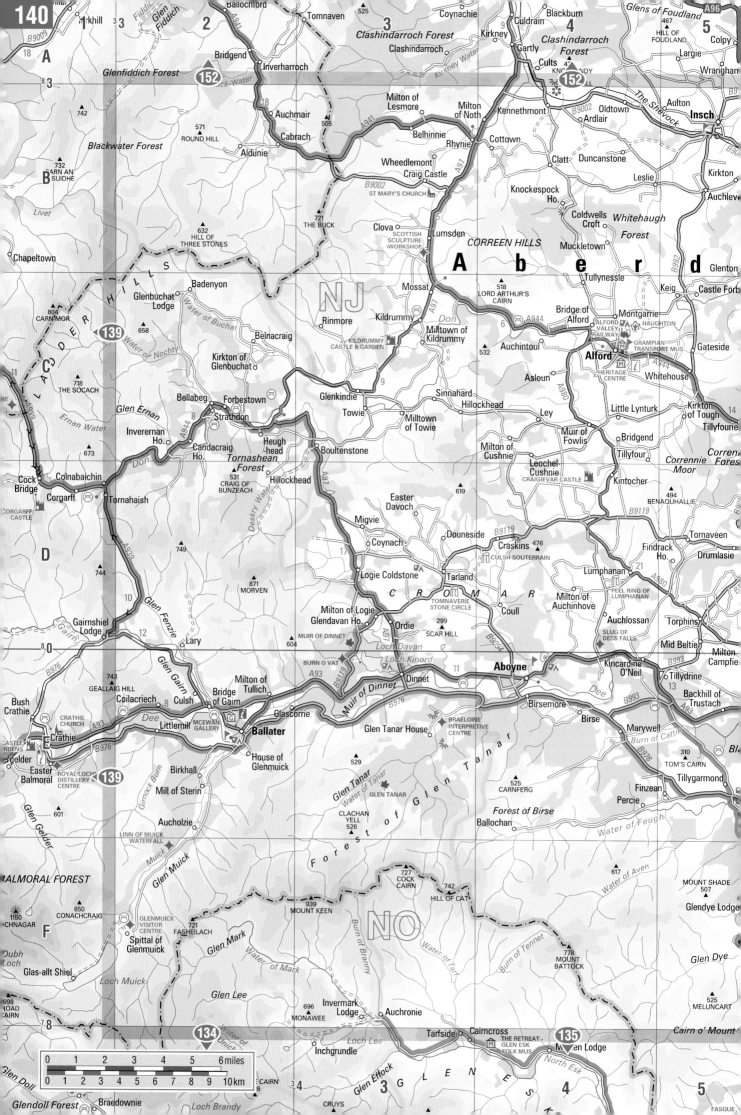

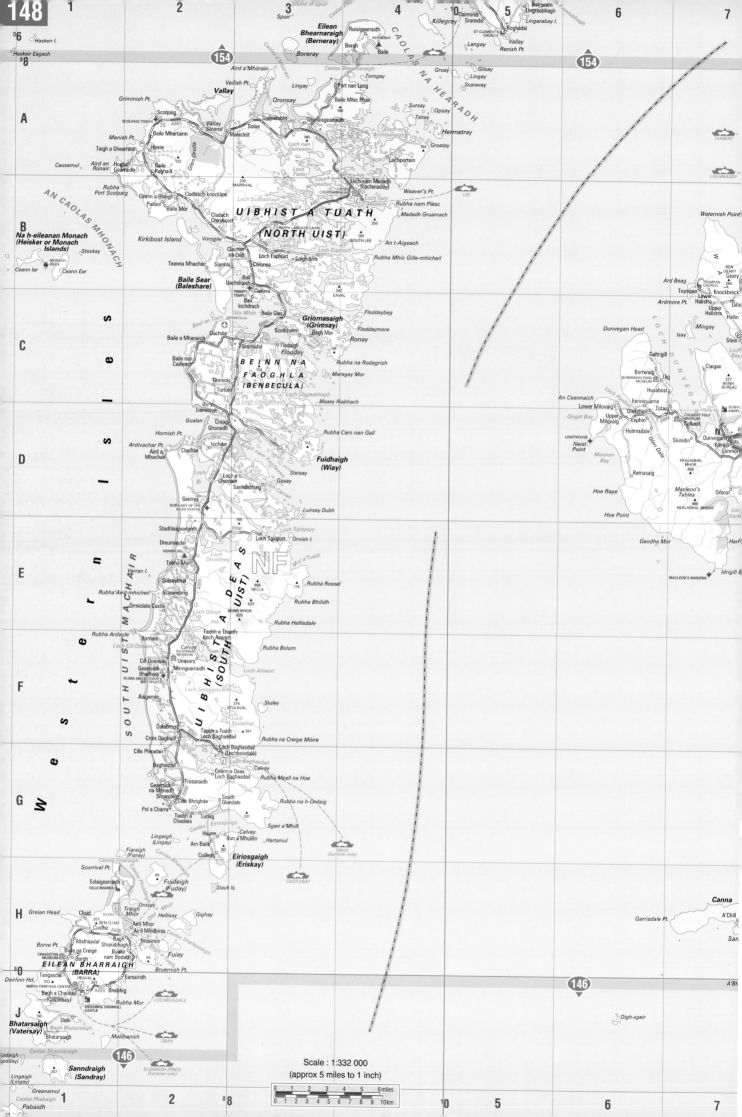

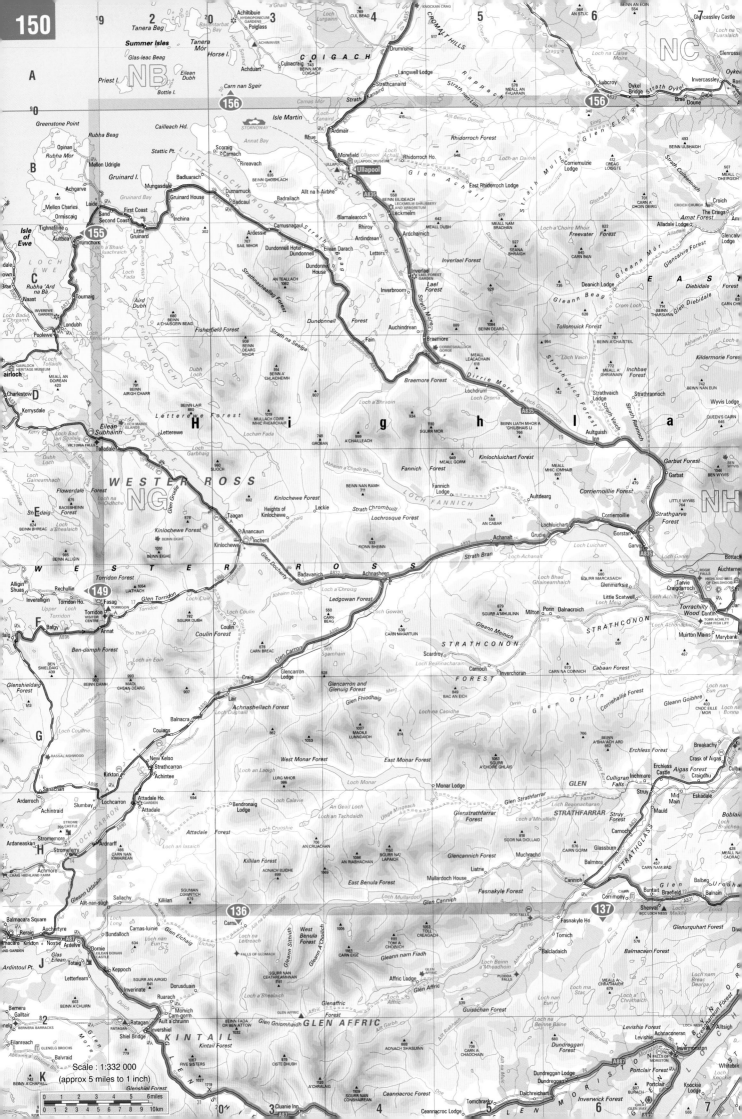

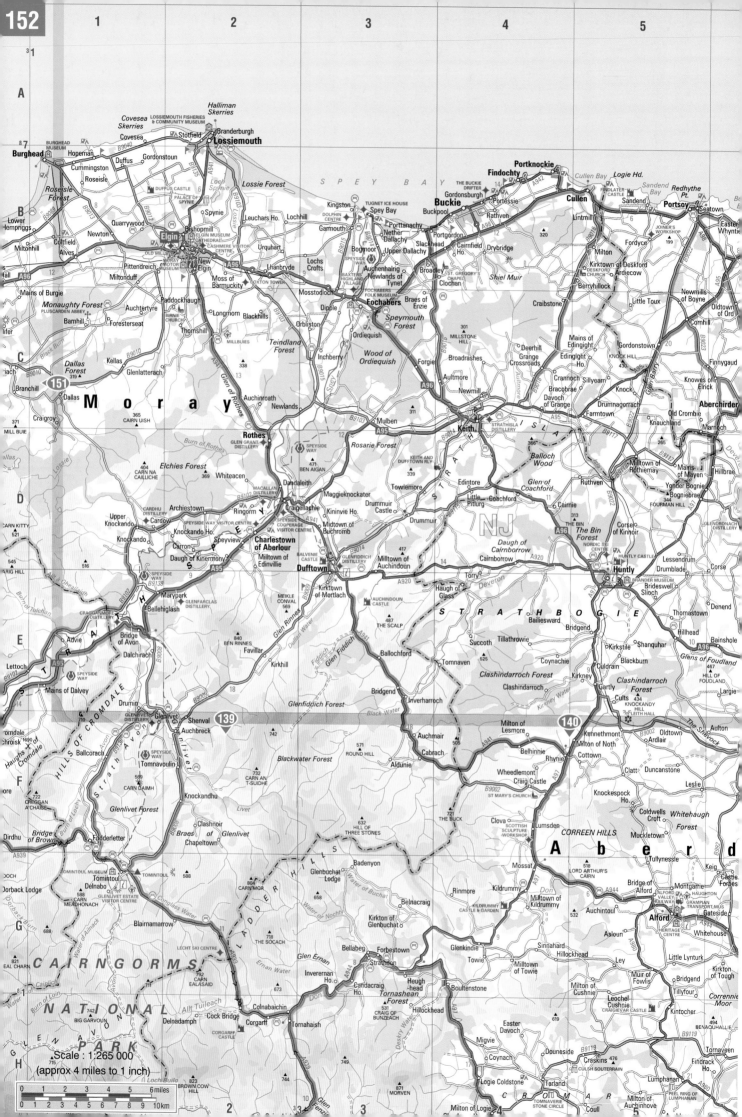

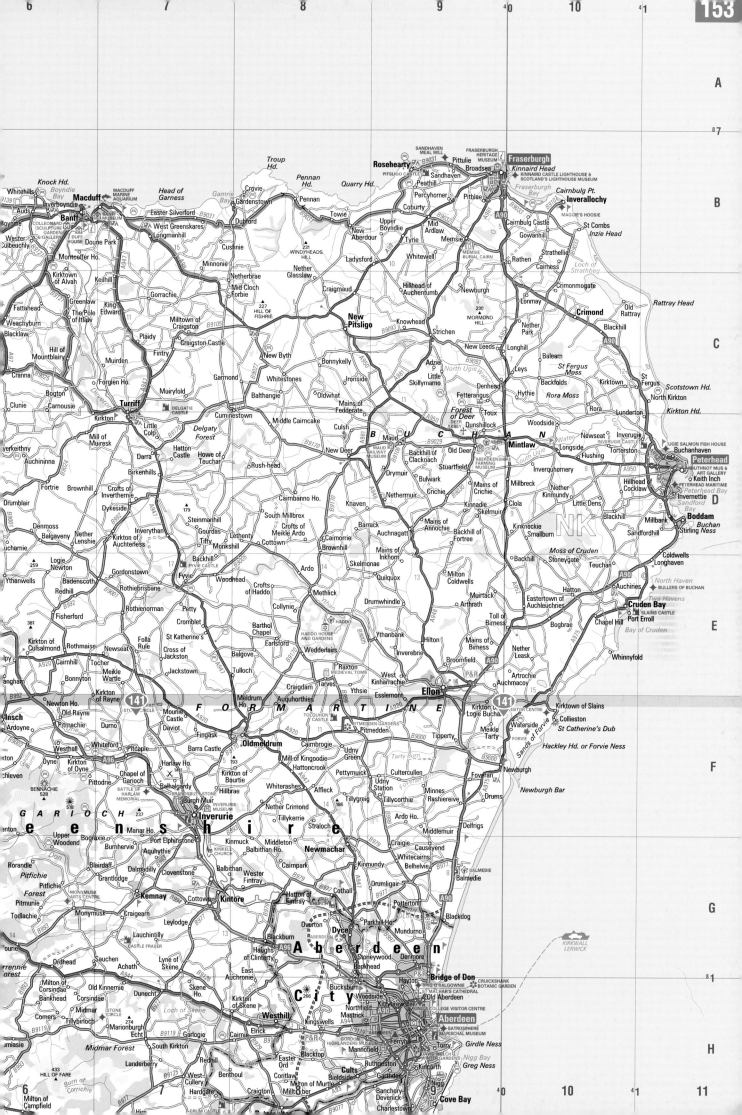

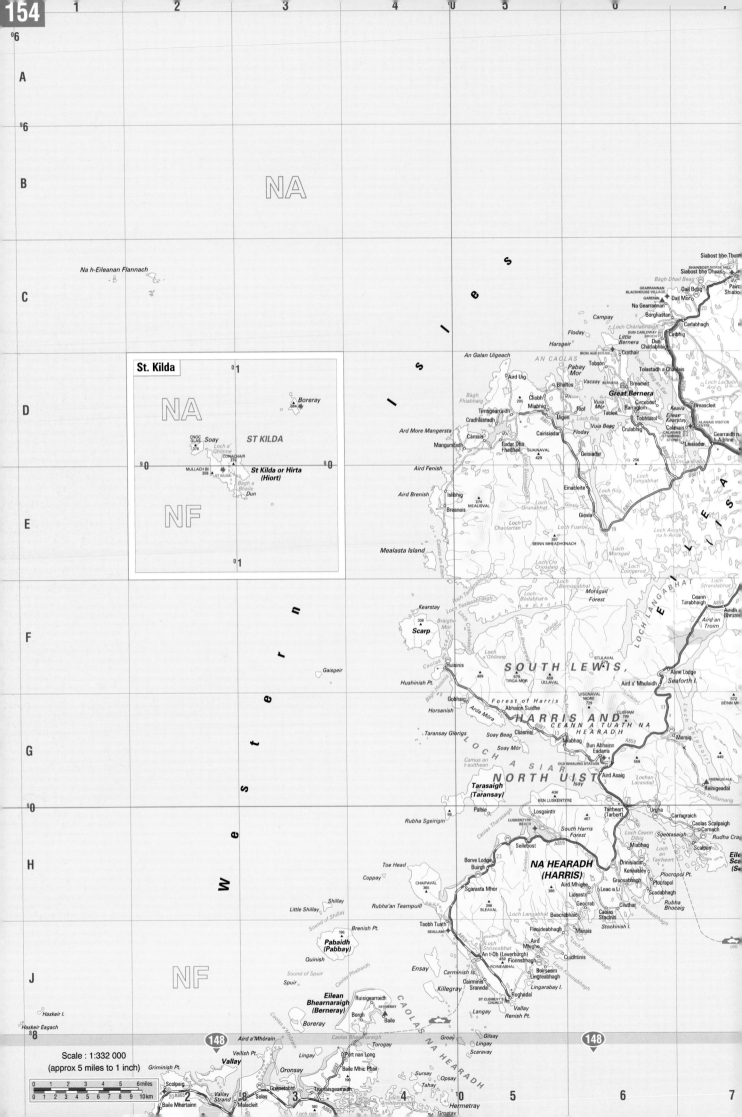

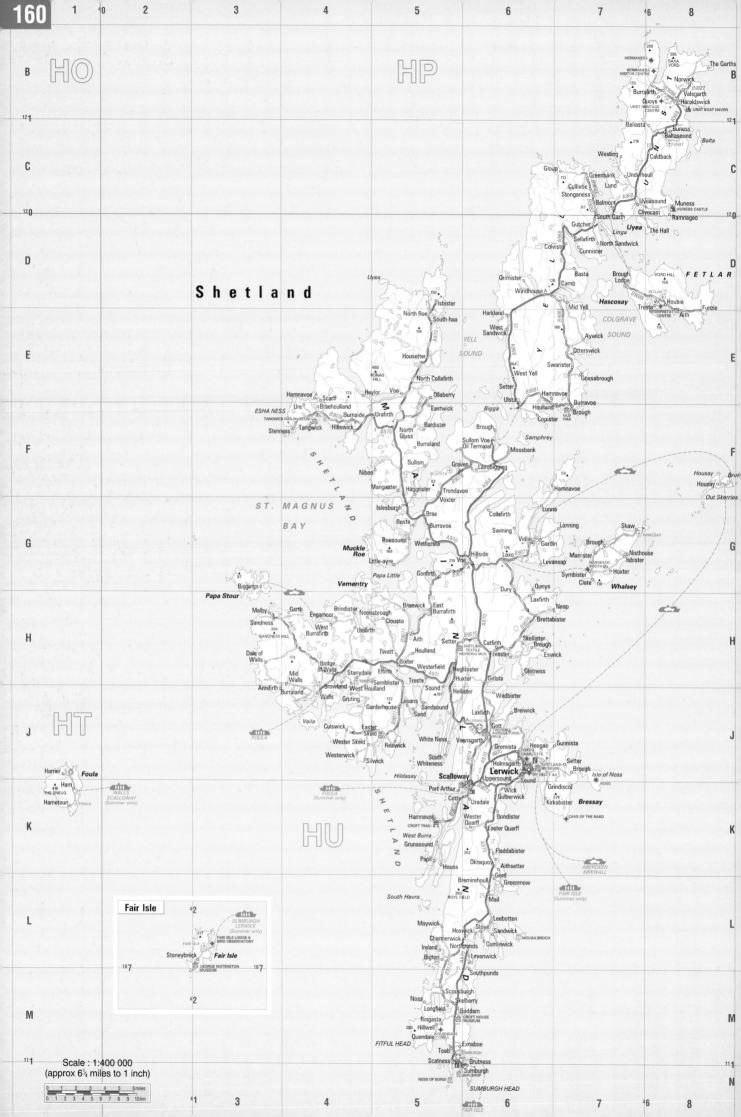

HO

HP

Shetland

Uyea

ESHA NESS

SHETLAND

ST. MAGNUS

BAY

Muckle Roe

Papa Stour

HT

Vaila

Foula

FOULA
WALLS
SCALLOWAY
(Summer only)

HU

Hildasay

FOULA
(Summer only)

SHETLAND

South Havra

West Burra

South Havra

Fair Isle

SUMBURGH
LERWICK
(Summer only)

FAIR ISLE

Stoneybreck *Fair Isle*

GEORGE WATERSTON
MUSEUM

FAIR ISLE
LODGE &
BIRD OBSERVATORY

FAIR ISLE
(Summer only)

ABERDEEN
KIRKWALL

FITFUL HEAD

SUMBURGH HEAD

FAIR ISLE

Scale : 1:400 000
(approx 6¼ miles to 1 inch)

0   1   2   3   4   5   6 miles
0 1 2 3 4 5 6 7 8 9 10km

UNST

HERMANESS
HERMANESS
VISITOR CENTRE
SAXA
VORD
200
285
The Garths
Norwick
Burrafirth
Quoys
Valsgarth
Haroldswick
UNST HERITAGE
CENTRE
UNST BOAT HAVEN
Baliasta
Buness
Baltasound
Balta
Westing
Caldback
UNST
216

Gloup
Greenbank
113
Cullivoe
Stonganess
Underhoull
Lund
A968
Belmont
Uyeasound
Muness
MUNESS CASTLE
97
South Garth
Clivocast
Ramnageo
Gutcher
Sellafirth
Linga
The Hall
Colvister
North Sandwick
Cunnister

Uyea

YELL

Grimister
126
Basta
Brough
Lodge
VORD HILL
158
FETLAR
Windhouse
Camb
Hascosay
Tresta
Houbie
Harkland
Mid Yell
INTERPRETATIVE
CENTRE
Aith
Funzie
West
Sandwick
186
Aywick
COLGRAVE
SOUND
115
10
West Yell
Otterswick
864
Swarister
B9081
Setter
Gossabrough
Ulsta
Hamnavoe
13
Burravoe
Houlland
Brough
OLD
HAA
Copister

Bigga

Samphrey

Brough
Housay
Bru
Sullom Voe
Oil Terminal
Mossbank
59
Housay
Hamnavoe
Out Skerries

North Roe
130
Isbister
South-haa
196

North Collafirth

450
RONAS
HILL
Heylor
Voe
Ollaberry

Hamnavoe
Scarff
173
Eastwick
Ure
Braehoulland
Burnside
Urafirth
TANGWICK HAA MUSEUM
Stenness
Tangwick
Hillswick
Bardister
North
Gluss
Burraland
Sullom
A970
Graven
Laxobigging
Nibon
82
SCATSTA
Mangaster
Haggrister
Trondavoe
Voxter
A970
Islesburgh
Brae
Collafirth
Lunna
Roesound
Busta
Burravoe
Swining
Lunning
Skaw
Little-ayre
Wethersta
Hillside
Vidlin
Gardin
Brough
Nisthouse
Isbister
Gonfirth
126
Laxo
B907
Marrister
Huxter
Papa Little
219
Voe
Levaneap
Symbister
WHALSAY
Vementry
A
Dury
Quoys
Clate
119
Whalsay
Braewick
East
Burrafirth
Laxfirth
Neap
Melby
Garth
Brindister
Noonsbrough
281
Brettabister
Sandness
Engamoor
Clousta
Skellister
Brough
249
West
Burrafirth
Unifirth
Aith
Setter
Catfirth
Eswick
SANDNESS HILL
B9071
Houlland
SHETLAND
TEXTILE
WORKING MUS
Heglibister
Freester
Gletness
Dale of
Walls
173
Twatt
Bixter
Westerfield
14
Bridge
of Walls
A971
Stanydale
Effirth
Tresta
Huxter
Girlsta
Mid
Walls
Browland
TEMPLE
Semblister
Sound
Hellister
Wadbister
Annifirth
Burraland
Walls
West Houlland
191
Gruting
Garderhouse
Leeans
Sandsound
Laxfirth
Breiwick
133
Sand
Gott
Gremista
ROYAL AGRICULTURAL
MUS
Gunnista
Culswick
Easter
Skeld
White Ness
Veensgarth
Heogan
Wester Skeld
Reawick
South
Whiteness
Holmsgarth
SHETLAND
MUSEUM
Setter
Brough
Westerwick
Silwick
Scalloway
Lerwick
Uppersound
HELEY AA
Isle of Noss
NOSS
Port Arthur
Cutts
Wick
Gulberwick
Grindiscol
Bressay
Harrier
Uradale
Kirkabister
Foula
Ham
Hamnavoe
Wester
Quarff
CAVE OF THE BARD
THE SNEUG
Hametoun
CROFT TRAIL
Easter Quarff
West Burra
Grunasound
Fladdabister
Papil
262
Aithsetter
Houss
A970
Bremirehoull
Gord
Greenmow
Mail
293
ROYL FIELD
2C
Leebotten
Maywick
Sandwick
MOUSA BROCH
Hoswick
Stove
Channerwick
Cumliewick
Ireland
Northpunds
Bigton
Levenwick
Southpunds
Noss
Scousburgh
Longfield
Skelberry
Boddam
Ringasta
CROFT HOUSE
MUSEUM
Hillwell
283
Quendale
QUENDALE
MILL
Exnaboe
Toab
Scatness
Grutness
NESS OF BURGI
Sumburgh
JARLSHOF

Edinburgh approaches

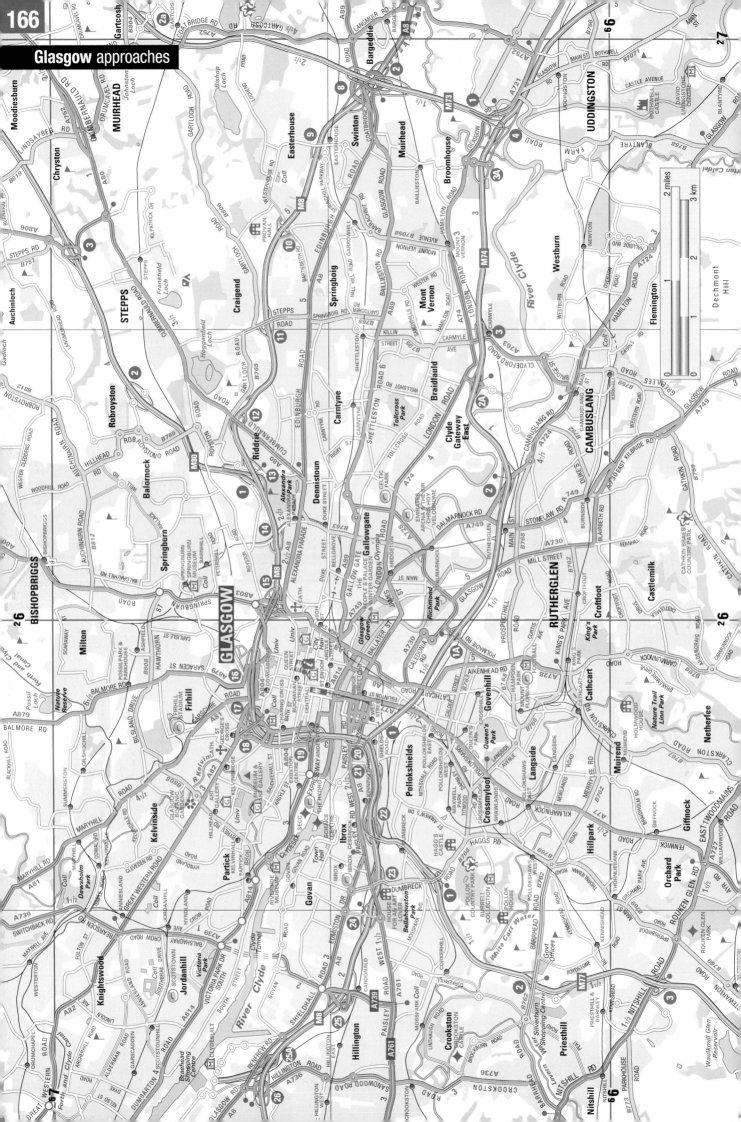

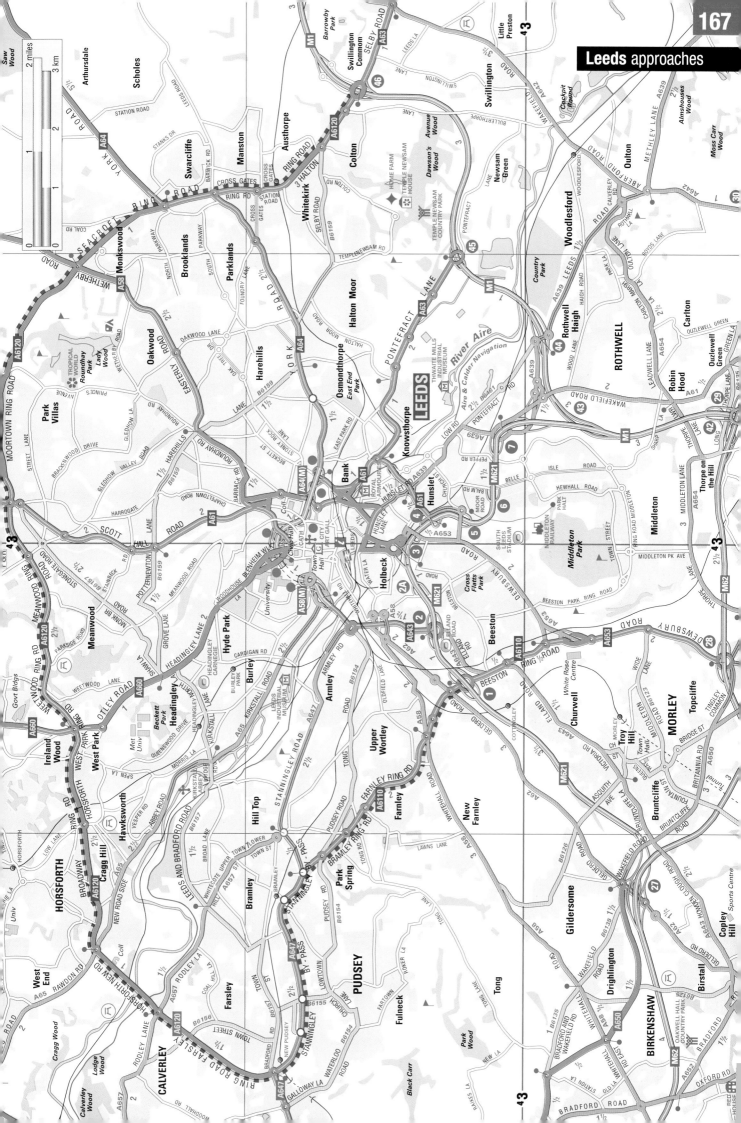

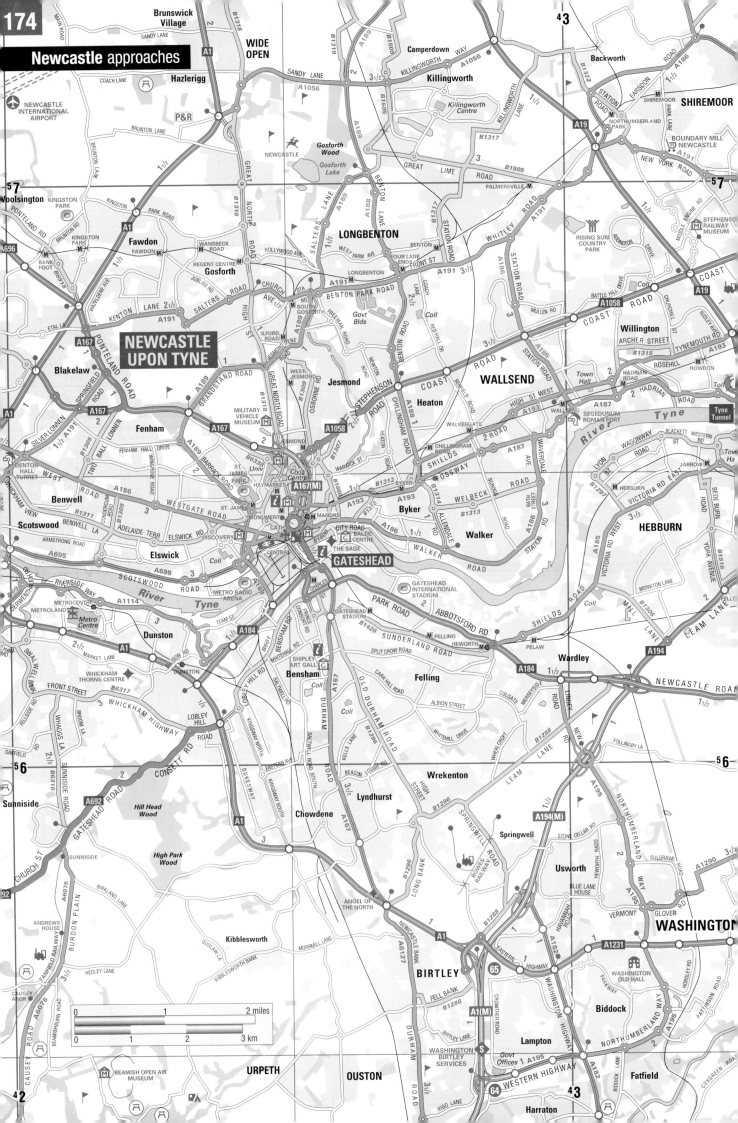

Town plan symbols

	Motorway
	Primary route – dual, single carriageway
	A road – dual, single carriageway
	B road – dual, single carriageway
	Minor through road
	One-way street
	Pedestrian roads
	Shopping streets
	Railway with station
	Tramway with station
	Underground or Metro station
Ⓗ	Hospital
Ⓟ	Parking
	Police, Post Office
	Shopmobility
▲	Youth hostel
	Bus or railway station building
	Shopping precinct or retail park
	Park
	Congestion charge zone

✝	Abbey or cathedral
	Ancient monument
	Aquarium
🅖	Art gallery
	Bird collection or aviary
	Building of interest
	Castle
	Church of interest
	Cinema
	Garden
	Historic ship
	House
	House and garden
Ⓜ	Museum
	Preserved railway
	Roman antiquity
	Safari park
	Theatre
🅘	Tourist information centre
	Zoo
✦	Other place of interest

Aberdeen

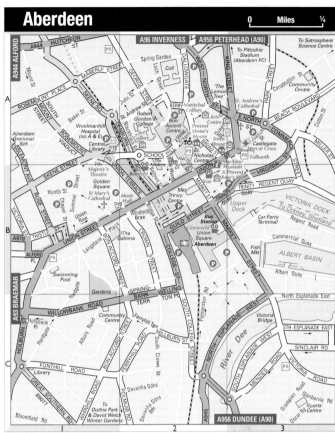

Bath

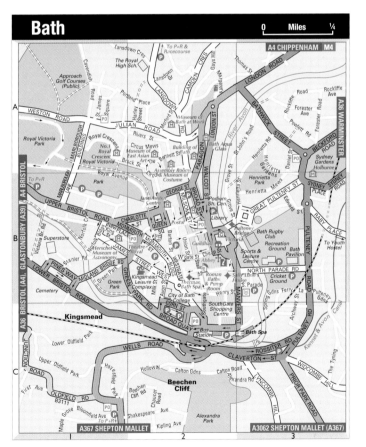

Blackpool

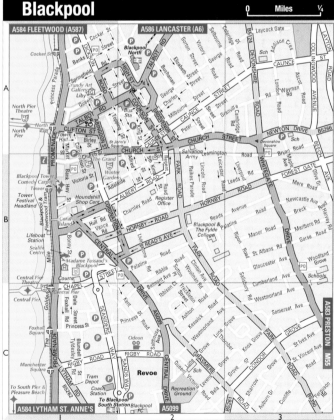

Birmingham

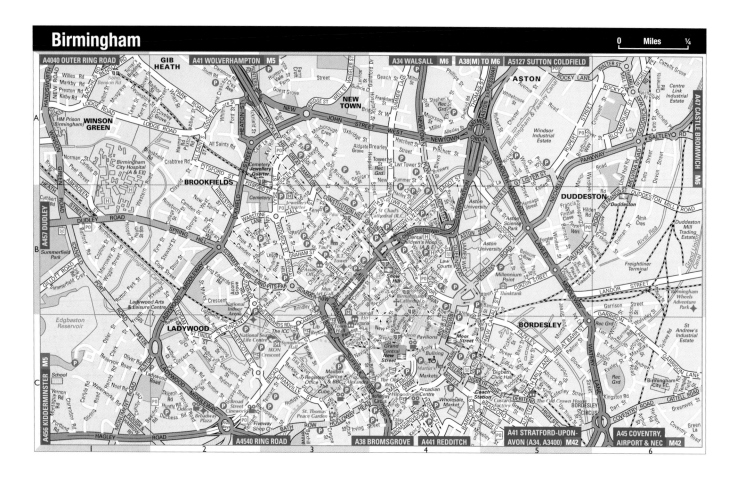

Bournemouth

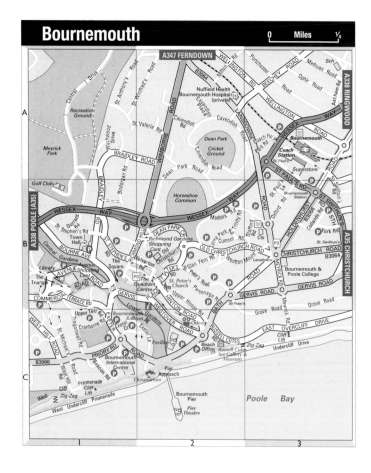

Bradford

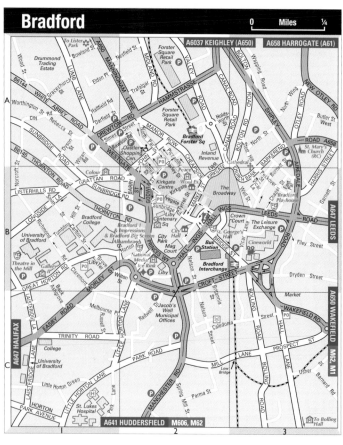

Bristol

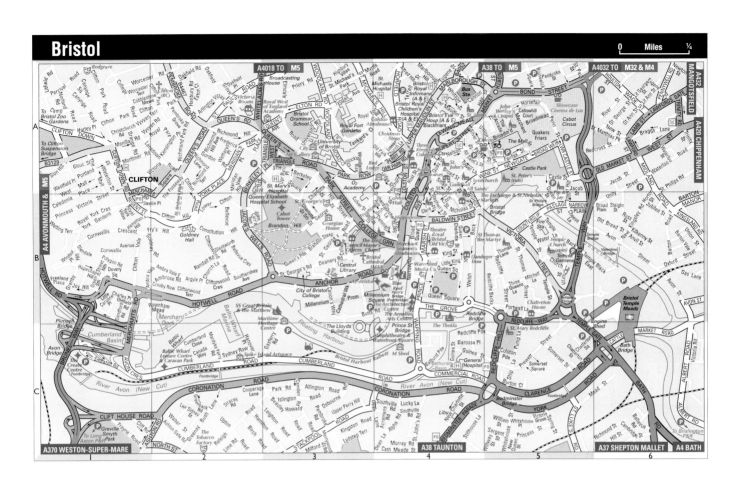

Brighton

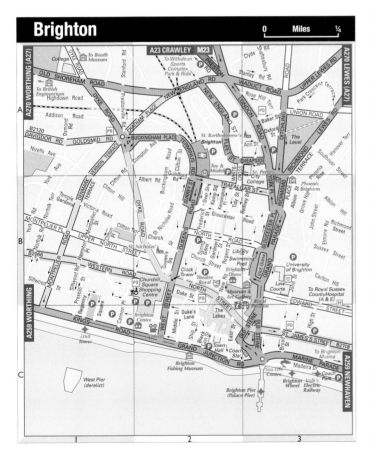

Cambridge

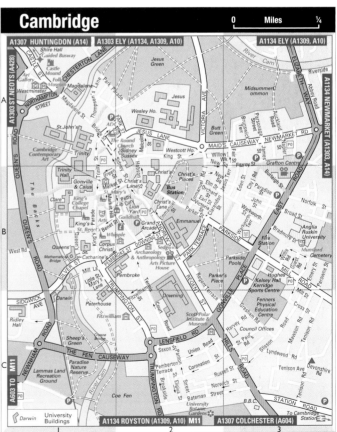

Canterbury

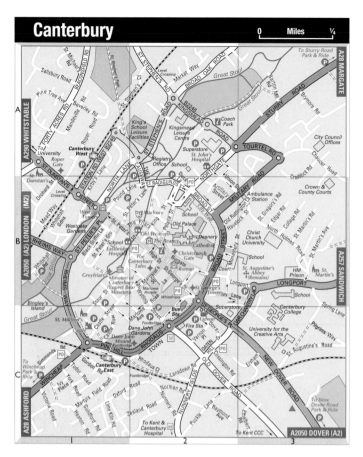

Cardiff / Caerdydd

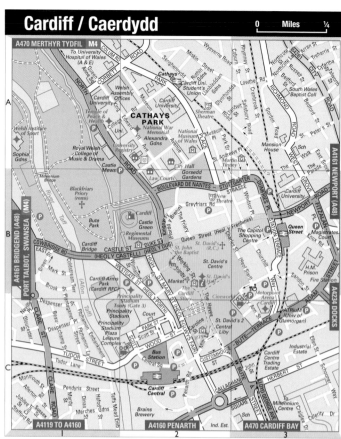

Cheltenham

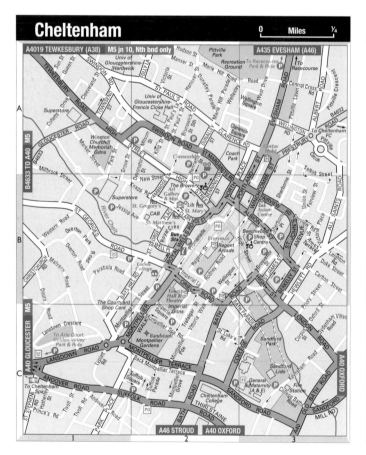

Chester

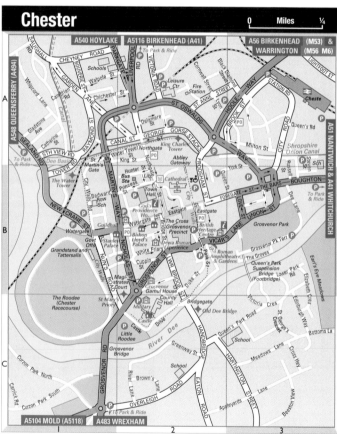

Colchester

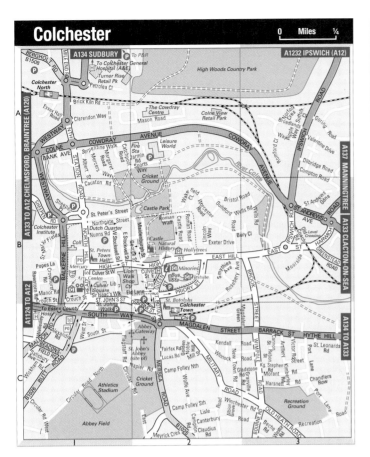

Coventry

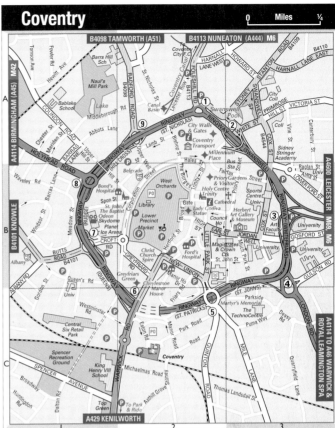

Derby

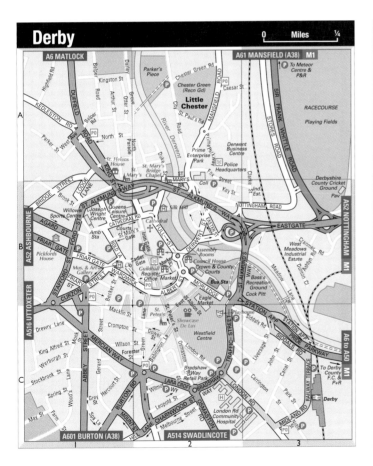

Dundee

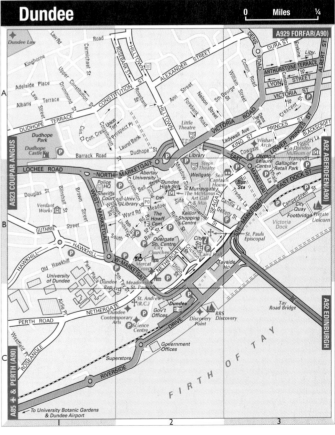

Edinburgh

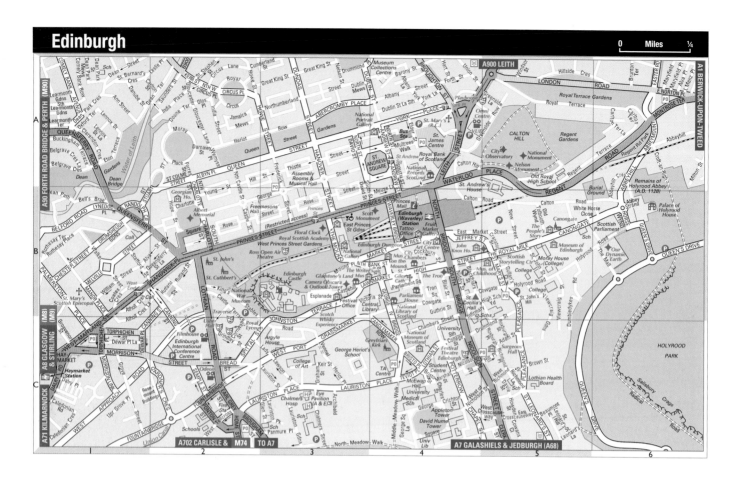

Durham

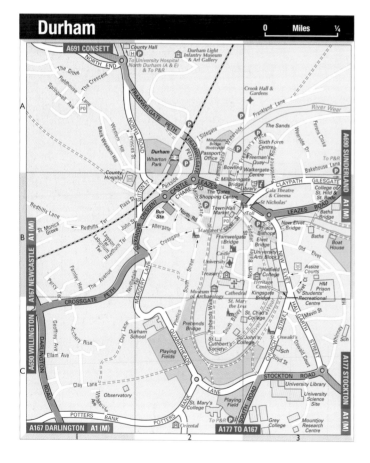

Exeter

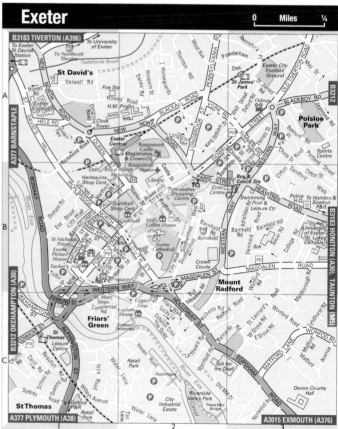

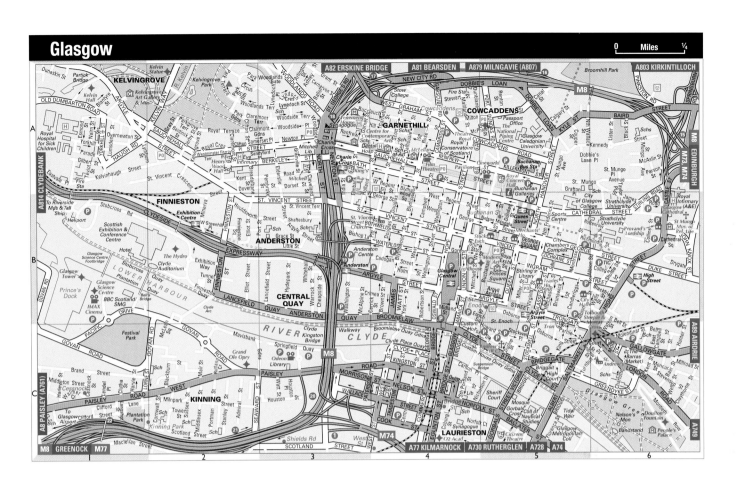

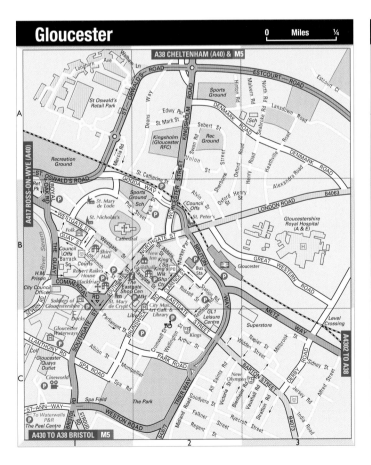

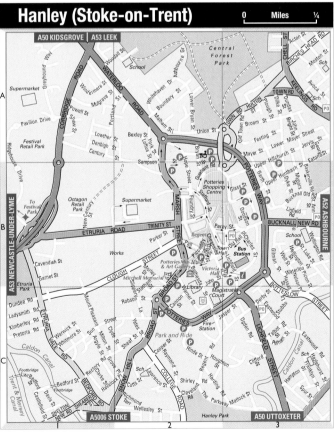

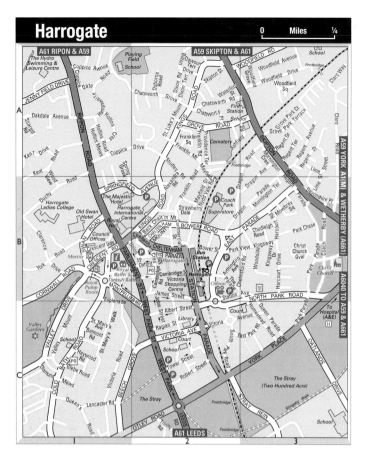

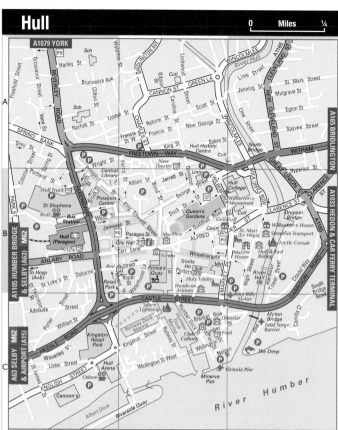

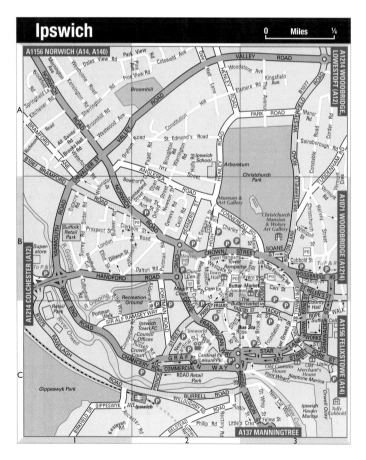

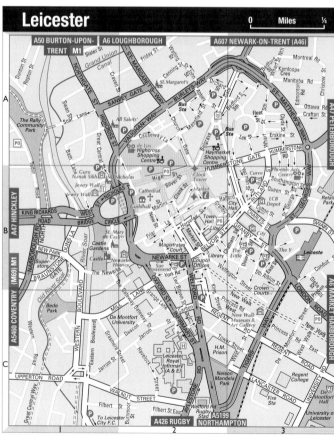

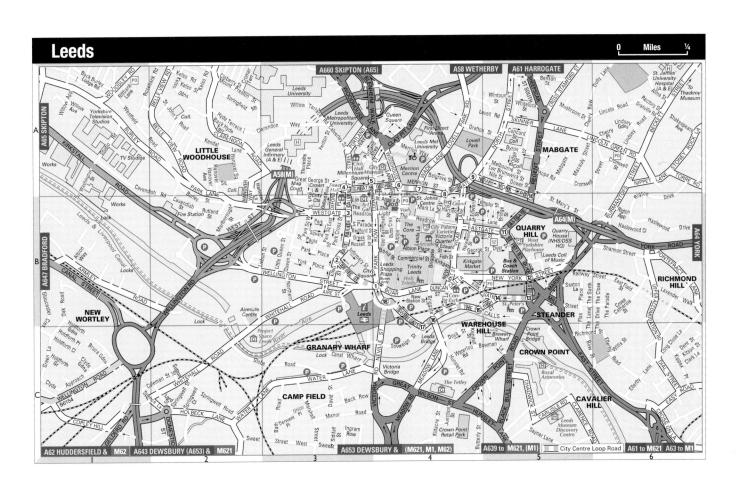

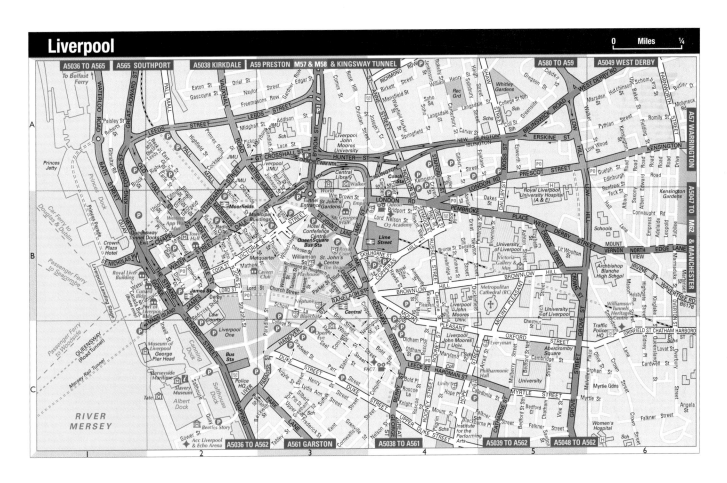

Congestion Charging Zone

London Docklands

0 Miles 1

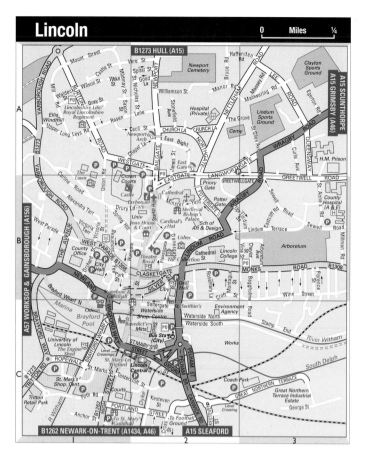

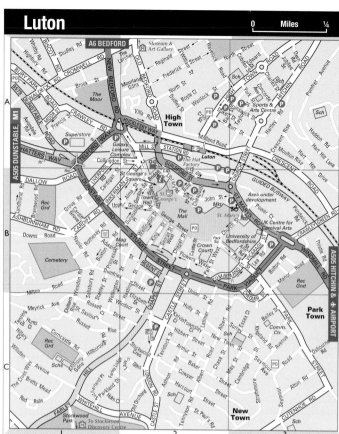

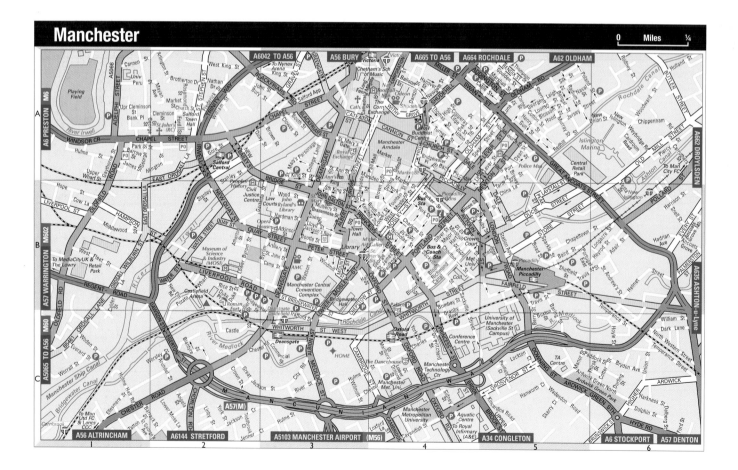

Maidstone

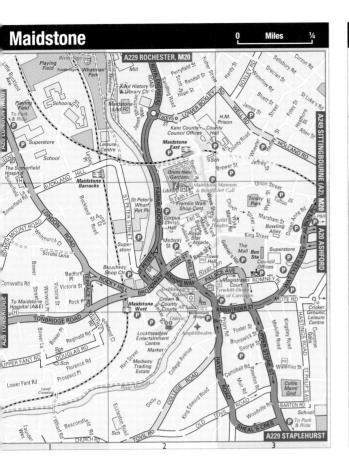

Middlesbrough

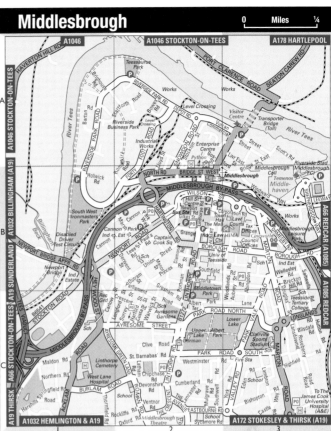

Milton Keynes

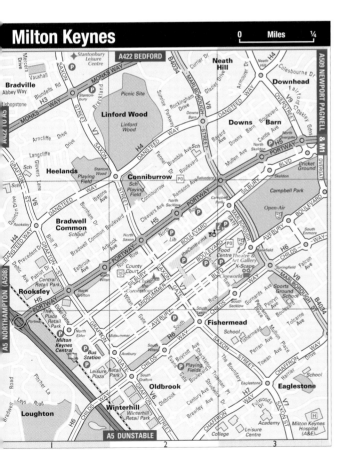

Newcastle upon Tyne

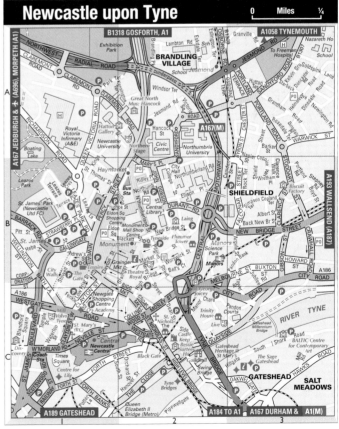

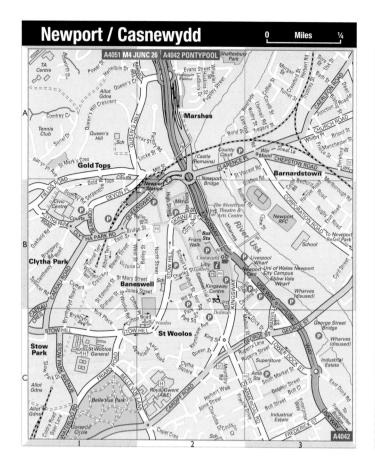

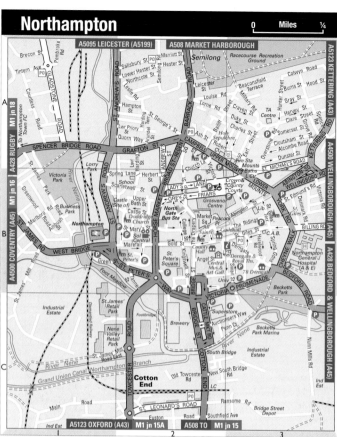

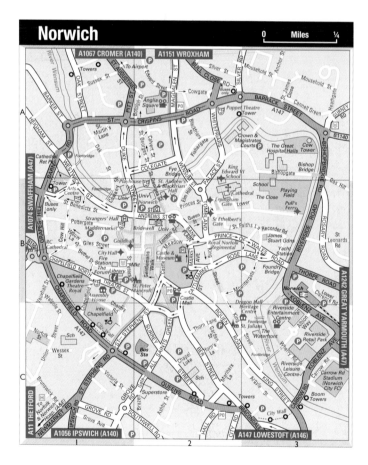

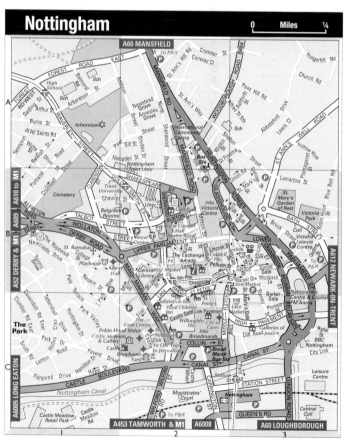

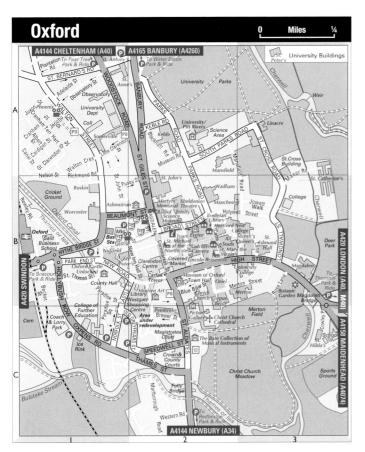

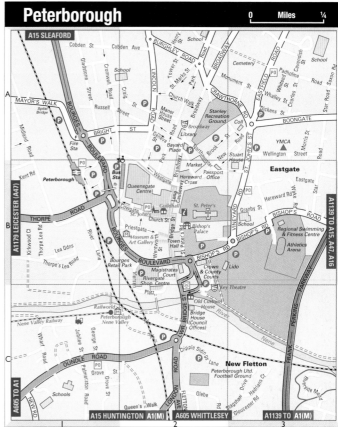

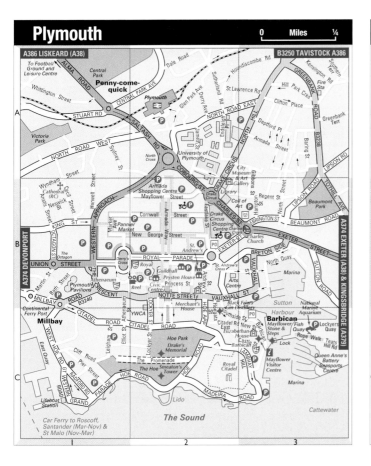

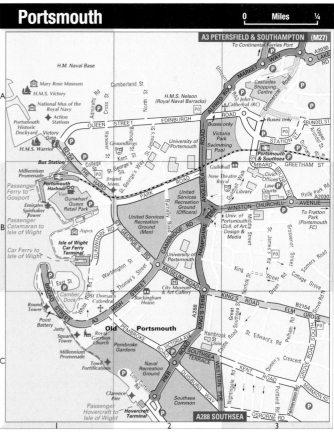

Reading

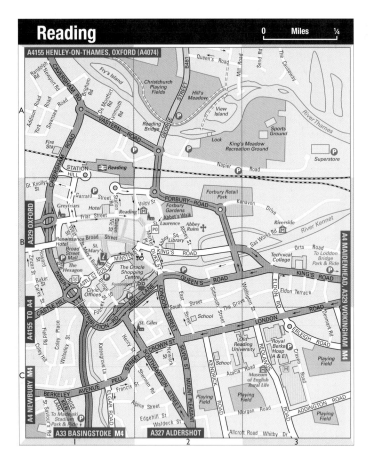

Salisbury

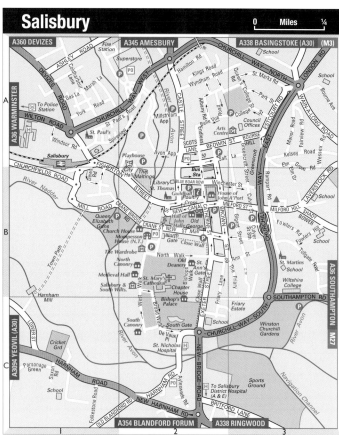

Scarborough

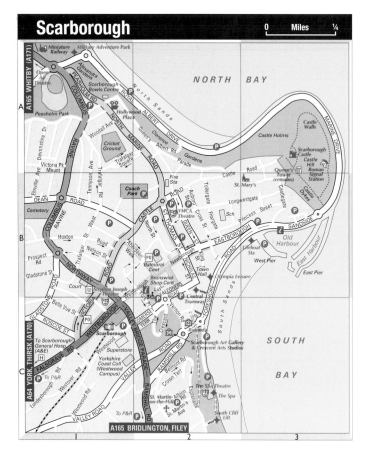

Southampton

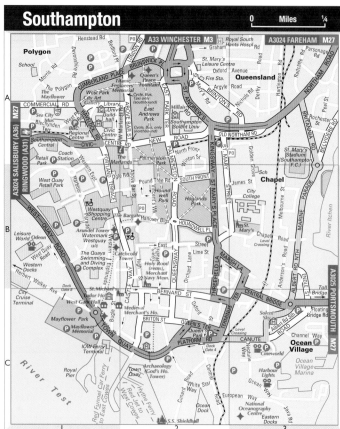

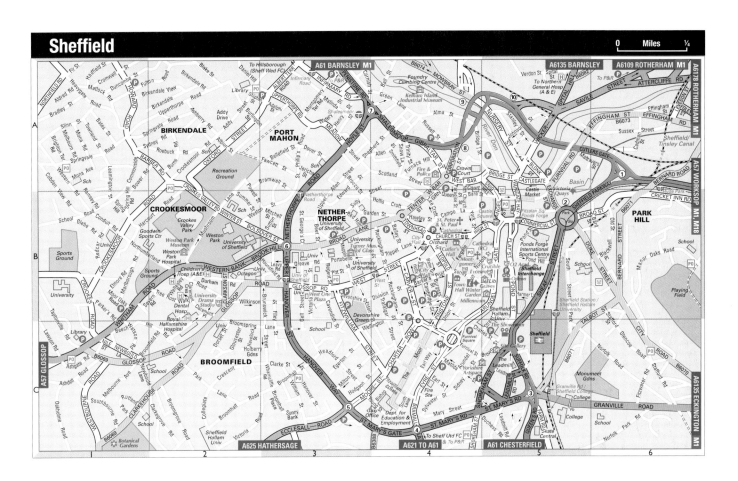

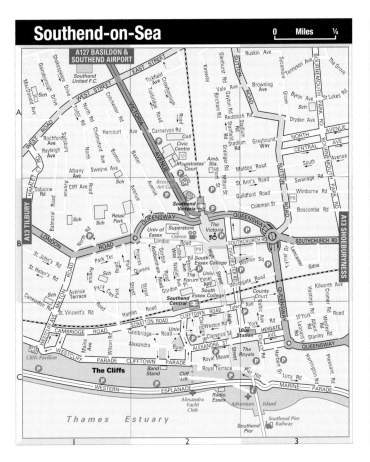

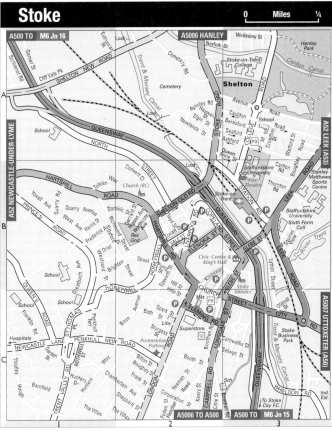

Stratford-upon-Avon

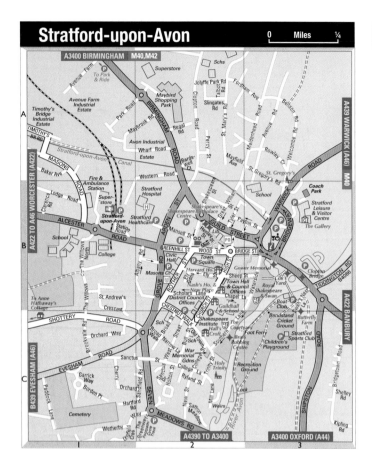

Sunderland

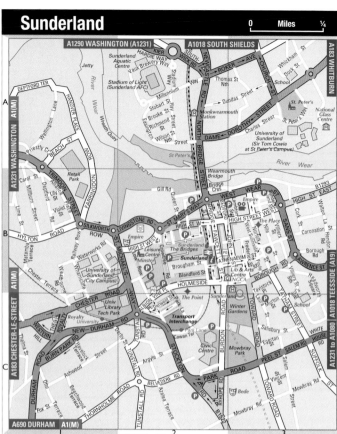

Swansea / Abertawe

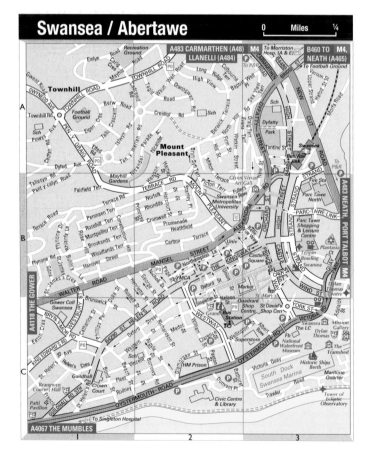

Swindon

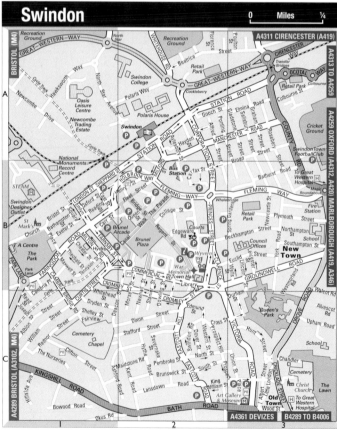

Taunton

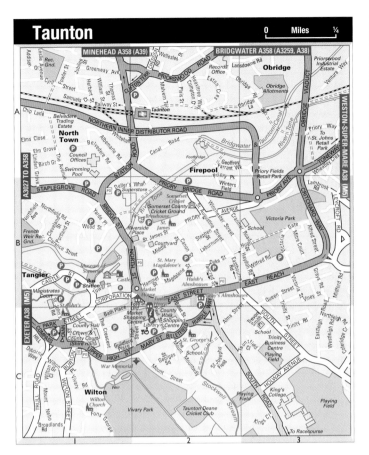

Telford

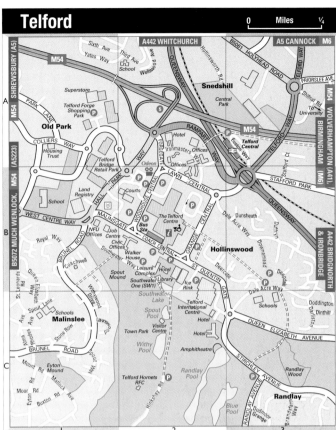

Winchester

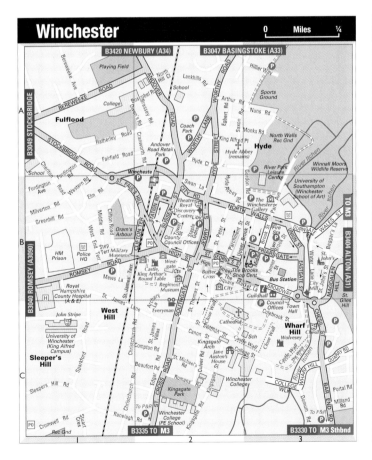

Windsor

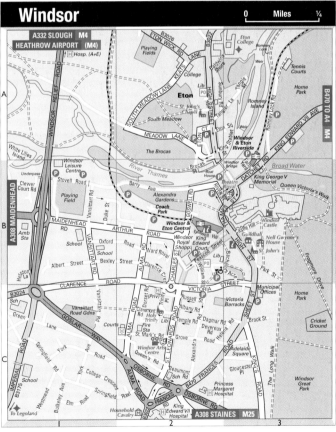

Wolverhampton

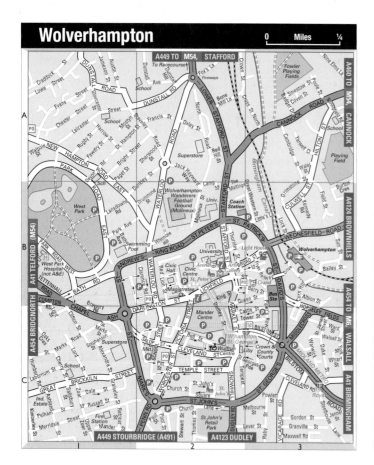

Worcester

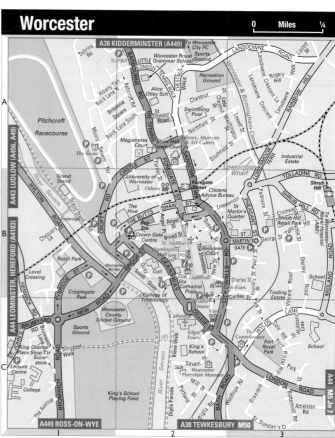

Wrexham

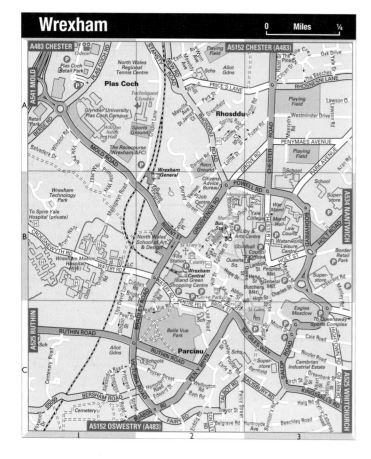

York

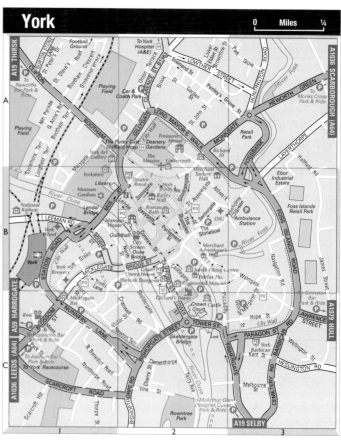

Town plan indexes

Chester • Colchester • Coventry • Derby • Dundee • Durham • Edinburgh 197

St C1
Hall & atre B2
send St A1
gar St C2
St B3
of Gloucestershire ncis Cl Hall) A2
of Gloucestershire rdwick) A1
ria Pl B3
ria St A2
ria Walk C2
l B2
esley Rd A2
ngton Rd A3
ngton Sq A3
ngton St B2
Drive A3
ern Rd B1
hcombe St B3
ton Churchill nl Gardens A1

ster 178

y Gateway A2
eyards La C3
The B3
ward Row B1
ton View C3
op Lloyd's Pal B2
k Diamond St A2
oms La C3
hton B3
erie St A1
ge St B2
gegate C2
sh Heritage tre B2
k St A3
n's La C2
Station B2
orian Rd A1
l St A2
ck Rd C1
e C2
e Dr C2
edral B2
erine St A1
ter A3
ney Rd A1
hester St A1
Rd A3
Walls B1/B2
Walls Rd B1
wall St A2
ty Hall C2
s Hey C3
s, The B2
oin St B2
on Park North C1
on Park South C1
Basin A1
La B3
mere St A2
a Roman erience B2
e St B2
gate B2
gate St B2
n Rd C2
burgh Way C3
beth Cr B3
Station A2
gate St B2
sham St B2
ul House B2
den La A1
rge St A2
stone Ave A1
s Providence use B2
se Stacks A2
nway St C2
venor Bridge C1
venor Mus B2
venor Park B3
venor Park Terr C1
venor Precinct B2
venor St B2
es Rd B3
es, The B3
dhall Museum B1
dbridge C2
ington St C3
le Way A2
ter St B2
rmation Ctr B2
g Charles' wer A2
St A2
ure Centre A2
ary B2
tfoot St A3
e Roodee C2
rpool Rd A2
e St B3
er Bridge St B2
er Park Rd B3
St A2
istrates Court B2
dows La C3
dows, The B3
tary Museum C2
on St A3
Crane St B1
olas St B2
thgate A2
thgate St A2
's Rd B1
Dee Bridge C2
rleigh Rd C2
k St B2
ce Station B2
t Office A2/A3/B2
cess St B2
en St B2
en's Park Rd C3
en's Rd A3
e Course B1
mond St A1
r La C2
nan Amphitheatre Gardens B2
dee, The (Chester cecourse) B1
sell St A3
nne St A2
eorge's Cr C3
artin's Gate A1
artin's Way B1
ary's Priory B2
swalds Way A2
ghall Rd A1
and Rd A1
th View Rd A1

Stanley Palace B1
Station Rd A3
Steven St A3
Tower Rd B1
Town Hall B2
Union St B3
Vicar's La B2
Victoria Cr C3
Victoria Rd A2
Walpole St A1
Water Tower St A1
Water Tower, The B1
Watergate B1
Watergate St B2
Whipcord La A1
White Friars B2
York St B3

Colchester 179

Abbey Gateway C2
Albert St A1
Albion Grove C2
Alexandra Rd C1
Artillery St C3
Arts Centre B1
Balkerne Hill B1
Barrack St C3
Beaconsfield Rd C1
Beche Rd C3
Bergholt Rd A1
Bourne Rd C3
Brick Kiln Rd A1
Bristol Rd B2
Broadlands Way A3
Brook St B3
Bury Cl B2
Bus Sta B2
Butt Rd C1
Camp Folley North C2
Camp Folley South C2
Campion Rd C2
Cannon St C3
Canterbury Rd C2
Castle B2
Castle Park B2
Castle Rd B2
Catchpool Rd A1
Causton Rd B1
Chandlers Row C3
Circular Rd East C2
Circular Rd North C1
Circular Rd West C1
Clarendon Way A1
Claudius Rd C2
Colchester A1
Colchester Camp Abbey Field C1
Colchester Institute B1
Colchester Town C2
Colne Bank Ave A1
Colne View Retail Pk A2
Compton Rd A3
Cowdray Ave A1/A2
Cowdray Ctr, The A2
Crouch St B1
Crowhurst Rd B1
Culver Square Sh Ctr B1
Culver St East B2
Culver St West B1
Dilbridge Rd A3
East Hill B2
East St B3
East Stockwell St B1
Eld La B1
Essex Hall Rd A1
Exeter Dr B2
Fairfax Rd C2
Fire Station A2
Firstsite B2
Flagstaff Rd C1
George St B2
Gladstone Rd C2
Golden Noble Hill C2
Goring Rd A3
Granville Rd C3
Greenstead Rd B3
Guildford Rd B2
Harsnett Rd C3
Harwich Rd B3
Head St B1
High St B1/B2
High Woods Ctry Pk A2
Hollytrees B2
Hythe Hill C3
Information Ctr B2
Ipswich Rd A3
Jarmin Rd A2
Kendall Rd C2
Kimberley Rd C3
King Stephen Rd C3
Leisure World A2
Library B1
Lincoln Way B2
Lion Walk Sh Ctr B1
Lisle Rd C2
Lucas Rd C2
Magdalen Green C3
Magdalen St C2
Maidenburgh St B2
Maldon Rd C1
Manor Rd B1
Margaret Rd A1
Mason Rd A2
Mercers Way A1
Mercury B1
Mersea Rd C2
Meyrick Cr C2
Mile End Rd A1
Military Rd C2
Mill St C2
Minories B2
Moorside B3
Morant Rd C3
Napier Rd C2
Natural History B2
New Town Rd C2
Norfolk Cr A3
North Hill B1
North Station Rd A1
Northgate St B1
Nunns Rd B1
Odeon B1
Old Coach Rd B3
Old Heath Rd C3
Osborne St B2
Petrolea Cl A1
Police Station C1
Popes La B1
Port La C3
Post Office B2/C1
Priory St B2
Queen St B2
Rawstorn Rd B1
Rebon St C3
Recreation Rd C3
Ripple Way A3
Roman Rd B2
Roman Wall B2
Romford Cl A3
Rosebery Ave B2
St Andrews Ave B3
St Andrews Gdns B3
St Botolph St B2
St Botolphs B2
St John's Abbey (site of) C2
St John's St B1
St Johns Walk Sh Ctr B1
St Leonards Rd C3
St Marys Fields B1
St Peter's St B1
St Peters B1
Salisbury Ave C1
Serpentine Walk A1
Sheepen Pl B1
Sheepen Rd B1
Sir Isaac's Walk B1
Smythies Ave B2
South St C1
South Way C1
Sports Way A2
Suffolk Cl A3
Town Hall B1
Turner Rise Retail Pk A1
Valentine Dr A3
Victor Rd C3
Wakefield Cl B2
Wellesley Rd C1
Wells Rd B2/B3
West St C1
West Stockwell St B1
Weston Rd C3
Westway A1
Wickham Rd C1
Wimpole Rd C3
Winchester Rd C2
Winnock Rd C2
Wolfe Ave C2
Worcester Rd B2

Coventry 179

Abbots La A1
Albany B1
Albany Rd B1
Alma St B3
Art Faculty B3
Asthill Grove C2
Bablake School A1
Barras La A1/B1
Barrs Hill School A1
Belgrade B2
Bishop St A2
Bond's Hospital B1
Broad Gate B2
Broadway C1
Burges, The B2
Bus Station A3
Butts Radial B1
Canal Basin A2
Canterbury St A3
Cathedral B3
Central Six Retail Pk C1
Chester St A1
Cheylesmore Manor House B2
Christ Church Spire B2
City Coll A3
City Walls & Gates A2
Corporation St B2
Council House B2
Coundon Rd A1
Coventry Station C2
Coventry Transport Museum A2
Cox St A3
Croft Rd B1
Dalton Rd C1
Deasy Rd C3
Earl St B2
Eaton Rd C2
Fairfax St B2
Foleshill Rd A2
Ford's Hospital B2
Fowler Rd A1
Friars Rd C2
Gordon St C1
Gosford St B3
Greyfriars Green B2
Greyfriars Rd B2
Gulson Rd B3
Hales St A2
Harnall Lane East A3
Harnall Lane West A2
Herbert Art Gallery & Museum B3
Hertford St B2
Hewitt Ave A1
High St B2
Hill St B1
Holy Trinity B2
Holyhead Rd A1
Howard St A3
Huntingdon Rd C1
Information Ctr B2
Jordan Well B3
King Henry VIII School C1
Lady Godiva Statue B2
Lamb St A2
Leicester Row A2
Library B2
Little Park St B2
London Rd C3
Lower Ford St B3
Lower Prec Shop Ctr B2
Magistrates & Crown Courts B2
Manor House Drive B2
Manor Rd C2
Market B2
Martyr's Memorial C2
Meadow St B1
Meriden St A1
Michaelmas Rd C2
Middleborough Rd A1
Mile La C3
Millennium Place A2
Much Park St B3
Naul's Mill Park A1
New Union B2
Odeon B1
Park Rd C2
Parkside C3
Planet Ice Arena B1
Post Office B2/C2
Primrose Hill St A3
Priory Gardens & Visitor Centre B2
Priory St B3
Puma Way C3
Quarryfield La C3
Queen's Rd B1
Quinton Rd C2
Radford Rd A2
Raglan St B3
Ringway (Hill Cross) A1
Ringway (Queens) B1
Ringway (Rudge) B1
Ringway (St Johns) B3
Ringway (St Nicholas) A2
Ringway (St Patricks) C2
Ringway (Swanswell) A2
Ringway (Whitefriars) B3
St John St B2
St John The Baptist B2
St Nicholas St A2
Sidney Stringer Academy A3
Skydome B1
Spencer Ave C1
Spencer Rec Gnd C1
Spon St B1
Sports Centre B3
Stoney Rd C2
Stoney Stanton Rd A3
Swanswell Pool A3
Technocentre, The C3
Thomas Landsdail St C2
Tomson Ave A1
Top Green C1
Trinity St B2
University B3
University Sports Ctr B3
Upper Hill St A1
Upper Well St A2
Victoria St A3
Vine St A3
Warwick Rd C2
Waveley Rd B1
West Orchards Sh Ctr B2
Westminster Rd C1
White St A3
Windsor St B1

Derby 179

Abbey St C1
Agard St B1
Albert St B2
Albion St B2
Ambulance Station B1
Arthur St A1
Ashlyn Rd B3
Assembly Rooms B2
Babington La C2
Becket St B1
Belper Rd A1
Bold La B1
Bradshaw Way C2
Bradshaw Way Ret Pk C2
Bridge St B1
Brook St B1
Burton Rd C1
Bus Station B2
Caesar St A2
Canal St C3
Carrington St C3
Cathedral B2
Cathedral Rd B1
Charnwood St C2
Chester Green Rd A2
City Rd A2
Clarke St A3
Cock Pitt B3
Council House B2
Courts B1
Cranmer Rd B3
Crompton St C1
Crown & County Courts B2
Curzon St B1
Darley Grove A1
Derby C3
Derbyshire County Cricket Ground B3
Derwent Bsns Ctr A2
Derwent St B2
Drewry La C1
Duffield Rd A1
Duke St A2
Dunton Cl B3
Eagle Market C2
East St B2
Eastgate B3
Exeter St B2
Farm St C1
Ford St B1
Forester St C1
Fox St A2
Friar Gate B1
Friary St B1
Full St B2
Gerard St C1
Gower St C2
Green La C2
Grey St C1
Guildhall B2
Harcourt St C1
Highfield Rd A1
Hill La C2
Information Ctr B2
Iron Gate B2
John St C3
Joseph Wright Ctr B1
Kedleston Rd A1
Key St B2
King Alfred St C1
King St A1
Kingston St A1
Lara Croft Way C2
Leopold St C2
Library B1
Liversage St C3
Lodge La B1
London Rd C2
London Rd Community Hospital C2
Macklin St C1
Mansfield Rd A2
Market B2
Market Pl B2
May St C1
Meadow La B3
Melbourne St C2
Mercian Way C1
Midland Rd C3
Monk St C1
Morledge B2
Mount St C1
Mus & Art Gallery B1
Noble St C3
North Parade A1
North St A1
Nottingham Rd B3
Osmaston Rd C2
Otter St A1
Park St C3
Parker St A1
Pickfords House B1
Playhouse C2
Police HQ A2
Police Station B2
Post Office A1/A2/B1/B2/C2/C3
Pride Parkway C3
Prime Enterprise Pk A2
Prime Parkway A2
Queens Leisure Ctr B1
Racecourse A3
Railway Terr C3
Register Office B2
Sadler Gate B1
St Alkmund's Way B1/B2
St Helens House A1
St Mary's A1
St Mary's Bridge A2
St Mary's Bridge Chapel A2
St Mary's Gate B1
St Paul's Rd A2
St Peter's C2
St Peter's St C2
Showcase De Lux C2
Siddals Rd C3
Silk Mill B2
Sir Frank Whittle Rd A3
Spa La C1
Spring St C1
Stafford St B1
Station Approach C3
Stockbrook St C1
Stores Rd A3
Traffic St C2
Wardwick B1
Werburgh St C1
West Ave A1
West Meadows Industrial Estate B3
Westfield Centre C2
Wharf Rd A2
Wilmot St C2
Wilson St C1
Wood's La C1

Dundee 179

Abertay University B2
Adelaide Pl A1
Airlie Pl C1
Albany Terr A1
Albert St A3
Alexander St A2
Ann St A2
Arthurstone Terr A3
Bank St B2
Barrack Rd A1
Barrack St B2
Bell St B2
Blackscroft A3
Blinshall St B1
Brown St B1
Bus Station B3
Caird Hall B2
Camperdown St B3
Candle La B3
Carmichael St A1
City Churches B2
City Quay B3
City Sq B2
Commercial St B2
Constable St A3
Constitution Cres A1
Constitution Ct A1
Constitution St A1/B2
Cotton Rd A3
Courthouse Sq B1
Cowgate A3
Crescent St A3
Crichton St B2
Dens Brae A3
Dens Rd A3
Discovery Point C2
Douglas St B1
Drummond St A1
Dudhope Castle A1
Dudhope St A2
Dudhope Terr A1
Dundee C2
Dundee Contemporary Arts C2
Dundee High School B2
Dundee Law A1
Dundee Repertory C2
Dunhope Park A1
Dura St A3
East Dock St B3
East Marketgait B3
East Whale La B3
Erskine St A3
Euclid Cr B2
Forebank Rd A2
Foundry La A3
Frigate Unicorn B3
Gallagher Retail Park B3
Gellatly St B3
Government Offices C2
Guthrie St B1
Hawkhill B1
Hilltown A2
Howff Cemetery, The B2
Information Ctr B2
Keiller Shopping Ctr B2
Keillor Ctr, The B2
King St A3
Kinghorne Rd A1
Ladywell Ave A3
Laurel Bank A2
Law Rd A1
Law St A1
Library A2/A3
Library and Steps Theatre A2
Little Theatre A2
Lochee Rd B1
Lower Princes St A3
Lyon St A3
McManus Museum & Art Gallery, The B2
Meadow Side B2
Meadowside St Pauls B2
Mercat Cross B2
Murraygate B2
Nelson St A2
Nethergate B2/C1
North Lindsay St B2
North Marketgait B2
Old Hawkhill B1
Olympia Leisure Ctr B3
Overgate Sh Ctr B2
Park Pl B1
Perth Rd C1
Police Station A2/B1
Post Office B2
Princes St A3
Prospect Pl A2
Reform St B2
Riverside Dr C2
Roseangle C1
Rosebank St A2
RRS Discovery C2
St Andrew's C2
St Pauls Episcopal B3
Science Centre C2
Seagate B2
Sheriffs Court B1
Shopmobility B2
South George St A2
South Marketgait B3
South Tay St B2
South Ward Rd B2
Tay Road Bridge C3
Tayside House B2
Trades La B3
Union St B2
Union Terr A1
University Library B2
University of Dundee B1
Upper Constitution St A1
Verdant Works B1
Victoria Dock B3
Victoria Rd A2
Victoria St A3
Ward Rd B1
Wellgate B2
West Bell St B1
West Marketgait B1/B2
Westfield Pl C1
William St A3
Wishart Arch A3

Durham 180

Alexander Cr B2
Allergate B2
Archery Rise C1
Assize Courts B3
Avenue, The B1
Back Western Hill A1
Bakehouse La A3
Baths B3
Baths Bridge B3
Boat House B3
Bowling A2
Boyd St C3
Bus Station B2
Castle B2
Castle Chare B2
Cathedral B2
Church St C3
Clay La C1
Claypath B3
College of St Hild & St Bede B3
County Hall A1
County Hospital B1
Crescent, The A1
Crook Hall & Gardens A3
Crossgate B2
Crossgate Peth C1
Darlington Rd C1
Durham A2
Durham Light Infantry Museum & Arts Gallery A2
Durham School C2
Ellam Ave C1
Elvet Bridge B3
Elvet Court B3
Farnley Hey B1
Ferens Cl A3
Fieldhouse La A1
Flass St B1
Framewelgate Bridge B2
Framwelgate A2
Framwelgate Peth A2
Framwelgate Waterside A2
Frankland La A3
Freeman's Pl A3
Freeman's Quay L Ctr A3
Gala Theatre & Cinema B3
Gates Sh Ctr, The B2
Geoffrey Ave C1
Gilesgate B3
Grey College C3
Grove, The A1
Hallgarth St C3
Hatfield College B3
Hawthorn Terr B1
Heritage Centre B3
HM Prison B3
Information Ctr B3
John St B1
Kingsgate Bridge B3
Laburnum Terr B1
Lawson Terr B1
Leazes Rd B2/B3
Library B2
Margery La B2
Market B2
Mavin St C3
Millburngate B2
Millburngate Bridge B2
Millennium Bridge (foot/cycle) A2
Mountjoy Research Centre C3
Museum of Archaeology B2
Nevilledale Terr B1
New Elvet B3
New Elvet Bridge B3
North Bailey B3
North End A1
North Rd A1/B2
Observatory C1
Old Elvet B3
Oriental Museum C2
Oswald Court C3
Parkside B2
Passport Office A2
Percy Terr B1
Pimlico C2
Police Station B3
Post Office A1/B2
Potters Bank C1/C2
Prebends Bridge C2
Prebends Walk C2
Prince Bishops Sh Ctr B3
Princes St A1
Providence Row A3
Quarryheads La C2
Redhills La B1
Redhills Terr B1
Saddler St B3
St Chad's College C3
St Cuthbert's Society C2
St John's College C2
St Margaret's B2
St Mary The Less C2
St Mary's College C2
St Monica Grove B1
St Nicholas' B3
St Oswald's C3
Sands, The A3
Sixth Form College A3
Sidegate A2
Silver St B2
South Bailey C2
South Rd C3
South St B2
Springwell Ave A1
Stockton Rd C3
Students' Rec Ctr B3
Sutton St B2
Town Hall B2
Treasury Museum B2
University B2
University Arts Block B3
University Library C3
Univ Science Site C3
Walkergate Centre A3
Wearside Dr A3
Western Hill A1
Wharton Park A2
Whinney Hill C3
Whitehouse Ave C1

Edinburgh 180

Abbey Strand B6
Abbeyhill A6
Abbeyhill Cr B6
Abbeymount A6
Abercromby Pl A3
Adam St C5
Albany La A4
Albany St A4
Albert Memorial B2
Albyn Pl A2
Alva Pl A6
Alva St B1
Ann St A1
Appleton Tower C4
Archibald Pl C3
Argyle House C3
Assembly Rooms & Musical Hall A3
Atholl Cr B1
Atholl Crescent La C1
Bank St B4
Barony St A4
Beaumont Pl C5
Belford Rd B1
Belgrave Cr A1
Belgrave Crescent La A1
Bell's Brae B1
Blackfriars St B4
Blair St B4
Bread St C2
Bristo Pl C4
Bristo St C4
Brougham St C2
Broughton St A4
Brown St C5
Brunton Terr A6
Buckingham Terr A1
Burial Ground A6
Bus Station A4
Caledonian Cr C1
Caledonian Rd C1
Calton Hill A4
Calton Hill A5
Calton Rd B4
Camera Obscura & Outlook Tower B3
Candlemaker Row C4
Canning St B2
Canongate B5
Canongate B5
Carlton St A1
Carlton Terr A6
Carlton Terrace La A6
Castle St B2
Castle Terr B2
Castlehill B3
Central Library B4
Chalmers Hospital C3
Chalmers St C3
Chambers St C4
Chapel St C4
Charles St C4
Charlotte Sq B2
Chester St B1
Circus La A2
Circus Pl A2
City Art Centre B4
City Chambers B4
City Observatory A5
Clarendon Cr A1
Clerk St C5
Coates Cr B1
Cockburn St B4
College of Art C3
Comely Bank Ave A1
Comely Bank Row A1
Cornwall St C2
Cowans Cl C5
Cowgate B4
Cranston St B5
Crichton St C4
Croft-An-Righ A6
Cumberland St A2
Dalry Pl C1
Dalry Rd C1
Danube St A1
Darnawy St A2
David Hume Tower C4
Davie St C5
Dean Bridge A1
Dean Gdns A1
Dean Park Cr A1
Dean Park Mews A1
Dean Park St A1
Dean Path B1
Dean St A1
Dean Terr A1
Dewar Pl C1
Dewar Place La C1
Doune Terr A2
Drummond Pl A3
Drummond St C5
Drumsheugh Gdns B1
Dublin Mews A3
Dublin St A4
Dublin St La South A4
Dumbiedykes Rd B5
Dundas St A3
Earl Grey St C2
East Crosscauseway C5
East Market St B4
East Norton Pl A6
East Princes St Gdns B3
Easter Rd A6
Edinburgh (Waverley) B4
Edinburgh Castle B3
Edinburgh Dungeon B4
Edinburgh Int Conference Ctr C2
Elder St A4
Esplanade B3
Eton Terr A1
Eye Pavilion C3
Festival Office B3
Festival Theatre Edinburgh C4
Filmhouse C2
Fire Station C2
Floral Clock B3
Forres St A2
Forth St A4
Fountainbridge C2
Frederick St A3
Freemasons' Hall B3
Fruit Market B4
Gardner's Cr C2
George Heriot's School C3
George IV Bridge B4
George Sq C4
George Sq La C4
George St B3
Georgian House B2
Gladstone's Land B3
Glen St C3
Gloucester La A2
Gloucester Pl A2
Gloucester St A2
Graham St C3
Grassmarket C3
Great King St A3
Great Stuart B1
Greenside La A5
Greenside Row A5
Greyfriars Kirk C4
Grindlay St C2
Grosvenor St C1
Grove St C1
Gullan's Cl B5
Guthrie St B4
Hanover St A3
Hart St A4
Haymarket C1
Haymarket Sta C1
Heriot Pl C3
Heriot Row A2
High School Yard B5
High St B4
Hill Pl C5
Hill St A2
Hillside Cr A5
Holyrood Abbey (remains of) A6
Holyrood Park C6
Holyrood Rd B5
Home St C2
Hope St B2
Horse Wynd B6
Howden St C5
Howe St A2
India Pl A2
India St A2
Infirmary St B4
Information Ctr B4
Jamaica Mews A2
Jeffrey St B4
John Knox House B4
Johnston Terr C3
Keir St C3
Kerr St A2
King's Stables Rd B2
Lady Lawson St C3
Lauriston Gdns C3
Lauriston Park C3
Lauriston Pl C3
Lauriston St C3
Lawnmarket B3
Learmonth Gdns A1
Learmonth Terr A1
Leith St A4
Lennox St A1
Lennox St La A1
Leslie Pl A2
London Rd A5
Lothian Health Board C5
Lothian Rd B2
Lothian St C4
Lower Menz Pl A6
Lynedoch Pl B1
Mall, The B6
Manor Pl B1
Market St B4
Marshall St C4
Maryfield A6
Maryfield Pl A6
McEwan Hall C4
Medical School C4
Melville St B1
Meuse La B4
Middle Meadow Walk C4
Milton St A6
Montrose Terr A6
Moray House (Coll) B5
Moray Place A2
Morrison Link C1
Morrison St C1
Mound Pl B3
Mound, The B3
Multrees Walk A4
Mus Collections Ctr A4
Museum of Childhood B5
Museum of Edinburgh B5
Museum on the Mound B4
National Museum of Scotland C4
National Gallery B3
National Library of Scotland B4
National Monument A5
National Portrait Gallery B4
National Records Scotland A4
Nelson Monument A5
Nelson St A3
New St B5
Nicolson Sq C4
Nicolson St C4
Niddry St B4
North Bank St B3
North Bridge B4
North Castle St A2
North Charlotte St A2
North Meadow Walk C3
North St Andrew St A4
North St David St A3
North West Circus Pl A2
Northumberland St A3
Odeon C2
Old Royal High School A5
Old Tolbooth Wynd B5
Omni Centre A4
Our Dynamic Earth B6
Oxford Terr A1
Palace of Holyrood House B6
Palmerston Pl B1
Panmure Pl C3
Parliament House B4
Parliament Sq B4
People's Story, The B5
Playhouse Theatre A4
Pleasance C5
Police Station A4
Ponton St C2
Post Office A3/A4/B5/C1/C2/C4/C5
Potterrow C4
Princes Mall B4
Princes St B3
Princes St B3
Queen St A2
Queen Street Gdns A3
Queen's Dr B6/C6
Queensferry Rd A1
Queensferry St B1
Queensferry St La B2
Radical Rd C6
Randolph Cr B1
Regent Gdns A5
Regent Rd B5
Regent Rd Park A6
Regent Terr A5
Richmond La C5
Richmond Pl C5
Rose St B2
Rosemount Bldgs C1
Ross Open Air Theatre B3
Rothesay Pl B1
Rothesay Terr B1
Roxburgh Pl C5
Roxburgh St C5
Royal Bank of Scotland A4
Royal Circus A2
Royal Lyceum C2
Royal Mile, The B5
Royal Scottish Academy B3
Royal Terr A5
Royal Terrace Gdns A5
Rutland Sq B2
Rutland St B2
St Andrew Sq A4
St Andrew Sq A4
St Andrew's House A4
St Bernard's Cr A1
St Cecilia's Hall B4
St Colme St A2
St Cuthbert's B2
St Giles' B4
St James Centre A4
St John St B5
St John's B2
St John's Hill B5
St Leonard's Hill C5
St Leonard's La C5
St Leonard's St C5
St Mary's
St Mary's Scottish Episcopal B1
St Mary's St B5
St Stephen St A2
Salisbury Crags C6
Saunders St A2
Scotch Whisky Experience B3
Scott Monument B4
Scottish Parliament B6
Scottish Storytelling Centre B5
Semple St C2
Shandwick Pl B2
South Bridge B4
South Charlotte St B2
South College St C4
South Learmonth Gdns A1
South St Andrew St A4
South St David St A3
Spittal St C2
Stafford St B1
Student Centre C4
Surgeons' Hall C5
TA Centre C4
Tattoo Office B4
Teviot Pl C4
Thistle St A3
Torphichen Pl C1
Torphichen St C1
Traverse Theatre B2
Tron Sq B4
Tron, The B4
Union St A4
University C4
University Library C4
Upper Grove Pl C1
Usher Hall C2
Vennel C3
Victoria St B3
Viewcraig Gdns B5
Viewcraig St B5
VUE A4
Walker St B1
Waterloo Pl A4
Waverley Bridge B4
Wemyss Pl A2
West Approach Rd C1
West Crosscauseway C5
West End B1
West Maitland St C1
West of Nicholson St C4
West Port C3
West Princes St Gdns B3
West Richmond St C5
West Tollcross C2
White Horse Cl B5
William St B1
Windsor St A5
Writer's Mus, The B4
York La A4
York Pl A4
York Pl A4
Young St B2

202 Oxford • Peterborough • Plymouth • Portsmouth • Reading • Salisbury • Scarborough • Sheffield

Burton St B2
Bus Station A2
Canal St C2
Carlton St B3
Carrington St C2
Castle C2
Castle Blvd C1
Castle Gate C2
Castle Meadow Rd C1
Castle Mdw Retail Pk C1
Castle Museum & Gallery C2
Castle Rd C2
Castle Wharf C2
Cavendish Rd East C1
Cemetery B1
Chaucer St B1
Cheapside B2
Church Rd A3
City Link C3
City of Caves C2
Clarendon St B1
Cliff Rd C3
Clumber Rd East C1
Clumber St B2
College St B1
Collin St C2
Conway Cl A2
Council House B2
Cranbrook St B3
Cranmer St A2
Cromwell St B1
Curzon St B3
Derby Rd B1
Dryden St A2
Exchange Ctr, The B2
Fishpond Dr C1
Fletcher Gate B3
Forest Rd East A1
Forest Rd West A1
Friar La C2
Galleries of Justice C3
Gedling Gr A1
Gedling St B3
George St B3
Gill St A2
Glasshouse St B2
Goldsmith St B2
Goose Gate B3
Great Freeman St A2
Guildhall B2
Hamilton Dr C1
Hampden St A1
Heathcote St B3
High Pavement C3
High School A1
Holles Cr C1
Hope Dr C1
Hungerhill Rd A3
Huntingdon Dr C1
Huntingdon St A2
Information Ctr B2
Instow Rise A3
Int Com Ctr A2
intu Broadmarsh C2
intu Victoria Centre B2
Kent St B3
King St B2
Lace Centre, The C2
Lace Market B3
Lace Mkt Theatre C3
Lamartine St B3
Leisure Ctr C3
Lenton Rd C1
Lewis Cl A3
Lincoln St B2
London Rd C3
Long Row B2
Low Pavement C2
Lower Parliament St B3
Magistrates' Court C2
Maid Marian Way B2
Mansfield Rd A2/B2
Middle Hill C2
Milton St B2
Mount St B2
National Ice Centre C3
Newcastle Dr B1
Newstead Gr A2
North Sherwood St A2
Nottingham Arena C3
Nottingham Sta C3
Nottingham Trent University A2/B2
Old Market Sq B2
Oliver St A1
Park Dr C1
Park Row C1
Park Terr B1
Park Valley C1
Park, The C1
Peas Hill Rd A3
Peel St A1
Pelham St B2
Peveril Dr C1
Plantagenet St A3
Playhouse Theatre B1
Plumptre St C3
Police Station B1/B2
Poplar St C3
Portland Rd B1
Post Office B2
Queen's Rd C3
Raleigh St A1
Regent St B1
Rick St B3
Robin Hood St B3
Robin Hood Statue C2
Ropewalk, The B1
Royal Centre B2
Royal Children Inn C2
Royal Concert Hall B2
St Ann's Hill Rd A2
St Ann's Way A2
St Ann's Well Rd A3
St Barnabas B1
St James' St B2
St Mark's St B3
St Mary's Gdn of Rest B3
St Mary's Gate B3
St Nicholas C2
St Peter's C2
St Peter's Gate B2
Salutation Inn C2
Shakespeare St B2
Shelton St A2
Shopmobility A2
South Pde B2
South Rd C1
South Sherwood St B2
Station St C3
Station Street C3
Stoney St B3
Talbot St B1
Tattershall Dr C1
Tennis Dr B1

Tennyson St A1
Theatre Royal B2
Trent St C3
Trent University B2
Union Rd B3
Upper Parliament St B2
Victoria Leisure Ctr B3
Victoria Park B3
Victoria St B2
Walter St A1
Warser Gate B3
Watkin St A2
Waverley St A1
Wheeler Gate B2
Wilford Rd C2
Wilford St C2
Willoughby House C2
Wollaton St B1
Woodborough Rd A2
Woolpack La B3
Ye Old Trip to Jerusalem C2
York St A2

Oxford 189
Adelaide St A1
Albert St A1
All Souls (Coll) B2
Ashmolean Mus B2
Balliol (Coll) B2
Banbury Rd A2
Bate Collection of Musical Instruments C2
Beaumont St B1
Becket St B1
Blackhall Rd A2
Blue Boar St B2
Bodleian Library B2
Botanic Garden B3
Brasenose (Coll) B2
Brewer St C2
Broad St B2
Burton-Taylor Theatre B2
Bus Station B1
Canal St A1
Cardigan St A1
Carfax Tower B2
Castle B1
Castle St B1
Catte St B2
Cemetery C1
Christ Church (Coll) B2
Christ Church Cath C2
Christ Church Mdw C2
Clarendon Centre B2
Coach & Lorry Park C1
College B3
Coll of Further Ed C1
Cornmarket St B2
Corpus Christi (Coll) B2
County Hall B1
Covered Market B2
Cowley Pl C3
Cranham St A1
Cranham Terr A1
Cricket Ground B1
Crown & County Courts C2
Deer Park B3
Exeter (Coll) B2
Folly Bridge C2
George St B1
Great Clarendon St A1
Hart St A1
Hertford (Coll) B2
High St B3
Hollybush Row B1
Holywell St B2
Hythe Bridge St B1
Ice Rink C1
Information Ctr B2
Jericho St A1
Jesus (Coll) B2
Jowett Walk B3
Juxon St A1
Keble (Coll) A2
Keble Rd A2
Library B2
Linacre (Coll) A3
Lincoln (Coll) B2
Little Clarendon St A1
Longwall St B3
Magdalen (Coll) B3
Magdalen Bridge B2
Magdalen St B2
Magistrate's Court C2
Manchester (Coll) B2
Manor Rd B3
Mansfield (Coll) A2
Mansfield Rd A3
Market B1
Marlborough Rd C2
Martyrs' Memorial B2
Merton (Coll) B3
Merton Field B3
Merton St B2
Mus of Modern Art B2
Museum of Oxford B2
Museum Rd A2
New College (Coll) B3
New Inn Hall St B2
New Rd B1
New Theatre B2
Norfolk St C1
Nuffield (Coll) B1
Observatory A1
Observatory St A1
Odeon B1/B2
Old Fire Station B1
Old Greyfriars St C2
Oriel (Coll) B2
Oxford Station B1
Oxford Story, The B2
Oxford University Research Centres A1
Oxpens Rd C1
Paradise Sq C1
Paradise St B1
Park End St B1
Parks Rd A2/B2
Pembroke (Coll) C2
Phoenix A1
Picture Gallery C2
Plantation Rd A1
Playhouse B2
Police Station C2
Post Office A1/B2
Pusey St B1
Queen's (Coll) B3
Queen's La B3
Radcliffe Camera B2
Rewley Rd B1
Richmond Rd A1
Rose La B3

Ruskin (Coll) B1
Saïd Business School B1
St Aldates C2
St Anne's (Coll) A1
St Antony's (Coll) A1
St Bernard's Rd A1
St Catherine's (Coll) B3
St Cross Building A3
St Cross Rd A3
St Edmund Hall (Coll) B3
St Giles St A2
St Hilda's (Coll) C3
St John St B2
St John's (Coll) B2
St Mary the Virgin B2
St Michael at the Northgate B2
St Peter's (Coll) B1
St Thomas St B1
Science Area A2
Science Museum B2
Sheldonian Theatre B2
Somerville (Coll) A1
South Parks Rd A2
Speedwell St C2
Sports Ground C3
Thames St C2
Town Hall B2
Trinity (Coll) B2
Turl St B2
University Coll (Coll) B3
Univ Mus & Pitt Rivers Mus A2
University Parks A2
Wadham (Coll) B2
Walton Cr A1
Walton St A1
Western Rd C2
Westgate Sh Ctr B2
Woodstock Rd A1
Worcester (Coll) B1

Peterborough 189
Athletics Arena B3
Bishop's Palace B2
Bishop's Rd B2/B3
Boongate A3
Bourges Boulevard A1
Bourges Retail Pk B1/B2
Bridge House (Council Offices) C2
Bridge St B2
Bright St A1
Broadway A2
Broadway A2
Brook St A2
Burghley Rd A2
Bus Station B2
Cavendish St A3
Charles St A3
Church St B2
Church Walk A2
Cobden Ave A1
Cobden St A1
Cowgate B2
Craig St A2
Crawthorne Rd A2
Cripple Sidings La C2
Cromwell Rd A1
Dickens St A3
Eastfield Rd A3
Eastgate B3
Fire Station A1
Fletton Ave C2
Frank Perkins Parkway C3
Geneva St A2
George St C1
Gladstone St A1
Glebe Rd C2
Gloucester Rd C3
Granby St B3
Grove St C1
Guildhall B2
Hadrians Ct C3
Henry St A2
Hereward Cross (Sh) B2
Hereward Rd B3
Information Ctr B2
Jubilee St C1
Kent Rd B1
Key Theatre C2
Kirkwood Cl B1
Lea Gdns B1
Library A2
Lincoln Rd A2
London Rd C2
Long Causeway B2
Lower Bridge St C2
Magistrates Court B2
Manor House St A2
Mayor's Walk A1
Midland Rd A1
Monument St A2
Morris St A3
Mus & Art Gallery B2
Nene Valley Railway C1
New Rd A2
New Rd C1
Northminster A2
Old Customs Ho C2
Oundle Rd C1
Padholme Rd A3
Palmerston Rd C1
Park Rd A2
Passport Office B2
Peterborough Nene Valley C1
Peterborough Sta B1
Peterborough United FC C2
Police Station B2
Post Office A3/B1/B2/B3/C1
Priestgate B2
Queen's Walk C2
Queensgate Centre B2
Railworld C1
Regional Swimming & Fitness Centre B3
River La B1
Rivergate Sh Ctr B2
Riverside Mead C3
Russell St A1
St John's B2
St John's St A3
St Marks St A2
St Peter's B2
St Peter's Rd B2
Saxon Rd A3
Spital Bridge A1
Stagshaw Dr C3
Star Rd B3
Thorpe Lea Rd B1

Thorpe Rd B1
Thorpe's Lea Rd B1
Tower St A2
Town Hall B2
Viersen Platz B2
Vineyard Rd B3
Wake Rd B3
Wellington St A3
Wentworth St B2
Westgate B2
Whalley St A3
Wharf Rd C1
Whitsed St A3
YMCA A3

Plymouth 189
Alma Rd A1
Anstis St B1
Armada Shop Ctr B2
Armada St A3
Armada Way B2
Arts Centre B2
Athenaeum St C1
Athenaeum B1
Barbican C3
Barbican C3
Baring St A3
Bath St B1
Beaumont Park B3
Beaumont Rd B3
Black Friars Gin Distillery C2
Breton Side B3
Castle St C3
Cathedral (RC) B1
Cecil St B1
Central Park A1
Central Park Ave A2
Charles Church B3
Charles Cross B3
Charles St B2
Citadel Rd C2
Citadel Rd East C2
City Museum & Art Gallery B2
Civic Centre B2
Cliff Rd C1
Clifton Pl A3
Cobourg St A2
College of Art B2
Continental Ferry Port B1
Cornwall St B2
Crescent, The B1
Dale Rd A2
Deptford Pl A3
Derry Ave A2
Derry's Cross B1
Drake Circus B2
Drake Cir Sh Ctr B2
Drake's Memorial C2
Eastlake St B2
Ebrington St B3
Elizabethan House C3
Elliot St C1
Endsleigh Pl A2
Exeter St B3
Fire Station A3
Fish Quay C3
Gibbons St A3
Glen Park Ave A2
Grand Pde C1
Great Western Rd C1
Greenbank Rd A3
Greenbank Terr A3
Guildhall B2
Hampton St B3
Harwell St B1
Hill Park Cr A3
Hoe Approach B2
Hoe Rd C2
Hoe, The C2
Hoegate St C2
Houndiscombe Rd A2
Information Ctr C3
James St A2
Kensington Rd A3
King St B1
Lambhay Hill C3
Leigham St C1
Library B2
Lipson Rd A3/B3
Lockyer St C2
Lockyers Quay C3
Madeira Rd C2
Marina B3
Market Ave B1
Martin St B1
Mayflower St B2
Mayflower Stone & Steps C3
Mayflower Visitor Centre C3
Merchant's House B2
Millbay Rd B1
National Marine Aquarium C3
Neswick St B1
New George St B2
New St C3
North Cross A2
North Hill A3
North Quay B2
North Rd East A2
North Rd West A1
North St B3
Notte St B2
Octagon, The B1
Octagon St B1
Pannier Market B1
Pennycomequick A1
Pier St C1
Plymouth Pavilions B1
Plymouth Station A2
Police Station B3
Post Office C2
Princess St B2
Promenade, The C2
Prysten House B2
Queen Anne's Battery Seasports Centre C3
Radford Rd C1
Reel B2
Regent St B3
Rope Walk C3
Royal Citadel C2
Royal Pde B2
Royal Theatre B2
St Andrew's B2
St Andrew's Cross B2
St Andrew's St B2
St Lawrence Rd A2
Saltash Rd A2
Shopmobility B2
Smeaton's Tower C2
Southern Terr A3

Southside St C2
Stuart Rd A1
Sutherland Rd A2
Sutton Rd B3
Sydney St A1
Teats Hill Rd C3
Tothill Ave B3
Union St B1
Univ of Plymouth A2
Vauxhall St B2/3
Victoria Park A1
West Hoe Rd C1
Western Approach B1
Whittington St A1
Wyndham St B1
YMCA B2
YWCA C2

Portsmouth 189
Action Stations C1
Admiralty Rd A1
Alfred Rd A2
Anglesea Rd B2
Arundel St B3
Aspex B1
Bishop St A2
Broad St C1
Buckingham Ho C2
Burnaby Rd B2
Bus Station B1
Camber Dock C1
Cambridge Rd B2
Car Ferry to Isle of Wight B1
Cascades Sh Ctr A3
Castle Rd C3
City Museum & Art Gallery B2
Civic Offices B3
Clarence Pier C2
College St B1
Commercial Rd A3
Cottage Gr B3
Cross St A1
Cumberland St A2
Duisburg Way C2
Durham St A3
East St B1
Edinburgh Rd A2
Elm Gr C3
Emirates Spinnaker Tower B1
Great Southsea St C3
Green Rd B3
Greetham St B3
Grosvenor St B3
Groundlings A2
Grove Rd North C3
Grove Rd South C3
Guildhall B3
Guildhall Walk B3
Gunwharf Quays Retail Park B1
Gunwharf Rd B1
Hambrook St C2
Hampshire Terr B2
Hanover St A1
Hard, The B1
High St C2
HM Naval Base A1
HMS Nelson (Royal Naval Barracks) A2
HMS Victory A1
HMS Warrior A1
Hovercraft Terminal C2
Hyde Park Rd B3
Information Ctr A1/B3
Isambard Brunel Rd B3
Isle of Wight Car Ferry Terminal B1
Kent Rd C3
Kent St A2
King St B3
King's Rd C3
King's Terr C2
Lake Rd A3
Law Courts B3
Library B3
Long Curtain Rd C2
Market Way A3
Marmion Rd C3
Mary Rose Mus A1
Middle St B3
Millennium Prom B1/C1
Museum Rd B2
National Museum of the Royal Navy A1
Naval Recreation Gd C2
Nightingale Rd C3
Norfolk St B3
North St A2
Osborne Rd C3
Park Rd B2
Passenger Catamaran to Isle of Wight B1
Passenger Ferry to Gosport B1
Pelham Rd C3
Pembroke Gdns C2
Pier Rd C2
Point Battery C1
Police Station B3
Portsmouth & Southsea A3
Portsmouth Harbour B1
Portsmouth Historic Dockyard A1
Post Office A2/A3/B1/B3/C3
Queen St A1
Queen's Cr C3
Round Tower C1
Royal Garrison Church C1
St Edward's Rd C3
St George's Rd B2
St George's Sq B1
St George's Way B2
St James's Rd B3
St James's St A2
St John's Cath (RC) A3
St Thomas's Cath C1
St Thomas's St B2
Somers Rd B3
Southsea Common C2
Southsea Terr C2
Square Tower C1
Station St A3
Swimming Pool A2
Town Fortifications C1
Unicorn Rd A2
United Services Recreation Ground B2

University of Portsmouth A2/B2
Univ of Portsmouth – Coll of Art, Design & Media B3
Upper Arundel St A3
Victoria Ave C2
Victoria Park A2
Victory Gate A1
Vue B1
Warblington St B1
Western Pde C2
White Hart Rd C1
Winston Churchill Ave B3

Reading 190
Abbey Ruins B2
Abbey Sq B2
Abbey St B2
Abbot's Walk B2
Acacia Rd C2
Addington Rd C3
Addison Rd A1
Allcroft Rd C3
Alpine St C2
Baker St B1
Berkeley Ave C1
Bridge St B1
Brigham Rd A1
Broad St B1
Broad Street Mall B1
Carey St B1
Castle Hill C1
Castle St B1
Causeway, The A3
Caversham Rd A1
Christchurch Playing Fields A2
Civic Offices B1
Coley Hill C1
Coley Pl C1
Craven Rd C3
Crown St C2
De Montfort Rd A1
Denmark Rd C3
Duke St B2
East St B2
Edgehill St C2
Eldon Rd B3
Eldon Terr B3
Elgar Rd C1
Erleigh Rd C3
Field Rd C1
Fire Station A1
Fobney St B1
Forbury Gdns B2
Forbury Rd B2
Forbury Retail Park B2
Francis St C1
Friar St B1
Garrard St B1
Gas Works Rd B3
George St A2
Great Knollys St B1
Greyfriars B1
Grove, The B2
Gun St B1
Henry St C1
Hexagon Theatre, The B1
Hill's Meadow A2
Howard St B1
Information Ctr B1
Inner Distribution Rd B1
Katesgrove La C1
Kenavon Dr B2
Kendrick Rd C2
King's Mdw Rec Gd A2
King's Rd B2
Library B2
London Rd C3
London St B2
Lynmouth Rd A1
Magistrate's Court B1
Market Pl B2
Mill La B2
Mill Rd A2
Minster St B1
Morgan Rd C3
Mount Pleasant C2
Museum of English Rural Life C3
Napier Rd A2
Newark St C2
Newport Rd A1
Old Reading Univ C3
Oracle Sh Ctr, The B1
Orts Rd B3
Pell St C1
Police Station B1
Post Office B2
Queen Victoria St B1
Queen's Rd A2
Queen's Rd B2
Randolph Rd A1
Reading Bridge A2
Reading Station A1
Redlands Rd C3
Renaissance Hotel B1
Riverside Museum B3
Rose Kiln La C1
Royal Berks Hospital (A&E) C3
St Giles C2
St Laurence B2
St Mary's B1
St Mary's Butts B1
St Saviour's Rd C1
Send Rd A3
Sherman Rd C2
Sidmouth St B2
Silver St C2
South St B2
Southampton St C2
Station Hill A1
Station Rd B1
Superstore A3
Swansea Rd A1
Technical College B3
Valpy St B2
Vastern Rd A1
Vue B2
Waldeck St C2
Watlington St B3
West St B1
Whitby Dr C3
Wolseley St C1
York Rd A1
Zinzan St B1

Salisbury 190
Albany Rd A2
Arts Centre A3
Ashley Rd A1

Avon Approach A2
Ayleswade Rd C2
Bedwin St A2
Belle Vue A2
Bishop's Palace C2
Bishops Walk B2
Blue Boar Row B2
Bourne Ave A3
Bourne Hill A3
Britford La C2
Broad Walk C2
Brown St B2
Bus Station B2
Castle St A2
Catherine St B2
Chapter House B2
Church House B2
Churchfields Rd B1
Churchill Way East B3
Churchill Way North A3
Churchill Way South C2
Churchill Way West A1
City Hall B2
Close Wall B2
Coldharbour La A1
College St A3
Council Offices A3
Court A1
Crane Bridge Rd B2
Crane St B2
Cricket Ground C1
Culver St South B3
De Vaux Pl C2
Devizes Rd A1
Dews Rd B1
Elm Grove B3
Elm Grove Rd A3
Endless St A2
Estcourt Rd A3
Exeter St C2
Fairview Rd A3
Fire Station A1
Fisherton St A1
Folkestone Rd C1
Fowlers Hill B3
Fowlers Rd B3
Friary Estate C3
Friary La B2
Friary, The B3
Gas La A1
Gigant St B3
Greencroft B3
Greencroft St A3
Guildhall B2
Hall of John Halle B2
Hamilton Rd A2
Harnham Mill B1
Harnham Rd C1/C2
High St B2
Hospital A1
Ho of John A'Port B2
Information Ctr B2
Kelsey Rd A3
King's Rd A2
Laverstock Rd B3
Library B2
London Rd A3
Lower St C1
Maltings, The B2
Manor Rd A3
Marsh La A1
Medieval Hall B2
Milford Hill B3
Milford St B3
Mill Rd B1
Millstream Approach A2
Mompesson House (NT) B2
New Bridge Rd C2
New Canal B2
New Harnham Rd C2
New St B2
North Canonry B2
North Gate B2
North Walk B2
Old Blandford Rd C1
Old Deanery B2
Old George Hall B2
Park St A3
Parsonage Green C1
Playhouse Theatre A2
Post Office A2/B2/C2
Poultry Cross B2
Queen Elizabeth Gdns B1
Queen's Rd A3
Rampart Rd B3
St Ann St B3
St Ann's Gate B2
St Marks Rd A3
St Martins B3
St Mary's Cath B2
St Nicholas Hospl C2
St Paul's A1
St Paul's Rd A1
St Thomas B2
Salisbury & South Wiltshire Mus B2
Salisbury General Hospital (A&E) C2
Salisbury Station A1
Salt La A3
Saxon Rd C1
Scots La A2
Shady Bower B3
South Canonry C2
South Gate C2
Southampton Rd B2
Spire View A1
Sports Ground C3
Tollgate Rd B3
Town Path B1
Wain-a-Long Rd A3
Wardrobe, The B2
Wessex Rd A3
West Walk C2
Wilton Rd A1
Wiltshire College B3
Winchester St B3
Windsor Rd A1
Winston Churchill Gdns C3
Wyndham Rd A2
YHA B3
York Rd A1

Scarborough 190
Aberdeen Walk B2
Albert Rd A2
Albion Rd C2
Alexandra Gardens A1
Auborough St B2
Balmoral Ctr B2
Belle Vue St C1
Belmont Rd C2
Brunswick Shop Ctr B2

Castle Dykes B3
Castle Hill A3
Castle Holms A3
Castle Rd B2
Castle Walls A3
Castlegate B3
Cemetery B1
Central Tramway B2
Clarence Gardens A2
Coach Park B1
Columbus Ravine A1
Court B1
Crescent, The C2
Cricket Ground A1
Cross St B2
Crown Terr C2
Dean Rd B1
Devonshire Dr A1
East Harbour B3
East Pier B3
Eastborough B2
Elmville Ave B1
Esplanade C2
Falconers Rd B2
Falsgrave Rd C1
Fire Station B2
Foreshore Rd B2
Friargate B2
Gladstone Rd B1
Gladstone St B1
Hollywood Plaza A1
Hoxton Rd B1
Information Ctr B2/B3
King St B2
Library B2
Lifeboat Station B3
Londesborough Rd C1
Longwestgate B3
Marine Dr A3
Military Adventure Park A1
Miniature Railway A1
Nelson St B1
Newborough B2
Nicolas St B2
North Marine Rd A1
North St B2
Northway B1
Old Harbour B3
Olympia Leisure B2
Peasholm Park A1
Peasholm Rd A1
Police Station B1
Post Office B2/C1
Princess St B3
Prospect Rd B1
Queen St B2
Queen's Parade A2
Queen's Tower (Remains) A3
Ramshill Rd C2
Roman Signal Sta A3
Roscoe St C1
Rotunda Museum C2
Royal Albert Dr A2
St Martin-on-the-Hill C2
St Martin's Ave C2
St Mary's B3
St Thomas St B2
Sandside B3
Scarborough C1
Scarborough Art Gallery and Crescent Art Studios C2
Scarborough Bowls Centre A1
Scarborough Castle A3
Shopmobility C2
Somerset Terr C2
South Cliff Lift C2
Spa Theatre, The C2
Spa, The C2
Stephen Joseph Theatre B1
Tennyson Ave B1
Tollergate B2
Town Hall B2
Trafalgar Rd B1
Trafalgar Square A1
Trafalgar St West B1
Valley Bridge Parade C2
Valley Rd C1
Vernon Rd C2
Victoria Park Mount A1
Victoria Rd B1
West Pier B3
Westborough C1
Westover Rd C1
Westwood C1
Woodall Ave A1
YMCA Theatre B2
York Pl B2
Yorkshire Coast College (Westwood Campus) C1

Sheffield 191
Addy Dr A2
Addy St A2
Adelphi St A3
Albert Terrace Rd A3
Albion St A2
Aldred Rd A1
Allen St A4
Alma St A4
Angel St B5
Arundel Gate B5
Arundel St C4
Ashberry Rd A2
Ashdell Rd C1
Ashgate Rd C1
Athletics Centre B2
Attercliffe Rd A6
Bailey St B4
Ball St A4
Balm Green B4
Bank St B4
Barber Rd A2
Bard St B5
Barker's Pool B4
Bates St A1
Beech Hill Rd C1
Beet St B3
Bellefield St A3
Bernard Rd A6
Bernard St B6
Birkendale A2
Birkendale Rd A2
Birkendale View A1
Bishop St C4
Blackwell Pl B6
Blake St A2
Blonk St A5
Bolsover St B2

Botanical Gdns
Bower Rd
Bradley St
Bramall La
Bramwell St
Bridge St
Brighton Terrace
Broad La
Broad St
Brocco St
Brook Hill
Broomfield Rd
Broomgrove Rd
Broomhall Pl
Broomhall Rd
Broomhall St
Broomspring La
Brown St
Brunswick St
Burgess St
Burlington St
Burns Rd
Cadman St
Cambridge St
Campo La
Carver St
Castle Market
Castle Square
Castlegate
Cathedral
Cathedral (RC)
Cavendish St
Charles St
Charter Row
Children's Hospita[l] (A&E)
Church St
City Hall
City Hall
City Rd
Claremont Cr
Claremont Pl
Clarke St
Clarkegrove Rd
Clarkehouse Rd
Clarkson St
Cobden View Rd
Collegiate Cr
Commercial St
Commonside
Conduit Rd
Cornish St
Corporation St
Court
Cricket Inn Rd
Cromwell St
Crookes Rd
Crookes Valley Pa[rk]
Crookes Valley Rd
Crookesmoor Rd
Crown Court
Crucible Theatre
Cutler's Hall
Cutlers Gate
Daniel Hill
Dental Hospital
Dept for Educatio[n] Employment
Devonshire Green
Devonshire St
Division St
Dorset St
Dover St
Duchess Rd
Duke St
Duncombe St
Durham Rd
Earl St
Earl Way
Ecclesall Rd
Edward St
Effingham Rd
Effingham St
Egerton St
Eldon St
Elmore Rd
Exchange St
Eyre St
Fargate
Farm Rd
Fawcett St
Filey St
Fir St
Fire & Police Mus
Fire Station
Fitzalan Sq/Ponds Forge
Fitzwater Rd
Fitzwilliam Gate
Fitzwilliam St
Flat St
Foley St
Foundry Climbing Centre
Fulton Rd
Furnace Hill
Furnival Rd
Furnival Sq
Furnival St
Garden St
Gell St
Gibraltar St
Glebe Rd
Glencoe Rd
Glossop Rd B2/
Gloucester St
Granville Rd
Granville Rd/Sheff College
Graves Gallery
Greave Rd
Green La
Hadfield St
Hanover St
Hanover Way
Harcourt Rd
Harmer La
Havelock St
Hawley St
Haymarket
Headford St
Heavygate Rd
Henry St
High St
Hodgson St
Holberry Gdns
Hollis Croft
Holly St
Hounsfield Rd
Howard Rd
Hoyle St
Hyde Park
Infirmary Rd
Infirmary Rd
Information Ctr
Jericho St
Johnson St

Southampton • Southend-on-Sea • Stoke • Stratford-upon-Avon • Sunderland • Swansea • Swindon 203

m Island
Mus A4
on Rd C1
nill Rd C5
nill St C5
nill, The C5
ington St A1
Rd B3
roft B4
old St B4
on St A6
ry A2
ry B5
ry C1
m Theatre B5
da St A3
avers St A5
r Oaks Rd B6
in St B3
oorough Rd B1
St C4
da St C4
ock Rd A1
ow St A3
ourn Rd A1
ourne Ave C1
nnium
eries B5
n St C3
nell St B3
a Ave A1
a Rd A1
gomery Terr Rd A3
gomery
atre B4
ument Gdns C6
Oaks Rd B1
, The C4
e St C3
bray St A4
nroom La B2
erthorpe Rd B3
erthorpe Rd B3
bould La C1
St C1
olk Park Rd C6
olk Rd C6
olk St B4
h Church St B4
nfield Rd A1
numberland Rd B1
ery St B5
cademy B5
olme Rd C1
gon B2
on B5
t B6
ard Square B4
rd St A2
dise St B4
La C2
Sq B5
er's Rd B1
son Building
iv) C2
stone Rd A3
one St B4
St B4
ce Station A4/B5
d Hill B5
d St B5
ds Forge Int
orts Ctr B5
obello St B3
Office
A1/A2/B3/B4/B5/
B6/C1/C3/C4/C6
ell St A2
en St B4
en's Rd C5
sey Rd B1
Hill B3
car Rd B1
ent St B3
kingham St B4
ouck Rd A2
al Hallamshire
spital C2
sell St A4
and Park C1
eorge's Cl A2
ary's Gate C3
ary's Rd C4/C5
eter & St Paul
thedral B4
hilip's Rd A3
le St A3
ool Rd B1
land St A4
ern Rd B5
esmoor A4
esmoor A3
af St B3
ffield Hallam Univ B5
ffield Ice Sports
– Skate Central C5
ffield
erchange B5
ffield Parkway A6
ffield Station C5
ffield Sta/Sheffield
llam Univ B5
ffield University B2
pherd St A3
ton St A2
reham St C4
wroom, The C5
ewsbury Rd C5
ey St C4
Gallery C5
n St A1
nfield A4
g Hill A5
w La A4
y St B3
th La C4
th Street Park B5
thbourne Rd C1
al Hill A5
al St A5
ng Hill B2
ng Hill Rd B1
ingvale Rd A1
ford Rd C6
ford St B4
nley St A5
folk Rd C5
nmer St B1
ny Bank C4
rey St B4
ssex St A6
son St B3
ney Rd A2
ester St C4
ot St B5
onville Rd C1
Office C4
Tenter St B4
Town Hall B4
Townend St A1
Townhead St B4
Trafalgar St B4
Tree Root Walk B2
Trinity St A4
Trippet La B4
Turner Museum
of Glass B3
Union St B4
Univ Drama Studio B2
Univ of Sheffield B3
Upper Allen St A3
Upper Hanover St B3
Upperthorpe Rd A2/A3
Verdon St A5
Victoria Quays B5
Victoria Rd C2
Victoria St B3
Waingate B5
Watery St A3
Watson Rd C1
Wellesley Rd B2
Wellington St C3
West Bar A4
West Bar Green A4
West One Plaza B3
West St B3
West St B4
Westbourne Rd C1
Western Bank B2
Western Rd A1
Weston Park B2
Weston Park Hospl B2
Weston Park Mus B2
Weston St A2
Wharncliffe Rd C3
Whitham Rd B1
Wicker A5
Wilkinson St B2
William St C3
Winter Garden B4
Winter St B2
York St B4
Yorkshire Artspace C5
Young St C4

Southampton 190

Above Bar St A2
Albert Rd North B3
Albert Rd South C3
Anderson's Rd B3
Archaeology Mus
(God's Ho Tower) C2
Argyle Rd A2
Arundel Tower B1
Bargate, The B2
BBC Regional Centre A1
Bedford Pl A1
Belvidere Rd A3
Bernard St C2
Blechynden Terr A1
Brinton's Rd A2
Britannia Rd A3
Briton St C2
Brunswick Pl A2
Bugle St C1
Canute Rd C3
Castle Way C2
Catchcold Tower B1
Central Bridge C3
Central Rd C2
Channel Way C3
Chapel Rd B3
Cineworld C3
City Art Gallery A1
City College B3
City Cruise Terminal C1
Civic Centre A1
Civic Centre Rd A1
Coach Station B1
Commercial Rd A1
Cumberland Pl A1
Cunard Rd C2
Derby Rd A3
Devonshire Rd A1
Dock Gate 4 C2
Dock Gate 8 B1
East Andrews Park A2
East Park Terr A2
East St B2
Endle St B3
European Way C2
Fire Station A2
Floating Bridge Rd C3
Golden Gr A3
Graham Rd A2
Guildhall A1
Hanover Bldgs B2
Harbour Lights C3
Harbour Pde B1
Hartington Rd A3
Havelock Rd A1
Henstead Rd A1
Herbert Walker Ave B1
High St B2
Hoglands Park B2
Holy Rood (Rems),
Merchant Navy
Memorial B2
Houndwell Park B2
Houndwell Pl B2
Hythe Ferry C2
Information Ctr A1
Isle of Wight Ferry
Terminal C1
James St B3
Java Rd C2
Kingsway A2
Leisure World B1
Library A1
Lime St B2
London Rd A2
Marine Pde B3
Marlands Shopping
Centre, The A1
Marsh La B2
Mayflower Meml C1
Mayflower Park C1
Mayflower Theatre,
The A1
Medieval Merchant's
House C1
Melbourne St B3
Millais A2
Morris Rd A1
National Oceanography
Centre C3
Neptune Way C3
New Rd A2
Nichols Rd A3
North Front A2
Northam Rd A3
Ocean Dock C2
Ocean Village Marina C3
Ocean Way C3
Odeon B1
Ogle Rd B1
Old Northam Rd A2
Orchard La B2
Oxford Ave A2
Oxford St C2
Palmerston Park A2
Palmerston Rd A2
Parsonage Rd A3
Peel St A3
Platform Rd C2
Polygon, The A1
Portland Terr B1
Post Office A2/A3/B2
Pound Tree Rd B2
Quays Swimming and
Diving Complex,
The B1
Queen's Park C2
Queen's Peace
Fountain A2
Queen's Terr C2
Queensway B2
Radcliffe Rd A3
Rochester St A3
Royal Pier C1
Royal South Hants
Hospital A2
St Andrew's Rd A2
St Mary St A2
St Mary's B3
St Mary's Leisure Ctr A2
St Mary's Pl B2
St Mary's Rd A2
St Mary's Stadium
(Southampton FC) A3
St Michael's C1
Sea City Mus A1
Solent Sky C3
South Front B2
Southampton Central
Station A1
Southampton Solent
University A2
SS Shieldhall C2
Terminus Terr C2
Threefield La B2
Titanic Engineers'
Memorial A2
Town Quay C1
Town Walls B2
Tudor House C1
Vincent's Walk B2
West Gate Hall C1
West Marlands Rd A1
West Park A1
West Park Rd A1
West Quay Rd B1
West Quay Retail Pk B1
Western Esplanade B1
Westquay Shop Ctr B1
White Star Way C2
Winton St A2

Southend-on-Sea 191

Adventure Island C3
Albany Ave A1
Albert Rd C3
Alexandra Rd C2
Alexandra St C2
Alexandra Yacht
Club C2
Ashburnham Rd B2
Ave Rd B1
Avenue Terr B1
Balmoral Rd B1
Baltic Ave B3
Baxter Ave A2/B2
Beecroft Art
Gallery B2
Bircham Rd A2
Boscombe Rd B3
Boston Ave A1/B2
Bournemouth Pk Rd A3
Browning Ave A3
Bus Station C3
Byron Ave A3
Cambridge Rd C1/C2
Canewdon Rd B1
Carnarvon Rd A2
Central Ave A3
Chelmsford Ave A1
Chichester Rd B2
Church Rd C3
Civic Centre A2
Clarence Rd C2
Clarence St C2
Cliff Ave B1
Cliffs Pavilion C1
Clifftown Parade C2
Clifftown Rd C2
Colchester Rd A1
Coleman St B3
College Way B2
County Court B3
Cromer Rd B3
Crowborough Rd A2
Dryden Ave A3
East St A2
Elmer App B2
Elmer Ave B2
Forum, The B2
Gainsborough Dr A1
Gayton Rd A2
Glenhurst Rd A2
Gordon Pl B2
Gordon Rd B2
Grainger Rd A2
Greyhound Way A3
Grove, The A3
Guildford Rd B3
Hamlet Ct Rd B1
Hamlet Rd C1
Harcourt Ave A1
Hartington Rd C3
Hastings Rd B3
Herbert Gr C3
Heygate Ave C3
High St B2/C2
Information Ctr C3
Kenway A2
Kilworth Ave B3
Lancaster Gdns B3
London Rd B1
Lucy Rd C3
MacDonald Ave A1
Magistrates' Court A2
Maine Ave C1
Maldon Rd A2
Marine Parade C3
Marine Rd C1
Milton Rd B1
Milton St B2
Napier Ave B2
North Ave A3
North Rd A1/B1
Odeon B2
Osborne Rd B1
Park Cres B1
Park Rd B1
Park St B1
Park Terr B1
Pier Hill C3
Pleasant Rd C3
Police Station A2
Post Office B2/B3
Princes St B2
Queens Rd B2
Queensway B2/B3/C3
Radio Essex C2
Rayleigh Ave A1
Redstock Rd A2
Rochford Ave A1
Royal Mews C2
Royal Terr C2
Royals Sh Ctr, The C3
Ruskin Ave A3
St Ann's Rd B3
St Helen's Rd B1
St John's Rd B1
St Leonard's Rd C3
St Lukes Rd A3
St Vincent's Rd C1
Salisbury Ave A1/B1
Scratton Rd C2
Shakespeare Dr A1
Shopmobility B2
Short St A2
South Ave A3
South Essex College B2
Southchurch Rd B3
Southend Central B2
Southend Pier
Railway C3
Southend United FC A1
Southend Victoria B2
Stadium Rd A2
Stanfield Rd A2
Stanley Rd C3
Sutton Rd A3/B3
Swanage Rd B3
Sweyne Ave A1
Sycamore Gr A3
Tennyson Ave A3
Tickfield Ave A2
Tudor Rd A1
Tunbridge Rd A2
Tylers Ave B3
Tyrrel Dr B3
Univ of Essex B2/C2
Vale Ave A2
Victoria Ave A2
Victoria Sh Ctr, The B2
Warrior Sq B3
Wesley Rd C3
West Rd A1
West St A1
Westcliff Ave C1
Westcliff Parade C1
Western Esplanade C1
Weston Rd C2
Whitegate Rd B3
Wilson Rd C1
Wimborne Rd B3
York Rd C3

Stoke 191

Ashford St A3
Avenue Rd A3
Aynsley Rd A2
Barnfield C1
Bath St C2
Beresford St A3
Bilton St C2
Boon Ave C2
Booth St C2
Boothen Rd C2/C3
Boughey St C2
Boughley Rd B3
Brighton St B1
Campbell Rd C2
Carlton Rd B3
Cauldon Rd A3
Cemetery A2
Cemetery Rd A2
Chamberlain Ave C1
Church (RC) B2
Church St C2
City Rd C3
Civic Centre &
King's Hall B3
Cliff Vale Pk A1
College Rd A3
Convent Cl B2
Copeland St B2
Cornwallis St C3
Corporation St C2
Crowther St A3
Dominic St B1
Elenora St B2
Elgin St B2
Epworth St A3
Etruscan St A1
Film Theatre B3
Fleming Rd C2
Fletcher Rd C2
Floyd St B2
Foden St C2
Frank St C2
Franklin Rd C1
Frederick Ave B1
Garden St C1
Garner St A1
Gerrard St B2
Glebe St B3
Greatbach Ave B1
Hanley Park A3
Harris St B1
Hartshill Rd B1
Hayward St A2
Hide St B2
Higson Ave B2
Hill St B2
Honeywall B2
Hunters Dr C1
Hunters Way C1
Keary St C2
Kingsway B2
Leek Rd B3
Library C2
Lime St C2
Liverpool Rd B2
London Rd C2
Lonsdale St C2
Lovatt St B2
Lytton St B3
Market C2
Newcastle La C1
Newlands St A2
Norfolk St A2
North St A1/B2
Northcote Ave B2
Oldmill St C3
Oriel St B1
Oxford St B1
Penkhull New Rd C1
Penkhull St C1
Police Station C2
Portmeirion
Pottery C2
Post Office A3
Prince's Rd B1
Pump St B2
Quarry Ave B1
Quarry Rd B1
Queen Anne St A3
Queen's Rd C1
Queensway A1/B2/C3
Richmond St B1
Rothwell St C1
St Peter's B3
St Thomas Pl C1
Scrivenor Rd A1
Seaford St A3
Selwyn St C3
Shelton New Rd A1
Shelton Old Rd B2
Sheppard St C2
Spark St C2
Spencer Rd B3
Spode St C2
Squires View B3
Staffordshire Univ B3
Stanley Matthews
Sports Centre B3
Station Rd B3
Stoke Business Park C3
Stoke Rd A2
Stoke-on-Trent Coll A3
Stoke-on-Trent
Station B3
Sturgess St C2
Thistley Hough C1
Thornton Rd B3
Tolkien Way B1
Trent Valley Rd C1
Vale St B2
Villas, The C1
Watford St A3
Wellesley St A3
West Ave B1
Westland St B1
Yeaman St C2
Yoxall Ave B1

Stratford-upon-Avon 192

Albany Rd B2
Alcester Rd B1
Ambulance Station B1
Arden St B2
Avenue Farm A1
Ave Farm Ind Est A1
Avenue Rd A3
Avon Industrial Est A2
Baker Ave A1
Bandstand C3
Benson Rd A3
Birmingham Rd A2
Boat Club B3
Borden Pl C1
Brass Rubbing Ctr C2
Bridge St B2
Bridgetown Rd C3
Bridgeway B3
Broad St C2
Broad Walk C2
Brookvale Rd C1
Bull St C2
Butterfly Farm C3
Cemetery C1
Chapel La B2
Cherry Orchard C1
Chestnut Walk B2
Children's
Playground C3
Church St C2
Civic Hall B2
Clarence Rd B1
Clopton Bridge B3
Clopton Rd A2
College B1
College La C2
College St C2
Com Sports Centre B1
Council Offices
(District) B2
Courtyard, The C2
Cox's Yard B3
Cricket Ground C3
Ely Gdns B2
Ely St B2
Evesham Rd C1
Fire Station B1
Foot Ferry C3
Fordham Ave A2
Gallery, The B3
Garrick Way C1
Gower Memorial B3
Great William St B2
Greenhill St B2
Greenway, The C2
Grove Rd B2
Guild St B2
Guildhall & School B2
Hall's Croft C2
Hartford Rd C1
Harvard House B2
Henley St B2
High St B2
Holton St C2
Holy Trinity C2
Information Ctr B3
Jolyffe Park Rd A2
Kipling Rd C3
Library B2
Lodge Rd B1
Maidenhead Rd A3
Mansell St B2
Masons Court B2
Masons Rd A1
Maybird Shopping Pk A2
Maybrook Rd A1
Mayfield Ave A2
Meer St B2
Mill La C2
Moat House Hotel B3
Narrow La C2
Nash's Ho &
New Pl B2
New St C2
Old Town C2
Orchard Way C1
Paddock La C1
Park Rd A1
Payton St B2
Percy St A2
Police Station B2
Post Office B2
Recreation Ground C2
Regal Road A2
Rother St B2
Rowley Cr A3
Royal Shakespeare
Theatre B3
Ryland St C2
Saffron Meadow C2
St Andrew's Cr B1
St Gregory's A3
St Gregory's Rd A3
St Mary's Rd A2
Sanctus Dr C2
Sanctus St C1
Sandfield Rd C2
Scholars La B2
Seven Meadows Rd C2
Shakespeare Ctr B2
Shakespeare Inst C2
Shakespeare St B2
Shakespeare's
Birthplace B2
Sheep St B2
Shelley Rd C3
Shipston Rd C3
Shottery Rd C1
Slingates Rd A2
Southern La C2
Station Rd B1
Stratford
Healthcare B2
Stratford Hospital B2
Stratford Leisure &
Visitor Centre B3
Stratford Sports Club B1
Stratford-upon-Avon
Station B1
Swan Theatre B3
Swan's Nest La B3
Talbot Rd A2
Tiddington Rd B3
Timothy's Bridge
Industrial Estate A1
Timothy's Bridge Rd A1
Town Hall & Council
Offices B2
Town Sq B2
Trinity St C2
Tyler St B2
War Memorial Gdns B3
Warwick Rd B3
Waterside B3
Welcombe Rd A3
West St C2
Western Rd A2
Wharf Rd A2
Willows North, The B1
Willows, The B1
Wood St B2

Sunderland 192

Albion Pl C2
Alliance Pl B1
Argyle St C2
Ashwood St C1
Athenaeum St B2
Azalea Terr C2
Beach St A1
Bede Theatre C3
Bedford St B2
Beechwood Terr C1
Belvedere Rd C2
Blandford St B2
Borough Rd B3
Bridge Cr B2
Bridge St B2
Bridges, The B2
Brooke St A2
Brougham St B2
Burdon Rd C2
Burn Park C1
Burn Park Rd C1
Burn Park Tech Park C1
Carol St B1
Charles St A3
Chester Rd C1
Chester Terr B1
Church St A3
Civic Centre C2
Cork St B3
Coronation St B3
Cowan Terr C2
Crowtree Rd B2
Dame Dorothy St A2
Deptford Rd B1
Deptford Terr A1
Derby St C2
Derwent St C2
Dock St A3
Dundas St A2
Durham Rd C1
Easington St A2
Egerton St C3
Empire B2
Empire Theatre B2
Farringdon Row B1
Fawcett St B2
Fox St C1
Foyle St B3
Frederick St B3
Gill Rd B2
Hanover Pl A1
Havelock Terr C1
Hay St A2
Headworth Sq B3
Hendon Rd B3
High St East B3
High St West B2/B3
Holmeside B2
Hylton Rd B1
Information Ctr B2
John St B3
Kier Hardie Way A2
Lambton St B3
Laura St C3
Lawrence St B3
Leisure Centre B2
Library & Arts Ctr B3
Lily St B1
Lime St B1
Livingstone Rd B2
Low Row B2
Matamba Terr B1
Millburn St B1
Millennium Way A2
Minster B2
Monkwearmouth
Station Museum A2
Mowbray Park C3
Mowbray Rd C3
Murton St C3
National Glass Ctr A3
New Durham Rd C1
Newcastle Rd A2
Nile St B3
Norfolk St B3
North Bridge St A2
Northern Gallery
for Contemporary
Art B3
Otto Terr C1
Park La C2
Park Lane C2
Park Rd C2
Paul's Rd B3
Peel St C3
Place, The B3
Police Station B2
Post Office B2
Priestly Cr A1
Queen St B2
Railway Row B1
Retail Park B1
Richmond St A2
Roker Ave A2
Royalty Theatre C1
Royalty, The C1
Ryhope Rd C2
St Mary's Way B2
St Michael's Way B2
St Peter's A3
St Peter's A2
St Peter's Way A3
St Vincent St C3
Salem Rd C3
Salem St C3
Salisbury St C3
Sans St B3
Silkworth Row B1
Southwick Rd A2
Stadium of Light
(Sunderland AFC) A2
Stadium Way A2
Stobart St A2
Stockton Rd C2
Suffolk St C3
Sunderland B2
Sunderland Aquatic
Centre A2
Sunderland Mus B3
Sunderland St B3
Sunderland Sta B2
Tatham St C3
Tavistock Pl B3
Thelma St C1
Thomas St North A2
Thornholme Rd C1
Toward Rd C3
Transport
Interchange C2
Trimdon St Way B1
Tunstall Rd C2
University C1
University Library C1
Univ of Sunderland
(City Campus) B1
Univ of Sunderland
(Sir Tom Cowle at St
Peter's Campus) A3
Vaux Brewery Way A2
Villiers St B3
Villiers St South B3
Vine Pl C2
Violet St B1
Walton La B3
Waterworks Rd B1
Wearmouth Bridge B2
Wellington La A1
West Sunniside B3
West Wear St B3
Westbourne Rd B1
Western Hill C1
Wharncliffe B1
Whickham St A3
White House Rd C3
Wilson St North A2
Winter Gdns C3
Wreath Quay A1

Swansea
Abertawe 192

Adelaide St C3
Albert Row C3
Alexandra Rd B3
Argyle St C1
Baptist Well Pl A2
Beach St C1
Belle Vue Way B3
Berw Rd A1
Berwick Terr A2
Bond St C1
Brangwyn Concert
Hall C1
Bridge St A3
Brookands Terr B1
Brunswick St C1
Bryn-Syfi Terr A2
Bryn-y-Mor Rd C1
Bullins La B1
Burrows Rd C1
Bus Station C2
Bus/Rail link A3
Cadfan Rd A1
Cadrawd Rd A1
Caer St B3
Carig Cr A1
Carlton Terr B2
Carmarthen Rd A3
Castle Square B3
Castle St B3
Catherine St C1
Cinema B3
Civic Ctr & Library C2
Clarence St C2
Colbourne Terr A2
Constitution Hill B1
Court B3
Creidiol Rd A2
Cromwell St B2
Crown Courts C1
Duke St B1
Dunvant Pl C2
Dyfatty Park A3
Dyfatty St A3
Dyfed Ave A1
Dylan Thomas Ctr B3
Dylan Thomas
Theatre C3
Eaton Cr C1
Eigen Cr A1
Elfed Rd A1
Emlyn Rd A1
Evans Terr A3
Fairfield Terr B1
Ffynone Dr B1
Ffynone Rd B1
Fire Station B3
Firm St A2
Fleet St C1
Francis St C1
Fullers Row B2
George St B2
Glamorgan St C2
Glynn Vivian Art
Gallery B3
Gower Coll Swansea C1
Graig Terr A3
Grand Theatre C2
Granogwen Rd A2
Guildhall C1
Guildhall Rd South C1
Gwent Rd A1
Gwynedd Ave A1
Hafod St A3
Hanover St B1
Harcourt St B2
Harries St A2
Heathfield B2
Henrietta St B1
Hewson St B2
High St A3/B3
High View A2
Hill St A2
Historic Ships
Berth C3
HM Prison C2
Information Ctr C2
Islwyn Rd A1
King Edward's Rd C1
Kingsway, The B2
LC, The C3
Long Ridge A2
Madoc St C2
Mansel St B2
Maritime Quarter C3
Market B3
Mayhill Gdns B1
Mayhill Rd A1
Milton Terr A2
Mission Gallery C3
Montpellier Terr B1
Morfa Rd A3
Mount Pleasant B2
National Waterfront
Museum C3
Nelson St C2
New Cut Rd A3
New St A3
Nicander Pde A2
Nicander Pl A2
Nicholl St B2
Norfolk St B2
North Hill Rd A2
Northampton La B2
Orchard St B3
Oxford St B2
Oystermouth Rd C1
Page St B2
Pant-y-Celyn Rd B1
Parc Tawe Link B3
Parc Tawe North B3
Parc Tawe Sh & L Ctr B3
Patti Pavilion C1
Paxton St C2
Pen-y-Graig Rd A1
Penmaen Terr B1
Phillips Pde C1
Picton Terr B2
Plantasia B3
Police Station B2
Post Office
A1/A2/C1/C2
Powys Ave A1
Primrose St B2
Princess Way B3
Promenade B2
Pryder Gdns A1
Quadrant Shop Ctr C2
Quay Park B3
Rhianfa La B1
Rhondda St B2
Richardson St C2
Rodney St C1
Rose Hill B1
Rosehill Terr B1
Russell St B1
St David's Shop Ctr C3
St Helen's Ave C1
St Helen's Cr C1
St Helen's Rd C1
St James Gdns B1
St James's Cr B1
St Mary's B3
Sea View Terr A3
Singleton St C2
South Dock C3
Stanley Pl B2
Strand B3
Swansea Castle B3
Swansea Metropolitan
University B2
Swansea Museum C3
Swansea Station A3
Taliesyn Rd B1
Tan y Marian Rd A1
Tegid Rd A2
Teilo Cr A1
Tenpin Bowling B3
Terrace Rd B1/B2
Tontine St A3
Tower of Ecliptic
Observatory C3
Townhill Rd A1
Tramshed, The C3
Trawler Rd C3
Union St B2
Upper Strand A3
Vernon St A3
Victoria Quay C3
Victoria Rd B3
Vincent St C1
Walter Rd B1
Watkin St A2
Waun-Wen Rd A2
Wellington St C2
Westbury St C1
Western St C1
Westway C2
William St C2
Wind St B3
Woodlands Terr B1
YMCA B2
York St C3

Swindon 192

Albert St C3
Albion St C1
Alfred St A2
Alvescot Rd C3
Art Gallery & Mus C3
Ashford Rd C1
Aylesbury St A2
Bath Rd C2
Bathampton St B1
Bathurst Rd B3
Beatrice St A2
Beckhampton St B3
Bowood Rd C1
Bristol St B1
Broad St A3
Brunel Arcade B2
Brunel Plaza B2
Brunswick St C2
Bus Station B2
Cambria Bridge Rd B1
Cambria Place B1
Canal Walk B2
Carfax St B2
Carr St B1
Cemetery C1/C3
Chandler Cl C3
Chapel C1
Chester St B1
Christ Church C3
Church Place B1
Cirencester Way A3
Clarence St B2
Clifton St C1
Cockleberry A2
Colbourne A3
Colbourne St A3
College St B2
Commercial Rd B2
Corporation St A2
Council Offices B3
County Rd A3
Courts B2
Cricket Ground A3
Cricklade Street C3
Crombey St B1/C2
Cross St C2
Curtis St B1
Deacon St C1
Designer Outlet
(Great Western) B1
Dixon St C2
Dover St C2
Dowling St C2
Drove Rd C3
Dryden St C1
Durham St C3
East St B1
Eastcott Hill C2
Eastcott Rd C2
Edgeware Rd B2
Edmund St C2
Elmina Rd A3
Emlyn Square B1
Euclid St B3
Exeter St B1
Fairview C1
Faringdon Rd B1
Farnsby St B1
Fire Station B3
Fleet St B2
Fleming Way B2/B3
Florence St A2
Gladstone St A3
Gooch St A2
Graham St A3
Great Western
Way A1/A2
Groundwell Rd B3
Hawksworth Way A1
Haydon St A2
Henry St B2
Hillside Ave C1
Holbrook Way B2
Hunt St C3
Hydro B1
Hythe Rd C2
Information Ctr B2
Joseph St C1
Kent Rd C2
King William St C2
Kingshill Rd C1
Lansdown Rd C2
Lawn, The C3
Leicester St B3
Library B2
Lincoln St B3
Little London C3
London St B1
Magic B3
Maidstone Rd C2
Manchester Rd A3
Maxwell St B1
Milford St B2
Milton Rd B1
Morse St C2
National Monuments
Record Centre B1
Newcastle St B3
Newcombe Drive A1
Newcombe Trading
Estate A1
Newhall St C2
North St C2
North Star A1
North Star Ave A1
Northampton St B3
Nurseries, The C1
Oasis Leisure Ctr A1
Ocotal Way A3
Okus Rd C1
Old Town C3
Oxford St B1
Parade, The B2
Park Lane B1
Park Lane A1
Park, The B1
Pembroke St C2
Plymouth St B3
Polaris House A2
Polaris Way A2
Police Station B2
Ponting St A2
Post Office
B1/B2/C1/C3
Poulton St A3
Princes St B2
Prospect Hill C2
Prospect Place C2
Queen St B2
Queen's Park C3
Radnor St C1
Read St C1
Reading St B1
Regent St B2
Retail Park A2/A3/B3
Rosebery St A3
St Mark's B1
Salisbury St A3
Savernake St C2
Shelley St C1
Sheppard St B1
South St C2
Southampton St B3
Spring Gardens B3
Stafford Street C2
Stanier St C2
Station Road A2

Index to road maps of Britain

Abbreviations used in the index

Aberdeen	Aberdeen City
Aberds	Aberdeenshire
Ald	Alderney
Anglesey	Isle of Anglesey
Angus	Angus
Argyll	Argyll and Bute
Bath	Bath and North East Somerset
Bedford	Bedford
Bl Gwent	Blaenau Gwent
Blackburn	Blackburn with Darwen
Blackpool	Blackpool
Bmouth	Bournemouth
Borders	Scottish Borders
Brack	Bracknell
Bridgend	Bridgend
Brighton	City of Brighton and Hove
Bristol	City and County of Bristol
Bucks	Buckinghamshire
C Beds	Central Bedfordshire
Caerph	Caerphilly
Cambs	Cambridgeshire
Cardiff	Cardiff
Carms	Carmarthenshire
Ceredig	Ceredigion
Ches E	Cheshire East
Ches W	Cheshire West and Chester
Clack	Clackmannanshire
Conwy	Conwy
Corn	Cornwall
Cumb	Cumbria
Darl	Darlington
Denb	Denbighshire
Derby	City of Derby
Derbys	Derbyshire
Devon	Devon
Dorset	Dorset
Dumfries	Dumfries and Galloway
Dundee	Dundee City
Durham	Durham
E Ayrs	East Ayrshire
E Dunb	East Dunbartonshire
E Loth	East Lothian
E Renf	East Renfrewshire
E Sus	East Sussex
E Yorks	East Riding of Yorkshire
Edin	City of Edinburgh
Essex	Essex
Falk	Falkirk
Fife	Fife
Flint	Flintshire
Glasgow	City of Glasgow
Glos	Gloucestershire
Gtr Man	Greater Manchester
Guern	Guernsey
Gwyn	Gwynedd
Halton	Halton
Hants	Hampshire
Hereford	Herefordshire
Herts	Hertfordshire
Highld	Highland
Hrtlpl	Hartlepool
Hull	Hull
IoM	Isle of Man
IoW	Isle of Wight
Invclyd	Inverclyde
Jersey	Jersey
Kent	Kent
Lancs	Lancashire
Leicester	City of Leicester
Leics	Leicestershire
Lincs	Lincolnshire
London	Greater London
Luton	Luton
M Keynes	Milton Keynes
M Tydf	Merthyr Tydfil
Mbro	Middlesbrough
Medway	Medway
Mers	Merseyside
Midloth	Midlothian
Mon	Monmouthshire
Moray	Moray
N Ayrs	North Ayrshire
N Lincs	North Lincolnshire
N Lanark	North Lanarkshire
N Som	North Somerset
N Yorks	North Yorkshire
NE Lincs	North East Lincolnshire
Neath	Neath Port Talbot
Newport	City and County of Newport
Norf	Norfolk
Northants	Northamptonshire
Northumb	Northumberland
Nottingham	City of Nottingham
Notts	Nottinghamshire
Orkney	Orkney
Oxon	Oxfordshire
Pboro	Peterborough
Pembs	Pembrokeshire
Perth	Perth and Kinross
Plym	Plymouth
Poole	Poole
Powys	Powys
Ptsmth	Portsmouth
Reading	Reading
Redcar	Redcar and Cleveland
Renfs	Renfrewshire
Rhondda	Rhondda Cynon Taff
Rutland	Rutland
S Ayrs	South Ayrshire
S Glos	South Gloucestershire
S Lanark	South Lanarkshire
S Yorks	South Yorkshire
Scilly	Scilly
Shetland	Shetland
Shrops	Shropshire
Slough	Slough
Som	Somerset
Soton	Southampton
Staffs	Staffordshire
Southend	Southend-on-Sea
Stirling	Stirling
Stockton	Stockton-on-Tees
Stoke	Stoke-on-Trent
Suff	Suffolk
Sur	Surrey
Swansea	Swansea
Swindon	Swindon
T&W	Tyne and Wear
Telford	Telford and Wrekin
Thurrock	Thurrock
Torbay	Torbay
Torf	Torfaen
V Glam	The Vale of Glamorgan
W Berks	West Berkshire
W Dunb	West Dunbartonshire
W Isles	Western Isles
W Loth	West Lothian
W Mid	West Midlands
W Sus	West Sussex
W Yorks	West Yorkshire
Warks	Warwickshire
Warr	Warrington
Wilts	Wiltshire
Windsor	Windsor and Maidenhead
Wokingham	Wokingham
Worcs	Worcestershire
Wrex	Wrexham
York	City of York

How to use the index

Example

Trudoxhill Som **24** E2

- grid square
- page number
- county or unitary authority

A

Ab Kettleby Leics 64 B4
Ab Lench Worcs 50 D5
Abbas Combe Som 12 B5
Abberley Worcs 50 C2
Abberton Essex 43 C6
Abberton Worcs 50 D4
Abberwick Northumb 117 C7
Abbess Roding Essex 42 C1
Abbey Devon 11 C6
Abbey-cwm-hir Powys 48 B2
Abbey Dore Hereford 49 F5
Abbey Field Essex 43 B5
Abbey Hulton Stoke 75 E6
Abbey St Bathans Borders 122 C3
Abbey Town Cumb 107 D8
Abbey Village Lancs 86 B4
Abbey Wood London 29 B5
Abbeydale S Yorks 88 F4
Abbeystead Lancs 93 D5
Abbots Bickington Devon 9 C5
Abbots Bromley Staffs 62 B4
Abbots Langley Herts 40 D3
Abbots Leigh N Som 23 B7
Abbots Morton Worcs 50 D5
Abbots Ripton Cambs 54 B3
Abbots Salford Warks 51 D5
Abbotsbury Dorset 12 F3
Abbotsham Devon 9 B6
Abbotskerswell Devon 7 C6
Abbotsley Cambs 54 D3
Abbotswood Hants 14 B4
Abbotts Ann Hants 25 E8
Abcott Shrops 49 B5
Abdon Shrops 61 F5
Aber Ceredig 46 E3
Aber-Arad Carms 46 F2
Aber-banc Ceredig 46 E2
Aber Cowarch Gwyn 59 C5
Aber-Giâr Carms 46 E4
Aber-gwynfi Neath 34 E2
Aber-Hirnant Gwyn 72 F3
Aber-nant Rhondda 34 D4
Aber-Rhiwlech Gwyn 59 B6
Aber-Village Powys 35 B5
Aberaeron Ceredig 46 C3
Aberaman Rhondda 34 D4
Aberangell Gwyn 58 C5
Aberarder Highld 137 F7
Aberarder House Highld 138 B2
Aberarder Lodge Highld 137 F8
Aberargie Perth 128 C3
Aberarth Ceredig 46 C3
Aberavon Neath 33 E8
Aberbeeg Bl Gwent 35 D6
Abercanaid M Tydf 34 D4
Abercarn Caerph 35 E6
Abercastle Pembs 44 B3
Abercegir Powys 58 D5
Aberchirder Aberds 152 C6
Abercraf Powys 34 C2
Abercrombie Fife 129 D7
Abercych Pembs 45 E4
Abercynafon Powys 34 C4
Abercynon Rhondda 34 E4
Aberdalgie Perth 128 B2
Aberdâr = Aberdare Rhondda 34 D3
Aberdare = Aberdâr Rhondda 34 D3
Aberdaron Gwyn 70 E2
Aberdaugleddau = Milford Haven Pembs 44 E4
Aberdeen Aberdeen 141 D8
Aberdesach Gwyn 82 F4
Aberdour Fife 128 F3
Aberdovey Gwyn 58 E3
Aberdulais Neath 34 D1
Aberedw Powys 48 E2
Abereiddy Pembs 44 B2
Abererch Gwyn 70 D4
Aberfan M Tydf 34 D4
Aberfeldy Perth 133 E5
Aberffraw Anglesey 82 E3
Aberffrwd Ceredig 47 B5
Aberford W Yorks 95 F7
Aberfoyle Stirling 126 D4
Abergavenny = Y Fenni Mon 35 C6
Abergele Conwy 72 B3
Abergorlech Carms 46 F4
Abergwaun = Fishguard Pembs 44 B4
Abergwesyn Powys 47 D7
Abergwili Carms 33 B5
Abergwynant Gwyn 58 C3
Abergwyngregyn Gwyn 83 D6
Abergynolwyn Gwyn 58 D3
Aberhonddu = Brecon Powys 34 B4
Aberhosan Powys 58 E5
Aberkenfig Bridgend 34 F2
Aberlady E Loth 129 F6
Aberlemno Angus 135 D5
Aberllefenni Gwyn 58 D4
Abermagwr Ceredig 47 B5
Abermaw = Barmouth Gwyn 58 C3
Abermeurig Ceredig 46 D4
Abermule Powys 59 E8
Abernaint Powys 59 B8
Abernant Carms 32 B4
Abernethy Perth 128 C3
Abernyte Perth 134 F2
Aberpennar = Mountain Ash Rhondda 34 E4
Aberporth Ceredig 45 D4
Abersoch Gwyn 70 E4
Abersychan Torf 35 D6
Abertawe = Swansea Swansea 33 E7
Aberteifi = Cardigan Ceredig 45 E3
Aberthin V Glam 22 B2
Abertillery = Abertyleri Bl Gwent 35 D6
Abertridwr Caerph 35 F5
Abertridwr Powys 59 C7
Abertyleri = Abertillery Bl Gwent 35 D6
Abertysswg Caerph 35 D5
Aberuthven Perth 127 C8
Aberyscir Powys 34 B3
Aberystwyth Ceredig 58 F2
Abhainn Suidhe W Isles 154 G5
Abingdon-on-Thames Oxon 38 E4
Abinger Common Sur 28 E2
Abinger Hammer Sur 27 E8
Abington S Lanark 114 B2
Abington Pigotts Cambs 54 E4
Ablington Glos 37 D8
Ablington Wilts 25 E6
Abney Derbys 75 B8
Aboyne Aberds 140 E4
Abram Gtr Man 86 D4
Abriachan Highld 151 H8
Abridge Essex 41 E7
Abronhill N Lanark 119 B7
Abson S Glos 24 B2
Abthorpe Northants 52 E4
Abune-the-Hill Orkney 159 F3
Aby Lincs 79 B7
Acaster Malbis York 95 E8
Acaster Selby N Yorks 95 E8
Accrington Lancs 87 B5
Acha Argyll 146 F4
Acha Mor W Isles 155 E8
Achabraid Argyll 145 E7
Achachork Highld 149 D9
Achafolla Argyll 124 D3
Achagary Highld 157 D10
Achahoish Argyll 144 F6
Achalader Perth 133 E8
Achallader Argyll 131 E7
Ach'an Todhair Highld 130 B4
Achanalt Highld 150 E5
Achanamara Argyll 144 E6
Achandunie Highld 151 D9
Achany Highld 157 J8
Achaphubuil Highld 130 B4
Acharacle Highld 147 E9
Acharn Highld 147 F10
Acharn Perth 132 E4
Acharole Highld 158 E4
Achath Aberds 141 C6
Achavanich Highld 158 F3
Achavraat Highld 151 G12
Achddu Carms 33 D5
Achduart Highld 156 J3
Achentoul Highld 157 F11
Achfary Highld 156 F5
Achgarve Highld 155 H13
Achiemore Highld 156 C6
Achiemore Highld 157 D11
A'Chill Highld 148 H7
Achiltibuie Highld 156 J3
Achina Highld 157 C10
Achinduich Highld 157 J8
Achinduin Argyll 124 B4
Achingills Highld 158 D3
Achintee Highld 131 B5
Achintee Highld 150 G2
Achintraid Highld 149 E13
Achlean Highld 138 E4
Achleck Argyll 146 G7
Achluachrach Highld 137 F5
Achlyness Highld 156 D5
Achmelvich Highld 156 G3
Achmore Highld 149 E13
Achmore Stirling 132 F2
Achnaba Argyll 124 B5
Achnaba Argyll 145 E8
Achnabat Highld 151 H8
Achnacarnin Highld 156 F3
Achnacarry Highld 136 F4
Achnacloich Argyll 125 B5
Achnacloich Highld 149 H10
Achnaconeran Highld 137 C7
Achnacraig Argyll 146 G7
Achnacroish Argyll 130 E2
Achnadrish Argyll 146 F7
Achnafalnich Argyll 125 C8
Achnagarron Highld 151 E9
Achnaha Highld 146 E7
Achnahanat Highld 151 B8
Achnahannet Highld 139 B5
Achnairn Highld 157 H8
Achnaluachrach Highld 157 J9
Achnasaul Highld 136 F4
Achnasheen Highld 150 F4
Achosnich Highld 146 E7
Achranich Highld 147 G10
Achreamie Highld 157 C13
Achriabhach Highld 131 C5
Achriesgill Highld 156 D5
Achrimsdale Highld 157 J12
Achtoty Highld 157 C9
Achurch Northants 65 F7
Achuvoldrach Highld 157 D8
Achvaich Highld 151 B10
Achvarasdal Highld 157 C12
Ackergill Highld 158 E5
Acklam Mbro 102 C2
Acklam N Yorks 96 C3
Ackleton Shrops 61 E7
Acklington Northumb 117 D8
Ackton W Yorks 88 B5
Ackworth Moor Top W Yorks 88 C5
Acle Norf 69 C7
Acock's Green W Mid 62 F5
Acol Kent 31 C7
Acomb Northumb 110 C2
Acomb York 95 D8
Aconbury Hereford 49 F7
Acre Lancs 87 B5
Acre Street W Sus 15 E8
Acrefair Wrex 73 E6
Acton Ches E 74 D3
Acton Dorset 13 G7
Acton London 41 F5
Acton Shrops 60 F3
Acton Suff 56 E2
Acton Wrex 73 D7
Acton Beauchamp Hereford 49 D8
Acton Bridge Ches W 74 B2
Acton Burnell Shrops 60 D5
Acton Green Hereford 49 D8
Acton Pigott Shrops 60 D5
Acton Round Shrops 61 E6
Acton Scott Shrops 60 F4
Acton Trussell Staffs 62 C3
Acton Turville S Glos 37 F5
Adbaston Staffs 61 B7
Adber Dorset 12 B3
Adderley Shrops 74 E3
Adderstone Northumb 123 F7
Addiewell W Loth 120 C2
Addingham W Yorks 94 E3
Addington Bucks 39 B7
Addington Kent 29 D7
Addington London 28 C4
Addinston Borders 121 D8
Addiscombe London 28 C4
Addlestone Sur 27 C8
Addlethorpe Lincs 79 C8
Adel W Yorks 95 F5
Adeney Telford 61 C7
Adfa Powys 59 D7
Adforton Hereford 49 B6
Adisham Kent 31 D6
Adlestrop Glos 38 B2
Adlingfleet E Yorks 90 B2
Adlington Lancs 86 C4
Admaston Staffs 62 B4
Admaston Telford 61 C6
Admington Warks 51 E7
Adstock Bucks 52 F5
Adstone Northants 52 D3
Adversane W Sus 16 B4
Advie Highld 152 E1
Adwalton W Yorks 88 B3
Adwell Oxon 39 E6
Adwick le Street S Yorks 89 D6
Adwick upon Dearne S Yorks 89 D5
Adziel Aberds 153 C9
Ae Village Dumfries 114 F2
Affleck Aberds 141 B7
Affpuddle Dorset 13 E6
Affric Lodge Highld 136 B4
Afon-wen Flint 72 B5
Afton IoW 14 F4
Agglethorpe N Yorks 101 F5
Agneash IoM 84 D4
Aigburth Mers 85 F4
Aiginis W Isles 155 D9
Aike E Yorks 97 E6
Aikerness Orkney 159 C5
Aikers Orkney 159 J5
Aiketgate Cumb 108 E4
Aikton Cumb 108 D2
Ailey Hereford 48 E5
Ailstone Warks 51 D7
Ailsworth Pboro 65 E8
Ainderby Quernhow N Yorks 102 F1
Ainderby Steeple N Yorks 101 E8
Aingers Green Essex 43 B7
Ainsdale Mers 85 C4
Ainsdale-on-Sea Mers 85 C4
Ainstable Cumb 108 E5
Ainsworth Gtr Man 87 C5
Ainthorpe N Yorks 103 D5
Aintree Mers 85 E4
Aird Argyll 124 E3
Aird Dumfries 104 C4
Aird Highld 149 A12
Aird W Isles 155 D10
Aird a Mhachair W Isles 148 D2
Aird a' Mhulaidh W Isles 154 F6
Aird Asaig W Isles 154 G6
Aird Dhail W Isles 155 A9
Aird Mhidhinis W Isles 148 H2
Aird Mhighe W Isles 154 H6
Aird Mhighe W Isles 154 J5
Aird Mhor W Isles 148 H2
Aird of Sleat Highld 149 H10
Aird Thunga W Isles 155 D9
Aird Uig W Isles 154 D5
Airdens Highld 151 B9
Airdrie N Lanark 119 C7
Airdtorrisdale Highld 157 C9
Airidh a Bhruaich W Isles 154 F7
Airieland Dumfries 106 D4
Airmyn E Yorks 89 B8
Airntully Perth 133 F7
Airor Highld 149 H12
Airth Falk 127 F7
Airton N Yorks 94 D2
Airyhassen Dumfries 105 E7
Aisby Lincs 78 F3
Aisby Lincs 90 E2
Aisgernis W Isles 148 F2
Aiskew N Yorks 101 F7
Aislaby N Yorks 103 D6
Aislaby N Yorks 103 F5
Aislaby Stockton 102 C2
Aisthorpe Lincs 78 A2
Aith Orkney 159 G3
Aith Shetland 160 D8
Aith Shetland 160 H5
Aithsetter Shetland 160 K6
Aitkenhead S Ayrs 112 D3
Aitnoch Highld 151 H12
Akeld Northumb 117 B5
Akeley Bucks 52 F5
Akenham Suff 56 E5
Albaston Corn 6 B2
Alberbury Shrops 60 C3
Albourne W Sus 17 C6
Albrighton Shrops 60 C4
Albrighton Shrops 62 D2
Alburgh Norf 69 F5
Albury Herts 41 B7
Albury Sur 27 E8
Albury End Herts 41 B7
Alby Hill Norf 81 D7
Alcaig Highld 151 F8
Alcaston Shrops 60 F4
Alcester Warks 51 D5
Alciston E Sus 18 E2
Alcombe Som 21 E8
Alcombe Wilts 24 C3
Alconbury Cambs 54 B2
Alconbury Weston Cambs 54 B2
Aldbar Castle Angus 135 D5
Aldborough N Yorks 95 C7
Aldborough Norf 81 D7
Aldbourne Wilts 25 B7
Aldbrough E Yorks 97 F8
Aldbrough St John N Yorks 101 C7
Aldbury Herts 40 C2
Aldcliffe Lancs 92 C4
Aldclune Perth 133 C6
Aldeburgh Suff 57 D8
Aldeby Norf 69 E7
Aldenham Herts 40 E4
Alderbury Wilts 14 B2
Aldercar Derbys 76 E4
Alderford Norf 68 C4
Alderholt Dorset 14 C2
Alderley Glos 36 E4
Alderley Edge Ches E 74 B5
Aldermaston W Berks 26 C3
Aldermaston Wharf W Berks 26 C4
Alderminster Warks 51 E7
Alder's End Hereford 49 E8
Aldersey Green Ches W 73 D8
Aldershot Hants 27 D6
Alderton Glos 50 F5
Alderton Northants 52 E5
Alderton Shrops 60 B4
Alderton Suff 57 E7
Alderton Wilts 37 F5
Alderwasley Derbys 76 D3
Aldfield N Yorks 95 C5
Aldford Ches W 73 D8
Aldham Essex 43 B5
Aldham Suff 56 E4
Aldie Highld 151 C10
Aldingbourne W Sus 16 D3
Aldingham Cumb 92 B2
Aldington Kent 19 B7
Aldington Worcs 51 E5
Aldington Frith Kent 19 B7
Aldochlay Argyll 126 E2
Aldreth Cambs 54 B5
Aldridge W Mid 62 D4
Aldringham Suff 57 C8
Aldsworth Glos 38 C1
Aldunie Moray 140 B2
Aldwark Derbys 76 D2
Aldwark N Yorks 95 C7
Aldwick W Sus 16 E3
Aldwincle Northants 65 F7
Aldworth W Berks 26 B3
Alexandria W Dunb 118 B3
Alfardisworthy Devon 8 C4
Alfington Devon 11 E6
Alfold Sur 27 F8
Alfold Bars W Sus 27 F8
Alfold Crossways Sur 27 F8
Alford Aberds 140 C4
Alford Lincs 79 B7
Alford Som 23 F8
Alfreton Derbys 76 D4
Alfrick Worcs 50 D2
Alfrick Pound Worcs 50 D2
Alfriston E Sus 18 E2
Algaltraig Argyll 145 F9
Algarkirk Lincs 79 F5
Alhampton Som 23 F8
Aline Lodge W Isles 154 F6
Alisary Highld 147 D10
Alkborough N Lincs 90 B2
Alkerton Oxon 51 E8
Alkham Kent 31 E6
Alkington Shrops 74 F2
Alkmonton Derbys 75 F8
All Cannings Wilts 25 C5
All Saints South Elmham Suff 69 F6
All Stretton Shrops 60 E4
Alladale Lodge Highld 150 C7
Allaleigh Devon 7 D6
Allanaquoich Aberds 139 E7
Allangrange Mains Highld 151 F9
Allanton Borders 122 D4
Allanton N Lanark 119 D8
Allathasdal W Isles 148 H1
Allendale Town Northumb 109 D8
Allenheads Northumb 109 E8
Allens Green Herts 41 C7
Allensford Durham 110 D3
Allensmore Hereford 49 F6
Allenton Derby 76 F3
Aller Som 12 B2
Allerby Cumb 107 F7
Allerford Som 21 E8
Allerston N Yorks 103 F6
Allerthorpe E Yorks 96 E3
Allerton Mers 86 F2
Allerton W Yorks 94 F4
Allerton Bywater W Yorks 88 B5
Allerton Mauleverer N Yorks 95 D7
Allesley W Mid 63 F7
Allestree Derby 76 F3
Allet Corn 3 B6
Allexton Leics 64 D5
Allgreave Ches E 75 C6
Allhallows Medway 30 B2
Allhallows-on-Sea Medway 30 B2
Alligin Shuas Highld 149 C13
Allimore Green Staffs 62 C2
Allington Lincs 77 E8
Allington Wilts 25 C5
Allington Wilts 25 F7
Allithwaite Cumb 92 B3
Alloa Clack 127 E7
Allonby Cumb 107 E7
Alloway S Ayrs 112 C3
Allt Carms 33 D6
Allt na h-Airbhe Highld 150 B4
Allt-nan-sùgh Highld 136 B2
Alltchaorunn Highld 131 D5
Alltforgan Powys 59 B6
Alltmawr Powys 48 E2
Alltnacaillich Highld 156 E7
Alltsigh Highld 137 C7
Alltwalis Carms 46 F3
Alltwen Neath 33 D8
Alltyblaca Ceredig 46 E4
Allwood Green Suff 56 B4
Almeley Hereford 48 D5
Almer Dorset 13 E7
Almholme S Yorks 89 D6
Almington Staffs 74 F4
Alminstone Cross Devon 8 B5
Almondbank Perth 128 B2
Almondbury W Yorks 88 C2
Almondsbury S Glos 36 F3
Alne N Yorks 95 C7
Alness Highld 151 E9
Alnham Northumb 117 C5
Alnmouth Northumb 117 C8
Alnwick Northumb 117 C7
Alperton London 40 F4
Alphamstone Essex 56 F2
Alpheton Suff 56 D2
Alphington Devon 10 E4
Alport Derbys 76 C2
Alpraham Ches E 74 D2
Alresford Essex 43 B6
Alrewas Staffs 63 C5
Alsager Ches E 74 D4
Alsagers Bank Staffs 74 E5
Alsop en le Dale Derbys 75 D8
Alston Cumb 109 E7
Alston Devon 11 D8
Alstone Glos 50 F4
Alstonefield Staffs 75 D8
Alswear Devon 10 B2
Altandhu Highld 156 H2
Altanduin Highld 157 G11
Altarnun Corn 8 F4
Altass Highld 156 J7
Alterwall Highld 158 D4
Altham Lancs 93 F7
Althorne Essex 43 E5
Althorpe N Lincs 90 D2
Alticry Dumfries 105 D6
Altnabreac Station Highld 157 E13
Altnacealgach Hotel Highld 156 H5
Altnacraig Argyll 124 C4
Altnafeadh Highld 131 D6
Altnaharra Highld 157 F8
Altofts W Yorks 88 B4
Alton Derbys 76 C3
Alton Hants 26 F5
Alton Staffs 75 E7
Alton Pancras Dorset 12 D5
Alton Priors Wilts 25 C6
Altrincham Gtr Man 87 F5
Altrua Highld 136 F5
Altskeith Stirling 126 D3
Altyre Ho. Moray 151 F13
Alva Clack 127 E7
Alvanley Ches W 73 B8
Alvaston Derby 76 F3
Alvechurch Worcs 50 B5
Alvecote Warks 63 D6
Alvediston Wilts 13 B7
Alveley Shrops 61 F7
Alverdiscott Devon 9 B7
Alverstoke Hants 15 E7
Alverstone IoW 15 F6
Alverton Notts 77 E7
Alves Moray 152 B1
Alvescot Oxon 38 D2
Alveston S Glos 36 F3
Alveston Warks 51 D7
Alvie Highld 138 D4
Alvingham Lincs 91 E7
Alvington Glos 36 D3
Alwalton Cambs 65 E8
Alweston Dorset 12 C4
Alwinton Northumb 116 D5
Alwoodley W Yorks 95 E5
Alyth Perth 134 E2
Am Baile W Isles 148 G2
Am Buth Argyll 124 C4
Amatnatua Highld 150 B7
Amber Hill Lincs 78 E5
Ambergate Derbys 76 D3
Amberley Glos 37 D5
Amberley W Sus 16 C4
Amble Northumb 117 D8
Amblecote W Mid 62 F2
Ambler Thorn W Yorks 87 B8
Ambleside Cumb 99 D5
Ambleston Pembs 44 C5
Ambrosden Oxon 39 C6
Amcotts N Lincs 90 C2
Amersham Bucks 40 E2
Amesbury Wilts 25 E6
Amington Staffs 63 D6
Amisfield Dumfries 114 F2
Amlwch Anglesey 82 B4
Amlwch Port Anglesey 82 B4
Ammanford = Rhydaman Carms 33 C7
Amod Argyll 143 E8
Amotherby N Yorks 96 B3
Ampfield Hants 14 B5
Ampleforth N Yorks 95 B8
Ampney Crucis Glos 37 D7
Ampney St Mary Glos 37 D7
Ampney St Peter Glos 37 D7
Amport Hants 25 E7
Ampthill C Beds 53 F8
Ampton Suff 56 B2
Amroth Pembs 32 D2
Amulree Perth 133 F5
An Caol Highld 149 C11
An Cnoc W Isles 155 D9
An Gleann Ur W Isles 155 D9
An t-Ob = Leverburgh W Isles 154 J5
Anagach Highld 139 B6
Anaheilt Highld 130 C2
Anancaun Highld 150 E3
Ancaster Lincs 78 E2
Anchor Shrops 59 F8
Anchorsholme Blackpool 92 E3
Ancroft Northumb 123 E5
Ancrum Borders 116 B2
Anderby Lincs 79 B8
Anderson Dorset 13 E6
Anderton Ches W 74 B3
Andover Hants 25 E8
Andover Down Hants 25 E8
Andoversford Glos 37 C7
Andreas IoM 84 C4
Anfield Mers 85 E4
Angersleigh Som 11 C6
Angle Pembs 44 E3
Angmering W Sus 16 D4
Angram N Yorks 95 E8
Angram N Yorks 100 E3
Anie Stirling 126 C4
Ankerville Highld 151 D11
Anlaby E Yorks 90 B4
Anmer Norf 80 E3
Anna Valley Hants 25 E8
Annan Dumfries 107 C8
Annat Argyll 125 C6
Annat Highld 149 C13
Annbank S Ayrs 112 B4
Annesley Notts 76 D5
Annesley Woodhouse Notts 76 D4
Annfield Plain Durham 110 D4
Annifirth Shetland 160 J3
Annitsford T&W 111 B5
Annscroft Shrops 60 D4
Ansdell Lancs 85 B4
Ansford Som 23 F8
Ansley Warks 63 E6
Anslow Staffs 63 B6
Anslow Gate Staffs 63 B5
Anstey Herts 54 F5
Anstey Leics 64 D2
Anstruther Easter Fife 129 D7
Anstruther Wester Fife 129 D7
Ansty Hants 26 E5
Ansty W Sus 17 B6
Ansty Warks 63 F7

Baulking Oxon 38 E3
Baumber Lincs 78 B5
Baunton Glos 37 D7
Baverstock Wilts 24 F5
Bawburgh Norf 68 D4
Bawdeswell Norf 81 E6
Bawdrip Som 22 F5
Bawdsey Suff 57 E7
Bawtry S Yorks 89 E7
Baxenden Lancs 87 B5
Baxterley Warks 63 E6
Baybridge Hants 15 B6
Baycliff Cumb 92 B2
Baydon Wilts 25 B7
Bayford Herts 41 D6
Bayford Som 12 B5
Bayles Cumb 109 E7
Baylham Suff 56 D5
Baynard's Green Oxon 39 B5
Bayston Hill Shrops 60 D4
Baythorn End Essex 55 E8
Bayton Worcs 49 B8
Beach Highld 130 D1
Beachampton Bucks 53 F5
Beachamwell Norf 67 D7
Beachans Moray 151 G13
Beacharr Argyll 143 D7
Beachborough Kent 19 B8
Beachley Glos 36 E2
Beacon Devon 11 D6
Beacon End Essex 43 B5
Beacon Hill Sur 27 F6
Beacon's Bottom Bucks 39 E7
Beaconsfield Bucks 40 F2
Beacrabhaic W Isles 154 H6
Beadlam N Yorks 102 F4
Beadlow C Beds 54 F2
Beadnell Northumb 117 B8
Beaford Devon 9 C7
Beal N Yorks 89 B6
Beal Northumb 123 E6
Beamhurst Staffs 75 F7
Beaminster Dorset 12 D2
Beamish Durham 110 D5
Beamsley N Yorks 94 D3
Bean Kent 29 B6
Beanacre Wilts 24 C4
Beanley Northumb 117 C6
Beaquoy Orkney 159 F4
Bear Cross Bmouth 13 E8
Beardwood Blackburn 86 B4
Beare Green Sur 28 E2
Bearley Warks 51 C6
Bearnus Argyll 146 G6
Bearpark Durham 110 E5
Bearsbridge Northumb 109 D7
Bearsden E Dunb 118 B5
Bearsted Kent 29 D8
Bearstone Shrops 74 F4
Bearwood Hereford 49 D5
Bearwood Poole 13 E8
Bearwood W Mid 62 F4
Beattock Dumfries 114 D3
Beauchamp Roding Essex 42 C1
Beauchief S Yorks 88 F4
Beaufort Bl Gwent 35 C5
Beaufort Castle Highld 151 G8
Beaulieu Hants 14 D4
Beauly Highld 151 G8
Beaumaris Anglesey 83 D6
Beaumont Cumb 108 D3
Beaumont Essex 43 B7
Beaumont Hill Darl 101 C7
Beausale Warks 51 B7
Beauworth Hants 15 B6
Beaworthy Devon 9 E6
Beazley End Essex 42 B3
Bebington Mers 85 F4
Bebside Northumb 117 F8
Beccles Suff 69 E7
Becconsall Lancs 86 B2
Beck Foot Cumb 99 E8
Beck Hole N Yorks 103 D6
Beck Row Suff 55 B7
Beck Side Cumb 98 F4
Beckbury Shrops 61 D7
Beckenham London 28 C4
Beckermet Cumb 98 D2
Beckfoot Cumb 98 D3
Beckfoot Cumb 107 E7
Beckford Worcs 50 F4
Beckhampton Wilts 25 C5
Beckingham Lincs 77 D8
Beckingham Notts 89 F8
Beckington Som 24 D3
Beckley E Sus 19 C5
Beckley Hants 14 E3
Beckley Oxon 39 C5
Beckton London 41 F7
Beckwithshaw N Yorks 95 D5
Becontree London 41 F7
Bed-y-coedwr Gwyn 71 E8
Bedale N Yorks 101 F7
Bedburn Durham 110 F4
Bedchester Dorset 13 C6
Beddau Rhondda 34 F4
Beddgelert Gwyn 71 C6
Beddingham E Sus 17 D8
Beddington London 28 C4
Bedfield Suff 57 C6
Bedford Bedford 53 D8
Bedham W Sus 16 B4
Bedhampton Hants 15 D8
Bedingfield Suff 57 C5
Bedlam N Yorks 95 C5
Bedlington Northumb 117 F8
Bedlington Station Northumb 117 F8
Bedlinog M Tydf 34 D4
Bedminster Bristol 23 B7
Bedmond Herts 40 D3
Bednall Staffs 62 C3
Bedrule Borders 116 C2
Bedstone Shrops 49 B5
Bedwas Caerph 35 F5
Bedworth Warks 63 F7
Bedworth Heath Warks 63 F7
Beeby Leics 64 D3
Beech Hants 26 F4
Beech Staffs 75 F5
Beech Hill Gtr Man 86 D3
Beech Hill W Berks 26 C4
Beechingstoke Wilts 25 D5
Beedon W Berks 26 B2
Beeford E Yorks 97 D7
Beeley Derbys 76 C2
Beelsby NE Lincs 91 D6
Beenham W Berks 26 C3
Beeny Corn 8 E3
Beer Devon 11 F7
Beer Hackett Dorset 12 C3
Beercrocombe Som 11 B8
Beesands Devon 7 E6
Beesby Lincs 91 F8
Beeson Devon 7 E6
Beeston C Beds 54 E2
Beeston Ches W 74 D2
Beeston Norf 68 C2
Beeston Notts 76 F5
Beeston W Yorks 95 F5
Beeston Regis Norf 81 C7
Beeswing Dumfries 107 C5
Beetham Cumb 92 B4
Beetley Norf 68 C2
Begbroke Oxon 38 C4
Begelly Pembs 32 D2
Beggar's Bush Powys 48 C4
Beguildy Powys 48 B3
Beighton Norf 69 D6
Beighton S Yorks 88 F5
Beighton Hill Derbys 76 D2
Beith N Ayrs 118 D3
Bekesbourne Kent 31 D5
Belaugh Norf 69 C5
Belbroughton Worcs 50 B4
Belchamp Otten Essex 56 E2
Belchamp St Paul Essex 55 E8
Belchamp Walter Essex 56 E2
Belchford Lincs 79 B5
Belford Northumb 123 F7
Belhaven E Loth 122 B2
Belhelvie Aberds 141 C8
Belhinnie Aberds 140 B3
Bell Bar Herts 41 D5
Bell Busk N Yorks 94 D2
Bell End Worcs 50 B4
Bell o'th'Hill Ches W 74 E2
Bellabeg Aberds 140 C2
Bellamore S Ayrs 112 F2
Bellanoch Argyll 144 D6
Bellaty Angus 134 D2
Belleau Lincs 79 B7
Bellehiglash Moray 152 E1
Bellerby N Yorks 101 E6
Bellever Devon 6 B4
Belliehill Angus 135 C5
Bellingdon Bucks 40 D2
Bellingham Northumb 116 F4
Belloch Argyll 143 E7
Bellochantuy Argyll 143 E7
Bells Yew Green E Sus 18 B3
Bellsbank E Ayrs 112 D4
Bellshill N Lanark 119 C7
Bellshill Northumb 123 F7
Bellspool Borders 120 F4
Bellsquarry W Loth 120 C3
Belmaduthy Highld 151 F9
Belmesthorpe Rutland 65 C7
Belmont Blackburn 86 C4
Belmont London 28 C3
Belmont S Ayrs 112 B3
Belmont Shetland 160 C7
Belnacraig Aberds 140 C2
Belowda Corn 4 C4
Belper Derbys 76 E3
Belper Lane End Derbys 76 E3
Belsay Northumb 110 B4
Belses Borders 115 B8
Belsford Devon 7 D5
Belstead Suff 56 E5
Belston S Ayrs 112 B3
Belstone Devon 9 E8
Belthorn Blackburn 86 B5
Beltinge Kent 31 C5
Beltoft N Lincs 90 D2
Belton Leics 63 B8
Belton Lincs 78 F2
Belton N Lincs 89 D8
Belton Norf 69 D7
Belton in Rutland Rutland 64 D5
Beltring Kent 29 E7
Belts of Collonach Aberds 141 E5
Belvedere London 29 B5
Belvoir Leics 77 F8
Bembridge IoW 15 F7
Bemersyde Borders 121 F8
Bemerton Wilts 25 F6
Bempton E Yorks 97 B7
Ben Alder Lodge Highld 132 B2
Ben Armine Lodge Highld 157 H10
Ben Casgro W Isles 155 E9
Benacre Suff 69 F8
Benbuie Dumfries 113 E7
Benderloch Argyll 124 B5
Bendronaig Lodge Highld 150 H3
Benenden Kent 18 B5
Benfield Dumfries 105 C7
Bengate Norf 69 B6
Bengeworth Worcs 50 E5
Benhall Green Suff 57 C7
Benhall Street Suff 57 C7
Benholm Aberds 135 C8
Beningbrough N Yorks 95 D8
Benington Herts 41 B5
Benington Lincs 79 E6
Benllech Anglesey 82 C5
Benmore Argyll 145 E10
Benmore Stirling 126 B3
Benmore Lodge Highld 156 H6
Bennacott Corn 8 E4
Bennan N Ayrs 143 F10
Benniworth Lincs 91 F6
Benover Kent 29 E8
Bensham T&W 110 C5
Benslie N Ayrs 118 E3
Benson Oxon 39 E6
Bent Aberds 135 B6
Bent Gate Lancs 87 B5
Benthall Northumb 117 B8
Benthall Shrops 61 D6
Bentham Glos 37 C6
Benthoul Aberdeen 141 D7
Bentlawnt Shrops 60 D3
Bentley E Yorks 97 F6
Bentley Hants 27 E5
Bentley S Yorks 89 D6
Bentley Suff 56 F5
Bentley Warks 63 E6
Bentley Worcs 50 C4
Bentley Heath W Mid 51 B6
Benton Devon 21 F5
Bentpath Dumfries 115 E6
Bents W Loth 120 C2
Bentworth Hants 26 E4
Benvie Dundee 134 F3
Benwick Cambs 66 E3
Beoley Worcs 51 C5
Beoraidbeg Highld 147 B9
Bepton W Sus 16 C2
Berden Essex 41 B7
Bere Alston Devon 6 C2
Bere Ferrers Devon 6 C2
Bere Regis Dorset 13 E6
Berepper Corn 3 D5
Bergh Apton Norf 69 D6
Berinsfield Oxon 39 E5
Berkeley Glos 36 E3
Berkhamsted Herts 40 D2
Berkley Som 24 E3
Berkswell W Mid 51 B7
Bermondsey London 28 B4
Bernera Highld 149 F13
Bernice Argyll 145 D10
Bernisdale Highld 149 C9
Berrick Salome Oxon 39 E6
Berriedale Highld 158 H3
Berrier Cumb 99 B5
Berriew Powys 59 D8
Berrington Northumb 123 E6
Berrington Shrops 60 D5
Berrow Som 22 D5
Berrow Green Worcs 50 D2
Berry Down Cross Devon 20 E4
Berry Hill Glos 36 C2
Berry Hill Pembs 45 E2
Berry Pomeroy Devon 7 C6
Berryhillock Moray 152 B5
Berrynarbor Devon 20 E4
Bersham Wrex 73 E7
Berstane Orkney 159 G5
Berwick E Sus 18 E2
Berwick Bassett Wilts 25 B5
Berwick Hill Northumb 110 B4
Berwick St James Wilts 25 F5
Berwick St John Wilts 13 B7
Berwick St Leonard Wilts 24 F4
Berwick-upon-Tweed Northumb 123 D5
Bescar Lancs 85 C4
Besford Worcs 50 E4
Bessacarr S Yorks 89 D7
Bessels Leigh Oxon 38 D4
Bessingby E Yorks 97 C7
Bessingham Norf 81 D7
Bestbeech Hill E Sus 18 B3
Besthorpe Norf 68 E3
Besthorpe Notts 77 C8
Bestwood Nottingham 77 E5
Bestwood Village Notts 77 E5
Beswick E Yorks 97 E6
Betchworth Sur 28 E3
Bethania Ceredig 46 C4
Bethania Gwyn 71 C8
Bethania Gwyn 83 F6
Bethel Anglesey 82 D3
Bethel Gwyn 72 F3
Bethel Gwyn 82 E5
Bethersden Kent 30 E3
Bethesda Gwyn 83 E6
Bethesda Pembs 32 C1
Bethlehem Carms 33 B7
Bethnal Green London 41 F6
Betley Staffs 74 E4
Betsham Kent 29 B7
Betteshanger Kent 31 D7
Bettiscombe Dorset 11 E8
Bettisfield Wrex 73 F8
Betton Shrops 60 D3
Betton Shrops 74 F3
Bettws Bridgend 34 F3
Bettws Mon 35 C6
Bettws Newport 35 E6
Bettws Cedewain Powys 59 E8
Bettws Gwerfil Goch Denb 72 E4
Bettws Ifan Ceredig 46 E2
Bettws Newydd Mon 35 D7
Bettws-y-crwyn Shrops 60 F2
Bettyhill Highld 157 C10
Betws Carms 33 C7
Betws Bledrws Ceredig 46 D4
Betws-Garmon Gwyn 82 F5
Betws-y-Coed Conwy 83 F7
Betws-yn-Rhos Conwy 72 B3
Beulah Ceredig 45 E4
Beulah Powys 47 D8
Bevendean Brighton 17 D7
Bevercotes Notts 77 B6
Beverley E Yorks 97 F6
Beverston Glos 37 E5
Bevington Glos 36 E3
Bewaldeth Cumb 108 F2
Bewcastle Cumb 109 B5
Bewdley Worcs 50 B2
Bewerley N Yorks 94 C4
Bewholme E Yorks 97 D7
Bexhill E Sus 18 E4
Bexley London 29 B5
Bexleyheath London 29 B5
Bexwell Norf 67 D6
Beyton Suff 56 C3
Bhaltos W Isles 154 D5
Bhatarsaigh W Isles 148 J1
Bibury Glos 37 D8
Bicester Oxon 39 B5
Bickenhall Som 11 C7
Bickenhill W Mid 63 F5
Bicker Lincs 78 F5
Bickershaw Gtr Man 86 D4
Bickerstaffe Lancs 86 D2
Bickerton Ches E 74 D2
Bickerton N Yorks 95 D7
Bickington Devon 7 B5
Bickington Devon 20 F4
Bickleigh Devon 6 C3
Bickleigh Devon 10 D4
Bickleton Devon 20 F4
Bickley London 28 C5
Bickley Moss Ches W 74 E2
Bicknacre Essex 42 D3
Bicknoller Som 22 F3
Bicknor Kent 30 D2
Bickton Hants 14 C2
Bicton Shrops 60 C4
Bicton Shrops 60 F2
Bidborough Kent 29 E6
Biddenden Kent 19 B5
Biddenham Bedford 53 E8
Biddestone Wilts 24 B3
Biddisham Som 23 D5
Biddlesden Bucks 52 E4
Biddlestone Northumb 117 D5
Biddulph Staffs 75 D5
Biddulph Moor Staffs 75 D6
Bideford Devon 9 B6
Bidford-on-Avon Warks 51 D6
Bidston Mers 85 E3
Bielby E Yorks 96 E3
Bieldside Aberdeen 141 D7
Bierley IoW 15 G6
Bierley W Yorks 94 F4
Bierton Bucks 39 C8
Big Sand Highld 149 A12
Bigbury Devon 6 E4
Bigbury on Sea Devon 6 E4
Bigby Lincs 90 D4
Biggar Cumb 92 C1
Biggar S Lanark 120 F3
Biggin Derbys 75 D8
Biggin Derbys 76 E2
Biggin N Yorks 95 F8
Biggin Hill London 28 D5
Biggings Shetland 160 G3
Biggleswade C Beds 54 E2
Bighouse Highld 157 C11
Bighton Hants 26 F4
Bignor W Sus 16 C3
Bigton Shetland 160 L5
Bilberry Corn 4 C5
Bilborough Nottingham 76 E5
Bilbrook Som 22 E2
Bilbrough N Yorks 95 E8
Bilbster Highld 158 E4
Bildershaw Durham 101 B7
Bildeston Suff 56 E3
Billericay Essex 42 E2
Billesdon Leics 64 D4
Billesley Warks 51 D6
Billingborough Lincs 78 F4
Billinge Mers 86 D3
Billingford Norf 81 E6
Billingham Stockton 102 B2
Billinghay Lincs 78 D4
Billingley S Yorks 88 D5
Billingshurst W Sus 16 B4
Billingsley Shrops 61 F7
Billington C Beds 40 B2
Billington Lancs 93 F7
Billockby Norf 69 C7
Billy Row Durham 110 F4
Bilsborrow Lancs 92 F5
Bilsby Lincs 79 B7
Bilsham W Sus 16 D3
Bilsington Kent 19 B7
Bilson Green Glos 36 C3
Bilsthorpe Notts 77 C6
Bilsthorpe Moor Notts 77 D6
Bilston Midloth 121 C5
Bilston W Mid 62 E3
Bilstone Leics 63 D7
Bilting Kent 30 E4
Bilton E Yorks 97 F7
Bilton Northumb 117 C8
Bilton Warks 52 B2
Bilton in Ainsty N Yorks 95 E7
Bimbister Orkney 159 G4
Binbrook Lincs 91 E6
Binchester Blocks Durham 110 F5
Bincombe Dorset 12 F4
Bindal Highld 151 C12
Binegar Som 23 E8
Binfield Brack 27 B6
Binfield Heath Oxon 26 B5
Bingfield Northumb 110 B2
Bingham Notts 77 F7
Bingley W Yorks 94 F4
Bings Heath Shrops 60 C5
Binham Norf 81 D5
Binley Hants 26 D2
Binley W Mid 51 B8
Binley Woods Warks 51 B8
Binniehill Falk 119 B8
Binsoe N Yorks 94 B5
Binstead IoW 15 E6
Binsted Hants 27 E5
Binton Warks 51 D6
Bintree Norf 81 E6
Binweston Shrops 60 D3
Birch Essex 43 C5
Birch Gtr Man 87 D6
Birch Green Essex 43 C5
Birch Heath Ches W 74 C2
Birch Hill Ches W 74 B2
Birch Vale Derbys 87 F8
Bircham Newton Norf 80 D3
Bircham Tofts Norf 80 D3
Birchanger Essex 41 B8
Birchencliffe W Yorks 88 C2
Bircher Hereford 49 C6
Birchgrove Cardiff 22 B3
Birchgrove Swansea 33 E8
Birchington Kent 31 C6
Birchmoor Warks 63 D6
Birchover Derbys 76 C2
Birchwood Lincs 78 C2
Birchwood Warr 86 E4
Bircotes Notts 89 E7
Birdbrook Essex 55 E8
Birdforth N Yorks 95 B7
Birdham W Sus 16 E2
Birdholme Derbys 76 C3
Birdingbury Warks 52 C2
Birdlip Glos 37 C6
Birds Edge W Yorks 88 D3
Birdsall N Yorks 96 C4
Birdsgreen Shrops 61 F7
Birdsmoor Gate Dorset 11 D8
Birdston E Dunb 119 B6
Birdwell S Yorks 88 D4
Birdwood Glos 36 C4
Birgham Borders 122 F3
Birkby N Yorks 101 D8
Birkdale Mers 85 C4
Birkenhead Mers 85 F4
Birkenhills Aberds 153 D7
Birkenshaw N Lanark 119 C6
Birkenshaw W Yorks 88 B3
Birkhall Aberds 140 E2
Birkhill Angus 134 F3
Birkhill Borders 114 C5
Birkholme Lincs 65 B6
Birkin N Yorks 89 B6
Birley Hereford 49 D6
Birling Kent 29 C7
Birling Northumb 117 D8
Birling Gap E Sus 18 F2
Birlingham Worcs 50 E4
Birmingham W Mid 62 F4
Birnam Perth 133 E7
Birse Aberds 140 E4
Birsemore Aberds 140 E4
Birstall Leics 64 D2
Birstall W Yorks 88 B3
Birstwith N Yorks 94 D5
Birthorpe Lincs 78 F4
Birtley Hereford 49 C5
Birtley Northumb 109 B8
Birtley T&W 111 D5
Birts Street Worcs 50 F2
Bisbrooke Rutland 65 E5
Biscathorpe Lincs 91 F6
Biscot Luton 40 B3
Bish Mill Devon 10 B2
Bisham Windsor 39 F8
Bishampton Worcs 50 D4
Bishop Auckland Durham 101 B7
Bishop Burton E Yorks 97 F5
Bishop Middleham Durham 111 F6
Bishop Monkton N Yorks 95 C6
Bishop Norton Lincs 90 E3
Bishop Sutton Bath 23 D7
Bishop Thornton N Yorks 95 C5
Bishop Wilton E Yorks 96 D3
Bishopbridge Lincs 90 E4
Bishopbriggs E Dunb 119 C6
Bishopmill Moray 152 B2
Bishops Cannings Wilts 24 C5
Bishop's Castle Shrops 60 F3
Bishop's Caundle Dorset 12 C4
Bishop's Cleeve Glos 37 B6
Bishops Frome Hereford 49 E8
Bishop's Green Essex 42 C2
Bishop's Hull Som 11 B7
Bishop's Itchington Warks 51 D8
Bishops Lydeard Som 11 B6
Bishops Nympton Devon 10 B2
Bishop's Offley Staffs 61 B7
Bishop's Stortford Herts 41 B7
Bishop's Sutton Hants 26 F4
Bishop's Tachbrook Warks 51 C8
Bishops Tawton Devon 20 F4
Bishop's Waltham Hants 15 C6
Bishop's Wood Staffs 62 D2
Bishopsbourne Kent 31 D5
Bishopsteignton Devon 7 B7
Bishopstoke Hants 15 C5
Bishopston Swansea 33 F6
Bishopstone Bucks 39 C8
Bishopstone E Sus 17 D8
Bishopstone Hereford 49 E6
Bishopstone Swindon 38 F2
Bishopstone Wilts 13 B8
Bishopstrow Wilts 24 E3
Bishopswood Som 11 C7
Bishopsworth Bristol 23 C7
Bishopthorpe York 95 E8
Bishopton Darl 102 B1
Bishopton Dumfries 105 E8
Bishopton N Yorks 95 B6
Bishopton Renfs 118 B4
Bishopton Warks 51 D6
Bishton Newport 35 F7
Bisley Glos 37 D6
Bisley Sur 27 D7
Bispham Blackpool 92 E3
Bispham Green Lancs 86 C2
Bissoe Corn 3 B6
Bisterne Close Hants 14 D3
Bitchfield Lincs 65 B6
Bittadon Devon 20 E4
Bittaford Devon 6 D4
Bittering Norf 68 C2
Bitterley Shrops 49 B7
Bitterne Soton 15 C5
Bitteswell Leics 64 F2
Bitton S Glos 23 C8
Bix Oxon 39 F7
Bixter Shetland 160 H5
Blaby Leics 64 E2
Black Bourton Oxon 38 D2
Black Callerton T&W 110 C4
Black Clauchrie S Ayrs 112 F2
Black Corries Lodge Highld 131 D6
Black Crofts Argyll 124 B5
Black Dog Devon 10 D3
Black Heddon Northumb 110 B3
Black Lane Gtr Man 87 D5
Black Marsh Shrops 60 E3
Black Mount Argyll 131 E6
Black Notley Essex 42 B3
Black Pill Swansea 33 E7
Black Tar Pembs 44 E4
Black Torrington Devon 9 D6
Blackacre Dumfries 114 E3
Blackadder West Borders 122 D4
Blackawton Devon 7 D6
Blackborough Devon 11 D5
Blackborough End Norf 67 C6
Blackboys E Sus 18 C2
Blackbrook Derbys 76 E3
Blackbrook Mers 86 E3
Blackbrook Staffs 74 F4
Blackburn Aberds 141 C7
Blackburn Aberds 152 E5
Blackburn Blackburn 86 B4
Blackburn W Loth 120 C2
Blackcraig Dumfries 113 F7
Blackden Heath Ches E 74 B4
Blackdog Aberds 141 C8
Blackfell T&W 111 D5
Blackfield Hants 14 D5
Blackford Cumb 108 C3
Blackford Perth 127 D7
Blackford Som 12 B4
Blackford Som 23 E6
Blackfordby Leics 63 C7
Blackgang IoW 15 G5
Blackhall Colliery Durham 111 F7
Blackhall Mill T&W 110 D4
Blackhall Rocks Durham 111 F7
Blackham E Sus 29 F5
Blackhaugh Borders 121 F7
Blackheath Essex 43 B6
Blackheath Suff 57 B8
Blackheath Sur 27 E8
Blackheath W Mid 62 F3
Blackhill Aberds 153 C10
Blackhill Aberds 153 D10
Blackhill Highld 149 C8
Blackhills Highld 151 F12
Blackhills Moray 152 C2
Blackhorse S Glos 23 B8
Blackland Wilts 24 C5
Blacklaw Aberds 153 C6
Blackley Gtr Man 87 D6
Blacklunans Perth 134 C1
Blackmill Bridgend 34 F3
Blackmoor Hants 27 F5
Blackmoor Gate Devon 21 E5
Blackmore Essex 42 D2
Blackmore End Essex 55 F8
Blackmore End Herts 40 C4
Blackness Falk 120 B3
Blacknest Hants 27 E5
Blacko Lancs 93 E8
Blackpool Blackpool 92 F3
Blackpool Devon 7 E6
Blackpool Pembs 32 C1
Blackpool Gate Cumb 108 B5
Blackridge W Loth 119 C8
Blackrock Argyll 142 B4
Blackrock Mon 35 C6
Blackrod Gtr Man 86 C4
Blackshaw Dumfries 107 C7
Blackshaw Head W Yorks 87 B7
Blacksmith's Green Suff 56 C5
Blackstone W Sus 17 C6
Blackthorn Oxon 39 C6
Blackthorpe Suff 56 C3
Blacktoft E Yorks 90 B2
Blacktop Aberdeen 141 D7
Blacktown Newport 35 F6
Blackwall Tunnel London 41 F6
Blackwater Corn 3 B6
Blackwater Hants 27 D6
Blackwater IoW 15 F6
Blackwaterfoot N Ayrs 143 F9
Blackwell Darl 101 C7
Blackwell Derbys 75 B8
Blackwell Derbys 76 D4
Blackwell W Sus 28 F4
Blackwell Warks 51 E7
Blackwell Worcs 50 B4
Blackwood = Coed Duon Caerph 35 E5
Blackwood S Lanark 119 E7
Blackwood Hill Staffs 75 D6
Blacon Ches W 73 C7
Bladnoch Dumfries 105 D8
Bladon Oxon 38 C4
Blaen-gwynfi Neath 34 E2
Blaen-waun Carms 32 B3
Blaen-y-coed Carms 32 B4
Blaen-y-Cwm Denb 72 F4
Blaen-y-cwm Gwyn 71 E8
Blaen-y-cwm Powys 59 B7
Blaenannerch Ceredig 45 E4
Blaenau Ffestiniog Gwyn 71 C8
Blaenavon Torf 35 D6
Blaencelyn Ceredig 46 D2
Blaendyryn Powys 47 F8
Blaenffos Pembs 45 F3
Blaengarw Bridgend 34 E3
Blaengwrach Neath 34 D2
Blaenpennal Ceredig 46 C5
Blaenplwyf Ceredig 46 B4
Blaenporth Ceredig 45 E4
Blaenrhondda Rhondda 34 D3
Blaenycwm Ceredig 47 B7
Blagdon N Som 23 D7
Blagdon Torbay 7 C6
Blagdon Hill Som 11 C7
Blagill Cumb 109 E7
Blaguegate Lancs 86 D2
Blaich Highld 130 B4
Blain Highld 147 E9
Blaina Bl Gwent 35 D6
Blair Atholl Perth 133 C5
Blair Drummond Stirling 127 E6
Blairbeg N Ayrs 143 E11
Blairdaff Aberds 141 C5
Blairglas Argyll 126 F2
Blairgowrie Perth 134 E1
Blairhall Fife 128 F2
Blairingone Perth 127 E8
Blairland N Ayrs 118 E3
Blairlogie Stirling 127 E7
Blairlomond Argyll 125 F7
Blairmore Argyll 145 E10
Blairnamarrow Moray 139 C8
Blairquhosh Stirling 126 F4
Blair's Ferry Argyll 145 G8
Blairskaith E Dunb 119 B5
Blaisdon Glos 36 C4
Blakebrook Worcs 50 B3
Blakedown Worcs 50 B3
Blakelaw Borders 122 F3
Blakeley Staffs 62 E2
Blakeley Lane Staffs 75 E6
Blakemere Hereford 49 E5
Blakeney Glos 36 D3
Blakeney Norf 81 C6
Blakenhall Ches E 74 E4
Blakenhall W Mid 62 E3
Blakeshall Worcs 62 F2
Blakesley Northants 52 D4
Blanchland Northumb 110 D2
Bland Hill N Yorks 94 D5
Blandford Forum Dorset 13 D6
Blandford St Mary Dorset 13 D6
Blanefield Stirling 119 B5
Blankney Lincs 78 C3
Blantyre S Lanark 119 D6
Blar a'Chaorainn Highld 131 C5
Blaran Argyll 124 D4
Blarghour Argyll 125 D5
Blarmachfoldach Highld 130 C4
Blarnalearoch Highld 150 B4
Blashford Hants 14 D2
Blaston Leics 64 E5
Blatherwycke Northants 65 E6
Blawith Cumb 98 F4
Blaxhall Suff 57 D7
Blaxton S Yorks 89 D7
Blaydon T&W 110 C4
Bleadon N Som 22 D5
Bleak Hey Nook Gtr Man 87 D8
Blean Kent 30 C5
Bleasby Lincs 90 F5
Bleasby Notts 77 E7
Bleasdale Lancs 93 E5
Bleatarn Cumb 100 C2
Blebocraigs Fife 129 C6
Bleddfa Powys 48 C4
Bledington Glos 38 B2
Bledlow Bucks 39 D7
Bledlow Ridge Bucks 39 E7
Blegbie E Loth 121 C7
Blencarn Cumb 109 F6
Blencogo Cumb 107 E8
Blendworth Hants 15 C8
Blenheim Park Norf 80 D4
Blennerhasset Cumb 107 E8
Blervie Castle Moray 151 F13
Bletchingdon Oxon 39 C5
Bletchingley Sur 28 D4
Bletchley M Keynes 53 F6
Bletchley Shrops 74 F3
Bletherston Pembs 32 B1
Bletsoe Bedford 53 D8
Blewbury Oxon 39 F5
Blickling Norf 81 E7
Blidworth Notts 77 D5
Blindburn Northumb 116 C4
Blindcrake Cumb 107 F8
Blindley Heath Sur 28 E4
Blisland Corn 5 B6
Bliss Gate Worcs 50 B2
Blissford Hants 14 C2
Blisworth Northants 52 D5
Blithbury Staffs 62 B4
Blitterlees Cumb 107 D8
Blockley Glos 51 F6
Blofield Norf 69 D6
Blofield Heath Norf 69 C6
Blo' Norton Norf 56 B4
Bloomfield Borders 115 B8
Blore Staffs 75 E8
Blount's Green Staffs 75 F7
Blowick Mers 85 C4
Bloxham Oxon 52 F2
Bloxholm Lincs 78 D3
Bloxwich W Mid 62 D3
Bloxworth Dorset 13 E6
Blubberhouses N Yorks 94 D4
Blue Anchor Som 22 E2
Blue Anchor Swansea 33 E6
Blue Row Essex 43 C6
Blundeston Suff 69 E8
Blunham C Beds 54 D2
Blunsdon St Andrew Swindon 37 F8
Bluntington Worcs 50 B3
Bluntisham Cambs 54 B4
Blunts Corn 5 C8
Blyborough Lincs 90 E3
Blyford Suff 57 B8
Blymhill Staffs 62 C2
Blyth Northumb 117 F9
Blyth Notts 89 F7
Blyth Bridge Borders 120 E4
Blythburgh Suff 57 B8
Blythe Borders 121 E8
Blythe Bridge Staffs 75 E6
Blyton Lincs 90 E2
Boarhills Fife 129 C7
Boarhunt Hants 15 D7
Boars Head Gtr Man 86 D3
Boars Hill Oxon 38 D4
Boarshead E Sus 18 B2
Boarstall Bucks 39 C6
Boasley Cross Devon 9 E6
Boat of Garten Highld 138 C5
Boath Highld 151 D8
Bobbing Kent 30 C2
Bobbington Staffs 62 E2
Bobbingworth Essex 41 D8
Bocaddon Corn 5 D6
Bochastle Stirling 126 D5
Bocking Essex 42 B3
Bocking Churchstreet Essex 42 B3
Boddam Aberds 153 D11
Boddam Shetland 160 M5
Boddington Glos 37 B5
Bodedern Anglesey 82 C3
Bodelwyddan Denb 72 B4
Bodenham Hereford 49 D7
Bodenham Wilts 14 B2
Bodenham Moor Hereford 49 D7
Bodermid Gwyn 70 E2
Bodewryd Anglesey 82 B3
Bodfari Denb 72 B4
Bodffordd Anglesey 82 D4
Bodham Norf 81 C7
Bodiam E Sus 18 C4
Bodicote Oxon 52 F2
Bodieve Corn 4 B4
Bodinnick Corn 5 D6
Bodle Street Green E Sus 18 D3
Bodmin Corn 5 C5
Bodney Norf 67 E8
Bodorgan Anglesey 82 E3
Bodsham Kent 30 E5
Boduan Gwyn 70 D4
Bodymoor Heath Warks 63 E5
Bogallan Highld 151 F9
Bogbrae Aberds 153 E10
Bogend Borders 122 E3
Bogend S Ayrs 118 F3
Boghall W Loth 120 C2
Boghead S Lanark 119 E7
Bogmoor Moray 152 B3
Bogniebrae Aberds 152 D5
Bognor Regis W Sus 16 E3
Bograxie Aberds 141 C6
Bogside N Lanark 119 D8
Bogton Aberds 153 C6
Bogue Dumfries 113 F6
Bohenie Highld 137 F5
Bohortha Corn 3 C7
Bohuntine Highld 137 F5
Boirseam W Isles 154 J5
Bojewyan Corn 2 C2
Bolam Durham 101 B6
Bolam Northumb 117 F6
Bolberry Devon 6 F4
Bold Heath Mers 86 F3
Boldon T&W 111 C6
Boldon Colliery T&W 111 C6
Boldre Hants 14 E4
Boldron Durham 101 C5
Bole Notts 89 F8
Bolehill Derbys 76 D2
Boleside Borders 121 F7
Bolham Devon 10 C4
Bolham Water Devon 11 C6
Bolingey Corn 4 D2
Bollington Ches E 75 B6
Bollington Cross Ches E 75 B6
Bolney W Sus 17 B6
Bolnhurst Bedford 53 D8
Bolshan Angus 135 D6
Bolsover Derbys 76 B4
Bolsterstone S Yorks 88 E3
Bolstone Hereford 49 F7
Boltby N Yorks 102 F2
Bolter End Bucks 39 E7
Bolton Cumb 99 B8
Bolton E Loth 121 B8
Bolton E Yorks 96 D3
Bolton Gtr Man 86 D5
Bolton Northumb 117 C7
Bolton Abbey N Yorks 94 D3
Bolton Bridge N Yorks 94 D3
Bolton-by-Bowland Lancs 93 E7
Bolton-le-Sands Lancs 92 C4
Bolton Low Houses Cumb 108 E2
Bolton-on-Swale N Yorks 101 E7
Bolton Percy N Yorks 95 E8
Bolton Town End Lancs 92 C4
Bolton upon Dearne S Yorks 89 D5
Boltonfellend Cumb 108 C4
Boltongate Cumb 108 E2
Bolventor Corn 5 B6
Bomere Heath Shrops 60 C4
Bon-y-maen Swansea 33 E7
Bonar Bridge Highld 151 B9
Bonawe Argyll 125 B6
Bonby N Lincs 90 C4
Boncath Pembs 45 F4
Bonchester Bridge Borders 115 C8
Bonchurch IoW 15 G6
Bondleigh Devon 9 D8
Bonehill Devon 6 B5
Bonehill Staffs 63 D5
Bo'ness Falk 127 F8
Bonhill W Dunb 118 B3
Boningale Shrops 62 D2
Bonjedward Borders 116 B2
Bonkle N Lanark 119 D8
Bonnavoulin Highld 147 F8
Bonnington Edin 120 C4
Bonnington Kent 19 B7
Bonnybank Fife 129 D5
Bonnybridge Falk 127 F7
Bonnykelly Aberds 153 C8
Bonnyrigg and Lasswade Midloth 121 C6
Bonnyton Aberds 153 E6
Bonnyton Angus 134 F3
Bonnyton Angus 135 D6
Bonsall Derbys 76 D2
Bonskeid House Perth 133 C5
Bont Mon 35 C7
Bont-Dolgadfan Powys 59 D5
Bont-goch Ceredig 58 F3
Bont-newydd Conwy 72 B4
Bont Newydd Gwyn 71 C8
Bont Newydd Gwyn 71 E8
Bontddu Gwyn 58 C3
Bonthorpe Lincs 79 B7
Bontnewydd Ceredig 46 C5
Bontnewydd Gwyn 82 F4
Bontuchel Denb 72 D4
Bonvilston V Glam 22 B2
Booker Bucks 39 E8
Boon Borders 121 E8
Boosbeck Redcar 102 C4
Boot Cumb 98 D3
Boot Street Suff 57 E6
Booth W Yorks 87 B8
Booth Wood W Yorks 87 C8
Boothby Graffoe Lincs 78 D2
Boothby Pagnell Lincs 78 F2
Boothen Stoke 75 E5
Boothferry E Yorks 89 B8
Boothville Northants 53 C5
Bootle Cumb 98 F3
Bootle Mers 85 E4
Booton Norf 81 E7
Boquhan Stirling 126 F4
Boraston Shrops 49 B8
Borden Kent 30 C2
Borden W Sus 16 B2
Bordley N Yorks 94 C2
Bordon Hants 27 F6
Bordon Camp Hants 27 F5
Boreham Essex 42 D3
Boreham Wilts 24 E3
Boreham Street E Sus 18 D3
Borehamwood Herts 40 E4
Boreland Dumfries 114 E4
Boreland Stirling 132 F2
Borgh W Isles 148 H1
Borgh W Isles 154 J4
Borghastan W Isles 154 C7
Borgie Highld 157 D9
Borgue Dumfries 106 E3
Borgue Highld 158 H3
Borley Essex 56 E2
Bornais W Isles 148 F2
Bornesketaig Highld 149 A8
Borness Dumfries 106 E3
Borough Green Kent 29 D7
Boroughbridge N Yorks 95 C6
Borras Head Wrex 73 D7
Borreraig Highld 148 C6
Borrobol Lodge Highld 157 G11
Borrowash Derbys 76 F4
Borrowby N Yorks 102 F2
Borrowdale Cumb 98 C4
Borrowfield Aberds 141 E7
Borth Ceredig 58 E3
Borth-y-Gest Gwyn 71 D6
Borthwickbrae Borders 115 C7
Borthwickshiels Borders 115 C7
Borve Highld 149 D9
Borve Lodge W Isles 154 H5
Borwick Lancs 92 B5
Bosavern Corn 2 C2
Bosbury Hereford 49 E8
Boscastle Corn 8 E3
Boscombe Bmouth 14 E2
Boscombe Wilts 25 F7
Boscoppa Corn 4 D5
Bosham W Sus 16 D2
Bosherston Pembs 44 F4
Boskenna Corn 2 D3
Bosley Ches E 75 C6
Bossall N Yorks 96 C3
Bossiney Corn 8 F2
Bossingham Kent 31 E5
Bossington Som 21 E7
Bostock Green Ches W 74 C3
Boston Lincs 79 E6
Boston Long Hedges Lincs 79 E6
Boston Spa W Yorks 95 E7
Boston West Lincs 79 E5
Boswinger Corn 3 B8
Botallack Corn 2 C2
Botany Bay London 41 E5
Botcherby Cumb 108 D4
Botcheston Leics 63 D8
Botesdale Suff 56 B4
Bothal Northumb 117 F8
Bothamsall Notts 77 B6
Bothel Cumb 107 F8
Bothenhampton Dorset 12 E2
Bothwell S Lanark 119 D7
Botley Bucks 40 D2
Botley Hants 15 C6
Botley Oxon 38 D4
Botolph Claydon Bucks 39 B7
Botolphs W Sus 17 D5
Bottacks Highld 150 E7
Bottesford Leics 77 F8
Bottesford N Lincs 90 D2
Bottisham Cambs 55 C6
Bottlesford Wilts 25 D6
Bottom Boat W Yorks 88 B4
Bottom House Staffs 75 D7
Bottom o'th'Moor Gtr Man 86 C4
Bottom of Hutton Lancs 86 B2
Bottomcraig Fife 129 B5
Botusfleming Corn 6 C2
Botwnnog Gwyn 70 D3
Bough Beech Kent 29 E5
Boughrood Powys 48 F3
Boughspring Glos 36 E2
Boughton Norf 67 D6
Boughton Northants 53 C5
Boughton Notts 77 C6
Boughton Aluph Kent 30 E4
Boughton Lees Kent 30 E4
Boughton Malherbe Kent 30 E2
Boughton Monchelsea Kent 29 D8
Boughton Street Kent 30 D4
Boulby Redcar 103 C5
Boulden Shrops 60 F5
Boulmer Northumb 117 C8
Boulston Pembs 44 D4
Boultenstone Aberds 140 C3
Boultham Lincs 78 C2
Bourn Cambs 54 D4
Bourne Lincs 65 B7
Bourne End Bucks 40 F1
Bourne End C Beds 53 E7
Bourne End Herts 40 D3
Bournemouth Bmouth 13 E8
Bournes Green Glos 37 D6
Bournes Green Southend 43 F5
Bournheath Worcs 50 B4
Bournmoor Durham 111 D6
Bournville W Mid 62 F4
Bourton Dorset 24 F2
Bourton N Som 23 C5
Bourton Oxon 38 F2
Bourton Shrops 61 E5
Bourton on Dunsmore Warks 52 B2
Bourton on the Hill Glos 51 F6
Bourton-on-the-Water Glos 38 B1
Bousd Argyll 146 E5
Boustead Hill Cumb 108 D2
Bouth Cumb 99 F5
Bouthwaite N Yorks 94 B4
Boveney Bucks 27 B7
Boverton V Glam 21 C8
Bovey Tracey Devon 7 B6
Bovingdon Herts 40 D3
Bovingdon Green Bucks 39 F8
Bovingdon Green Herts 40 D3
Bovinger Essex 41 D8
Bovington Camp Dorset 13 F6
Bow Borders 121 E7
Bow Devon 10 D2
Bow Orkney 159 J4
Bow Brickhill M Keynes 53 F7
Bow of Fife Fife 128 C5
Bow Street Ceredig 58 F3
Bowbank Durham 100 B4
Bowburn Durham 111 F6
Bowcombe IoW 15 F5
Bowd Devon 11 E6
Bowden Borders 121 F8
Bowden Devon 7 E6
Bowden Hill Wilts 24 C4
Bowderdale Cumb 100 D1
Bowdon Gtr Man 87 F5
Bower Northumb 116 F3
Bower Hinton Som 12 C2
Bowerchalke Wilts 13 B8
Bowerhill Wilts 24 C4
Bowermadden Highld 158 D4
Bowers Gifford Essex 42 F3
Bowershall Fife 128 E2
Bowertower Highld 158 D4
Bowes Durham 100 C4
Bowgreave Lancs 92 E4
Bowgreen Gtr Man 87 F5
Bowhill Borders 115 B7
Bowhouse Dumfries 107 C7
Bowland Bridge Cumb 99 F6
Bowley Hereford 49 D7
Bowlhead Green Sur 27 F7
Bowling W Dunb 118 B4
Bowling W Yorks 94 F4
Bowling Bank Wrex 73 E7
Bowling Green Worcs 50 D3
Bowmanstead Cumb 99 E5
Bowmore Argyll 142 C4
Bowness-on-Solway Cumb 108 C2
Bowness-on-Windermere Cumb 99 E6
Bowsden Northumb 123 E5
Bowside Lodge Highld 157 C11
Bowston Cumb 99 E6
Bowthorpe Norf 68 D4
Box Glos 37 D5
Box Wilts 24 C3
Box End Bedford 53 E8
Boxbush Glos 36 C4
Boxford Suff 56 E3
Boxford W Berks 26 B2
Boxgrove W Sus 16 D3
Boxley Kent 29 D8
Boxmoor Herts 40 D3
Boxted Essex 56 F4
Boxted Suff 56 D2
Boxted Cross Essex 56 F4
Boxted Heath Essex 56 F4
Boxworth Cambs 54 C4
Boxworth End Cambs 54 C4
Boyden Gate Kent 31 C6
Boylestone Derbys 75 F8
Boyndie Aberds 153 B6
Boynton E Yorks 97 C7
Boysack Angus 135 E6
Boyton Corn 8 E5
Boyton Suff 57 E7
Boyton Wilts 24 F4
Boyton Cross Essex 42 D2
Boyton End Suff 55 E8
Bozeat Northants 53 D7

uxton Norf 81 E8
uxworth Derbys 87 F8
wcle = Buckley Flint 73 C6
wlch Powys 35 B5
wlch-Llan Ceredig 46 D4
wlch-y-cibau Powys 59 C8
wlch-y-fadfa Ceredig 46 E3
wlch-y-ffridd Powys 59 E7
wlch-y-sarnau Powys 48 B2
wlchgwyn Wrex 73 D6
wlchnewydd Carms 32 B4
wlchtocyn Gwyn 70 E4
wlchyddar Powys 59 B8
wlchygroes Pembs 45 F4
yermoor T&W 110 D4
yers Green Durham 110 F5
yfield Northants 52 D3
yfleet Sur 27 C8
yford Hereford 49 E5
ygrave Herts 54 F3
yker T&W 111 C5
ylchau Conwy 72 C3
yley Ches W 74 C4
ynea Carms 33 E6
yrness Northumb 116 D3
ythorn Cambs 53 B8
yton Hereford 49 C5
yworth W Sus 16 B3

C

abharstadh W Isles 155 E8
ablea Perth 133 F6
abourne Lincs 90 D5
abrach Argyll 144 G3
abrach Moray 140 B2
abrich Highld 151 G8
abus Lancs 92 E4
ackle Street E Sus 17 B8
adbury Devon 10 D4
adbury Barton Devon 9 C8
adder E Dunb 119 B6
addington C Beds 40 C3
addonfoot Borders 121 F7
ade Street E Sus 18 C3
adeby Leics 63 D8
adeby S Yorks 89 D6
adeleigh Devon 10 D4
adgwith Corn 3 E6
adham Fife 128 D4
adishead Gtr Man 86 E5
adle Swansea 33 E7
adley Lancs 92 F5
adley Wilts 25 C7
adley Wilts 25 D7
admore End Bucks 39 E7
adnam Hants 14 C3
adney N Lincs 90 D4
adole Flint 73 C6
adoxton V Glam 22 C3
adoxton-Juxta-Neath Neath 34 E1
adshaw Blackburn 86 C5
adzow S Lanark 119 D7
aeathro Gwyn 82 E4
aehopkin Powys 34 C2
aenby Lincs 90 F4
aenby Corner Lincs 90 F3
aér-bryn Carms 33 C6
aer Llan Mon 36 D1
aerau Bridgend 34 E2
aerau Cardiff 22 B3
aerdeon Gwyn 58 C3
aerdydd = Cardiff Cardiff 22 B3
Caerfarchell Pembs 44 C2
Caerffili = Caerphilly Caerph 35 F5
Caerfyrddin = Carmarthen Carms 33 B5
Caergeiliog Anglesey 82 D3
Caergwrle Flint 73 D7
Caergybi = Holyhead Anglesey 82 C2
Caerleon = Caerllion Newport 35 E7
Caerllion = Caerleon Newport 35 E7
Caernarfon Gwyn 82 E4
Caerphilly = Caerffili Caerph 35 F5
Caersws Powys 59 E7
Caerwedros Ceredig 46 D2
Caerwent Mon 36 E1
Caerwych Gwyn 71 D7
Caerwys Flint 72 B5
Caethle Gwyn 58 E3
Caim Anglesey 83 C6
Caio Carms 47 F5
Cairinis W Isles 148 B3
Cairisiadar W Isles 154 D5
Cairminis W Isles 154 J5
Cairnbaan Argyll 145 D7
Cairnbanno Ho. Aberds 153 D8
Cairnborrow Aberds 152 D4
Cairnbrogie Aberds 141 B7
Cairnbulg Castle Aberds 153 B10
Cairncross Angus 134 B4
Cairncross Borders 122 C4
Cairndow Argyll 125 D7
Cairness Aberds 153 B10
Cairneyhill Fife 128 F2
Cairnfield Ho. Moray 152 B4
Cairngaan Dumfries 104 F5
Cairngarroch Dumfries 104 E4
Cairnhill Aberds 153 E6
Cairnie Aberds 141 D7
Cairnie Aberds 152 D4
Cairnorrie Aberds 153 D8
Cairnpark Aberds 141 C7
Cairnryan Dumfries 104 C4
Cairnton Orkney 159 H4
Caister-on-Sea Norf 69 C8
Caistor Lincs 90 D5
Caistor St Edmund Norf 68 D5
Caistron Northumb 117 D5
Caitha Bowland Borders 121 E7
Calais Street Suff 56 F3
Calanais W Isles 154 D7
Calbost W Isles 155 F9
Calbourne IoW 14 F5
Calceby Lincs 79 B6
Calcot Row W Berks 26 B4
Calcott Kent 31 C5
Caldback Shetland 160 C8
Caldbeck Cumb 108 F3
Caldbergh N Yorks 101 F5
Caldecote Cambs 54 D4
Caldecote Cambs 65 F8
Caldecote Herts 54 F3
Caldecote Northants 52 D4
Caldecott Northants 53 C7
Caldecott Oxon 38 E4
Caldecott Rutland 65 E5
Calder Bridge Cumb 98 D2
Calder Hall Cumb 98 D2
Calder Mains Highld 158 E2
Calder Vale Lancs 92 E5
Calderbank N Lanark 119 C7
Calderbrook Gtr Man 87 C7
Caldercruix N Lanark 119 C8
Caldermill S Lanark 119 E6
Calderwood S Lanark 119 D6
Caldhame Angus 134 E4
Caldicot Mon 36 F1
Caldwell Derbys 63 C6
Caldwell N Yorks 101 C6
Caldy Mers 85 F3
Caledrhydiau Ceredig 46 D3
Calfsound Orkney 159 E6
Calgary Argyll 146 F6
Califer Moray 151 F13
California Falk 120 B2
California Norf 69 C8
Calke Derbys 63 B7
Callakille Highld 149 C11
Callaly Northumb 117 D6
Callander Stirling 126 D5
Callaughton Shrops 61 E6
Callestick Corn 4 D2
Calligarry Highld 149 H11
Callington Corn 5 C8
Callow Hereford 49 F6
Callow End Worcs 50 E3
Callow Hill Wilts 37 F7
Callow Hill Worcs 50 B2
Callows Grave Worcs 49 C7
Calmore Hants 14 C4
Calmsden Glos 37 D7
Calne Wilts 24 B5
Calow Derbys 76 B4
Calshot Hants 15 D5
Calstock Corn 6 C2
Calstone Wellington Wilts 24 C5
Calthorpe Norf 81 D7
Calthwaite Cumb 108 E4
Calton N Yorks 94 D2
Calton Staffs 75 D8
Calveley Ches E 74 D2
Calver Derbys 76 B2
Calver Hill Hereford 49 E5
Calverhall Shrops 74 F3
Calverleigh Devon 10 C4
Calverley W Yorks 94 F5
Calvert Bucks 39 B6
Calverton M Keynes 53 F5
Calverton Notts 77 E6
Calvine Perth 133 C5
Calvo Cumb 107 D8
Cam Glos 36 E4
Camas-luinie Highld 136 B2
Camasnacroise Highld 130 D2
Camastianavaig Highld 149 E10
Camasunary Highld 149 G10
Camault Muir Highld 151 G8
Camb Shetland 160 D7
Camber E Sus 19 D6
Camberley Sur 27 C6
Camberwell London 28 B4
Camblesforth N Yorks 89 B7
Cambo Northumb 117 F6
Cambois Northumb 117 F9
Camborne Corn 3 B5
Cambourne Cambs 54 D4
Cambridge Cambs 55 D5
Cambridge Glos 36 D4
Cambridge Town Southend 43 F5
Cambus Clack 127 E7
Cambusavie Farm Highld 151 B10
Cambusbarron Stirling 127 E6
Cambuskenneth Stirling 127 E7
Cambuslang S Lanark 119 C6
Cambusmore Lodge Highld 151 B10
Camden London 41 F5
Camelford Corn 8 F3
Camelsdale Sur 27 F6
Camerory Highld 151 H13
Camer's Green Worcs 50 F2
Camerton Bath 23 D8
Camerton Cumb 107 F7
Camerton E Yorks 91 B6
Camghouran Perth 132 D2
Cammachmore Aberds 141 E8
Cammeringham Lincs 90 F3
Camore Highld 151 B10
Camp Hill Warks 63 E7
Campbeltown Argyll 143 F8
Camperdown T&W 111 B5
Campmuir Perth 134 F2
Campsall S Yorks 89 C6
Campsey Ash Suff 57 D7
Campton C Beds 54 F2
Camptown Borders 116 C2
Camrose Pembs 44 C4
Camserney Perth 133 E5
Camster Highld 158 F4
Camuschoirk Highld 130 C1
Camuscross Highld 149 G11
Camusnagaul Highld 130 B4
Camusnagaul Highld 150 C3
Camusrory Highld 147 B11
Camusteel Highld 149 D12
Camusterrach Highld 149 D12
Camusvrachan Perth 132 E3
Canada Hants 14 C3
Canadia E Sus 18 D4
Canal Side S Yorks 89 C7
Candacraig Ho. Aberds 140 C2
Candlesby Lincs 79 C7
Candy Mill S Lanark 120 E3
Cane End Oxon 26 B4
Canewdon Essex 42 E4
Canford Bottom Dorset 13 D8
Canford Cliffs Poole 13 F8
Canford Magna Poole 13 E8
Canham's Green Suff 56 C4
Canholes Derbys 75 B7
Canisbay Highld 158 C5
Cann Dorset 13 B6
Cann Common Dorset 13 B6
Cannard's Grave Som 23 E8
Cannich Highld 150 H6
Cannington Som 22 F4
Cannock Staffs 62 D3
Cannock Wood Staffs 62 C4
Canon Bridge Hereford 49 E6
Canon Frome Hereford 49 E8
Canon Pyon Hereford 49 E6
Canonbie Dumfries 108 B3
Canons Ashby Northants 52 D3
Canonstown Corn 2 C4
Canterbury Kent 30 D5
Cantley Norf 69 D6
Cantley S Yorks 89 D7
Cantlop Shrops 60 D5
Canton Cardiff 22 B3
Cantraybruich Highld 151 G10
Cantraydoune Highld 151 G10
Cantraywood Highld 151 G10
Cantsfield Lancs 93 B6
Canvey Island Essex 42 F3
Canwick Lincs 78 C2
Canworthy Water Corn 8 E4
Caol Highld 131 B5
Caol Ila Argyll 142 A5
Caolas Argyll 146 G3
Caolas Scalpaigh W Isles 154 H7
Caolas Stocinis W Isles 154 H6
Capel Sur 28 E2
Capel Bangor Ceredig 58 F3
Capel Betws Lleucu Ceredig 46 D5
Capel Carmel Gwyn 70 E2
Capel Coch Anglesey 82 C4
Capel Curig Conwy 83 F7
Capel Cynon Ceredig 46 E2
Capel Dewi Carms 33 B5
Capel Dewi Ceredig 46 E3
Capel Dewi Ceredig 58 F3
Capel Garmon Conwy 83 F8
Capel-gwyn Anglesey 82 D3
Capel Gwyn Carms 33 B5
Capel Gwynfe Carms 33 B8
Capel Hendre Carms 33 C6
Capel Hermon Gwyn 71 E8
Capel Isaac Carms 33 B6
Capel Iwan Carms 45 F4
Capel le Ferne Kent 31 F6
Capel Llanilltern Cardiff 34 F4
Capel Mawr Anglesey 82 D4
Capel St Andrew Suff 57 E7
Capel St Mary Suff 56 F4
Capel Seion Ceredig 46 B5
Capel Tygwydd Ceredig 45 E4
Capel Uchaf Gwyn 70 C5
Capel-y-graig Gwyn 82 E5
Capelulo Conwy 83 D7
Capenhurst Ches W 73 B7
Capernwray Lancs 92 B5
Capheaton Northumb 117 F6
Cappercleuch Borders 115 B5
Capplegill Dumfries 114 D4
Capton Devon 7 D6
Caputh Perth 133 F7
Car Colston Notts 77 E7
Carbis Bay Corn 2 C4
Carbost Highld 149 D9
Carbost Highld 149 E8
Carbrook S Yorks 88 F4
Carbrooke Norf 68 D2
Carburton Notts 77 B6
Carcant Borders 121 D6
Carcary Angus 135 D6
Carclaze Corn 4 D5
Carcroft S Yorks 89 C6
Cardenden Fife 128 E4
Cardeston Shrops 60 C3
Cardiff = Caerdydd Cardiff 22 B3
Cardigan = Aberteifi Ceredig 45 E3
Cardington Bedford 53 E8
Cardington Shrops 60 E5
Cardinham Corn 5 C6
Cardonald Glasgow 118 C5
Cardow Moray 152 D1
Cardrona Borders 121 F6
Cardross Argyll 118 B3
Cardurnock Cumb 107 D8
Careby Lincs 65 C7
Careston Castle Angus 135 D5
Carew Pembs 32 D1
Carew Cheriton Pembs 32 D1
Carew Newton Pembs 32 D1
Carey Hereford 49 F7
Carfrae E Loth 121 C8
Cargenbridge Dumfries 107 B6
Cargill Perth 134 F1
Cargo Cumb 108 D3
Cargreen Corn 6 C2
Carham Northumb 122 F4
Carhampton Som 22 E2
Carharrack Corn 3 B6
Carie Perth 132 D3
Carie Perth 132 F3
Carines Corn 4 D2
Carisbrooke IoW 15 F5
Cark Cumb 92 B3
Carlabhagh W Isles 154 C7
Carland Cross Corn 4 D3
Carlby Lincs 65 C7
Carlecotes S Yorks 88 D2
Carlesmoor N Yorks 94 B4
Carleton Cumb 99 B7
Carleton Cumb 108 D4
Carleton Lancs 92 F3
Carleton N Yorks 94 E2
Carleton Forehoe Norf 68 D3
Carleton Rode Norf 68 E4
Carlin How Redcar 103 C5
Carlingcott Bath 23 D8
Carlisle Cumb 108 D4
Carlops Borders 120 D4
Carlton Bedford 53 D7
Carlton Cambs 55 D7
Carlton Leics 63 D7
Carlton N Yorks 89 B7
Carlton N Yorks 101 C6
Carlton N Yorks 101 F5
Carlton N Yorks 102 F4
Carlton Notts 77 E6
Carlton S Yorks 88 C4
Carlton Stockton 102 B1
Carlton Suff 57 C7
Carlton W Yorks 88 B4
Carlton Colville Suff 69 F8
Carlton Curlieu Leics 64 E3
Carlton Husthwaite N Yorks 95 B7
Carlton in Cleveland N Yorks 102 D3
Carlton in Lindrick Notts 89 F6
Carlton le Moorland Lincs 78 D2
Carlton Miniott N Yorks 102 F1
Carlton on Trent Notts 77 C7
Carlton Scroop Lincs 78 E2
Carluke S Lanark 119 D8
Carmarthen = Caerfyrddin Carms 33 B5
Carmel Anglesey 82 C3
Carmel Carms 33 C6
Carmel Flint 73 B5
Carmel Guern 16
Carmel Gwyn 82 F4
Carmont Aberds 141 F7
Carmunnock Glasgow 119 D6
Carmyle Glasgow 119 C6
Carmyllie Angus 135 E5
Carn-gorm Highld 136 B2
Carnaby E Yorks 97 C7
Carnach Highld 136 B3
Carnach Highld 150 B3
Carnach W Isles 154 H7
Carnachy Highld 157 D10
Càrnais W Isles 154 D5
Carnbee Fife 129 D7
Carnbo Perth 128 D2
Carnbrea Corn 3 B5
Carnduff S Lanark 119 E6
Carnduncan Argyll 142 B3
Carne Corn 3 C8
Carnforth Lancs 92 B4
Carnhedryn Pembs 44 C3
Carnhell Green Corn 2 C5
Carnkie Corn 3 C5
Carnkie Corn 3 C6
Carno Powys 59 E6
Carnoch Highld 150 F5
Carnoch Highld 150 H6
Carnock Fife 128 F2
Carnon Downs Corn 3 B6
Carnousie Aberds 153 C6
Carnoustie Angus 135 F5
Carnwath S Lanark 120 E2
Carnyorth Corn 2 C2
Carperby N Yorks 101 F5
Carpley Green N Yorks 100 F4
Carr S Yorks 89 E6
Carr Hill T&W 111 C5
Carradale Argyll 143 E9
Carragraich W Isles 154 H6
Carrbridge Highld 138 B5
Carrefour Selous Jersey 17
Carreg-wen Pembs 45 E4
Carreglefn Anglesey 82 C3
Carrick Argyll 145 E8
Carrick Fife 129 C6
Carrick Castle Argyll 145 D10
Carrick Ho. Orkney 159 E6
Carriden Falk 128 F2
Carrington Gtr Man 86 E5
Carrington Lincs 79 D6
Carrington Midloth 121 C6
Carrog Conwy 71 C8
Carrog Denb 72 E5
Carron Falk 127 F7
Carron Moray 152 D2
Carron Bridge Stirling 127 F6
Carronbridge Dumfries 113 E8
Carronshore Falk 127 F7
Carrshield Northumb 109 E8
Carrutherstown Dumfries 107 B8
Carrville Durham 111 E6
Carsaig Argyll 144 E6
Carsaig Argyll 147 J8
Carscreugh Dumfries 105 D6
Carse Gray Angus 134 D4
Carse Ho. Argyll 144 G6
Carsegowan Dumfries 105 D8
Carseriggan Dumfries 105 C7
Carsethorn Dumfries 107 D6
Carshalton London 28 C3
Carsington Derbys 76 D2
Carskiey Argyll 143 H7
Carsluith Dumfries 105 D8
Carsphairn Dumfries 113 E5
Carstairs S Lanark 120 E2
Carstairs Junction S Lanark 120 E2
Carswell Marsh Oxon 38 E3
Carter's Clay Hants 14 B4
Carterton Oxon 38 D2
Carterway Heads Northumb 110 D3
Carthew Corn 4 D5
Carthorpe N Yorks 101 F8
Cartington Northumb 117 D6
Cartland S Lanark 119 E8
Cartmel Cumb 92 B3
Cartmel Fell Cumb 99 F6
Carway Carms 33 D5
Cary Fitzpaine Som 12 B3
Cas-gwent = Chepstow Mon 36 E2
Cascob Powys 48 C4
Cashlie Perth 132 E1
Cashmoor Dorset 13 C7
Casnewydd = Newport Newport 35 F7
Cassey Compton Glos 37 C7
Cassington Oxon 38 C4
Cassop Durham 111 F6
Castell Denb 72 C5
Castell-Howell Ceredig 46 E3
Castell-Nedd = Neath Neath 33 E8
Castell Newydd Emlyn = Newcastle Emlyn Carms 46 E2
Castell-y-bwch Torf 35 E6
Castellau Rhondda 34 F4
Casterton Cumb 93 B6
Castle Acre Norf 67 C8
Castle Ashby Northants 53 D6
Castle Bolton N Yorks 101 E5
Castle Bromwich W Mid 62 F5
Castle Bytham Lincs 65 C6
Castle Caereinion Powys 59 D8
Castle Camps Cambs 55 E7
Castle Carrock Cumb 108 D5
Castle Cary Som 23 F8
Castle Combe Wilts 24 B3
Castle Donington Leics 63 B8
Castle Douglas Dumfries 106 C4
Castle Eaton Swindon 37 E8
Castle Eden Durham 111 F7
Castle Forbes Aberds 140 C5
Castle Frome Hereford 49 E8
Castle Green Sur 27 C7
Castle Gresley Derbys 63 C6
Castle Heaton Northumb 122 E5
Castle Hedingham Essex 55 F8
Castle Hill Kent 29 E7
Castle Huntly Perth 128 B5
Castle Kennedy Dumfries 104 D5
Castle O'er Dumfries 115 E5
Castle Pulverbatch Shrops 60 D4
Castle Rising Norf 67 B6
Castle Stuart Highld 151 G10
Castlebay = Bagh a Chaisteil W Isles 148 J1
Castlebythe Pembs 32 B1
Castlecary N Lanark 119 B7
Castlecraig Highld 151 E11
Castlefairn Dumfries 113 F7
Castleford W Yorks 88 B5
Castlehill Borders 120 F5
Castlehill Highld 158 D3
Castlehill W Dunb 118 B3
Castlemaddy Dumfries 113 F5
Castlemartin Pembs 44 F4
Castlemilk Dumfries 107 B8
Castlemilk Glasgow 119 D6
Castlemorris Pembs 44 B4
Castlemorton Worcs 50 F2
Castleside Durham 110 E3
Castlethorpe M Keynes 53 E6
Castleton Angus 134 E3
Castleton Argyll 145 E7
Castleton Derbys 88 F2
Castleton Gtr Man 87 C6
Castleton N Yorks 102 D4
Castleton Newport 35 F6
Castletown Ches W 73 D8
Castletown Highld 151 G10
Castletown Highld 158 D3
Castletown IoM 84 F2
Castletown T&W 111 D6
Castleweary Borders 115 D7
Castley N Yorks 95 E5
Caston Norf 68 E2
Castor Pboro 65 E8
Catacol N Ayrs 143 D10
Catbrain S Glos 36 F2
Catbrook Mon 36 D2
Catchall Corn 2 D3
Catchems Corner W Mid 51 B7
Catchgate Durham 110 D4
Catcleugh Northumb 116 D3
Catcliffe S Yorks 88 F5
Catcott Som 23 F5
Caterham Sur 28 D4
Catfield Norf 69 B6
Catfirth Shetland 160 H6
Catford London 28 B4
Catforth Lancs 92 F4
Cathays Cardiff 22 B3
Cathcart Glasgow 119 C5
Cathedine Powys 35 B5
Catherington Hants 15 C7
Catherton Shrops 49 B8
Catlodge Highld 138 E2
Catlowdy Cumb 108 B4
Catmore W Berks 38 F4
Caton Lancs 92 C5
Caton Green Lancs 92 C5
Catrine E Ayrs 113 B5
Cat's Ash Newport 35 E7
Catsfield E Sus 18 D4
Catshill Worcs 50 B4
Cattal N Yorks 95 D7
Cattawade Suff 56 F5
Catterall Lancs 92 E4
Catterick N Yorks 101 E7
Catterick Bridge N Yorks 101 E7
Catterick Garrison N Yorks 101 E6
Catterlen Cumb 108 F4
Catterline Aberds 135 B8
Catterton N Yorks 95 E8
Catthorpe Leics 52 B3
Cattistock Dorset 12 E3
Catton N Yorks 95 B6
Catton Northumb 109 D8
Catwick E Yorks 97 E7
Catworth Cambs 53 B8
Caudlesprings Norf 68 D2
Caulcott Oxon 39 B5
Cauldcots Angus 135 E6
Cauldhame Stirling 126 E5
Cauldmill Borders 115 C8
Cauldon Staffs 75 E7
Caulkerbush Dumfries 107 D6
Caulside Dumfries 115 F7
Caunsall Worcs 62 F2
Caunton Notts 77 D7
Causeway End Dumfries 105 C8
Causeway Foot W Yorks 94 F3
Causeway-head Stirling 127 E6
Causewayend S Lanark 120 F3
Causewayhead Cumb 107 D8
Causey Park Bridge Northumb 117 E7
Causeyend Aberds 141 C8
Cautley Cumb 100 E1
Cavendish Suff 56 E2
Cavendish Bridge Leics 63 B8
Cavenham Suff 55 C8
Caversfield Oxon 39 B5
Caversham Reading 26 B5
Caverswall Staffs 75 E6
Cavil E Yorks 96 F3
Cawdor Highld 151 F11
Cawkwell Lincs 79 B5
Cawood N Yorks 95 F8
Cawsand Corn 6 D2
Cawston Norf 81 E7
Cawthorne S Yorks 88 D3
Cawthorpe Lincs 65 B7
Cawton N Yorks 96 B2
Caxton Cambs 54 D4
Caynham Shrops 49 B7
Caythorpe Lincs 78 E2
Caythorpe Notts 77 E6
Cayton N Yorks 103 F8
Ceann a Bhaigh W Isles 148 B2
Ceann a Deas Loch Baghasdail W Isles 148 G2
Ceann Shiphoirt W Isles 155 F7
Ceann Tarabhaigh W Isles 154 F7
Ceannacroc Lodge Highld 136 C5
Cearsiadair W Isles 155 E8
Cefn Berain Conwy 72 C3
Cefn-brith Conwy 72 D3
Cefn Canol Powys 73 F6
Cefn-coch Conwy 83 E8
Cefn Coch Powys 59 B8
Cefn-coed-y-cymmer M Tydf 34 D4
Cefn Cribbwr Bridgend 34 F2
Cefn Cross Bridgend 34 F2
Cefn-ddwysarn Gwyn 72 F3
Cefn Einion Shrops 60 F2
Cefn-gorwydd Powys 47 E8
Cefn-mawr Wrex 73 E6
Cefn-y-bedd Flint 73 D7
Cefn-y-pant Carms 32 B2
Cefneithin Carms 33 C6
Cei-bach Ceredig 46 D3
Ceinewydd = New Quay Ceredig 46 D2
Ceint Anglesey 82 D4
Cellan Ceredig 46 E5
Cellarhead Staffs 75 E6
Cemaes Anglesey 82 B3
Cemmaes Powys 58 D5
Cemmaes Road Powys 58 D5
Cenarth Carms 45 E4
Cenin Gwyn 71 C5
Central Invclyd 118 B2
Ceos W Isles 155 E8
Ceres Fife 129 C6
Cerne Abbas Dorset 12 D4
Cerney Wick Glos 37 E7
Cerrigceinwen Anglesey 82 D4
Cerrigydrudion Conwy 72 E3
Cessford Borders 116 B3
Ceunant Gwyn 82 E5
Chaceley Glos 50 F3
Chacewater Corn 3 B6
Chackmore Bucks 52 F4
Chacombe Northants 52 E2
Chad Valley W Mid 62 F4
Chadderton Gtr Man 87 D7
Chadderton Fold Gtr Man 87 D6
Chaddesden Derby 76 F3
Chaddesley Corbett Worcs 50 B3
Chaddleworth W Berks 26 B2
Chadlington Oxon 38 B3
Chadshunt Warks 51 D8
Chadwell Leics 64 B4
Chadwell St Mary Thurrock 29 B7
Chadwick End W Mid 51 B7
Chadwick Green Mers 86 E3
Chaffcombe Som 11 C8
Chagford Devon 10 F2
Chailey E Sus 17 C7
Chain Bridge Lincs 79 E6
Chainbridge Cambs 66 D4
Chainhurst Kent 29 E8
Chalbury Dorset 13 D8
Chalbury Common Dorset 13 D8
Chaldon Sur 28 D4
Chaldon Herring Dorset 13 F5
Chale IoW 15 G5
Chale Green IoW 15 G5
Chalfont Common Bucks 40 E3
Chalfont St Giles Bucks 40 E2
Chalfont St Peter Bucks 40 E3
Chalford Glos 37 D5
Chalgrove Oxon 39 E6
Chalk Kent 29 B7
Challacombe Devon 21 E5
Challoch Dumfries 105 C7
Challock Kent 30 D4
Chalton C Beds 40 B3
Chalton Hants 15 C8
Chalvington E Sus 18 E2
Chancery Ceredig 46 B4
Chandler's Ford Hants 14 B5
Channel Tunnel Kent 19 B8
Channerwick Shetland 160 L6
Chantry Som 24 E2
Chantry Suff 56 E5
Chapel Fife 128 E4
Chapel Allerton Som 23 D6
Chapel Allerton W Yorks 95 F6
Chapel Amble Corn 4 B4
Chapel Brampton Northants 52 C5
Chapel Chorlton Staffs 74 F5
Chapel-en-le-Frith Derbys 87 F8
Chapel End Warks 63 E7
Chapel Green Warks 52 C2
Chapel Green Warks 63 F6
Chapel Haddlesey N Yorks 89 B6
Chapel Head Cambs 66 F3
Chapel Hill Aberds 153 E10
Chapel Hill Lincs 78 D5
Chapel Hill Mon 36 E2
Chapel Hill N Yorks 95 E6
Chapel Lawn Shrops 48 B5
Chapel-le-Dale N Yorks 93 B7
Chapel Milton Derbys 87 F8
Chapel of Garioch Aberds 141 B6
Chapel Row W Berks 26 C3
Chapel St Leonards Lincs 79 B8
Chapel Stile Cumb 99 D5
Chapelgate Lincs 66 B4
Chapelhall N Lanark 119 C7
Chapelhill Dumfries 114 E3
Chapelhill Highld 151 D11
Chapelhill N Ayrs 118 E2
Chapelhill Perth 128 B4
Chapelhill Perth 133 F7
Chapelknowe Dumfries 108 B3
Chapelton Angus 135 E6
Chapelton Devon 9 B7
Chapelton Highld 138 C5
Chapelton S Lanark 119 E6
Chapeltown Blackburn 86 C5
Chapeltown Moray 139 B8
Chapeltown S Yorks 88 E4
Chapmans Well Devon 9 E5
Chapmanslade Wilts 24 E3
Chapmore End Herts 41 C6
Chappel Essex 42 B4
Chard Som 11 D8
Chardstock Devon 11 D8
Charfield S Glos 36 E4
Charford Worcs 50 C4
Charing Kent 30 E3
Charing Cross Dorset 14 C2
Charing Heath Kent 30 E3
Charingworth Glos 51 F7
Charlbury Oxon 38 C3
Charlcombe Bath 24 C2
Charlecote Warks 51 D7
Charles Devon 21 F5
Charles Tye Suff 56 D4
Charlesfield Dumfries 107 C8
Charleston Angus 134 E3
Charleston Renfs 118 C4
Charlestown Aberdeen 141 D8
Charlestown Corn 4 D5
Charlestown Derbys 87 E8
Charlestown Dorset 12 G4
Charlestown Fife 128 F2
Charlestown Gtr Man 87 D6
Charlestown Highld 149 A13
Charlestown Highld 151 G9
Charlestown W Yorks 87 B7
Charlestown of Aberlour Moray 152 D2
Charlesworth Derbys 87 E8
Charleton Devon 7 E5
Charlton Hants 25 E8
Charlton Herts 40 B4
Charlton London 28 B5
Charlton Northants 52 F3
Charlton Northumb 116 F4
Charlton Som 23 D8
Charlton Telford 61 C5
Charlton W Sus 16 C2
Charlton Wilts 13 B7
Charlton Wilts 25 D6
Charlton Wilts 37 F6
Charlton Worcs 50 E5
Charlton Abbots Glos 37 B7
Charlton Adam Som 12 B3
Charlton-All-Saints Wilts 14 B2
Charlton Down Dorset 12 E4
Charlton Horethorne Som 12 B4
Charlton Kings Glos 37 B6
Charlton Mackerell Som 12 B3
Charlton Marshall Dorset 13 D6
Charlton Musgrove Som 12 B5
Charlton on Otmoor Oxon 39 C5
Charltons Redcar 102 C4
Charlwood Sur 28 E3
Charlynch Som 22 F4
Charminster Dorset 12 E4
Charmouth Dorset 11 E8
Charndon Bucks 39 B6
Charney Bassett Oxon 38 E3
Charnock Richard Lancs 86 C3
Charsfield Suff 57 D6
Chart Corner Kent 29 D8
Chart Sutton Kent 30 E2
Charter Alley Hants 26 D3
Charterhouse Som 23 D6
Charterville Allotments Oxon 38 C3
Chartham Kent 30 D5
Chartham Hatch Kent 30 D5
Chartridge Bucks 40 D2
Charvil Wokingham 27 B5
Charwelton Northants 52 D3
Chasetown Staffs 62 D4
Chastleton Oxon 38 B2
Chasty Devon 8 D5
Chatburn Lancs 93 E7
Chatcull Staffs 74 F4
Chatham Medway 29 C8
Chathill Northumb 117 B7
Chattenden Medway 29 B8
Chatteris Cambs 66 F3
Chattisham Suff 56 E4
Chatto Borders 116 C3
Chatton Northumb 117 B6
Chawleigh Devon 10 C2
Chawley Oxon 38 D4
Chawston Bedford 54 D2
Chawton Hants 26 F5
Cheadle Gtr Man 87 F6
Cheadle Staffs 75 E7
Cheadle Heath Gtr Man 87 F6
Cheadle Hulme Gtr Man 87 F6
Cheam London 28 C3
Cheapside Sur 27 D8
Chearsley Bucks 39 C7
Chebsey Staffs 62 B2
Checkendon Oxon 39 F6
Checkley Ches E 74 E4
Checkley Hereford 49 F7
Checkley Staffs 75 F7
Chedburgh Suff 55 D8
Cheddar Som 23 D6
Cheddington Bucks 40 C2
Cheddleton Staffs 75 D6
Cheddon Fitzpaine Som 11 B7
Chedglow Wilts 37 E6
Chedgrave Norf 69 E6
Chedington Dorset 12 D2
Chediston Suff 57 B7
Chedworth Glos 37 C7
Chedzoy Som 22 F5
Cheeklaw Borders 122 D3
Cheeseman's Green Kent 19 B7
Cheglinch Devon 20 E4
Cheldon Devon 10 C2
Chelford Ches E 74 B5
Chell Heath Stoke 75 D5
Chellaston Derby 76 F3
Chellington Bedford 53 D7
Chelmarsh Shrops 61 F7
Chelmer Village Essex 42 D3
Chelmondiston Suff 57 F6
Chelmorton Derbys 75 C8
Chelmsford Essex 42 D3
Chelsea London 28 B3
Chelsfield London 29 C5
Chelsworth Suff 56 E3
Cheltenham Glos 37 B6
Chelveston Northants 53 C7
Chelvey N Som 23 C6
Chelwood Bath 23 C8
Chelwood Common E Sus 17 B8
Chelwood Gate E Sus 17 B8
Chelworth Wilts 37 E6
Chelworth Green Wilts 37 E7
Chemistry Shrops 74 E2
Chenies Bucks 40 E3
Cheny Longville Shrops 60 F4
Chepstow = Cas-gwent Mon 36 E2
Chequerfield W Yorks 89 B5
Cherhill Wilts 24 B5
Cherington Glos 37 E6
Cherington Warks 51 F7
Cheriton Devon 21 E6
Cheriton Hants 15 B6
Cheriton Kent 19 B8
Cheriton Swansea 33 E5
Cheriton Bishop Devon 10 E2
Cheriton Fitzpaine Devon 10 D3
Cheriton or Stackpole Elidor Pembs 44 F4
Cherrington Telford 61 B6
Cherry Burton E Yorks 97 E5
Cherry Hinton Cambs 55 D5
Cherry Orchard Worcs 50 D3
Cherry Willingham Lincs 78 B3
Cherrybank Perth 128 B3
Chertsey Sur 27 C8
Cheselbourne Dorset 13 E5
Chesham Bucks 40 D2
Chesham Bois Bucks 40 E2
Cheshunt Herts 41 D6
Cheslyn Hay Staffs 62 D3
Chessington London 28 C2
Chester Ches W 73 C8
Chester-Le-Street Durham 111 D5
Chester Moor Durham 111 E5
Chesterblade Som 23 E8
Chesterfield Derbys 76 B3
Chesters Borders 116 B2
Chesters Borders 116 C2
Chesterton Cambs 55 C5
Chesterton Cambs 65 E8
Chesterton Glos 37 D7
Chesterton Oxon 39 B5
Chesterton Shrops 61 E7
Chesterton Staffs 74 E5
Chesterton Warks 51 D8
Chesterwood Northumb 109 C8
Chestfield Kent 30 C5
Cheston Devon 6 D4
Cheswardine Shrops 61 B7
Cheswick Northumb 123 E6
Chetnole Dorset 12 D4
Chettiscombe Devon 10 C4
Chettisham Cambs 66 F5
Chettle Dorset 13 C7
Chetton Shrops 61 E6
Chetwode Bucks 39 B6
Chetwynd Aston Telford 61 C7
Cheveley Cambs 55 C7
Chevening Kent 29 D5
Chevington Suff 55 D8
Chevithorne Devon 10 C4
Chew Magna Bath 23 C7
Chew Stoke Bath 23 C7
Chewton Keynsham Bath 23 C8
Chewton Mendip Som 23 D7
Chicheley M Keynes 53 E7
Chichester W Sus 16 D2
Chickerell Dorset 12 F4
Chicklade Wilts 24 F4
Chicksgrove Wilts 24 F4
Chidden Hants 15 C7
Chiddingfold Sur 27 F7
Chiddingly E Sus 18 D2
Chiddingstone Kent 29 E5
Chiddingstone Causeway Kent 29 E6
Chiddingstone Hoath Kent 29 E5
Chideock Dorset 12 E2
Chidham W Sus 15 D8
Chidswell W Yorks 88 B3
Chieveley W Berks 26 B2
Chignall Smealy Essex 42 C2
Chignall St James Essex 42 D2
Chigwell Essex 41 E7
Chigwell Row Essex 41 E7
Chilbolton Hants 25 F8
Chilcomb Hants 15 B6
Chilcombe Dorset 12 E3
Chilcompton Som 23 D8
Chilcote Leics 63 C6
Child Okeford Dorset 13 C6
Childer Thornton Ches W 73 B7
Childrey Oxon 38 F3
Child's Ercall Shrops 61 B6
Childswickham Worcs 51 F5
Childwall Mers 86 F2
Childwick Green Herts 40 C4
Chilfrome Dorset 12 E3
Chilgrove W Sus 16 C2
Chilham Kent 30 D4
Chilhampton Wilts 25 F5
Chilla Devon 9 D6
Chillaton Devon 9 F6
Chillenden Kent 31 D6
Chillerton IoW 15 F5
Chillesford Suff 57 D7
Chillingham Northumb 117 B6
Chillington Devon 7 E5
Chillington Som 11 C8
Chilmark Wilts 24 F4
Chilson Oxon 38 C3
Chilsworthy Corn 6 B2
Chilsworthy Devon 8 D5
Chilthorne Domer Som 12 C3
Chiltington E Sus 17 C7
Chilton Bucks 39 C6
Chilton Durham 101 B7
Chilton Oxon 38 F4
Chilton Cantelo Som 12 B3
Chilton Foliat Wilts 25 B8
Chilton Lane Durham 111 F6
Chilton Polden Som 23 F5
Chilton Street Suff 55 E8
Chilton Trinity Som 22 F4
Chilvers Coton Warks 63 F7
Chilwell Notts 76 F5
Chilworth Hants 14 C5
Chilworth Sur 27 E8
Chimney Oxon 38 D3
Chineham Hants 26 D4
Chingford London 41 E6
Chinley Derbys 87 F8
Chinley Head Derbys 87 F8
Chinnor Oxon 39 D7
Chipnall Shrops 74 F4
Chippenhall Green Suff 57 B6
Chippenham Cambs 55 C7
Chippenham Wilts 24 B4
Chipperfield Herts 40 D3
Chipping Herts 54 F4
Chipping Lancs 93 E6
Chipping Campden Glos 51 F6
Chipping Hill Essex 42 C4
Chipping Norton Oxon 38 B3
Chipping Ongar Essex 42 D1
Chipping Sodbury S Glos 36 F4
Chipping Warden Northants 52 E2
Chipstable Som 10 B5
Chipstead Kent 29 D5
Chipstead Sur 28 D3
Chirbury Shrops 60 E2
Chirk = Y Waun Wrex 73 F6
Chirk Bank Shrops 73 F6
Chirmorrie S Ayrs 105 B6
Chirnside Borders 122 D4
Chirnsidebridge Borders 122 D4
Chirton Wilts 25 D5
Chisbury Wilts 25 C7
Chiselborough Som 12 C2
Chiseldon Swindon 25 B6
Chiserley W Yorks 87 B8
Chislehampton Oxon 39 E5
Chislehurst London 28 B5
Chislet Kent 31 C6
Chiswell Green Herts 40 D4
Chiswick London 28 B3
Chiswick End Cambs 54 E4
Chisworth Derbys 87 E7
Chithurst W Sus 16 B2
Chittering Cambs 55 B5
Chitterne Wilts 24 E4
Chittlehamholt Devon 9 B8
Chittlehampton Devon 9 B8
Chittoe Wilts 24 C4
Chivenor Devon 20 F4
Chobham Sur 27 C7
Choicelee Borders 122 D3
Cholderton Wilts 25 E7
Cholesbury Bucks 40 D2
Chollerford Northumb 110 B2
Chollerton Northumb 110 B2
Cholmondeston Ches E 74 C3
Cholsey Oxon 39 F5
Cholstrey Hereford 49 D6
Chop Gate N Yorks 102 E3
Choppington Northumb 117 F8
Chopwell T&W 110 D4
Chorley Ches E 74 D2
Chorley Lancs 86 C3
Chorley Shrops 61 F6
Chorley Staffs 62 C4
Chorleywood Herts 40 E3
Chorlton cum Hardy Gtr Man 87 E6
Chorlton Lane Ches W 73 E8
Choulton Shrops 60 F3
Chowdene T&W 111 D5
Chowley Ches W 73 D8
Chrishall Essex 54 F5
Christchurch Cambs 66 E4
Christchurch Dorset 14 E2
Christchurch Glos 36 C2
Christchurch Newport 35 F7
Christian Malford Wilts 24 B4
Christleton Ches W 73 C8
Christmas Common Oxon 39 E7
Christon N Som 23 D5
Christon Bank Northumb 117 B8
Christow Devon 10 F3
Chryston N Lanark 119 B6
Chudleigh Devon 7 B6
Chudleigh Knighton Devon 7 B6
Chulmleigh Devon 9 C8
Chunal Derbys 87 E8
Church Lancs 86 B5
Church Aston Telford 61 C7
Church Brampton Northants 52 C5
Church Broughton Derbys 76 F2
Church Crookham Hants 27 D6
Church Eaton Staffs 62 C2
Church End C Beds 40 B2
Church End C Beds 53 F7
Church End C Beds 54 F2
Church End Cambs 66 D3
Church End Cambs 66 F2
Church End E Yorks 97 D6
Church End Essex 42 B3
Church End Essex 55 E6
Church End Hants 26 D4
Church End Lincs 78 F5
Church End Warks 63 E6
Church End Warks 63 E6
Church End Wilts 24 B5
Church Enstone Oxon 38 B3
Church Fenton N Yorks 95 F8
Church Green Devon 11 E6
Church Green Norf 68 E3
Church Gresley Derbys 63 C6
Church Hanborough Oxon 38 C4
Church Hill Ches W 74 C3
Church Houses N Yorks 102 E4
Church Knowle Dorset 13 F7
Church Laneham Notts 77 B8
Church Langton Leics 64 E4
Church Lawford Warks 52 B2
Church Lawton Ches E 74 D5
Church Leigh Staffs 75 F7
Church Lench Worcs 50 D5
Church Mayfield Staffs 75 E8
Church Minshull Ches E 74 C3
Church Norton W Sus 16 E2
Church Preen Shrops 60 E5
Church Pulverbatch Shrops 60 D4
Church Stoke Powys 60 E2
Church Stowe Northants 52 D4
Church Street Kent 29 B8
Church Stretton Shrops 60 E4
Church Town N Lincs 89 D8
Church Town Sur 28 D4
Church Village Rhondda 34 F4
Church Warsop Notts 77 C5
Churcham Glos 36 C4
Churchbank Shrops 48 B4
Churchbridge Staffs 62 D3
Churchdown Glos 37 C5
Churchend Essex 42 B2
Churchend Essex 43 E6
Churchend S Glos 36 E4
Churchfield W Mid 62 E4
Churchgate Street Essex 41 C7
Churchill Devon 11 D8
Churchill Devon 20 E4
Churchill N Som 23 D6
Churchill Oxon 38 B2
Churchill Worcs 50 B3
Churchill Worcs 50 D4
Churchinford Som 11 C7
Churchover Warks 64 F2
Churchstanton Som 11 C6
Churchstow Devon 6 E5
Churchtown Derbys 76 C2
Churchtown IoM 84 C4
Churchtown Lancs 92 E4

ofton Wilts 25 C7
ofts of Benachielt Highld 158 G3
ofts of Haddo Aberds 153 E8
ofts of Inverthernie Aberds 153 D7
ofts of Meikle Ardo Aberds 153 D8
ofty Swansea 33 E6
oggan Argyll 124 C3
oglin Cumb 109 E5
oich Highld 150 B7
ois Dughaill W Isles 148 F2
omarty Highld 151 E10
omblet Aberds 153 E7
omdale Highld 139 B6
omer Herts 41 B5
omer Norf 81 C8
omford Derbys 76 D2
omhall S Glos 36 E3
omhall Common Glos 36 F3
omor W Isles 155 E9
omra Highld 137 E8
omwell Notts 77 C7
onberry E Ayrs 113 B6
ondall Hants 27 E5
onk-y-Voddy IoM 84 D3
onton Mers 86 F2
ook Cumb 99 E6
ook Durham 110 F4
ook of Devon Perth 128 D2
ookedholm E Ayrs 118 F4
ookes S Yorks 88 F4
ookham Northumb 122 F5
ookham W Berks 26 C3
ookham Village Hants 27 D5
ookhaugh Borders 114 B4
ookhouse Borders 116 B3
ooklands Cumb 99 F7
opredy Oxon 52 E2
opston Leics 64 C2
opthorne Worcs 50 E4
opton N Yorks 103 F5
opwell Bishop Notts 77 F6
opwell Butler Notts 77 F6
os W Isles 155 A10
osbost W Isles 155 E8
osby Cumb 107 F7
osby IoM 84 E3
osby N Lincs 90 C2
osby Garrett Cumb 100 D2
osby Ravensworth Cumb 99 C8
osby Villa Cumb 107 F7
oscombe Som 23 E7
oss Som 23 D6
oss Ash Mon 35 C8
oss-at-Hand Kent 29 E8
oss Green Devon 9 F5
oss Green Suff 56 D2
oss Green Suff 56 D3
oss Green Warks 51 D8
oss-hands Carms 32 B2
oss Hands Carms 33 C6
oss Hands Pembs 32 C1
oss Hill Derbys 76 E4
oss Houses Shrops 60 D5
oss in Hand E Sus 18 C2
oss in Hand Leics 64 F2
oss Inn Ceredig 46 C4
oss Inn Ceredig 46 D2
oss Inn Rhondda 34 F4
oss Keys Kent 29 D6
oss Lane Head Shrops 61 E7
oss Lanes Corn 3 D5
oss Lanes N Yorks 95 C8
oss Lanes Wrex 73 E7
oss Oak Powys 35 B5
oss of Jackston Aberds 153 E7
oss o'th'hands Derbys 76 E2
oss Street Suff 57 B5
ossaig Argyll 143 C9
ossal Highld 149 E9
ossapol Argyll 146 G2
ossburn Falk 119 B8
ossbush W Sus 16 D4
osscanonby Cumb 107 F7
ossdale Street Norf 81 D8
ossens Mers 85 C4
ossflatts W Yorks 94 E4
ossford Fife 128 F2
ossford S Lanark 119 E8
ossgate Lincs 66 B2
ossgatehall E Loth 121 C6
ossgates Fife 128 F3
ossgates Powys 48 C2
ossgill Lancs 93 C5
osshill E Ayrs 112 B4
osshill Fife 128 E3
osshill S Ayrs 112 D3
osshouse E Ayrs 118 F3
ossings Cumb 108 B5
osskeys Caerph 35 E6
osskirk Highld 157 B13
osslanes Shrops 60 C3
osslee Borders 115 C6
osslee Renfs 118 C4
ossmichael Dumfries 106 C4
Crossmoor Lancs 92 F4
Crossroads Aberds 141 E6
Crossroads E Ayrs 118 F4
Crossway Hereford 49 F8
Crossway Mon 35 C8
Crossway Powys 48 D2
Crossway Green Worcs 50 C3
Crossways Dorset 13 F5
Crosswell Pembs 45 F3
Crosswood Ceredig 47 B5
Crosthwaite Cumb 99 E6
Croston Lancs 86 C2
Crostwick Norf 69 C5
Crostwight Norf 69 B6
Crothair W Isles 154 D6
Crouch Kent 29 D7
Crouch Hill Dorset 12 C5
Crouch House Green Kent 28 E5
Croucheston Wilts 13 B8
Croughton Northants 52 F3
Crovie Aberds 153 B8
Crow Edge S Yorks 88 D2
Crow Hill Hereford 36 B3
Crowan Corn 2 C5
Crowborough E Sus 18 B2
Crowcombe Som 22 F3
Crowdecote Derbys 75 C8
Crowden Derbys 87 E8
Crowell Oxon 39 E7
Crowfield Northants 52 E4
Crowfield Suff 56 D5
Crowhurst E Sus 18 D4
Crowhurst Sur 28 E4
Crowhurst Lane End Sur 28 E4
Crowland Lincs 66 C2
Crowlas Corn 2 C4
Crowle N Lincs 89 C8
Crowle Worcs 50 D4
Crowmarsh Gifford Oxon 39 F6
Crown Corner Suff 57 B6
Crownhill Plym 6 D2
Crownland Suff 56 C4
Crownthorpe Norf 68 D3
Crowntown Corn 2 C5
Crows-an-wra Corn 2 D2
Crowshill Norf 68 D2
Crowsnest Shrops 60 D3
Crowthorne Brack 27 C6
Crowton Ches W 74 B2
Croxall Staffs 63 C5
Croxby Lincs 91 E5
Croxdale Durham 111 F5
Croxden Staffs 75 F7
Croxley Green Herts 40 E3
Croxton Cambs 54 C3
Croxton N Lincs 90 C4
Croxton Norf 67 F8
Croxton Staffs 74 F4
Croxton Kerrial Leics 64 B5
Croxtonbank Staffs 74 F4
Croy Highld 151 G10
Croy N Lanark 119 B7
Croyde Devon 20 F3
Croydon Cambs 54 E4
Croydon London 28 C4
Crubenmore Lodge Highld 138 E2
Cruckmeole Shrops 60 D4
Cruckton Shrops 60 C4
Cruden Bay Aberds 153 E10
Crudgington Telford 61 C6
Crudwell Wilts 37 E6
Crug Powys 48 B3
Crugmeer Corn 4 B4
Crugybar Carms 47 F5
Crulabhig W Isles 154 D6
Crumlin = Crymlyn Caerph 35 E6
Crumpsall Gtr Man 87 D6
Crundale Kent 30 E4
Crundale Pembs 44 D4
Cruwys Morchard Devon 10 C3
Crux Easton Hants 26 D2
Crwbin Carms 33 C5
Crya Orkney 159 H4
Cryers Hill Bucks 40 E1
Crymlyn = Crumlin Caerph 35 E6
Crymlyn Gwyn 83 D6
Crymych Pembs 45 F3
Crynant Neath 34 D1
Crynfryn Ceredig 46 C4
Cuaig Highld 149 C12
Cuan Argyll 124 D3
Cubbington Warks 51 C8
Cubeck N Yorks 100 F4
Cubert Corn 4 D2
Cubley S Yorks 88 D3
Cubley Common Derbys 75 F8
Cublington Bucks 39 B8
Cublington Hereford 49 F6
Cuckfield W Sus 17 B7
Cucklington Som 13 B5
Cuckney Notts 77 B5
Cuckoo Hill Notts 89 E8
Cuddesdon Oxon 39 D6
Cuddington Bucks 39 C7
Cuddington Ches W 74 B3
Cuddington Heath Ches W 73 E8
Cuddy Hill Lancs 92 F4
Cudham London 28 D5
Cudliptown Devon 6 B3
Cudworth S Yorks 88 D4
Cudworth Som 11 C8
Cuffley Herts 41 D6
Cuiashader W Isles 155 B10
Cuidhir W Isles 148 H1
Cuidhtinis W Isles 154 J5
Culbo Highld 151 E9
Culbokie Highld 151 F9
Culburnie Highld 150 G7
Culcabock Highld 151 G9
Culcairn Highld 151 E9
Culcharry Highld 151 F11
Culcheth Warr 86 E4
Culdrain Aberds 152 E5
Culduie Highld 149 D12
Culford Suff 56 B2
Culgaith Cumb 99 B8
Culham Oxon 39 E5
Culkein Highld 156 F3
Culkein Drumbeg Highld 156 F4
Culkerton Glos 37 E6
Cullachie Highld 139 B5
Cullen Moray 152 B5
Cullercoats T&W 111 B6
Cullicudden Highld 151 E9
Cullingworth W Yorks 94 F3
Cullipool Argyll 124 D3
Cullivoe Shetland 160 C7
Culloch Perth 127 C6
Culloden Highld 151 G10
Cullompton Devon 10 D5
Culmaily Highld 151 B11
Culmazie Dumfries 105 D7
Culmington Shrops 60 F4
Culmstock Devon 11 C6
Culnacraig Highld 156 J3
Culnaknock Highld 149 B10
Culpho Suff 57 E6
Culrain Highld 151 B8
Culross Fife 127 F8
Culroy S Ayrs 112 C3
Culsh Aberds 140 E2
Culsh Aberds 153 D8
Culshabbin Dumfries 105 D7
Culswick Shetland 160 J4
Cultercullen Aberds 141 B8
Cults Aberdeen 141 D7
Cults Aberds 152 E5
Cults Dumfries 105 E8
Culverstone Green Kent 29 C7
Culverthorpe Lincs 78 E3
Culworth Northants 52 E3
Culzie Lodge Highld 151 D8
Cumbernauld N Lanark 119 B7
Cumbernauld Village N Lanark 119 B7
Cumberworth Lincs 79 B8
Cuminestown Aberds 153 C8
Cumlewick Shetland 160 L6
Cummersdale Cumb 108 D3
Cummertrees Dumfries 107 C8
Cummingston Moray 152 B1
Cumnock E Ayrs 113 B5
Cumnor Oxon 38 D4
Cumrew Cumb 108 D5
Cumwhinton Cumb 108 D4
Cumwhitton Cumb 108 D5
Cundall N Yorks 95 B7
Cunninghamhead N Ayrs 118 E3
Cunnister Shetland 160 D7
Cupar Fife 129 C5
Cupar Muir Fife 129 C5
Cupernham Hants 14 B4
Curbar Derbys 76 B2
Curbridge Hants 15 C6
Curbridge Oxon 38 D3
Curdridge Hants 15 C6
Curdworth Warks 63 E5
Curland Som 11 C7
Curlew Green Suff 57 C7
Currarie S Ayrs 112 E1
Curridge W Berks 26 B2
Currie Edin 120 C4
Curry Mallet Som 11 B8
Curry Rivel Som 11 B8
Curtisden Green Kent 29 E8
Curtisknowle Devon 6 D5
Cury Corn 3 D5
Cushnie Aberds 153 B7
Cushuish Som 22 F3
Cusop Hereford 48 E4
Cutcloy Dumfries 105 F8
Cutcombe Som 21 F8
Cutgate Gtr Man 87 C6
Cutiau Gwyn 58 C3
Cutlers Green Essex 55 F6
Cutnall Green Worcs 50 C3
Cutsdean Glos 51 F5
Cutthorpe Derbys 76 B3
Cutts Shetland 160 K6
Cuxham Oxon 39 E6
Cuxton Medway 29 C8
Cuxwold Lincs 91 D5
Cwm Bl Gwent 35 D5
Cwm Denb 72 B4
Cwm Swansea 33 E7
Cwm-byr Carms 46 F5
Cwm-Cewydd Gwyn 59 C5
Cwm-cou Ceredig 45 E4
Cwm-Dulais Swansea 33 D7
Cwm-felin-fach Caerph 35 E5
Cwm Ffrwd-oer Torf 35 D6
Cwm-hesgen Gwyn 71 E8
Cwm-hwnt Rhondda 34 D3
Cwm Irfon Powys 47 E7
Cwm-Llinau Powys 58 D5
Cwm-mawr Carms 33 C6
Cwm-parc Rhondda 34 E3
Cwm Penmachno Conwy 71 C8
Cwm-y-glo Carms 33 C6
Cwm-y-glo Gwyn 82 E5
Cwmafan Neath 34 E1
Cwmaman Rhondda 34 E4
Cwmann Carms 46 E4
Cwmavon Torf 35 D6
Cwmbâch Rhondda 34 D4
Cwmbach Carms 32 B3
Cwmbach Carms 33 D5
Cwmbach Powys 48 D2
Cwmbach Powys 48 F3
Cwmbelan Powys 59 F6
Cwmbrân = Cwmbran Torf 35 E6
Cwmbran = Cwmbrân Torf 35 E6
Cwmbrwyno Ceredig 58 F4
Cwmcarn Caerph 35 E6
Cwmcarvan Mon 36 D1
Cwmcych Carms 45 F4
Cwmdare Rhondda 34 D3
Cwmderwen Powys 59 D6
Cwmdu Carms 46 F5
Cwmdu Powys 35 B5
Cwmdu Swansea 33 E7
Cwmduad Carms 46 F2
Cwmdwr Carms 47 F6
Cwmfelin Bridgend 34 F2
Cwmfelin M Tydf 34 D4
Cwmfelin Boeth Carms 32 C2
Cwmfelin Mynach Carms 32 B3
Cwmffrwd Carms 33 C5
Cwmgiedd Powys 34 C1
Cwmgors Neath 33 C8
Cwmgwili Carms 33 C6
Cwmgwrach Neath 34 D2
Cwmhiraeth Carms 46 F2
Cwmifor Carms 33 B7
Cwmisfael Carms 33 C5
Cwmllynfell Neath 33 C8
Cwmorgan Pembs 45 F4
Cwmpengraig Carms 46 F2
Cwmrhos Powys 35 B5
Cwmsychpant Ceredig 46 E3
Cwmtillery Bl Gwent 35 D6
Cwmwysg Powys 34 B2
Cwmyoy Mon 35 B6
Cwmystwyth Ceredig 47 B6
Cwrt Gwyn 58 D3
Cwrt-newydd Ceredig 46 E3
Cwrt-y-cadno Carms 47 E5
Cwrt-y-gollen Powys 35 C6
Cydweli = Kidwelly Carms 33 D5
Cyffordd Llandudno = Llandudno Junction Conwy 83 D7
Cyffylliog Denb 72 D4
Cyfronydd Powys 59 D8
Cymer Neath 34 E2
Cyncoed Cardiff 35 F5
Cynghordy Carms 47 E7
Cynheidre Carms 33 D5
Cynwyd Denb 72 E4
Cynwyl Elfed Carms 32 B4
Cywarch Gwyn 59 C5

D

Dacre Cumb 99 B6
Dacre N Yorks 94 C4
Dacre Banks N Yorks 94 C4
Daddry Shield Durham 109 F8
Dadford Bucks 52 F4
Dadlington Leics 63 E8
Dafarn Faig Gwyn 71 C5
Dafen Carms 33 D6
Daffy Green Norf 68 D2
Dagenham London 41 F7
Daglingworth Glos 37 D6
Dagnall Bucks 40 C2
Dail Beag W Isles 154 C7
Dail bho Dheas W Isles 155 A9
Dail bho Thuath W Isles 155 A9
Dail Mor W Isles 154 C7
Daill Argyll 142 B4
Dailly S Ayrs 112 D2
Dairsie or Osnaburgh Fife 129 C6
Daisy Hill Gtr Man 86 D4
Dalabrog W Isles 148 F2
Dalavich Argyll 125 D5
Dalbeattie Dumfries 106 C5
Dalblair E Ayrs 113 C6
Dalbog Angus 135 B5
Dalbury Derbys 76 F2
Dalby IoM 84 E2
Dalby N Yorks 96 B2
Dalchalloch Perth 132 C4
Dalchalm Highld 157 J12
Dalchenna Argyll 125 E6
Dalchirach Moray 152 E1
Dalchork Highld 157 H8
Dalchreichart Highld 137 C5
Dalchruin Perth 127 C6
Dalderby Lincs 78 C5
Dale Pembs 44 E3
Dale Abbey Derbys 76 F4
Dale Head Cumb 99 C6
Dale of Walls Shetland 160 H3
Dalelia Highld 147 E10
Daless Highld 151 H11
Dalfaber Highld 138 C5
Dalgarven N Ayrs 118 E2
Dalgety Bay Fife 128 F3
Dalginross Perth 127 B6
Dalguise Perth 133 E6
Dalhalvaig Highld 157 D11
Dalham Suff 55 C8
Dalinlongart Argyll 145 E10
Dalkeith Midloth 121 C6
Dallam Warr 86 E3
Dallas Moray 151 F14
Dalleagles E Ayrs 113 C5
Dallinghoo Suff 57 D6
Dallington E Sus 18 D3
Dallington Northants 52 C5
Dallow N Yorks 94 B4
Dalmadilly Aberds 141 C6
Dalmally Argyll 125 C7
Dalmarnock Glasgow 119 C6
Dalmary Stirling 126 E4
Dalmellington E Ayrs 112 D4
Dalmeny Edin 120 B4
Dalmigavie Highld 138 C3
Dalmigavie Lodge Highld 138 B3
Dalmore Highld 151 E9
Dalmuir W Dunb 118 B4
Dalnabreck Highld 147 E9
Dalnacardoch Lodge Perth 132 B4
Dalnacroich Highld 150 F6
Dalnaglar Castle Perth 133 C8
Dalnahaitnach Highld 138 B4
Dalnaspidal Lodge Perth 132 B3
Dalnavaid Perth 133 C7
Dalnavie Highld 151 D9
Dalnawillan Lodge Highld 157 E13
Dalness Highld 131 D5
Dalnessie Highld 157 H9
Dalqueich Perth 128 D2
Dalreavoch Highld 157 J10
Dalry N Ayrs 118 E2
Dalrymple E Ayrs 112 C3
Dalserf S Lanark 119 D8
Dalston Cumb 108 D3
Dalswinton Dumfries 114 F2
Dalton Dumfries 107 B8
Dalton Lancs 86 D2
Dalton N Yorks 95 B7
Dalton N Yorks 101 D6
Dalton Northumb 110 B4
Dalton Northumb 110 D2
Dalton S Yorks 89 E5
Dalton-in-Furness Cumb 92 B2
Dalton-le-Dale Durham 111 E7
Dalton-on-Tees N Yorks 101 D7
Dalton Piercy Hrtlpl 111 F7
Dalveich Stirling 126 B5
Dalvina Lodge Highld 157 E9
Dalwhinnie Highld 138 F2
Dalwood Devon 11 D7
Dalwyne S Ayrs 112 E3
Dam Green Norf 68 F3
Dam Side Lancs 92 E4
Damerham Hants 14 C2
Damgate Norf 69 D7
Damnaglaur Dumfries 104 F5
Damside Borders 120 E4
Danbury Essex 42 D3
Danby N Yorks 103 D5
Danby Wiske N Yorks 101 E8
Dandaleith Moray 152 D2
Danderhall Midloth 121 C6
Dane End Herts 41 B6
Danebridge Ches E 75 C6
Danehill E Sus 17 B8
Danemoor Green Norf 68 D3
Danesford Shrops 61 E7
Daneshill Hants 26 D4
Dangerous Corner Lancs 86 C3
Danskine E Loth 121 C8
Darcy Lever Gtr Man 86 D5
Darenth Kent 29 B6
Daresbury Halton 86 F3
Darfield S Yorks 88 D5
Darfoulds Notts 77 B5
Dargate Kent 30 C4
Darite Corn 5 C7
Darlaston W Mid 62 E3
Darley N Yorks 94 D5
Darley Bridge Derbys 76 C2
Darley Head N Yorks 94 D4
Darlingscott Warks 51 E7
Darlington Darl 101 C7
Darliston Shrops 74 F2
Darlton Notts 77 B7
Darnall S Yorks 88 F4
Darnick Borders 121 F8
Darowen Powys 58 D5
Darra Aberds 153 D7
Darracott Devon 20 F3
Darras Hall Northumb 110 B4
Darrington W Yorks 89 B5
Darsham Suff 57 C8
Dartford Kent 29 B6
Dartford Crossing Kent 29 B6
Dartington Devon 7 C5
Dartmeet Devon 6 B4
Dartmouth Devon 7 D6
Darton S Yorks 88 D4
Darvel E Ayrs 119 F5
Darwell Hole E Sus 18 D3
Darwen Blackburn 86 B4
Datchet Windsor 27 B7
Datchworth Herts 41 C5
Datchworth Green Herts 41 C5
Daubhill Gtr Man 86 D5
Daugh of Kinermony Moray 152 D2
Dauntsey Wilts 37 F6
Dava Moray 151 H13
Davenham Ches W 74 B3
Davenport Green Ches E 74 B5
Daventry Northants 52 C3
David's Well Powys 48 B2
Davidson's Mains Edin 120 B5
Davidstow Corn 8 F3
Davington Dumfries 115 D5
Daviot Aberds 141 B6
Daviot Highld 151 H10
Davoch of Grange Moray 152 C4
Davyhulme Gtr Man 87 E5
Daw's House Corn 8 F5
Dawley Telford 61 D6
Dawlish Devon 7 B7
Dawlish Warren Devon 7 B7
Dawn Conwy 83 D8
Daws Heath Essex 42 F4
Daw's House Corn 8 F5
Dawsmere Lincs 79 F7
Dayhills Staffs 75 F6
Daylesford Glos 38 B2
Ddôl-Cownwy Powys 59 C7
Ddrydwy Anglesey 82 D3
Deadwater Northumb 116 E2
Deaf Hill Durham 111 F6
Deal Kent 31 D7
Deal Hall Essex 43 E6
Dean Cumb 98 B2
Dean Devon 6 C5
Dean Devon 20 E4
Dean Dorset 13 C7
Dean Hants 15 C6
Dean Som 23 E8
Dean Prior Devon 6 C5
Dean Row Ches E 87 F6
Deanburnhaugh Borders 115 C6
Deane Gtr Man 86 D4
Deane Hants 26 D3
Deanich Lodge Highld 150 C6
Deanland Dorset 13 C7
Deans W Loth 120 C3
Deanscales Cumb 98 B2
Deanshanger Northants 53 F5
Deanston Stirling 127 D6
Dearham Cumb 107 F7
Debach Suff 57 D6
Debden Essex 41 E7
Debden Essex 55 F6
Debden Cross Essex 55 F6
Debenham Suff 57 C5
Dechmont W Loth 120 B3
Deddington Oxon 52 F2
Dedham Essex 56 F4
Dedham Heath Essex 56 F4
Deebank Aberds 141 E5
Deene Northants 65 E6
Deenethorpe Northants 65 E6
Deepcar S Yorks 88 E3
Deepcut Sur 27 D7
Deepdale Cumb 100 F2
Deeping Gate Lincs 65 D8
Deeping St James Lincs 65 D8
Deeping St Nicholas Lincs 66 C2
Deerhill Moray 152 C4
Deerhurst Glos 37 B5
Deerness Orkney 159 H6
Defford Worcs 50 E4
Defynnog Powys 34 B3
Deganwy Conwy 83 D7
Deighton N Yorks 102 D1
Deighton W Yorks 88 C2
Deighton York 96 E2
Deiniolen Gwyn 83 E5
Delabole Corn 8 F2
Delamere Ches W 74 C2
Delfrigs Aberds 141 B8
Dell Lodge Highld 139 C6
Delliefure Highld 151 H13
Delnabo Moray 139 C7
Delnadamph Aberds 139 D8
Delph Gtr Man 87 D7
Delves Durham 110 E4
Delvine Perth 133 E8
Dembleby Lincs 78 F3
Denaby Main S Yorks 89 E5
Denbigh = Dinbych Denb 72 C4
Denbury Devon 7 C6
Denby Derbys 76 E3
Denby Dale W Yorks 88 D3
Denchworth Oxon 38 E3
Dendron Cumb 92 B2
Denel End C Beds 53 F8
Denend Aberds 152 E6
Denford Northants 53 B7
Dengie Essex 43 D5
Denham Bucks 40 F3
Denham Suff 55 C8
Denham Suff 57 B5
Denham Street Suff 57 B5
Denhead Aberds 153 C9
Denhead Fife 129 C6
Denhead of Arbilot Angus 135 E5
Denhead of Gray Dundee 134 F3
Denholm Borders 115 C8
Denholme W Yorks 94 F3
Denholme Clough W Yorks 94 F3
Denio Gwyn 70 D4
Denmead Hants 15 C7
Denmore Aberdeen 141 C8
Denmoss Aberds 153 D6
Dennington Suff 57 C6
Denny Falk 127 F7
Denny Lodge Hants 14 D4
Dennyloanhead Falk 127 F7
Denshaw Gtr Man 87 C7
Denside Aberds 141 E7
Densole Kent 31 E6
Denston Suff 55 D8
Denstone Staffs 75 E8
Dent Cumb 100 F2
Denton Cambs 65 F8
Denton Darl 101 C7
Denton E Sus 17 D8
Denton Gtr Man 87 E7
Denton Kent 31 E6
Denton Lincs 77 F8
Denton N Yorks 94 E4
Denton Norf 69 F5
Denton Northants 53 D6
Denton Oxon 39 D5
Denton's Green Mers 86 E2
Denver Norf 67 D6
Denwick Northumb 117 C8
Deopham Norf 68 D3
Deopham Green Norf 68 E3
Depden Suff 55 D8
Depden Green Suff 55 D8
Deptford London 28 B4
Deptford Wilts 24 F5
Derby Derby 76 F3
Derbyhaven IoM 84 F2
Dereham Norf 68 C2
Deri Caerph 35 D5
Derril Devon 8 D5
Derringstone Kent 31 E6
Derrington Staffs 62 B2
Derriton Devon 8 D5
Derry Hill Wilts 24 B4
Derryguaig Argyll 146 H7
Derrythorpe N Lincs 90 D2
Dersingham Norf 80 D2
Dervaig Argyll 146 F7
Derwen Denb 72 D4
Derwenlas Powys 58 E4
Desborough Northants 64 F5
Desford Leics 63 D8
Detchant Northumb 123 F6
Detling Kent 29 D8
Deuddwr Powys 60 C2
Devauden Mon 36 E1
Devil's Bridge Ceredig 47 B6
Devizes Wilts 24 C5
Devol Invclyd 118 B3
Devonport Plym 6 D2
Devonside Clack 127 E8
Devoran Corn 3 C6
Dewar Borders 121 E6
Dewlish Dorset 13 E5
Dewsbury W Yorks 88 B3
Dewsbury Moor W Yorks 88 B3
Dewshall Court Hereford 49 F6
Dhoon IoM 84 D4
Dhoor IoM 84 C4
Dhowin IoM 84 B4
Dial Post W Sus 17 C5
Dibden Hants 14 D5
Dibden Purlieu Hants 14 D5
Dickleburgh Norf 68 F4
Didbrook Glos 51 F5
Didcot Oxon 39 F5
Diddington Cambs 54 C2
Diddlebury Shrops 60 F5
Didley Hereford 49 F6
Didling W Sus 16 C2
Didmarton Glos 37 F5
Didsbury Gtr Man 87 E6
Didworthy Devon 6 C4
Digby Lincs 78 D3
Digg Highld 149 B9
Diggle Gtr Man 87 D8
Digmoor Lancs 86 D2
Digswell Park Herts 41 C5
Dihewyd Ceredig 46 D3
Dilham Norf 69 B6
Dilhorne Staffs 75 E6
Dillarburn S Lanark 119 E8
Dillington Cambs 54 C2
Dilston Northumb 110 C2
Dilton Marsh Wilts 24 E3
Dilwyn Hereford 49 D6
Dinas Carms 45 F4
Dinas Gwyn 70 D3
Dinas Cross Pembs 45 F2
Dinas Dinlle Gwyn 82 F4
Dinas-Mawddwy Gwyn 59 C5
Dinas Powys V Glam 22 B3
Dinbych = Denbigh Denb 72 C4
Dinbych-Y-Pysgod = Tenby Pembs 32 D2
Dinder Som 23 E7
Dinedor Hereford 49 F7
Dingestow Mon 36 C1
Dingle Mers 85 F4
Dingleden Kent 18 B5
Dingley Northants 64 F4
Dingwall Highld 151 F8
Dinlabyre Borders 115 E8
Dinmael Conwy 72 E4
Dinnet Aberds 140 E3
Dinnington S Yorks 89 F6
Dinnington Som 12 C2
Dinnington T&W 110 B5
Dinorwic Gwyn 83 E5
Dinton Bucks 39 C7
Dinton Wilts 24 F5
Dinwoodie Mains Dumfries 114 E4
Dinworthy Devon 8 C5
Dippen N Ayrs 143 F11
Dippenhall Sur 27 E6
Dipple Moray 152 C3
Dipple S Ayrs 112 D2
Diptford Devon 6 D5
Dipton Durham 110 D4
Dirdhu Highld 139 B6
Dirleton E Loth 129 F7
Dirt Pot Northumb 109 E8
Discoed Powys 48 C4
Diseworth Leics 63 B8
Dishes Orkney 159 F7
Dishforth N Yorks 95 B6
Disley Ches E 87 F7
Diss Norf 56 B5
Disserth Powys 48 D2
Distington Cumb 98 B2
Ditchampton Wilts 25 F5
Ditcheat Som 23 F8
Ditchingham Norf 69 E6
Ditchling E Sus 17 C7
Ditherington Shrops 60 C5
Dittisham Devon 7 D6
Ditton Halton 86 F2
Ditton Kent 29 D8
Ditton Green Cambs 55 D7
Ditton Priors Shrops 61 F6
Divach Highld 137 B7
Divlyn Carms 47 F6
Dixton Glos 50 F4
Dixton Mon 36 C2
Dobcross Gtr Man 87 D7
Dobwalls Corn 5 C7
Doc Penfro = Pembroke Dock Pembs 44 E4
Doccombe Devon 10 F2
Dochfour Ho. Highld 151 H9
Dochgarroch Highld 151 G9
Docking Norf 80 D3
Docklow Hereford 49 D7
Dockray Cumb 99 B5
Dockroyd W Yorks 94 F3
Dodburn Borders 115 D7
Doddinghurst Essex 42 E1
Doddington Cambs 66 E3
Doddington Kent 30 D3
Doddington Lincs 78 B2
Doddington Northumb 123 F5
Doddington Shrops 49 B8
Doddiscombsleigh Devon 10 F3
Dodford Northants 52 C4
Dodford Worcs 50 B4
Dodington S Glos 24 A2
Dodleston Ches W 73 C7
Dods Leigh Staffs 75 F7
Dodworth S Yorks 88 D4
Doe Green Warr 86 F3
Doe Lea Derbys 76 C4
Dog Village Devon 10 E4
Dogdyke Lincs 78 D5
Dogmersfield Hants 27 D5
Dogridge Wilts 37 F7
Dogsthorpe Pboro 65 D8
Dol-fôr Powys 58 D5
Dôl-y-Bont Ceredig 58 F3
Dol-y-cannau Powys 48 E4
Dolanog Powys 59 C7
Dolau Powys 48 C3
Dolau Rhondda 34 F3
Dolbenmaen Gwyn 71 C6
Dolfach Powys 59 D6
Dolfor Powys 59 F8
Dolgarrog Conwy 83 E7
Dolgellau Gwyn 58 C4
Dolgran Carms 46 F3
Dolhendre Gwyn 72 F2
Doll Highld 157 J11
Dollar Clack 127 E8
Dolley Green Powys 48 C4
Dollwen Ceredig 58 F3
Dolphin Flint 73 B5
Dolphinholme Lancs 92 D5
Dolphinton S Lanark 120 E4
Dolton Devon 9 C7
Dolwen Conwy 83 D8
Dolwen Powys 59 D6
Dolwyd Conwy 83 D8
Dolwyddelan Conwy 83 F7
Dolyhir Powys 48 D4
Doncaster S Yorks 89 D6
Dones Green Ches W 74 B3
Donhead St Andrew Wilts 13 B7
Donhead St Mary Wilts 13 B7
Donibristle Fife 128 F3
Donington Lincs 78 F5
Donington on Bain Lincs 91 F6
Donington South Ing Lincs 78 F5
Donisthorpe Leics 63 C7
Donkey Town Sur 27 C7
Donnington Glos 38 B1
Donnington Hereford 50 F2
Donnington Shrops 61 D5
Donnington Telford 61 C7
Donnington W Berks 26 C2
Donnington W Sus 16 D2
Donnington Wood Telford 61 C7
Donyatt Som 11 C8
Doonfoot S Ayrs 112 C3
Dorback Lodge Highld 139 C6
Dorchester Dorset 12 E4
Dorchester Oxon 39 E5
Dordon Warks 63 D6
Dore S Yorks 88 F4
Dores Highld 151 H8
Dorking Sur 28 E2
Dormansland Sur 28 E5
Dormanstown Redcar 102 B3
Dormington Hereford 49 E7
Dormston Worcs 50 D4
Dornal S Ayrs 105 B6
Dorney Bucks 27 B7
Dornie Highld 149 F13
Dornoch Highld 151 C10
Dornock Dumfries 108 C2
Dorrery Highld 158 E2
Dorridge W Mid 51 B6
Dorrington Lincs 78 D3
Dorrington Shrops 60 D4
Dorsington Warks 51 E6
Dorstone Hereford 48 E5
Dorton Bucks 39 C6
Dorusduain Highld 136 B2
Dosthill Staffs 63 E6
Dottery Dorset 12 E2
Doublebois Corn 5 C6
Dougarie N Ayrs 143 E9
Doughton Glos 37 E5
Douglas IoM 84 E3
Douglas S Lanark 119 F8
Douglas & Angus Dundee 134 F4
Douglas Water S Lanark 119 F8
Douglas West S Lanark 119 F8
Douglastown Angus 134 E4
Doulting Som 23 E8
Dounby Orkney 159 F3
Doune Highld 156 J7
Doune Stirling 127 D6
Doune Park Aberds 153 B7
Douneside Aberds 140 D3
Dounie Highld 151 B8
Dounreay Highld 157 C12
Dousland Devon 6 C3
Dovaston Shrops 60 B3
Dove Holes Derbys 75 B7
Dovenby Cumb 107 F7
Dover Kent 31 E7
Dovercourt Essex 57 F6
Doverdale Worcs 50 C3
Doveridge Derbys 75 F8
Doversgreen Sur 28 E3
Dowally Perth 133 E7
Dowbridge Lancs 92 F4
Dowdeswell Glos 37 C6
Dowlais M Tydf 34 D4
Dowland Devon 9 C7
Dowlish Wake Som 11 C8
Down Ampney Glos 37 E8
Down Hatherley Glos 37 B5
Down St Mary Devon 10 D2
Down Thomas Devon 6 D3
Downcraig Ferry N Ayrs 145 H10
Downderry Corn 5 D8
Downe London 28 C5
Downend IoW 15 F6
Downend S Glos 23 B8
Downend W Berks 26 B2
Downfield Dundee 134 F3
Downgate Corn 5 B8
Downham Essex 42 E3
Downham Lancs 93 E7
Downham Northumb 122 F4
Downham Market Norf 67 D6
Downhead Som 23 E8
Downhill Perth 133 F7
Downhill T&W 111 D6
Downholland Cross Lancs 85 D4
Downholme N Yorks 101 E6
Downies Aberds 141 E8
Downley Bucks 39 E8
Downside Som 23 E8
Downside Sur 28 D2
Downton Hants 14 E3
Downton Wilts 14 B2
Downton on the Rock Hereford 49 B6
Dowsby Lincs 65 B8
Dowsdale Lincs 66 C2
Dowthwaitehead Cumb 99 B5
Doxey Staffs 62 B3
Doxford Northumb 117 B7
Doxford Park T&W 111 D6
Doynton S Glos 24 B2
Draffan S Lanark 119 E7
Dragonby N Lincs 90 C3
Drakeland Corner Devon 6 D3
Drakemyre N Ayrs 118 D2
Drake's Broughton Worcs 50 E4
Drakes Cross Worcs 51 B5
Drakewalls Corn 6 B2
Draughton N Yorks 94 D3
Draughton Northants 53 B5
Drax N Yorks 89 B7
Draycote Warks 52 B2
Draycott Derbys 76 F4
Draycott Glos 51 F6
Draycott Som 23 D6
Draycott in the Clay Staffs 63 B5
Draycott in the Moors Staffs 75 E6
Drayford Devon 10 C2
Drayton Leics 64 E5
Drayton Lincs 78 F5
Drayton Norf 68 C4
Drayton Oxon 38 E4
Drayton Oxon 52 E2
Drayton Ptsmth 15 D7
Drayton Som 12 B2
Drayton Worcs 50 B4
Drayton Bassett Staffs 63 D5
Drayton Beauchamp Bucks 40 C2
Drayton Parslow Bucks 39 B8
Drayton St Leonard Oxon 39 E5
Dre-fach Carms 33 C7
Dre-fach Ceredig 46 E4
Drebley N Yorks 94 D3
Dreemskerry IoM 84 C4
Dreenhill Pembs 44 D4
Drefach Carms 33 C6
Drefach Carms 46 F2
Drefelin Carms 46 F2
Dreghorn N Ayrs 118 F3
Drellingore Kent 31 E6
Drem E Loth 121 B8
Dresden Stoke 75 E6
Dreumasdal W Isles 148 E2
Drewsteignton Devon 10 E2
Driby Lincs 79 B6
Driffield E Yorks 97 D6
Driffield Glos 37 E7
Drigg Cumb 98 E2
Drighlington W Yorks 88 B3
Drimnin Highld 147 F8
Drimpton Dorset 12 D2
Drimsynie Argyll 125 E7
Drinisiadar W Isles 154 H6
Drinkstone Suff 56 C3
Drinkstone Green Suff 56 C3
Drishaig Argyll 125 D7
Drissaig Argyll 124 D5
Drochil Borders 120 E4
Drointon Staffs 62 B4
Droitwich Spa Worcs 50 C3
Droman Highld 156 D4
Dron Perth 128 C3
Dronfield Derbys 76 B3
Dronfield Woodhouse Derbys 76 B3
Drongan E Ayrs 112 C4
Dronley Angus 134 F3
Droxford Hants 15 C7
Droylsden Gtr Man 87 E7
Druid Denb 72 E4
Druidston Pembs 44 D3
Druimarbin Highld 130 B4
Druimavuic Argyll 130 E4
Druimdrishaig Argyll 144 F6
Druimindarroch Highld 147 C9
Druimyeon More Argyll 143 C7
Drum Argyll 145 F8
Drum Perth 128 D2
Drumbeg Highld 156 F4
Drumblade Aberds 152 D5
Drumblair Aberds 153 D6
Drumbuie Dumfries 113 F5
Drumbuie Highld 149 E12
Drumburgh Cumb 108 D2
Drumburn Dumfries 107 C6
Drumchapel Glasgow 118 B5
Drumchardine Highld 151 G8
Drumchork Highld 155 J13
Drumclog S Lanark 119 F6
Drumderfit Highld 151 F9
Drumeldrie Fife 129 D6
Drumelzier Borders 120 F4
Drumfearn Highld 149 G11
Drumgask Highld 138 E2
Drumgley Angus 134 D4
Drumguish Highld 138 E3
Drumin Moray 152 E1
Drumlasie Aberds 140 D5
Drumlemble Argyll 143 G7
Drumligair Aberds 141 C8
Drumlithie Aberds 141 F6
Drummoddie Dumfries 105 E7
Drummond Highld 151 E9
Drummore Dumfries 104 F5
Drummuir Moray 152 D3
Drummuir Castle Moray 152 D3
Drumnadrochit Highld 137 B8
Drumnagorrach Moray 152 C5
Drumoak Aberds 141 E6
Drumpark Dumfries 107 A5
Drumphail Dumfries 105 C6
Drumrash Dumfries 106 B3
Drumrunie Highld 156 J4
Drums Aberds 141 B8
Drumsallie Highld 130 B3
Drumstinchall Dumfries 107 D5
Drumsturdy Angus 134 F4
Drumtochty Castle Aberds 135 B6
Drumtroddan Dumfries 105 E7
Drumuie Highld 149 D9
Drumuillie Highld 138 B5
Drumvaich Stirling 127 D5
Drumwhindle Aberds 153 E9
Drunkendub Angus 135 E6
Drury Flint 73 C6
Drury Square Norf 68 C2
Dry Doddington Lincs 77 E8
Dry Drayton Cambs 54 C4
Drybeck Cumb 100 C1
Drybridge Moray 152 B4
Drybridge N Ayrs 118 F3
Drybrook Glos 36 C3
Dryburgh Borders 121 F8
Dryhope Borders 115 B5
Drylaw Edin 120 B5
Drym Corn 2 C5
Drymen Stirling 126 F3
Drymuir Aberds 153 D9
Drynoch Highld 149 E9
Dryslwyn Carms 33 B6
Dryton Shrops 61 D5
Dubford Aberds 153 B8
Dubton Angus 135 D5
Duchally Highld 156 H6
Duchlage Argyll 126 F2
Duck Corner Suff 57 E7
Duckington Ches W 73 D8
Ducklington Oxon 38 D3
Duckmanton Derbys 76 B4
Duck's Cross Bedford 54 D2
Duddenhoe End Essex 55 F5
Duddingston Edin 121 B5
Duddington Northants 65 D6
Duddleswell E Sus 17 B8
Duddo Northumb 122 E5
Duddon Ches W 74 C2
Duddon Bridge Cumb 98 F4
Dudleston Shrops 73 F7
Dudleston Heath Shrops 73 F7
Dudley T&W 111 B5
Dudley W Mid 62 E3
Dudley Port W Mid 62 E3
Duffield Derbys 76 E3
Duffryn Neath 34 E2
Duffryn Newport 35 F6
Dufftown Moray 152 E3
Duffus Moray 152 B1
Dufton Cumb 100 B1
Duggleby N Yorks 96 C4
Duirinish Highld 149 E12
Duisdalemore Highld 149 G12
Duisky Highld 130 B4
Dukestown Bl Gwent 35 C5
Dukinfield Gtr Man 87 E7
Dulas Anglesey 82 C4
Dulcote Som 23 E7
Dulford Devon 11 D5
Dull Perth 133 E5
Dullatur N Lanark 119 B7
Dullingham Cambs 55 D7
Dulnain Bridge Highld 139 B5
Duloe Bedford 54 C2
Duloe Corn 5 D7
Dulsie Highld 151 G12
Dulverton Som 10 B4
Dulwich London 28 B4
Dumbarton W Dunb 118 B3
Dumbleton Glos 50 F5
Dumcrieff Dumfries 114 D4
Dumfries Dumfries 107 B6
Dumgoyne Stirling 126 F4
Dummer Hants 26 E3
Dumpford W Sus 16 B2
Dumpton Kent 31 C7
Dun Angus 135 D6
Dun Charlabhaigh W Isles 154 C6
Dunain Ho. Highld 151 G9
Dunalastair Perth 132 D4
Dunan Highld 149 F10
Dunans Argyll 145 D9
Dunball Som 22 E5
Dunbar E Loth 122 B2
Dunbeath Highld 158 H3
Dunbeg Argyll 124 B4
Dunblane Stirling 127 D6
Dunbog Fife 128 C4
Duncanston Highld 151 F8
Duncanstone Aberds 140 B4
Dunchurch Warks 52 B2
Duncote Northants 52 D4
Duncow Dumfries 114 F2
Duncraggan Stirling 126 D4
Duncrievie Perth 128 D3
Duncton W Sus 16 C3
Dundas Ho. Orkney 159 K5
Dundee Dundee 134 F4
Dundeugh Dumfries 113 F5
Dundon Som 23 F6
Dundonald S Ayrs 118 F3
Dundonnell Highld 150 C3
Dundonnell Hotel Highld 150 C3
Dundonnell House Highld 150 C4
Dundraw Cumb 108 E2
Dundreggan Highld 137 C6
Dundreggan Lodge Highld 137 C6
Dundrennan Dumfries 106 E4
Dundry N Som 23 C7
Dunecht Aberds 141 D6
Dunfermline Fife 128 F2
Dunfield Glos 37 E8
Dunford Bridge S Yorks 88 D2
Dungworth S Yorks 88 F3
Dunham Notts 77 B8
Dunham-on-the-Hill Ches W 73 B8

Dunham Town Gtr Man 86 F5
Dunhampton Worcs 50 C3
Dunholme Lincs 78 B3
Dunino Fife 129 C7
Dunipace Falk 127 F7
Dunira Perth 127 B6
Dunkeld Perth 133 E7
Dunkerton Bath 24 D2
Dunkeswell Devon 11 D6
Dunkeswick N Yorks 95 E6
Dunkirk Kent 30 D4
Dunkirk Norf 81 E8
Dunk's Green Kent 29 D7
Dunlappie Angus 135 C5
Dunley Hants 26 D2
Dunley Worcs 50 C2
Dunlichity Lodge Highld 151 H9
Dunlop E Ayrs 118 E4
Dunmaglass Lodge Highld 137 B8
Dunmore Argyll 144 G6
Dunmore Falk 127 F7
Dunnet Highld 158 C4
Dunnichen Angus 135 E5
Dunninald Angus 135 D7
Dunning Perth 128 C2
Dunnington E Yorks 97 D7
Dunnington Warks 51 D5
Dunnington York 96 D2
Dunnockshaw Lancs 87 B6
Dunollie Argyll 124 B4
Dunoon Argyll 145 F10
Dunragit Dumfries 105 D5
Dunrostan Argyll 144 E6
Duns Borders 122 D3
Duns Tew Oxon 38 B4
Dunsby Lincs 65 B8
Dunscore Dumfries 113 F8
Dunscroft S Yorks 89 D7
Dunsdale Redcar 102 C4
Dunsden Green Oxon 26 B5
Dunsfold Sur 27 F8
Dunsford Devon 10 F3
Dunshalt Fife 128 C4
Dunshillock Aberds 153 D9
Dunskey Ho. Dumfries 104 D4
Dunsley N Yorks 103 C6
Dunsmore Bucks 40 D1
Dunsop Bridge Lancs 93 D6
Dunstable C Beds 40 B3
Dunstall Staffs 63 B5
Dunstall Common Worcs 50 E3
Dunstall Green Suff 55 C8
Dunstan Northumb 117 C8
Dunstan Steads Northumb 117 B8
Dunster Som 21 E8
Dunston Lincs 78 C3
Dunston Norf 68 D5
Dunston Staffs 62 C3
Dunston T&W 110 C5
Dunsville S Yorks 89 D7
Dunswell E Yorks 97 F6
Dunsyre S Lanark 120 E3
Dunterton Devon 5 B8
Duntisbourne Abbots Glos 37 D6
Duntisbourne Leer Glos 37 D6
Duntisbourne Rouse Glos 37 D6
Duntish Dorset 12 D4
Duntocher W Dunb 118 B4
Dunton Bucks 39 B8
Dunton C Beds 54 E3
Dunton Norf 80 D4
Dunton Bassett Leics 64 E2
Dunton Green Kent 29 D6
Dunton Wayletts Essex 42 E2
Duntulm Highld 149 A9
Dunure S Ayrs 112 C2
Dunvant Swansea 33 E6
Dunvegan Highld 148 D7
Dunwich Suff 57 B8
Dunwood Staffs 75 D6
Dupplin Castle Perth 128 C2
Durdar Cumb 108 D4
Durgates E Sus 18 B3
Durham Durham 111 E5
Durisdeer Dumfries 113 D8
Durisdeermill Dumfries 113 D8
Durkar W Yorks 88 C4
Durleigh Som 22 F4
Durley Hants 15 C6
Durley Wilts 25 C7
Durnamuck Highld 150 B3
Durness Highld 156 C7
Durno Aberds 141 B6
Duror Highld 130 D3
Durran Argyll 125 E5
Durran Highld 158 D3
Durrington W Sus 16 D5
Durrington Wilts 25 E6
Dursley Glos 36 E4
Durston Som 11 B7
Durweston Dorset 13 D6
Dury Shetland 160 G6
Duston Northants 52 C5
Duthil Highld 138 B5
Dutlas Powys 48 B4
Duton Hill Essex 42 B2
Dutson Corn 8 F5
Dutton Ches W 74 B2
Duxford Cambs 55 E5
Duxford Oxon 38 E3
Dwygyfylchi Conwy 83 D7
Dwyran Anglesey 82 E4
Dyce Aberdeen 141 C7
Dye House Northumb 110 D2
Dyffryn Bridgend 34 E2
Dyffryn Carms 32 B4
Dyffryn Pembs 44 B4
Dyffryn Ardudwy Gwyn 71 E6
Dyffryn Castell Ceredig 58 F4
Dyffryn Ceidrych Carms 33 B8
Dyffryn Cellwen Neath 34 D2
Dyke Lincs 65 B8
Dyke Moray 151 F12
Dykehead Angus 134 C3
Dykehead N Lanark 119 D8
Dykehead Stirling 126 E4
Dykelands Aberds 135 C7
Dykends Angus 134 D2
Dykeside Aberds 153 D7
Dykesmains N Ayrs 118 E2
Dylife Powys 59 E5
Dymchurch Kent 19 C7
Dymock Glos 50 F2
Dyrham S Glos 24 B2
Dysart Fife 128 E5
Dyserth Denb 72 B4

E

Eachwick Northumb 110 B4
Eadar Dha Fhadhail W Isles 154 D5
Eagland Hill Lancs 92 E4
Eagle Lincs 77 C8
Eagle Barnsdale Lincs 77 C8
Eagle Moor Lincs 77 C8
Eaglescliffe Stockton 102 C2
Eaglesfield Cumb 98 B2
Eaglesfield Dumfries 108 B2
Eaglesham E Renf 119 D5
Eaglethorpe Northants 65 E7
Eairy IoM 84 E2
Eakley Lanes M Keynes 53 D6
Eakring Notts 77 C6
Ealand N Lincs 89 C8
Ealing London 40 F4
Eals Northumb 109 D6
Eamont Bridge Cumb 99 B7
Earby Lancs 94 E2
Earcroft Blackburn 86 B4
Eardington Shrops 61 E7
Eardisland Hereford 49 D6
Eardisley Hereford 48 E5
Eardiston Shrops 60 B3
Eardiston Worcs 49 C8
Earith Cambs 54 B4
Earl Shilton Leics 63 E8
Earl Soham Suff 57 C6
Earl Sterndale Derbys 75 C7
Earl Stonham Suff 56 D5
Earle Northumb 117 B5
Earley Wokingham 27 B5
Earlham Norf 68 D5
Earlish Highld 149 B8
Earls Barton Northants 53 C6
Earls Colne Essex 42 B4
Earl's Croome Worcs 50 E3
Earl's Green Suff 56 C4
Earlsdon W Mid 51 B8
Earlsferry Fife 129 E6
Earlsfield Lincs 78 F2
Earlsford Aberds 153 E8
Earlsheaton W Yorks 88 B3
Earlsmill Moray 151 F12
Earlston Borders 121 F8
Earlston E Ayrs 118 F4
Earlswood Mon 36 E1
Earlswood Sur 28 E3
Earlswood Warks 51 B6
Earnley W Sus 16 E2
Earsairidh W Isles 148 J2
Earsdon T&W 111 B6
Earsham Norf 69 F6
Earswick York 96 D2
Eartham W Sus 16 D3
Easby N Yorks 101 D6
Easby N Yorks 102 D3
Easdale Argyll 124 D3
Easebourne W Sus 16 B2
Easenhall Warks 52 B2
Eashing Sur 27 E7
Easington Bucks 39 C6
Easington Durham 111 E7
Easington E Yorks 91 C7
Easington Northumb 123 F7
Easington Oxon 39 E6
Easington Oxon 52 F2
Easington Redcar 103 C5
Easington Colliery Durham 111 E7
Easington Lane T&W 111 E6
Easingwold N Yorks 95 C8
Easole Street Kent 31 D6
Eassie Angus 134 E3
East Aberthaw V Glam 22 C2
East Adderbury Oxon 52 F2
East Allington Devon 7 E5
East Anstey Devon 10 B3
East Appleton N Yorks 101 E7
East Ardsley W Yorks 88 B4
East Ashling W Sus 16 D2
East Auchronie Aberds 141 D7
East Ayton N Yorks 103 F7
East Bank Bl Gwent 35 D6
East Barkwith Lincs 91 F5
East Barming Kent 29 D8
East Barnby N Yorks 103 C6
East Barnet London 41 E5
East Barns E Loth 122 B3
East Barsham Norf 80 D5
East Beckham Norf 81 D7
East Bedfont London 27 B8
East Bergholt Suff 56 F4
East Bilney Norf 68 C2
East Blatchington E Sus 17 D8
East Boldre Hants 14 D4
East Brent Som 22 D5
East Bridgford Notts 77 E6
East Buckland Devon 21 F5
East Budleigh Devon 11 F5
East Burrafirth Shetland 160 H5
East Burton Dorset 13 F6
East Butsfield Durham 110 E4
East Butterwick N Lincs 90 D2
East Cairnbeg Aberds 135 B7
East Calder W Loth 120 C3
East Carleton Norf 68 D4
East Carlton Northants 64 F5
East Carlton W Yorks 94 E5
East Chaldon Dorset 13 F5
East Challow Oxon 38 F3
East Chiltington E Sus 17 C7
East Chinnock Som 12 C2
East Chisenbury Wilts 25 D6
East Clandon Sur 27 D8
East Claydon Bucks 39 B7
East Clyne Highld 157 J12
East Coker Som 12 C3
East Combe Som 22 F3
East Common N Yorks 96 F2
East Compton Som 23 E8
East Cottingwith E Yorks 96 E3
East Cowes IoW 15 E6
East Cowick E Yorks 89 B7
East Cowton N Yorks 101 D8
East Cramlington Northumb 111 B5
East Cranmore Som 23 E8
East Creech Dorset 13 F7
East Croachy Highld 138 B2
East Croftmore Highld 139 C5
East Curthwaite Cumb 108 E3
East Dean E Sus 18 F2
East Dean Hants 14 B3
East Dean W Sus 16 C3
East Down Devon 20 E5
East Drayton Notts 77 B7
East Ella Hull 90 B4
East End Dorset 13 E7
East End E Yorks 91 B6
East End Hants 14 E4
East End Hants 15 B7
East End Hants 26 C2
East End Herts 41 B7
East End Kent 18 B5
East End N Som 23 B6
East End Oxon 38 C3
East Farleigh Kent 29 D8
East Farndon Northants 64 F4
East Ferry Lincs 90 E2
East Fortune E Loth 121 B8
East Garston W Berks 25 B8
East Ginge Oxon 38 F4
East Goscote Leics 64 C3
East Grafton Wilts 25 C7
East Grimstead Wilts 14 B3
East Grinstead W Sus 28 F4
East Guldeford E Sus 19 C6
East Haddon Northants 52 C4
East Hagbourne Oxon 39 F5
East Halton N Lincs 90 C5
East Ham London 41 F7
East Hanney Oxon 38 E4
East Hanningfield Essex 42 D3
East Hardwick W Yorks 89 C5
East Harling Norf 68 F2
East Harlsey N Yorks 102 E2
East Harnham Wilts 14 B2
East Harptree Bath 23 D7
East Hartford Northumb 111 B5
East Harting W Sus 15 C8
East Hatley Cambs 54 D3
East Hauxwell N Yorks 101 E6
East Haven Angus 135 F5
East Heckington Lincs 78 E4
East Hedleyhope Durham 110 E4
East Hendred Oxon 38 F4
East Herrington T&W 111 D6
East Heslerton N Yorks 96 B5
East Hoathly E Sus 18 D2
East Horrington Som 23 E7
East Horsley Sur 27 D8
East Horton Northumb 123 F6
East Huntspill Som 22 E5
East Hyde C Beds 40 C4
East Ilkerton Devon 21 E6
East Ilsley W Berks 38 F4
East Keal Lincs 79 C6
East Kennett Wilts 25 C6
East Keswick W Yorks 95 E6
East Kilbride S Lanark 119 D6
East Kirkby Lincs 79 C6
East Knapton N Yorks 96 B4
East Knighton Dorset 13 F6
East Knoyle Wilts 24 F3
East Kyloe Northumb 123 F6
East Lambrook Som 12 C2
East Lamington Highld 151 D10
East Langdon Kent 31 E7
East Langton Leics 64 E4
East Langwell Highld 157 J10
East Lavant W Sus 16 D2
East Lavington W Sus 16 C3
East Layton N Yorks 101 D6
East Leake Notts 64 B2
East Learmouth Northumb 122 F4
East Leigh Devon 9 D8
East Lexham Norf 67 C8
East Lilburn Northumb 117 B6
East Linton E Loth 121 B8
East Liss Hants 15 B8
East Looe Corn 5 D7
East Lound N Lincs 89 E8
East Lulworth Dorset 13 F6
East Lutton N Yorks 96 C5
East Lydford Som 23 F7
East Mains Aberds 141 E5
East Malling Kent 29 D8
East March Angus 134 F4
East Marden W Sus 16 C2
East Markham Notts 77 B7
East Marton N Yorks 94 D2
East Meon Hants 15 B7
East Mere Devon 10 C4
East Mersea Essex 43 C6
East Mey Highld 158 C5
East Molesey Sur 28 C2
East Morden Dorset 13 E7
East Morton W Yorks 94 E3
East Ness N Yorks 96 B2
East Newton E Yorks 97 F8
East Norton Leics 64 D4
East Nynehead Som 11 B6
East Oakley Hants 26 D3
East Ogwell Devon 7 B6
East Orchard Dorset 13 C6
East Ord Northumb 123 D5
East Panson Devon 9 E5
East Peckham Kent 29 E7
East Pennard Som 23 F7
East Perry Cambs 54 C2
East Portlemouth Devon 6 F5
East Prawle Devon 7 F5
East Preston W Sus 16 D4
East Putford Devon 9 C5
East Quantoxhead Som 22 E3
East Rainton T&W 111 E6
East Ravendale NE Lincs 91 E6
East Raynham Norf 80 E4
East Rhidorroch Lodge Highld 150 B5
East Rigton W Yorks 95 E6
East Rounton N Yorks 102 D2
East Row N Yorks 103 C6
East Rudham Norf 80 E4
East Runton Norf 81 C7
East Ruston Norf 69 B6
East Saltoun E Loth 121 C7
East Sleekburn Northumb 117 F8
East Somerton Norf 69 C7
East Stockwith Lincs 89 E8
East Stoke Dorset 13 F6
East Stoke Notts 77 E7
East Stour Dorset 13 B6
East Stourmouth Kent 31 C6
East Stowford Devon 9 B8
East Stratton Hants 26 F3
East Studdal Kent 31 E7
East Suisnish Highld 149 E10
East Taphouse Corn 5 C6
East-the-Water Devon 9 B6
East Thirston Northumb 117 E7
East Tilbury Thurrock 29 B7
East Tisted Hants 26 F5
East Torrington Lincs 90 F5
East Tuddenham Norf 68 C3
East Tytherley Hants 14 B3
East Tytherton Wilts 24 B4
East Village Devon 10 D3
East Wall Shrops 60 E5
East Walton Norf 67 C7
East Wellow Hants 14 B4
East Wemyss Fife 128 E5
East Whitburn W Loth 120 C2
East Williamston Pembs 32 D1
East Winch Norf 67 C6
East Winterslow Wilts 25 F7
East Wittering W Sus 15 E8
East Witton N Yorks 101 F6
East Woodburn Northumb 116 F5
East Woodhay Hants 26 C2
East Worldham Hants 26 F5
East Worlington Devon 10 C2
East Worthing W Sus 17 D5
Eastbourne E Sus 18 F3
Eastbridge Suff 57 C8
Eastburn W Yorks 94 E3
Eastbury London 40 E3
Eastbury W Berks 25 B8
Eastby N Yorks 94 D3
Eastchurch Kent 30 B3
Eastcombe Glos 37 D5
Eastcote London 40 F4
Eastcote Northants 52 D4
Eastcote W Mid 51 B6
Eastcott Corn 8 C4
Eastcott Wilts 24 D5
Eastcourt Wilts 25 C7
Eastcourt Wilts 37 E6
Easter Ardross Highld 151 D9
Easter Balmoral Aberds 139 E8
Easter Boleskine Highld 137 B8
Easter Compton S Glos 36 F2
Easter Cringate Stirling 127 F6
Easter Davoch Aberds 140 D3
Easter Earshaig Dumfries 114 D3
Easter Fearn Highld 151 C9
Easter Galcantray Highld 151 G11
Easter Howgate Midloth 120 C5
Easter Howlaws Borders 122 E3
Easter Kinkell Highld 151 F8
Easter Lednathie Angus 134 C3
Easter Milton Highld 151 G12
Easter Moniack Highld 151 G8
Easter Ord Aberdeen 141 D7
Easter Quarff Shetland 160 K6
Easter Rhynd Perth 128 C3
Easter Row Stirling 127 E6
Easter Silverford Aberds 153 B7
Easter Skeld Shetland 160 J5
Easter Whyntie Aberds 152 B6
Eastergate W Sus 16 D3
Easterhouse Glasgow 119 C6
Eastern Green W Mid 63 F6
Easterton Wilts 24 D5
Eastertown Som 22 D5
Eastertown of Auchleuchries Aberds 153 E10
Eastfield N Lanark 119 C8
Eastfield N Yorks 103 F8
Eastfield Hall Northumb 117 D8
Eastgate Durham 110 F2
Eastgate Norf 81 E7
Eastham Mers 85 F4
Eastham Ferry Mers 85 F4
Easthampstead Brack 27 C6
Eastheath Wokingham 27 C6
Easthope Shrops 61 E5
Easthorpe Essex 43 B5
Easthorpe Leics 77 F8
Easthorpe Notts 77 D7
Easthouses Midloth 121 C6
Eastington Devon 10 D2
Eastington Glos 36 D4
Eastington Glos 37 C8
Eastleach Martin Glos 38 D2
Eastleach Turville Glos 38 D1
Eastleigh Devon 9 B6
Eastleigh Hants 14 C5
Eastling Kent 30 D3
Eastmoor Derbys 76 B3
Eastmoor Norf 67 D7
Eastney Ptsmth 15 E7
Eastnor Hereford 50 F2
Eastoft N Lincs 90 C2
Eastoke Hants 15 E8
Easton Cambs 54 B2
Easton Cumb 108 B4
Easton Cumb 108 D2
Easton Devon 10 F2
Easton Dorset 12 G4
Easton Hants 26 F3
Easton Lincs 65 B6
Easton Norf 68 C4
Easton Som 23 E7
Easton Suff 57 D6
Easton Wilts 24 B3
Easton Grey Wilts 37 F5
Easton-in-Gordano N Som 23 B7
Easton Maudit Northants 53 D6
Easton on the Hill Northants 65 D7
Easton Royal Wilts 25 C7
Eastpark Dumfries 107 C7
Eastrea Cambs 66 E2
Eastriggs Dumfries 108 C2
Eastrington E Yorks 89 B8
Eastry Kent 31 D7
Eastville Bristol 23 B8
Eastville Lincs 79 D7
Eastwell Leics 64 B4
Eastwick Herts 41 C7
Eastwick Shetland 160 F5
Eastwood Notts 76 E4
Eastwood Southend 42 F4
Eastwood W Yorks 87 B7
Eathorpe Warks 51 C8
Eaton Ches E 75 C5
Eaton Ches W 74 C2
Eaton Leics 64 B4
Eaton Norf 68 D5
Eaton Notts 77 B7
Eaton Oxon 38 D4
Eaton Shrops 60 F3
Eaton Shrops 60 F5
Eaton Bishop Hereford 49 F6
Eaton Bray C Beds 40 B2
Eaton Constantine Shrops 61 D5
Eaton Green C Beds 40 B2
Eaton Hastings Oxon 38 E2
Eaton on Tern Shrops 61 B6
Eaton Socon Cambs 54 D2
Eavestone N Yorks 94 C5
Ebberston N Yorks 103 F6
Ebbesbourne Wake Wilts 13 B7
Ebbw Vale = Glyn Ebwy Bl Gwent 35 D5
Ebchester Durham 110 D4
Ebford Devon 10 F4
Ebley Glos 37 D5
Ebnal Ches W 73 E8
Ebrington Glos 51 E6
Ecchinswell Hants 26 D2
Ecclaw Borders 122 C3
Ecclefechan Dumfries 107 B8
Eccles Borders 122 E3
Eccles Gtr Man 87 E5
Eccles Kent 29 C8
Eccles on Sea Norf 69 B7
Eccles Road Norf 68 E3
Ecclesall S Yorks 88 F4
Ecclesfield S Yorks 88 E4
Ecclesgreig Aberds 135 C7
Eccleshall Staffs 62 B2
Eccleshill W Yorks 94 F4
Ecclesmachan W Loth 120 B3
Eccleston Ches W 73 C8
Eccleston Lancs 86 C3
Eccleston Mers 86 E2
Eccleston Park Mers 86 E2
Eccup W Yorks 95 E5
Echt Aberds 141 D6
Eckford Borders 116 B3
Eckington Derbys 76 B4
Eckington Worcs 50 E4
Ecton Northants 53 C6
Edale Derbys 88 F2
Edburton W Sus 17 C6
Edderside Cumb 107 E7
Edderton Highld 151 C10
Eddistone Devon 8 B4
Eddleston Borders 120 E5
Eden Park London 28 C4
Edenbridge Kent 28 E5
Edenfield Lancs 87 C5
Edenhall Cumb 109 F5
Edenham Lincs 65 B7
Edensor Derbys 76 C2
Edentaggart Argyll 126 E2
Edenthorpe S Yorks 89 D7
Edentown Cumb 108 D3
Ederline Argyll 124 E4
Edern Gwyn 70 D3
Edgarley Som 23 F7
Edgbaston W Mid 62 F4
Edgcott Bucks 39 B6
Edgcott Som 21 F7
Edge Shrops 60 D3
Edge End Glos 36 C2
Edge Green Ches W 73 D8
Edge Hill Mers 85 F4
Edgebolton Shrops 61 B5
Edgefield Norf 81 D6
Edgefield Street Norf 81 D6
Edgeside Lancs 87 B6
Edgeworth Glos 37 D6
Edgmond Telford 61 C7
Edgmond Marsh Telford 61 B7
Edgton Shrops 60 F3
Edgware London 40 E4
Edgworth Blackburn 86 C5
Edinample Stirling 126 B4
Edinbane Highld 149 C8
Edinburgh Edin 121 B5
Edingale Staffs 63 C6
Edingight Ho. Moray 152 C5
Edingley Notts 77 D6
Edingthorpe Norf 69 A6
Edingthorpe Green Norf 69 A6
Edington Som 23 F5
Edington Wilts 24 D4
Edintore Moray 152 D4
Edith Weston Rutland 65 D6
Edithmead Som 22 E5
Edlesborough Bucks 40 C2
Edlingham Northumb 117 D7
Edlington Lincs 78 B5
Edmondsham Dorset 13 C8
Edmondsley Durham 110 E5
Edmondthorpe Leics 65 C5
Edmonstone Orkney 159 F6
Edmonton London 41 E6
Edmundbyers Durham 110 D3
Ednam Borders 122 F3
Ednaston Derbys 76 E2
Edradynate Perth 133 D5
Edrom Borders 122 D4
Edstaston Shrops 74 F2
Edstone Warks 51 C6
Edvin Loach Hereford 49 D8
Edwalton Notts 77 F5
Edwardstone Suff 56 E3
Edwinsford Carms 46 F5
Edwinstowe Notts 77 C6
Edworth C Beds 54 E3
Edwyn Ralph Hereford 49 D8
Edzell Angus 135 C5
Efail Isaf Rhondda 34 F4
Efailnewydd Gwyn 70 D4
Efailwen Carms 32 B2
Efenechtyd Denb 72 D5
Effingham Sur 28 D2
Effirth Shetland 160 H5
Efford Devon 10 D3
Egdon Worcs 50 D4
Egerton Gtr Man 86 C5
Egerton Kent 30 E3
Egerton Forstal Kent 30 E2
Eggborough N Yorks 89 B6
Eggbuckland Plym 6 D3
Eggington C Beds 40 B2
Egginton Derbys 63 B6
Egglescliffe Stockton 102 C2
Eggleston Durham 100 B4
Egham Sur 27 B8
Egleton Rutland 65 D5
Eglingham Northumb 117 C7
Egloshayle Corn 4 B5
Egloskerry Corn 8 F4
Eglwys-Brewis V Glam 22 C2
Eglwys Cross Wrex 73 E8
Eglwys Fach Ceredig 58 E3
Eglwysbach Conwy 83 D8
Eglwyswen Pembs 45 F3
Eglwyswrw Pembs 45 F3
Egmanton Notts 77 C7
Egremont Cumb 98 C2
Egremont Mers 85 E4
Egton N Yorks 103 D6
Egton Bridge N Yorks 103 D6
Eight Ash Green Essex 43 B5
Eignaig Highld 130 E1
Eil Highld 138 C4
Eilanreach Highld 149 G13
Eilean Darach Highld 150 C4
Eileanach Lodge Highld 151 E8
Einacleite W Isles 154 E6
Eisgean W Isles 155 F8
Eisingrug Gwyn 71 D7
Elan Village Powys 47 C8
Elberton S Glos 36 F3
Elburton Plym 6 D3
Elcho Perth 128 B3
Elcombe Swindon 37 F8
Eldernell Cambs 66 E3
Eldersfield Worcs 50 F3
Elderslie Renfs 118 C4
Eldon Durham 101 B7
Eldrick S Ayrs 112 F2
Eldroth N Yorks 93 C7
Eldwick W Yorks 94 E4
Elfhowe Cumb 99 E6
Elford Northumb 123 F7
Elford Staffs 63 C5
Elgin Moray 152 B2
Elgol Highld 149 G10
Elham Kent 31 E5
Elie Fife 129 D6
Elim Anglesey 82 C3
Eling Hants 14 C4
Elishader Highld 149 B10
Elishaw Northumb 116 E4
Elkesley Notts 77 B6
Elkstone Glos 37 C6
Ellan Highld 138 B4
Elland W Yorks 88 B2
Ellary Argyll 144 F6
Ellastone Staffs 75 E8
Ellemford Borders 122 C3
Ellenbrook IoM 84 E3
Ellenhall Staffs 62 B2
Ellen's Green Sur 27 F8
Ellerbeck N Yorks 102 E2
Ellerburn N Yorks 103 F6
Ellerby N Yorks 103 C5
Ellerdine Heath Telford 61 B6
Ellerhayes Devon 10 D4
Elleric Argyll 130 E4
Ellerker E Yorks 90 B3
Ellerton E Yorks 96 F3
Ellerton Shrops 61 B7
Ellesborough Bucks 39 D8
Ellesmere Shrops 73 F8
Ellesmere Port Ches W 73 B8
Ellingham Norf 69 E6
Ellingham Northumb 117 B7
Ellingstring N Yorks 101 F6
Ellington Cambs 54 B2
Ellington Northumb 117 E8
Elliot Angus 135 F6
Ellisfield Hants 26 E4
Ellistown Leics 63 C8
Ellon Aberds 153 E9
Ellonby Cumb 108 F4
Ellough Suff 69 F7
Elloughton E Yorks 90 B3
Ellwood Glos 36 D2
Elm Cambs 66 D4
Elm Hill Dorset 13 B6
Elm Park London 41 F8
Elmbridge Worcs 50 C4
Elmdon Essex 55 F5
Elmdon W Mid 63 F5
Elmdon Heath W Mid 63 F5
Elmers End London 28 C4
Elmesthorpe Leics 63 E8
Elmfield IoW 15 E7
Elmhurst Staffs 62 C5
Elmley Castle Worcs 50 E4
Elmley Lovett Worcs 50 C3
Elmore Glos 36 C4
Elmore Back Glos 36 C4
Elmscott Devon 8 B4
Elmsett Suff 56 E4
Elmstead Market Essex 43 B6
Elmsted Kent 30 E5
Elmstone Kent 31 C6
Elmstone Hardwicke Glos 37 B6
Elmswell E Yorks 97 D5
Elmswell Suff 56 C3
Elmton Derbys 76 B5
Elphin Highld 156 H5
Elphinstone E Loth 121 B6
Elrick Aberds 141 D7
Elrig Dumfries 105 E7
Elsdon Northumb 117 E5
Elsecar S Yorks 88 E4
Elsenham Essex 41 B8
Elsfield Oxon 39 C5
Elsham N Lincs 90 C4
Elsing Norf 68 C3
Elslack N Yorks 94 E2
Elson Shrops 73 F7
Elsrickle S Lanark 120 E3
Elstead Sur 27 E7
Elsted W Sus 16 C2
Elsthorpe Lincs 65 B7
Elstob Durham 101 B8
Elston Notts 77 E7
Elston Wilts 25 E5
Elstone Devon 9 C8
Elstow Bedford 53 E8
Elstree Herts 40 E4
Elstronwick E Yorks 97 F8
Elswick Lancs 92 F4
Elsworth Cambs 54 C4
Elterwater Cumb 99 D5
Eltham London 28 B5
Eltisley Cambs 54 D3
Elton Cambs 65 E7
Elton Ches W 73 B8
Elton Derbys 76 C2
Elton Glos 36 C4
Elton Hereford 49 B6
Elton Notts 77 F7
Elton Stockton 102 C2
Elton Green Ches W 73 B8
Elvanfoot S Lanark 114 C2
Elvaston Derbys 76 F4
Elveden Suff 56 B2
Elvingston E Loth 121 B7
Elvington Kent 31 D6
Elvington York 96 E2
Elwick Hrtlpl 111 F7
Elwick Northumb 123 F7
Elworth Ches E 74 C4
Elworthy Som 22 F2
Ely Cambs 66 F5
Ely Cardiff 22 B3
Emberton M Keynes 53 E6
Embleton Cumb 107 F8
Embleton Northumb 117 B8
Embo Highld 151 B11
Embo Street Highld 151 B11
Emborough Som 23 D8
Embsay N Yorks 94 D3
Emery Down Hants 14 D3
Emley W Yorks 88 C3
Emmbrook Wokingham 27 C5
Emmer Green Reading 26 B5
Emmington Oxon 39 D7
Emneth Norf 66 D4
Emneth Hungate Norf 66 D5
Empingham Rutland 65 D6
Empshott Hants 27 F5
Emstrey Shrops 60 C5
Emsworth Hants 15 D8
Enborne W Berks 26 C2
Enchmarsh Shrops 60 E5
Enderby Leics 64 E2
Endmoor Cumb 99 F7
Endon Staffs 75 D6
Endon Bank Staffs 75 D6
Enfield London 41 E6
Enfield Wash London 41 E6
Enford Wilts 25 D6
Engamoor Shetland 160 H4
Engine Common S Glos 36 F3
Englefield W Berks 26 B4
Englefield Green Sur 27 B7
Englesea-brook Ches E 74 D4
English Bicknor Glos 36 C2
English Frankton Shrops 60 B4
Englishcombe Bath 24 C2
Enham Alamein Hants 25 E8
Enmore Som 22 F4
Ennerdale Bridge Cumb 98 C2
Enoch Dumfries 113 D8
Enochdhu Perth 133 C7
Ensay Argyll 146 G6
Ensbury Bmouth 13 E8
Ensdon Shrops 60 C4
Ensis Devon 9 B7
Enstone Oxon 38 B3
Enterkinfoot Dumfries 113 D8
Enterpen N Yorks 102 D2
Enville Staffs 62 F2
Eolaigearraidh W Isles 148 H2
Eorabus Argyll 146 J6
Eòropaidh W Isles 155 A10
Epperstone Notts 77 E6
Epping Essex 41 D7
Epping Green Essex 41 D7
Epping Green Herts 41 D5
Epping Upland Essex 41 D7
Eppleby N Yorks 101 C6
Eppleworth E Yorks 97 F6
Epsom Sur 28 C3
Epwell Oxon 51 E8
Epworth N Lincs 89 D8
Epworth Turbary N Lincs 89 D8
Erbistock Wrex 73 E7
Erbusaig Highld 149 F12
Erchless Castle Highld 150 G7
Erdington W Mid 62 E5
Eredine Argyll 125 E5
Eriboll Highld 156 D7
Ericstane Dumfries 114 C3
Eridge Green E Sus 18 B2
Erines Argyll 145 F7
Eriswell Suff 55 B8
Erith London 29 B6
Erlestoke Wilts 24 D4
Ermine Lincs 78 B2
Ermington Devon 6 D4
Erpingham Norf 81 D7
Errogie Highld 137 B8
Errol Perth 128 B4
Erskine Renfs 118 B4
Erskine Bridge Renfs 118 B4
Ervie Dumfries 104 C4
Erwarton Suff 57 F6
Erwood Powys 48 E2
Eryholme N Yorks 101 D8
Eryrys Denb 73 D6
Escomb Durham 101 B6
Escrick N Yorks 96 E2
Esgairdawe Carms 46 E5
Esgairgeiliog Powys 58 D4
Esh Durham 110 E4
Esh Winning Durham 110 E4
Esher Sur 28 C2
Esholt W Yorks 94 E4
Eshott Northumb 117 E8
Eshton N Yorks 94 D2
Esk Valley N Yorks 103 D6
Eskadale Highld 150 H7
Eskbank Midloth 121 C6
Eskdale Green Cumb 98 D3
Eskdalemuir Dumfries 115 E5
Eske E Yorks 97 E6
Eskham Lincs 91 E7
Esprick Lancs 92 F4
Essendine Rutland 65 C7
Essendon Herts 41 D5
Essich Highld 151 H9
Essington Staffs 62 D3
Esslemont Aberds 141 B8
Eston Redcar 102 C3
Eswick Shetland 160 H6
Etal Northumb 122 F5
Etchilhampton Wilts 24 C5
Etchingham E Sus 18 C4
Etchinghill Kent 19 B8
Etchinghill Staffs 62 C4
Ethie Castle Angus 135 E6
Ethie Mains Angus 135 E6
Etling Green Norf 68 C3
Eton Windsor 27 B7
Eton Wick Windsor 27 B7
Etteridge Highld 138 E2
Ettersgill Durham 100 B3
Ettingshall W Mid 62 E3
Ettington Warks 51 E7
Etton E Yorks 97 E5
Etton Pboro 65 D8
Ettrick Borders 115 C5
Ettrickbridge Borders 115 B6
Ettrickhill Borders 115 C5
Etwall Derbys 76 F2
Euston Suff 56 B2
Euximoor Drove Cambs 66 E4
Euxton Lancs 86 C3
Evanstown Bridgend 34 F3
Evanton Highld 151 E9
Evedon Lincs 78 E3
Evelix Highld 151 B10
Evenjobb Powys 48 C4
Evenley Northants 52 F3
Evenlode Glos 38 B2
Evenwood Durham 101 B6
Evenwood Gate Durham 101 B6
Everbay Orkney 159 F7
Evercreech Som 23 F8
Everdon Northants 52 D3
Everingham E Yorks 96 E4
Everleigh Wilts 25 D7
Everley N Yorks 103 F7
Eversholt C Beds 53 F7
Evershot Dorset 12 D3
Eversley Hants 27 C5
Eversley Cross Hants 27 C5
Everthorpe E Yorks 96 F5
Everton C Beds 54 D3
Everton Hants 14 E3
Everton Mers 85 E4
Everton Notts 89 E7
Evertown Dumfries 108 B3
Evesbatch Hereford 49 E8
Evesham Worcs 50 E5
Evington Leicester 64 D3
Ewden Village S Yorks 88 E3
Ewell Sur 28 C3
Ewell Minnis Kent 31 E6
Ewelme Oxon 39 E6
Ewen Glos 37 E7
Ewenny V Glam 21 B8
Ewerby Lincs 78 E4
Ewerby Thorpe Lincs 78 E4
Ewes Dumfries 115 E6
Ewesley Northumb 117 E6
Ewhurst Sur 27 E8
Ewhurst Green E Sus 18 C4
Ewhurst Green Sur 27 F8
Ewloe Flint 73 C7
Ewloe Green Flint 73 C6
Ewood Blackburn 86 B4
Eworthy Devon 9 E6
Ewshot Hants 27 E6
Ewyas Harold Hereford 35 B7
Exbourne Devon 9 D8
Exbury Hants 14 E5
Exebridge Devon 10 B4
Exelby N Yorks 101 F7
Exeter Devon 10 E4
Exford Som 21 F7
Exhall Warks 51 D6
Exley Head W Yorks 94 F3
Exminster Devon 10 F4
Exmouth Devon 10 F5
Exnaboe Shetland 160 M5
Exning Suff 55 C7
Exton Devon 10 F4
Exton Hants 15 B7
Exton Rutland 65 C6
Exton Som 21 F8
Exwick Devon 10 E4
Eyam Derbys 76 B2
Eydon Northants 52 D3
Eye Hereford 49 C6
Eye Pboro 66 D2
Eye Suff 56 B5
Eye Green Pboro 66 D2
Eyemouth Borders 122 C5
Eyeworth C Beds 54 E3
Eyhorne Street Kent 30 D2
Eyke Suff 57 D7
Eynesbury Cambs 54 D2
Eynort Highld 149 F8
Eynsford Kent 29 C6
Eynsham Oxon 38 D4
Eype Dorset 12 E2
Eyre Highld 149 C9
Eyre Highld 149 E10
Eythorne Kent 31 E6
Eyton Hereford 49 C6
Eyton Shrops 60 F3
Eyton Wrex 73 E7
Eyton upon the Weald Moors Telford 61 C6

F

Faccombe Hants 25 D8
Faceby N Yorks 102 D2
Facit Lancs 87 C6
Faddiley Ches E 74 D2
Fadmoor N Yorks 102 F4
Faerdre Swansea 33 D7
Failand N Som 23 B7
Failford S Ayrs 112 B4
Failsworth Gtr Man 87 D6
Fain Highld 150 D4
Fair Green Norf 67 C6
Fair Hill Cumb 108 F5
Fair Oak Hants 15 C5
Fair Oak Green Hants 26 C4
Fairbourne Gwyn 58 C3
Fairburn N Yorks 89 B5
Fairfield Derbys 75 B7
Fairfield Stockton 102 C2
Fairfield Worcs 50 B4
Fairfield Worcs 50 E5
Fairford Glos 38 D1
Fairhaven Lancs 85 B4
Fairlie N Ayrs 118 D2
Fairlight E Sus 19 D5
Fairlight Cove E Sus 19 D5
Fairmile Devon 11 E5
Fairmilehead Edin 120 C5
Fairoak Staffs 74 F4
Fairseat Kent 29 C7
Fairstead Essex 42 C3
Fairstead Norf 67 C6
Fairwarp E Sus 17 B8
Fairy Cottage IoM 84 D4
Fairy Cross Devon 9 B6
Fakenham Norf 80 E5
Fakenham Magna Suff 56 B3
Fala Midloth 121 C7
Fala Dam Midloth 121 C7
Falahill Borders 121
Falcon Hereford 49
Faldingworth Lincs 90
Falfield S Glos 36
Falkenham Suff 57
Falkirk Falk 119
Falkland Fife 128
Falla Borders 116
Fallgate Derbys 76
Fallin Stirling 127
Fallowfield Gtr Man 87
Fallsidehill Borders 122
Falmer E Sus 17
Falmouth Corn 3
Falsgrave N Yorks 103
Falstone Northumb 116
Fanagmore Highld 156
Fangdale Beck N Yorks 102
Fangfoss E Yorks 96
Fankerton Falk 127
Fanmore Argyll 146
Fannich Lodge Highld 150
Fans Borders 122
Far Bank S Yorks 89
Far Bletchley M Keynes 53
Far Cotton Northants 52
Far Forest Worcs 50
Far Laund Derbys 76
Far Sawrey Cumb 99
Farcet Cambs 66
Farden Shrops 49
Fareham Hants 15
Farewell Staffs 62
Farforth Lincs 79
Faringdon Oxon 38
Farington Lancs 86
Farlam Cumb 109
Farlary Highld 157
Farleigh N Som 23
Farleigh Sur 28
Farleigh Hungerford Som 24
Farleigh Wallop Hants 26
Farlesthorpe Lincs 79
Farleton Cumb 99
Farleton Lancs 93
Farley Shrops 60
Farley Staffs 75
Farley Wilts 14
Farley Green Sur 27
Farley Hill Luton 40
Farley Hill Wokingham 26
Farleys End Glos 36
Farlington N Yorks 96
Farlow Shrops 61
Farmborough Bath 23
Farmcote Glos 37
Farmcote Shrops 61
Farmington Glos 37
Farmoor Oxon 38
Farmtown Moray 152
Farnborough Hants 27
Farnborough London 28
Farnborough W Berks 38
Farnborough Warks 52
Farnborough Green Hants 27
Farncombe Sur 27
Farndish Bedford 53
Farndon Ches W 73
Farndon Notts 77
Farnell Angus 135
Farnham Dorset 13
Farnham Essex 41
Farnham N Yorks 95
Farnham Suff 57
Farnham Sur 27
Farnham Common Bucks 40
Farnham Green Essex 41
Farnham Royal Bucks 40
Farnhill N Yorks 94
Farningham Kent 29
Farnley N Yorks 94
Farnley W Yorks 95
Farnley Tyas W Yorks 88
Farnsfield Notts 77
Farnworth Gtr Man 86
Farnworth Halton 86
Farr Highld 138
Farr Highld 151
Farr Highld 157
Farr House Highld 151
Farringdon Devon 10
Farrington Gurney Bath 23
Farsley W Yorks 94
Farthinghoe Northants 52
Farthingloe Kent 31
Farthingstone Northants 52
Fartown W Yorks 88
Farway Devon 11
Fasag Highld 149
Fascadale Highld 147
Faslane Port Argyll 145
Fasnacloich Argyll 130
Fasnakyle Ho Highld 137
Fassfern Highld 130
Fatfield T&W 111
Fattahead Aberds 153
Faugh Cumb 108
Fauldhouse W Loth 120
Faulkbourne Essex 42
Faulkland Som 24
Fauls Shrops 74
Faversham Kent 30
Favillar Moray 152
Fawdington N Yorks 95
Fawfieldhead Staffs 75
Fawkham Green Kent 29
Fawler Oxon 38
Fawley Bucks 39
Fawley Hants 15
Fawley W Berks 38
Fawley Chapel Hereford 36
Faxfleet E Yorks 90
Faygate W Sus 28
Fazakerley Mers 85
Fazeley Staffs 63
Fearby N Yorks 101
Fearn Highld 151 D
Fearn Lodge Highld 151
Fearn Station Highld 151 D
Fearnan Perth 132
Fearnbeg Highld 149 C
Fearnhead Warr 86
Fearnmore Highld 149 B
Featherstone Staffs 62
Featherstone W Yorks 88
Featherwood Northumb 116
Feckenham Worcs 50
Feering Essex 42
Feetham N Yorks 100
Feizor N Yorks 93
Felbridge Sur 28
Felbrigg Norf 81
Felcourt Sur 28
Felden Herts 40
Felin-Crai Powys 34
Felindre Carms 33
Felindre Carms 33
Felindre Carms 46
Felindre Carms 47
Felindre Ceredig 46
Felindre Powys 59
Felindre Swansea 33
Felindre Farchog Pembs 45
Felinfach Ceredig 46
Felinfach Powys 48
Felinfoel Carms 33
Felingwm isaf Carms 33

Golden Hill Hants 14 E3
Golden Pot Hants 26 E5
Golden Valley Glos 37 B6
Goldenhill Stoke 75 D5
Golders Green London 41 F5
Goldhanger Essex 43 D5
Golding Shrops 60 D5
Goldington Bedford 53 D8
Goldsborough N Yorks 95 D6
Goldsborough N Yorks 103 C6
Goldsithney Corn 2 C4
Goldsworthy Devon 9 B5
Goldthorpe S Yorks 89 D5
Gollanfield Highld 151 F11
Golspie Highld 157 J11
Golval Highld 157 C11
Gomeldon Wilts 25 F6
Gomersal W Yorks 88 B3
Gomshall Sur 27 E8
Gonalston Notts 77 E6
Gonfirth Shetland 160 G5
Good Easter Essex 42 C2
Gooderstone Norf 67 D7
Goodleigh Devon 20 F5
Goodmanham E Yorks 96 E4
Goodnestone Kent 30 C4
Goodnestone Kent 31 D6
Goodrich Hereford 36 C2
Goodrington Torbay 7 D6
Goodshaw Lancs 87 B6
Goodwick = Wdig Pembs 44 B4
Goodworth Clatford Hants 25 E8
Goole E Yorks 89 B8
Goonbell Corn 3 B6
Goonhavern Corn 4 D2
Goose Eye W Yorks 94 E3
Goose Green Gtr Man 86 D3
Goose Green Norf 68 F4
Goose Green W Sus 16 C5
Gooseham Corn 8 C4
Goosey Oxon 38 E3
Goosnargh Lancs 93 F5
Goostrey Ches E 74 B4
Gorcott Hill Warks 51 C5
Gord Shetland 160 L6
Gordon Borders 122 E2
Gordonbush Highld 157 J11
Gordonsburgh Moray 152 B4
Gordonstoun Moray 152 B1
Gordonstown Aberds 152 C5
Gordonstown Aberds 153 E7
Gore Kent 31 D7
Gore Cross Wilts 24 D5
Gore Pit Essex 42 C4
Gorebridge Midloth 121 C6
Gorefield Cambs 66 C4
Gorey Jersey 17
Gorgie Edin 120 B5
Goring Oxon 39 F6
Goring-by-Sea W Sus 16 D5
Goring Heath Oxon 26 B4
Gorleston-on-Sea Norf 69 D8
Gornalwood W Mid 62 E3
Gorrachie Aberds 153 C7
Gorran Churchtown Corn 3 B8
Gorran Haven Corn 3 B9
Gorrenberry Borders 115 E7
Gors Ceredig 46 B5
Gorse Hill Swindon 38 F1
Gorsedd Flint 73 B5
Gorseinon Swansea 33 E6
Gorseness Orkney 159 G5
Gorsgoch Ceredig 46 D3
Gorslas Carms 33 C6
Gorsley Glos 36 B3
Gorstan Highld 150 E6
Gorstanvorran Highld 130 B2
Gorsteyhill Staffs 74 D4
Gorsty Hill Staffs 62 B5
Gortantaoid Argyll 142 A4
Gorton Gtr Man 87 E6
Gosbeck Suff 57 D5
Gosberton Lincs 78 F5
Gosberton Clough Lincs 65 B8
Gosfield Essex 42 B3
Gosford Hereford 49 C7
Gosforth Cumb 98 D2
Gosforth T&W 110 C5
Gosmore Herts 40 B4
Gosport Hants 15 E7
Gossabrough Shetland 160 E7
Gossington Glos 36 D4
Goswick Northumb 123 E6
Gotham Notts 76 F5
Gotherington Glos 37 B6
Gott Shetland 160 J6
Goudhurst Kent 18 B4
Goulceby Lincs 79 B5
Gourdas Aberds 153 D7
Gourdon Aberds 135 B8
Gourock Invclyd 118 B2
Govan Glasgow 119 C5
Govanhill Glasgow 119 C5
Goveton Devon 7 E5
Govilon Mon 35 C6
Gowanhill Aberds 153 B10
Gowdall E Yorks 89 B7
Gowerton Swansea 33 E6
Gowkhall Fife 128 F2
Gowthorpe E Yorks 96 D3
Goxhill E Yorks 97 E7
Goxhill N Lincs 90 B5
Goxhill Haven N Lincs 90 B5
Goytre Neath 34 F1
Grabhair W Isles 155 F8
Graby Lincs 65 B7
Grade Corn 3 E6
Graffham W Sus 16 C3
Grafham Cambs 54 C2
Grafham Sur 27 E8
Grafton Hereford 49 F6
Grafton N Yorks 95 C7
Grafton Oxon 38 D2
Grafton Shrops 60 C4
Grafton Worcs 49 C7
Grafton Flyford Worcs 50 D4
Grafton Regis Northants 53 E5
Grafton Underwood Northants 65 F6
Grafty Green Kent 30 E2
Graianrhyd Denb 73 D6
Graig Conwy 83 D8
Graig Denb 72 B4
Graig-fechan Denb 72 D5
Grain Medway 30 B2
Grainsby Lincs 91 E6
Grainthorpe Lincs 91 E7
Grampound Corn 3 B8
Grampound Road Corn 4 D4
Gramsdal W Isles 148 C3
Granborough Bucks 39 B7
Granby Notts 77 F7
Grandborough Warks 52 C2
Grandtully Perth 133 D6
Grange Cumb 98 C4
Grange E Ayrs 118 F4
Grange Medway 29 C8
Grange Mers 85 F3
Grange Perth 128 B4
Grange Crossroads Moray 152 C4
Grange Hall Moray 151 E13
Grange Hill Essex 41 E7
Grange Moor W Yorks 88 C3
Grange of Lindores Fife 128 C4
Grange-over-Sands Cumb 92 B4
Grange Villa Durham 110 D5
Grangemill Derbys 76 D2
Grangemouth Falk 127 F8
Grangepans Falk 128 F2
Grangetown Cardiff 22 B3
Grangetown Redcar 102 B3
Granish Highld 138 C5
Gransmoor E Yorks 97 D7
Granston Pembs 44 B3
Grantchester Cambs 54 D5
Grantham Lincs 78 F2
Grantley N Yorks 94 C5
Grantlodge Aberds 141 C6
Granton Dumfries 114 D3
Granton Edin 120 B5
Grantown-on-Spey Highld 139 B6
Grantshouse Borders 122 C4
Grappenhall Warr 86 F4
Grasby Lincs 90 D4
Grasmere Cumb 99 D5
Grasscroft Gtr Man 87 D7
Grassendale Mers 85 F4
Grassholme Durham 100 B4
Grassington N Yorks 94 C3
Grassmoor Derbys 76 C4
Grassthorpe Notts 77 C7
Grateley Hants 25 E7
Gratwich Staffs 75 F7
Graveley Cambs 54 C3
Graveley Herts 41 B5
Gravelly Hill W Mid 62 E5
Gravels Shrops 60 D3
Graven Shetland 160 F6
Graveney Kent 30 C4
Gravesend Herts 41 B7
Gravesend Kent 29 B7
Grayingham Lincs 90 E3
Grayrigg Cumb 99 E7
Grays Thurrock 29 B7
Grayshott Hants 27 F6
Grayswood Sur 27 F7
Graythorp Hrtlpl 102 B3
Grazeley Wokingham 26 C4
Greasbrough S Yorks 88 E5
Greasby Mers 85 F3
Great Abington Cambs 55 E6
Great Addington Northants 53 B7
Great Alne Warks 51 D6
Great Altcar Lancs 85 D4
Great Amwell Herts 41 C6
Great Asby Cumb 100 C1
Great Ashfield Suff 56 C3
Great Ayton N Yorks 102 C3
Great Baddow Essex 42 D3
Great Bardfield Essex 55 F7
Great Barford Bedford 54 D2
Great Barr W Mid 62 E4
Great Barrington Glos 38 C2
Great Barrow Ches W 73 C8
Great Barton Suff 56 C2
Great Barugh N Yorks 96 B3
Great Bavington Northumb 117 F5
Great Bealings Suff 57 E6
Great Bedwyn Wilts 25 C7
Great Bentley Essex 43 B7
Great Billing Northants 53 C6
Great Bircham Norf 80 D3
Great Blakenham Suff 56 D5
Great Blencow Cumb 108 F4
Great Bolas Telford 61 B6
Great Bookham Sur 28 D2
Great Bourton Oxon 52 E2
Great Bowden Leics 64 F4
Great Bradley Suff 55 D7
Great Braxted Essex 42 C4
Great Bricett Suff 56 D4
Great Brickhill Bucks 53 F7
Great Bridge W Mid 62 E3
Great Bridgeford Staffs 62 B2
Great Brington Northants 52 C4
Great Bromley Essex 43 B6
Great Broughton Cumb 107 F7
Great Broughton N Yorks 102 D3
Great Budworth Ches W 74 B3
Great Burdon Darl 101 C8
Great Burgh Sur 28 D3
Great Burstead Essex 42 E2
Great Busby N Yorks 102 D3
Great Canfield Essex 42 C1
Great Carlton Lincs 91 F8
Great Casterton Rutland 65 D7
Great Chart Kent 30 E3
Great Chatwell Staffs 61 C7
Great Chesterford Essex 55 E6
Great Cheverell Wilts 24 D4
Great Chishill Cambs 54 F5
Great Clacton Essex 43 C7
Great Cliff W Yorks 88 C4
Great Clifton Cumb 98 B2
Great Coates NE Lincs 91 D6
Great Comberton Worcs 50 E4
Great Corby Cumb 108 D4
Great Cornard Suff 56 E2
Great Cowden E Yorks 97 E8
Great Coxwell Oxon 38 E2
Great Crakehall N Yorks 101 E7
Great Cransley Northants 53 B6
Great Cressingham Norf 67 D8
Great Crosby Mers 85 E4
Great Cubley Derbys 75 F8
Great Dalby Leics 64 C4
Great Denham Bedford 53 E8
Great Doddington Northants 53 C6
Great Dunham Norf 67 C8
Great Dunmow Essex 42 B2
Great Durnford Wilts 25 F6
Great Easton Essex 42 B2
Great Easton Leics 64 E5
Great Eccleston Lancs 92 E4
Great Edstone N Yorks 103 F5
Great Ellingham Norf 68 E3
Great Elm Som 24 E2
Great Eversden Cambs 54 D4
Great Fencote N Yorks 101 E7
Great Finborough Suff 56 D4
Great Fransham Norf 67 C8
Great Gaddesden Herts 40 C3
Great Gidding Cambs 65 F8
Great Givendale E Yorks 96 D4
Great Glemham Suff 57 C7
Great Glen Leics 64 E3
Great Gonerby Lincs 77 F8
Great Gransden Cambs 54 D3
Great Green Norf 69 F5
Great Green Suff 56 D3
Great Habton N Yorks 96 B3
Great Hale Lincs 78 E4
Great Hallingbury Essex 41 C8
Great Hampden Bucks 39 D8
Great Harrowden Northants 53 B6
Great Harwood Lancs 93 F7
Great Haseley Oxon 39 D6
Great Hatfield E Yorks 97 E7
Great Haywood Staffs 62 B4
Great Heath W Mid 63 F7
Great Heck N Yorks 89 B6
Great Henny Essex 56 F2
Great Hinton Wilts 24 D4
Great Hockham Norf 68 E2
Great Holland Essex 43 C8
Great Horkesley Essex 56 F3
Great Hormead Herts 41 B6
Great Horton W Yorks 94 F4
Great Horwood Bucks 53 F5
Great Houghton Northants 53 D5
Great Houghton S Yorks 88 D5
Great Hucklow Derbys 75 B8
Great Kelk E Yorks 97 D7
Great Kimble Bucks 39 D8
Great Kingshill Bucks 40 E1
Great Langton N Yorks 101 E7
Great Leighs Essex 42 C3
Great Lever Gtr Man 86 D5
Great Limber Lincs 90 D5
Great Linford M Keynes 53 E6
Great Livermere Suff 56 B2
Great Longstone Derbys 76 B2
Great Lumley Durham 111 E5
Great Lyth Shrops 60 D4
Great Malvern Worcs 50 E2
Great Maplestead Essex 56 F2
Great Marton Blackpool 92 F3
Great Massingham Norf 80 E3
Great Melton Norf 68 D4
Great Milton Oxon 39 D6
Great Missenden Bucks 40 D1
Great Mitton Lancs 93 F7
Great Mongeham Kent 31 D7
Great Moulton Norf 68 E4
Great Munden Herts 41 B6
Great Musgrave Cumb 100 C2
Great Ness Shrops 60 C3
Great Notley Essex 42 B3
Great Oakley Essex 43 B7
Great Oakley Northants 65 F5
Great Offley Herts 40 B4
Great Ormside Cumb 100 C2
Great Orton Cumb 108 D3
Great Ouseburn N Yorks 95 C7
Great Oxendon Northants 64 F4
Great Oxney Green Essex 42 D2
Great Palgrave Norf 67 C8
Great Parndon Essex 41 D7
Great Paxton Cambs 54 C3
Great Plumpton Lancs 92 F3
Great Plumstead Norf 69 C6
Great Ponton Lincs 78 F2
Great Preston W Yorks 88 B5
Great Raveley Cambs 66 F2
Great Rissington Glos 38 C1
Great Rollright Oxon 51 F8
Great Ryburgh Norf 81 E5
Great Ryle Northumb 117 C6
Great Ryton Shrops 60 D4
Great Saling Essex 42 B3
Great Salkeld Cumb 109 F5
Great Sampford Essex 55 F7
Great Sankey Warr 86 F3
Great Saxham Suff 55 C8
Great Shefford W Berks 25 B8
Great Shelford Cambs 55 D5
Great Smeaton N Yorks 101 D8
Great Snoring Norf 80 D5
Great Somerford Wilts 37 F6
Great Stainton Darl 101 B8
Great Stambridge Essex 42 E4
Great Staughton Cambs 54 C2
Great Steeping Lincs 79 C7
Great Stonar Kent 31 D7
Great Strickland Cumb 99 B7
Great Stukeley Cambs 54 B3
Great Sturton Lincs 78 B5
Great Sutton Ches W 73 B7
Great Sutton Shrops 60 F5
Great Swinburne Northumb 110 B2
Great Tew Oxon 38 B3
Great Tey Essex 42 B4
Great Thurkleby N Yorks 95 B7
Great Thurlow Suff 55 D7
Great Torrington Devon 9 C6
Great Tosson Northumb 117 D6
Great Totham Essex 42 C4
Great Totham Essex 42 C4
Great Tows Lincs 91 E6
Great Urswick Cumb 92 B2
Great Wakering Essex 43 F5
Great Waldingfield Suff 56 E3
Great Walsingham Norf 80 D5
Great Waltham Essex 42 C2
Great Warley Essex 42 E1
Great Washbourne Glos 50 F4
Great Weldon Northants 65 F6
Great Welnetham Suff 56 D2
Great Wenham Suff 56 F4
Great Whittington Northumb 110 B3
Great Wigborough Essex 43 C5
Great Wilbraham Cambs 55 D6
Great Wishford Wilts 25 F5
Great Witcombe Glos 37 C6
Great Witley Worcs 50 C2
Great Wolford Warks 51 F7
Great Wratting Suff 55 E7
Great Wymondley Herts 41 B5
Great Wyrley Staffs 62 D3
Great Wytheford Shrops 61 C5
Great Yarmouth Norf 69 D8
Great Yeldham Essex 55 F8
Greater Doward Hereford 36 C2
Greatford Lincs 65 C7
Greatgate Staffs 75 E7
Greatham Hants 27 F5
Greatham Hrtlpl 102 B2
Greatham W Sus 16 C4
Greatstone on Sea Kent 19 C7
Greatworth Northants 52 E3
Greave Lancs 87 B6
Greeba IoM 84 D3
Green Denb 72 C4
Green End Bedford 54 D2
Green Hammerton N Yorks 95 D7
Green Lane Powys 59 E8
Green Ore Som 23 D7
Green St Green London 29 C5
Green Street Herts 40 E4
Greenbank Shetland 160 C7
Greenburn W Loth 120 C2
Greendikes Northumb 117 B6
Greenfield C Beds 53 F8
Greenfield Flint 73 B5
Greenfield Gtr Man 87 D7
Greenfield Highld 136 D5
Greenfield Oxon 39 E7
Greenford London 40 F4
Greengairs N Lanark 119 B7
Greenham W Berks 26 C2
Greenhaugh Northumb 116 F3
Greenhead Northumb 109 C6
Greenhill Falk 119 B8
Greenhill Kent 31 C5
Greenhill Leics 63 C8
Greenhill London 40 F4
Greenhills N Ayrs 118 D3
Greenhithe Kent 29 B6
Greenholm E Ayrs 118 F5
Greenholme Cumb 99 D7
Greenhouse Borders 115 B8
Greenhow Hill N Yorks 94 C4
Greenigoe Orkney 159 H5
Greenland Highld 158 D4
Greenlands Bucks 39 F7
Greenlaw Aberds 153 C6
Greenlaw Borders 122 E3
Greenlea Dumfries 107 B7
Greenloaning Perth 127 D7
Greenmount Gtr Man 87 C5
Greenmow Shetland 160 L6
Greenock Invclyd 118 B2
Greenock West Invclyd 118 B2
Greenodd Cumb 99 F5
Greenrow Cumb 107 D8
Greens Norton Northants 52 E4
Greenside T&W 110 C4
Greensidehill Northumb 117 C5
Greenstead Green Essex 42 B4
Greensted Essex 41 D8
Greenwich London 28 B4
Greet Glos 50 F5
Greete Shrops 49 B7
Greetham Lincs 79 B6
Greetham Rutland 65 C6
Greetland W Yorks 87 B8
Gregg Hall Cumb 99 E6
Gregson Lane Lancs 86 B3
Greinetobht W Isles 148 A3
Greinton Som 23 F6
Gremista Shetland 160 J6
Grenaby IoM 84 E2
Grendon Northants 53 C6
Grendon Warks 63 D6
Grendon Common Warks 63 E6
Grendon Green Hereford 49 D7
Grendon Underwood Bucks 39 B6
Grenofen Devon 6 B2
Grenoside S Yorks 88 E4
Greosabhagh W Isles 154 H6
Gresford Wrex 73 D7
Gresham Norf 81 D7
Greshornish Highld 149 C8
Gressenhall Norf 68 C2
Gressingham Lancs 93 C5
Gresty Green Ches E 74 D4
Greta Bridge Durham 101 C5
Gretna Dumfries 108 C3
Gretna Green Dumfries 108 C3
Gretton Glos 50 F5
Gretton Northants 65 E5
Gretton Shrops 60 E5
Grewelthorpe N Yorks 94 B5
Grey Green N Lincs 89 D8
Greygarth N Yorks 94 B4
Greynor Carms 33 D6
Greysouthen Cumb 98 B2
Greystoke Cumb 108 F4
Greystone Angus 135 E5
Greystone Dumfries 107 B6
Greywell Hants 26 D5
Griais W Isles 155 C9
Grianan W Isles 155 D9
Gribthorpe E Yorks 96 F3
Gridley Corner Devon 9 E5
Griff Warks 63 F7
Griffithstown Torf 35 E6
Grimbister Orkney 159 G4
Grimblethorpe Lincs 91 F6
Grimeford Village Lancs 86 C4
Grimethorpe S Yorks 88 D5
Griminis W Isles 148 C2
Grimister Shetland 160 D6
Grimley Worcs 50 C3
Grimness Orkney 159 J5
Grimoldby Lincs 91 F7
Grimpo Shrops 60 B3
Grimsargh Lancs 93 F5
Grimsbury Oxon 52 E2
Grimsby NE Lincs 91 C6
Grimscote Northants 52 D4
Grimscott Corn 8 D4
Grimsthorpe Lincs 65 B7
Grimston E Yorks 97 F8
Grimston Leics 64 B3
Grimston Norf 80 E3
Grimston York 96 D2
Grimstone Dorset 12 E4
Grinacombe Moor Devon 9 E6
Grindale E Yorks 97 B7
Grindigar Orkney 159 H6
Grindiscol Shetland 160 K6
Grindle Shrops 61 D7
Grindleford Derbys 76 B2
Grindleton Lancs 93 E7
Grindley Staffs 62 B4
Grindley Brook Shrops 74 E2
Grindlow Derbys 75 B8
Grindon Northumb 122 E5
Grindon Staffs 75 D7
Grindonmoor Gate Staffs 75 D7
Gringley on the Hill Notts 89 E8
Grinsdale Cumb 108 D3
Grinshill Shrops 60 B5
Grinton N Yorks 101 E5
Griomsidar W Isles 155 E8
Grishipoll Argyll 146 F4
Grisling Common E Sus 17 B8
Gristhorpe N Yorks 103 F8
Griston Norf 68 E2
Gritley Orkney 159 H6
Grittenham Wilts 37 F7
Grittleton Wilts 37 F5
Grizebeck Cumb 98 F4
Grizedale Cumb 99 E5
Grobister Orkney 159 F7
Groby Leics 64 D2
Groes Conwy 72 C4
Groes Neath 34 F1
Groes-faen Rhondda 34 F4
Groes-lwyd Powys 60 C2
Groesffordd Marli Denb 72 B4
Groeslon Gwyn 82 E5
Groeslon Gwyn 82 F4
Grogport Argyll 143 D9
Gromford Suff 57 D7
Gronant Flint 72 A4
Groombridge E Sus 18 B2
Grosmont Mon 35 B8
Grosmont N Yorks 103 D6
Groton Suff 56 E3
Grougfoot Falk 120 B3
Grouville Jersey 17
Grove Dorset 12 G5
Grove Kent 31 C6
Grove Notts 77 B7
Grove Oxon 38 E4
Grove Park London 28 B5
Grove Vale W Mid 62 E4
Grovesend Swansea 33 D6
Grudie Highld 150 E6
Gruids Highld 157 J8
Gruinard House Highld 150 B2
Grula Highld 149 F8
Gruline Argyll 147 G8
Grunasound Shetland 160 K5
Grundisburgh Suff 57 D6
Grunsagill Lancs 93 D7
Gruting Shetland 160 J4
Grutness Shetland 160 N6
Gualachulain Highld 131 E5
Gualin Ho. Highld 156 D6
Guardbridge Fife 129 C6
Guarlford Worcs 50 E3
Guay Perth 133 E7
Guestling Green E Sus 19 D5
Guestling Thorn E Sus 18 D5
Guestwick Norf 81 E6
Guestwick Green Norf 81 E6
Guide Blackburn 86 B5
Guide Post Northumb 117 F8
Guilden Morden Cambs 54 E3
Guilden Sutton Ches W 73 C8
Guildford Sur 27 E7
Guildtown Perth 133 F8
Guilsborough Northants 52 B4
Guilsfield Powys 60 C2
Guilton Kent 31 D6
Guineaford Devon 20 F4
Guisborough Redcar 102 C4
Guiseley W Yorks 94 E4
Guist Norf 81 E5
Guith Orkney 159 E6
Guiting Power Glos 37 B7
Gulberwick Shetland 160 K6
Gullane E Loth 129 F6
Gulval Corn 2 C3
Gulworthy Devon 6 B2
Gumfreston Pembs 32 D2
Gumley Leics 64 E3
Gummow's Shop Corn 4 D3
Gun Hill E Sus 18 D2
Gunby E Yorks 96 F3
Gunby Lincs 65 B6
Gundleton Hants 26 F4
Gunn Devon 20 F5
Gunnerside N Yorks 100 E4
Gunnerton Northumb 110 B2
Gunness N Lincs 90 C2
Gunnislake Corn 6 B2
Gunnista Shetland 160 J7
Gunthorpe Norf 81 D6
Gunthorpe Notts 77 E6
Gunthorpe Pboro 65 D8
Gunville IoW 15 F5
Gunwalloe Corn 3 D5
Gurnard IoW 15 E5
Gurnett Ches E 75 B6
Gurney Slade Som 23 E8
Gurnos Powys 34 D1
Gussage All Saints Dorset 13 C8
Gussage St Michael Dorset 13 C7
Guston Kent 31 E7
Gutcher Shetland 160 D7
Guthrie Angus 135 D5
Guyhirn Cambs 66 D3
Guyhirn Gull Cambs 66 D3
Guy's Head Lincs 66 B4
Guy's Marsh Dorset 13 B6
Guyzance Northumb 117 D8
Gwaenysgor Flint 72 A4
Gwalchmai Anglesey 82 D3
Gwaun-Cae-Gurwen Neath 33 C8
Gwaun-Leision Neath 33 C8
Gwbert Ceredig 45 E3
Gweek Corn 3 D6
Gwehelog Mon 35 D7
Gwenddwr Powys 48 E2
Gwennap Corn 3 C6
Gwenter Corn 3 E6
Gwernaffield Flint 73 C6
Gwernesney Mon 35 D8
Gwernogle Carms 46 F4
Gwernymynydd Flint 73 C6
Gwersyllt Wrex 73 D7
Gwespyr Flint 85 F2
Gwithian Corn 2 B4
Gwredog Anglesey 82 C4
Gwyddelwern Denb 72 E4
Gwyddgrug Carms 46 F3
Gwydyr Uchaf Conwy 83 E7
Gwynfryn Wrex 73 D6
Gwystre Powys 48 C2
Gwytherin Conwy 83 E8
Gyfelia Wrex 73 E7
Gyffin Conwy 83 D7
Gyre Orkney 159 H4
Gyrn-goch Gwyn 70 C5

H

Habberley Shrops 60 D3
Habergham Lancs 93 F8
Habrough NE Lincs 90 C5
Haceby Lincs 78 F3
Hacheston Suff 57 D7
Hackbridge London 28 C3
Hackenthorpe S Yorks 88 F5
Hackford Norf 68 D3
Hackforth N Yorks 101 E7
Hackland Orkney 159 F4
Hackleton Northants 53 D6
Hackness N Yorks 103 E7
Hackness Orkney 159 J4
Hackney London 41 F6
Hackthorn Lincs 90 F3
Hackthorpe Cumb 99 B7
Haconby Lincs 65 B8
Hacton London 41 F8
Hadden Borders 122 F3
Haddenham Bucks 39 D7
Haddenham Cambs 55 B5
Haddington E Loth 121 B8
Haddington Lincs 78 C2
Haddiscoe Norf 69 E7
Haddon Cambs 65 E8
Haddon Ches E 75 C6
Hade Edge W Yorks 88 D2
Hademore Staffs 63 D5
Hadfield Derbys 87 E8
Hadham Cross Herts 41 C7
Hadham Ford Herts 41 B7
Hadleigh Essex 42 F4
Hadleigh Suff 56 E4
Hadley Telford 61 C6
Hadley End Staffs 62 B5
Hadlow Kent 29 E7
Hadlow Down E Sus 18 C2
Hadnall Shrops 60 C5
Hadstock Essex 55 E6
Hady Derbys 76 B3
Hadzor Worcs 50 C4
Haffenden Quarter Kent 30 E2
Hafod-Dinbych Conwy 83 F8
Hafod-lom Conwy 83 D8
Haggate Lancs 93 F8
Haggbeck Cumb 108 B4
Haggerston Northumb 123 E6
Haggrister Shetland 160 F5
Hagley Hereford 49 E7
Hagley Worcs 62 F3
Hagworthingham Lincs 79 C6
Haigh Gtr Man 86 D4
Haigh S Yorks 88 C3
Haigh Moor W Yorks 88 B3
Haighton Green Lancs 93 F5
Hail Weston Cambs 54 C2
Haile Cumb 98 D2
Hailes Glos 50 F5
Hailey Herts 41 C6
Hailey Oxon 38 C3
Hailsham E Sus 18 E2
Haimer Highld 158 D3
Hainault London 41 E7
Hainford Norf 68 C5
Hainton Lincs 91 F5
Hairmyres S Lanark 119 D6
Haisthorpe E Yorks 97 C7
Hakin Pembs 44 E3
Halam Notts 77 D6
Halbeath Fife 128 F3
Halberton Devon 10 C5
Halcro Highld 158 D4
Hale Gtr Man 87 F5
Hale Halton 86 F2
Hale Hants 14 C2
Hale Bank Halton 86 F2
Hale Street Kent 29 E7
Halebarns Gtr Man 87 F5
Hales Norf 69 E6
Hales Staffs 74 F4
Hales Place Kent 30 D5
Halesfield Telford 61 D7
Halesgate Lincs 66 B3
Halesowen W Mid 62 F3
Halesworth Suff 57 B7
Halewood Mers 86 F2
Halford Shrops 60 F4
Halford Warks 51 E7
Halfpenny Furze Carms 32 C3
Halfpenny Green Staffs 62 E2
Halfway Carms 46 F5
Halfway Carms 47 F7
Halfway W Berks 26 C2
Halfway Bridge W Sus 16 B3
Halfway House Shrops 60 C3
Halfway Houses Kent 30 B3
Halifax W Yorks 87 B8
Halket E Ayrs 118 D4
Halkirk Highld 158 E3
Halkyn Flint 73 B6
Hall Dunnerdale Cumb 98 E4
Hall Green W Mid 62 F5
Hall Green W Yorks 88 C4
Hall Grove Herts 41 C5
Hall of Tankerness Orkney 159 H6
Hall of the Forest Shrops 60 F2
Halland E Sus 18 D2
Hallaton Leics 64 E4
Hallatrow Bath 23 D8
Hallbankgate Cumb 109 D5
Hallen S Glos 36 F2
Halliburton Borders 122 E2
Hallin Highld 148 C7
Halling Medway 29 C8
Hallington Lincs 91 F7
Hallington Northumb 110 B2
Halliwell Gtr Man 86 C5
Halloughton Notts 77 D6
Hallow Worcs 50 D3
Hallrule Borders 115 C8
Halls E Loth 122 B2
Hall's Green Herts 41 B5
Hallsands Devon 7 F6
Hallthwaites Cumb 98 F3
Hallworthy Corn 8 F3
Hallyburton House Perth 134 F2
Hallyne Borders 120 E4
Halmer End Staffs 74 E4
Halmore Glos 36 D3
Halmyre Mains Borders 120 E4
Halnaker W Sus 16 D3
Halsall Lancs 85 C4
Halse Northants 52 E3
Halse Som 11 B6
Halsetown Corn 2 C4
Halsham E Yorks 91 B6
Halsinger Devon 20 F4
Halstead Essex 56 F2
Halstead Kent 29 C5
Halstead Leics 64 D4
Halstock Dorset 12 D3
Haltham Lincs 78 C5
Haltoft End Lincs 79 E6
Halton Bucks 40 C1
Halton Halton 86 F3
Halton Lancs 92 C5
Halton Northumb 110 C2
Halton W Yorks 95 F6
Halton Wrex 73 F7
Halton East N Yorks 94 D3
Halton Gill N Yorks 93 B8
Halton Holegate Lincs 79 C7
Halton Lea Gate Northumb 109 D6
Halton West N Yorks 93 D8
Haltwhistle Northumb 109 C7
Halvergate Norf 69 D7
Halwell Devon 7 D5
Halwill Devon 9 E6
Halwill Junction Devon 9 D6
Ham Devon 11 D7
Ham Glos 36 E3
Ham Highld 158 C4
Ham Kent 31 D7
Ham London 28 B2
Ham Shetland 160 K1
Ham Wilts 25 C8
Ham Common Dorset 13 B6
Ham Green Hereford 50 E2
Ham Green Kent 19 C5
Ham Green Kent 30 C2
Ham Green N Som 23 B7
Ham Green Worcs 50 C5
Ham Street Som 23 F7
Hamble-le-Rice Hants 15 D5
Hambleden Bucks 39 F7
Hambledon Hants 15 C7
Hambledon Sur 27 F7
Hambleton Lancs 92 E3
Hambleton N Yorks 95 F8
Hambridge Som 11 B8
Hambrook S Glos 23 B8
Hambrook W Sus 15 D8
Hameringham Lincs 79 C6
Hamerton Cambs 54 B2
Hametoun Shetland 160 K1
Hamilton S Lanark 119 D7
Hammer W Sus 27 F6
Hammerpot W Sus 16 D4
Hammersmith London 28 B3
Hammerwich Staffs 62 D4
Hammerwood E Sus 28 F5
Hammond Street Herts 41 D6
Hammoon Dorset 13 C6
Hamnavoe Shetland 160 E4
Hamnavoe Shetland 160 E6
Hamnavoe Shetland 160 F6
Hamnavoe Shetland 160 K5
Hampden Park E Sus 18 E3
Hamperden End Essex 55 F6
Hampnett Glos 37 C7
Hampole S Yorks 89 C6
Hampreston Dorset 13 E8
Hampstead London 41 F5
Hampstead Norreys W Berks 26 B3
Hampsthwaite N Yorks 95 D5
Hampton London 28 C2
Hampton Shrops 61 F7
Hampton Worcs 50 E5
Hampton Bishop Hereford 49 F7
Hampton Heath Ches W 73 E8
Hampton in Arden W Mid 63 F6
Hampton Loade Shrops 61 F7
Hampton Lovett Worcs 50 C3
Hampton Lucy Warks 51 D7
Hampton on the Hill Warks 51 C7
Hampton Poyle Oxon 39 C5
Hamrow Norf 80 E5
Hamsey E Sus 17 C8
Hamsey Green London 28 D4
Hamstall Ridware Staffs 62 C5
Hamstead IoW 14 E5
Hamstead W Mid 62 E4
Hamstead Marshall W Berks 26 C2
Hamsterley Durham 110 D4
Hamsterley Durham 110 F4
Hamstreet Kent 19 B7
Hamworthy Poole 13 E7
Hanbury Staffs 63 B5
Hanbury Worcs 50 C4
Hanbury Woodend Staffs 63 B5
Hanby Lincs 78 F3
Hanchurch Staffs 74 E5
Handbridge Ches W 73 C8
Handcross W Sus 17 B6
Handforth Ches E 87 F6
Handley Ches W 73 D8
Handsacre Staffs 62 C4
Handsworth S Yorks 88 F5
Handsworth W Mid 62 E4
Handy Cross Devon 9 B6
Hanford Stoke 75 E5
Hanging Langford Wilts 24 F5
Hangleton W Sus 16 D4
Hanham S Glos 23 B8
Hankelow Ches E 74 E3
Hankerton Wilts 37 E6
Hankham E Sus 18 E3
Hanley Stoke 75 E5
Hanley Castle Worcs 50 E3
Hanley Child Worcs 49 C8
Hanley Swan Worcs 50 E3
Hanley William Worcs 49 C8
Hanlith N Yorks 94 C2
Hanmer Wrex 73 F8
Hannah Lincs 79 B8
Hannington Hants 26 D3
Hannington Northants 53 B6
Hannington Swindon 38 E1
Hannington Wick Swindon 38 E1
Hansel Village S Ayrs 118 F3
Hanslope M Keynes 53 E6
Hanthorpe Lincs 65 B7
Hanwell London 40 F4
Hanwell Oxon 52 E2
Hanwood Shrops 60 D4
Hanworth London 28 B2
Hanworth Norf 81 D7
Happendon S Lanark 119 F8
Happisburgh Norf 69 A6
Happisburgh Common Norf 69 B6
Hapsford Ches W 73 B8
Hapton Lancs 93 F7
Hapton Norf 68 E4
Harberton Devon 7 D5
Harbertonford Devon 7 D5
Harbledown Kent 30 D5
Harborne W Mid 62 F4
Harborough Magna Warks 52 B2
Harbottle Northumb 117 D5
Harbury Warks 51 D8
Harby Leics 77 F7
Harby Notts 77 B8
Harcombe Devon 11 E6
Harden W Mid 62 D4
Harden W Yorks 94 F3
Hardenhuish Wilts 24 B4
Hardgate Aberds 141 D6
Hardham W Sus 16 C4
Hardingham Norf 68 D3
Hardingstone Northants 53 D5
Hardington Som 24 D2
Hardington Mandeville Som 12 C3
Hardington Marsh Som 12 D3
Hardley Hants 14 D5
Hardley Street Norf 69 D6
Hardmead M Keynes 53 E7
Hardrow N Yorks 100 E3
Hardstoft Derbys 76 C4
Hardway Hants 15 D7
Hardway Som 24 F2
Hardwick Bucks 39 C8
Hardwick Cambs 54 D4
Hardwick Norf 67 C6
Hardwick Norf 68 F5
Hardwick Northants 53 C6
Hardwick Notts 77 B6
Hardwick Oxon 38 D3
Hardwick Oxon 39 B5
Hardwick W Mid 62 E4
Hardwicke Glos 36 C4
Hardwicke Glos 37 B6
Hardwicke Hereford 48 E4
Hardy's Green Essex 43 B5
Hare Green Essex 43 B6
Hare Hatch Wokingham 27 B6
Hare Street Herts 41 B6
Hareby Lincs 79 C6
Hareden Lancs 93 D6
Harefield London 40 E3
Harehills W Yorks 95 F6
Harehope Northumb 117 B6
Haresceugh Cumb 109 E6
Harescombe Glos 37 C5
Haresfield Glos 37 C5
Hareshaw N Lanark 119 C8
Hareshaw Head Northumb 116 F4
Harewood W Yorks 95 E6
Harewood End Hereford 36 B2
Harford Carms 46 E5
Harford Devon 6 D4
Hargate Norf 68 E4
Hargatewall Derbys 75 B8
Hargrave Ches W 73 C8
Hargrave Northants 53 B8
Hargrave Suff 55 D8
Harker Cumb 108 C3
Harkland Shetland 160 E6
Harkstead Suff 57 F5
Harlaston Staffs 63 C6
Harlaw Ho. Aberds 141 B6
Harlaxton Lincs 77 F8
Harle Syke Lancs 93 F8
Harlech Gwyn 71 D6
Harlequin Notts 77 F6
Harlescott Shrops 60 C5
Harlesden London 41 F5
Harleston Devon 7 E5
Harleston Norf 68 F5
Harleston Suff 56 D4
Harlestone Northants 52 C5
Harley S Yorks 88 E4
Harley Shrops 61 D5
Harleyholm S Lanark 120 F2
Harlington C Beds 53 F8
Harlington London 27 B8
Harlington S Yorks 89 D5
Harlosh Highld 149 D7
Harlow Essex 41 C7
Harlow Hill N Yorks 95 D
Harlow Hill Northumb 110 C
Harlthorpe E Yorks 96 F
Harlton Cambs 54 D
Harman's Cross Dorset 13 F
Harmby N Yorks 101 F
Harmer Green Herts 41 C
Harmer Hill Shrops 60 B
Harmondsworth London 27 B
Harmston Lincs 78 C
Harnham Northumb 110 B
Harnhill Glos 37 D
Harold Hill London 41 E
Harold Wood London 41 E
Haroldston West Pembs 44 D
Haroldswick Shetland 160 B
Harome N Yorks 102 F
Harpenden Herts 40 C
Harpford Devon 11 E
Harpham E Yorks 97 C
Harpley Norf 80 E
Harpley Worcs 49 C
Harpole Northants 52 C
Harpsdale Highld 158 E
Harpsden Oxon 39 F
Harpswell Lincs 90 F
Harpur Hill Derbys 75 B
Harpurhey Gtr Man 87 D
Harraby Cumb 108 D
Harrapool Highld 149 F1
Harrier Shetland 160 J
Harrietfield Perth 127 B
Harrietsham Kent 30 D
Harrington Cumb 98 B
Harrington Lincs 79 B
Harrington Northants 64 F
Harringworth Northants 65 E
Harris Highld 146 B
Harrogate N Yorks 95 D
Harrold Bedford 53 D
Harrow London 40 F
Harrow on the Hill London 40 F
Harrow Street Suff 56 F
Harrow Weald London 40 E
Harrowbarrow Corn 5 C
Harrowden Bedford 53 E
Harrowgate Hill Darl 101 C
Harston Cambs 54 D
Harston Leics 77 F
Harswell E Yorks 96 E
Hart Hrtlpl 111 F
Hart Common Gtr Man 86 D
Hart Hill Luton 40 B
Hart Station Hrtlpl 111 F
Hartburn Northumb 117 F
Hartburn Stockton 102 C
Hartest Suff 56 D
Hartfield E Sus 29 F
Hartford Cambs 54 B
Hartford Ches W 74 B
Hartford End Essex 42 C
Hartfordbridge Hants 27 D
Hartforth N Yorks 101 D
Harthill Ches W 74 D
Harthill N Lanark 120 C
Harthill S Yorks 89 F
Hartington Derbys 75 C
Hartland Devon 8 B
Hartlebury Worcs 50 B
Hartlepool Hrtlpl 111 F
Hartley Cumb 100 D
Hartley Kent 18 E
Hartley Kent 29 C
Hartley Northumb 111 B
Hartley Westpall Hants 26 D
Hartley Wintney Hants 27 D
Hartlip Kent 30 C
Hartoft End N Yorks 103 E
Harton N Yorks 96 C
Harton Shrops 60 F
Harton T&W 111 C
Hartpury Glos 36 B
Hartshead W Yorks 88 B
Hartshill Warks 63 E
Hartshorne Derbys 63 B
Hartsop Cumb 99 C
Hartwell Northants 53 D
Hartwood N Lanark 119 D
Harvieston Stirling 126 F
Harvington Worcs 51 E
Harvington Cross Worcs 51 E
Harwell Oxon 38 F
Harwich Essex 57 F
Harwood Durham 109 F
Harwood Gtr Man 86 C
Harwood Dale N Yorks 103 E
Harworth Notts 89 E
Hasbury W Mid 62 F
Hascombe Sur 27 E
Haselbech Northants 52 B
Haselbury Plucknett Som 12 C
Haseley Warks 51 C
Haselor Warks 51 D
Hasfield Glos 37 B
Hasguard Pembs 44 E
Haskayne Lancs 85 D
Hasketon Suff 57 D
Hasland Derbys 76 C
Haslemere Sur 27 F
Haslingden Lancs 87 B
Haslingfield Cambs 54 D
Haslington Ches E 74 D
Hassall Ches E 74 D
Hassall Green Ches E 74 D
Hassell Street Kent 30 E
Hassendean Borders 115 B
Hassingham Norf 69 D
Hassocks W Sus 17 C
Hassop Derbys 76 B
Hastigrow Highld 158 D
Hastingleigh Kent 30 E
Hastings E Sus 18 E
Hastingwood Essex 41 D
Hastoe Herts 40 D
Haswell Durham 111 E
Haswell Plough Durham 111 E
Hatch C Beds 54 E
Hatch Hants 26 D
Hatch Wilts 13 E
Hatch Beauchamp Som 11 B
Hatch End London 40 E
Hatch Green Som 11 C
Hatchet Gate Hants 14 D
Hatching Green Herts 40 C
Hatchmere Ches W 74 E
Hatcliffe NE Lincs 91 D
Hatfield Hereford 49 D
Hatfield Herts 41 D
Hatfield S Yorks 89 D
Hatfield Worcs 50 D
Hatfield Broad Oak Essex 41 C
Hatfield Garden Village Herts 41 D
Hatfield Heath Essex 41 C
Hatfield Hyde Herts 41 C
Hatfield Peverel Essex 42 C
Hatfield Woodhouse S Yorks 89 D
Hatford Oxon 38 E
Hatherden Hants 25 D
Hatherleigh Devon 9 D
Hathern Leics 63 E
Hatherop Glos 38 D
Hathersage Derbys 88 F
Hathershaw Gtr Man 87 D

Hulme End Staffs 75 D8
Hulme Walfield Ches E 74 C5
Hulver Street Suff 69 F7
Hulverstone IoW 14 F4
Humber Hereford 49 D7
Humber Bridge N Lincs 90 B4
Humberston NE Lincs 91 D7
Humbie E Loth 121 C7
Humbleton E Yorks 97 F8
Humbleton Northumb 117 B5
Humby Lincs 78 F3
Hume Borders 122 E3
Humshaugh Northumb 110 B2
Huna Highld 158 C5
Huncoat Lancs 93 F7
Huncote Leics 64 E2
Hundalee Borders 116 C2
Hunderthwaite Durham 100 B4
Hundle Houses Lincs 79 D5
Hundleby Lincs 79 C6
Hundleton Pembs 44 E4
Hundon Suff 55 E8
Hundred Acres Hants 15 C6
Hundred End Lancs 86 B2
Hundred House Powys 48 D3
Hungarton Leics 64 D3
Hungerford Hants 14 C2
Hungerford W Berks 25 C8
Hungerford Newtown W Berks 25 B8
Hungerton Lincs 65 B5
Hungladder Highld 149 A8
Hunmanby N Yorks 97 B6
Hunmanby Moor N Yorks 97 B7
Hunningham Warks 51 C8
Hunny Hill IoW 15 F5
Hunsdon Herts 41 C7
Hunsingore N Yorks 95 D7
Hunslet W Yorks 95 F6
Hunsonby Cumb 109 F5
Hunspow Highld 158 C4
Hunstanton Norf 80 C2
Hunstanworth Durham 110 E2
Hunsterson Ches E 74 E3
Hunston Suff 56 C3
Hunston W Sus 16 D2
Hunstrete Bath 23 C8
Hunt End Worcs 50 C5
Hunter's Quay Argyll 145 F10
Hunthill Lodge Angus 134 B4
Hunting-tower Perth 128 B2
Huntingdon Cambs 54 B3
Huntingfield Suff 57 B7
Huntingford Dorset 24 F3
Huntington E Loth 121 B7
Huntington Hereford 48 D4
Huntington Staffs 62 C3
Huntington York 96 D2
Huntley Glos 36 C4
Huntly Aberds 152 E5
Huntlywood Borders 122 E2
Hunton Kent 29 E8
Hunton N Yorks 101 E6
Hunt's Corner Norf 68 F3
Hunt's Cross Mers 86 F2
Huntsham Devon 10 B5
Huntspill Som 22 E5
Huntworth Som 22 F5
Hunwick Durham 110 F4
Hunworth Norf 81 D6
Hurdsfield Ches E 75 B6
Hurley Warks 63 E6
Hurley Windsor 39 F8
Hurlford E Ayrs 118 F4
Hurliness Orkney 159 K3
Hurn Dorset 14 E2
Hurn's End Lincs 79 E7
Hursley Hants 14 B5
Hurst N Yorks 101 D5
Hurst Som 12 C2
Hurst Wokingham 27 B5
Hurst Green E Sus 18 C4
Hurst Green Lancs 93 F6
Hurst Wickham W Sus 17 C6
Hurstbourne Priors Hants 26 E2
Hurstbourne Tarrant Hants 25 D8
Hurstpierpoint W Sus 17 C6
Hurstwood Lancs 93 F8
Hurtmore Sur 27 E7
Hurworth Place Darl 101 D7
Hury Durham 100 C4
Husabost Highld 148 C7
Husbands Bosworth Leics 64 F3
Husborne Crawley C Beds 53 F7
Husthwaite N Yorks 95 B8
Hutchwns Bridgend 21 B7
Huthwaite Notts 76 D4
Huttoft Lincs 79 B8
Hutton Borders 122 D5
Hutton Cumb 99 B6
Hutton E Yorks 97 D6
Hutton Essex 42 E2
Hutton Lancs 86 B2
Hutton N Som 22 D5
Hutton Buscel N Yorks 103 F7
Hutton Conyers N Yorks 95 B6
Hutton Cranswick E Yorks 97 D6
Hutton End Cumb 108 F4
Hutton Gate Redcar 102 C3
Hutton Henry Durham 111 F7
Hutton-le-Hole N Yorks 103 E5
Hutton Magna Durham 101 C6
Hutton Roof Cumb 93 B5
Hutton Roof Cumb 108 F3
Hutton Rudby N Yorks 102 D2
Hutton Sessay N Yorks 95 B7
Hutton Village Redcar 102 C3
Hutton Wandesley N Yorks 95 D8
Huxley Ches W 74 C2
Huxter Shetland 160 G7
Huxter Shetland 160 H5
Huxton Borders 122 C4
Huyton Mers 86 E2
Hwlffordd = Haverfordwest Pembs 44 D4
Hycemoor Cumb 98 F2
Hyde Glos 37 D5
Hyde Gtr Man 87 E7
Hyde Hants 14 C2
Hyde Heath Bucks 40 D2
Hyde Park S Yorks 89 D6
Hydestile Sur 27 E7
Hylton Castle T&W 111 D6
Hyndford Bridge S Lanark 120 E2
Hynish Argyll 146 H2
Hyssington Powys 60 E3
Hythe Hants 14 D5
Hythe Kent 19 B8
Hythe End Windsor 27 B8
Hythie Aberds 153 C10

I

Ibberton Dorset 13 D5
Ible Derbys 76 D2
Ibsley Hants 14 D2
Ibstock Leics 63 C8
Ibstone Bucks 39 E7
Ibthorpe Hants 25 D8
Ibworth Hants 26 D3
Ichrachan Argyll 125 B6
Ickburgh Norf 67 E8
Ickenham London 40 F3
Ickford Bucks 39 D6
Ickham Kent 31 D6
Ickleford Herts 54 F2
Icklesham E Sus 19 D5
Ickleton Cambs 55 E5
Icklingham Suff 55 B8
Ickwell Green C Beds 54 E2
Icomb Glos 38 B2
Idbury Oxon 38 C2
Iddesleigh Devon 9 D7
Ide Devon 10 E3
Ide Hill Kent 29 D5
Ideford Devon 7 B6
Iden E Sus 19 C6
Iden Green Kent 18 B4
Iden Green Kent 18 B5
Idle W Yorks 94 F4
Idlicote Warks 51 E7
Idmiston Wilts 25 F6
Idole Carms 33 C5
Idridgehay Derbys 76 E2
Idrigill Highld 149 B8
Idstone Oxon 38 F2
Idvies Angus 135 E5
Iffley Oxon 39 D5
Ifield W Sus 28 F3
Ifold W Sus 27 F8
Iford E Sus 17 D8
Ifton Heath Shrops 73 F7
Ightfield Shrops 74 F2
Ightham Kent 29 D6
Iken Suff 57 D8
Ilam Staffs 75 D8
Ilchester Som 12 B3
Ilderton Northumb 117 B6
Ilford London 41 F7
Ilfracombe Devon 20 E4
Ilkeston Derbys 76 E4
Ilketshall St Andrew Suff 69 F6
Ilketshall St Lawrence Suff 69 F6
Ilketshall St Margaret Suff 69 F6
Ilkley W Yorks 94 E4
Illey W Mid 62 F3
Illingworth W Yorks 87 B8
Illogan Corn 3 B5
Illston on the Hill Leics 64 E4
Ilmer Bucks 39 D7
Ilmington Warks 51 E7
Ilminster Som 11 C8
Ilsington Devon 7 B5
Ilston Swansea 33 E6
Ilton N Yorks 94 B4
Ilton Som 11 C8
Imachar N Ayrs 143 D9
Imeraval Argyll 142 D4
Immingham NE Lincs 91 C5
Impington Cambs 54 C5
Ince Ches W 73 B8
Ince Blundell Mers 85 D4
Ince in Makerfield Gtr Man 86 D3
Inch of Arnhall Aberds 135 B6
Inchbare Angus 135 C6
Inchberry Moray 152 C3
Inchbraoch Angus 135 D7
Incheril Highld 150 E3
Inchgrundle Angus 134 B4
Inchina Highld 150 B2
Inchinnan Renfs 118 C4
Inchkinloch Highld 157 E8
Inchlaggan Highld 136 D4
Inchlumpie Highld 151 D8
Inchmore Highld 150 G6
Inchnacardoch Hotel Highld 137 C6
Inchnadamph Highld 156 G5
Inchree Highld 130 C4
Inchture Perth 128 B4
Inchyra Perth 128 B3
Indian Queens Corn 4 D4
Inerval Argyll 142 D4
Ingatestone Essex 42 E2
Ingbirchworth S Yorks 88 D3
Ingestre Staffs 62 B3
Ingham Lincs 90 F3
Ingham Norf 69 B6
Ingham Suff 56 B2
Ingham Corner Norf 69 B6
Ingleborough Norf 66 C4
Ingleby Derbys 63 B7
Ingleby Lincs 77 B8
Ingleby Arncliffe N Yorks 102 D2
Ingleby Barwick Stockton 102 C2
Ingleby Greenhow N Yorks 102 D3
Inglemire Hull 97 F6
Inglesbatch Bath 24 C2
Inglesham Swindon 38 E2
Ingleton Durham 101 B6
Ingleton N Yorks 93 B6
Inglewhite Lancs 92 E5
Ingliston Edin 120 B4
Ingoe Northumb 110 B3
Ingol Lancs 92 F5
Ingoldisthorpe Norf 80 D2
Ingoldmells Lincs 79 C8
Ingoldsby Lincs 78 F3
Ingon Warks 51 D7
Ingram Northumb 117 C6
Ingrow W Yorks 94 F3
Ings Cumb 99 E6
Ingst S Glos 36 F2
Ingworth Norf 81 E7
Inham's End Cambs 66 E2
Inkberrow Worcs 50 D5
Inkpen W Berks 25 C8
Inkstack Highld 158 C4
Inn Cumb 99 D6
Innellan Argyll 145 F10
Innerleithen Borders 121 F6
Innerleven Fife 129 D5
Innermessan Dumfries 104 C4
Innerwick E Loth 122 B3
Innerwick Perth 132 E2
Innis Chonain Argyll 125 C7
Insch Aberds 140 B5
Insh Highld 138 D4
Inshore Highld 156 C6
Inskip Lancs 92 F4
Instoneville S Yorks 89 C6
Instow Devon 20 F3
Intake S Yorks 89 D6
Inver Aberds 139 E8
Inver Highld 151 C11
Inver Perth 133 E7
Inver Mallie Highld 136 F4
Inverailort Highld 147 C10
Inveraldie Angus 134 F4
Inveralligin Highld 149 C13
Inverallochy Aberds 153 B10
Inveran Highld 151 B8
Inveraray Argyll 125 E6
Inverarish Highld 149 E10
Inverarity Angus 134 E4
Inverarnan Stirling 126 C2
Inverasdale Highld 155 J13
Inverbeg Argyll 126 E2
Inverbervie Aberds 135 B8
Inverboyndie Aberds 153 B6
Inverbroom Highld 150 C4
Invercassley Highld 156 J7
Invercauld House Aberds 139 E7
Inverchaolain Argyll 145 F9
Invercharnan Highld 131 E5
Inverchoran Highld 150 F5
Invercreran Argyll 130 E4
Inverdruie Highld 138 C5
Inverebrie Aberds 153 E9
Invereck Argyll 145 E10
Inverernan Ho. Aberds 140 C2
Invereshie House Highld 138 D4
Inveresk E Loth 121 B6
Inverey Aberds 139 F6
Inverfarigaig Highld 137 B8
Invergarry Highld 137 D6
Invergelder Aberds 139 E8
Invergeldie Perth 127 B6
Invergordon Highld 151 E10
Invergowrie Perth 134 F3
Inverguseran Highld 149 H12
Inverhadden Perth 132 D3
Inverharroch Moray 152 E3
Inverherive Stirling 126 B2
Inverie Highld 147 B10
Inverinan Argyll 125 D5
Inverinate Highld 136 B2
Inverkeilor Angus 135 E6
Inverkeithing Fife 128 F3
Inverkeithny Aberds 153 D6
Inverkip Invclyd 118 B2
Inverkirkaig Highld 156 H3
Inverlael Highld 150 C4
Inverlochlarig Stirling 126 C3
Inverlochy Argyll 125 C7
Inverlochy Highld 131 B5
Inverlussa Argyll 144 E5
Invermark Lodge Angus 140 F3
Invermoidart Highld 147 D9
Invermoriston Highld 137 C7
Invernaver Highld 157 C10
Inverneill Argyll 145 E7
Inverness Highld 151 G9
Invernettie Aberds 153 D11
Invernoaden Argyll 125 F7
Inveroran Hotel Argyll 131 E6
Inverpolly Lodge Highld 156 H3
Inverquharity Angus 134 D4
Inverquhomery Aberds 153 D10
Inverroy Highld 137 F5
Inversanda Highld 130 D3
Invershiel Highld 136 C2
Invershin Highld 151 B8
Inversnaid Hotel Stirling 126 D2
Inverugie Aberds 153 D11
Inveruglas Argyll 126 D2
Inveruglass Highld 138 D4
Inverurie Aberds 141 B6
Invervar Perth 132 E3
Inverythan Aberds 153 D7
Inwardleigh Devon 9 E7
Inworth Essex 42 C4
Iochdar W Isles 148 D2
Iping W Sus 16 B2
Ipplepen Devon 7 C6
Ipsden Oxon 39 F6
Ipsley Worcs 51 C5
Ipstones Staffs 75 D7
Ipswich Suff 57 E5
Irby Mers 85 F3
Irby in the Marsh Lincs 79 C7
Irby upon Humber NE Lincs 91 D5
Irchester Northants 53 C7
Ireby Cumb 108 F2
Ireby Lancs 93 B6
Ireland Orkney 159 H4
Ireland Shetland 160 L5
Ireland's Cross Shrops 74 E4
Ireleth Cumb 92 B2
Ireshopeburn Durham 109 F8
Irlam Gtr Man 86 E5
Irnham Lincs 65 B7
Iron Acton S Glos 36 F3
Iron Cross Warks 51 D5
Ironbridge Telford 61 D6
Irongray Dumfries 107 B6
Ironmacannie Dumfries 106 B3
Ironside Aberds 153 C8
Ironville Derbys 76 D4
Irstead Norf 69 B6
Irthington Cumb 108 C4
Irthlingborough Northants 53 B7
Irton N Yorks 103 F8
Irvine N Ayrs 118 F3
Isauld Highld 157 C12
Isbister Orkney 159 F3
Isbister Orkney 159 G4
Isbister Shetland 160 D5
Isbister Shetland 160 G7
Isfield E Sus 17 C8
Isham Northants 53 B6
Isle Abbotts Som 11 B8
Isle Brewers Som 11 B8
Isle of Whithorn Dumfries 105 F8
Isleham Cambs 55 B7
Isleornsay Highld 149 G12
Islesburgh Shetland 160 G5
Islesteps Dumfries 107 B6
Isleworth London 28 B2
Isley Walton Leics 63 B8
Islibhig W Isles 154 E4
Islington London 41 F6
Islip Northants 53 B7
Islip Oxon 39 C5
Istead Rise Kent 29 C7
Isycoed Wrex 73 D8
Itchen Soton 14 C5
Itchen Abbas Hants 26 F3
Itchen Stoke Hants 26 F3
Itchingfield W Sus 16 B5
Itchington S Glos 36 F3
Itteringham Norf 81 D7
Itton Devon 9 E8
Itton Common Mon 36 E1
Ivegill Cumb 108 E4
Iver Bucks 40 F3
Iver Heath Bucks 40 F3
Iveston Durham 110 D4
Ivinghoe Bucks 40 C2
Ivinghoe Aston Bucks 40 C2
Ivington Hereford 49 D6
Ivington Green Hereford 49 D6
Ivy Chimneys Essex 41 D7
Ivy Cross Dorset 13 B6
Ivy Hatch Kent 29 D6
Ivybridge Devon 6 D4
Ivychurch Kent 19 C7
Iwade Kent 30 C3
Iwerne Courtney or Shroton Dorset 13 C6
Iwerne Minster Dorset 13 C6
Ixworth Suff 56 B3
Ixworth Thorpe Suff 56 B3

J

Jack Hill N Yorks 94 D5
Jack in the Green Devon 10 E5
Jacksdale Notts 76 D4
Jackstown Aberds 153 E7
Jacobstow Corn 8 E3
Jacobstowe Devon 9 D7
Jameston Pembs 32 E1
Jamestown Dumfries 115 E6
Jamestown Highld 150 F7
Jamestown W Dunb 126 F2
Jarrow T&W 111 C6
Jarvis Brook E Sus 18 C2
Jasper's Green Essex 42 B3
Java Argyll 124 B3
Jawcraig Falk 119 B8
Jaywick Essex 43 C7
Jealott's Hill Brack 27 B6
Jedburgh Borders 116 B2
Jeffreyston Pembs 32 D1
Jellyhill E Dunb 119 B6
Jemimaville Highld 151 E10
Jersey Farm Herts 40 D4
Jesmond T&W 111 C5
Jevington E Sus 18 E2
Jockey End Herts 40 C3
John o'Groats Highld 158 C5
Johnby Cumb 108 F4
John's Cross E Sus 18 C4
Johnshaven Aberds 135 C7
Johnston Pembs 44 D4
Johnstone Renfs 118 C4
Johnstonebridge Dumfries 114 E3
Johnstown Carms 33 C5
Johnstown Wrex 73 E7
Joppa Edin 121 B6
Joppa S Ayrs 112 C4
Jordans Bucks 40 E2
Jordanthorpe S Yorks 88 F4
Jump S Yorks 88 D4
Jumpers Green Dorset 14 E2
Juniper Green Edin 120 C4
Jurby East IoM 84 C3
Jurby West IoM 84 C3

K

Kaber Cumb 100 C2
Kaimend S Lanark 120 E2
Kaimes Edin 121 C5
Kalemouth Borders 116 B3
Kames Argyll 124 D4
Kames Argyll 145 F8
Kames E Ayrs 113 B6
Kea Corn 3 B7
Keadby N Lincs 90 C2
Keal Cotes Lincs 79 C6
Kearsley Gtr Man 87 D5
Kearstwick Cumb 99 F8
Kearton N Yorks 100 E4
Kearvaig Highld 156 B5
Keasden N Yorks 93 C7
Keckwick Halton 86 F3
Keddington Lincs 91 F7
Kedington Suff 55 E8
Kedleston Derbys 76 E3
Keelby Lincs 91 C5
Keele Staffs 74 E5
Keeley Green Bedford 53 E8
Keeston Pembs 44 D4
Keevil Wilts 24 D4
Kegworth Leics 63 B8
Kehelland Corn 2 B5
Keig Aberds 140 C5
Keighley W Yorks 94 E3
Keil Highld 130 D3
Keilarsbrae Clack 127 E7
Keilhill Aberds 153 C7
Keillmore Argyll 144 E5
Keillor Perth 134 E2
Keillour Perth 127 B8
Keills Argyll 142 B5
Keils Argyll 144 G4
Keinton Mandeville Som 23 F7
Keir Mill Dumfries 113 E8
Keisby Lincs 65 B7
Keiss Highld 158 D5
Keith Moray 152 C4
Keith Inch Aberds 153 D11
Keithock Angus 135 C6
Kelbrook Lancs 94 E2
Kelby Lincs 78 E3
Keld Cumb 99 C7
Keld N Yorks 100 D3
Keldholme N Yorks 103 F5
Kelfield N Lincs 90 D2
Kelfield N Yorks 95 F8
Kelham Notts 77 D7
Kellan Argyll 147 G8
Kellas Angus 134 F4
Kellas Moray 152 C1
Kellaton Devon 7 F6
Kelleth Cumb 100 D1
Kelleythorpe E Yorks 97 D5
Kelling Norf 81 C6
Kellingley N Yorks 89 B6
Kellington N Yorks 89 B6
Kelloe Durham 111 F6
Kelloholm Dumfries 113 C7
Kelly Devon 9 F5
Kelly Bray Corn 5 B8
Kelmarsh Northants 52 B5
Kelmscot Oxon 38 E2
Kelsale Suff 57 C7
Kelsall Ches W 74 C2
Kelsall Hill Ches W 74 C2
Kelshall Herts 54 F4
Kelsick Cumb 107 D8
Kelso Borders 122 F3
Kelstedge Derbys 76 C3
Kelstern Lincs 91 E6
Kelston Bath 24 C2
Keltneyburn Perth 132 E4
Kelton Dumfries 107 B6
Kelty Fife 128 E3
Kelvedon Essex 42 C4
Kelvedon Hatch Essex 42 E1
Kelvin S Lanark 119 D6
Kelvinside Glasgow 119 C5
Kelynack Corn 2 C2
Kemback Fife 129 C6
Kemberton Shrops 61 D7
Kemble Glos 37 E6
Kemerton Worcs 50 F4
Kemeys Commander Mon 35 D7
Kemnay Aberds 141 C6
Kemp Town Brighton 17 D7
Kempley Glos 36 B3
Kemps Green Warks 51 B6
Kempsey Worcs 50 E3
Kempsford Glos 38 E1
Kempshott Hants 26 D4
Kempston Bedford 53 E8
Kempston Hardwick Bedford 53 E8
Kempton Shrops 60 F3
Kemsing Kent 29 D6
Kemsley Kent 30 C3
Kenardington Kent 19 B6
Kenchester Hereford 49 E6
Kencot Oxon 38 D2
Kendal Cumb 99 E7
Kendoon Dumfries 113 F6
Kendray S Yorks 88 D4
Kenfig Bridgend 34 F2
Kenfig Hill Bridgend 34 F2
Kenilworth Warks 51 B7
Kenknock Stirling 132 F1
Kenley London 28 D4
Kenley Shrops 61 D5
Kenmore Highld 149 C12
Kenmore Perth 132 E4
Kenn Devon 10 F4
Kenn N Som 23 C6
Kennacley W Isles 154 H6
Kennacraig Argyll 145 G7
Kennerleigh Devon 10 D3
Kennet Clack 127 E8
Kennethmont Aberds 140 B4
Kennett Cambs 55 C7
Kennford Devon 10 F4
Kenninghall Norf 68 F3
Kenninghall Heath Norf 68 F3
Kennington Kent 30 E4
Kennington Oxon 39 D5
Kennoway Fife 129 D5
Kenny Hill Suff 55 B7
Kennythorpe N Yorks 96 C3
Kenovay Argyll 146 G2
Kensaleyre Highld 149 C9
Kensington London 28 B3
Kensworth C Beds 40 C3
Kensworth Common C Beds 40 C3
Kent's Oak Hants 14 B4
Kent Street E Sus 18 D4
Kent Street Kent 29 D7
Kent Street W Sus 17 B6
Kentallen Highld 130 D4
Kentchurch Hereford 35 B8
Kentford Suff 55 C8
Kentisbeare Devon 11 D5
Kentisbury Devon 20 E5
Kentisbury Ford Devon 20 E5
Kentmere Cumb 99 D6
Kenton Devon 10 F4
Kenton Suff 57 C5
Kenton T&W 110 C5
Kenton Bankfoot T&W 110 C5
Kentra Highld 147 E9
Kents Bank Cumb 92 B3
Kent's Green Glos 36 B4
Kenwick Shrops 73 F8
Kenwyn Corn 3 B7
Keoldale Highld 156 C6
Keppanach Highld 130 C4
Keppoch Highld 136 B2
Keprigan Argyll 143 G7
Kepwick N Yorks 102 E2
Kerchesters Borders 122 F3
Keresley W Mid 63 F7
Kernborough Devon 7 E5
Kerne Bridge Hereford 36 C2
Kerris Corn 2 D3
Kerry Powys 59 F8
Kerrycroy Argyll 145 G10
Kerry's Gate Hereford 49 F5
Kerrysdale Highld 149 A13
Kersall Notts 77 C7
Kersey Suff 56 E4
Kershopefoot Cumb 115 F7
Kersoe Worcs 50 F4
Kerswell Devon 11 D5
Kerswell Green Worcs 50 E3
Kesgrave Suff 57 E6
Kessingland Suff 69 F8
Kessingland Beach Suff 69 F8
Kessington E Dunb 119 B5
Kestle Corn 3 B8
Kestle Mill Corn 4 D3
Keston London 28 C5
Keswick Cumb 98 B4
Keswick Norf 68 D5
Keswick Norf 81 D9
Ketley Telford 61 C6
Ketley Bank Telford 61 C6
Ketsby Lincs 79 B6
Kettering Northants 53 B6
Ketteringham Norf 68 D4
Kettins Perth 134 F2
Kettlebaston Suff 56 D3
Kettlebridge Fife 128 D5
Kettleburgh Suff 57 C6
Kettlehill Fife 128 D5
Kettleholm Dumfries 107 B8
Kettleness N Yorks 103 C6
Kettleshume Ches E 75 B6
Kettlesing Bottom N Yorks 94 D5
Kettlesing Head N Yorks 94 D5
Kettlestone Norf 81 D5
Kettlethorpe Lincs 77 B8
Kettletoft Orkney 159 E7
Kettlewell N Yorks 94 B2
Ketton Rutland 65 D6
Kew London 28 B2
Kew Br. London 28 B2
Kewstoke N Som 22 C5
Kexbrough S Yorks 88 D4
Kexby Lincs 90 F2
Kexby York 96 D3
Key Green Ches E 75 C5
Keyham Leics 64 D3
Keyhaven Hants 14 E4
Keyingham E Yorks 91 B6
Keymer W Sus 17 C7
Keynsham Bath 23 C8
Keysoe Bedford 53 C8
Keysoe Row Bedford 53 C8
Keyston Cambs 53 B8
Keyworth Notts 77 F6
Kibblesworth T&W 110 D5
Kibworth Beauchamp Leics 64 E3
Kibworth Harcourt Leics 64 E3
Kidbrooke London 28 B5
Kiddemore Green Staffs 62 D2
Kidderminster Worcs 50 B3
Kiddington Oxon 38 B4
Kidlington Oxon 38 C4
Kidmore End Oxon 26 B4
Kidsgrove Staffs 74 D5
Kidstones N Yorks 100 F4
Kidwelly = Cydweli Carms 33 D5
Kiel Crofts Argyll 124 B5
Kielder Northumb 116 E3
Kierfiold Ho Orkney 159 G3
Kilbagie Fife 127 F8
Kilbarchan Renfs 118 C4
Kilbeg Highld 149 H11
Kilberry Argyll 144 G6
Kilbirnie N Ayrs 118 D3
Kilbride Argyll 124 C4
Kilbride Argyll 124 C5
Kilbride Highld 149 F10
Kilburn Angus 134 C3
Kilburn Derbys 76 E3
Kilburn London 41 F5
Kilburn N Yorks 95 B8
Kilby Leics 64 E3
Kilchamaig Argyll 145 G7
Kilchattan Argyll 144 D2
Kilchattan Bay Argyll 145 H10
Kilchenzie Argyll 143 F7
Kilcheran Argyll 124 B4
Kilchiaran Argyll 142 B3
Kilchoan Argyll 124 D3
Kilchoan Highld 146 E7
Kilchoman Argyll 142 B3
Kilchrenan Argyll 125 C6
Kilconquhar Fife 129 D6
Kilcot Glos 36 B3
Kilcoy Highld 151 F8
Kilcreggan Argyll 145 E11
Kildale N Yorks 102 D4
Kildalloig Argyll 143 G8
Kildary Highld 151 D10
Kildermorie Lodge Highld 151 D8
Kildonan N Ayrs 143 F11
Kildonan Lodge Highld 157 G12
Kildonnan Highld 146 C7
Kildrummy Aberds 140 C3
Kildwick N Yorks 94 E3
Kilfinan Argyll 145 F8
Kilfinnan Highld 137 E5
Kilgetty Pembs 32 D2
Kilgwrrwg Common Mon 36 E1
Kilham E Yorks 97 C6
Kilham Northumb 122 F4
Kilkenneth Argyll 146 G2
Kilkerran Argyll 143 G8
Kilkhampton Corn 8 C4
Killamarsh Derbys 89 F5
Killay Swansea 33 E7
Killbeg Argyll 147 G9
Killean Argyll 143 D7
Killearn Stirling 126 F4
Killen Highld 151 F9
Killerby Darl 101 C6
Killichonan Perth 132 D2
Killiechonate Highld 136 F5
Killiechronan Argyll 147 G8
Killiecrankie Perth 133 C6
Killiemor Argyll 146 H7
Killiemore House Argyll 146 J7
Killilan Highld 150 H2
Killimster Highld 158 E5
Killin Stirling 132 F2
Killin Lodge Highld 137 D8
Killinallan Argyll 142 A4
Killinghall N Yorks 95 D5
Killington Cumb 99 F8
Killingworth T&W 111 B5
Killmahumaig Argyll 144 D6
Killochyett Borders 121 E7
Killocraw Argyll 143 E7
Killundine Highld 147 G8
Kilmacolm Invclyd 118 C3
Kilmaha Argyll 124 E5
Kilmahog Stirling 126 D5
Kilmalieu Highld 130 D2
Kilmaluag Highld 149 A9
Kilmany Fife 129 B5
Kilmarie Highld 149 G10
Kilmarnock E Ayrs 118 F4
Kilmaron Castle Fife 129 C5
Kilmartin Argyll 124 F4
Kilmaurs E Ayrs 118 E4
Kilmelford Argyll 124 D4
Kilmeny Argyll 142 B4
Kilmersdon Som 23 D8
Kilmeston Hants 15 B6
Kilmichael Argyll 143 F7
Kilmichael Glassary Argyll 145 D7
Kilmichael of Inverlussa Argyll 144 E6
Kilmington Devon 11 E7
Kilmington Wilts 24 F2
Kilmonivaig Highld 136 F4
Kilmorack Highld 150 G7
Kilmore Argyll 124 C4
Kilmore Highld 149 H11
Kilmory Argyll 144 F6
Kilmory Highld 147 D8
Kilmory Highld 149 H8
Kilmory N Ayrs 143 F10
Kilmuir Highld 148 D7
Kilmuir Highld 149 A8
Kilmuir Highld 151 D10
Kilmuir Highld 151 G9
Kilmun Argyll 124 D5
Kilmun Argyll 145 E10
Kiln Pit Hill Northumb 110 D3
Kilncadzow S Lanark 119 E8
Kilndown Kent 18 B4
Kilnhurst S Yorks 89 E5
Kilninian Argyll 146 G6
Kilninver Argyll 124 C4
Kilnsea E Yorks 91 C8
Kilnsey N Yorks 94 C2
Kilnwick E Yorks 97 E5
Kilnwick Percy E Yorks 96 D4
Kiloran Argyll 144 D2
Kilpatrick N Ayrs 143 F10
Kilpeck Hereford 49 F6
Kilphedir Highld 157 H12
Kilpin E Yorks 89 B8
Kilpin Pike E Yorks 89 B8
Kilrenny Fife 129 D7
Kilsby Northants 52 B3
Kilspindie Perth 128 B4
Kilsyth N Lanark 119 B7
Kiltarlity Highld 151 G8
Kilton Notts 77 B5
Kilton Som 22 E3
Kilton Thorpe Redcar 102 C4
Kilvaxter Highld 149 B8
Kilve Som 22 E3
Kilvington Notts 77 E7
Kilwinning N Ayrs 118 E3
Kimber worth S Yorks 88 E5
Kimberley Norf 68 D3
Kimberley Notts 76 E5
Kimble Wick Bucks 39 D8
Kimblesworth Durham 111 E5
Kimbolton Cambs 53 C8
Kimbolton Hereford 49 C7
Kimcote Leics 64 F2
Kimmeridge Dorset 13 G7
Kimmerston Northumb 123 F5
Kimpton Hants 25 E7
Kimpton Herts 40 C4
Kinbrace Highld 157 F11
Kinbuck Stirling 127 D6
Kincaple Fife 129 C6
Kincardine Fife 127 F8
Kincardine Highld 151 C9
Kincardine Bridge Falk 127 F8
Kincardine O'Neil Aberds 140 E4
Kinclaven Perth 134 F1
Kincorth Aberdeen 141 D8
Kincorth Ho. Moray 151 E13
Kincraig Highld 138 D4
Kincraigie Perth 133 E6
Kindallachan Perth 133 E6
Kineton Glos 37 B7
Kineton Warks 51 D8
Kinfauns Perth 128 B3
King Edward Aberds 153 C7
King Sterndale Derbys 75 B7
Kingairloch Highld 130 D2
Kingarth Argyll 145 H9
Kingcoed Mon 35 D8
Kingerby Lincs 90 E4
Kingham Oxon 38 B2
Kingholm Quay Dumfries 107 B6
Kinghorn Fife 128 F4
Kingie Highld 136 D4
Kinglassie Fife 128 E4
Kingoodie Perth 128 B5
King's Acre Hereford 49 E6
King's Bromley Staffs 62 C5
King's Caple Hereford 36 B2
King's Cliffe Northants 65 E7
King's Coughton Warks 51 D5
King's Heath W Mid 62 F4
Kings Hedges Cambs 55 C5
Kings Langley Herts 40 D3
King's Hill Kent 29 D7
King's Lynn Norf 67 B6
King's Meaburn Cumb 99 B8
King's Mills Wrex 73 E7
Kings Muir Borders 121 F5
King's Newnham Warks 52 B2
King's Newton Derbys 63 B7
King's Norton Leics 64 D3
King's Norton W Mid 51 B5
King's Nympton Devon 9 C8
King's Pyon Hereford 49 D6
King's Ripton Cambs 54 B3
King's Somborne Hants 25 F8
King's Stag Dorset 12 C5
King's Stanley Glos 37 D5
King's Sutton Northants 52 F2
King's Thorn Hereford 49 F7
King's Walden Herts 40 B4
Kings Worthy Hants 26 F2
Kingsand Corn 6 D2
Kingsbarns Fife 129 C7
Kingsbridge Devon 6 E5
Kingsbridge Som 21 F8
Kingsburgh Highld 149 C8
Kingsbury London 41 F5
Kingsbury Warks 63 E6
Kingsbury Episcopi Som 12 B2
Kingsclere Hants 26 D3
Kingscote Glos 37 E5
Kingscott Devon 9 C7
Kingscross N Ayrs 143 F11
Kingsdon Som 12 B3
Kingsdown Kent 31 E7
Kingseat Fife 128 E3
Kingsey Bucks 39 D7
Kingsfold W Sus 28 F2
Kingsford E Ayrs 118 E4
Kingsford Worcs 62 F2
Kingsforth N Lincs 90 C4
Kingsgate Kent 31 B7
Kingsheanton Devon 20 F4
Kingshouse Hotel Highld 131 D6
Kingside Hill Cumb 107 D8
Kingskerswell Devon 7 C6
Kingskettle Fife 128 D5
Kingsland Anglesey 82 C2
Kingsland Hereford 49 C6
Kingsley Ches W 74 B2
Kingsley Hants 27 F5
Kingsley Staffs 75 E7
Kingsley Green W Sus 27 F6
Kingsley Holt Staffs 75 E7
Kingsley Park Northants 53 C5
Kingsmuir Angus 134 E4
Kingsmuir Fife 129 D7
Kingsnorth Kent 19 B7
Kingstanding W Mid 62 E4
Kingsteignton Devon 7 B6
Kingsthorpe Northants 53 C5
Kingston Cambs 54 D4
Kingston Devon 6 E4
Kingston Dorset 13 D5
Kingston Dorset 13 G7
Kingston E Loth 129 F7
Kingston Hants 14 D2
Kingston IoW 15 F5
Kingston Kent 31 D5
Kingston Moray 152 B3
Kingston Bagpuize Oxon 38 E4
Kingston Blount Oxon 39 E7
Kingston by Sea W Sus 17 D6
Kingston Deverill Wilts 24 F3
Kingston Gorse W Sus 16 D4
Kingston Lisle Oxon 38 F3
Kingston Maurward Dorset 12 E5
Kingston near Lewes E Sus 17 D7
Kingston on Soar Notts 64 B2
Kingston Russell Dorset 12 E3
Kingston Seymour N Som 23 C6
Kingston St Mary Som 11 B7
Kingston Upon Hull Hull 90 B4
Kingston upon Thames London 28 C2
Kingston Vale London 28 B3
Kingstone Hereford 49 F6
Kingstone Som 11 C8
Kingstone Staffs 62 B4
Kingstown Cumb 108 D3
Kingswear Devon 7 D6
Kingswells Aberdeen 141 D7
Kingswinford W Mid 62 F2
Kingswood Bucks 39 C6
Kingswood Glos 36 E4
Kingswood Hereford 48 D4
Kingswood Kent 30 D2
Kingswood Powys 60 D2
Kingswood S Glos 23 B8
Kingswood Sur 28 D3
Kingswood Warks 51 B6
Kingthorpe Lincs 78 B4
Kington Hereford 48 D4
Kington Worcs 50 D4
Kington Langley Wilts 24 B4
Kington Magna Dorset 13 B5
Kington St Michael Wilts 24 B4
Kingussie Highld 138 D3
Kingweston Som 23 F7
Kininvie Ho. Moray 152 D3
Kinkell Bridge Perth 127 C8
Kinknockie Aberds 153 D10
Kinlet Shrops 61 F7
Kinloch Fife 128 C4
Kinloch Highld 146 B6
Kinloch Highld 149 G11
Kinloch Highld 156 F6
Kinloch Perth 133 E8
Kinloch Perth 134 E2
Kinloch Hourn Highld 136 D2
Kinloch Laggan Highld 137 F8
Kinloch Lodge Highld 157 D8
Kinloch Rannoch Perth 132 D3
Kinlochan Highld 130 C2
Kinlochard Stirling 126 D3
Kinlochbeoraid Highld 147 C11
Kinlochbervie Highld 156 D5
Kinlocheil Highld 130 B3
Kinlochewe Highld 150 E3
Kinlochleven Highld 131 C5
Kinlochmoidart Highld 147 D10
Kinlochmorar Highld 147 B11
Kinlochmore Highld 131 C5
Kinlochspelve Argyll 124 C2
Kinloid Highld 147 C9
Kinloss Moray 151 E13
Kinmel Bay Conwy 72 A3
Kinmuck Aberds 141 C7
Kinmundy Aberds 141 C7
Kinnadie Aberds 153 D9
Kinnaird Perth 128 B4
Kinnaird Castle Angus 135 D6
Kinneff Aberds 135 B8
Kinnelhead Dumfries 114 D3
Kinnell Angus 135 D6
Kinnerley Shrops 60 B3
Kinnersley Hereford 48 E5
Kinnersley Worcs 50 E3
Kinnerton Powys 48 C4
Kinnesswood Perth 128 D3
Kinninvie Durham 101 B5
Kinnordy Angus 134 D3
Kinoulton Notts 77 F6
Kinross Perth 128 D3
Kinrossie Perth 134 F1
Kinsbourne Green Herts 40 C4
Kinsey Heath Ches E 74 E3
Kinsham Hereford 49 C5
Kinsham Worcs 50 F4
Kinsley W Yorks 88 C5
Kinson Bmouth 13 E8
Kintbury W Berks 25 C8
Kintessack Moray 151 E12
Kintillo Perth 128 C3
Kintocher Aberds 140 D4
Kinton Hereford 49 B6
Kinton Shrops 60 C3
Kintore Aberds 141 C6
Kintour Argyll 142 C5
Kintra Argyll 142 D4
Kintra Argyll 146 J6
Kintraw Argyll 124 E4
Kinuachdrachd Argyll 124 F3
Kinveachy Highld 138 C5
Kinver Staffs 62 F2
Kippax W Yorks 95 F7
Kippen Stirling 127 E5
Kippford or Scaur Dumfries 106 D5
Kirbister Orkney 159 F7
Kirbister Orkney 159 H4
Kirbuster Orkney 159 F3
Kirby Bedon Norf 69 D5
Kirby Bellars Leics 64 C4
Kirby Cane Norf 69 E6
Kirby Cross Essex 43 B8
Kirby Grindalythe N Yorks 96 C5
Kirby Hill N Yorks 95 C6
Kirby Hill N Yorks 101 D6
Kirby Knowle N Yorks 102 F2
Kirby-le-Soken Essex 43 B8
Kirby Misperton N Yorks 96 B3
Kirby Muxloe Leics 64 D2
Kirby Row Norf 69 E6
Kirby Sigston N Yorks 102 E2
Kirby Underdale E Yorks 96 D4
Kirby Wiske N Yorks 102 F1
Kirdford W Sus 16 B4
Kirk Highld 158 E4
Kirk Bramwith S Yorks 89 C7
Kirk Deighton N Yorks 95 D6
Kirk Ella E Yorks 90 B4
Kirk Hallam Derbys 76 E4
Kirk Hammerton N Yorks 95 D7
Kirk Ireton Derbys 76 D2
Kirk Langley Derbys 76 F2
Kirk Merrington Durham 111 F5
Kirk Michael IoM 84 C3
Kirk of Shotts N Lanark 119 C8
Kirk Sandall S Yorks 89 D7
Kirk Smeaton N Yorks 89 C6
Kirk Yetholm Borders 116 B4
Kirkabister Shetland 160 K6
Kirkandrews Dumfries 106 E3
Kirkandrews upon Eden Cumb 108 D3
Kirkbampton Cumb 108 D3
Kirkbean Dumfries 107 D6
Kirkbride Cumb 108 D2
Kirkbuddo Angus 135 E5
Kirkburn Borders 121 F5
Kirkburn E Yorks 97 D5
Kirkburton W Yorks 88 C2
Kirkby Lincs 90 E4
Kirkby Mers 86 E2
Kirkby N Yorks 102 D3
Kirkby Fleetham N Yorks 101 E7
Kirkby Green Lincs 78 D3
Kirkby In Ashfield Notts 76 D5
Kirkby-in-Furness Cumb 98 F4
Kirkby la Thorpe Lincs 78 E3
Kirkby Lonsdale Cumb 93 B6
Kirkby Malham N Yorks 93 C8
Kirkby Mallory Leics 63 D8
Kirkby Malzeard N Yorks 94 B5
Kirkby Mills N Yorks 103 F5
Kirkby on Bain Lincs 78 C5
Kirkby Overflow N Yorks 95 E6
Kirkby Stephen Cumb 100 D2
Kirkby Thore Cumb 99 B8
Kirkby Underwood Lincs 65 B7
Kirkby Wharfe N Yorks 95 E8
Kirkbymoorside N Yorks 102 F4
Kirkcaldy Fife 128 E4
Kirkcambeck Cumb 108 C5
Kirkcarswell Dumfries 106 E4
Kirkcolm Dumfries 104 C4
Kirkconnel Dumfries 113 C7
Kirkconnell Dumfries 107 C6
Kirkcowan Dumfries 105 C7
Kirkcudbright Dumfries 106 D3
Kirkdale Mers 85 E4
Kirkfieldbank S Lanark 119 E8
Kirkgunzeon Dumfries 107 C5
Kirkham Lancs 92 F4
Kirkham N Yorks 96 C3
Kirkhamgate W Yorks 88 B3
Kirkharle Northumb 117 F6
Kirkheaton Northumb 110 B3
Kirkheaton W Yorks 88 C2
Kirkhill Angus 135 C6
Kirkhill Highld 151 G8
Kirkhill Midloth 120 C5
Kirkhill Moray 152 E2
Kirkhope Borders 115 B6
Kirkhouse Borders 121 F6
Kirkiboll Highld 157 D8
Kirkibost Highld 149 G10
Kirkinch Angus 134 E3
Kirkinner Dumfries 105 D8
Kirkintilloch E Dunb 119 B6
Kirkland Cumb 98 C2
Kirkland Cumb 109 F6
Kirkland Dumfries 113 C7
Kirkland Dumfries 113 E8
Kirkleatham Redcar 102 B3
Kirklevington Stockton 102 D2
Kirkley Suff 69 E8
Kirklington N Yorks 101 F8
Kirklington Notts 77 D6
Kirklinton Cumb 108 C4
Kirkliston Edin 120 B4
Kirkmaiden Dumfries 104 F5
Kirkmichael Perth 133 D7
Kirkmichael S Ayrs 112 D3
Kirkmuirhill S Lanark 119 E7
Kirknewton Northumb 122 F5
Kirknewton W Loth 120 C4
Kirkney Aberds 152 E5
Kirkoswald Cumb 109 E5
Kirkoswald S Ayrs 112 D2
Kirkpatrick Durham Dumfries 106 B4
Kirkpatrick-Fleming Dumfries 108 B2
Kirksanton Cumb 98 F3
Kirkstall W Yorks 95 F5
Kirkstead Lincs 78 C4
Kirkstile Aberds 152 E5
Kirkstyle Highld 158 C5
Kirkton Aberds 140 B5
Kirkton Aberds 153 D6
Kirkton Angus 134 E4
Kirkton Angus 134 F4
Kirkton Borders 115 C8
Kirkton Dumfries 114 F2
Kirkton Fife 129 B5
Kirkton Highld 149 F13
Kirkton Highld 150 G2
Kirkton Highld 151 B10
Kirkton Highld 151 F10
Kirkton Perth 127 C8
Kirkton S Lanark 114 B2
Kirkton Stirling 126 D4
Kirkton Manor Borders 120 F5
Kirkton of Airlie Angus 134 D3

Manar Ho. Aberds 141 B6
Manaton Devon 10 F2
Manby Lincs 91 F7
Mancetter Warks 63 E7
Manchester Gtr Man 87 E6
Manchester Airport Gtr Man 87 F6
Mancot Flint 73 C7
Mandally Highld 137 D5
Manea Cambs 66 F4
Manfield N Yorks 101 C7
Mangaster Shetland 160 F5
Mangotsfield S Glos 23 B8
Mangurstadh W Isles 154 D5
Mankinholes W Yorks 87 B7
Manley Ches W 74 B2
Mannal Argyll 146 G2
Mannerston W Loth 120 B3
Manningford Bohune Wilts 25 D6
Manningford Bruce Wilts 25 D6
Manningham W Yorks 94 F4
Mannings Heath W Sus 17 B6
Mannington Dorset 13 D8
Manningtree Essex 56 F4
Mannofield Aberdeen 141 D8
Manor London 41 F7
Manor Estate S Yorks 88 F4
Manorbier Pembs 32 E1
Manordeilo Carms 33 B7
Manorhill Borders 122 F2
Manorowen Pembs 44 B4
Mansel Lacy Hereford 49 E6
Mansell Gamage Hereford 49 E5
Mansergh Cumb 99 F8
Mansfield E Ayrs 113 C6
Mansfield Notts 76 C5
Mansfield Woodhouse Notts 76 C5
Mansriggs Cumb 98 F4
Manston Dorset 13 C6
Manston Kent 31 C7
Manston W Yorks 95 F6
Manswood Dorset 13 D7
Manthorpe Lincs 65 C7
Manthorpe Lincs 78 F2
Manton N Lincs 90 D3
Manton Notts 77 B5
Manton Rutland 65 D5
Manton Wilts 25 C6
Manuden Essex 41 B7
Maperton Som 12 B4
Maple Cross Herts 40 E3
Maplebeck Notts 77 C7
Mapledurham Oxon 26 B4
Mapledurwell Hants 26 D4
Maplehurst W Sus 17 B5
Maplescombe Kent 29 C6
Mapleton Derbys 75 E8
Mapperley Derbys 76 E4
Mapperley Park Nottingham 77 E5
Mapperton Dorset 12 E3
Mappleborough Green Warks 51 C5
Mappleton E Yorks 97 E8
Mappowder Dorset 12 D5
Mar Lodge Aberds 139 E6
Maraig W Isles 154 G6
Marazanvose Corn 4 D3
Marazion Corn 2 C4
Marbhig W Isles 155 F9
Marbury Ches E 74 E2
March Cambs 66 E4
March S Lanark 114 C2
Marcham Oxon 38 E4
Marchamley Shrops 61 B5
Marchington Staffs 75 F8
Marchington Woodlands Staffs 62 B5
Marchroes Gwyn 70 E4
Marchwiel Wrex 73 E7
Marchwood Hants 14 C4
Marcross V Glam 21 C8
Marden Hereford 49 E7
Marden Kent 29 E8
Marden T&W 111 B6
Marden Wilts 25 D5
Marden Beech Kent 29 E8
Marden Thorn Kent 29 E8
Mardy Mon 35 C7
Marefield Leics 64 D4
Mareham le Fen Lincs 79 C5
Mareham on the Hill Lincs 79 C5
Marehay Derbys 76 E3
Marehill W Sus 16 C4
Maresfield E Sus 17 B8
Marfleet Hull 90 B5
Marford Wrex 73 D7
Margam Neath 34 F1
Margaret Marsh Dorset 13 C6
Margaret Roding Essex 42 C1
Margaretting Essex 42 D2
Margate Kent 31 B7
Margnaheglish N Ayrs 143 E11
Margrove Park Redcar 102 C4
Marham Norf 67 C7
Marhamchurch Corn 8 D4
Marholm Pboro 65 D8
Mariandyrys Anglesey 83 C6
Marianglas Anglesey 82 C5
Mariansleigh Devon 10 B2
Marionburgh Aberds 141 D6
Marishader Highld 149 B9
Marjoriebanks Dumfries 114 F3
Mark Dumfries 104 D5
Mark S Ayrs 104 B4
Mark Som 23 E5
Mark Causeway Som 23 E5
Mark Cross E Sus 17 C8
Mark Cross E Sus 18 B2
Markbeech Kent 29 E5
Markby Lincs 79 B7
Market Bosworth Leics 63 D8
Market Deeping Lincs 65 D8
Market Drayton Shrops 74 F3
Market Harborough Leics 64 F4
Market Lavington Wilts 24 D5
Market Overton Rutland 65 C5
Market Rasen Lincs 90 F5
Market Stainton Lincs 78 B5
Market Warsop Notts 77 C5
Market Weighton E Yorks 96 E4
Market Weston Suff 56 B3
Markethill Perth 134 F2
Markfield Leics 63 C8
Markham Caerph 35 D5
Markham Moor Notts 77 B7
Markinch Fife 128 D4
Markington N Yorks 95 C5
Marks Tey Essex 43 B5
Marksbury Bath 23 C8
Markyate Herts 40 C3
Marland Gtr Man 87 C6
Marlborough Wilts 25 C6
Marlbrook Hereford 49 D7
Marlbrook Worcs 50 B4
Marlcliff Warks 51 D5
Marldon Devon 7 C6
Marlesford Suff 57 D7
Marley Green Ches E 74 E2
Marley Hill T&W 110 D5
Marley Mount Hants 14 E3
Marlingford Norf 68 D4
Marloes Pembs 44 E2
Marlow Bucks 39 F8
Marlow Hereford 49 B6
Marlow Bottom Bucks 40 F1
Marlpit Hill Kent 28 E5
Marlpool Derbys 76 E4
Marnhull Dorset 13 C5
Marnoch Aberds 152 C5
Marnock N Lanark 119 C7
Marple Gtr Man 87 F7
Marple Bridge Gtr Man 87 F7
Marr S Yorks 89 D6
Marrel Highld 157 H13
Marrick N Yorks 101 E5
Marrister Shetland 160 G7
Marros Carms 32 D3
Marsden T&W 111 C6
Marsden W Yorks 87 C8
Marsett N Yorks 100 F4
Marsh Devon 11 C7
Marsh W Yorks 94 F3
Marsh Baldon Oxon 39 E5
Marsh Gibbon Bucks 39 B6
Marsh Green Devon 10 E5
Marsh Green Kent 28 E5
Marsh Green Staffs 75 D5
Marsh Lane Derbys 76 B4
Marsh Street Som 21 E8
Marshall's Heath Herts 40 C4
Marshalsea Dorset 11 D8
Marshalswick Herts 40 D4
Marsham Norf 81 E7
Marshaw Lancs 93 D5
Marshborough Kent 31 D7
Marshbrook Shrops 60 F4
Marshchapel Lincs 91 E7
Marshfield Newport 35 F6
Marshfield S Glos 24 B2
Marshgate Corn 8 E3
Marshland St James Norf 66 D5
Marshside Mers 85 C4
Marshwood Dorset 11 E8
Marske N Yorks 101 D6
Marske-by-the-Sea Redcar 102 B4
Marston Ches W 74 B3
Marston Hereford 49 D5
Marston Lincs 77 E8
Marston Oxon 39 D5
Marston Staffs 62 B3
Marston Staffs 62 C2
Marston Warks 63 E6
Marston Wilts 24 D4
Marston Doles Warks 52 D2
Marston Green W Mid 63 F5
Marston Magna Som 12 B3
Marston Meysey Wilts 37 E8
Marston Montgomery Derbys 75 F8
Marston Moretaine C Beds 53 E7
Marston on Dove Derbys 63 B6
Marston St Lawrence Northants 52 E3
Marston Stannett Hereford 49 D7
Marston Trussell Northants 64 F3
Marstow Hereford 36 C2
Marsworth Bucks 40 C2
Marten Wilts 25 D7
Marthall Ches E 74 B5
Martham Norf 69 C7
Martin Hants 13 C8
Martin Kent 31 E7
Martin Lincs 78 C5
Martin Lincs 78 D4
Martin Dales Lincs 78 C4
Martin Drove End Hants 13 B8
Martin Hussingtree Worcs 50 C3
Martin Mill Kent 31 E7
Martinhoe Devon 21 E5
Martinhoe Cross Devon 21 E5
Martinscroft Warr 86 F4
Martinstown Dorset 12 F4
Martlesham Suff 57 E6
Martlesham Heath Suff 57 E6
Martletwy Pembs 32 C1
Martley Worcs 50 D2
Martock Som 12 C2
Marton Ches E 75 C5
Marton E Yorks 97 F7
Marton Lincs 90 F2
Marton Mbro 102 C3
Marton N Yorks 95 C7
Marton N Yorks 103 F5
Marton Shrops 60 B4
Marton Shrops 60 D2
Marton Warks 52 C2
Marton-le-Moor N Yorks 95 B6
Martyr Worthy Hants 26 F3
Martyr's Green Sur 27 D8
Marwick Orkney 159 F3
Marwood Devon 20 F4
Mary Tavy Devon 6 B3
Marybank Highld 150 F7
Maryburgh Highld 151 F8
Maryhill Glasgow 119 C5
Marykirk Aberds 135 C6
Marylebone Gtr Man 86 D3
Marypark Moray 152 E1
Maryport Cumb 107 F7
Maryport Dumfries 104 F5
Maryton Angus 135 D6
Marywell Aberds 140 E4
Marywell Aberds 141 E8
Marywell Angus 135 E6
Masham N Yorks 101 F7
Mashbury Essex 42 C2
Masongill N Yorks 93 B6
Masonhill S Ayrs 112 B3
Mastin Moor Derbys 76 B4
Mastrick Aberdeen 141 D7
Matching Essex 41 C8
Matching Green Essex 41 C8
Matching Tye Essex 41 C8
Matfen Northumb 110 B3
Matfield Kent 29 E7
Mathern Mon 36 E2
Mathon Hereford 50 E2
Mathry Pembs 44 B3
Matlaske Norf 81 D7
Matlock Derbys 76 C2
Matlock Bath Derbys 76 D2
Matson Glos 37 C5
Matterdale End Cumb 99 B5
Mattersey Notts 89 F7
Mattersey Thorpe Notts 89 F7
Mattingley Hants 26 D5
Mattishall Norf 68 C3
Mattishall Burgh Norf 68 C3
Mauchline E Ayrs 112 B4
Maud Aberds 153 D9
Maugersbury Glos 38 B2
Maughold IoM 84 C4
Mauld Highld 150 H7
Maulden C Beds 53 F8
Maulds Meaburn Cumb 99 C8
Maunby N Yorks 102 F1
Maund Bryan Hereford 49 D7
Maundown Som 11 B5
Mautby Norf 69 C7
Mavis Enderby Lincs 79 C6
Maw Green Ches E 74 D4
Mawbray Cumb 107 E7
Mawdesley Lancs 86 C2
Mawdlam Bridgend 34 F2
Mawgan Corn 3 D6
Mawla Corn 3 B6
Mawnan Corn 3 D6
Mawnan Smith Corn 3 D6
Mawsley Northants 53 B6
Maxey Pboro 65 D8
Maxstoke Warks 63 F6
Maxton Borders 122 F2
Maxton Kent 31 E7
Maxwellheugh Borders 122 F3
Maxwelltown Dumfries 107 B6
Maxworthy Corn 8 E4
May Bank Staffs 75 E5
Mayals Swansea 33 E7
Maybole S Ayrs 112 D3
Mayfield E Sus 18 C2
Mayfield Midloth 121 C6
Mayfield Staffs 75 E8
Mayfield W Loth 120 C2
Mayford Sur 27 D7
Mayland Essex 43 D5
Maynard's Green E Sus 18 D2
Maypole Mon 36 C1
Maypole Scilly 2 E4
Maypole Green Essex 43 B5
Maypole Green Norf 69 E7
Maypole Green Suff 57 C6
Maywick Shetland 160 L5
Meadle Bucks 39 D8
Meadowtown Shrops 60 D3
Meaford Staffs 75 F5
Meal Bank Cumb 99 E7
Mealabost W Isles 155 D9
Mealabost Bhuirgh W Isles 155 B9
Mealsgate Cumb 108 E2
Meanwood W Yorks 95 F5
Mearbeck N Yorks 93 C8
Meare Som 23 E6
Meare Green Som 11 B8
Mears Ashby Northants 53 C6
Measham Leics 63 C7
Meath Green Sur 28 E3
Meathop Cumb 99 F6
Meaux E Yorks 97 F6
Meavy Devon 6 C3
Medbourne Leics 64 E4
Medburn Northumb 110 B4
Meddon Devon 8 C4
Meden Vale Notts 77 C5
Medlam Lincs 79 D6
Medmenham Bucks 39 F8
Medomsley Durham 110 D4
Medstead Hants 26 F4
Meer End W Mid 51 B7
Meerbrook Staffs 75 C6
Meers Bridge Lincs 91 F8
Meesden Herts 54 F5
Meeth Devon 9 D7
Meggethead Borders 114 B4
Meidrim Carms 32 B3
Meifod Denb 72 D4
Meifod Powys 59 C8
Meigle N Ayrs 118 C1
Meigle Perth 134 E2
Meikle Earnock S Lanark 119 D7
Meikle Ferry Highld 151 C10
Meikle Forter Angus 134 C1
Meikle Gluich Highld 151 C9
Meikle Pinkerton E Loth 122 B3
Meikle Strath Aberds 135 B6
Meikle Tarty Aberds 141 B8
Meikle Wartle Aberds 153 E7
Meikleour Perth 134 F1
Meinciau Carms 33 C5
Meir Stoke 75 E6
Meir Heath Staffs 75 E6
Melbourn Cambs 54 E4
Melbourne Derbys 63 B7
Melbourne E Yorks 96 E3
Melbourne S Lanark 120 E3
Melbury Abbas Dorset 13 B6
Melbury Bubb Dorset 12 D3
Melbury Osmond Dorset 12 D3
Melbury Sampford Dorset 12 D3
Melby Shetland 160 H3
Melchbourne Bedford 53 C8
Melcombe Bingham Dorset 13 D5
Melcombe Regis Dorset 12 F4
Meldon Devon 9 E7
Meldon Northumb 117 F7
Meldreth Cambs 54 E4
Meldrum Ho. Aberds 141 B7
Melfort Argyll 124 D4
Melgarve Highld 137 E7
Meliden Denb 72 A4
Melin-y-coed Conwy 83 E8
Melin-y-ddôl Powys 59 D7
Melin-y-grug Powys 59 D7
Melin-y-Wig Denb 72 E4
Melinbyrhedyn Powys 58 E5
Melincourt Neath 34 D2
Melkinthorpe Cumb 99 B7
Melkridge Northumb 109 C7
Melksham Wilts 24 C4
Melldalloch Argyll 145 F8
Melling Lancs 93 B5
Melling Mers 85 D4
Melling Mount Mers 86 D2
Mellis Suff 56 B5
Mellon Charles Highld 155 H13
Mellon Udrigle Highld 155 H13
Mellor Gtr Man 87 F7
Mellor Lancs 93 F6
Mellor Brook Lancs 93 F6
Mells Som 24 E2
Melmerby Cumb 109 F6
Melmerby N Yorks 95 B6
Melmerby N Yorks 101 F5
Melplash Dorset 12 E2
Melrose Borders 121 F8
Melsetter Orkney 159 K3
Melsonby N Yorks 101 D6
Meltham W Yorks 88 C2
Melton Suff 57 D6
Melton Constable Norf 81 D6
Melton Mowbray Leics 64 C4
Melton Ross N Lincs 90 C4
Meltonby E Yorks 96 D3
Melvaig Highld 155 J12
Melverley Shrops 60 C3
Melverley Green Shrops 60 C3
Melvich Highld 157 C11
Membury Devon 11 D7
Memsie Aberds 153 B9
Memus Angus 134 D4
Menabilly Corn 5 D5
Menai Bridge = Porthaethwy Anglesey 83 D5
Mendham Suff 69 F5
Mendlesham Suff 56 C5
Mendlesham Green Suff 56 C4
Menheniot Corn 5 C7
Mennock Dumfries 113 D8
Menston W Yorks 94 E4
Menstrie Clack 127 E7
Menthorpe N Yorks 96 F2
Mentmore Bucks 40 C2
Meoble Highld 147 C10
Meole Brace Shrops 60 C4
Meols Mers 85 E3
Meonstoke Hants 15 C7
Meopham Kent 29 C7
Meopham Station Kent 29 C7
Mepal Cambs 66 F4
Meppershall C Beds 54 F2
Merbach Hereford 48 E5
Mere Ches E 86 F5
Mere Wilts 24 F3
Mere Brow Lancs 86 C2
Mere Green W Mid 62 E5
Mereclough Lancs 93 F8
Mereside Blackpool 92 F3
Mereworth Kent 29 D7
Mergie Aberds 141 F6
Meriden W Mid 63 F6
Merkadale Highld 149 E8
Merkland Dumfries 106 B4
Merkland S Ayrs 112 E2
Merkland Lodge Highld 156 G7
Merley Poole 13 E8
Merlin's Bridge Pembs 44 D4
Merrington Shrops 60 B4
Merrion Pembs 44 F4
Merriott Som 12 C2
Merrivale Devon 6 B3
Merrow Sur 27 D8
Merrymeet Corn 5 C7
Mersham Kent 19 B7
Merstham Sur 28 D3
Merston W Sus 16 D2
Merstone IoW 15 F6
Merther Corn 3 B7
Merthyr Carms 32 B4
Merthyr Cynog Powys 47 F8
Merthyr-Dyfan V Glam 22 C3
Merthyr Mawr Bridgend 21 B7
Merthyr Tudful = Merthyr Tydfil M Tydf 34 D4
Merthyr Tydfil = Merthyr Tudful M Tydf 34 D4
Merthyr Vale M Tydf 34 E4
Merton Devon 9 C7
Merton London 28 B3
Merton Norf 68 E2
Merton Oxon 39 C5
Mervinslaw Borders 116 C2
Meshaw Devon 10 C2
Messing Essex 42 C4
Messingham N Lincs 90 D2
Metfield Suff 69 F5
Metheringham Lincs 78 C3
Methil Fife 129 E5
Methlem Gwyn 70 D2
Methley W Yorks 88 B4
Methlick Aberds 153 E8
Methven Perth 128 B2
Methwold Norf 67 E7
Methwold Hythe Norf 67 E7
Mettingham Suff 69 F6
Mevagissey Corn 3 B9
Mewith Head N Yorks 93 C7
Mexborough S Yorks 89 D5
Mey Highld 158 C4
Meysey Hampton Glos 37 E8
Miabhag W Isles 154 G5
Miabhag W Isles 154 H6
Miabhig W Isles 154 D5
Michaelchurch Hereford 36 B2
Michaelchurch Escley Hereford 48 F5
Michaelchurch on Arrow Powys 48 D4
Michaelston-le-Pit V Glam 22 B3
Michaelston-y-Fedw Newport 35 F6
Michaelstow Corn 5 B5
Michealston-super-Ely Cardiff 22 B3
Micheldever Hants 26 F3
Michelmersh Hants 14 B4
Mickfield Suff 56 C5
Mickle Trafford Ches W 73 C8
Micklebring S Yorks 89 E6
Mickleby N Yorks 103 C6
Mickleham Sur 28 D2
Mickleover Derby 76 F3
Micklethwaite W Yorks 94 E4
Mickleton Durham 100 B4
Mickleton Glos 51 E6
Mickletown W Yorks 88 B4
Mickley N Yorks 95 B5
Mickley Square Northumb 110 C3
Mid Ardlaw Aberds 153 B9
Mid Auchinlech Invclyd 118 B3
Mid Beltie Aberds 140 D5
Mid Calder W Loth 120 C3
Mid Cloch Forbie Aberds 153 C7
Mid Clyth Highld 158 G4
Mid Lavant W Sus 16 D2
Mid Main Highld 150 H7
Mid Urchany Highld 151 G11
Mid Walls Shetland 160 H4
Mid Yell Shetland 160 D7
Midbea Orkney 159 D5
Middle Assendon Oxon 39 F7
Middle Aston Oxon 38 B4
Middle Barton Oxon 38 B4
Middle Cairncake Aberds 153 D8
Middle Claydon Bucks 39 B7
Middle Drums Angus 135 D5
Middle Handley Derbys 76 B4
Middle Littleton Worcs 51 E5
Middle Maes-coed Hereford 48 F5
Middle Mill Pembs 44 C3
Middle Rasen Lincs 90 F4
Middle Rigg Perth 128 D2
Middle Tysoe Warks 51 E8
Middle Wallop Hants 25 F7
Middle Winterslow Wilts 25 F7
Middle Woodford Wilts 25 F6
Middlebie Dumfries 108 B2
Middleforth Green Lancs 86 B3
Middleham N Yorks 101 F6
Middlehope Shrops 60 F4
Middlemarsh Dorset 12 D4
Middlemuir Aberds 141 B8
Middlesbrough Mbro 102 B2
Middleshaw Cumb 99 F7
Middleshaw Dumfries 107 B8
Middlesmoor N Yorks 94 B3
Middlestone Durham 111 F5
Middlestone Moor Durham 110 F5
Middlestown W Yorks 88 C3
Middlethird Borders 122 E2
Middleton Aberds 141 C7
Middleton Argyll 146 G2
Middleton Cumb 99 F8
Middleton Derbys 75 C8
Middleton Derbys 76 D2
Middleton Essex 56 F2
Middleton Gtr Man 87 D6
Middleton Hants 26 E2
Middleton Hereford 49 C7
Middleton Lancs 92 D4
Middleton Midloth 121 D6
Middleton N Yorks 94 E4
Middleton N Yorks 103 F5
Middleton Norf 67 C6
Middleton Northants 64 F5
Middleton Northumb 117 F6
Middleton Northumb 123 F7
Middleton Perth 128 D3
Middleton Perth 133 E8
Middleton Shrops 49 B7
Middleton Shrops 60 B3
Middleton Shrops 60 E2
Middleton Suff 57 C8
Middleton Swansea 33 F5
Middleton W Yorks 88 B3
Middleton Warks 63 E5
Middleton Cheney Northants 52 E2
Middleton Green Staffs 75 F6
Middleton Hall Northumb 117 B5
Middleton-in-Teesdale Durham 100 B4
Middleton Moor Suff 57 C8
Middleton-on-Leven N Yorks 102 D2
Middleton-on-Sea W Sus 16 D3
Middleton on the Hill Hereford 49 C7
Middleton-on-the-Wolds E Yorks 96 E5
Middleton One Row Darl 102 C1
Middleton Priors Shrops 61 E6
Middleton Quernham N Yorks 95 B6
Middleton Scriven Shrops 61 F6
Middleton St George Darl 101 C8
Middleton Stoney Oxon 39 B5
Middleton Tyas N Yorks 101 D7
Middletown Cumb 98 D1
Middletown Powys 60 C3
Middlewich Ches E 74 C3
Middlewood Green Suff 56 C4
Middlezoy Som 23 F5
Middridge Durham 101 B7
Midfield Highld 157 C8
Midge Hall Lancs 86 B3
Midgeholme Cumb 109 D6
Midgham W Berks 26 C3
Midgley W Yorks 87 B8
Midgley W Yorks 88 C3
Midhopestones S Yorks 88 E3
Midhurst W Sus 16 B2
Midlem Borders 115 B8
Midmar Aberds 141 D5
Midsomer Norton Bath 23 D8
Midton Invclyd 118 B2
Midtown Highld 155 J13
Midtown Highld 157 C8
Midtown of Buchromb Moray 152 D3
Midville Lincs 79 D6
Midway Ches E 87 F7
Migdale Highld 151 B9
Migvie Aberds 140 D3
Milarrochy Stirling 126 E3
Milborne Port Som 12 C4
Milborne St Andrew Dorset 13 E6
Milborne Wick Som 12 B4
Milbourne Northumb 110 B4
Milburn Cumb 100 B1
Milbury Heath S Glos 36 E3
Milcombe Oxon 52 F2
Milden Suff 56 E3
Mildenhall Suff 55 B8
Mildenhall Wilts 25 C7
Mile Cross Norf 68 C5
Mile Elm Wilts 24 C4
Mile End Essex 43 B5
Mile End Glos 36 C2
Mile Oak Brighton 17 D6
Milebrook Powys 48 B5
Milebush Kent 29 E8
Mileham Norf 68 C2
Milesmark Fife 128 F2
Milfield Northumb 122 F5
Milford Derbys 76 E3
Milford Devon 8 B4
Milford Powys 59 E7
Milford Staffs 62 B3
Milford Sur 27 E7
Milford Wilts 14 B2
Milford Haven = Aberdaugleddau Pembs 44 E4
Milford on Sea Hants 14 E3
Milkwall Glos 36 D2
Milkwell Wilts 13 B7
Mill Bank W Yorks 87 B8
Mill Common Suff 69 F7
Mill End Bucks 39 F7
Mill End Herts 54 F4
Mill Green Essex 42 D2
Mill Green Norf 68 F4
Mill Green Suff 56 E3
Mill Hill London 41 E5
Mill Lane Hants 27 D5
Mill of Kingoodie Aberds 141 B7
Mill of Muiresk Aberds 153 D6
Mill of Sterin Aberds 140 E2
Mill of Uras Aberds 141 F7
Mill Place N Lincs 90 D3
Mill Side Cumb 99 F6
Mill Street Norf 68 C3
Milland W Sus 16 B2
Millarston Renfs 118 C4
Millbank Aberds 153 D11
Millbank Highld 158 D3
Millbeck Cumb 98 B4
Millbounds Orkney 159 E6
Millbreck Aberds 153 D10
Millbridge Sur 27 E6
Millbrook C Beds 53 F8
Millbrook Corn 6 D2
Millbrook Soton 14 C4
Millburn S Ayrs 112 B4
Millcombe Devon 7 E6
Millcorner E Sus 18 C5
Milldale Staffs 75 D8
Millden Lodge Angus 135 B5
Milldens Angus 135 D5
Millerhill Midloth 121 C6
Miller's Dale Derbys 75 B8
Miller's Green Derbys 76 D2
Millgreen Shrops 61 B6
Millhalf Hereford 48 E4
Millhayes Devon 11 D7
Millhead Lancs 92 B4
Millheugh S Lanark 119 D7
Millholme Cumb 99 E7
Millhouse Argyll 145 F8
Millhouse Cumb 108 F3
Millhouse Green S Yorks 88 D3
Millhousebridge Dumfries 114 F4
Millhouses S Yorks 88 F4
Millikenpark Renfs 118 C4
Millin Cross Pembs 44 D4
Millington E Yorks 96 D4
Millmeece Staffs 74 F5
Millom Cumb 98 F3
Millook Corn 8 E3
Millpool Corn 5 B6
Millport N Ayrs 145 H10
Millquarter Dumfries 113 F6
Millthorpe Lincs 78 F4
Millthrop Cumb 100 E1
Milltimber Aberdeen 141 D7
Milltown Corn 5 D6
Milltown Derbys 76 C3
Milltown Devon 20 F4
Milltown Dumfries 108 B3
Milltown of Aberdalgie Perth 128 B2
Milltown of Auchindoun Moray 152 D3
Milltown of Craigston Aberds 153 C7
Milltown of Edinvillie Moray 152 D2
Milltown of Kildrummy Aberds 140 C3
Milltown of Rothiemay Moray 152 D5
Milltown of Towie Aberds 140 C3
Milnathort Perth 128 D3
Milner's Heath Ches W 73 C8
Milngavie E Dunb 119 B5
Milnrow Gtr Man 87 C7
Milnshaw Lancs 87 B5
Milnthorpe Cumb 99 F6
Milo Carms 33 C6
Milson Shrops 49 B8
Milstead Kent 30 D3
Milston Wilts 25 E6
Milton Angus 134 E3
Milton Cambs 55 C5
Milton Cumb 109 C5
Milton Derbys 63 B7
Milton Dumfries 105 D6
Milton Dumfries 106 B5
Milton Dumfries 113 F8
Milton Highld 150 F6
Milton Highld 150 H7
Milton Highld 151 D10
Milton Highld 151 G8
Milton Highld 158 E5
Milton Moray 152 B5
Milton N Som 22 C5
Milton Notts 77 B7
Milton Oxon 38 E4
Milton Oxon 52 F2
Milton Pembs 32 D1
Milton Perth 127 C8
Milton Ptsmth 15 E7
Milton Stirling 126 D4
Milton Stoke 75 D6
Milton W Dunb 118 B4
Milton Abbas Dorset 13 D6
Milton Abbot Devon 6 B2
Milton Bridge Midloth 120 C5
Milton Bryan C Beds 53 F7
Milton Clevedon Som 23 F8
Milton Coldwells Aberds 153 E9
Milton Combe Devon 6 C2
Milton Damerel Devon 9 C5
Milton End Glos 37 D8
Milton Ernest Bedford 53 D8
Milton Green Ches W 73 D8
Milton Hill Oxon 38 E4
Milton Keynes M Keynes 53 F6
Milton Keynes Village M Keynes 53 F6
Milton Lilbourne Wilts 25 C6
Milton Malsor Northants 52 D5
Milton Morenish Perth 132 F3
Milton of Auchinhove Aberds 140 D4
Milton of Balgonie Fife 128 D5
Milton of Buchanan Stirling 126 E3
Milton of Campfield Aberds 140 D5
Milton of Campsie E Dunb 119 B6
Milton of Corsindae Aberds 141 D5
Milton of Cushnie Aberds 140 C4
Milton of Dalcapon Perth 133 D6
Milton of Edradour Perth 133 D6
Milton of Gollanfield Highld 151 F10
Milton of Lesmore Aberds 140 B3
Milton of Logie Aberds 140 D3
Milton of Murtle Aberdeen 141 D7
Milton of Noth Aberds 140 B4
Milton of Tullich Aberds 140 E2
Milton on Stour Dorset 13 B5
Milton Regis Kent 30 C3
Milton under Wychwood Oxon 38 C2
Miltonduff Moray 152 B1
Miltonhill Moray 151 E13
Miltonise Dumfries 105 B5
Milverton Som 11 B6
Milverton Warks 51 C8
Milwich Staffs 75 F6
Minard Argyll 125 F5
Minchinhampton Glos 37 D5
Mindrum Northumb 122 F4
Minehead Som 21 E8
Minera Wrex 73 D6
Minety Wilts 37 E7
Minffordd Gwyn 58 C4
Minffordd Gwyn 71 D6
Minffordd Gwyn 83 D5
Miningsby Lincs 79 C6
Minions Corn 5 B7
Minishant S Ayrs 112 C3
Minllyn Gwyn 59 C5
Minnes Aberds 141 B8
Minngearraidh W Isles 148 F2
Minnigaff Dumfries 105 C8
Minnonie Aberds 153 B7
Minskip N Yorks 95 C6
Minstead Hants 14 C3
Minsted W Sus 16 B2
Minster Kent 30 B3
Minster Kent 31 C7
Minster Lovell Oxon 38 C3
Minsterley Shrops 60 D3
Minsterworth Glos 36 C4
Minterne Magna Dorset 12 D4
Minting Lincs 78 B4
Mintlaw Aberds 153 D9
Minto Borders 115 B8
Minton Shrops 60 E4
Minwear Pembs 32 C1
Minworth W Mid 63 E5
Mirbister Orkney 159 F4
Mirehouse Cumb 98 C1
Mireland Highld 158 D5
Mirfield W Yorks 88 C3
Miserden Glos 37 D6
Miskin Rhondda 34 F4
Misson Notts 89 E7
Misterton Leics 64 F2
Misterton Notts 89 E8
Misterton Som 12 D2
Mistley Essex 56 F5
Mitcham London 28 C3
Mitchel Troy Mon 36 C1
Mitcheldean Glos 36 C3
Mitchell Corn 4 D3
Mitcheltroy Common Mon 36 D1
Mitford Northumb 117 F7
Mithian Corn 4 D2
Mitton Staffs 62 C2
Mixbury Oxon 52 F4
Moat Cumb 108 B4
Moats Tye Suff 56 D4
Mobberley Ches E 74 B4
Mobberley Staffs 75 E7
Moccas Hereford 49 E5
Mochdre Conwy 83 D8
Mochdre Powys 59 F7
Mochrum Dumfries 105 E7
Mockbeggar Hants 14 D2
Mockerkin Cumb 98 B2
Modbury Devon 6 D4
Moddershall Staffs 75 F6
Moelfre Anglesey 82 C5
Moelfre Powys 59 B8
Moffat Dumfries 114 D3
Moggerhanger C Beds 54 E2
Moira Leics 63 C7
Mol-chlach Highld 149 G9
Molash Kent 30 D4
Mold = Yr Wyddgrug Flint 73 C6
Moldgreen W Yorks 88 C2
Molehill Green Essex 42 B1
Molescroft E Yorks 97 E6
Molesden Northumb 117 F7
Molesworth Cambs 53 B8
Moll Highld 149 E10
Molland Devon 10 B3
Mollington Ches W 73 B7
Mollington Oxon 52 E2
Mollinsburn N Lanark 119 B7
Monachty Ceredig 46 C4
Monachylemore Stirling 126 C3
Monar Lodge Highld 150 G5
Monaughty Powys 48 C4
Monboddo House Aberds 135 B7
Mondynes Aberds 135 B7
Monevechadan Argyll 125 E7
Monewden Suff 57 D6
Moneydie Perth 128 B2
Moniaive Dumfries 113 E7
Monifieth Angus 134 F4
Monikie Angus 135 F4
Monimail Fife 128 C4
Monington Pembs 45 E3
Monk Bretton S Yorks 88 D4
Monk Fryston N Yorks 89 B6
Monk Sherborne Hants 26 D4
Monk Soham Suff 57 C6
Monk Street Essex 42 B2
Monken Hadley London 41 E5
Monkhopton Shrops 61 E6
Monkland Hereford 49 D6
Monkleigh Devon 9 B6
Monknash V Glam 21 B8
Monkokehampton Devon 9 D7
Monks Eleigh Suff 56 E3
Monk's Gate W Sus 17 B6
Monks Heath Ches E 74 B5
Monks Kirby Warks 63 F8
Monks Risborough Bucks 39 D8
Monkseaton T&W 111 B6
Monkshill Aberds 153 D7
Monksilver Som 22 F2
Monkspath W Mid 51 B6
Monkswood Mon 35 D7
Monkton Devon 11 D6
Monkton Kent 31 C6
Monkton Pembs 44 E4
Monkton S Ayrs 112 B3
Monkton Combe Bath 24 C2
Monkton Deverill Wilts 24 F3
Monkton Farleigh Wilts 24 C3
Monkton Heathfield Som 11 B7
Monkton Up Wimborne Dorset 13 C8
Monkwearmouth T&W 111 D6
Monkwood Hants 26 F4
Monmouth = Trefynwy Mon 36 C2
Monmouth Cap Mon 35 B7
Monnington on Wye Hereford 49 E5
Monreith Dumfries 105 E7
Monreith Mains Dumfries 105 E7
Mont Saint Guern 16
Montacute Som 12 C2
Montcoffer Ho. Aberds 153 B6
Montford Argyll 145 G10
Montford Shrops 60 C4
Montford Bridge Shrops 60 C4
Montgarrie Aberds 140 C4
Montgomery = Trefaldwyn Powys 60 E2
Montrave Fife 129 D5
Montrose Angus 135 D7
Montsale Essex 43 E6
Monxton Hants 25 E8
Monyash Derbys 75 C8
Monymusk Aberds 141 C5
Monzie Perth 127 B7
Monzie Castle Perth 127 B7
Moodiesburn N Lanark 119 B6
Moonzie Fife 128 C5
Moor Allerton W Yorks 95 F5
Moor Crichel Dorset 13 D7
Moor End E Yorks 96 F4
Moor End York 96 D2
Moor Monkton N Yorks 95 D8
Moor of Granary Moray 151 F13
Moor of Ravenstone Dumfries 105 E7
Moor Row Cumb 98 C2
Moor Street Kent 30 C2
Moorby Lincs 79 C5
Moordown Bmouth 13 E8
Moore Halton 86 F3
Moorend Glos 36 D4
Moorends S Yorks 89 C7
Moorgate S Yorks 88 E5
Moorgreen Notts 76 E4
Moorhall Derbys 76 B3
Moorhampton Hereford 49 E5
Moorhead W Yorks 94 F4
Moorhouse Cumb 108 D3
Moorhouse Notts 77 C7
Moorlinch Som 23 F5
Moorsholm Redcar 102 C4
Moorside Gtr Man 87 D7
Moorthorpe W Yorks 89 C5
Moortown Hants 14 D2
Moortown IoW 14 F5
Moortown Lincs 90 E4
Morangie Highld 151 C10
Morar Highld 147 B9
Morborne Cambs 65 E8
Morchard Bishop Devon 10 D2
Morcombelake Dorset 12 E2
Morcott Rutland 65 D6
Morda Shrops 60 B2
Morden Dorset 13 E7
Morden London 28 C3
Mordiford Hereford 49 F7
Mordon Durham 101 B8
More Shrops 60 E3
Morebath Devon 10 B4
Morebattle Borders 116 B3
Morecambe Lancs 92 C4
Morefield Highld 150 B4
Moreleigh Devon 7 D5
Morenish Perth 132 F2
Moresby Cumb 98 B1
Moresby Parks Cumb 98 C1
Morestead Hants 15 B6
Moreton Dorset 13 F6
Moreton Essex 41 D8
Moreton Mers 85 E3
Moreton Oxon 39 D6
Moreton Staffs 61 C7
Moreton Corbet Shrops 61 B5
Moreton-in-Marsh Glos 51 F7
Moreton Jeffries Hereford 49 E8
Moreton Morrell Warks 51 D8
Moreton on Lugg Hereford 49 E7
Moreton Pinkney Northants 52 E3
Moreton Say Shrops 74 F3
Moreton Valence Glos 36 D4
Moretonhampstead Devon 10 F2
Morfa Carms 33 C6
Morfa Carms 33 E6
Morfa Bach Carms 32 C4
Morfa Bychan Gwyn 71 D6
Morfa Dinlle Gwyn 82 F4
Morfa Glas Neath 34 D2
Morfa Nefyn Gwyn 70 C3
Morfydd Denb 72 E5
Morgan's Vale Wilts 14 B2
Moriah Ceredig 46 B5
Morland Cumb 99 B7
Morley Derbys 76 E3
Morley Durham 101 B6
Morley W Yorks 88 B3
Morley Green Ches E 87 F6
Morley St Botolph Norf 68 E3
Morningside Edin 120 B5
Morningside N Lanark 119 D8
Morningthorpe Norf 68 E5
Morpeth Northumb 117 F8
Morphie Aberds 135 C7
Morrey Staffs 62 C5
Morris Green Essex 55 F8
Morriston Swansea 33 E7
Morston Norf 81 C6
Mortehoe Devon 20 E3
Mortimer W Berks 26 C4
Mortimer West End Hants 26 C4
Mortimer's Cross Hereford 49 C6
Mortlake London 28 B3
Morton Cumb 108 D3
Morton Derbys 76 C4
Morton Lincs 65 B7
Morton Lincs 77 C8
Morton Lincs 90 E2
Morton Norf 68 C4
Morton Notts 77 D7
Morton S Glos 36 E3
Morton Shrops 60 B2
Morton Bagot Warks 51 C6
Morton-on-Swale N Yorks 101 E8
Morvah Corn 2 C3
Morval Corn 5 D7
Morvich Highld 136 B2
Morvich Highld 157 J10
Morville Shrops 61 E6
Morville Heath Shrops 61 E6
Morwenstow Corn 8 C4
Mosborough S Yorks 88 F5
Moscow E Ayrs 118 E4
Mosedale Cumb 108 F3
Moseley W Mid 62 E3
Moseley W Mid 62 F4
Moseley Worcs 50 D3
Moss Argyll 146 G2
Moss Highld 147 E9
Moss S Yorks 89 C6
Moss Wrex 73 D7
Moss Bank Mers 86 E3
Moss Edge Lancs 92 E4
Moss End Brack 27 B6
Moss of Barmuckity Moray 152 B2
Moss Pit Staffs 62 B3
Moss-side Highld 151 F11
Moss Side Lancs 92 F3
Mossat Aberds 140 C3
Mossbank Shetland 160 F6
Mossbay Cumb 98 B1
Mossblown S Ayrs 112 B4
Mossbrow Gtr Man 86 F5
Mossburnford Borders 116 C2
Mossdale Dumfries 106 B3
Mossend N Lanark 119 C7
Mosser Cumb 98 B3
Mossfield Highld 151 D9
Mossgiel E Ayrs 112 B4
Mosside Angus 134 D4
Mossley Ches E 75 C5
Mossley Gtr Man 87 D7
Mossley Hill Mers 85 F4
Mosstodloch Moray 152 B3
Mosston Angus 135 E5
Mossy Lea Lancs 86 C3
Mosterton Dorset 12 D2
Moston Gtr Man 87 D6
Moston Shrops 61 B5
Moston Green Ches E 74 C4
Mostyn Flint 85 F2
Mostyn Quay Flint 85 F2
Motcombe Dorset 13 B6
Mothecombe Devon 6 E4
Motherby Cumb 99 B6
Motherwell N Lanark 119 D7
Mottingham London 28 B5
Mottisfont Hants 14 B4
Mottistone IoW 14 F5
Mottram in Longdendale Gtr Man 87 E7
Mottram St Andrew Ches E 75 B5
Mouilpied Guern 16
Mouldsworth Ches W 74 B2
Moulin Perth 133 D6
Moulsecoomb Brighton 17 D7
Moulsford Oxon 39 F5
Moulsoe M Keynes 53 E7
Moulton Ches W 74 C3
Moulton Lincs 66 B3
Moulton N Yorks 101 D7
Moulton Northants 53 C5
Moulton Suff 55 C7
Moulton V Glam 22 B2
Moulton Chapel Lincs 66 C2
Moulton Eaugate Lincs 66 C3
Moulton Seas End Lincs 66 B3
Moulton St Mary Norf 69 D6
Mounie Castle Aberds 141 B6
Mount Corn 4 D2
Mount Corn 5 C6
Mount Highld 151 G12
Mount Bures Essex 56 F3
Mount Canisp Highld 151 D10
Mount Hawke Corn 3 B6
Mount Pleasant Ches E 74 D5
Mount Pleasant Derbys 63 C6
Mount Pleasant Derbys 76 E3
Mount Pleasant Flint 73 B6
Mount Pleasant Hants 14 E3
Mount Pleasant W Yorks 88 B3
Mount Sorrel Wilts 13 B8
Mount Tabor W Yorks 87 B8
Mountain W Yorks 94 F3
Mountain Ash = Aberpennar Rhondda 34 E4
Mountain Cross Borders 120 E4

Mountain Water Pembs 44 C4
Mountbenger Borders 115 B6
Mountfield E Sus 18 C4
Mountgerald Highld 151 E8
Mountjoy Corn 4 C3
Mountnessing Essex 42 E2
Mounton Mon 36 E2
Mountsorrel Leics 64 C2
Mousehole Corn 2 D3
Mousen Northumb 123 F7
Mouswald Dumfries 107 B7
Mow Cop Ches E 75 D5
Mowhaugh Borders 116 B4
Mowsley Leics 64 F3
Moxley W Mid 62 E3
Moy Highld 137 F7
Moy Highld 151 H10
Moy Hall Highld 151 H10
Moy Ho. Moray 151 E13
Moy Lodge Highld 137 F7
Moyles Court Hants 14 D2
Moylgrove Pembs 45 E3
Muasdale Argyll 143 D7
Much Birch Hereford 49 F7
Much Cowarne Hereford 49 E8
Much Dewchurch Hereford 49 F6
Much Hadham Herts 41 C7
Much Hoole Lancs 86 B2
Much Marcle Hereford 49 F8
Much Wenlock Shrops 61 D6
Muchalls Aberds 141 E8
Muchelney Som 12 B2
Muchlarnick Corn 5 D7
Muchrachd Highld 150 H5
Muckernich Highld 151 F8
Mucking Thurrock 42 F2
Muckleford Dorset 12 E4
Mucklestone Staffs 74 F4
Muckleton Shrops 61 B5
Muckletown Aberds 140 B4
Muckley Corner Staffs 62 D4
Muckton Lincs 91 F7
Mudale Highld 157 F8
Muddiford Devon 20 F4
Mudeford Dorset 14 E2
Mudford Som 12 C3
Mudgley Som 23 E6
Mugdock Stirling 119 B5
Mugeary Highld 149 E9
Mugginton Derbys 76 E2
Muggleswick Durham 110 E3
Muie Highld 157 J9
Muir Aberds 139 F6
Muir of Fairburn Highld 150 F7
Muir of Fowlis Aberds 140 C4
Muir of Ord Highld 151 F8
Muir of Pert Angus 134 F4
Muirden Aberds 153 C7
Muirdrum Angus 135 F5
Muirhead Angus 134 F3
Muirhead Fife 128 D4
Muirhead N Lanark 119 C6
Muirhead S Ayrs 118 F3
Muirhouselaw Borders 116 B2
Muirhouses Falk 128 F2
Muirkirk E Ayrs 113 B6
Muirmill Stirling 127 F6
Muirshearlich Highld 136 F4
Muirskie Aberds 141 E7
Muirtack Aberds 153 E9
Muirton Highld 151 E10
Muirton Perth 127 C8
Muirton Perth 128 B3
Muirton Mains Highld 150 F7
Muirton of Ardblair Perth 134 E1
Muirton of Ballochy Angus 135 C6
Muiryfold Aberds 153 C7
Muker N Yorks 100 E4
Mulbarton Norf 68 D4
Mulben Moray 152 C3
Mulindry Argyll 142 C4
Mullardoch House Highld 150 H5
Mullion Corn 3 E5
Mullion Cove Corn 3 E5
Mumby Lincs 79 B8
Munderfield Row Hereford 49 D8
Munderfield Stocks Hereford 49 D8
Mundesley Norf 81 D9
Mundford Norf 67 E8
Mundham Norf 69 E6
Mundon Essex 42 D4
Mundurno Aberdeen 141 C8
Munerigie Highld 137 D5
Muness Shetland 160 C8
Mungasdale Highld 150 B2
Mungrisdale Cumb 108 F3
Munlochy Highld 151 F9
Munsley Hereford 49 E8
Munslow Shrops 60 F5
Murchington Devon 9 F8
Murcott Oxon 39 C5
Murkle Highld 158 D3
Murlaggan Highld 136 E3
Murlaggan Highld 137 F6
Murra Orkney 159 H3
Murrayfield Edin 120 B5
Murrow Cambs 66 D3
Mursley Bucks 39 B8
Murthill Angus 134 D4
Murthly Perth 133 F7
Murton Cumb 100 B2
Murton Durham 111 E6
Murton Northumb 123 E5
Murton York 96 D2
Musbury Devon 11 E7
Muscoates N Yorks 102 F4
Musdale Argyll 124 C5
Musselburgh E Loth 121 B6
Muston Leics 77 F8
Muston N Yorks 97 B6
Mustow Green Worcs 50 B3
Mutehill Dumfries 106 E3
Mutford Suff 69 F7
Muthill Perth 127 C7
Mutterton Devon 10 D5
Muxton Telford 61 C7
Mybster Highld 158 E3
Myddfai Carms 34 B1
Myddle Shrops 60 B4
Mydroilyn Ceredig 46 D3
Myerscough Lancs 92 F4
Mylor Bridge Corn 3 C7
Mynachlog-ddu Pembs 45 F3
Myndtown Shrops 60 F3
Mynydd Bach Ceredig 47 B6
Mynydd-bach Mon 36 E1
Mynydd Bodafon Anglesey 82 C4
Mynydd-isa Flint 73 C6
Mynyddygarreg Carms 33 D5
Mynytho Gwyn 70 D4
Myrebird Aberds 141 E6
Myrelandhorn Highld 158 E4
Myreside Perth 128 B4
Myrtle Hill Carms 47 F6
Mytchett Sur 27 D6
Mytholm W Yorks 87 B7
Mytholmroyd W Yorks 87 B8
Myton-on-Swale N Yorks 95 C7
Mytton Shrops 60 C4

N

Na Gearrannan W Isles 154 C6
Naast Highld 155 J13
Naburn York 95 E8
Nackington Kent 31 D5
Nacton Suff 57 E6
Nafferton E Yorks 97 D6
Nailbridge Glos 36 C3
Nailsbourne Som 11 B7
Nailsea N Som 23 B6
Nailstone Leics 63 D8
Nailsworth Glos 37 E5
Nairn Highld 151 F11
Nalderswood Sur 28 E3
Nancegollan Corn 2 C5
Nancledra Corn 2 C3
Nanhoron Gwyn 70 D3
Nannau Gwyn 71 E8
Nannerch Flint 73 C5
Nanpantan Leics 64 C2
Nanpean Corn 4 D4
Nanstallon Corn 4 C5
Nant-ddu Powys 34 C4
Nant-glas Powys 47 C8
Nant Peris Gwyn 83 F6
Nant Uchaf Denb 72 D4
Nant-y-Bai Carms 47 E6
Nant-y-cafn Neath 34 D2
Nant-y-derry Mon 35 D7
Nant-y-ffin Carms 46 F4
Nant-y-moel Bridgend 34 E3
Nant-y-pandy Conwy 83 D6
Nanternis Ceredig 46 D2
Nantgaredig Carms 33 B5
Nantgarw Rhondda 35 F5
Nantglyn Denb 72 C4
Nantgwyn Powys 47 B8
Nantlle Gwyn 82 F5
Nantmawr Shrops 60 B2
Nantmel Powys 48 C2
Nantmor Gwyn 71 C7
Nantwich Ches E 74 D3
Nantycaws Carms 33 C5
Nantyffyllon Bridgend 34 E2
Nantyglo Bl Gwent 35 C5
Naphill Bucks 39 E8
Nappa N Yorks 93 D8
Napton on the Hill Warks 52 C2
Narberth = Arberth Pembs 32 C2
Narborough Leics 64 E2
Narborough Norf 67 C7
Nasareth Gwyn 82 F4
Naseby Northants 52 B4
Nash Bucks 53 F5
Nash Hereford 48 C5
Nash Newport 35 F7
Nash Shrops 49 B8
Nash Lee Bucks 39 D8
Nassington Northants 65 E7
Nasty Herts 41 B6
Nateby Cumb 100 D2
Nateby Lancs 92 E4
Natland Cumb 99 F7
Naughton Suff 56 E4
Naunton Glos 37 B8
Naunton Worcs 50 F3
Naunton Beauchamp Worcs 50 D4
Navenby Lincs 78 D2
Navestock Heath Essex 41 E8
Navestock Side Essex 42 E1
Navidale Highld 157 H13
Nawton N Yorks 102 F4
Nayland Suff 56 F3
Nazeing Essex 41 D7
Neacroft Hants 14 E2
Neal's Green Warks 63 F7
Neap Shetland 160 H7
Near Sawrey Cumb 99 E5
Neasham Darl 101 C8
Neath = Castell-Nedd Neath 33 E8
Neath Abbey Neath 33 E8
Neatishead Norf 69 B6
Nebo Anglesey 82 B4
Nebo Ceredig 46 C4
Nebo Conwy 83 F8
Nebo Gwyn 82 F4
Necton Norf 67 D8
Nedd Highld 156 F4
Nedderton Northumb 117 F8
Nedging Tye Suff 56 E4
Needham Norf 68 F5
Needham Market Suff 56 D4
Needingworth Cambs 54 B4
Needwood Staffs 63 B5
Neen Savage Shrops 49 B8
Neen Sollars Shrops 49 B8
Neenton Shrops 61 F6
Nefyn Gwyn 70 C4
Neilston E Renf 118 D4
Neinthirion Powys 59 D6
Neithrop Oxon 52 E2
Nelly Andrews Green Powys 60 D2
Nelson Caerph 35 E5
Nelson Lancs 93 F8
Nelson Village Northumb 111 B5
Nemphlar S Lanark 119 E8
Nempnett Thrubwell N Som 23 C7
Nene Terrace Lincs 66 D2
Nenthall Cumb 109 E7
Nenthead Cumb 109 E7
Nenthorn Borders 122 F2
Nerabus Argyll 142 C3
Nercwys Flint 73 C6
Nerston S Lanark 119 D6
Nesbit Northumb 123 F5
Ness Ches W 73 B7
Nesscliffe Shrops 60 C3
Neston Ches W 73 B6
Neston Wilts 24 C3
Nether Alderley Ches E 74 B5
Nether Blainslie Borders 121 E8
Nether Booth Derbys 88 F2
Nether Broughton Leics 64 B3
Nether Burrow Lancs 93 B6
Nether Cerne Dorset 12 E4
Nether Compton Dorset 12 C3
Nether Crimond Aberds 141 B7
Nether Dalgliesh Borders 115 D5
Nether Dallachy Moray 152 B3
Nether Exe Devon 10 D4
Nether Glasslaw Aberds 153 C8
Nether Handwick Angus 134 E3
Nether Haugh S Yorks 88 E5
Nether Heage Derbys 76 D3
Nether Heyford Northants 52 D4
Nether Hindhope Borders 116 C3
Nether Howecleuch S Lanark 114 C3
Nether Kellet Lancs 92 C5
Nether Kinmundy Aberds 153 D10
Nether Langwith Notts 76 B5
Nether Leask Aberds 153 E10
Nether Lenshie Aberds 153 D6
Nether Monynut Borders 122 C3
Nether Padley Derbys 76 B2
Nether Park Aberds 153 C10
Nether Poppleton York 95 D8
Nether Silton N Yorks 102 E2
Nether Stowey Som 22 F3
Nether Urquhart Fife 128 D3
Nether Wallop Hants 25 F8
Nether Wasdale Cumb 98 D3
Nether Whitacre Warks 63 E6
Nether Worton Oxon 52 F2
Netheravon Wilts 25 E6
Netherbrae Aberds 153 C7
Netherbrough Orkney 159 G4
Netherburn S Lanark 119 E8
Netherbury Dorset 12 E2
Netherby Cumb 108 B3
Netherby N Yorks 95 E6
Nethercote Warks 52 C3
Nethercott Devon 20 F3
Netherend Glos 36 D2
Netherfield E Sus 18 D4
Netherhampton Wilts 14 B2
Netherlaw Dumfries 106 E4
Netherley Aberds 141 E7
Netherley Mers 86 F2
Nethermill Dumfries 114 F3
Nethermuir Aberds 153 D9
Netherplace E Renf 118 D5
Netherseal Derbys 63 C6
Netherthird E Ayrs 113 C5
Netherthong W Yorks 88 D2
Netherthorpe S Yorks 89 F6
Netherton Angus 135 D5
Netherton Devon 7 B6
Netherton Hants 25 D8
Netherton Mers 85 D4
Netherton Northumb 117 D5
Netherton Oxon 38 E4
Netherton Perth 133 D8
Netherton Stirling 119 B5
Netherton W Mid 62 F3
Netherton W Yorks 88 C2
Netherton W Yorks 88 C3
Netherton Worcs 50 E4
Nethertown Cumb 98 D1
Nethertown Highld 158 C5
Netherwitton Northumb 117 E7
Netherwood E Ayrs 113 B6
Nethy Bridge Highld 139 B6
Netley Hants 15 D5
Netley Marsh Hants 14 C4
Netteswell Essex 41 C7
Nettlebed Oxon 39 F7
Nettlebridge Som 23 E8
Nettlecombe Dorset 12 E3
Nettleden Herts 40 C3
Nettleham Lincs 78 B3
Nettlestead Kent 29 D7
Nettlestead Green Kent 29 D7
Nettlestone IoW 15 E7
Nettlesworth Durham 111 E5
Nettleton Lincs 90 D5
Nettleton Wilts 24 B3
Neuadd Carms 33 B7
Nevendon Essex 42 E3
Nevern Pembs 45 E2
New Abbey Dumfries 107 C6
New Aberdour Aberds 153 B8
New Addington London 28 C4
New Alresford Hants 26 F3
New Alyth Perth 134 E2
New Arley Warks 63 F6
New Ash Green Kent 29 C7
New Barn Kent 29 C7
New Barnetby N Lincs 90 C4
New Barton Northants 53 C6
New Bewick Northumb 117 B6
New-bigging Angus 134 E2
New Bilton Warks 52 B2
New Bolingbroke Lincs 79 D6
New Boultham Lincs 78 B2
New Bradwell M Keynes 53 E6
New Brancepeth Durham 110 E5
New Bridge Wrex 73 E6
New Brighton Flint 73 C6
New Brighton Mers 85 E4
New Brinsley Notts 76 D4
New Broughton Wrex 73 D7
New Buckenham Norf 68 E3
New Byth Aberds 153 C8
New Catton Norf 68 C5
New Cheriton Hants 15 B6
New Costessey Norf 68 C4
New Cowper Cumb 107 E8
New Cross Ceredig 46 B5
New Cross London 28 B4
New Cumnock E Ayrs 113 C6
New Deer Aberds 153 D8
New Delaval Northumb 111 B5
New Duston Northants 52 C5
New Earswick York 96 D2
New Edlington S Yorks 89 E6
New Elgin Moray 152 B2
New Ellerby E Yorks 97 F7
New Eltham London 28 B5
New End Worcs 51 D5
New Farnley W Yorks 94 F5
New Ferry Mers 85 F4
New Fryston W Yorks 89 B5
New Galloway Dumfries 106 B3
New Gilston Fife 129 D6
New Grimsby Scilly 2 E3
New Hainford Norf 68 C5
New Hartley Northumb 111 B6
New Haw Sur 27 C8
New Hedges Pembs 32 D2
New Herrington T&W 111 D6
New Hinksey Oxon 39 D5
New Holkham Norf 80 D4
New Holland N Lincs 90 B4
New Houghton Derbys 76 C4
New Houghton Norf 80 E3
New Houses N Yorks 93 B8
New Humberstone Leicester 64 D3
New Hutton Cumb 99 E7
New Hythe Kent 29 D8
New Inn Carms 46 F3
New Inn Mon 36 D1
New Inn Pembs 45 F2
New Inn Torf 35 E7
New Invention Shrops 48 B4
New Invention W Mid 62 D3
New Kelso Highld 150 G2
New Kingston Notts 64 B2
New Lanark S Lanark 119 E8
New Lane Lancs 86 C2
New Lane End Warr 86 E4
New Leake Lincs 79 D7
New Leeds Aberds 153 C9
New Longton Lancs 86 B3
New Luce Dumfries 105 C5
New Malden London 28 C3
New Marske Redcar 102 B4
New Marton Shrops 73 F7
New Micklefield W Yorks 95 F7
New Mill Aberds 141 F6
New Mill Herts 40 C2
New Mill W Yorks 88 D2
New Mill Wilts 25 C6
New Mills Ches E 87 F5
New Mills Corn 4 D3
New Mills Derbys 87 F7
New Mills Powys 59 D7
New Milton Hants 14 E3
New Moat Pembs 32 B1
New Ollerton Notts 77 C6
New Oscott W Mid 62 E4
New Park N Yorks 95 D5
New Pitsligo Aberds 153 C8
New Polzeath Corn 4 B4
New Quay = Ceinewydd Ceredig 46 D2
New Rackheath Norf 69 C5
New Radnor Powys 48 C4
New Rent Cumb 108 F4
New Ridley Northumb 110 D3
New Road Side N Yorks 94 E2
New Romney Kent 19 C7
New Rossington S Yorks 89 E7
New Row Ceredig 47 B6
New Row Lancs 93 F6
New Row N Yorks 102 C4
New Sarum Wilts 25 F6
New Silksworth T&W 111 D6
New Stevenston N Lanark 119 D7
New Street Staffs 75 D7
New Street Lane Shrops 74 F3
New Swanage Dorset 13 F8
New Totley S Yorks 76 B3
New Town E Loth 121 B7
New Tredegar = Tredegar Newydd Caerph 35 D5
New Trows S Lanark 119 F8
New Ulva Argyll 144 E6
New Walsoken Cambs 66 D4
New Waltham NE Lincs 91 D6
New Whittington Derbys 76 B3
New Wimpole Cambs 54 E4
New Winton E Loth 121 B7
New Yatt Oxon 38 C3
New York Lincs 78 D5
New York N Yorks 94 C4
Newall W Yorks 94 E4
Newark Orkney 159 D8
Newark Pboro 66 D2
Newark-on-Trent Notts 77 D7
Newarthill N Lanark 119 D7
Newbarns Cumb 92 B2
Newbattle Midloth 121 C6
Newbiggin Cumb 92 C2
Newbiggin Cumb 98 E2
Newbiggin Cumb 99 B6
Newbiggin Cumb 99 B8
Newbiggin Cumb 109 E5
Newbiggin Durham 100 B4
Newbiggin N Yorks 100 E4
Newbiggin N Yorks 100 F4
Newbiggin-by-the-Sea Northumb 117 F9
Newbiggin-on-Lune Cumb 100 D2
Newbigging Angus 134 F4
Newbigging Angus 134 F4
Newbigging S Lanark 120 E3
Newbold Derbys 76 B3
Newbold Leics 63 C8
Newbold on Avon Warks 52 B2
Newbold on Stour Warks 51 E7
Newbold Pacey Warks 51 D7
Newbold Verdon Leics 63 D8
Newborough Anglesey 82 E4
Newborough Pboro 66 D2
Newborough Staffs 62 B5
Newbottle Northants 52 F3
Newbottle T&W 111 D6
Newbourne Suff 57 E6
Newbridge Caerph 35 E6
Newbridge Ceredig 46 D4
Newbridge Corn 2 C3
Newbridge Corn 5 C8
Newbridge Dumfries 107 B6
Newbridge Edin 120 B4
Newbridge Hants 14 C3
Newbridge IoW 14 F5
Newbridge Pembs 44 B4
Newbridge Green Worcs 50 F3
Newbridge-on-Usk Mon 35 E7
Newbridge on Wye Powys 48 D2
Newbrough Northumb 109 C8
Newbuildings Devon 10 D2
Newburgh Aberds 141 B8
Newburgh Aberds 153 C9
Newburgh Borders 115 C6
Newburgh Fife 128 C4
Newburgh Lancs 86 C2
Newburn T&W 110 C4
Newbury W Berks 26 C2
Newbury Park London 41 F7
Newby Cumb 99 B7
Newby Lancs 93 E8
Newby N Yorks 93 B7
Newby N Yorks 102 C3
Newby N Yorks 103 E8
Newby Bridge Cumb 99 F5
Newby East Cumb 108 D4
Newby West Cumb 108 D3
Newby Wiske N Yorks 102 F1
Newcastle Mon 35 C8
Newcastle Shrops 60 F2
Newcastle Emlyn = Castell Newydd Emlyn Carms 46 E2
Newcastle-under-Lyme Staffs 74 E5
Newcastle Upon Tyne T&W 110 C5
Newcastleton or Copshaw Holm Borders 115 F7
Newchapel Pembs 45 F4
Newchapel Powys 59 F6
Newchapel Staffs 75 D5
Newchapel Sur 28 E4
Newchurch Carms 32 B4
Newchurch IoW 15 F6
Newchurch Kent 19 B7
Newchurch Lancs 93 F8
Newchurch Mon 36 E1
Newchurch Powys 48 D4
Newchurch Staffs 62 B5
Newcott Devon 11 D7
Newcraighall Edin 121 B6
Newdigate Sur 28 E2
Newell Green Brack 27 B6
Newenden Kent 18 C5
Newent Glos 36 B4
Newerne Glos 36 D3
Newfield Durham 110 F5
Newfield Highld 151 D10
Newford Scilly 2 E4
Newfound Hants 26 D3
Newgale Pembs 44 C3
Newgate Norf 81 C6
Newgate Street Herts 41 D6
Newhall Ches E 74 E3
Newhall Derbys 63 B6
Newhall House Highld 151 E9
Newhall Point Highld 151 E10
Newham Northumb 117 B7
Newham Hall Northumb 117 B7
Newhaven Derbys 75 D8
Newhaven E Sus 17 D8
Newhaven Edin 121 B5
Newhey Gtr Man 87 C7
Newholm N Yorks 103 C6
Newhouse N Lanark 119 C7
Newick E Sus 17 B8
Newingreen Kent 19 B8
Newington Kent 19 B8
Newington Kent 30 C2
Newington Kent 31 C7
Newington Notts 89 E7
Newington Oxon 39 E6
Newington Shrops 60 F4
Newland Glos 36 D2
Newland Hull 97 F6
Newland N Yorks 89 B7
Newland Worcs 50 E2
Newlandrig Midloth 121 C6
Newlands Borders 115 E8
Newlands Highld 151 G10
Newlands Moray 152 C3
Newlands Northumb 110 D3
Newland's Corner Sur 27 E8
Newlands of Geise Highld 158 D2
Newlands of Tynet Moray 152 B3
Newlands Park Anglesey 82 C2
Newlandsmuir S Lanark 119 D6
Newlot Orkney 159 G6
Newlyn Corn 2 D3
Newmachar Aberds 141 C7
Newmains N Lanark 119 D8
Newmarket Suff 55 C7
Newmarket W Isles 155 D9
Newmill Borders 115 C7
Newmill Corn 2 C3
Newmill Moray 152 C4
Newmill of Inshewan Angus 134 C4
Newmills of Boyne Aberds 152 C5
Newmiln Perth 133 F8
Newmilns E Ayrs 118 F5
Newnham Cambs 54 D5
Newnham Glos 36 C3
Newnham Hants 26 D5
Newnham Herts 54 F3
Newnham Kent 30 D3
Newnham Northants 52 D3
Newnham Bridge Worcs 49 C8
Newpark Fife 129 C6
Newport Devon 20 F4
Newport E Yorks 96 F4
Newport Essex 55 F6
Newport Highld 158 H3
Newport IoW 15 F6
Newport = Casnewydd Newport 35 F7
Newport Norf 69 C8
Newport = Trefdraeth Pembs 45 F2
Newport Telford 61 C7
Newport-on-Tay Fife 129 B6
Newport Pagnell M Keynes 53 E6
Newpound Common W Sus 16 B4
Newquay Corn 4 C3
Newsbank Ches E 74 C5
Newseat Aberds 153 D10
Newseat Aberds 153 E7
Newsham N Yorks 101 C6
Newsham N Yorks 102 F1
Newsham Northumb 111 B6
Newsholme E Yorks 89 B8
Newsholme Lancs 93 D8
Newsome W Yorks 88 C2
Newstead Borders 121 F8
Newstead Northumb 117 B7
Newstead Notts 76 D5
Newthorpe N Yorks 95 F7
Newton Argyll 125 F6
Newton Borders 116 B2
Newton Bridgend 21 B7
Newton Cambs 54 E5
Newton Cambs 66 C4
Newton Cardiff 22 B4
Newton Ches W 73 C8
Newton Ches W 74 B2
Newton Ches W 74 D2
Newton Cumb 92 B2
Newton Derbys 76 D4
Newton Dorset 13 C5
Newton Dumfries 108 B2
Newton Dumfries 114 E4
Newton Gtr Man 87 E7
Newton Hereford 48 F5
Newton Hereford 49 D7
Newton Highld 151 E10
Newton Highld 151 G10
Newton Highld 156 F5
Newton Highld 158 F5
Newton Lancs 92 F4
Newton Lancs 93 B5
Newton Lancs 93 D6
Newton Lincs 78 F3
Newton Moray 152 B1
Newton Norf 67 C8
Newton Northants 65 F5
Newton Northumb 110 C3
Newton Notts 77 E6
Newton Perth 133 F5
Newton S Lanark 119 C6
Newton S Lanark 120 F2
Newton S Yorks 89 D6
Newton Staffs 62 B4
Newton Suff 56 E3
Newton Swansea 33 F7
Newton W Loth 120 B3
Newton Warks 52 B3
Newton Wilts 14 B3
Newton Abbot Devon 7 B6
Newton Arlosh Cumb 107 D8
Newton Aycliffe Durham 101 B7
Newton Bewley Hrtlpl 102 B2
Newton Blossomville M Keynes 53 D7
Newton Bromswold Northants 53 C7
Newton Burgoland Leics 63 D7
Newton by Toft Lincs 90 F4
Newton Ferrers Devon 6 E3
Newton Flotman Norf 68 E5
Newton Hall Northumb 110 C3
Newton Harcourt Leics 64 E3
Newton Heath Gtr Man 87 D6
Newton Ho. Aberds 141 B5
Newton Kyme N Yorks 95 E7
Newton-le-Willows Mers 86 E3
Newton-le-Willows N Yorks 101 F7
Newton Longville Bucks 53 F6
Newton Mearns E Renf 118 D5
Newton Morrell N Yorks 101 D7
Newton Mulgrave N Yorks 103 C5
Newton of Ardtoe Highld 147 D9
Newton of Balcanquhal Perth 128 C3
Newton of Falkland Fife 128 D4
Newton on Ayr S Ayrs 112 B3
Newton on Ouse N Yorks 95 D8
Newton-on-Rawcliffe N Yorks 103 E6
Newton-on-the-Moor Northumb 117 D7
Newton on Trent Lincs 77 B8
Newton Park Argyll 145 G10
Newton Poppleford Devon 11 F5
Newton Purcell Oxon 52 F4
Newton Regis Warks 63 D6
Newton Reigny Cumb 108 F4
Newton Solney Derbys 63 B6
Newton St Cyres Devon 10 E3
Newton St Faith Norf 68 C5
Newton St Loe Bath 24 C2
Newton St Petrock Devon 9 C6
Newton Stacey Hants 26 E2
Newton Stewart Dumfries 105 C8
Newton Tony Wilts 25 E7
Newton Tracey Devon 9 B7
Newton under Roseberry Redcar 102 C3
Newton upon Derwent E Yorks 96 E3
Newton Valence Hants 26 F5
Newtonairds Dumfries 113 F8
Newtongrange Midloth 121 C6
Newtonhill Aberds 141 E8
Newtonhill Highld 151 G8
Newtonmill Angus 135 C6
Newtonmore Highld 138 E3
Newtown Argyll 125 E6
Newtown Ches W 74 B2
Newtown Corn 3 D6
Newtown Cumb 107 E7
Newtown Cumb 108 C5
Newtown Derbys 87 F7
Newtown Devon 10 B2
Newtown Glos 36 D3
Newtown Glos 50 F4
Newtown Hants 14 B4
Newtown Hants 14 C3
Newtown Hants 15 C6
Newtown Hants 15 C7
Newtown Hants 15 D5
Newtown Hants 26 C2
Newtown Hereford 49 E8
Newtown Highld 137 D6
Newtown IoM 84 E3
Newtown IoW 14 E5
Newtown Northumb 117 B6
Newtown Northumb 117 D6
Newtown Northumb 123 F5
Newtown Poole 13 E8
Newtown = Y Drenewydd Powys 59 E8
Newtown Shrops 73 F8
Newtown Staffs 75 C6
Newtown Staffs 75 C7
Newtown Wilts 13 B7
Newtown Linford Leics 64 D2
Newtown St Boswells Borders 121 F8
Newtown Unthank Leics 63 D8
Newtyle Angus 134 E2
Neyland Pembs 44 E4
Niarbyl IoM 84 E2
Nibley S Glos 36 F3
Nibley Green Glos 36 E4
Nibon Shetland 160 F5
Nicholashayne Devon 11 C6
Nicholaston Swansea 33 F6
Nidd N Yorks 95 C6
Nigg Aberdeen 141 D8
Nigg Highld 151 D11
Nigg Ferry Highld 151 E10
Nightcott Som 10 B3
Nilig Denb 72 D4
Nine Ashes Essex 42 D1
Nine Mile Burn Midloth 120 D4
Nine Wells Pembs 44 C2
Ninebanks Northumb 109 D7
Ninfield E Sus 18 D4
Ningwood IoW 14 F4
Nisbet Borders 116 B2
Nisthouse Orkney 159 G4
Nisthouse Shetland 160 G7
Niton IoW 15 G6
Nitshill Glasgow 118 C5
No Man's Heath Ches W 74 E2
No Man's Heath Warks 63 D6
Noak Hill London 41 E8
Noblethorpe S Yorks 88 D3
Nobottle Northants 52 C4
Nocton Lincs 78 C3
Noke Oxon 39 C5
Nolton Pembs 44 D3
Nolton Haven Pembs 44 D3
Nomansland Devon 10 C3
Nomansland Wilts 14 C3
Noneley Shrops 60 B4
Nonikiln Highld 151 D9
Nonington Kent 31 D6
Noonsbrough Shetland 160 H4
Norbreck Blackpool 92 E3
Norbridge Hereford 50 E2
Norbury Ches E 74 E2
Norbury Derbys 75 E8
Norbury Shrops 60 E3
Norbury Staffs 61 B7
Nordelph Norf 67 D5
Norden Gtr Man 87 C6
Norden Heath Dorset 13 F7
Nordley Shrops 61 E6
Norham Northumb 122 E5
Norley Ches W 74 B2
Norleywood Hants 14 E4
Norman Cross Cambs 65 E8
Normanby N Lincs 90 C2
Normanby N Yorks 103 F5
Normanby Redcar 102 C3
Normanby-by-Spital Lincs 90 F4
Normanby by Stow Lincs 90 F2
Normanby le Wold Lincs 90 E5
Normandy Sur 27 D7
Norman's Bay E Sus 18 E3
Norman's Green Devon 11 D5
Normanstone Suff 69 E8
Normanton Derby 76 F3
Normanton Leics 77 E8
Normanton Lincs 78 E2
Normanton Notts 77 D7
Normanton Rutland 65 D6
Normanton W Yorks 88 B4
Normanton le Heath Leics 63 C7
Normanton on Soar Notts 64 B2
Normanton-on-the-Wolds Notts 77 F6
Normanton on Trent Notts 77 C7
Normoss Lancs 92 F3
Norney Sur 27 E7
Norrington Common Wilts 24 C3
Norris Green Mers 85 E4
Norris Hill Leics 63 C7
North Anston S Yorks 89 F6
North Aston Oxon 38 B4
North Baddesley Hants 14 C4
North Ballachulish Highld 130 C4
North Barrow Som 12 B4
North Barsham Norf 80 D5
North Benfleet Essex 42 F3
North Bersted W Sus 16 D3
North Berwick E Loth 129 F7
North Boarhunt Hants 15 C7
North Bovey Devon 10 F2
North Bradley Wilts 24 D3
North Brentor Devon 9 F6
North Brewham Som 24 F2
North Buckland Devon 20 E3
North Burlingham Norf 69 C6
North Cadbury Som 12 B4
North Cairn Dumfries 104 B3
North Carlton Lincs 78 B2
North Carrine Argyll 143 H7
North Cave E Yorks 96 F4
North Cerney Glos 37 D7
North Charford Wilts 14 C2
North Charlton Northumb 117 B7
North Cheriton Som 12 B4
North Cliff E Yorks 97 E8
North Cliffe E Yorks 96 F4
North Clifton Notts 77 B8
North Cockerington Lincs 91 E7
North Coker Som 12 C3
North Collafirth Shetland 160 E5
North Common E Sus 17 B7
North Connel Argyll 124 B5
North Cornelly Bridgend 34 F2
North Cotes Lincs 91 D7
North Cove Suff 69 F7
North Cowton N Yorks 101 D7
North Crawley M Keynes 53 E7
North Cray London 29 B5
North Creake Norf 80 D4
North Curry Som 11 B8
North Dalton E Yorks 96 D5
North Dawn Orkney 159 H5
North Deighton N Yorks 95 D6
North Duffield N Yorks 96 F2
North Elkington Lincs 91 E6
North Elmham Norf 81 E5
North Elmshall W Yorks 89 C5
North End Bucks 39 B8
North End E Yorks 97 F8
North End Essex 42 C2
North End Hants 26 C2
North End Lincs 78 E5
North End N Som 23 C6
North End Ptsmth 15 D7
North End Som 11 B7
North End W Sus 16 D5
North Erradale Highld 155 J12
North Fambridge Essex 42 E4
North Fearns Highld 149 E10
North Featherstone W Yorks 88 B5
North Ferriby E Yorks 90 B3
North Frodingham E Yorks 97 D7
North Gluss Shetland 160 F5
North Gorley Hants 14 C2
North Green Norf 68 F5
North Green Suff 57 C7
North Greetwell Lincs 78 B3
North Grimston N Yorks 96 C4
North Halley Orkney 159 H6
North Halling Medway 29 C8
North Hayling Hants 15 D8
North Hazelrigg Northumb 123 F6
North Heasley Devon 21 F6
North Heath W Sus 16 B4
North Hill Cambs 55 B5
North Hill Corn 5 B7
North Hinksey Oxon 38 D4
North Holmwood Sur 28 E2
North Howden E Yorks 96 F3
North Huish Devon 6 D5
North Hykeham Lincs 78 C2
North Johnston Pembs 44 D4
North Kelsey Lincs 90 D4
North Kelsey Moor Lincs 90 D4
North Kessock Highld 151 G9
North Killingholme N Lincs 90 C5
North Kilvington N Yorks 102 F2
North Kilworth Leics 64 F3
North Kirkton Aberds 153 C11
North Kiscadale N Ayrs 143 F11
North Kyme Lincs 78 D4
North Lancing W Sus 17 D5
North Lee Bucks 39 D8
North Leigh Oxon 38 C3
North Leverton with Habblesthorpe Notts 89 F8
North Littleton Worcs 51 E5
North Lopham Norf 68 F3
North Luffenham Rutland 65 D6
North Marden W Sus 16 C2
North Marston Bucks 39 B7
North Middleton Midloth 121 D6
North Middleton Northumb 117 B6
North Molton Devon 10 B2
North Moreton Oxon 39 F5
North Mundham W Sus 16 D2
North Muskham Notts 77 D7
North Newbald E Yorks 96 F5
North Newington Oxon 52 F2
North Newnton Wilts 25 D6
North Newton Som 22 F4
North Nibley Glos 36 E4
North Oakley Hants 26 D3
North Ockendon London 42 F1
North Ormesby Mbro 102 B3
North Ormsby Lincs 91 E6
North Otterington N Yorks 102 F1
North Owersby Lincs 90 E4
North Perrott Som 12 D2
North Petherton Som 22 F4
North Petherwin Corn 8 F4
North Pickenham Norf 67 D8
North Piddle Worcs 50 D4
North Poorton Dorset 12 E3
North Port Argyll 125 C6
North Queensferry Fife 128 F3
North Radworthy Devon 21 F6
North Rauceby Lincs 78 E3
North Reston Lincs 91 F7
North Rigton N Yorks 95 E5
North Rode Ches E 75 C5
North Roe Shetland 160 E5
North Runcton Norf 67 C6
North Sandwick Shetland 160 D7
North Scale Cumb 92 C1
North Scarle Lincs 77 C8
North Seaton Northumb 117 F8
North Shian Argyll 130 E3
North Shields T&W 111 C6
North Shoebury Southend 43 F5
North Shore Blackpool 92 F3
North Side Cumb 98 B2
North Side Pboro 66 E2
North Skelton Redcar 102
North Somercotes Lincs 91
North Stainley N Yorks 95
North Stainmore Cumb 100
North Stifford Thurrock 42
North Stoke Bath 24
North Stoke Oxon 39
North Stoke W Sus 16
North Street Hants 26
North Street Kent 30
North Street Medway 30
North Street W Berks 26
North Sunderland Northumb 123
North Tamerton Corn 8
North Tawton Devon 9
North Thoresby Lincs 91
North Tidworth Wilts 25
North Togston Northumb 117
North Tuddenham Norf 68
North Walbottle T&W 110
North Walsham Norf 81
North Waltham Hants 26
North Warnborough Hants 26
North Water Bridge Angus 135
North Watten Highld 158
North Weald Bassett Essex 41
North Wheatley Notts 89
North Whilborough Devon 7
North Wick Bath 23
North Willingham Lincs 91
North Wingfield Derbys 76
North Witham Lincs 65
North Woolwich London 28
North Wootton Dorset 12
North Wootton Norf 67
North Wootton Som 23
North Wraxall Wilts 24
North Wroughton Swindon 38
Northacre Norf 68
Northallerton N Yorks 102
Northam Devon 9
Northam Soton 14
Northampton Northants 53
Northaw Herts 41
Northbeck Lincs 78
Northborough Pboro 65 D8
Northbourne Kent 31
Northbridge Street E Sus 18
Northchapel W Sus 16
Northchurch Herts 40
Northcott Devon 8
Northdown Kent 31
Northdyke Orkney 159
Northend Bath 24 C2
Northend Bucks 39 E7
Northend Warks 51 D8
Northenden Gtr Man 87 E6
Northfield Aberdeen 141 D8
Northfield Borders 122 C5
Northfield E Yorks 90 B4
Northfield W Mid 50 B5
Northfields Lincs 65 D7
Northfleet Kent 29 B7
Northgate Lincs 65 B8
Northhouse Borders 115 D7
Northiam E Sus 18 C5
Northill C Beds 54 E2
Northington Hants 26 F3
Northlands Lincs 79 D6
Northlea Durham 111 D7
Northleach Glos 37 C8
Northleigh Devon 11 E6
Northlew Devon 9 E7
Northmoor Oxon 38 D4
Northmoor Green or Moorland Som 22 F5
Northmuir Angus 134 D3
Northney Hants 15 D8
Northolt London 40 F4
Northop Flint 73 C6
Northop Hall Flint 73 C6
Northorpe Lincs 65 C7
Northorpe Lincs 78 F5
Northorpe Lincs 90 E2
Northover Som 12 B3
Northover Som 23 F6
Northowram W Yorks 88 B2
Northport Dorset 13 F7
Northpunds Shetland 160 L6
Northrepps Norf 81 D8
Northtown Orkney 159 J5
Northway Glos 50 F4
Northwich Ches W 74 B3
Northwick S Glos 36 F2
Northwold Norf 67 E7
Northwood Derbys 76 C2
Northwood IoW 15 E5
Northwood Kent 31 C7
Northwood London 40 E3
Northwood Shrops 73 F8
Northwood Green Glos 36 C4
Norton E Sus 17 D8
Norton Glos 37 B5
Norton Halton 86 F3
Norton Herts 54 F3
Norton IoW 14 F4
Norton Mon 35 C8
Norton Northants 52 C4
Norton Notts 77 B5
Norton Powys 48 C5
Norton S Yorks 89 C6
Norton Shrops 60 F4
Norton Shrops 61 D5
Norton Shrops 61 D7
Norton Stockton 102 B2
Norton Suff 56 C3
Norton W Sus 16 D3
Norton W Sus 16 E2
Norton Wilts 37 F5
Norton Worcs 50 D3
Norton Worcs 50 E5
Norton Bavant Wilts 24 E4
Norton Bridge Staffs 75 F5
Norton Canes Staffs 62 D4
Norton Canon Hereford 49 E5
Norton Corner Norf 81 E6
Norton Disney Lincs 77 D8
Norton East Staffs 62 D4
Norton Ferris Wilts 24 F2
Norton Fitzwarren Som 11 B6
Norton Green IoW 14 F4
Norton Hawkfield Bath 23 C7
Norton Heath Essex 42 D2
Norton in Hales Shrops 74 F4
Norton-in-the-Moors Stoke 75 D5
Norton-Juxta-Twycross Leics 63 D7
Norton-le-Clay N Yorks 95 B7
Norton Lindsey Warks 51 C7
Norton Malreward Bath 23 C8
Norton Mandeville Essex 42 D1
Norton-on-Derwent N Yorks 96 B3
Norton St Philip Som 24 D2
Norton sub Hamdon Som 12 C2
Norton Woodseats S Yorks 88 F4

Norwell Notts 77 C7
Norwell Woodhouse Notts 77 C7
Norwich Norf 68 D5
Norwick Shetland 160 B8
Norwood Derbys 89 F5
Norwood Hill Sur 28 E3
Norwoodside Cambs 66 E4
Noseley Leics 64 E4
Noss Shetland 160 M5
Noss Mayo Devon 6 E3
Nosterfield N Yorks 101 F7
Nostie Highld 149 F13
Notgrove Glos 37 B8
Nottage Bridgend 21 B7
Nottingham Nottingham 77 F5
Nottington Dorset 12 F4
Notton W Yorks 88 C4
Notton Wilts 24 C4
Nounsley Essex 42 C3
Noutard's Green Worcs 50 C2
Novar House Highld 151 E9
Nox Shrops 60 C4
Nuffield Oxon 39 F6
Nun Hills Lancs 87 B6
Nun Monkton N Yorks 95 D8
Nunburnholme E Yorks 96 E4
Nuncargate Notts 76 D5
Nuneaton Warks 63 E7
Nuneham Courtenay Oxon 39 E5
Nunney Som 24 E2
Nunnington N Yorks 96 B2
Nunnykirk Northumb 117 E6
Nunsthorpe NE Lincs 91 D6
Nunthorpe Mbro 102 C3
Nunthorpe York 96 D2
Nunton Wilts 14 B2
Nunwick N Yorks 95 B6
Nupend Glos 36 D4
Nursling Hants 14 C4
Nursted Hants 15 B8
Nutbourne W Sus 15 D8
Nutbourne W Sus 16 C4
Nutfield Sur 28 D4
Nuthall Notts 76 E5
Nuthampstead Herts 54 F5
Nuthurst W Sus 17 B5
Nutley E Sus 17 B8
Nutley Hants 26 E4
Nutwell S Yorks 89 D7
Nybster Highld 158 D5
Nyetimber W Sus 16 E2
Nyewood W Sus 16 B2
Nymet Rowland Devon 10 D2
Nymet Tracey Devon 10 D2
Nympsfield Glos 37 D5
Nynehead Som 11 B6
Nyton W Sus 16 D3

O

Oad Street Kent 30 C2
Oadby Leics 64 D3
Oak Cross Devon 9 E7
Oakamoor Staffs 75 E7
Oakbank W Loth 120 C3
Oakdale Caerph 35 E5
Oake Som 11 B6
Oaken Staffs 62 D2
Oakenclough Lancs 92 E5
Oakengates Telford 61 C7
Oakenholt Flint 73 B6
Oakenshaw Durham 110 F5
Oakenshaw W Yorks 88 B2
Oakerthorpe Derbys 76 D3
Oakes W Yorks 88 C2
Oakfield Torf 35 E7
Oakford Ceredig 46 D3
Oakford Devon 10 B4
Oakfordbridge Devon 10 B4
Oakgrove Ches E 75 C6
Oakham Rutland 65 D5
Oakhanger Hants 27 F5
Oakhill Som 23 E8
Oakhurst Kent 29 D6
Oakington Cambs 54 C5
Oaklands Herts 41 C5
Oaklands Powys 48 D2
Oakle Street Glos 36 C4
Oakley Bedford 53 D8
Oakley Bucks 39 C6
Oakley Fife 128 F2
Oakley Hants 26 D3
Oakley Oxon 39 D7
Oakley Poole 13 E8
Oakley Suff 57 B5
Oakley Green Windsor 27 B7
Oakley Park Powys 59 F6
Oakmere Ches W 74 C2
Oakridge Glos 37 D6
Oakridge Hants 26 D4
Oaks Shrops 60 D4
Oaks Green Derbys 75 F8
Oaksey Wilts 37 E6
Oakthorpe Leics 63 C7
Oakwoodhill Sur 28 F2
Oakworth W Yorks 94 F3
Oape Highld 156 J7
Oare Kent 30 C4
Oare Som 21 E7
Oare W Berks 26 B3
Oare Wilts 25 C6
Oasby Lincs 78 F3
Oathlaw Angus 134 D4
Oatlands N Yorks 95 D6
Oban Argyll 124 C4
Oban Highld 147 C11
Oborne Dorset 12 C4
Obthorpe Lincs 65 C7
Occlestone Green Ches W 74 C3
Occold Suff 57 B5
Ochiltree E Ayrs 112 B5
Ochtermuthill Perth 127 C7
Ochtertyre Perth 127 B7
Ockbrook Derbys 76 F4
Ockham Sur 27 D8
Ockle Highld 147 D8
Ockley Sur 28 F2
Ocle Pychard Hereford 49 E7
Octon E Yorks 97 C6
Octon Cross Roads E Yorks 97 C6
Odcombe Som 12 C3
Odd Down Bath 24 C2
Oddendale Cumb 99 C7
Odder Lincs 78 B2
Oddingley Worcs 50 D4
Oddington Glos 38 B2
Oddington Oxon 39 C5
Odell Bedford 53 D7
Odie Orkney 159 F7
Odiham Hants 26 D5
Odstock Wilts 14 B2
Odstone Leics 63 D7
Offchurch Warks 51 C8
Offenham Worcs 51 E5
Offham E Sus 17 C7
Offham Kent 29 D7
Offham W Sus 16 D4
Offord Cluny Cambs 54 C3
Offord Darcy Cambs 54 C3
Offton Suff 56 E4
Offwell Devon 11 E6
Ogbourne Maizey Wilts 25 B6
Ogbourne St Andrew Wilts 25 B6
Ogbourne St George Wilts 25 B7
Ogil Angus 134 C4
Ogle Northumb 110 B4
Ogmore V Glam 21 B7
Ogmore-by-Sea V Glam 21 B7
Ogmore Vale Bridgend 34 E3
Okeford Fitzpaine Dorset 13 C6
Okehampton Devon 9 E7
Okehampton Camp Devon 9 E7
Okraquoy Shetland 160 K6
Old Northants 53 B5
Old Aberdeen Aberdeen 141 D8
Old Alresford Hants 26 F3
Old Arley Warks 63 E6
Old Basford Nottingham 76 E5
Old Basing Hants 26 D4
Old Bewick Northumb 117 B6
Old Bolingbroke Lincs 79 C6
Old Bramhope W Yorks 94 E5
Old Brampton Derbys 76 B3
Old Bridge of Tilt Perth 133 C5
Old Bridge of Urr Dumfries 106 C4
Old Buckenham Norf 68 E3
Old Burghclere Hants 26 D2
Old Byland N Yorks 102 F3
Old Cassop Durham 111 F6
Old Castleton Borders 115 E8
Old Catton Norf 68 C5
Old Clee NE Lincs 91 D6
Old Cleeve Som 22 E2
Old Clipstone Notts 77 C6
Old Colwyn Conwy 83 D8
Old Coulsdon London 28 D4
Old Crombie Aberds 152 C5
Old Dailly S Ayrs 112 E2
Old Dalby Leics 64 B3
Old Deer Aberds 153 D9
Old Denaby S Yorks 89 E5
Old Edlington S Yorks 89 E6
Old Eldon Durham 101 B7
Old Ellerby E Yorks 97 F7
Old Felixstowe Suff 57 F7
Old Fletton Pboro 65 E8
Old Glossop Derbys 87 E8
Old Goole E Yorks 89 B8
Old Hall Powys 59 F6
Old Heath Essex 43 B6
Old Heathfield E Sus 18 C2
Old Hill W Mid 62 F3
Old Hunstanton Norf 80 C2
Old Hurst Cambs 54 B3
Old Hutton Cumb 99 F7
Old Kea Corn 3 B7
Old Kilpatrick W Dunb 118 B4
Old Kinnernie Aberds 141 D6
Old Knebworth Herts 41 B5
Old Langho Lancs 93 F7
Old Laxey IoM 84 D4
Old Leake Lincs 79 D7
Old Malton N Yorks 96 B3
Old Micklefield W Yorks 95 F7
Old Milton Hants 14 E3
Old Milverton Warks 51 C7
Old Monkland N Lanark 119 C7
Old Netley Hants 15 D5
Old Philpstoun W Loth 120 B3
Old Quarrington Durham 111 F6
Old Radnor Powys 48 D4
Old Rattray Aberds 153 C10
Old Rayne Aberds 141 B5
Old Romney Kent 19 C7
Old Sodbury S Glos 36 F4
Old Somerby Lincs 78 F2
Old Stratford Northants 53 E5
Old Thirsk N Yorks 102 F2
Old Town Cumb 99 F7
Old Town Cumb 108 E4
Old Town Northumb 116 E4
Old Town Scilly 2 E4
Old Trafford Gtr Man 87 E6
Old Tupton Derbys 76 C3
Old Warden C Beds 54 E2
Old Weston Cambs 53 B8
Old Whittington Derbys 76 B3
Old Wick Highld 158 E5
Old Windsor Windsor 27 B7
Old Wives Lees Kent 30 D4
Old Woking Sur 27 D8
Old Woodhall Lincs 78 C5
Oldany Highld 156 F4
Oldberrow Warks 51 C6
Oldborough Devon 10 D2
Oldbury Shrops 61 E7
Oldbury W Mid 62 F3
Oldbury Warks 63 E7
Oldbury-on-Severn S Glos 36 E3
Oldbury on the Hill Glos 37 F5
Oldcastle Bridgend 21 B8
Oldcastle Mon 35 B7
Oldcotes Notts 89 F6
Oldfallow Staffs 62 C3
Oldfield Worcs 50 C3
Oldford Som 24 D2
Oldham Gtr Man 87 D7
Oldhamstocks E Loth 122 B3
Oldland S Glos 23 B8
Oldmeldrum Aberds 141 B7
Oldshore Beg Highld 156 D4
Oldshoremore Highld 156 D5
Oldstead N Yorks 102 F3
Oldtown Aberds 140 B4
Oldtown of Ord Aberds 152 C6
Oldway Swansea 33 F6
Oldways End Devon 10 B3
Oldwhat Aberds 153 C8
Olgrinmore Highld 158 E2
Oliver's Battery Hants 15 B5
Ollaberry Shetland 160 E5
Ollerton Ches E 74 B4
Ollerton Notts 77 C6
Ollerton Shrops 61 B6
Olmarch Ceredig 46 D5
Olney M Keynes 53 D6
Olrig Ho. Highld 158 D3
Olton W Mid 62 F5
Olveston S Glos 36 F3
Olwen Ceredig 46 E4
Ombersley Worcs 50 C3
Ompton Notts 77 C6
Onchan IoM 84 E3
Onecote Staffs 75 D7
Onen Mon 35 C8
Ongar Hill Norf 67 B5
Ongar Street Hereford 49 C5
Onibury Shrops 49 B6
Onich Highld 130 C4
Onllwyn Neath 34 C2
Onneley Staffs 74 E4
Onslow Village Sur 27 E7
Onthank E Ayrs 118 E4
Openwoodgate Derbys 76 E3
Opinan Highld 149 A12
Opinan Highld 155 H13
Orange Lane Borders 122 E3
Orange Row Norf 66 B5
Orasaigh W Isles 155 F8
Orbliston Moray 152 C3
Orbost Highld 148 D7
Orby Lincs 79 C7
Orchard Hill Devon 9 B6
Orchard Portman Som 11 B7
Orcheston Wilts 25 E5
Orcop Hereford 36 B1
Orcop Hill Hereford 36 B1
Ord Highld 149 G11
Ordhead Aberds 141 C5
Ordie Aberds 140 D3
Ordiequish Moray 152 C3
Ordsall Notts 89 F7
Ore E Sus 18 D5
Oreton Shrops 61 F6
Orford Suff 57 E8
Orford Warr 86 E4
Orgreave Staffs 63 C5
Orlestone Kent 19 B6
Orleton Hereford 49 C6
Orleton Worcs 49 C8
Orlingbury Northants 53 B6
Ormesby Redcar 102 C3
Ormesby St Margaret Norf 69 C7
Ormesby St Michael Norf 69 C7
Ormiclate Castle W Isles 148 E2
Ormiscaig Highld 155 H13
Ormiston E Loth 121 C7
Ormsaigbeg Highld 146 E7
Ormsaigmore Highld 146 E7
Ormsary Argyll 144 F6
Ormsgill Cumb 92 B1
Ormskirk Lancs 86 D2
Orpington London 29 C5
Orrell Gtr Man 86 D3
Orrell Mers 85 E4
Orrisdale IoM 84 C3
Orroland Dumfries 106 E4
Orsett Thurrock 42 F2
Orslow Staffs 62 C2
Orston Notts 77 E7
Orthwaite Cumb 108 F2
Ortner Lancs 92 D5
Orton Cumb 99 D8
Orton Northants 53 B6
Orton Longueville Pboro 65 E8
Orton-on-the-Hill Leics 63 D7
Orton Waterville Pboro 65 E8
Orwell Cambs 54 D4
Osbaldeston Lancs 93 F6
Osbaldwick York 96 D2
Osbaston Shrops 60 B3
Osbournby Lincs 78 F3
Oscroft Ches W 74 C2
Ose Highld 149 D8
Osgathorpe Leics 63 C8
Osgodby Lincs 90 E4
Osgodby N Yorks 96 F2
Osgodby N Yorks 103 F8
Oskaig Highld 149 E10
Oskamull Argyll 146 G7
Osmaston Derby 76 F3
Osmaston Derbys 76 E2
Osmington Dorset 12 F5
Osmington Mills Dorset 12 F5
Osmotherley N Yorks 102 E2
Ospisdale Highld 151 C10
Ospringe Kent 30 C4
Ossett W Yorks 88 B3
Ossington Notts 77 C7
Ostend Essex 43 E5
Oswaldkirk N Yorks 96 B2
Oswaldtwistle Lancs 86 B5
Oswestry Shrops 60 B2
Otford Kent 29 D6
Otham Kent 29 D8
Othery Som 23 F5
Otley Suff 57 D6
Otley W Yorks 94 E5
Otter Ferry Argyll 145 E8
Otterbourne Hants 15 B5
Otterburn N Yorks 93 D8
Otterburn Northumb 116 E4
Otterburn Camp Northumb 116 E4
Otterham Corn 8 E3
Otterhampton Som 22 E4
Ottershaw Sur 27 C8
Otterswick Shetland 160 E7
Otterton Devon 11 F5
Ottery St Mary Devon 11 E6
Ottinge Kent 31 E5
Ottringham E Yorks 91 B6
Oughterby Cumb 108 D2
Oughtershaw N Yorks 100 F3
Oughterside Cumb 107 E8
Oughtibridge S Yorks 88 E4
Oughtrington Warr 86 F4
Oulston N Yorks 95 B8
Oulton Cumb 108 D2
Oulton Norf 81 E7
Oulton Staffs 75 F6
Oulton Suff 69 E8
Oulton W Yorks 88 B4
Oulton Broad Suff 69 E8
Oulton Street Norf 81 E7
Oundle Northants 65 F7
Ousby Cumb 109 F6
Ousdale Highld 158 H2
Ousden Suff 55 D8
Ousefleet E Yorks 90 B2
Ouston Durham 111 D5
Ouston Northumb 110 B3
Out Newton E Yorks 91 B7
Out Rawcliffe Lancs 92 E4
Outertown Orkney 159 G3
Outgate Cumb 99 E5
Outhgill Cumb 100 D2
Outlane W Yorks 87 C8
Outwell Norf 66 D5
Outwick Hants 14 C2
Outwood Sur 28 E4
Outwood W Yorks 88 B4
Outwoods Staffs 61 C7
Ovenden W Yorks 87 B8
Ovenscloss Borders 121 F7
Over Cambs 54 B4
Over Ches W 74 C3
Over S Glos 36 F2
Over Compton Dorset 12 C3
Over Green W Mid 63 E5
Over Haddon Derbys 76 C2
Over Hulton Gtr Man 86 D4
Over Kellet Lancs 92 B5
Over Kiddington Oxon 38 B4
Over Knutsford Ches E 74 B4
Over Monnow Mon 36 C2
Over Norton Oxon 38 B3
Over Peover Ches E 74 B4
Over Silton N Yorks 102 E2
Over Stowey Som 22 F3
Over Stratton Som 12 C2
Over Tabley Ches E 86 F5
Over Wallop Hants 25 F7
Over Whitacre Warks 63 E6
Over Worton Oxon 38 B4
Overbister Orkney 159 D7
Overbury Worcs 50 F4
Overcombe Dorset 12 F4
Overgreen Derbys 76 B3
Overleigh Som 23 F6
Overley Green Warks 51 D5
Overpool Ches W 73 B7
Overscaig Hotel Highld 156 G7
Overseal Derbys 63 C6
Oversland Kent 30 D4
Overstone Northants 53 C6
Overstrand Norf 81 C8
Overthorpe Northants 52 E2
Overton Aberdeen 141 C7
Overton Ches W 74 B2
Overton Dumfries 107 C6
Overton Hants 26 E3
Overton Lancs 92 D4
Overton N Yorks 95 D8
Overton Shrops 49 B7
Overton Swansea 33 F5
Overton W Yorks 88 C3
Overton = Owrtyn Wrex 73 E7
Overton Bridge Wrex 73 E7
Overtown N Lanark 119 D8
Oving Bucks 39 B7
Oving W Sus 16 D3
Ovingdean Brighton 17 D7
Ovingham Northumb 110 C3
Ovington Durham 101 C6
Ovington Essex 55 E8
Ovington Hants 26 F3
Ovington Norf 68 D2
Ovington Northumb 110 C3
Ower Hants 14 C4
Owermoigne Dorset 13 F5
Owlbury Shrops 60 E3
Owler Bar Derbys 76 B2
Owlerton S Yorks 88 F4
Owl's Green Suff 57 C6
Owlswick Bucks 39 D7
Owmby Lincs 90 D4
Owmby-by-Spital Lincs 90 F4
Owrtyn = Overton Wrex 73 E7
Owslebury Hants 15 B6
Owston Leics 64 D4
Owston S Yorks 89 C6
Owston Ferry N Lincs 90 D2
Owstwick E Yorks 97 F8
Owthorne E Yorks 91 B7
Owthorpe Notts 77 F6
Oxborough Norf 67 D7
Oxcombe Lincs 79 B6
Oxen Park Cumb 99 F5
Oxenholme Cumb 99 F7
Oxenhope W Yorks 94 F3
Oxenton Glos 50 F4
Oxenwood Wilts 25 D8
Oxford Oxon 39 D5
Oxhey Herts 40 E4
Oxhill Warks 51 E8
Oxley W Mid 62 D3
Oxley Green Essex 43 C5
Oxley's Green E Sus 18 C3
Oxnam Borders 116 C2
Oxshott Sur 28 C2
Oxspring S Yorks 88 D3
Oxted Sur 28 D4
Oxton Borders 121 D7
Oxton Notts 77 D6
Oxwich Swansea 33 F5
Oxwick Norf 80 E5
Oykel Bridge Highld 156 J6
Oyne Aberds 141 B5

P

Pabail Iarach W Isles 155 D10
Pabail Uarach W Isles 155 D10
Pace Gate N Yorks 94 D4
Packington Leics 63 C7
Padanaram Angus 134 D4
Padbury Bucks 52 F5
Paddington London 41 F5
Paddlesworth Kent 19 B8
Paddock Wood Kent 29 E7
Paddockhaugh Moray 152 C2
Paddockhole Dumfries 115 F5
Padfield Derbys 87 E8
Padiham Lancs 93 F7
Padog Conwy 83 F8
Padside N Yorks 94 D4
Padstow Corn 4 B4
Padworth W Berks 26 C4
Page Bank Durham 110 F5
Pagham W Sus 16 E2
Paglesham Churchend Essex 43 E5
Paglesham Eastend Essex 43 E5
Paibeil W Isles 148 B2
Paible W Isles 154 H5
Paignton Torbay 7 C6
Pailton Warks 63 F8
Painscastle Powys 48 E3
Painshawfield Northumb 110 C3
Painsthorpe E Yorks 96 D4
Painswick Glos 37 D5
Pairc Shiaboist W Isles 154 C7
Paisley Renfs 118 C4
Pakefield Suff 69 E8
Pakenham Suff 56 C3
Pale Gwyn 72 F3
Palestine Hants 25 E7
Paley Street Windsor 27 B6
Palfrey W Mid 62 E4
Palgowan Dumfries 112 F3
Palgrave Suff 56 B5
Pallion T&W 111 D6
Palmarsh Kent 19 B8
Palnackie Dumfries 106 D5
Palnure Dumfries 105 C8
Palterton Derbys 76 C4
Pamber End Hants 26 D4
Pamber Green Hants 26 D4
Pamber Heath Hants 26 C4
Pamphill Dorset 13 D7
Pampisford Cambs 55 E5
Pan Orkney 159 J4
Panbride Angus 135 F5
Pancrasweek Devon 8 D4
Pandy Gwyn 58 D3
Pandy Mon 35 B7
Pandy Powys 59 D6
Pandy Wrex 73 F5
Pandy Tudur Conwy 83 E8
Panfield Essex 42 B3
Pangbourne W Berks 26 B4
Pannal N Yorks 95 D6
Panshanger Herts 41 C5
Pant Shrops 60 B2
Pant-glâs Powys 58 E4
Pant-glas Carms 33 B6
Pant-glas Gwyn 71 C5
Pant-glas Shrops 73 F6
Pant-lasau Swansea 33 E7
Pant Mawr Powys 59 F5
Pant-teg Carms 33 B5
Pant-y-Caws Carms 32 B2
Pant-y-dwr Powys 47 B8
Pant-y-ffridd Powys 59 D8
Pant-y-Wacco Flint 72 B5
Pant-yr-awel Bridgend 34 F3
Pantgwyn Carms 33 B6
Pantgwyn Ceredig 45 E4
Panton Lincs 78 B4
Pantperthog Gwyn 58 D4
Pantyffynnon Carms 33 C7
Pantymwyn Flint 73 C5
Panxworth Norf 69 C6
Papcastle Cumb 107 F8
Papigoe Highld 158 E5
Papil Shetland 160 K5
Papley Orkney 159 J5
Papple E Loth 121 B8
Papplewick Notts 76 D5
Papworth Everard Cambs 54 C3
Papworth St Agnes Cambs 54 C3
Par Corn 5 D5
Parbold Lancs 86 C2
Parbrook Som 23 F7
Parbrook W Sus 16 B4
Parc Gwyn 72 F2
Parc-Seymour Newport 35 E8
Parc-y-rhôs Carms 46 E4
Parcllyn Ceredig 45 D4
Pardshaw Cumb 98 B2
Parham Suff 57 C7
Park Dumfries 114 E2
Park Corner Oxon 39 F6
Park Corner Windsor 40 F1
Park End Mbro 102 C3
Park End Northumb 109 B8
Park Gate Hants 15 D6
Park Hill N Yorks 95 C6
Park Hill Notts 77 D6
Park Street W Sus 28 F2
Parkend Glos 36 D3
Parkeston Essex 57 F6
Parkgate Ches W 73 B6
Parkgate Dumfries 114 F3
Parkgate Kent 19 B5
Parkgate Sur 28 E3
Parkham Devon 9 B5
Parkham Ash Devon 9 B5
Parkhill Ho. Aberds 141 C7
Parkhouse Mon 36 D1
Parkhouse Green Derbys 76 C4
Parkhurst IoW 15 E5
Parkmill Swansea 33 F6
Parkneuk Aberds 135 B7
Parkstone Poole 13 E8
Parley Cross Dorset 13 E8
Parracombe Devon 21 E5
Parrog Pembs 45 F2
Parsley Hay Derbys 75 C8
Parson Cross S Yorks 88 E4
Parson Drove Cambs 66 D3
Parsonage Green Essex 42 D3
Parsonby Cumb 107 F8
Parson's Heath Essex 43 B6
Partick Glasgow 119 C5
Partington Gtr Man 86 E5
Partney Lincs 79 C7
Parton Cumb 98 B1
Parton Dumfries 106 B3
Parton Glos 37 B5
Partridge Green W Sus 17 C5
Parwich Derbys 75 D8
Passenham Northants 53 F5
Paston Norf 81 D9
Patchacott Devon 9 E6
Patcham Brighton 17 D7
Patching W Sus 16 D4
Patchole Devon 20 E5
Pateley Bridge N Yorks 94 C4
Paternoster Heath Essex 43 C5
Path of Condie Perth 128 C2
Pathe Som 23 F5
Pathhead Aberds 135 C7
Pathhead E Ayrs 113 C6
Pathhead Fife 128 E4
Pathhead Midloth 121 C6
Pathstruie Perth 128 C2
Patna E Ayrs 112 C4
Patney Wilts 25 D5
Patrick IoM 84 D2
Patrick Brompton N Yorks 101 E7
Patrington E Yorks 91 B7
Patrixbourne Kent 31 D5
Patterdale Cumb 99 C5
Pattingham Staffs 62 E2
Pattishall Northants 52 D4
Pattiswick Green Essex 42 B4
Patton Bridge Cumb 99 E7
Paul Corn 2 D3
Paulerspury Northants 52 E5
Paull E Yorks 91 B5
Paulton Bath 23 D8
Pavenham Bedford 53 D7
Pawlett Som 22 E5
Pawston Northumb 122 F4
Paxford Glos 51 F6
Paxton Borders 122 D5
Payhembury Devon 11 D5
Paythorne Lancs 93 D8
Peacehaven E Sus 17 D8
Peak Dale Derbys 75 B7
Peak Forest Derbys 75 B8
Peakirk Pboro 65 D8
Pearsie Angus 134 D3
Pease Pottage W Sus 28 F3
Peasedown St John Bath 24 D2
Peasemore W Berks 26 B2
Peasenhall Suff 57 C7
Peaslake Sur 27 E8
Peasley Cross Mers 86 E3
Peasmarsh E Sus 19 C5
Peaston E Loth 121 C7
Peastonbank E Loth 121 C7
Peat Inn Fife 129 D6
Peathill Aberds 153 B9
Peatling Magna Leics 64 E2
Peatling Parva Leics 64 F2
Peaton Shrops 60 F5
Peats Corner Suff 57 C5
Pebmarsh Essex 56 F2
Pebworth Worcs 51 E6
Pecket Well W Yorks 87 B7
Peckforton Ches E 74 D2
Peckham London 28 B4
Peckleton Leics 63 D8
Pedlinge Kent 19 B8
Pedmore W Mid 62 F3
Pedwell Som 23 F6
Peebles Borders 121 E5
Peel IoM 84 D2
Peel Common Hants 15 D6
Peel Park S Lanark 119 D6
Peening Quarter Kent 19 C5
Pegsdon C Beds 54 F2
Pegswood Northumb 117 F8
Pegwell Kent 31 C7
Peinchorran Highld 149 E10
Peinlich Highld 149 C9
Pelaw T&W 111 C5
Pelcomb Bridge Pembs 44 D4
Pelcomb Cross Pembs 44 D4
Peldon Essex 43 C5
Pellon W Yorks 87 B8
Pelsall W Mid 62 D4
Pelton Durham 111 D5
Pelutho Cumb 107 E8
Pelynt Corn 5 D7
Pemberton Gtr Man 86 D3
Pembrey Carms 33 D5
Pembridge Hereford 49 D5
Pembroke = Penfro Pembs 44 E4
Pembroke Dock = Doc Penfro Pembs 44 E4
Pembury Kent 29 E7
Pen-bont Rhydybeddau Ceredig 58 F3
Pen-clawdd Swansea 33 E6
Pen-ffordd Pembs 32 B1
Pen-groes-oped Mon 35 D7
Pen-llyn Anglesey 82 C3
Pen-lon Anglesey 82 E4
Pen-sarn Gwyn 70 C5
Pen-sarn Gwyn 71 E6
Pen-twyn Mon 36 D2
Pen-y-banc Carms 33 B7
Pen-y-bont Carms 32 B4
Pen-y-bont Gwyn 58 D4
Pen-y-bont Gwyn 71 E7
Pen-y-bont Powys 60 B2
Pen-Y-Bont Ar Ogwr = Bridgend Bridgend 21 B8
Pen-y-bryn Gwyn 58 C3
Pen-y-bryn Pembs 45 E3
Pen-y-cae Powys 34 C2
Pen-y-cae-mawr Mon 35 E8
Pen-y-cefn Flint 72 B5
Pen-y-clawdd Mon 36 D1
Pen-y-coedcae Rhondda 34 F4
Pen-y-fai Bridgend 34 F2
Pen-y-garn Carms 46 F4
Pen-y-garn Ceredig 58 F3
Pen-y-garnedd Anglesey 82 D5
Pen-y-gop Conwy 72 E3
Pen-y-graig Gwyn 70 D2
Pen-y-groes Carms 33 C6
Pen-y-groeslon Gwyn 70 D3
Pen-y-Gwryd Hotel Gwyn 83 F6
Pen-y-stryt Denb 73 D5
Pen-yr-heol Mon 35 C8
Pen-yr-Heolgerrig M Tydf 34 D4
Penallt Mon 36 C2
Penally Pembs 32 E2
Penalt Hereford 36 B2
Penare Corn 3 B8
Penarlâg = Hawarden Flint 73 C7
Penarth V Glam 22 B3
Penbryn Ceredig 45 D4
Pencader Carms 46 F3
Pencaenewydd Gwyn 70 C5
Pencaitland E Loth 121 C7
Pencarnisiog Anglesey 82 D3
Pencarreg Carms 46 E4
Pencelli Powys 34 B4
Pencoed Bridgend 34 F3
Pencombe Hereford 49 D7
Pencoyd Hereford 36 B2
Pencraig Hereford 36 B2
Pencraig Powys 59 B7
Pendeen Corn 2 C2
Penderyn Rhondda 34 D3
Pendine Carms 32 D3
Pendlebury Gtr Man 87 D5
Pendleton Lancs 93 F7
Pendock Worcs 50 F2
Pendoggett Corn 4 B5
Pendomer Som 12 C3
Pendoylan V Glam 22 B2
Pendre Bridgend 34 F3
Penegoes Powys 58 D4
Penfro = Pembroke Pembs 44 E4
Pengam Caerph 35 E5
Penge London 28 B4
Pengenffordd Powys 48 F3
Pengorffwysfa Anglesey 82 B4
Pengover Green Corn 5 C7
Penhale Corn 3 E5
Penhale Corn 4 D4
Penhalvaen Corn 3 C6
Penhill Swindon 38 F1
Penhow Newport 35 E8
Penhurst E Sus 18 D3
Peniarth Gwyn 58 D3
Penicuik Midloth 120 C5
Peniel Carms 33 B5
Peniel Denb 72 C4
Penifiler Highld 149 D9
Peninver Argyll 143 F8
Penisarwaun Gwyn 83 E5
Penistone S Yorks 88 D3
Penjerrick Corn 3 C6
Penketh Warr 86 F3
Penkill S Ayrs 112 E2
Penkridge Staffs 62 C3
Penley Wrex 73 F8
Penllergaer Swansea 33 E7
Penllyn V Glam 21 B8
Penmachno Conwy 83 F7
Penmaen Swansea 33 F6
Penmaenan Conwy 83 D7
Penmaenmawr Conwy 83 D7
Penmaenpool Gwyn 58 C3
Penmark V Glam 22 C2
Penmarth Corn 3 C6
Penmon Anglesey 83 C6
Penmore Mill Argyll 146 F7
Penmorfa Ceredig 46 D2
Penmorfa Gwyn 71 C6
Penmynydd Anglesey 82 D5
Penn Bucks 40 E2
Penn W Mid 62 E2
Penn Street Bucks 40 E2
Pennal Gwyn 58 D4
Pennan Aberds 153 B8
Pennant Ceredig 46 C4
Pennant Denb 72 D4
Pennant Denb 72 F4
Pennant Powys 59 E5
Pennant Melangell Powys 59 B7
Pennar Pembs 44 E4
Pennard Swansea 33 F6
Pennerley Shrops 60 E3
Pennington Cumb 92 B2
Pennington Gtr Man 86 E4
Pennington Hants 14 E4
Penny Bridge Cumb 99 F5
Pennycross Argyll 147 J8
Pennygate Norf 69 B6
Pennygown Argyll 147 G8
Pennymoor Devon 10 C3
Pennywell T&W 111 D6
Penparc Ceredig 45 E4
Penparc Pembs 44 B3
Penparcau Ceredig 58 F2
Penperlleni Mon 35 D7
Penpillick Corn 5 D5
Penpol Corn 3 C7
Penpoll Corn 5 D6
Penpont Dumfries 113 E8
Penpont Powys 34 B3
Penrhôs Mon 35 C8
Penrherber Carms 45 F4
Penrhiw goch Carms 33 C6
Penrhiw-llan Ceredig 46 E2
Penrhiw-pâl Ceredig 46 E2
Penrhiwceiber Rhondda 34 E4
Penrhos Gwyn 70 D4
Penrhos Powys 34 C1
Penrhosfeilw Anglesey 82 C2
Penrhyn Bay Conwy 83 C8
Penrhyn-coch Ceredig 58 F3
Penrhyndeudraeth Gwyn 71 D7
Penrhynside Conwy 83 C8
Penrice Swansea 33 F5
Penrith Cumb 108 F5
Penrose Corn 4 B3
Penruddock Cumb 99 B6
Penryn Corn 3 C6
Pensarn Carms 33 C5
Pensarn Conwy 72 B3
Pensax Worcs 50 C2
Pensby Mers 85 F3
Penselwood Som 24 F2
Pensford Bath 23 C8
Penshaw T&W 111 D6
Penshurst Kent 29 E6
Pensilva Corn 5 C7
Penston E Loth 121 B7
Pentewan Corn 3 B9
Pentir Gwyn 83 E5
Pentire Corn 4 C2
Pentlow Essex 56 E2
Pentney Norf 67 C7
Penton Mewsey Hants 25 E8
Pentraeth Anglesey 82 D5
Pentre Carms 33 C6
Pentre Powys 59 F7
Pentre Powys 60 E2
Pentre Rhondda 34 E3
Pentre Shrops 60 C3
Pentre Wrex 72 F5
Pentre Wrex 73 E6
Pentre-bâch Ceredig 46 E4
Pentre-bach Powys 47 F8
Pentre Berw Anglesey 82 D4
Pentre-bont Conwy 83 F7
Pentre-celyn Denb 72 D5
Pentre-Celyn Powys 59 D5
Pentre-chwyth Swansea 33 E7
Pentre-cwrt Carms 46 F2
Pentre Dolau-Honddu Powys 47 E8
Pentre-dwr Swansea 33 E7
Pentre-galar Pembs 45 F3
Pentre-Gwenlais Carms 33 C7
Pentre Gwynfryn Gwyn 71 E6
Pentre Halkyn Flint 73 B6
Pentre-Isaf Conwy 83 E8
Pentre Llanrhaeadr Denb 72 C4
Pentre-llwyn-llŵyd Powys 47 D8
Pentre-llyn Ceredig 46 B5
Pentre-llyn cymmer Conwy 72 D3
Pentre Meyrick V Glam 21 B8
Pentre-poeth Newport 35 F6
Pentre-rhew Ceredig 47 D5
Pentre-tafarn-y-fedw Conwy 83 E8
Pentre-ty-gwyn Carms 47 F7
Pentrebach M Tydf 34 D4
Pentrebach Swansea 33 D7
Pentrebeirdd Powys 59 C8
Pentrecagal Carms 46 E2
Pentredwr Denb 73 E5
Pentrefelin Carms 33 B6
Pentrefelin Ceredig 46 E5
Pentrefelin Conwy 83 D8
Pentrefelin Gwyn 71 D6
Pentrefoelas Conwy 83 F8
Pentregat Ceredig 46 D2
Pentreheyling Shrops 60 E2
Pentre'r Felin Conwy 83 E8
Pentre'r-felin Powys 47 F8
Pentrich Derbys 76 D3
Pentridge Dorset 13 C8
Pentyrch Cardiff 35 F5
Penuchadre V Glam 21 B7
Penuwch Ceredig 46 C4
Penwithick Corn 4 D5
Penwyllt Powys 34 C2
Penybanc Carms 33 C7
Penybont Powys 48 C3
Penybontfawr Powys 59 B7
Penycae Wrex 73 E6
Penycwm Pembs 44 C3
Penyffordd Flint 73 C7
Penyffridd Gwyn 82 F5
Penygarnedd Powys 59 B8
Penygraig Rhondda 34 E3
Penygroes Gwyn 82 F4
Penygroes Pembs 45 F3
Penyrheol Caerph 35 F5
Penysarn Anglesey 82 B4
Penywaun Rhondda 34 D3
Penzance Corn 2 C3
Peopleton Worcs 50 D4
Peover Heath Ches E 74 B4
Peper Harow Sur 27 E7
Perceton N Ayrs 118 E3
Percie Aberds 140 E4
Percyhorner Aberds 153 B9
Periton Som 21 E8
Perivale London 40 F4
Perkinsville Durham 111 D5
Perlethorpe Notts 77 B6
Perranarworthal Corn 3 C6
Perranporth Corn 4 D2
Perranuthnoe Corn 2 D4
Perranzabuloe Corn 4 D2
Perry Barr W Mid 62 E4
Perry Green Herts 41 C7
Perry Green Wilts 37 F6
Perry Street Kent 29 B7
Perryfoot Derbys 88 F2
Pershall Staffs 74 F5
Pershore Worcs 50 E4
Pert Angus 135 C6
Pertenhall Bedford 53 C8
Perth Perth 128 B3
Perthy Shrops 73 F7
Perton Staffs 62 E2
Pertwood Wilts 24 F3
Peter Tavy Devon 6 B3
Peterborough Pboro 65 E8
Peterburn Highld 155 J12
Peterchurch Hereford 48 F5
Peterculter Aberdeen 141 D7
Peterhead Aberds 153 D11
Peterlee Durham 111 E7
Peter's Green Herts 40 C4
Peters Marland Devon 9 C6
Petersfield Hants 15 B8
Peterston super-Ely V Glam 22 B2
Peterstone Wentlooge Newport 35 F6
Peterstow Hereford 36 B2
Petertown Orkney 159 H4
Petham Kent 30 D5
Petrockstow Devon 9 D7
Pett E Sus 19 D5
Pettaugh Suff 57 D5
Petteridge Kent 29 E7
Pettinain S Lanark 120 E2
Pettistree Suff 57 D6
Petton Devon 10 B5
Petton Shrops 60 B4
Petts Wood London 28 C5
Petty Aberds 153 E7
Pettycur Fife 128 F4
Pettymuick Aberds 141 B8
Petworth W Sus 16 B3
Pevensey E Sus 18 E3
Pevensey Bay E Sus 18 E3
Pewsey Wilts 25 C6
Philham Devon 8 B4
Philiphaugh Borders 115 B7
Phillack Corn 2 C4
Philleigh Corn 3 C7
Philpstoun W Loth 120 B3
Phocle Green Hereford 36 B3
Phoenix Green Hants 27 D5
Pica Cumb 98 B2
Piccotts End Herts 40 D3
Pickering N Yorks 103 F5
Picket Piece Hants 25 E8
Picket Post Hants 14 D2
Pickhill N Yorks 101 F8
Picklescott Shrops 60 E4
Pickletillem Fife 129 B6
Pickmere Ches E 74 B3
Pickney Som 11 B6
Pickstock Telford 61 B7
Pickwell Devon 20 E3
Pickwell Leics 64 C4
Pickworth Lincs 78 F3
Pickworth Rutland 65 C6
Picton Ches W 73 B8
Picton Flint 85 F2
Picton N Yorks 102 D2
Piddinghoe E Sus 17 D8
Piddington Northants 53 D6
Piddington Oxon 39 C6
Piddlehinton Dorset 12 E5
Piddletrenthide Dorset 12 E5
Pidley Cambs 54 B4
Piercebridge Darl 101 C7
Pierowall Orkney 159 D5
Pigdon Northumb 117 F7
Pikehall Derbys 75 D8
Pilgrims Hatch Essex 42 E1
Pilham Lincs 90 E2
Pill N Som 23 B7
Pillaton Corn 5 C8
Pillerton Hersey Warks 51 E8
Pillerton Priors Warks 51 E7
Pilleth Powys 48 C4
Pilley Hants 14 E4
Pilley S Yorks 88 D4
Pilling Lancs 92 E4
Pilling Lane Lancs 92 E3
Pillowell Glos 36 D3
Pillwell Dorset 13 C5
Pilning S Glos 36 F2
Pilsbury Derbys 75 C8
Pilsdon Dorset 12 E2
Pilsgate Pboro 65 D7
Pilsley Derbys 76 B2
Pilsley Derbys 76 C4
Pilton Devon 20 F4
Pilton Northants 65 F7
Pilton Rutland 65 D6
Pilton Som 23 E7
Pilton Green Swansea 33 F5
Pimperne Dorset 13 D7
Pin Mill Suff 57 F6
Pinchbeck Lincs 66 B2
Pinchbeck Bars Lincs 65 B8
Pinchbeck West Lincs 66 B2
Pincheon Green S Yorks 89 C7
Pinehurst Swindon 38 F1
Pinfold Lancs 85 C4
Pinged Carms 33 D5
Pinhoe Devon 10 E4
Pinkneys Green Windsor 40 F1
Pinley W Mid 51 B8
Pinminnoch S Ayrs 112 E1
Pinmore S Ayrs 112 E2
Pinmore Mains S Ayrs 112 E2
Pinner London 40 F4
Pinvin Worcs 50 E4
Pinwherry S Ayrs 112 F1
Pinxton Derbys 76 D4
Pipe and Lyde Hereford 49 E7
Pipe Gate Shrops 74 E4
Piperhill Highld 151 F11
Piper's Pool Corn 8 F4
Pipewell Northants 64 F5
Pippacott Devon 20 F4
Pipton Powys 48 F3
Pirbright Sur 27 D7
Pirnmill N Ayrs 143 D9
Pirton Herts 54 F2
Pirton Worcs 50 E3
Pisgah Ceredig 47 B5
Pisgah Stirling 127 D6
Pishill Oxon 39 F7
Pistyll Gwyn 70 C4
Pitagowan Perth 133 C5
Pitblae Aberds 153 B9
Pitcairngreen Perth 128 B2
Pitcalnie Highld 151 D11
Pitcaple Aberds 141 B6
Pitch Green Bucks 39 D7
Pitch Place Sur 27 D7
Pitchcombe Glos 37 D5
Pitchcott Bucks 39 B7
Pitchford Shrops 60 D5
Pitcombe Som 23 F8
Pitcorthie Fife 129 D7
Pitcox E Loth 122 B2
Pitcur Perth 134 F2
Pitfichie Aberds 141 C5
Pitforthie Aberds 135 B8
Pitgrudy Highld 151 B10
Pitkennedy Angus 135 D5
Pitkevy Fife 128 D4
Pitkierie Fife 129 D7
Pitlessie Fife 128 D5
Pitlochry Perth 133 D6
Pitmachie Aberds 141 B5
Pitmain Highld 138 D3
Pitmedden Aberds 141 B7
Pitminster Som 11 C7
Pitmuies Angus 135 E5
Pitmunie Aberds 141 C5
Pitney Som 12 B2
Pitscottie Fife 129 C6
Pitsea Essex 42 F3
Pitsford Northants 53 C5
Pitsmoor S Yorks 88 F4
Pitstone Bucks 40 C2
Pitstone Green Bucks 40 C2
Pittendreich Moray 152 B1
Pittentrail Highld 157 J10
Pittenweem Fife 129 D7
Pittington Durham 111 E6
Pittodrie Aberds 141 B5
Pitton Wilts 25 F7
Pittswood Kent 29 E7
Pittulie Aberds 153 B9
Pity Me Durham 111 E5
Pityme Corn 4 B4
Pityoulish Highld 138 C5
Pixey Green Suff 57 B6
Pixham Sur 28 D2
Pixley Hereford 49 F8
Place Newton N Yorks 96 B4
Plaidy Aberds 153 C7
Plains N Lanark 119 C7
Plaish Shrops 60 E5
Plaistow W Sus 27 F8
Plaitford Wilts 14 C3
Plank Lane Gtr Man 86 E4
Plas-canol Gwyn 58 C2
Plas Gogerddan Ceredig 58 F3
Plas Llwyngwern Powys 58 D4
Plas Nantyr Wrex 73 F5
Plas-yn-Cefn Denb 72 B4
Plastow Green Hants 26 C3
Platt Kent 29 D7
Platt Bridge Gtr Man 86 D4
Platts Common S Yorks 88 D4
Plawsworth Durham 111 E5
Plaxtol Kent 29 D7
Play Hatch Oxon 26 B5
Playden E Sus 19 C6
Playford Suff 57 E6
Playing Place Corn 3 B7
Playley Green Glos 50 F2
Plealey Shrops 60 D4
Plean Stirling 127 F7
Pleasington Blackburn 86 B4
Pleasley Derbys 76 C5
Pleckgate Blackburn 93 F6
Plenmeller Northumb 109 C7
Pleshey Essex 42 C2
Plockton Highld 149 E13
Plocrapol W Isles 154 H6
Ploughfield Hereford 49 E5
Plowden Shrops 60 F3
Ploxgreen Shrops 60 D3
Pluckley Kent 30 E3
Pluckley Thorne Kent 30 E3
Plumbland Cumb 107 F8
Plumley Ches E 74 B4
Plumpton Cumb 108 F4
Plumpton E Sus 17 C7
Plumpton Green E Sus 17 C7
Plumpton Head Cumb 108 F5
Plumstead London 29 B5
Plumstead Norf 81 D7
Plumtree Notts 77 F6
Plungar Leics 77 F7
Plush Dorset 12 D5
Plwmp Ceredig 46 D2
Plymouth Plym 6 D2
Plympton Plym 6 D3

Plymstock Plym 6 D3
Plymtree Devon 11 D5
Pockley N Yorks 102 F4
Pocklington E Yorks 96 E4
Pode Hole Lincs 66 B2
Podimore Som 12 B3
Podington Bedford 53 C7
Podmore Staffs 74 F4
Point Clear Essex 43 C6
Pointon Lincs 78 F4
Pokesdown Bmouth 14 E2
Pol a Charra W Isles 148 G2
Polbae Dumfries 105 B6
Polbain Highld 156 H2
Polbathic Corn 5 D8
Polbeth W Loth 120 C3
Polchar Highld 138 D4
Pole Elm Worcs 50 E3
Polebrook Northants 65 F7
Polegate E Sus 18 E2
Poles Highld 151 B10
Polesworth Warks 63 D6
Polgigga Corn 2 D2
Polglass Highld 156 J3
Polgooth Corn 4 D4
Poling W Sus 16 D4
Polkerris Corn 5 D5
Polla Highld 156 D6
Pollington E Yorks 89 C7
Polloch Highld 130 C1
Pollok Glasgow 118 C5
Pollokshields Glasgow 119 C5
Polmassick Corn 3 B8
Polmont Falk 120 B2
Polnessan E Ayrs 112 C4
Polnish Highld 147 C10
Polperro Corn 5 D7
Polruan Corn 5 D6
Polsham Som 23 E7
Polstead Suff 56 F3
Poltalloch Argyll 124 F4
Poltimore Devon 10 E4
Polton Midloth 121 C5
Polwarth Borders 122 D3
Polyphant Corn 8 F4
Polzeath Corn 4 B4
Ponders End London 41 E6
Pondersbridge Cambs 66 E2
Pondtail Hants 27 D6
Ponsanooth Corn 3 C6
Ponsworthy Devon 6 B5
Pont Aber Carms 33 B8
Pont Aber-Geirw Gwyn 71 E8
Pont-ar-gothi Carms 33 B6
Pont ar Hydfer Powys 34 B2
Pont-ar-llechau Carms 33 B8
Pont Cwm Pydew Denb 72 F4
Pont Cyfyng Conwy 83 F7
Pont Cysyllte Wrex 73 E6
Pont Dolydd Prysor Gwyn 71 D8
Pont-faen Powys 47 F8
Pont Fronwydd Gwyn 58 B5
Pont-gareg Pembs 45 E3
Pont-Henri Carms 33 D5
Pont-Llogel Powys 59 C7
Pont Pen-y-benglog Gwyn 83 E6
Pont Rhyd-goch Conwy 83 E6
Pont-Rhyd-sarn Gwyn 59 B5
Pont Rhyd-y-cyff Bridgend 34 F2
Pont-rhyd-y-groes Ceredig 47 B6
Pont-rug Gwyn 82 E5
Pont Senni = Sennybridge Powys 34 B3
Pont-siân Ceredig 46 E3
Pont-y-gwaith Rhondda 34 E4
Pont-Y-Pŵl = Pontypool Torf 35 D6
Pont-y-pant Conwy 83 F7
Pont y Pennant Gwyn 59 B6
Pont yr Afon-Gam Gwyn 71 C8
Pont-yr-hafod Pembs 44 C4
Pontamman Carms 33 C7
Pontantwn Carms 33 C5
Pontardawe Neath 33 D8
Pontarddulais Swansea 33 D6
Pontarsais Carms 33 B5
Pontblyddyn Flint 73 C6
Pontbren Araeth Carms 33 B7
Pontbren Llwyd Rhondda 34 D3
Pontefract W Yorks 89 B5
Ponteland Northumb 110 B4
Ponterwyd Ceredig 58 F4
Pontesbury Shrops 60 D3
Pontfadog Wrex 73 F6
Pontfaen Pembs 45 F2
Pontgarreg Ceredig 46 D2
Ponthir Torf 35 E7
Ponthirwaun Ceredig 45 E4
Pontllanfraith Caerph 35 E5
Pontlliw Swansea 33 D7
Pontllyfni Gwyn 82 F4
Pontlottyn Caerph 35 D5
Pontneddfechan Powys 34 D3
Pontnewydd Torf 35 E6
Pontrhydfendigaid Ceredig 47 C6
Pontrhydyfen Neath 34 E1
Pontrilas Hereford 35 B7
Pontrobert Powys 59 C8
Ponts Green E Sus 18 D3
Pontshill Hereford 36 B3
Pontsticill M Tydf 34 C4
Pontwgan Conwy 83 D7
Pontyates Carms 33 D5
Pontyberem Carms 33 C6
Pontyclun Rhondda 34 F4
Pontycymer Bridgend 34 E3
Pontyglasier Pembs 45 F3
Pontypool = Pont-Y-Pŵl Torf 35 D6
Pontypridd Rhondda 34 F4
Pontywaun Caerph 35 E6
Pooksgreen Hants 14 C4
Pool Corn 3 B5
Pool W Yorks 94 E5
Pool o'Muckhart Clack 128 D2
Pool Quay Powys 60 C2
Poole Poole 13 E8
Poole Keynes Glos 37 E6
Poolend Staffs 75 D6
Poolewe Highld 155 J13
Pooley Bridge Cumb 99 B6
Poolfold Staffs 75 D5
Poolhill Glos 36 B4
Poolsbrook Derbys 76 B4
Pootings Kent 29 E5
Pope Hill Pembs 44 D4
Popeswood Brack 27 C6
Popham Hants 26 E3
Poplar London 41 F6
Popley Hants 26 D4
Porchester Nottingham 77 E5
Porchfield IoW 14 E5
Porin Highld 150 F6
Poringland Norf 69 D5
Porkellis Corn 3 C5
Porlock Som 21 E7
Porlock Weir Som 21 E7
Port Ann Argyll 145 E8
Port Appin Argyll 130 E3
Port Arthur Shetland 160 K5
Port Askaig Argyll 142 B5
Port Bannatyne Argyll 145 G9
Port Carlisle Cumb 108 C2
Port Charlotte Argyll 142 C3
Port Clarence Stockton 102 B2
Port Driseach Argyll 145 F8
Port e Vullen IoM 84 C4
Port Ellen Argyll 142 D4
Port Elphinstone Aberds 141 C6
Port Erin IoM 84 F1
Port Erroll Aberds 153 E10
Port-Eynon Swansea 33 F5
Port Gaverne Corn 8 F2
Port Glasgow Invclyd 118 B3
Port Henderson Highld 149 A12
Port Isaac Corn 4 A4
Port Lamont Argyll 145 F9
Port Lion Pembs 44 E4
Port Logan Dumfries 104 E4
Port Mholair W Isles 155 D10
Port Mor Highld 146 D7
Port Mulgrave N Yorks 103 C5
Port Nan Giùran W Isles 155 D10
Port nan Long W Isles 148 A3
Port Nis W Isles 155 A10
Port of Menteith Stirling 126 D4
Port Quin Corn 4 A4
Port Ramsay Argyll 130 E2
Port St Mary IoM 84 F2
Port Sunlight Mers 85 F4
Port Talbot Neath 34 E1
Port Tennant Swansea 33 E7
Port Wemyss Argyll 142 C2
Port William Dumfries 105 E7
Portachoillan Argyll 144 H6
Portavadie Argyll 145 G8
Portbury N Som 23 B7
Portchester Hants 15 D7
Portclair Highld 137 C7
Portencalzie Dumfries 104 B4
Portencross N Ayrs 118 E1
Portesham Dorset 12 F4
Portessie Moray 152 B4
Portfield Gate Pembs 44 D4
Portgate Devon 9 F6
Portgordon Moray 152 B3
Portgower Highld 157 H13
Porth Corn 4 C3
Porth Rhondda 34 E4
Porth Navas Corn 3 D6
Porth Tywyn = Burry Port Carms 33 D5
Porth-y-waen Shrops 60 B2
Porthaethwy = Menai Bridge Anglesey 83 D5
Porthallow Corn 3 D6
Porthallow Corn 5 D7
Porthcawl Bridgend 21 B7
Porthcothan Corn 4 B3
Porthcurno Corn 2 D2
Porthgain Pembs 44 B3
Porthill Shrops 60 C4
Porthkerry V Glam 22 C2
Porthleven Corn 2 D5
Porthllechog Anglesey 82 B4
Porthmadog Gwyn 71 D6
Porthmeor Corn 2 C3
Portholland Corn 3 B8
Porthoustock Corn 3 D7
Porthpean Corn 4 D5
Porthtowan Corn 3 B5
Porthyrhyd Carms 33 C6
Porthyrhyd Carms 47 F6
Portincaple Argyll 145 D11
Portington E Yorks 96 F3
Portinnisherrich Argyll 125 D5
Portinscale Cumb 98 B4
Portishead N Som 23 B6
Portkil Argyll 145 E11
Portknockie Moray 152 B4
Portlethen Aberds 141 E8
Portling Dumfries 107 D5
Portloe Corn 3 C8
Portmahomack Highld 151 C12
Portmeirion Gwyn 71 D6
Portmellon Corn 3 B9
Portmore Hants 14 E4
Portnacroish Argyll 130 E3
Portnahaven Argyll 142 C2
Portnalong Highld 149 E8
Portnaluchaig Highld 147 C9
Portnancon Highld 156 C7
Portnellan Stirling 126 B3
Portobello Edin 121 B6
Porton Wilts 25 F6
Portpatrick Dumfries 104 D4
Portreath Corn 3 B5
Portree Highld 149 D9
Portscatho Corn 3 C7
Portsea Ptsmth 15 D7
Portskerra Highld 157 C11
Portskewett Mon 36 F2
Portslade Brighton 17 D6
Portslade-by-Sea Brighton 17 D6
Portsmouth Ptsmth 15 D7
Portsmouth W Yorks 87 B7
Portsonachan Argyll 125 C6
Portsoy Aberds 152 B5
Portswood Soton 14 C5
Porttanachy Moray 152 B3
Portuairk Highld 146 E7
Portway Hereford 49 F6
Portway Worcs 51 B5
Portwrinkle Corn 5 D8
Poslingford Suff 55 E8
Postbridge Devon 6 B4
Postcombe Oxon 39 E7
Postling Kent 19 B8
Postwick Norf 69 D5
Potholm Dumfries 115 F6
Potsgrove C Beds 40 B2
Pott Row Norf 80 E3
Pott Shrigley Ches E 75 B6
Potten End Herts 40 D3
Potter Brompton N Yorks 97 B5
Potter Heigham Norf 69 C7
Potter Street Essex 41 D7
Potterhanworth Lincs 78 C3
Potterhanworth Booths Lincs 78 C3
Potterne Wilts 24 D4
Potterne Wick Wilts 24 D5
Potternewton W Yorks 95 F6
Potters Bar Herts 41 D5
Potter's Cross Staffs 62 F2
Potterspury Northants 53 E5
Potterton Aberds 141 C8
Potterton W Yorks 95 F7
Potto N Yorks 102 D2
Potton C Beds 54 E3
Poughill Corn 8 D4
Poughill Devon 10 D3
Poulshot Wilts 24 D4
Poulton Glos 37 D8
Poulton Mers 85 E4
Poulton-le-Fylde Lancs 92 F3
Pound Bank Worcs 50 B2
Pound Green E Sus 18 C2
Pound Green IoW 14 F4
Pound Green Worcs 50 B2
Pound Hill W Sus 28 F3
Poundfield E Sus 18 B2
Poundland S Ayrs 112 F1
Poundon Bucks 39 B6
Poundsgate Devon 6 B5
Poundstock Corn 8 E4
Powburn Northumb 117 C6
Powderham Devon 10 F4
Powerstock Dorset 12 E3
Powfoot Dumfries 107 C8
Powick Worcs 50 D3
Powmill Perth 128 E2
Poxwell Dorset 12 F5
Poyle Slough 27 B8
Poynings W Sus 17 C6
Poyntington Dorset 12 C4
Poynton Ches E 87 F7
Poynton Green Telford 61 C5
Poystreet Green Suff 56 D3
Praa Sands Corn 2 D4
Pratt's Bottom London 29 C5
Praze Corn 2 C4
Praze-an-Beeble Corn 2 C5
Predannack Wollas Corn 3 E5
Prees Shrops 74 F2
Prees Green Shrops 74 F2
Prees Heath Shrops 74 F2
Prees Higher Heath Shrops 74 F2
Prees Lower Heath Shrops 74 F2
Preesall Lancs 92 E3
Preesgweene Shrops 73 F6
Prenderguest Borders 122 D5
Prendwick Northumb 117 C6
Prengwyn Ceredig 46 E3
Prenteg Gwyn 71 C6
Prenton Mers 85 F4
Prescot Mers 86 E2
Prescott Shrops 60 B4
Pressen Northumb 122 F4
Prestatyn Denb 72 A4
Prestbury Ches E 75 B6
Prestbury Glos 37 B6
Presteigne = Llanandras Powys 48 C5
Presthope Shrops 61 E5
Prestleigh Som 23 E8
Preston Borders 122 D3
Preston Brighton 17 D7
Preston Devon 7 B6
Preston Dorset 12 F5
Preston E Loth 121 B8
Preston E Yorks 97 F7
Preston Glos 37 D7
Preston Glos 49 F8
Preston Herts 40 B4
Preston Kent 30 C4
Preston Kent 31 C6
Preston Lancs 86 B3
Preston Northumb 117 B7
Preston Rutland 65 D5
Preston Shrops 60 C5
Preston Wilts 24 B5
Preston Wilts 25 B7
Preston Bagot Warks 51 C6
Preston Bissett Bucks 39 B6
Preston Bowyer Som 11 B6
Preston Brockhurst Shrops 60 B5
Preston Brook Halton 86 F3
Preston Candover Hants 26 E4
Preston Capes Northants 52 D3
Preston Crowmarsh Oxon 39 E6
Preston Gubbals Shrops 60 C4
Preston on Stour Warks 51 E7
Preston on the Hill Halton 86 F3
Preston on Wye Hereford 49 E5
Preston Plucknett Som 12 C3
Preston St Mary Suff 56 D3
Preston-under-Scar N Yorks 101 E5
Preston upon the Weald Moors Telford 61 C6
Preston Wynne Hereford 49 E7
Prestonmill Dumfries 107 D6
Prestonpans E Loth 121 B6
Prestwich Gtr Man 87 D6
Prestwick Northumb 110 B4
Prestwick S Ayrs 112 B3
Prestwood Bucks 40 D1
Price Town Bridgend 34 E3
Prickwillow Cambs 67 F5
Priddy Som 23 D7
Priest Hutton Lancs 92 B5
Priest Weston Shrops 60 E2
Priesthaugh Borders 115 D7
Primethorpe Leics 64 E2
Primrose Green Norf 68 C3
Primrose Valley N Yorks 97 B7
Primrosehill Herts 40 D3
Princes Gate Pembs 32 C2
Princes Risborough Bucks 39 D8
Princethorpe Warks 52 B2
Princetown Caerph 35 C5
Princetown Devon 6 B3
Prion Denb 72 C4
Prior Muir Fife 129 C7
Prior Park Northumb 123 D5
Priors Frome Hereford 49 F7
Priors Hardwick Warks 52 D2
Priors Marston Warks 52 D2
Priorslee Telford 61 C7
Priory Wood Hereford 48 E4
Priston Bath 23 C8
Pristow Green Norf 68 F4
Prittlewell Southend 42 F4
Privett Hants 15 B7
Prixford Devon 20 F4
Probus Corn 3 B7
Proncy Highld 151 B10
Prospect Cumb 107 E8
Prudhoe Northumb 110 C3
Ptarmigan Lodge Stirling 126 D2
Pubil Perth 132 E1
Puckeridge Herts 41 B6
Puckington Som 11 C8
Pucklechurch S Glos 23 B8
Pucknall Hants 14 B4
Puckrup Glos 50 F3
Puddinglake Ches W 74 C4
Puddington Ches W 73 B7
Puddington Devon 10 C3
Puddledock Norf 68 E3
Puddletown Dorset 13 E5
Pudleston Hereford 49 D7
Pudsey W Yorks 94 F5
Pulborough W Sus 16 C4
Puleston Telford 61 B7
Pulford Ches W 73 D7
Pulham Dorset 12 D5
Pulham Market Norf 68 F4
Pulham St Mary Norf 68 F5
Pulloxhill C Beds 53 F8
Pumpherston W Loth 120 C3
Pumsaint Carms 47 E5
Puncheston Pembs 32 B1
Puncknowle Dorset 12 F3
Punnett's Town E Sus 18 C3
Purbrook Hants 15 D7
Purewell Dorset 14 E2
Purfleet Thurrock 29 B6
Puriton Som 22 E5
Purleigh Essex 42 D4
Purley London 28 C4
Purley W Berks 26 B4
Purlogue Shrops 48 B4
Purls Bridge Cambs 66 F4
Purse Caundle Dorset 12 C4
Purslow Shrops 60 F3
Purston Jaglin W Yorks 88 C5
Purton Glos 36 D3
Purton Glos 36 D3
Purton Wilts 37 F7
Purton Stoke Wilts 37 E7
Pury End Northants 52 E5
Pusey Oxon 38 E3
Putley Hereford 49 F8
Putney London 28 B3
Putsborough Devon 20 E3
Puttenham Herts 40 C1
Puttenham Sur 27 E7
Puxton N Som 23 C6
Pwll Carms 33 D5
Pwll-glas Denb 72 D5
Pwll-trap Carms 32 C3
Pwll-y-glaw Neath 34 E1
Pwllcrochan Pembs 44 E4
Pwllgloyw Powys 48 F2
Pwllheli Gwyn 70 D4
Pwllmeyric Mon 36 E2
Pye Corner Newport 35 F7
Pye Green Staffs 62 C3
Pyecombe W Sus 17 C6
Pyewipe NE Lincs 91 C6
Pyle = Y Pîl Bridgend 34 F2
Pyle IoW 15 G5
Pylle Som 23 F8
Pymoor Cambs 66 F4
Pyrford Sur 27 D8
Pyrton Oxon 39 E6
Pytchley Northants 53 B6
Pyworthy Devon 8 D5

Q

Quabbs Shrops 60 F2
Quadring Lincs 78 F5
Quainton Bucks 39 C7
Quarley Hants 25 E7
Quarndon Derbys 76 E3
Quarrier's Homes Invclyd 118 C3
Quarrington Lincs 78 E3
Quarrington Hill Durham 111 F6
Quarry Bank W Mid 62 F3
Quarryford E Loth 121 C8
Quarryhill Highld 151 C10
Quarrywood Moray 152 B1
Quarter S Lanark 119 D7
Quatford Shrops 61 E7
Quatt Shrops 61 F7
Quebec Durham 110 E4
Quedgeley Glos 37 C5
Queen Adelaide Cambs 67 F5
Queen Camel Som 12 B3
Queen Charlton Bath 23 C8
Queen Dart Devon 10 C3
Queen Oak Dorset 24 F2
Queen Street Kent 29 E7
Queen Street Wilts 37 F7
Queenborough Kent 30 B3
Queenhill Worcs 50 F3
Queen's Head Shrops 60 B3
Queen's Park Bedford 53 E8
Queen's Park Northants 53 C5
Queensbury W Yorks 94 F4
Queensferry Edin 120 B4
Queensferry Flint 73 C7
Queenstown Blackpool 92 F3
Queenzieburn N Lanark 119 B6
Quemerford Wilts 24 C5
Quendale Shetland 160 M5
Quendon Essex 55 F6
Queniborough Leics 64 C3
Quenington Glos 37 D8
Quernmore Lancs 92 D5
Quethiock Corn 5 C8
Quholm Orkney 159 G3
Quicks Green W Berks 26 B3
Quidenham Norf 68 F3
Quidhampton Hants 26 D3
Quidhampton Wilts 25 F6
Quilquox Aberds 153 E9
Quina Brook Shrops 74 F2
Quindry Orkney 159 J5
Quinton Northants 53 D5
Quinton W Mid 62 F3
Quintrell Downs Corn 4 C3
Quixhill Staffs 75 E8
Quoditch Devon 9 E6
Quoig Perth 127 B7
Quorndon Leics 64 C2
Quothquan S Lanark 120 F2
Quoyloo Orkney 159 F3
Quoyness Orkney 159 H3
Quoys Shetland 160 B8
Quoys Shetland 160 G6

R

Raasay Ho. Highld 149 E10
Rabbit's Cross Kent 29 E8
Raby Mers 73 B7
Rachan Mill Borders 120 F4
Rachub Gwyn 83 E6
Rackenford Devon 10 C3
Rackham W Sus 16 C4
Rackheath Norf 69 C5
Racks Dumfries 107 B7
Rackwick Orkney 159 D5
Rackwick Orkney 159 J3
Radbourne Derbys 76 F2
Radcliffe Gtr Man 87 D5
Radcliffe Northumb 117 D8
Radcliffe on Trent Notts 77 F6
Radclive Bucks 52 F4
Radcot Oxon 38 E2
Raddery Highld 151 F10
Radernie Fife 129 D6
Radford Semele Warks 51 C8
Radipole Dorset 12 F4
Radlett Herts 40 E4
Radley Oxon 39 E5
Radmanthwaite Notts 76 C5
Radmoor Shrops 61 B6
Radmore Green Ches E 74 D2
Radnage Bucks 39 E7
Radstock Bath 23 D8
Radstone Northants 52 E3
Radway Warks 51 E8
Radway Green Ches E 74 D4
Radwell Bedford 53 D8
Radwell Herts 54 F3
Radwinter Essex 55 F7
Radyr Cardiff 35 F5
Rafford Moray 151 F13
Ragdale Leics 64 C3
Raglan Mon 35 D8
Ragnall Notts 77 B8
Rahane Argyll 145 E11
Rainford Mers 86 D2
Rainford Junction Mers 86 D2
Rainham London 41 F8
Rainham Medway 30 C2
Rainhill Mers 86 E2
Rainhill Stoops Mers 86 E3
Rainow Ches E 75 B6
Rainton N Yorks 95 B6
Rainworth Notts 77 D5
Raisbeck Cumb 99 D8
Raise Cumb 109 E7
Rait Perth 128 B4
Raithby Lincs 79 C6
Raithby Lincs 91 F7
Rake W Sus 16 B2
Rakewood Gtr Man 87 C7
Ram Carms 46 E4
Ram Lane Kent 30 E3
Ramasaig Highld 148 D6
Rame Corn 3 C6
Rame Corn 6 E2
Rameldry Mill Bank Fife 128 D5
Ramnageo Shetland 160 C8
Rampisham Dorset 12 D3
Rampside Cumb 92 C2
Rampton Cambs 54 C5
Rampton Notts 77 B7
Ramsbottom Gtr Man 87 C5
Ramsbury Wilts 25 B7
Ramscraigs Highld 158 H3
Ramsdean Hants 15 B8
Ramsdell Hants 26 D3
Ramsden Oxon 38 C3
Ramsden Bellhouse Essex 42 E3
Ramsden Heath Essex 42 E3
Ramsey Cambs 66 F2
Ramsey Essex 57 F6
Ramsey IoM 84 C4
Ramsey Forty Foot Cambs 66 F3
Ramsey Heights Cambs 66 F2
Ramsey Island Essex 43 D5
Ramsey Mereside Cambs 66 F2
Ramsey St Mary's Cambs 66 F2
Ramseycleuch Borders 115 C5
Ramsgate Kent 31 C7
Ramsgill N Yorks 94 B4
Ramshorn Staffs 75 E7
Ramsnest Common Sur 27 F7
Ranais W Isles 155 E9
Ranby Lincs 78 B5
Ranby Notts 89 F7
Rand Lincs 78 B4
Randwick Glos 37 D5
Ranfurly Renfs 118 C3
Rangag Highld 158 F3
Rangemore Staffs 63 B5
Rangeworthy S Glos 36 F3
Rankinston E Ayrs 112 C4
Ranmoor S Yorks 88 F4
Ranmore Common Sur 28 D2
Rannerdale Cumb 98 C3
Rannoch Station Perth 131 D8
Ranochan Highld 147 C11
Ranskill Notts 89 F7
Ranton Staffs 62 B2
Ranworth Norf 69 C6
Raploch Stirling 127 E6
Rapness Orkney 159 D6
Rascal Moor E Yorks 96 F4
Rascarrel Dumfries 106 E4
Rashiereive Aberds 141 B8
Raskelf N Yorks 95 B7
Rassau Bl Gwent 35 C5
Rastrick W Yorks 88 B2
Ratagan Highld 136 C2
Ratby Leics 64 D2
Ratcliffe Culey Leics 63 E7
Ratcliffe on Soar Leics 63 B8
Ratcliffe on the Wreake Leics 64 C3
Rathen Aberds 153 B10
Rathillet Fife 129 B5
Rathmell N Yorks 93 D8
Ratho Edin 120 B4
Ratho Station Edin 120 B4
Rathven Moray 152 B4
Ratley Warks 51 E8
Ratlinghope Shrops 60 E4
Rattar Highld 158 C4
Ratten Row Lancs 92 E4
Rattery Devon 6 C5
Rattlesden Suff 56 D3
Rattray Perth 134 E1
Raughton Head Cumb 108 E3
Raunds Northants 53 B7
Ravenfield S Yorks 89 E5
Ravenglass Cumb 98 E2
Raveningham Norf 69 E6
Ravenscar N Yorks 103 D7
Ravenscraig Invclyd 118 B2
Ravensdale IoM 84 C3
Ravensden Bedford 53 D8
Ravenseat N Yorks 100 D3
Ravenshead Notts 77 D5
Ravensmoor Ches E 74 D3
Ravensthorpe Northants 52 B4
Ravensthorpe W Yorks 88 B3
Ravenstone Leics 63 C8
Ravenstone M Keynes 53 D6
Ravenstonedale Cumb 100 D2
Ravenstown Cumb 92 B3
Ravenstruther S Lanark 120 E2
Ravensworth N Yorks 101 D6
Raw N Yorks 103 D7
Rawcliffe E Yorks 89 B7
Rawcliffe York 95 D8
Rawcliffe Bridge E Yorks 89 B7
Rawdon W Yorks 94 F5
Rawmarsh S Yorks 88 E5
Rawreth Essex 42 E3
Rawridge Devon 11 D7
Rawtenstall Lancs 87 B6
Raxton Aberds 153 E8
Raydon Suff 56 F4
Raylees Northumb 117 E5
Rayleigh Essex 42 E4
Rayne Essex 42 B3
Rayners Lane London 40 F4
Raynes Park London 28 C3
Reach Cambs 55 C6
Read Lancs 93 F7
Reading Reading 26 B5
Reading Street Kent 19 B6
Reagill Cumb 99 C8
Rearquhar Highld 151 B10
Rearsby Leics 64 C3
Reaster Highld 158 D4
Reawick Shetland 160 J5
Reay Highld 157 C12
Rechullin Highld 149 C13
Reculver Kent 31 C6
Red Dial Cumb 108 E2
Red Hill Worcs 50 D3
Red Houses Jersey 17
Red Lodge Suff 55 B7
Red Rail Hereford 36 B2
Red Rock Gtr Man 86 D3
Red Roses Carms 32 C3
Red Row Northumb 117 E8
Red Street Staffs 74 D5
Red Wharf Bay Anglesey 82 C5
Redberth Pembs 32 D1
Redbourn Herts 40 C4
Redbourne N Lincs 90 E3
Redbrook Mon 36 C2
Redbrook Wrex 74 E2
Redburn Highld 151 E8
Redburn Highld 151 G12
Redburn Northumb 109 C7
Redcar Redcar 102 B4
Redcastle Angus 135 D6
Redcastle Highld 151 G8
Redcliff Bay N Som 23 B6
Redding Falk 120 B2
Reddingmuirhead Falk 120 B2
Reddish Gtr Man 87 E6
Redditch Worcs 50 C5
Rede Suff 56 D2
Redenhall Norf 69 F5
Redesdale Camp Northumb 116 E4
Redesmouth Northumb 116 F4
Redford Aberds 135 B7
Redford Angus 135 E5
Redford Durham 110 F3
Redfordgreen Borders 115 C6
Redgorton Perth 128 B2
Redgrave Suff 56 B4
Redhill Aberds 141 D6
Redhill Aberds 153 E6
Redhill N Som 23 C7
Redhill Sur 28 D3
Redhouse Argyll 145 G7
Redhouses Argyll 142 B4
Redisham Suff 69 F7
Redland Bristol 23 B7
Redland Orkney 159 F4
Redlingfield Suff 57 B5
Redlynch Som 23 F9
Redlynch Wilts 14 B3
Redmarley D'Abitot Glos 50 F2
Redmarshall Stockton 102 B1
Redmile Leics 77 F7
Redmire N Yorks 101 E5
Redmoor Corn 5 C5
Rednal Shrops 60 B3
Redpath Borders 121 F8
Redpoint Highld 149 B12
Redruth Corn 3 B5
Redvales Gtr Man 87 D6
Redwick Newport 35 F8
Redwick S Glos 36 F2
Redworth Darl 101 B7
Reed Herts 54 F4
Reedham Norf 69 D7
Reedness E Yorks 89 B8
Reeds Beck Lincs 78 C5
Reepham Lincs 78 B3
Reepham Norf 81 E6
Reeth N Yorks 101 E5
Regaby IoM 84 C4
Regoul Highld 151 F11
Reiff Highld 156 H2
Reigate Sur 28 D3
Reighton N Yorks 97 B7
Reighton Gap N Yorks 97 B7
Reinigeadal W Isles 154 G7
Reiss Highld 158 E5
Rejerrah Corn 4 D2
Releath Corn 3 C5
Relubbus Corn 2 C4
Relugas Moray 151 G12
Remenham Wokingham 39 F7
Remenham Hill Wokingham 39 F7
Remony Perth 132 E4
Rempstone Notts 64 B2
Rendcomb Glos 37 D7
Rendham Suff 57 C7
Rendlesham Suff 57 D7
Renfrew Renfs 118 C5
Renhold Bedford 53 D8
Renishaw Derbys 76 B4
Rennington Northumb 117 C8
Renton W Dunb 118 B3
Renwick Cumb 109 E5
Repps Norf 69 C7
Repton Derbys 63 B7
Reraig Highld 149 F13
Rescobie Angus 135 D5
Resipole Highld 147 E10
Resolis Highld 151 E9
Resolven Neath 34 D2
Reston Borders 122 C4
Reswallie Angus 135 D5
Retew Corn 4 D4
Retford Notts 89 F8
Rettendon Essex 42 E3
Rettendon Place Essex 42 E3
Revesby Lincs 79 C5
Revesby Bridge Lincs 79 C6
Rew Street IoW 15 E5
Rewe Devon 10 E4
Reydon Suff 57 B8
Reydon Smear Suff 57 B8
Reymerston Norf 68 D3
Reynalton Pembs 32 D1
Reynoldston Swansea 33 E5
Rezare Corn 5 B8
Rhaeadr Gwy = Rhayader Powys 47 C8
Rhandirmwyn Carms 47 E6
Rhayader = Rhaeadr Gwy Powys 47 C8
Rhedyn Gwyn 70 D3
Rhemore Highld 147 F8
Rhencullen IoM 84 C3
Rhes-y-cae Flint 73 B5
Rhewl Denb 72 C5
Rhewl Denb 73 E5
Rhian Highld 157 H8
Rhicarn Highld 156 G3
Rhiconich Highld 156 D5
Rhicullen Highld 151 D9
Rhidorroch Ho. Highld 150 B4
Rhifail Highld 157 E10
Rhigos Rhondda 34 D3
Rhilochan Highld 157 J10
Rhiroy Highld 150 C4
Rhisga = Risca Caerph 35 E6
Rhiw Gwyn 70 E3
Rhiwabon = Ruabon Wrex 73 E7
Rhiwbina Cardiff 35 F5
Rhiwbryfdir Gwyn 71 C7
Rhiwderin Newport 35 F6
Rhiwlas Gwyn 72 F3
Rhiwlas Gwyn 83 E5
Rhiwlas Powys 73 F5
Rhodes Gtr Man 87 D6
Rhodes Minnis Kent 31 E5
Rhodesia Notts 77 B5
Rhodiad Pembs 44 C2
Rhondda Rhondda 34 E3
Rhonehouse or Kelton Hill Dumfries 106 D4
Rhoose = Y Rhws V Glam 22 C2
Rhôs Carms 46 F2
Rhôs Neath 33 D8
Rhos-fawr Gwyn 70 D4
Rhos-goch Powys 48 E3
Rhos-hill Pembs 45 E3
Rhos-on-Sea Conwy 83 C8
Rhos-y-brithdir Powys 59 B8
Rhos-y-garth Ceredig 46 B5
Rhos-y-gwaliau Gwyn 72 F3
Rhos-y-llan Gwyn 70 D3
Rhos-y-Madoc Wrex 73 E7
Rhos-y-meirch Powys 48 C4
Rhosaman Carms 33 C8
Rhosbeirio Anglesey 82 B3
Rhoscefnhir Anglesey 82 D5
Rhoscolyn Anglesey 82 D2
Rhoscrowther Pembs 44 E4
Rhosesmor Flint 73 C6
Rhosgadfan Gwyn 82 F5
Rhosgoch Anglesey 82 C4
Rhoshirwaun Gwyn 70 E2
Rhoslan Gwyn 71 C5
Rhoslefain Gwyn 58 D2
Rhosllanerchrugog Wrex 73 E6
Rhosmaen Carms 33 B7
Rhosmeirch Anglesey 82 D4
Rhosneigr Anglesey 82 D3
Rhosnesni Wrex 73 D7
Rhosrobin Wrex 73 D7
Rhossili Swansea 33 F5
Rhosson Pembs 44 C2
Rhostryfan Gwyn 82 F4
Rhostyllen Wrex 73 E7
Rhosybol Anglesey 82 C4
Rhu Argyll 145 E11
Rhu Argyll 145 G7
Rhuallt Denb 72 B4
Rhuddall Heath Ches W 74 C2
Rhuddlan Ceredig 46 E3
Rhuddlan Denb 72 B4
Rhue Highld 150 B3
Rhulen Powys 48 E3
Rhunahaorine Argyll 143 D8
Rhuthun = Ruthin Denb 72 D5
Rhyd Gwyn 71 C7
Rhyd Powys 59 D6
Rhyd-Ddu Gwyn 83 F5
Rhyd-moel-ddu Powys 48 B2
Rhyd-Rosser Ceredig 46 C4
Rhyd-uchaf Gwyn 72 F3
Rhyd-wen Gwyn 58 C4
Rhyd-y-clafdy Gwyn 70 D4
Rhyd-y-foel Conwy 72 B3
Rhyd-y-fro Neath 33 D8
Rhyd-y-gwin Swansea 33 D7
Rhyd-y-meirch Mon 35 D7
Rhyd-y-meudwy Denb 72 D5
Rhyd-y-pandy Swansea 33 D7
Rhyd-y-sarn Gwyn 71 C7
Rhyd-yr-onen Gwyn 58 D3
Rhydaman = Ammanford Carms 33 C7
Rhydargaeau Carms 33 B5
Rhydcymerau Carms 46 F4
Rhydd Worcs 50 E3
Rhydding Neath 33 E8
Rhydfudr Ceredig 46 C4
Rhydlewis Ceredig 46 E2
Rhydlios Gwyn 70 D2
Rhydlydan Conwy 83 F8
Rhydness Powys 48 E3
Rhydowen Ceredig 46 E3
Rhydspence Hereford 48 E4
Rhydtalog Flint 73 D6
Rhydwyn Anglesey 82 C3
Rhydycroesau Powys 73 F6
Rhydyfelin Ceredig 46 B4
Rhydyfelin Rhondda 34 F4
Rhydymain Gwyn 58 B5
Rhydymwyn Flint 73 C6
Rhyl = Y Rhyl Denb 72 A4
Rhymney = Rhymni Caerph 35 D5
Rhymni = Rhymney Caerph 35 D5
Rhynd Fife 129 B6
Rhynd Perth 128 B3
Rhynie Aberds 140 B3
Rhynie Highld 151 D11
Ribbesford Worcs 50 B2
Ribblehead N Yorks 93 B7
Ribbleton Lancs 93 F5
Ribchester Lancs 93 F6
Ribigill Highld 157 D8
Riby Lincs 91 D5
Riby Cross Roads Lincs 91 D5
Riccall N Yorks 96 F2
Riccarton E Ayrs 118 F4
Richards Castle Hereford 49 C6
Richings Park Bucks 27 B8
Richmond London 28 B2
Richmond N Yorks 101 D6
Rickarton Aberds 141 F7
Rickinghall Suff 56 B4
Rickleton T&W 111 D5
Rickling Essex 55 F5
Rickmansworth Herts 40 E3
Riddings Cumb 108 B4
Riddings Derbys 76 D4
Riddlecombe Devon 9 C8
Riddlesden W Yorks 94 E3
Riddrie Glasgow 119 C6
Ridge Dorset 13 F7
Ridge Hants 14 C4
Ridge Wilts 24 F4
Ridge Green Sur 28 E4
Ridge Lane Warks 63 E6
Ridgebourne Powys 48 C2
Ridgehill N Som 23 C7
Ridgeway Cross Hereford 50 E2
Ridgewell Essex 55 E8
Ridgewood E Sus 17 C8
Ridgmont C Beds 53 F7
Riding Mill Northumb 110 C3
Ridleywood Wrex 73 D8
Ridlington Norf 69 A6
Ridlington Rutland 64 D5
Ridsdale Northumb 116 F5
Riechip Perth 133 E7
Riemore Perth 133 E7
Rienachait Highld 156 F3
Rievaulx N Yorks 102 F3
Rift House Hrtlpl 111 F7
Rigg Dumfries 108 C2
Rigside N Lanark 119 B7
Rigsby Lincs 79 B7
Rigside S Lanark 119 F8
Riley Green Lancs 86 B4
Rileyhill Staffs 62 C5
Rilla Mill Corn 5 B7
Rillington N Yorks 96 B4
Rimington Lancs 93 E8
Rimpton Som 12 B4
Rimswell E Yorks 91 B7
Rinaston Pembs 44 C4
Ringasta Shetland 160 M5
Ringford Dumfries 106 D3
Ringinglow S Yorks 88 F3
Ringland Norf 68 C4
Ringles Cross E Sus 17 B8
Ringmer E Sus 17 C8
Ringmore Devon 6 E4
Ringorm Moray 152 D2
Ring's End Cambs 66 D3
Ringsfield Suff 69 F7
Ringsfield Corner Suff 69 F7
Ringshall Herts 40 C2
Ringshall Suff 56 D4
Ringshall Stocks Suff 56 D4
Ringstead Norf 80 C3
Ringstead Northants 53 B7
Ringwood Hants 14 D2
Ringwould Kent 31 E7
Rinmore Aberds 140 C3
Rinnigill Orkney 159 J4
Rinsey Corn 2 D4
Riof W Isles 154 D6
Ripe E Sus 18 D2
Ripley Derbys 76 D3
Ripley Hants 14 E2
Ripley N Yorks 95 C5
Ripley Sur 27 D8
Riplingham E Yorks 97 F5
Ripon N Yorks 95 B6
Rippingale Lincs 65 B7
Ripple Kent 31 E7
Ripple Worcs 50 F3
Ripponden W Yorks 87 C8
Rireavach Highld 150 B3
Risabus Argyll 142 D4
Risbury Hereford 49 D7
Risby Suff 55 C8
Risca = Rhisga Caerph 35 E6
Rise E Yorks 97 E7
Riseden E Sus 18 B3
Risegate Lincs 66 B2
Riseholme Lincs 78 B2
Riseley Bedford 53 C8
Riseley Wokingham 26 C5
Rishangles Suff 57 C5
Rishton Lancs 93 F7
Rishworth W Yorks 87 C8
Rising Bridge Lancs 87 B5
Risley Derbys 76 F4
Risley Warr 86 E4
Risplith N Yorks 94 C5
Rispond Highld 156 C7
Rivar Wilts 25 C8
Rivenhall End Essex 42 C4
River Bank Cambs 55 C6
Riverhead Kent 29 D6
Rivington Lancs 86 C4
Roa Island Cumb 92 C2
Roachill Devon 10 B3
Road Green Norf 69 E5
Roade Northants 53 D5
Roadhead Cumb 108 B5
Roadmeetings S Lanark 119 E8
Roadside Highld 158 D3
Roadside of Catterline Aberds 135 B8
Roadside of Kinneff Aberds 135 B8
Roadwater Som 22 F2
Roag Highld 149 D7
Roath Cardiff 22 B3
Roberton Borders 115 C7
Roberton S Lanark 114 B2
Robertsbridge E Sus 18 C4
Roberttown W Yorks 88 B2
Robeston Cross Pembs 44 E3
Robeston Wathen Pembs 32 C1
Robin Hood W Yorks 88 B4
Robin Hood's Bay N Yorks 103 D7
Roborough Devon 6 C3
Roborough Devon 9 C7
Roby Mers 86 E2
Roby Mill Lancs 86 D3
Rocester Staffs 75 F8
Roch Pembs 44 C3
Roch Gate Pembs 44 C3
Rochdale Gtr Man 87 C6
Roche Corn 4 C4
Rochester Medway 29 C8
Rochester Northumb 116 E4
Rochford Essex 42 E4
Rock Corn 4 B4
Rock Northumb 117 B8
Rock W Sus 16 C5
Rock Worcs 50 B2
Rock Ferry Mers 85 F4
Rockbeare Devon 10 E5
Rockbourne Hants 14 C2
Rockcliffe Cumb 108 C3
Rockcliffe Dumfries 107 D5
Rockfield Highld 151 C12
Rockfield Mon 36 C1
Rockford Hants 14 D2
Rockhampton S Glos 36 E3
Rockingham Northants 65 E5
Rockland All Saints Norf 68 E2
Rockland St Mary Norf 69 D6
Rockland St Peter Norf 68 E2
Rockley Wilts 25 B6
Rockwell End Bucks 39 F7
Rockwell Green Som 11 B6
Rodborough Glos 37 D5
Rodbourne Swindon 37 F8
Rodbourne Wilts 37 F6
Rodbourne Cheney Swindon 37 F8
Rodd Hereford 48 C5
Roddam Northumb 117 B6
Rodden Dorset 12 F4
Rode Som 24 D3
Rode Heath Ches E 74 D5
Rodeheath Ches E 75 C5
Roden Telford 61 C5
Rodhuish Som 22 F2
Rodington Telford 61 C5
Rodley Glos 36 C4
Rodley W Yorks 94 F5
Rodmarton Glos 37 E6
Rodmell E Sus 17 D8
Rodmersham Kent 30 C3
Rodney Stoke Som 23 D6
Rodsley Derbys 76 E2
Rodway Som 22 F4
Rodwell Dorset 12 G4
Roe Green Herts 54 F4
Roecliffe N Yorks 95 C6
Roehampton London 28 B3
Roesound Shetland 160 G5
Roffey W Sus 28 F2
Rogart Highld 157 J10
Rogart Station Highld 157 J10
Rogate W Sus 16 B2
Rogerstone Newport 35 F6
Roghadal W Isles 154 J5
Rogiet Mon 36 F1
Rogue's Alley Cambs 66 D3
Roke Oxon 39 E6
Roker T&W 111 D7
Rollesby Norf 69 C7
Rolleston Leics 64 D4
Rolleston Notts 77 D7
Rolleston-on-Dove Staffs 63 B6
Rolston E Yorks 97 E8
Rolvenden Kent 18 B5
Rolvenden Layne Kent 19 B5
Romaldkirk Durham 100 B4
Romanby N Yorks 102 E1
Romannobridge Borders 120 E4
Romansleigh Devon 10 B2
Romford London 41 F8
Romiley Gtr Man 87 E7
Romsey Hants 14 B4
Romsey Town Cambs 55 D5
Romsley Shrops 61 F7
Romsley Worcs 50 B4
Ronague IoM 84 E2
Rookhope Durham 110 E2
Rookley IoW 15 F6
Rooks Bridge Som 23 D5
Roos E Yorks 97 F8
Roosebeck Cumb 92 C2
Rootham's Green Bedford 54 D2
Rootpark S Lanark 120 D2
Ropley Hants 26 F4
Ropley Dean Hants 26 F4
Ropsley Lincs 78 F2
Rora Aberds 153 C10
Rorandle Aberds 141 C5
Rorrington Shrops 60 D3
Roscroggan Corn 3 B5
Rose Corn 4 D2
Rose Ash Devon 10 B2
Rose Green W Sus 16 E3
Rose Grove Lancs 93 F8
Rose Hill E Sus 17 C8
Rose Hill Lancs 93 F8
Rose Hill Suff 57 E5
Roseacre Kent 29 D8
Roseacre Lancs 92 F4
Rosebank S Lanark 119 E8
Rosebrough Northumb 117 B7
Rosebush Pembs 32 B1
Rosecare Corn 8 E3
Rosedale Abbey N Yorks 103 E5
Roseden Northumb 117 B6
Rosefield Highld 151 F11

Ros–Shi 223

osehall Highld 156 J7
osehaugh Mains
Highld 151 F9
osehearty Aberds 153 B9
osehill Shrops 74 F3
oseisle Moray 152 B1
oselands E Sus 18 E3
osemarket Pembs 44 E4
osemarkie Highld 151 F10
Rosemary Lane Devon 11 C6
Rosemount Perth 134 E1
Rosenannon Corn 4 C4
Rosewell Midloth 121 C5
Roseworth Stockton 102 B2
Roseworthy Corn 2 C5
Rosgill Cumb 99 C7
Roshven Highld 147 D10
Roskhill Highld 149 D7
Roskill House Highld 151 F9
Rosley Cumb 108 E3
Roslin Midloth 121 C5
Rosliston Derbys 63 C6
Rosneath Argyll 145 E11
Ross Dumfries 106 E3
Ross Northumb 123 F7
Ross Perth 127 B6
Ross-on-Wye Hereford 36 B3
Rossett Wrex 73 D7
Rossett Green N Yorks 95 D6
Rossie Ochill Perth 128 C2
Rossie Priory Perth 134 F2
Rossington S Yorks 89 E7
Rosskeen Highld 151 E9
Rossland Renfs 118 B4
Roster Highld 158 G4
Rostherne Ches E 86 F5
Rosthwaite Cumb 98 C4
Roston Derbys 75 E8
Rosyth Fife 128 F3
Rothbury Northumb 117 D6
Rotherby Leics 64 C3
Rotherfield E Sus 18 C2
Rotherfield Greys Oxon 39 F7
Rotherfield Peppard
Oxon 39 F7
Rotherham S Yorks 88 E5
Rothersthorpe
Northants 52 D5
Rotherwick Hants 26 D5
Rothes Moray 152 D2
Rothesay Argyll 145 G9
Rothiebrisbane
Aberds 153 E7
Rothienorman Aberds 153 E7
Rothiesholm Orkney 159 F7
Rothley Leics 64 C2
Rothley Northumb 117 F6
Rothley Shield East
Northumb 117 E6
Rothmaise Aberds 153 E6
Rothwell Lincs 91 E5
Rothwell Northants 64 F5
Rothwell W Yorks 88 B4
Rothwell Haigh W Yorks 88 B4
Rotsea E Yorks 97 D6
Rottal Angus 134 C3
Rotten End Suff 57 C7
Rottingdean Brighton 17 D7
Rottington Cumb 98 C1
Roud IoW 15 F6
Rough Close Staffs 75 F6
Rough Common Kent 30 D5
Rougham Norf 80 E4
Rougham Suff 56 C3
Rougham Green Suff 56 C3
Roughburn Highld 137 F6
Roughlee Lancs 93 E8
Roughley W Mid 62 E5
Roughsike Cumb 108 B5
Roughton Lincs 78 C5
Roughton Norf 81 D8
Roughton Shrops 61 E7
Roughton Moor Lincs 78 C5
Roundhay W Yorks 95 F6
Roundstonefoot
Dumfries 114 D4
Roundstreet
Common W Sus 16 B4
Roundway Wilts 24 C5
Rous Lench Worcs 50 D5
Rousdon Devon 11 E7
Routenburn N Ayrs 118 C1
Routh E Yorks 97 E6
Row Corn 5 B5
Row Cumb 99 F6
Row Heath Essex 43 C7
Rowanburn Dumfries 108 B4
Rowardennan Stirling 126 E2
Rowde Wilts 24 C4
Rowen Conwy 83 D7
Rowfoot Northumb 109 C6
Rowhedge Essex 43 B6
Rowhook W Sus 28 F2
Rowington Warks 51 C7
Rowland Derbys 76 B2
Rowlands Castle
Hants 15 C8
Rowlands Gill T&W 110 D4
Rowledge Sur 27 E6
Rowlestone Hereford 35 B7
Rowley E Yorks 97 F5
Rowley Shrops 60 D3
Rowley Hill W Yorks 88 C2
Rowley Regis W Mid 62 F3
Rowly Sur 27 E8
Rowney Green Worcs 50 B5
Rownhams Hants 14 C4
Rowrah Cumb 98 C2
Rowsham Bucks 39 C8
Rowsley Derbys 76 C2
Rowstock Oxon 38 F4
Rowston Lincs 78 D3
Rowton Ches W 73 C8
Rowton Shrops 60 C3
Rowton Telford 61 C6
Roxburgh Borders 122 F3
Roxby N Lincs 90 C3
Roxby N Yorks 103 C5
Roxton Bedford 54 D2
Roxwell Essex 42 D2
Royal Leamington
Spa Warks 51 C8
Royal Oak Darl 101 B7
Royal Oak Lancs 86 D2
Royal Tunbridge
Wells Kent 18 B2
Royal Wootton
Bassett Wilts 37 F7
Roybridge Highld 137 F5
Roydhouse W Yorks 88 C3
Roydon Essex 41 D7
Roydon Norf 68 F3
Roydon Norf 80 E3
Roydon Hamlet Essex 41 D7
Royston Herts 54 E4
Royston S Yorks 88 C4
Royton Gtr Man 87 D7
Rozel Jersey 17
Ruabon = Rhiwabon Wrex 73 E7
Ruaig Argyll 146 G3
Ruan Lanihorne Corn 3 B7
Ruan Minor Corn 3 E6
Ruarach Highld 136 B2
Ruardean Glos 36 C3
Ruardean Woodside Glos 36 C3
Rubery Worcs 50 B4
Ruckcroft Cumb 108 E5
Ruckhall Hereford 49 F6
Ruckinge Kent 19 B7
Ruckland Lincs 79 B6
Ruckley Shrops 60 D5
Rudbaxton Pembs 44 C4
Rudby N Yorks 102 D2
Ruddington Notts 77 F5
Rudford Glos 36 B4
Rudge Shrops 62 E2
Rudge Som 24 D3
Rudgeway S Glos 36 F3
Rudgwick W Sus 27 F8
Rudhall Hereford 36 B3
Rudheath Ches W 74 B3
Rudley Green Essex 42 D4
Rudry Caerph 35 F5
Rudston E Yorks 97 C6
Rudyard Staffs 75 D6
Rufford Lancs 86 C2
Rufforth York 95 D8
Rugby Warks 52 B3
Rugeley Staffs 62 C4
Ruglen S Ayrs 112 D2
Ruilick Highld 151 G8
Ruishton Som 11 B7
Ruisigearraidh
W Isles 154 J4
Ruislip London 40 F3
Ruislip Common
London 40 F3
Rumbling Bridge
Perth 128 E2
Rumburgh Suff 69 F6
Rumford Corn 4 B3
Rumney Cardiff 22 B4
Runcorn Halton 86 F3
Runcton W Sus 16 D2
Runcton Holme Norf 67 D6
Rundlestone Devon 6 B3
Runfold Sur 27 E6
Runhall Norf 68 D3
Runham Norf 69 C7
Runham Norf 69 D8
Runnington Som 11 B6
Runsell Green Essex 42 D3
Runswick Bay N Yorks 103 C6
Runwell Essex 42 E3
Ruscombe Wokingham 27 B5
Rush Green London 41 F8
Rush-head Aberds 153 D8
Rushall Hereford 49 F8
Rushall Norf 68 F4
Rushall W Mid 62 D4
Rushall Wilts 25 D6
Rushbrooke Suff 56 C2
Rushbury Shrops 60 E5
Rushden Herts 54 F4
Rushden Northants 53 C7
Rushenden Kent 30 B3
Rushford Norf 68 F2
Rushlake Green E Sus 18 D3
Rushmere Suff 69 F7
Rushmere St
Andrew Suff 57 E6
Rushmoor Sur 27 E6
Rushock Worcs 50 B3
Rusholme Gtr Man 87 E6
Rushton Ches W 74 C2
Rushton Northants 64 F5
Rushton Shrops 61 D6
Rushton Spencer
Staffs 75 C6
Rushwick Worcs 50 D3
Rushyford Durham 101 B7
Ruskie Stirling 126 D5
Ruskington Lincs 78 D3
Rusland Cumb 99 F5
Rusper W Sus 28 F3
Ruspidge Glos 36 C3
Russell's Water Oxon 39 F7
Russel's Green Suff 57 B6
Rusthall Kent 18 B2
Rustington W Sus 16 D4
Ruston N Yorks 103 F7
Ruston Parva E Yorks 97 C6
Ruswarp N Yorks 103 D6
Rutherford Borders 122 F2
Rutherglen S Lanark 119 C6
Ruthernbridge Corn 4 C5
Ruthin = Rhuthun
Denb 72 D5
Ruthrieston Aberdeen 141 D8
Ruthven Aberds 152 D5
Ruthven Angus 134 E2
Ruthven Highld 138 E3
Ruthven Highld 151 H11
Ruthven House Angus 134 E3
Ruthvoes Corn 4 C4
Ruthwell Dumfries 107 C7
Ruyton-XI-Towns
Shrops 60 B3
Ryal Northumb 110 B3
Ryal Fold Blackburn 86 B4
Ryall Dorset 12 E2
Ryarsh Kent 29 D7
Rydal Cumb 99 D5
Ryde IoW 15 E6
Rye E Sus 19 C6
Rye Foreign E Sus 19 C5
Rye Harbour E Sus 19 D6
Rye Park Herts 41 C6
Rye Street Worcs 50 F2
Ryecroft Gate Staffs 75 C6
Ryehill E Yorks 91 B6
Ryhall Rutland 65 C7
Ryhill W Yorks 88 C4
Ryhope T&W 111 D7
Rylstone N Yorks 94 D2
Ryme Intrinseca Dorset 12 C3
Ryther N Yorks 95 F8
Ryton Glos 50 F2
Ryton N Yorks 96 B3
Ryton Shrops 61 D7
Ryton T&W 110 C4
Ryton-on-Dunsmore
Warks 51 B8

S

Sabden Lancs 93 F7
Sacombe Herts 41 C6
Sacriston Durham 110 E5
Sadberge Darl 101 C8
Saddell Argyll 143 E8
Saddington Leics 64 E3
Saddle Bow Norf 67 C6
Saddlescombe W Sus 17 C6
Sadgill Cumb 99 D6
Saffron Walden
Essex 55 F6
Sageston Pembs 32 D1
Saham Hills Norf 68 D2
Saham Toney Norf 68 D2
Saighdinis W Isles 148 B3
Saighton Ches W 73 C8
St Abbs Borders 122 C5
St Abb's Haven
Borders 122 C5
St Agnes Corn 4 D2
St Agnes Scilly 2 F3
St Albans Herts 40 D4
St Allen Corn 4 D3
St Andrews Fife 129 C7
St Andrew's Major
V Glam 22 B3
St Anne Ald 16
St Annes Lancs 85 B4
St Ann's Dumfries 114 E3
St Ann's Chapel Corn 6 B2
St Ann's Chapel Devon 6 E4
St Anthony-in-
Meneage Corn 3 D6
St Anthony's Hill E Sus 18 E3
St Arvans Mon 36 E2
St Asaph = Llanelwy
Denb 72 B4
St Athan V Glam 22 C2
St Aubin Jersey 17
St Austell Corn 4 D5
St Bees Cumb 98 C1
St Blazey Corn 5 D5
St Boswells Borders 121 F8
St Brelade Jersey 17
St Breock Corn 4 B4
St Breward Corn 5 B5
St Briavels Glos 36 D2
St Bride's Pembs 44 D3
St Brides Major V Glam 21 B7
St Bride's
Netherwent Mon 35 F8
St Brides super Ely
V Glam 22 B2
St Brides Wentlooge
Newport 35 F6
St Budeaux Plym 6 D2
St Buryan Corn 2 D3
St Catherine Bath 24 B2
St Catherine's Argyll 125 E7
St Clears = Sanclêr
Carms 32 C3
St Cleer Corn 5 C7
St Clement Corn 3 B7
St Clements Jersey 17
St Clether Corn 8 F4
St Colmac Argyll 145 G9
St Columb Major Corn 4 C4
St Columb Minor Corn 4 C3
St Columb Road Corn 4 D4
St Combs Aberds 153 B10
St Cross South
Elmham Suff 69 F5
St Cyrus Aberds 135 C7
St David's Perth 127 B8
St David's = Tyddewi
Pembs 44 C2
St Day Corn 3 B6
St Dennis Corn 4 D4
St Devereux Hereford 49 F6
St Dogmaels Pembs 45 E3
St Dogwells Pembs 44 C4
St Dominick Corn 6 C2
St Donat's V Glam 21 C8
St Edith's Wilts 24 C4
St Endellion Corn 4 B4
St Enoder Corn 4 D3
St Erme Corn 4 D3
St Erney Corn 5 D8
St Erth Corn 2 C4
St Ervan Corn 4 B3
St Eval Corn 4 C3
St Ewe Corn 3 B8
St Fagans Cardiff 22 B3
St Fergus Aberds 153 C10
St Fillans Perth 127 B5
St Florence Pembs 32 D1
St Genny's Corn 8 E3
St George Conwy 72 B3
St George's V Glam 22 B2
St Germans Corn 5 D8
St Giles Lincs 78 B2
St Giles in the
Wood Devon 9 C7
St Giles on the
Heath Devon 9 E5
St Harmon Powys 47 B8
St Helen Auckland
Durham 101 B6
St Helena Warks 63 D6
St Helen's E Sus 18 D5
St Helens IoW 15 F7
St Helens Mers 86 E3
St Helier Jersey 17
St Helier London 28 C3
St Hilary Corn 2 C4
St Hilary V Glam 22 B2
Saint Hill W Sus 28 F4
St Illtyd Bl Gwent 35 D6
St Ippollytts Herts 40 B4
St Ishmael's Pembs 44 E3
St Issey Corn 4 B4
St Ive Corn 5 C8
St Ives Cambs 54 B4
St Ives Corn 2 B4
St Ives Dorset 14 D2
St James South
Elmham Suff 69 F6
St Jidgey Corn 4 C4
St John Corn 6 D2
St John's IoM 84 D2
St John's Jersey 17
St John's Sur 27 D7
St John's Worcs 50 D3
St John's Chapel
Durham 109 F8
St John's Fen End
Norf 66 C5
St John's Highway
Norf 66 C5
St John's Town of
Dalry Dumfries 113 F6
St Judes IoM 84 C3
St Just Corn 2 C2
St Just in Roseland
Corn 3 C7
St Katherine's Aberds 153 E7
St Keverne Corn 3 D6
St Kew Corn 4 B5
St Kew Highway Corn 4 B5
St Keyne Corn 5 C7
St Lawrence Corn 4 C5
St Lawrence Essex 43 D5
St Lawrence IoW 15 G6
St Leonard's Bucks 40 D2
St Leonards Dorset 14 D2
St Leonards E Sus 18 E4
Saint Leonards
S Lanark 119 D6
St Levan Corn 2 D2
St Lythans V Glam 22 B3
St Mabyn Corn 4 B5
St Madoes Perth 128 B3
St Margaret's Hereford 49 F5
St Margarets Herts 41 C6
St Margaret's at
Cliffe Kent 31 E7
St Margaret's Hope
Orkney 159 J5
St Margaret South
Elmham Suff 69 F6
St Mark's IoM 84 E2
St Martin Corn 5 D7
St Martins Corn 3 D6
St Martin's Jersey 17
St Martins Perth 134 F1
St Martin's Shrops 73 F7
St Mary Bourne
Hants 26 D2
St Mary Church
V Glam 22 B2
St Mary Cray London 29 C5
St Mary Hill V Glam 21 B8
St Mary Hoo Medway 30 B2
St Mary in the
Marsh Kent 19 C7
St Mary's Jersey 17
St Mary's Orkney 159 H5
St Mary's Bay Kent 19 C7
St Maughans Mon 36 C1
St Mawes Corn 3 C7
St Mawgan Corn 4 C3
St Mellion Corn 5 C8
St Mellons Cardiff 35 F6
St Merryn Corn 4 B3
St Mewan Corn 4 D4
St Michael
Caerhays Corn 3 B8
St Michael
Penkevil Corn 3 B7
St Michael South
Elmham Suff 69 F6
St Michael's Kent 19 B5
St Michaels Worcs 49 C7
St Michael's on
Wyre Lancs 92 E4
St Minver Corn 4 B4
St Monans Fife 129 D7
St Neot Corn 5 C6
St Neots Cambs 54 C2
St Newlyn East Corn 4 D3
St Nicholas Pembs 44 B3
St Nicholas V Glam 22 B2
St Nicholas at Wade
Kent 31 C6
St Ninians Stirling 127 E6
St Osyth Essex 43 C7
St Osyth Heath Essex 43 C7
St Ouens Jersey 17
St Owens Cross
Hereford 36 B2
St Paul's Cray London 29 C5
St Paul's Walden
Herts 40 B4
St Peter Port Guern 16
St Peter's Jersey 17
St Peter's Kent 31 C7
St Petrox Pembs 44 F4
St Pinnock Corn 5 C7
St Quivox S Ayrs 112 B3
St Ruan Corn 3 E6
St Sampson Guern 16
St Stephen Corn 4 D4
St Stephen's Corn 8 F5
St Stephens Corn 6 D2
St Stephens Herts 40 D4
St Teath Corn 8 F2
St Thomas Devon 10 E4
St Tudy Corn 5 B5
St Twynnells Pembs 44 F4
St Veep Corn 5 D6
St Vigeans Angus 135 E6
St Wenn Corn 4 C4
St Weonards Hereford 36 B1
Saintbury Glos 51 F6
Salcombe Devon 6 F5
Salcombe Regis
Devon 11 F6
Salcott Essex 43 C5
Sale Gtr Man 87 E5
Sale Green Worcs 50 D4
Saleby Lincs 79 B7
Salehurst E Sus 18 C4
Salem Carms 33 B7
Salem Ceredig 58 F3
Salen Argyll 147 G8
Salen Highld 147 E9
Salesbury Lancs 93 F6
Salford C Beds 53 F7
Salford Gtr Man 87 E6
Salford Oxon 38 B2
Salford Priors Warks 51 D5
Salfords Sur 28 E3
Salhouse Norf 69 C6
Saline Fife 128 E2
Salisbury Wilts 14 B2
Sallachan Highld 130 C3
Sallachy Highld 150 H2
Sallachy Highld 157 J8
Salle Norf 81 E7
Salmonby Lincs 79 B6
Salmond's Muir
Angus 135 F5
Salperton Glos 37 B7
Salph End Bedford 53 D8
Salsburgh N Lanark 119 C8
Salt Staffs 62 B3
Salt End E Yorks 91 B5
Saltaire W Yorks 94 F4
Saltash Corn 6 D2
Saltburn Highld 151 E10
Saltburn-by-the-
Sea Redcar 102 B4
Saltby Leics 65 B5
Saltcoats Cumb 98 E2
Saltcoats N Ayrs 118 E2
Saltdean Brighton 17 D7
Salter Lancs 93 C6
Salterforth Lancs 93 E8
Salterswall Ches W 74 C3
Saltfleet Lincs 91 E8
Saltfleetby All
Saints Lincs 91 E8
Saltfleetby
St Clements Lincs 91 E8
Saltfleetby St Peter
Lincs 91 F8
Saltford Bath 23 C8
Salthouse Norf 81 C6
Saltmarshe E Yorks 89 B8
Saltney Flint 73 C7
Salton N Yorks 96 B3
Saltwick Northumb 110 B4
Saltwood Kent 19 B8
Salum Argyll 146 G3
Salvington W Sus 16 D5
Salwarpe Worcs 50 C3
Salwayash Dorset 12 E2
Sambourne Warks 51 C5
Sambrook Telford 61 B7
Samhla W Isles 148 B2
Samlesbury Lancs 93 F5
Samlesbury
Bottoms Lancs 86 B4
Sampford Arundel
Som 11 C6
Sampford Brett Som 22 E2
Sampford Courtenay
Devon 9 D8
Sampford Peverell
Devon 10 C5
Sampford Spiney
Devon 6 B3
Sampool Bridge Cumb 99 F6
Samuelston E Loth 121 B7
Sanachan Highld 149 D13
Sanaigmore Argyll 142 A3
Sanclêr = St Clears
Carms 32 C3
Sancreed Corn 2 D3
Sancton E Yorks 96 F5
Sand Highld 150 B2
Sand Shetland 160 J5
Sand Hole E Yorks 96 F4
Sand Hutton N Yorks 96 D2
Sandaig Highld 149 H12
Sandal Magna
W Yorks 88 C4
Sandale Cumb 108 E2
Sandbach Ches E 74 C4
Sandbank Argyll 145 E10
Sandbanks Poole 13 F8
Sandend Aberds 152 B5
Sanderstead London 28 C4
Sandfields Glos 37 B6
Sandford Cumb 100 C2
Sandford Devon 10 D3
Sandford Dorset 13 F7
Sandford IoW 15 F6
Sandford N Som 23 D6
Sandford S Lanark 119 E7
Sandford Shrops 74 F2
Sandford on
Thames Oxon 39 D5
Sandford Orcas
Dorset 12 B4
Sandford St Martin
Oxon 38 B4
Sandfordhill Aberds 153 D11
Sandgate Kent 19 B8
Sandgreen Dumfries 106 D2
Sandhaven Aberds 153 B9
Sandhead Dumfries 104 E4
Sandhills Sur 27 F7
Sandhoe Northumb 110 C2
Sandholme E Yorks 96 F4
Sandholme Lincs 79 F6
Sandhurst Brack 27 C6
Sandhurst Glos 37 B5
Sandhurst Kent 18 C4
Sandhurst Cross Kent 18 C4
Sandhutton N Yorks 102 F1
Sandiacre Derbys 76 F4
Sandilands Lincs 91 F9
Sandilands S Lanark 119 F8
Sandiway Ches W 74 B3
Sandleheath Hants 14 C2
Sandling Kent 29 D8
Sandlow Green Ches E 74 C4
Sandness Shetland 160 H3
Sandon Essex 42 D3
Sandon Herts 54 F4
Sandon Staffs 75 F6
Sandown IoW 15 F6
Sandplace Corn 5 D7
Sandridge Herts 40 C4
Sandridge Wilts 24 C4
Sandringham Norf 67 B6
Sandsend N Yorks 103 C6
Sandside Ho. Highld 157 C12
Sandsound Shetland 160 J5
Sandtoft N Lincs 89 D8
Sandway Kent 30 D2
Sandwell W Mid 62 F4
Sandwich Kent 31 D7
Sandwick Cumb 99 C6
Sandwick Orkney 159 K5
Sandwick Shetland 160 L6
Sandwith Cumb 98 C1
Sandy C Beds 54 E2
Sandy Carms 33 D5
Sandy Bank Lincs 79 D5
Sandy Haven Pembs 44 E3
Sandy Lane Wilts 24 C4
Sandy Lane Wrex 73 E7
Sandycroft Flint 73 C7
Sandyford Dumfries 114 E5
Sandyford Stoke 75 D5
Sandygate IoM 84 C3
Sandyhills Dumfries 107 D5
Sandylands Lancs 92 C4
Sandypark Devon 10 F2
Sandysike Cumb 108 C3
Sangobeg Highld 156 C7
Sangomore Highld 156 C7
Sanna Highld 146 E7
Sanndabhaig W Isles 148 D3
Sanndabhaig W Isles 155 D9
Sannox N Ayrs 143 D11
Sanquhar Dumfries 113 D7
Santon N Lincs 90 C3
Santon Bridge Cumb 98 D3
Santon Downham Suff 67 F8
Sapcote Leics 63 E8
Sapey Common
Hereford 50 C2
Sapiston Suff 56 B3
Sapley Cambs 54 B3
Sapperton Glos 37 D6
Sapperton Lincs 78 F3
Saracen's Head Lincs 66 B3
Sarclet Highld 158 F5
Sardis Carms 33 D6
Sarn Bridgend 34 F3
Sarn Powys 60 E2
Sarn Bach Gwyn 70 E4
Sarn Meyllteyrn Gwyn 70 D3
Sarnau Carms 32 C4
Sarnau Ceredig 46 D2
Sarnau Gwyn 72 F3
Sarnau Powys 48 F2
Sarnau Powys 60 C2
Sarnesfield Hereford 49 D5
Saron Carms 33 C7
Saron Carms 46 F2
Saron Denb 72 C4
Saron Gwyn 82 E5
Saron Gwyn 82 F4
Sarratt Herts 40 E3
Sarre Kent 31 C6
Sarsden Oxon 38 B2
Sarsgrum Highld 156 C6
Satley Durham 110 E4
Satron N Yorks 100 E4
Satterleigh Devon 9 B8
Satterthwaite Cumb 99 E5
Satwell Oxon 39 F7
Sauchen Aberds 141 C5
Saucher Perth 134 F1
Sauchie Clack 127 E7
Sauchieburn Aberds 135 C6
Saughall Ches W 73 B7
Saughtree Borders 115 E8
Saul Glos 36 D4
Saundby Notts 89 F8
Saundersfoot Pembs 32 D2
Saunderton Bucks 39 D7
Saunton Devon 20 F3
Sausthorpe Lincs 79 C6
Saval Highld 157 J8
Savary Highld 147 G9
Savile Park W Yorks 87 B8
Sawbridge Warks 52 C3
Sawbridgeworth
Herts 41 C7
Sawdon N Yorks 103 F7
Sawley Derbys 76 F4
Sawley Lancs 93 E7
Sawley N Yorks 94 C5
Sawston Cambs 55 E5
Sawtry Cambs 65 F8
Saxby Leics 64 C5
Saxby Lincs 90 F4
Saxby All Saints N Lincs 90 C3
Saxelbye Leics 64 B4
Saxham Street Suff 56 C4
Saxilby Lincs 77 B8
Saxlingham Norf 81 D6
Saxlingham Green
Norf 68 E5
Saxlingham
Nethergate Norf 68 E5
Saxlingham Thorpe
Norf 68 E5
Saxmundham Suff 57 C7
Saxon Street Cambs 55 D7
Saxondale Notts 77 F6
Saxtead Suff 57 C6
Saxtead Green Suff 57 C6
Saxthorpe Norf 81 D7
Saxton N Yorks 95 F7
Sayers Common
W Sus 17 C6
Scackleton N Yorks 96 B2
Scadabhagh W Isles 154 H6
Scaftworth Notts 89 E7
Scagglethorpe N Yorks 96 B4
Scaitcliffe Lancs 87 B5
Scalasaig Argyll 144 D2
Scalby E Yorks 90 B2
Scalby N Yorks 103 E8
Scaldwell Northants 53 B5
Scale Houses Cumb 109 E5
Scaleby Cumb 108 C4
Scaleby Hill Cumb 108 C4
Scales Cumb 92 B2
Scales Cumb 99 B5
Scales Lancs 92 F4
Scalford Leics 64 B4
Scaling Redcar 103 C5
Scallastle Argyll 124 B2
Scalloway Shetland 160 K6
Scalpay W Isles 154 H7
Scalpay Ho. Highld 149 F11
Scalpsie Argyll 145 H9
Scamadale Highld 147 B10
Scamblesby Lincs 79 B5
Scamodale Highld 130 B2
Scampston N Yorks 96 B4
Scampton Lincs 78 B2
Scapa Orkney 159 H5
Scapegoat Hill
W Yorks 87 C8
Scar Orkney 159 D7
Scarborough N Yorks 103 F8
Scarcliffe Derbys 76 C4
Scarcroft W Yorks 95 E6
Scarcroft Hill W Yorks 95 E6
Scardroy Highld 150 F5
Scarff Shetland 160 E4
Scarfskerry Highld 158 C4
Scargill Durham 101 C5
Scarinish Argyll 146 G3
Scarisbrick Lancs 85 C4
Scarning Norf 68 C2
Scarrington Notts 77 E7
Scartho NE Lincs 91 D6
Scarwell Orkney 159 F3
Scatness Shetland 160 M5
Scatraig Highld 151 H10
Scawby N Lincs 90 D3
Scawsby S Yorks 89 D6
Scawton N Yorks 102 F3
Scayne's Hill W Sus 17 B7
Scethrog Powys 35 B5
Scholar Green Ches E 74 D5
Scholes W Yorks 88 B2
Scholes W Yorks 88 D2
Scholes W Yorks 95 F6
School Green Ches W 74 C3
Scleddau Pembs 44 B4
Sco Ruston Norf 81 E8
Scofton Notts 89 F7
Scole Norf 56 B5
Scolpaig W Isles 148 A2
Scone Perth 128 B3
Sconser Highld 149 E10
Scoonie Fife 129 D5
Scoor Argyll 146 K7
Scopwick Lincs 78 D3
Scoraig Highld 150 B3
Scorborough E Yorks 97 E6
Scorrier Corn 3 B6
Scorton Lancs 92 E5
Scorton N Yorks 101 D7
Scotbheinn W Isles 148 C3
Scotby Cumb 108 D4
Scotch Corner N Yorks 101 D7
Scotforth Lancs 92 D4
Scothern Lincs 78 B3
Scotland Gate
Northumb 117 F8
Scotlandwell Perth 128 D3
Scotsburn Highld 151 D10
Scotscalder
Station Highld 158 E2
Scotscraig Fife 129 B6
Scots' Gap Northumb 117 F6
Scotston Aberds 135 B7
Scotston Perth 133 E6
Scotstoun Glasgow 118 C5
Scotstown Highld 130 C2
Scotswood T&W 110 C4
Scottas Highld 149 H12
Scotter Lincs 90 D2
Scotterthorpe Lincs 90 D2
Scottlethorpe Lincs 65 B7
Scotton Lincs 90 E2
Scotton N Yorks 95 D6
Scotton N Yorks 101 E6
Scottow Norf 81 E8
Scoughall E Loth 129 F8
Scoulag Argyll 145 H10
Scoulton Norf 68 D2
Scourie Highld 156 E4
Scourie More Highld 156 E4
Scousburgh Shetland 160 M5
Scrabster Highld 158 C2
Scrafield Lincs 79 C6
Scrainwood Northumb 117 D5
Scrane End Lincs 79 E6
Scraptoft Leics 64 D3
Scratby Norf 69 C8
Scrayingham N Yorks 96 C3
Scredington Lincs 78 E3
Scremby Lincs 79 C7
Scremerston Northumb 123 E6
Screveton Notts 77 E7
Scrivelsby Lincs 79 C5
Scriven N Yorks 95 D6
Scrooby Notts 89 E7
Scropton Derbys 75 F8
Scrub Hill Lincs 78 D5
Scruton N Yorks 101 E7
Sculcoates Hull 97 F6
Sculthorpe Norf 80 D4
Scunthorpe N Lincs 90 C2
Scurlage Swansea 33 F5
Sea Palling Norf 69 B7
Seaborough Dorset 12 D2
Seacombe Mers 85 E4
Seacroft Lincs 79 C8
Seacroft W Yorks 95 F6
Seadyke Lincs 79 F6
Seafield S Ayrs 112 B3
Seafield W Loth 120 C3
Seaford E Sus 17 E8
Seaforth Mers 85 E4
Seagrave Leics 64 C3
Seaham Durham 111 E7
Seahouses Northumb 123 F8
Seal Kent 29 D6
Sealand Flint 73 C7
Seale Sur 27 E6
Seamer N Yorks 102 C2
Seamer N Yorks 103 F8
Seamill N Ayrs 118 E2
Searby Lincs 90 D4
Seasalter Kent 30 C4
Seascale Cumb 98 D2
Seathorne Lincs 79 C8
Seathwaite Cumb 98 C4
Seathwaite Cumb 98 E4
Seatoller Cumb 98 C4
Seaton Corn 5 D8
Seaton Cumb 107 F7
Seaton Devon 11 F7
Seaton Durham 111 D6
Seaton E Yorks 97 E7
Seaton Northumb 111 B6
Seaton Rutland 65 E6
Seaton Burn T&W 110 B5
Seaton Carew Hrtlpl 102 B3
Seaton Delaval
Northumb 111 B6
Seaton Ross E Yorks 96 E3
Seaton Sluice
Northumb 111 B6
Seatown Aberds 152 B5
Seatown Dorset 12 E2
Seave Green N Yorks 102 D3
Seaview IoW 15 E7
Seaville Cumb 107 D8
Seavington St
Mary Som 12 C2
Seavington St
Michael Som 12 C2
Sebergham Cumb 108 E3
Seckington Warks 63 D6
Second Coast Highld 150 B2
Sedbergh Cumb 100 E1
Sedbury Glos 36 E2
Sedbusk N Yorks 100 E3
Sedgeberrow Worcs 50 F5
Sedgebrook Lincs 77 F8
Sedgefield Durham 102 B1
Sedgeford Norf 80 D3
Sedgehill Wilts 13 B6
Sedgley W Mid 62 E3
Sedgwick Cumb 99 F7
Sedlescombe E Sus 18 D4
Sedlescombe
Street E Sus 18 D4
Seend Wilts 24 C4
Seend Cleeve Wilts 24 C4
Seer Green Bucks 40 E2
Seething Norf 69 E6
Sefton Mers 85 D4
Seghill Northumb 111 B5
Seifton Shrops 60 F4
Seighford Staffs 62 B2
Seilebost W Isles 154 H5
Seion Gwyn 82 E5
Seisdon Staffs 62 E2
Seisiadar W Isles 155 D10
Selattyn Shrops 73 F6
Selborne Hants 26 F5
Selby N Yorks 96 F2
Selham W Sus 16 B3
Selhurst London 28 C4
Selkirk Borders 115 B7
Sellack Hereford 36 B2
Sellafirth Shetland 160 D7
Sellibister Orkney 159 D8
Sellindge Kent 19 B7
Sellindge Lees Kent 19 B8
Selling Kent 30 D4
Sells Green Wilts 24 C4
Selly Oak W Mid 62 F4
Selmeston E Sus 18 E2
Selsdon London 28 C4
Selsey W Sus 16 E2
Selsfield Common
W Sus 28 F4
Selsted Kent 31 E6
Selston Notts 76 D4
Selworthy Som 21 E8
Semblister Shetland 160 H5
Semer Suff 56 E3
Semington Wilts 24 C3
Semley Wilts 13 B6
Send Sur 27 D8
Send Marsh Sur 27 D8
Senghenydd Caerph 35 E5
Sennen Corn 2 D2
Sennen Cove Corn 2 D2
Sennybridge =
Pont Senni Powys 34 B3
Serlby Notts 89 F7
Sessay N Yorks 95 B7
Setchey Norf 67 C6
Setley Hants 14 D4
Setter Shetland 160 E6
Setter Shetland 160 H5
Setter Shetland 160 J7
Settiscarth Orkney 159 G4
Settle N Yorks 93 C8
Settrington N Yorks 96 B4
Seven Kings London 41 F7
Seven Sisters Neath 34 D2
Sevenhampton Glos 37 B7
Sevenoaks Kent 29 D6
Sevenoaks Weald
Kent 29 D6
Severn Beach S Glos 36 F2
Severn Stoke Worcs 50 E3
Severnhampton
Swindon 38 E2
Sevington Kent 30 E4
Sewards End Essex 55 F6
Sewardstone Essex 41 E6
Sewardstonebury
Essex 41 E6
Sewerby E Yorks 97 C7
Seworgan Corn 3 C6
Sewstern Leics 65 B5
Sezincote Glos 51 F6
Sgarasta Mhor
W Isles 154 H5
Sgiogarstaigh
W Isles 155 A10
Shabbington Bucks 39 D6
Shackerstone Leics 63 D7
Shackleford Sur 27 E7
Shade W Yorks 87 B7
Shadforth Durham 111 E6
Shadingfield Suff 69 F7
Shadoxhurst Kent 19 B6
Shadsworth Blackburn 86 B5
Shadwell Norf 68 F2
Shadwell W Yorks 95 F6
Shaftesbury Dorset 13 B6
Shafton S Yorks 88 C4
Shalbourne Wilts 25 C8
Shalcombe IoW 14 F4
Shalden Hants 26 E4
Shaldon Devon 7 B7
Shalfleet IoW 14 F5
Shalford Essex 42 B3
Shalford Sur 27 E8
Shalford Green Essex 42 B3
Shallowford Devon 21 E6
Shalmsford Street
Kent 30 D4
Shalstone Bucks 52 F4
Shamley Green Sur 27 E8
Shandon Argyll 145 E11
Shandwick Highld 151 D11
Shangton Leics 64 E4
Shankhouse Northumb 111 B5
Shanklin IoW 15 F6
Shanquhar Aberds 152 E5
Shanzie Perth 134 D2
Shap Cumb 99 C7
Shapwick Dorset 13 D7
Shapwick Som 23 F6
Shardlow Derbys 76 F4
Shareshill Staffs 62 D3
Sharlston W Yorks 88 C4
Sharlston Common
W Yorks 88 C4
Sharnbrook Bedford 53 D7
Sharnford Leics 63 E8
Sharoe Green Lancs 92 F5
Sharow N Yorks 95 B6
Sharp Street Norf 69 B6
Sharpenhoe C Beds 53 F8
Sharperton Northumb 117 D5
Sharpness Glos 36 D3
Sharpthorne W Sus 28 F4
Sharrington Norf 81 D6
Shatterford Worcs 61 F7
Shaugh Prior Devon 6 C3
Shavington Ches E 74 D4
Shaw Gtr Man 87 D7
Shaw W Berks 26 C2
Shaw Wilts 24 C3
Shaw Green Lancs 86 C3
Shaw Mills N Yorks 95 C5
Shawbury Shrops 61 B5
Shawdon Hall
Northumb 117 C6
Shawell Leics 64 F2
Shawford Hants 15 B5
Shawforth Lancs 87 B6
Shawhead Dumfries 107 B5
Shawhill Dumfries 108 C2
Shawton S Lanark 119 E6
Shawtonhill S Lanark 119 E6
Shear Cross Wilts 24 E3
Shearington Dumfries 107 C7
Shearsby Leics 64 E3
Shebbear Devon 9 D6
Shebdon Staffs 61 B7
Shebster Highld 157 C13
Sheddens E Renf 119 D5
Shedfield Hants 15 C6
Sheen Staffs 75 C8
Sheepscar W Yorks 95 F6
Sheepscombe Glos 37 C5
Sheepstor Devon 6 C3
Sheepwash Devon 9 D6
Sheepway N Som 23 B6
Sheepy Magna Leics 63 D7
Sheepy Parva Leics 63 D7
Sheering Essex 41 C8
Sheerness Kent 30 B3
Sheet Hants 15 B8
Sheffield S Yorks 88 F4
Sheffield Bottom
W Berks 26 C4
Sheffield Green E Sus 17 B8
Shefford C Beds 54 F2
Shefford Woodlands
W Berks 25 B8
Sheigra Highld 156 C4
Sheinton Shrops 61 D6
Shelderton Shrops 49 B6
Sheldon Derbys 75 C8
Sheldon Devon 11 D6
Sheldon W Mid 63 F5
Sheldwich Kent 30 D4
Shelf W Yorks 88 B2
Shelfanger Norf 68 F4
Shelfield W Mid 62 D4
Shelfield Warks 51 C6
Shelford Notts 77 E6
Shellacres Northumb 122 E4
Shelley Essex 42 D1
Shelley Suff 56 F4
Shelley W Yorks 88 C3
Shellingford Oxon 38 E3
Shellow Bowells Essex 42 D2
Shelsley Beauchamp
Worcs 50 C2
Shelsley Walsh Worcs 50 C2
Shelthorpe Leics 64 C2
Shelton Bedford 53 C8
Shelton Norf 68 E5
Shelton Notts 77 E7
Shelton Shrops 60 C4
Shelton Green Norf 68 E5
Shelve Shrops 60 E3
Shelwick Hereford 49 E7
Shenfield Essex 42 E2
Shenington Oxon 51 E8
Shenley Herts 40 D4
Shenley Brook End
M Keynes 53 F6
Shenley Church End
M Keynes 53 E6
Shenleybury Herts 40 D4
Shenmore Hereford 49 F5
Shennanton Dumfries 105 C7
Shenstone Staffs 62 D5
Shenstone Worcs 50 B3
Shenton Leics 63 D7
Shenval Highld 137 B7
Shenval Moray 139 B8
Shepeau Stow Lincs 66 C3
Shephall Herts 41 B5
Shepherd's Green
Oxon 39 F7
Shepherd's Port Norf 80 D2
Shepherdswell Kent 31 E6
Shepley W Yorks 88 D2
Shepperdine S Glos 36 E3
Shepperton Sur 27 C8
Shepreth Cambs 54 E4
Shepshed Leics 63 C8
Shepton Beauchamp
Som 12 C2
Shepton Mallet Som 23 E8
Shepton Montague
Som 23 F8
Shepway Kent 29 D8
Sheraton Durham 111 F7
Sherborne Dorset 12 C4
Sherborne Glos 38 C1
Sherborne St John
Hants 26 D4
Sherbourne Warks 51 C7
Sherburn Durham 111 E6
Sherburn N Yorks 97 B5
Sherburn Hill Durham 111 E6
Sherburn in Elmet
N Yorks 95 F7
Shere Sur 27 E8
Shereford Norf 80 E4
Sherfield English
Hants 14 B3
Sherfield on Loddon
Hants 26 D4
Sherford Devon 7 E5
Sheriff Hutton N Yorks 96 C2
Sheriffhales Shrops 61 C7
Sheringham Norf 81 C7
Sherington M Keynes 53 E6
Shernal Green Worcs 50 C4
Shernborne Norf 80 D3
Sherrington Wilts 24 F4
Sherston Wilts 37 F5
Sherwood Green
Devon 9 B7
Shettleston Glasgow 119 C6
Shevington Gtr Man 86 D3
Shevington Moor
Gtr Man 86 C3
Shevington Vale
Gtr Man 86 D3
Sheviock Corn 5 D8
Shide IoW 15 F5
Shiel Bridge Highld 136 C2
Shieldaig Highld 149 A13
Shieldaig Highld 149 C13
Shieldhill Dumfries 114 F3
Shieldhill Falk 119 B8
Shieldhill S Lanark 120 E3
Shielfoot Highld 147 E9
Shielhill Angus 134 D4
Shielhill Involyd 118 B2
Shifford Oxon 38 D3
Shifnal Shrops 61 D7
Shilbottle Northumb 117 D7
Shildon Durham 101 B7
Shillingford Devon 10 B4
Shillingford Oxon 39 E5
Shillingford St
George Devon 10 F4
Shillingstone Dorset 13 C6
Shillington C Beds 54 F2
Shillmoor Northumb 116 D4
Shilton Oxon 38 D2
Shilton Warks 63 F8
Shilvington Northumb 117 F7
Shimpling Norf 68 F4
Shimpling Suff 56 D2
Shimpling Street Suff 56 D2
Shincliffe Durham 111 E5
Shiney Row T&W 111 D6
Shinfield Wokingham 26 C5
Shingham Norf 67 D7
Shingle Street Suff 57 E7
Shinner's Bridge
Devon 7 C5
Shinness Highld 157 H8
Shipbourne Kent 29 D6
Shipdham Norf 68 D2
Shipham Som 23 D6
Shiphay Torbay 7 C6
Shiplake Oxon 27 B5
Shipley Derbys 76 E4
Shipley Northumb 117 C7
Shipley Shrops 62 E2
Shipley W Sus 16 B5
Shipley W Yorks 94 F4
Shipley Shiels
Northumb 116 E3
Shipmeadow Suff 69 F6
Shippea Hill Station
Cambs 67 F6
Shippon Oxon 38 E4
Shipston-on-Stour
Warks 51 E7
Shipton Glos 37 C7
Shipton N Yorks 95 D8
Shipton Shrops 61 E5
Shipton Bellinger
Hants 25 E7
Shipton Gorge Dorset 12 E2
Shipton Green W Sus 16 D2
Shipton Moyne Glos 37 F5
Shipton on Cherwell
Oxon 38 C4
Shipton Solers Glos 37 C7
Shipton-under-
Wychwood Oxon 38 C2
Shiptonthorpe E Yorks 96 E4
Shirburn Oxon 39 E6
Shirdley Hill Lancs 85 C4
Shirebrook Derbys 76 C5

oke sub Hamdon
om 12 C2
toke Talmage Oxon 39 E6
oke Trister Som 12 B5
oke Wake Dorset 13 D5
okeford Dorset 13 F6
okeham Notts 77 B7
okeinteignhead
Devon 7 B7
okenchurch Bucks 39 E7
okenham Devon 7 E6
okesay Shrops 60 F4
okesby Norf 69 C7
okesley N Yorks 102 D3
olford Som 22 E4
on Easton Som 23 D8
ondon Massey Essex 42 D1
one Bucks 39 C7
one Glos 36 E3
one Kent 19 C6
one Kent 29 B6
one S Yorks 89 F6
one Staffs 75 F6
one Worcs 50 B3
one Allerton Som 23 D6
one Bridge
Corner Pboro 66 D2
tone Chair W Yorks 88 B2
tone Cross E Sus 18 E3
tone Cross Kent 31 D7
tone-edge Batch
N Som 23 B6
tone House Cumb 100 F2
tone Street Kent 29 D6
tone Street Suff 56 F3
tone Street Suff 69 F6
tonebroom Derbys 76 D4
toneferry Hull 97 F7
tonefield S Lanark 119 D6
tonegate E Sus 18 C3
tonegate N Yorks 103 D5
tonegrave N Yorks 96 B2
tonehaugh Northumb 109 B7
tonehaven Aberds 141 F7
tonehouse Glos 37 D5
tonehouse Northumb 109 D6
tonehouse S Lanark 119 E7
toneleigh Warks 51 B8
tonely Cambs 54 C2
toner Hill Hants 15 B8
tone's Green Essex 43 B7
tonesby Leics 64 B5
tonesfield Oxon 38 C3
tonethwaite Cumb 98 C4
toney Cross Hants 14 C3
toney Middleton
Derbys 76 B2
toney Stanton Leics 63 E8
toney Stoke Som 24 F2
toney Stratton Som 23 F8
toney Stretton Shrops 60 D3
toneybreck Shetland 160 N8
toneyburn W Loth 120 C2
toneygate Aberds 153 E10
toneygate Leicester 64 D3
toneyhills Essex 43 E5
toneykirk Dumfries 104 D4
toneywood Aberdeen 141 C7
toneywood Falk 127 F6
tonganess Shetland 160 C7
tonham Aspal Suff 56 D5
tonnall Staffs 62 D4
tonor Oxon 39 F7
tonton Wyville Leics 64 E4
tony Cross Hereford 50 E2
tony Stratford
M Keynes 53 E5
tonyfield Highld 151 D9
toodleigh Devon 10 C4
topes S Yorks 88 F3
topham W Sus 16 C4
topsley Luton 40 B4
tores Corner Suff 57 E7
toreton Mers 85 F4
tornoway W Isles 155 D9
torridge Hereford 50 E2
torrington W Sus 16 C4
torrs Cumb 99 E5
torth Cumb 99 F6
torwood E Yorks 96 E3
totfield Moray 152 A2
totfold C Beds 54 F3
tottesdon Shrops 61 F6
toughton Leics 64 D3
toughton Sur 27 D7
toughton W Sus 16 C2
toul Highld 147 B10
toulton Worcs 50 E4
tour Provost Dorset 13 B5
tour Row Dorset 13 B6
tourbridge W Mid 62 F3
tourpaine Dorset 13 D6
tourport on Severn
Worcs 50 B3
tourton Staffs 62 F2
tourton Warks 51 F7
tourton Wilts 24 F2
tourton Caundle
Dorset 12 C5
tove Orkney 159 E7
tove Shetland 160 L6
toven Suff 69 F7
tow Borders 121 E7
tow Lincs 78 F3
tow Lincs 90 F2
tow Bardolph Norf 67 D6
tow Bedon Norf 68 E2
tow cum Quy Cambs 55 C6
tow Longa Cambs 54 B2
tow Maries Essex 42 E4
tow-on-the-Wold
Glos 38 B1
towbridge Norf 67 D6
towe Shrops 48 B5
towe-by-Chartley
Staffs 62 B4
towe Green Glos 36 D2
towell Som 12 B4
towford Devon 9 F6
towlangtoft Suff 56 C3
towmarket Suff 56 D4
towting Kent 30 E5
towupland Suff 56 D4
traad Argyll 145 G9
trachan Aberds 141 E5
tradbroke Suff 57 B6
tradishall Suff 55 D8
tradsett Norf 67 D6
tragglethorpe Lincs 78 D2
traid S Ayrs 112 E1
traith Dumfries 113 F8
traiton Edin 121 C5
traiton S Ayrs 112 D3
traloch Aberds 141 B7
traloch Perth 133 C7
tramshall Staffs 75 F7
trang IoM 84 E3
tranraer Dumfries 104 C4
tratfield Mortimer
W Berks 26 C4
tratfield Saye Hants 26 C4
tratfield Turgis Hants 26 D4
tratford London 41 F6
tratford St Andrew
Suff 57 C7
tratford St Mary Suff 56 F4
tratford Sub Castle
Wilts 25 F6
tratford Tony Wilts 13 B8
tratford-upon-
Avon Warks 51 D6
trath Highld 149 A12
trath Highld 158 E4
trathan Highld 136 E2
trathan Highld 156 G3
Strathan Highld 157 C8
Strathaven S Lanark 119 E7
Strathblane Stirling 119 B5
Strathcanaird Highld 156 J4
Strathcarron Highld 150 G2
Strathcoil Argyll 124 B2
Strathdon Aberds 140 C2
Strathellie Aberds 153 B10
Strathkinness Fife 129 C6
Strathmashie
House Highld 137 E8
Strathmiglo Fife 128 C4
Strathmore Lodge
Highld 158 F3
Strathpeffer Highld 150 F7
Strathrannoch Highld 150 D6
Strathtay Perth 133 D6
Strathvaich Lodge
Highld 150 D6
Strathwhillan N Ayrs 143 E11
Strathy Highld 157 C11
Strathyre Stirling 126 C4
Stratton Corn 8 D4
Stratton Dorset 12 E4
Stratton Glos 37 D7
Stratton Audley Oxon 39 B6
Stratton on the
Fosse Som 23 D8
Stratton St
Margaret Swindon 38 F1
Stratton St Michael
Norf 68 E5
Stratton Strawless
Norf 81 E8
Stravithie Fife 129 C7
Streat E Sus 17 C7
Streatham London 28 B4
Streatley C Beds 40 B3
Streatley W Berks 39 F5
Street Lancs 92 D5
Street N Yorks 103 D5
Street Som 23 F6
Street Dinas Shrops 73 F7
Street End Kent 30 D5
Street End W Sus 16 E2
Street Gate T&W 110 D5
Street Lydan Wrex 73 F8
Streethay Staffs 62 C5
Streetlam N Yorks 101 E8
Streetly W Mid 62 E4
Streetly End Cambs 55 E7
Strefford Shrops 60 F4
Strelley Notts 76 E5
Strensall York 96 C2
Stretcholt Som 22 E4
Strete Devon 7 E6
Stretford Gtr Man 87 E6
Strethall Essex 55 F5
Stretham Cambs 55 B6
Strettington W Sus 16 D2
Stretton Ches W 73 D8
Stretton Derbys 76 C3
Stretton Rutland 65 C6
Stretton Staffs 62 C2
Stretton Staffs 63 B6
Stretton Warr 86 F4
Stretton Grandison
Hereford 49 E8
Stretton-on-
Dunsmore Warks 52 B2
Stretton-on-Fosse
Warks 51 F7
Stretton Sugwas
Hereford 49 E6
Stretton under
Fosse Warks 63 F8
Stretton Westwood
Shrops 61 E5
Strichen Aberds 153 C9
Strines Gtr Man 87 F7
Stringston Som 22 E3
Strixton Northants 53 C7
Stroat Glos 36 E2
Stromeferry Highld 149 E13
Stromemore Highld 149 E13
Stromness Orkney 159 H3
Stronaba Highld 136 F5
Stronachlachar
Stirling 126 C3
Stronchreggan
Highld 130 B4
Stronchrubie Highld 156 H5
Strone Argyll 145 E10
Strone Highld 136 F4
Strone Highld 137 B8
Strone Invclyd 118 B2
Stronmilchan Argyll 125 C7
Strontian Highld 130 C2
Strood Medway 29 C8
Strood Green Sur 28 E3
Strood Green W Sus 16 B4
Strood Green W Sus 28 F2
Stroud Glos 37 D5
Stroud Hants 15 B8
Stroud Green Essex 42 E4
Stroxton Lincs 78 F2
Struan Highld 149 E8
Struan Perth 133 C5
Strubby Lincs 91 F8
Strumpshaw Norf 69 D6
Strutherhill S Lanark 119 E7
Struy Highld 150 H6
Stryt-issa Wrex 73 E6
Stuartfield Aberds 153 D9
Stub Place Cumb 98 E2
Stubbington Hants 15 D6
Stubbins Lancs 87 C5
Stubbs Cross Kent 19 B6
Stubb's Green Norf 69 E5
Stubbs Green Norf 69 E6
Stubhampton Dorset 13 C7
Stubton Lincs 77 E8
Stuckgowan Argyll 126 D2
Stuckton Hants 14 C2
Stud Green Windsor 27 B6
Studham C Beds 40 C3
Studland Dorset 13 F8
Studley Warks 51 C5
Studley Wilts 24 B4
Studley Roger N Yorks 95 B5
Stump Cross Essex 55 E6
Stuntney Cambs 55 B6
Sturbridge Staffs 74 F5
Sturmer Essex 55 E7
Sturminster
Marshall Dorset 13 D7
Sturminster
Newton Dorset 13 C5
Sturry Kent 31 C5
Sturton N Lincs 90 D3
Sturton by Stow Lincs 90 F2
Sturton le Steeple
Notts 89 F8
Stuston Suff 56 B5
Stutton N Yorks 95 E7
Stutton Suff 57 F5
Styal Ches E 87 F6
Styrrup Notts 89 E7
Suainebost W Isles 155 A10
Suardail W Isles 155 D9
Succoth Aberds 152 E4
Succoth Argyll 125 E8
Suckley Worcs 50 D2
Suckquoy Orkney 159 K5
Sudborough Northants 65 F6
Sudbourne Suff 57 D8
Sudbrook Lincs 78 E2
Sudbrook Mon 36 F2
Sudbrooke Lincs 78 B3
Sudbury Derbys 75 F8
Sudbury London 40 F4
Sudbury Suff 56 E2
Suddie Highld 151 F9
Sudgrove Glos 37 D6
Suffield N Yorks 103 E7
Suffield Norf 81 D8
Sugnall Staffs 74 F4
Suladale Highld 149 C8
Sulaisiadar W Isles 155 D10
Sulby IoM 84 C3
Sulgrave Northants 52 E3
Sulham W Berks 26 B4
Sulhamstead W Berks 26 C4
Sulland Orkney 159 D6
Sullington W Sus 16 C4
Sullom Shetland 160 F5
Sullom Voe Oil
Terminal Shetland 160 F5
Sully V Glam 22 C3
Sumburgh Shetland 160 N6
Summer Bridge
N Yorks 94 C5
Summer-house Darl 101 C7
Summercourt Corn 4 D3
Summerfield Norf 80 D3
Summergangs Hull 97 F7
Summerleaze Mon 35 F8
Summersdale W Sus 16 D2
Summerseat Gtr Man 87 C5
Summertown Oxon 39 D5
Summit Gtr Man 87 D7
Sunbury-on-
Thames Sur 28 C2
Sundaywell Dumfries 113 F8
Sunderland Argyll 142 B3
Sunderland Cumb 107 F8
Sunderland T&W 111 D6
Sunderland Bridge
Durham 111 F5
Sundhope Borders 115 B6
Sundon Park Luton 40 B3
Sundridge Kent 29 D5
Sunipol Argyll 146 F6
Sunk Island E Yorks 91 C6
Sunningdale Windsor 27 C7
Sunninghill Windsor 27 C7
Sunningwell Oxon 38 D4
Sunniside Durham 110 F4
Sunniside T&W 110 D5
Sunnyhurst Blackburn 86 B4
Sunnylaw Stirling 127 E6
Sunnyside W Sus 28 F4
Sunton Wilts 25 D7
Surbiton London 28 C2
Surby IoM 84 E2
Surfleet Lincs 66 B2
Surfleet Seas End
Lincs 66 B2
Surlingham Norf 69 D6
Sustead Norf 81 D7
Susworth Lincs 90 D2
Sutcombe Devon 8 C5
Suton Norf 68 E3
Sutors of
Cromarty Highld 151 E11
Sutterby Lincs 79 B6
Sutterton Lincs 79 F5
Sutton C Beds 54 E3
Sutton Cambs 54 B5
Sutton Kent 31 E7
Sutton London 28 C3
Sutton Mers 86 E3
Sutton N Yorks 89 B5
Sutton Norf 69 B6
Sutton Notts 77 F7
Sutton Notts 89 F7
Sutton Oxon 38 D4
Sutton Pboro 65 E7
Sutton S Yorks 89 C6
Sutton Shrops 61 F7
Sutton Shrops 74 F3
Sutton Som 23 F8
Sutton Staffs 61 B7
Sutton Suff 57 E7
Sutton Sur 27 E8
Sutton W Sus 16 C3
Sutton at Hone Kent 29 B6
Sutton Bassett
Northants 64 E4
Sutton Benger Wilts 24 B4
Sutton Bonington
Notts 64 B2
Sutton Bridge Lincs 66 B4
Sutton Cheney Leics 63 D8
Sutton Coldfield
W Mid 62 E5
Sutton Courtenay
Oxon 39 E5
Sutton Crosses Lincs 66 B4
Sutton Grange N Yorks 95 B5
Sutton Green Sur 27 D8
Sutton Howgrave
N Yorks 95 B6
Sutton In Ashfield
Notts 76 D4
Sutton-in-Craven
N Yorks 94 E3
Sutton in the Elms
Leics 64 E2
Sutton Ings Hull 97 F7
Sutton Lane Ends
Ches E 75 B6
Sutton Leach Mers 86 E3
Sutton Maddock
Shrops 61 D7
Sutton Mallet Som 23 F5
Sutton Mandeville
Wilts 13 B7
Sutton Manor Mers 86 E3
Sutton Montis Som 12 B4
Sutton on Hull Hull 97 F7
Sutton on Sea Lincs 91 F9
Sutton-on-the-
Forest N Yorks 95 C8
Sutton on the Hill
Derbys 76 F2
Sutton on Trent Notts 77 C7
Sutton Scarsdale
Derbys 76 C4
Sutton Scotney Hants 26 F2
Sutton St Edmund
Lincs 66 C3
Sutton St James Lincs 66 C3
Sutton St Nicholas
Hereford 49 E7
Sutton under Brailes
Warks 51 F8
Sutton-under-
Whitestonecliffe
N Yorks 102 F2
Sutton upon Derwent
E Yorks 96 E3
Sutton Valence Kent 30 E2
Sutton Veny Wilts 24 E3
Sutton Waldron Dorset 13 C6
Sutton Weaver Ches W 74 B2
Sutton Wick Bath 23 D7
Swaby Lincs 79 B6
Swadlincote Derbys 63 C7
Swaffham Norf 67 D8
Swaffham Bulbeck
Cambs 55 C6
Swaffham Prior
Cambs 55 C6
Swafield Norf 81 D8
Swainby N Yorks 102 D2
Swainshill Hereford 49 E6
Swainsthorpe Norf 68 D5
Swainswick Bath 24 C2
Swalcliffe Oxon 51 F8
Swalecliffe Kent 30 C5
Swallow Lincs 91 D5
Swallowcliffe Wilts 13 B7
Swallowfield
Wokingham 26 C5
Swallownest S Yorks 89 F5
Swallows Cross Essex 42 E2
Swan Green Ches W 74 B4
Swan Green Suff 57 B6
Swanage Dorset 13 G8
Swanbister Orkney 159 H4
Swanbourne Bucks 39 B8
Swanland E Yorks 90 B3
Swanley Kent 29 C6
Swanley Village Kent 29 C6
Swanmore Hants 15 C6
Swannington Leics 63 C8
Swannington Norf 68 C4
Swanscombe Kent 29 B7
Swansea = Abertawe
Swansea 33 E7
Swanton Abbott Norf 81 E8
Swanton Morley Norf 68 C3
Swanton Novers Norf 81 D6
Swanton Street Kent 30 D2
Swanwick Derbys 76 D4
Swanwick Hants 15 D6
Swarby Lincs 78 E3
Swardeston Norf 68 D5
Swarister Shetland 160 E7
Swarkestone Derbys 63 B7
Swarland Northumb 117 D7
Swarland Estate
Northumb 117 D7
Swarthmoor Cumb 92 B2
Swathwick Derbys 76 C3
Swaton Lincs 78 F4
Swavesey Cambs 54 C4
Sway Hants 14 E3
Swayfield Lincs 65 B6
Swaythling Soton 14 C5
Sweet Green Worcs 49 C8
Sweetham Devon 10 E3
Sweethouse Corn 5 C5
Sweffling Suff 57 C7
Swepstone Leics 63 C7
Swerford Oxon 51 F8
Swettenham Ches E 74 C5
Swetton N Yorks 94 B4
Swffryd Caerph 35 E6
Swiftsden E Sus 18 C4
Swilland Suff 57 D5
Swillington W Yorks 95 F6
Swimbridge Devon 9 B8
Swimbridge
Newland Devon 20 F5
Swinbrook Oxon 38 C2
Swinderby Lincs 77 C8
Swindon Glos 37 B6
Swindon Staffs 62 E2
Swindon Swindon 38 F1
Swine E Yorks 97 F7
Swinefleet E Yorks 89 B8
Swineshead Bedford 53 C8
Swineshead Lincs 78 E5
Swineshead Bridge
Lincs 78 E5
Swiney Highld 158 G4
Swinford Leics 52 B3
Swinford Oxon 38 D4
Swingate Notts 76 E5
Swingfield Minnis
Kent 31 E6
Swingfield Street
Kent 31 E6
Swinhoe Northumb 117 B8
Swinhope Lincs 91 E6
Swining Shetland 160 G6
Swinithwaite N Yorks 101 F5
Swinnow Moor
W Yorks 94 F5
Swinscoe Staffs 75 E8
Swinside Hall Borders 116 C3
Swinstead Lincs 65 B7
Swinton Borders 122 E4
Swinton Gtr Man 87 D5
Swinton N Yorks 94 B5
Swinton N Yorks 96 B3
Swinton S Yorks 88 E5
Swintonmill Borders 122 E4
Swithland Leics 64 C2
Swordale Highld 151 E8
Swordland Highld 147 B10
Swordly Highld 157 C10
Sworton Heath Ches E 86 F4
Swydd-ffynnon
Ceredig 47 C5
Swynnerton Staffs 75 F5
Swyre Dorset 12 F3
Sychtyn Powys 59 D6
Syde Glos 37 C6
Sydenham London 28 B4
Sydenham Oxon 39 D7
Sydenham Damerel
Devon 6 B2
Syderstone Norf 80 D4
Sydling St Nicholas
Dorset 12 E4
Sydmonton Hants 26 D2
Syerston Notts 77 E7
Syke Gtr Man 87 C6
Sykehouse S Yorks 89 C7
Sykes Lancs 93 D6
Syleham Suff 57 B6
Sylen Carms 33 D6
Symbister Shetland 160 G7
Symington S Ayrs 118 F3
Symington S Lanark 120 F2
Symonds Yat Hereford 36 C2
Symondsbury Dorset 12 E2
Synod Inn Ceredig 46 D3
Syre Highld 157 E9
Syreford Glos 37 B7
Syresham Northants 52 E4
Syston Leics 64 C3
Syston Lincs 78 E2
Sytchampton Worcs 50 C3
Sywell Northants 53 C6

T

Taagan Highld 150 E3
Tàbost W Isles 155 A10
Tabost W Isles 155 F8
Tackley Oxon 38 B4
Tacleit W Isles 154 D6
Tacolneston Norf 68 E4
Tadcaster N Yorks 95 E7
Taddington Derbys 75 B8
Taddiport Devon 9 C6
Tadley Hants 26 C4
Tadlow C Beds 54 E3
Tadmarton Oxon 51 F8
Tadworth Sur 28 D3
Tafarn-y-gelyn Denb 73 C5
Tafarnau-bach
Bl Gwent 35 C5
Taff's Well Rhondda 35 F5
Tafolwern Powys 59 D5
Tai Conwy 83 E7
Tai-bach Powys 59 B8
Tai-mawr Conwy 72 E3
Tai-Ucha Denb 72 D4
Taibach Neath 34 F1
Taigh a Ghearraidh
W Isles 148 A2
Tain Highld 151 C10
Tain Highld 158 D4
Tainant Wrex 73 E6
Tainlon Gwyn 82 F4
Tairbeart = Tarbert
W Isles 154 G6
Tai'r-Bull Powys 34 B3
Tairgwaith Neath 33 C8
Takeley Essex 42 B1
Takeley Street Essex 41 B8
Tal-sarn Ceredig 46 D4
Tal-y-bont Ceredig 58 F3
Tal-y-Bont Conwy 83 E7
Tal-y-bont Gwyn 71 E6
Tal-y-bont Gwyn 83 D6
Tal-y-cafn Conwy 83 D7
Tal-y-llyn Gwyn 58 D4
Tal-y-wern Powys 58 D5
Talachddu Powys 48 F2
Talacre Flint 85 F2
Talardd Gwyn 59 B5
Talaton Devon 11 E5
Talbenny Pembs 44 D3
Talbot Green Rhondda 34 F4
Talbot Village Poole 13 E8
Tale Devon 11 D5
Talerddig Powys 59 D6
Talgarreg Ceredig 46 D3
Talgarth Powys 48 F3
Talisker Highld 149 E8
Talke Staffs 74 D5
Talkin Cumb 109 D5
Talla Linnfoots
Borders 114 B4
Talladale Highld 150 D2
Tallarn Green Wrex 73 E8
Tallentire Cumb 107 F8
Talley Carms 46 F5
Tallington Lincs 65 D7
Talmine Highld 157 C8
Talog Carms 32 B4
Talsarn Carms 34 B1
Talsarnau Gwyn 71 D7
Talskiddy Corn 4 C4
Talwrn Anglesey 82 D4
Talwrn Wrex 73 E6
Talybont-on-Usk
Powys 35 B5
Talygarn Rhondda 34 F4
Talyllyn Powys 35 B5
Talysarn Gwyn 82 F4
Talywain Torf 35 D6
Tame Bridge N Yorks 102 D3
Tamerton Foliot Plym 6 C2
Tamworth Staffs 63 D6
Tan Hinon Powys 59 F5
Tan-lan Conwy 83 E7
Tan-lan Gwyn 71 C7
Tan-y-bwlch Gwyn 71 C7
Tan-y-fron Conwy 72 C3
Tan-y-graig Anglesey 82 D5
Tan-y-graig Gwyn 70 D4
Tan-y-groes Ceredig 45 E4
Tan-y-pistyll Powys 59 B7
Tan-yr-allt Gwyn 82 F4
Tandem W Yorks 88 C2
Tanden Kent 19 B6
Tandridge Sur 28 D4
Tanerdy Carms 33 B5
Tanfield Durham 110 D4
Tanfield Lea Durham 110 D4
Tangasdal W Isles 148 J1
Tangiers Pembs 44 D4
Tangley Hants 25 D8
Tanglwst Carms 46 F2
Tangmere W Sus 16 D3
Tangwick Shetland 160 F4
Tankersley S Yorks 88 D4
Tankerton Kent 30 C5
Tannach Highld 158 F5
Tannachie Aberds 141 F6
Tannadice Angus 134 D4
Tannington Suff 57 C6
Tansley Derbys 76 D3
Tansley Knoll Derbys 76 C3
Tansor Northants 65 E7
Tantobie Durham 110 D4
Tanton N Yorks 102 C3
Tanworth-in-Arden
Warks 51 B6
Tanygrisiau Gwyn 71 C7
Tanyrhydiau Ceredig 47 C6
Taobh a Chaolais
W Isles 148 G2
Taobh a Thuath
Loch Aineort W Isles 148 F2
Taobh a Tuath Loch
Baghasdail W Isles 148 F2
Taobh a'Ghlinne
W Isles 155 F8
Taobh Tuath W Isles 154 J4
Taplow Bucks 40 F2
Tapton Derbys 76 B3
Tarbat Ho. Highld 151 D10
Tarbert Argyll 143 C7
Tarbert Argyll 144 E5
Tarbert Argyll 145 G7
Tarbert =
Tairbeart W Isles 154 G6
Tarbet Argyll 126 D2
Tarbet Highld 147 B10
Tarbet Highld 156 E4
Tarbock Green Mers 86 F2
Tarbolton S Ayrs 112 B4
Tarbrax S Lanark 120 D3
Tardebigge Worcs 50 C5
Tarfside Angus 134 B4
Tarland Aberds 140 D3
Tarleton Lancs 86 B2
Tarlogie Highld 151 C10
Tarlscough Lancs 86 C2
Tarlton Glos 37 E6
Tarnbrook Lancs 93 D5
Tarporley Ches W 74 C2
Tarr Som 22 F3
Tarrant Crawford
Dorset 13 D7
Tarrant Gunville
Dorset 13 C7
Tarrant Hinton Dorset 13 C7
Tarrant Keyneston
Dorset 13 D7
Tarrant
Launceston Dorset 13 D7
Tarrant Monkton
Dorset 13 D7
Tarrant Rawston
Dorset 13 D7
Tarrant Rushton
Dorset 13 D7
Tarrel Highld 151 C11
Tarring Neville E Sus 17 D8
Tarrington Hereford 49 E8
Tarsappie Perth 128 B3
Tarskavaig Highld 149 H10
Tarves Aberds 153 E8
Tarvie Highld 150 F7
Tarvie Perth 133 C7
Tarvin Ches W 73 C8
Tasburgh Norf 68 E5
Tasley Shrops 61 E6
Taston Oxon 38 B3
Tatenhill Staffs 63 B6
Tathall End M Keynes 53 E6
Tatham Lancs 93 C6
Tathwell Lincs 91 F7
Tatling End Bucks 40 F3
Tatsfield Sur 28 D5
Tattenhall Ches W 73 D8
Tattenhoe M Keynes 53 F6
Tatterford Norf 80 E4
Tattersett Norf 80 D4
Tattershall Lincs 78 D5
Tattershall Bridge
Lincs 78 D4
Tattershall Thorpe
Lincs 78 D5
Tattingstone Suff 56 F5
Tatworth Som 11 D8
Taunton Som 11 B7
Taverham Norf 68 C4
Tavernspite Pembs 32 C2
Tavistock Devon 6 B2
Taw Green Devon 9 E8
Tawstock Devon 9 B7
Taxal Derbys 75 B7
Tay Bridge Dundee 129 B6
Tayinloan Argyll 143 D7
Taymouth Castle
Perth 132 E4
Taynish Argyll 144 E6
Taynton Glos 36 B4
Taynton Oxon 38 C2
Taynuilt Argyll 125 B6
Tayport Fife 129 B6
Tayvallich Argyll 144 E6
Tealby Lincs 91 E5
Tealing Angus 134 F4
Teangue Highld 149 H11
Teanna Mhachair
W Isles 148 B2
Tebay Cumb 99 D8
Tebworth C Beds 40 B2
Tedburn St Mary
Devon 10 E3
Teddington Glos 50 F4
Teddington London 28 B2
Tedstone Delamere
Hereford 49 D8
Tedstone Wafre
Hereford 49 D8
Teeton Northants 52 B4
Teffont Evias Wilts 24 F4
Teffont Magna Wilts 24 F4
Tegryn Pembs 45 F4
Teigh Rutland 65 C5
Teigncombe Devon 9 F8
Teigngrace Devon 7 B6
Teignmouth Devon 7 B7
Telford Telford 61 D6
Telham E Sus 18 D4
Tellisford Som 24 D3
Telscombe E Sus 17 D8
Telscombe Cliffs
E Sus 17 D7
Templand Dumfries 114 F3
Temple Corn 5 B6
Temple Glasgow 118 C5
Temple Midloth 121 D6
Temple Balsall W Mid 51 B7
Temple Bar Carms 33 C6
Temple Bar Ceredig 46 D4
Temple Cloud Bath 23 D8
Temple Combe Som 12 B5
Temple Ewell Kent 31 E6
Temple Grafton Warks 51 D6
Temple Guiting Glos 37 B7
Temple Herdewyke
Warks 51 D8
Temple Hirst N Yorks 89 B7
Temple Normanton
Derbys 76 C4
Temple Sowerby Cumb 99 B8
Templehall Fife 128 E4
Templeton Devon 10 C3
Templeton Pembs 32 C2
Templeton Bridge
Devon 10 C3
Templetown Durham 110 D4
Tempsford C Beds 54 D2
Ten Mile Bank Norf 67 E6
Tenbury Wells Worcs 49 C7
Tenby = Dinbych-Y-
Pysgod Pembs 32 D2
Tendring Essex 43 B7
Tendring Green Essex 43 B7
Tenston Orkney 159 G3
Tenterden Kent 19 B5
Terling Essex 42 C3
Ternhill Shrops 74 F3
Terregles Banks
Dumfries 107 B6
Terrick Bucks 39 D8
Terrington N Yorks 96 B2
Terrington St
Clement Norf 66 C5
Terrington St John
Norf 66 C5
Teston Kent 29 D8
Testwood Hants 14 C4
Tetbury Glos 37 E5
Tetbury Upton Glos 37 E5
Tetchill Shrops 73 F7
Tetcott Devon 8 E5
Tetford Lincs 79 B6
Tetney Lincs 91 D7
Tetney Lock Lincs 91 D7
Tetsworth Oxon 39 D6
Tettenhall W Mid 62 E2
Teuchan Aberds 153 E10
Teversal Notts 76 C4
Teversham Cambs 55 D5
Teviothead Borders 115 D7
Tewel Aberds 141 F7
Tewin Herts 41 C5
Tewkesbury Glos 50 F3
Teynham Kent 30 C3
Thackthwaite Cumb 98 B3
Thainston Aberds 135 B6
Thakeham W Sus 16 C5
Thame Oxon 39 D7
Thames Ditton Sur 28 C2
Thames Haven Thurrock 42 F3
Thamesmead London 41 F7
Thanington Kent 30 D5
Thankerton S Lanark 120 F2
Tharston Norf 68 E4
Thatcham W Berks 26 C3
Thatto Heath Mers 86 E3
Thaxted Essex 55 F7
The Aird Highld 149 C9
The Arms Norf 67 E8
The Bage Hereford 48 E4
The Balloch Perth 127 C7
The Barony Orkney 159 F3
The Bog Shrops 60 E3
The Bourne Sur 27 E6
The Braes Highld 149 E10
The Broad Hereford 49 C6
The Butts Som 24 E2
The Camp Glos 37 D6
The Camp Herts 40 D4
The Chequer Wrex 73 E8
The City Bucks 39 E7
The Common Wilts 25 F7
The Craigs Highld 150 B7
The Cronk IoM 84 C3
The Dell Suff 69 E7
The Den N Ayrs 118 D3
The Eals Northumb 116 F3
The Eaves Glos 36 D3
The Flatt Cumb 109 B5
The Four Alls Shrops 74 F3
The Garths Shetland 160 B8
The Green Cumb 98 F3
The Green Wilts 24 F3
The Grove Dumfries 107 B6
The Hall Shetland 160 D8
The Haven W Sus 27 F8
The Heath Norf 81 E7
The Heath Suff 56 F5
The Hill Cumb 98 F3
The Howe Cumb 99 F6
The Howe IoM 84 F1
The Hundred Hereford 49 C7
The Lee Bucks 40 D2
The Lhen IoM 84 B3
The Marsh Powys 60 E3
The Marsh Wilts 37 F7
The Middles Durham 110 D5
The Moor Kent 18 C4
The Mumbles =
Y Mwmbwls Swansea 33 F7
The Murray S Lanark 119 D6
The Neuk Aberds 141 E6
The Oval Bath 24 C2
The Pole of Itlaw
Aberds 153 C6
The Quarry Glos 36 E4
The Rhos Pembs 32 C1
The Rock Telford 61 D6
The Ryde Herts 41 D5
The Sands Sur 27 E6
The Stocks Kent 19 C6
The Throat Wokingham 27 C6
The Vauld Hereford 49 E7
The Wyke Shrops 61 D7
Theakston N Yorks 101 F8
Thealby N Lincs 90 C2
Theale Som 23 E6
Theale W Berks 26 B4
Thearne E Yorks 97 F6
Theberton Suff 57 C8
Theddingworth Leics 64 F3
Theddlethorpe
All Saints Lincs 91 F8
Theddlethorpe
St Helen Lincs 91 F8
Thelbridge Barton
Devon 10 C2
Thelnetham Suff 56 B4
Thelveton Norf 68 F4
Thelwall Warr 86 F4
Themelthorpe Norf 81 E6
Thenford Northants 52 E3
Therfield Herts 54 F4
Thetford Lincs 65 C8
Thetford Norf 67 F8
Theydon Bois Essex 41 E7
Thickwood Wilts 24 B3
Thimbleby Lincs 78 C5
Thimbleby N Yorks 102 E2
Thingwall Mers 85 F3
Thirdpart N Ayrs 118 E1
Thirlby N Yorks 102 F2
Thirlestane Borders 121 E8
Thirn N Yorks 101 F7
Thirsk N Yorks 102 F2
Thirtleby E Yorks 97 F7
Thistleton Lancs 92 F4
Thistleton Rutland 65 C6
Thistley Green Suff 55 B7
Thixendale N Yorks 96 C4
Thockrington
Northumb 110 B2
Tholomas Drove
Cambs 66 D3
Tholthorpe N Yorks 95 C7
Thomas Chapel Pembs 32 D2
Thomas Close Cumb 108 E4
Thomastown Aberds 152 E5
Thompson Norf 68 E2
Thomshill Moray 152 C2
Thong Kent 29 B7
Thongsbridge W Yorks 88 D2
Thoralby N Yorks 101 F5
Thoresway Lincs 91 E5
Thorganby Lincs 91 E6
Thorganby N Yorks 96 E2
Thorgill N Yorks 103 E5
Thorington Suff 57 B8
Thorington Street
Suff 56 F4
Thorlby N Yorks 94 D2
Thorley Herts 41 C7
Thorley Street Herts 41 C7
Thorley Street IoW 14 F4
Thormanby N Yorks 95 B7
Thornaby-on-Tees
Stockton 102 C2
Thornage Norf 81 D6
Thornborough Bucks 52 F5
Thornborough N Yorks 95 B5
Thornbury Devon 9 D6
Thornbury Hereford 49 D8
Thornbury S Glos 36 E3
Thornbury W Yorks 94 F4
Thornby Northants 52 B4
Thorncliffe Staffs 75 D7
Thorncombe Dorset 11 D8
Thorncombe Dorset 13 D6
Thorncombe
Street Sur 27 E8
Thorncote
Green C Beds 54 E2
Thorncross IoW 14 F5
Thorndon Suff 56 C5
Thorndon Cross Devon 9 E7
Thorne S Yorks 89 C7
Thorne St
Margaret Som 11 B5
Thorner W Yorks 95 E6
Thorney Notts 77 B8
Thorney Pboro 66 D2
Thorney Crofts E Yorks 91 B6
Thorney Green Suff 56 C4
Thorney Hill Hants 14 E2
Thorney Toll Pboro 66 D3
Thornfalcon Som 11 B7
Thornford Dorset 12 C4
Thorngumbald E Yorks 91 B6
Thornham Norf 80 C3
Thornham Magna Suff 56 B5
Thornham Parva Suff 56 B5
Thornhaugh Pboro 65 D7
Thornhill Cardiff 35 F5
Thornhill Cumb 98 D2
Thornhill Derbys 88 F2
Thornhill Dumfries 113 E8
Thornhill Soton 15 C5
Thornhill Stirling 127 E5
Thornhill W Yorks 88 C3
Thornhill Edge
W Yorks 88 C3
Thornhill Lees
W Yorks 88 C3
Thornholme E Yorks 97 C7
Thornley Durham 110 F4
Thornley Durham 111 F6
Thornliebank E Renf 118 D5
Thorns Suff 55 D8
Thorns Green Ches E 87 F5
Thornsett Derbys 87 F8
Thornthwaite Cumb 98 B4
Thornthwaite N Yorks 94 D4
Thornton Angus 134 E3
Thornton Bucks 53 F5
Thornton E Yorks 96 E3
Thornton Fife 128 E4
Thornton Lancs 92 E3
Thornton Leics 63 D8
Thornton Lincs 78 C5
Thornton Mbro 102 C2
Thornton Mers 85 D4
Thornton Northumb 123 E5
Thornton Pembs 44 E4
Thornton W Yorks 94 F4
Thornton Curtis
N Lincs 90 C4
Thornton Heath
London 28 C4
Thornton Hough Mers 85 F4
Thornton in Craven
N Yorks 94 E2
Thornton-le-Beans
N Yorks 102 E1
Thornton-le-Clay
N Yorks 96 C2
Thornton-le-Dale
N Yorks 103 F6
Thornton le Moor
Lincs 90 E4
Thornton-le-Moor
N Yorks 102 F1
Thornton-le-Moors
Ches W 73 B8
Thornton-le-Street
N Yorks 102 F2
Thornton Rust N Yorks 100 F4
Thornton Steward
N Yorks 101 F6
Thornton Watlass
N Yorks 101 F7
Thorntonhall
S Lanark 119 D5
Thorntonloch E Loth 122 B3
Thorntonpark
Northumb 122 E5
Thornwood
Common Essex 41 D7
Thornydykes Borders 122 E2
Thoroton Notts 77 E7
Thorp Arch W Yorks 95 E7
Thorpe Derbys 75 D8
Thorpe E Yorks 97 E5
Thorpe Lincs 91 F8
Thorpe N Yorks 94 C3
Thorpe Norf 69 E7
Thorpe Notts 77 E7
Thorpe Sur 27 C8
Thorpe Abbotts Norf 57 B5
Thorpe Acre Leics 64 B2
Thorpe Arnold Leics 64 B4
Thorpe Audlin W Yorks 89 C5
Thorpe Bassett
N Yorks 96 B4
Thorpe Bay Southend 43 F5
Thorpe by Water
Rutland 65 E5
Thorpe Common Suff 57 F6
Thorpe Constantine
Staffs 63 D6
Thorpe Culvert Lincs 79 C7
Thorpe End Norf 69 C5
Thorpe Fendykes
Lincs 79 C7
Thorpe Green Essex 43 B7
Thorpe Green Suff 56 D3
Thorpe Hesley S Yorks 88 E4
Thorpe in Balne
S Yorks 89 C6
Thorpe in the
Fallows Lincs 90 F3
Thorpe Langton Leics 64 E4
Thorpe Larches
Durham 102 B1
Thorpe-le-Soken
Essex 43 B7
Thorpe le Street
E Yorks 96 E4
Thorpe Malsor
Northants 53 B6
Thorpe Mandeville
Northants 52 E3
Thorpe Market Norf 81 D8
Thorpe Marriot Norf 68 C4
Thorpe Morieux Suff 56 D3
Thorpe on the Hill
Lincs 78 C2
Thorpe Salvin S Yorks 89 F6
Thorpe Satchville
Leics 64 C4
Thorpe St Andrew
Norf 69 D5
Thorpe St Peter Lincs 79 C7
Thorpe Thewles
Stockton 102 B2
Thorpe Tilney Lincs 78 D4
Thorpe Underwood
N Yorks 95 D7
Thorpe Waterville
Northants 65 F7
Thorpe Willoughby
N Yorks 95 F8
Thorpeness Suff 57 D8
Thorrington Essex 43 C6
Thorverton Devon 10 D4
Thrandeston Suff 56 B5
Thrapston Northants 53 B7
Thrashbush N Lanark 119 C7
Threapland Cumb 107 F8
Threapland N Yorks 94 C2
Threapwood Ches W 73 E8
Threapwood Staffs 75 E7
Three Ashes Hereford 36 B2
Three Bridges W Sus 28 F3
Three Burrows Corn 3 B6
Three Chimneys Kent 18 B5
Three Cocks Powys 48 F3
Three Crosses Swansea 33 E6
Three Cups Corner
E Sus 18 C3
Three Holes Norf 66 D5
Three Leg Cross E Sus 18 B3
Three Legged Cross
Dorset 13 D8
Three Oaks E Sus 18 D5
Threehammer
Common Norf 69 C6
Threekingham Lincs 78 F3
Threemile Cross
Wokingham 26 C5
Threemilestone Corn 3 B6
Threemiletown
W Loth 120 B3
Threlkeld Cumb 99 B5
Threshfield N Yorks 94 C2
Thrigby Norf 69 C7
Thringarth Durham 100 B4
Thringstone Leics 63 C8
Thrintoft N Yorks 101 E8
Thriplow Cambs 54 E5
Throckenholt Lincs 66 D3
Throcking Herts 54 F4
Throckley T&W 110 C4
Throckmorton Worcs 50 E4
Throphill Northumb 117 F7
Thropton Northumb 117 D6
Throsk Stirling 127 E7
Throwleigh Devon 9 E8
Throwley Kent 30 D3
Thrumpton Notts 76 F5
Thrumster Highld 158 F5
Thrunton Northumb 117 C6
Thrupp Glos 37 D5
Thrupp Oxon 38 C4
Thrushelton Devon 9 F6
Thrussington Leics 64 C3
Thruxton Hants 25 E7
Thruxton Hereford 49 F6
Thrybergh S Yorks 89 E5
Thulston Derbys 76 F4
Thundergay N Ayrs 143 D9
Thundersley Essex 42 F3
Thundridge Herts 41 C6
Thurcaston Leics 64 C2
Thurcroft S Yorks 89 F5
Thurgarton Norf 81 D7
Thurgarton Notts 77 E6
Thurgoland S Yorks 88 D3
Thurlaston Leics 64 E2
Thurlaston Warks 52 B2
Thurlbear Som 11 B7
Thurlby Lincs 65 C8
Thurlby Lincs 78 C2
Thurleigh Bedford 53 D8
Thurlestone Devon 6 E4
Thurloxton Som 22 F4
Thurlstone S Yorks 88 D3
Thurlton Norf 69 E7
Thurlwood Ches E 74 D5
Thurmaston Leics 64 D3
Thurnby Leics 64 D3
Thurne Norf 69 C7
Thurnham Kent 30 D2
Thurnham Lancs 92 D4
Thurning Norf 81 E6
Thurning Northants 65 F7
Thurnscoe S Yorks 89 D5
Thurnscoe East
S Yorks 89 D5
Thursby Cumb 108 D3
Thursford Norf 81 D5
Thursley Sur 27 F7
Thurso Highld 158 D3
Thurso East Highld 158 D3
Thurstaston Mers 85 F3
Thurston Suff 56 C3
Thurstonfield Cumb 108 D3
Thurstonland W Yorks 88 C2
Thurton Norf 69 D6
Thurvaston Derbys 76 F2
Thuxton Norf 68 D3
Thwaite N Yorks 100 E3

Thwaite Suff 56 C5
Thwaite St Mary Norf 69 E6
Thwaites W Yorks 94 E3
Thwaites Brow W Yorks 94 E3
Thwing E Yorks 97 B6
Tibbermore Perth 128 B2
Tibberton Glos 36 B4
Tibberton Telford 61 B6
Tibberton Worcs 50 D4
Tibenham Norf 68 F4
Tibshelf Derbys 76 C4
Tibthorpe E Yorks 97 D5
Ticehurst E Sus 18 B3
Tichborne Hants 26 F3
Tickencote Rutland 65 D6
Tickenham N Som 23 B6
Tickhill S Yorks 89 E6
Ticklerton Shrops 60 E4
Ticknall Derbys 63 B7
Tickton E Yorks 97 E6
Tidcombe Wilts 25 D7
Tiddington Oxon 39 D6
Tiddington Warks 51 D7
Tidebrook E Sus 18 C3
Tideford Corn 5 D8
Tideford Cross Corn 5 C8
Tidenham Glos 36 E2
Tideswell Derbys 75 B8
Tidmarsh W Berks 26 B4
Tidmington Warks 51 F7
Tidpit Hants 13 C8
Tidworth Wilts 25 E7
Tiers Cross Pembs 44 D4
Tiffield Northants 52 D4
Tifty Aberds 153 D7
Tigerton Angus 135 C5
Tigh-na-Blair Perth 127 C6
Tighnabruaich Argyll 145 F8
Tighnafiline Highld 155 J13
Tigley Devon 7 C5
Tilbrook Cambs 53 C8
Tilbury Thurrock 29 B7
Tilbury Juxta Clare Essex 55 E8
Tile Cross W Mid 63 F5
Tile Hill W Mid 51 B7
Tilehurst Reading 26 B4
Tilford Sur 27 E6
Tilgate W Sus 28 F3
Tilgate Forest Row W Sus 28 F3
Tillathrowie Aberds 152 E4
Tilley Shrops 60 B5
Tillicoultry Clack 127 E8
Tillingham Essex 43 D5
Tillington Hereford 49 E6
Tillington W Sus 16 B3
Tillington Common Hereford 49 E6
Tillyarblet Angus 135 C5
Tillybirloch Aberds 141 D5
Tillycorthie Aberds 141 B8
Tillydrine Aberds 140 E5
Tillyfour Aberds 140 C4
Tillyfourie Aberds 140 C5
Tillygarmond Aberds 140 E5
Tillygreig Aberds 141 B7
Tillykerrie Aberds 141 B7
Tilmanstone Kent 31 D7
Tilney All Saints Norf 67 C5
Tilney High End Norf 67 C5
Tilney St Lawrence Norf 66 C5
Tilshead Wilts 24 E5
Tilstock Shrops 74 F2
Tilston Ches W 73 D8
Tilstone Fearnall Ches W 74 C2
Tilsworth C Beds 40 B2
Tilton on the Hill Leics 64 D4
Timberland Lincs 78 D4
Timbersbrook Ches E 75 C5
Timberscombe Som 21 E8
Timble N Yorks 94 D4
Timperley Gtr Man 87 F5
Timsbury Bath 23 D8
Timsbury Hants 14 B4
Timsgearraidh W Isles 154 D5
Timworth Green Suff 56 C2
Tincleton Dorset 13 E5
Tindale Cumb 109 D6
Tingewick Bucks 52 F4
Tingley W Yorks 88 B3
Tingrith C Beds 53 F8
Tingwall Orkney 159 F4
Tinhay Devon 9 F5
Tinshill W Yorks 95 F5
Tinsley S Yorks 88 E5
Tintagel Corn 8 F2
Tintern Parva Mon 36 D2
Tintinhull Som 12 C3
Tintwistle Derbys 87 E8
Tinwald Dumfries 114 F3
Tinwell Rutland 65 D7
Tipperty Aberds 141 B8
Tipsend Norf 66 E5
Tipton W Mid 62 E3
Tipton St John Devon 11 E5
Tiptree Essex 42 C4
Tir-y-dail Carms 33 C7
Tirabad Powys 47 E7
Tiraghoil Argyll 146 J6
Tirley Glos 37 B5
Tirphil Caerph 35 D5
Tirril Cumb 99 B7
Tisbury Wilts 13 B7
Tisman's Common W Sus 27 F8
Tissington Derbys 75 D8
Titchberry Devon 8 B4
Titchfield Hants 15 D6
Titchmarsh Northants 53 B8
Titchwell Norf 80 C3
Tithby Notts 77 F6
Titley Hereford 48 C5
Titlington Northumb 117 C7
Titsey Sur 28 D5
Tittensor Staffs 75 F5
Tittleshall Norf 80 E4
Tiverton Ches W 74 C2
Tiverton Devon 10 C4
Tivetshall St Margaret Norf 68 F4
Tivetshall St Mary Norf 68 F4
Tividale W Mid 62 E3
Tivy Dale S Yorks 88 D3
Tixall Staffs 62 B3
Tixover Rutland 65 D6
Toab Orkney 159 H6
Toab Shetland 160 M5
Toadmoor Derbys 76 D3
Tobermory Argyll 147 F8
Toberonochy Argyll 124 E3
Tobha Mor W Isles 148 E2
Tobhtarol W Isles 154 D6
Tobson W Isles 154 D6
Tocher Aberds 153 E6
Tockenham Wilts 24 B5
Tockenham Wick Wilts 37 F7
Tockholes Blackburn 86 B4
Tockington S Glos 36 F3
Tockwith N Yorks 95 D7
Todber Dorset 13 B6
Todding Hereford 49 B6
Toddington C Beds 40 B3
Toddington Glos 50 F5
Todenham Glos 51 F7
Todhills Cumb 108 C3
Todlachie Aberds 141 C5
Todmorden W Yorks 87 B7
Todrig Borders 115 C7
Todwick S Yorks 89 F5
Toft Cambs 54 D4
Toft Lincs 65 C7
Toft Hill Durham 101 B6
Toft Hill Lincs 78 C5
Toft Monks Norf 69 E7
Toft next Newton Lincs 90 F4
Toftrees Norf 80 E4
Tofts Highld 158 D5
Toftwood Norf 68 C2
Togston Northumb 117 D8
Tokavaig Highld 149 G11
Tokers Green Oxon 26 B5
Tolastadh a Chaolais W Isles 154 D6
Tolastadh bho Thuath W Isles 155 C10
Toll Bar S Yorks 89 D6
Toll End W Mid 62 E3
Toll of Birness Aberds 153 E10
Tolland Som 22 F3
Tollard Royal Wilts 13 C7
Tollbar End W Mid 51 B8
Toller Fratrum Dorset 12 E3
Toller Porcorum Dorset 12 E3
Tollerton N Yorks 95 C8
Tollerton Notts 77 F6
Tollesbury Essex 43 C5
Tolleshunt D'Arcy Essex 43 C5
Tolleshunt Major Essex 43 C5
Tolm W Isles 155 D9
Tolpuddle Dorset 13 E5
Tolvah Highld 138 E4
Tolworth London 28 C2
Tomatin Highld 138 B4
Tombreck Highld 151 H9
Tomchrasky Highld 137 C5
Tomdoun Highld 136 D4
Tomich Highld 137 B6
Tomich Highld 151 D9
Tomich House Highld 151 G8
Tomintoul Aberds 139 E7
Tomintoul Moray 139 C7
Tomnaven Moray 152 E4
Tomnavoulin Moray 139 B8
Ton-Pentre Rhondda 34 E3
Tonbridge Kent 29 E6
Tondu Bridgend 34 F2
Tonfanau Gwyn 58 D2
Tong Shrops 61 D7
Tong W Yorks 94 F5
Tong Norton Shrops 61 D7
Tonge Leics 63 B8
Tongham Sur 27 E6
Tongland Dumfries 106 D3
Tongue Highld 157 D8
Tongue End Lincs 65 C8
Tongwynlais Cardiff 35 F5
Tonna Neath 34 E1
Tonwell Herts 41 C6
Tonypandy Rhondda 34 E3
Tonyrefail Rhondda 34 F4
Toot Baldon Oxon 39 D5
Toot Hill Essex 41 D8
Toothill Hants 14 C4
Top of Hebers Gtr Man 87 D6
Topcliffe N Yorks 95 B7
Topcroft Norf 69 E5
Topcroft Street Norf 69 E5
Toppesfield Essex 55 F8
Toppings Gtr Man 86 C5
Topsham Devon 10 F4
Torbay Torbay 7 D7
Torbeg N Ayrs 143 F10
Torboll Farm Highld 151 B10
Torbrex Stirling 127 E6
Torbryan Devon 7 C6
Torcross Devon 7 E6
Tore Highld 151 F9
Torinturk Argyll 145 G7
Torksey Lincs 77 B8
Torlum W Isles 148 C2
Torlundy Highld 131 B5
Tormarton S Glos 24 B2
Tormisdale Argyll 142 C2
Tormitchell S Ayrs 112 E2
Tormore N Ayrs 143 E9
Tornagrain Highld 151 G10
Tornahaish Aberds 139 D8
Tornaveen Aberds 140 D5
Torness Highld 137 B8
Toronto Durham 110 F4
Torpenhow Cumb 108 F2
Torphichen W Loth 120 B2
Torphins Aberds 140 D5
Torpoint Corn 6 D2
Torquay Torbay 7 C7
Torquhan Borders 121 E7
Torran Argyll 124 E4
Torran Highld 149 D10
Torran Highld 151 D10
Torrance E Dunb 119 B6
Torrans Argyll 146 J7
Torranyard N Ayrs 118 E3
Torre Torbay 7 C7
Torridon Highld 150 F2
Torridon Ho. Highld 149 C13
Torrin Highld 149 F10
Torrisdale Highld 157 C9
Torrisdale-Square Argyll 143 E8
Torrish Highld 157 H12
Torrisholme Lancs 92 C4
Torroble Highld 157 J8
Torry Aberdeen 141 D8
Torry Aberds 152 E4
Torryburn Fife 128 F2
Torterston Aberds 153 D10
Torthorwald Dumfries 107 B7
Tortington W Sus 16 D4
Tortworth S Glos 36 E4
Torvaig Highld 149 D9
Torver Cumb 98 E4
Torwood Falk 127 F7
Torworth Notts 89 F7
Tosberry Devon 8 B4
Toscaig Highld 149 E12
Toseland Cambs 54 C3
Tosside N Yorks 93 D7
Tostock Suff 56 C3
Totaig Highld 148 C7
Totaig Highld 149 F13
Tote Highld 149 D9
Totegan Highld 157 C11
Tothill Lincs 91 F8
Totland IoW 14 F4
Totnes Devon 7 C6
Toton Notts 76 F5
Totronald Argyll 146 F4
Totscore Highld 149 B8
Tottenham London 41 E6
Tottenhill Norf 67 C6
Tottenhill Row Norf 67 C6
Totteridge London 41 E5
Totternhoe C Beds 40 B2
Tottington Gtr Man 87 C5
Totton Hants 14 C4
Touchen End Windsor 27 B6
Tournaig Highld 155 J13
Toux Aberds 153 C9
Tovil Kent 29 D8
Tow Law Durham 110 F4
Toward Argyll 145 G10
Towcester Northants 52 E4
Towednack Corn 2 C3
Tower End Norf 67 C6
Towersey Oxon 39 D7
Towie Aberds 140 C3
Towie Aberds 153 B8
Towiemore Moray 152 D3
Town End Cambs 66 E4
Town End Cumb 99 F6
Town Row E Sus 18 B2
Town Yetholm Borders 116 B4
Townend W Dunb 118 B4
Towngate Lincs 65 C8
Townhead Cumb 108 F5
Townhead Dumfries 106 E3
Townhead S Ayrs 112 D2
Townhead S Yorks 88 D2
Townhead of Greenlaw Dumfries 106 C4
Townhill Fife 128 F3
Townsend Bucks 39 D7
Townsend Herts 40 D4
Townshend Corn 2 C4
Towthorpe York 96 D2
Towton N Yorks 95 F7
Towyn Conwy 72 B3
Toxteth Mers 85 F4
Toynton All Saints Lincs 79 C6
Toynton Fen Side Lincs 79 C6
Toynton St Peter Lincs 79 C7
Toy's Hill Kent 29 D5
Trabboch E Ayrs 112 B4
Traboe Corn 3 D6
Tradespark Highld 151 F11
Tradespark Orkney 159 H5
Trafford Park Gtr Man 87 E5
Trallong Powys 34 B3
Tranent E Loth 121 B7
Tranmere Mers 85 F4
Trantlebeg Highld 157 D11
Trantlemore Highld 157 D11
Tranwell Northumb 117 F7
Trapp Carms 33 C7
Traprain E Loth 121 B8
Traquair Borders 121 F6
Trawden Lancs 94 F2
Trawsfynydd Gwyn 71 D8
Tre-Gibbon Rhondda 34 D3
Tre-Taliesin Ceredig 58 E3
Tre-vaughan Carms 32 B4
Tre-wyn Mon 35 B7
Trealaw Rhondda 34 E4
Treales Lancs 92 F4
Trearddur Anglesey 82 D2
Treaslane Highld 149 C8
Trebanog Rhondda 34 E4
Trebanos Neath 33 D8
Trebartha Corn 5 B7
Trebarwith Corn 8 F2
Trebetherick Corn 4 B4
Treborough Som 22 F2
Trebudannon Corn 4 C3
Trebullett Corn 5 B8
Treburley Corn 5 B8
Trebyan Corn 5 C5
Trecastle Powys 34 B2
Trecenydd Caerph 35 F5
Trecwn Pembs 44 B4
Trecynon Rhondda 34 D3
Tredavoe Corn 2 D3
Treddiog Pembs 44 C3
Tredegar Bl Gwent 35 D5
Tredegar = Newydd Tredegar Caerph 35 D5
Tredington Glos 37 B6
Tredington Warks 51 E7
Tredinnick Corn 4 B4
Tredomen Powys 48 F3
Tredunnock Mon 35 E7
Tredustan Powys 48 F3
Treen Corn 2 D2
Treeton S Yorks 88 F5
Tref-Y-Clawdd = Knighton Powys 48 B4
Trefaldwyn = Montgomery Powys 60 E2
Trefasser Pembs 44 B3
Trefdraeth Anglesey 82 D4
Trefdraeth = Newport Pembs 45 F2
Trefecca Powys 48 F3
Trefechan Ceredig 58 F2
Trefeglwys Powys 59 E6
Trefenter Ceredig 46 C5
Treffgarne Pembs 44 C4
Treffynnon = Holywell Flint 73 B5
Treffynnon Pembs 44 C3
Trefgarn Owen Pembs 44 C3
Trefil Bl Gwent 35 C5
Trefilan Ceredig 46 D4
Trefin Pembs 44 B3
Treflach Shrops 60 B2
Trefnanney Powys 60 C2
Trefnant Denb 72 B4
Trefonen Shrops 60 B2
Trefor Anglesey 82 C3
Trefor Gwyn 70 C4
Treforest Rhondda 34 F4
Trefriw Conwy 83 E7
Trefynwy = Monmouth Mon 36 C2
Tregadillett Corn 8 F4
Tregaian Anglesey 82 D4
Tregare Mon 35 C8
Tregaron Ceredig 47 D5
Tregarth Gwyn 83 E6
Tregeare Corn 8 F4
Tregeiriog Wrex 73 F5
Tregele Anglesey 82 B3
Tregidden Corn 3 D6
Treglemais Pembs 44 C3
Tregole Corn 8 E3
Tregonetha Corn 4 C4
Tregony Corn 3 B8
Tregoss Corn 4 C4
Tregoyd Powys 48 F4
Tregroes Ceredig 46 E3
Tregurrian Corn 4 C3
Tregynon Powys 59 E7
Trehafod Rhondda 34 E4
Treharris M Tydf 34 E4
Treherbert Rhondda 34 E3
Trekenner Corn 5 B8
Treknow Corn 8 F2
Trelan Corn 3 E6
Trelash Corn 8 E3
Trelassick Corn 4 D3
Trelawnyd Flint 72 B4
Trelech Carms 45 F4
Treleddyd-fawr Pembs 44 C2
Trelewis M Tydf 35 E5
Treligga Corn 8 F2
Trelights Corn 4 B4
Trelill Corn 4 B5
Trelissick Corn 3 C7
Trellech Mon 36 D2
Trelleck Grange Mon 36 D1
Trelogan Flint 85 F2
Trelystan Powys 60 D2
Tremadog Gwyn 71 C6
Tremail Corn 8 F3
Tremain Ceredig 45 E4
Tremaine Corn 8 F4
Tremar Corn 5 C7
Trematon Corn 5 D8
Tremeirchion Denb 72 B4
Trenance Corn 4 C3
Trenarren Corn 3 B9
Trench Telford 61 C6
Treneglos Corn 8 F4
Trenewan Corn 5 D6
Trent Dorset 12 C3
Trent Vale Stoke 75 E5
Trentham Stoke 75 E5
Trentishoe Devon 20 E5
Treoes V Glam 21 B8
Treorchy = Treorci Rhondda 34 E3
Treorci = Treorchy Rhondda 34 E3
Tre'r-ddôl Ceredig 58 E3
Trerulefoot Corn 5 D8
Tresaith Ceredig 45 D4
Tresawle Corn 3 B7
Trescott Staffs 62 E2
Trescowe Corn 2 C4
Tresham Glos 36 E4
Tresillian Corn 3 B7
Tresinwen Pembs 44 A4
Treskinnick Cross Corn 8 E4
Tresmeer Corn 8 F4
Tresparrett Corn 8 E3
Tresparrett Posts Corn 8 E3
Tressait Perth 133 C5
Tresta Shetland 160 D8
Tresta Shetland 160 H5
Treswell Notts 77 B7
Trethosa Corn 4 D4
Trethurgy Corn 4 D5
Tretio Pembs 44 C2
Tretire Hereford 36 B2
Tretower Powys 35 B5
Treuddyn Flint 73 D6
Trevalga Corn 8 F2
Trevalyn Wrex 73 D7
Trevanson Corn 4 B4
Trevarren Corn 4 C4
Trevarrian Corn 4 C3
Trevarrick Corn 3 B8
Trevaughan Carms 32 C2
Treveighan Corn 5 B5
Trevellas Corn 4 D2
Treverva Corn 3 C7
Trevethin Torf 35 D6
Trevigro Corn 5 C8
Treviscoe Corn 4 D4
Trevone Corn 4 B3
Trewarmett Corn 8 F2
Trewassa Corn 8 F3
Trewellard Corn 2 C2
Trewen Corn 8 F4
Trewennack Corn 3 D5
Trewern Powys 60 C2
Trewethern Corn 4 B5
Trewidland Corn 5 D7
Trewint Corn 8 E3
Trewint Corn 8 F4
Trewithian Corn 3 C7
Trewoofe Corn 2 D3
Trewoon Corn 4 D4
Treworga Corn 3 B7
Treworlas Corn 3 C7
Treyarnon Corn 4 B3
Treyford W Sus 16 C2
Trezaise Corn 4 D4
Triangle W Yorks 87 B8
Trickett's Cross Dorset 13 D8
Triffleton Pembs 44 C4
Trimdon Durham 111 F6
Trimdon Colliery Durham 111 F6
Trimdon Grange Durham 111 F6
Trimingham Norf 81 D8
Trimley Lower Street Suff 57 F6
Trimley St Martin Suff 57 F6
Trimley St Mary Suff 57 F6
Trimpley Worcs 50 B2
Trimsaran Carms 33 D5
Trimstone Devon 20 E3
Trinafour Perth 132 C4
Trinant Caerph 35 D6
Tring Herts 40 C2
Tring Wharf Herts 40 C2
Trinity Angus 135 C6
Trinity Jersey 17
Trisant Ceredig 47 B6
Trislaig Highld 130 B4
Trispen Corn 4 D3
Tritlington Northumb 117 E8
Trochry Perth 133 E6
Trodigal Argyll 143 F7
Troed-rhiwdalar Powys 47 D8
Troedyraur Ceredig 46 E2
Troedyrhiw M Tydf 34 D4
Tromode IoM 84 E3
Trondavoe Shetland 160 F5
Troon Corn 3 C5
Troon S Ayrs 118 F3
Trosaraidh W Isles 148 G2
Trossachs Hotel Stirling 126 D4
Troston Suff 56 B2
Trottiscliffe Kent 29 C7
Trotton W Sus 16 B2
Troutbeck Cumb 99 B5
Troutbeck Cumb 99 D6
Troutbeck Bridge Cumb 99 D6
Trow Green Glos 36 D2
Trowbridge Wilts 24 D3
Trowell Notts 76 F4
Trowle Common Wilts 24 D3
Trowley Bottom Herts 40 C3
Trows Borders 122 F2
Trowse Newton Norf 68 D5
Trudoxhill Som 24 E2
Trull Som 11 B7
Trumaisgearraidh W Isles 148 A3
Trumpan Highld 148 B7
Trumpet Hereford 49 F8
Trumpington Cambs 54 D5
Trunch Norf 81 D8
Trunnah Lancs 92 E3
Truro Corn 3 B7
Trusham Devon 10 F3
Trusley Derbys 76 F2
Trusthorpe Lincs 91 F9
Trysull Staffs 62 E2
Tubney Oxon 38 E4
Tuckenhay Devon 7 D6
Tuckhill Shrops 61 F7
Tuckingmill Corn 3 B5
Tuddenham Suff 55 B8
Tuddenham St Martin Suff 57 E5
Tudeley Kent 29 E7
Tudhoe Durham 111 F5
Tudorville Hereford 36 B2
Tudweiliog Gwyn 70 D3
Tuesley Sur 27 E7
Tuffley Glos 37 C5
Tufton Hants 26 E2
Tufton Pembs 32 B1
Tugby Leics 64 D4
Tugford Shrops 61 F5
Tullibardine Perth 127 C8
Tullibody Clack 127 E7
Tullich Argyll 125 D6
Tullich Highld 138 B2
Tullich Muir Highld 151 D10
Tulliemet Perth 133 D6
Tulloch Aberds 135 B7
Tulloch Aberds 153 E8
Tulloch Perth 128 B2
Tulloch Castle Highld 151 E8
Tullochgorm Argyll 125 F5
Tulloes Angus 135 E5
Tullybannocher Perth 127 B6
Tullybelton Perth 133 F7
Tullyfergus Perth 134 E2
Tullymurdoch Perth 134 D1
Tullynessle Aberds 140 C4
Tumble Carms 33 C6
Tumby Woodside Lincs 79 D5
Tummel Bridge Perth 132 D4
Tunga W Isles 155 D9
Tunstall E Yorks 97 F9
Tunstall Kent 30 C2
Tunstall Lancs 93 B6
Tunstall N Yorks 101 E7
Tunstall Norf 69 D7
Tunstall Stoke 75 D5
Tunstall Suff 57 D7
Tunstall T&W 111 D6
Tunstead Derbys 75 B8
Tunstead Gtr Man 87 D8
Tunstead Norf 81 E8
Tunworth Hants 26 E4
Tupsley Hereford 49 E7
Tupton Derbys 76 C3
Tur Langton Leics 64 E4
Turgis Green Hants 26 D4
Turin Angus 135 D5
Turkdean Glos 37 C8
Turleigh Wilts 24 C3
Turn Lancs 87 C6
Turnastone Hereford 49 F5
Turnberry S Ayrs 112 D2
Turnditch Derbys 76 E2
Turners Hill W Sus 28 F4
Turners Puddle Dorset 13 E6
Turnford Herts 41 D6
Turnhouse Edin 120 B4
Turnworth Dorset 13 D6
Turriff Aberds 153 C7
Turton Bottoms Blackburn 86 C5
Turves Cambs 66 E3
Turvey Bedford 53 D7
Turville Bucks 39 E7
Turville Heath Bucks 39 E7
Turweston Bucks 52 F4
Tushielaw Borders 115 C6
Tutbury Staffs 63 B6
Tutnall Worcs 50 B4
Tutshill Glos 36 E2
Tuttington Norf 81 E8
Tutts Clump W Berks 26 B3
Tuxford Notts 77 B7
Twatt Orkney 159 F3
Twatt Shetland 160 H5
Twechar E Dunb 119 B7
Tweedmouth Northumb 123 D5
Tweedsmuir Borders 114 B3
Twelve Heads Corn 3 B6
Twemlow Green Ches E 74 C4
Twenty Lincs 65 B8
Twerton Bath 24 C2
Twickenham London 28 B2
Twigworth Glos 37 B5
Twineham W Sus 17 C6
Twinhoe Bath 24 D2
Twinstead Essex 56 F2
Twinstead Green Essex 56 F2
Twiss Green Warr 86 E4
Twiston Lancs 93 E8
Twitchen Devon 21 F6
Twitchen Shrops 49 B5
Two Bridges Devon 6 B4
Two Dales Derbys 76 C2
Two Mills Ches W 73 B7
Twycross Leics 63 D7
Twyford Bucks 39 B6
Twyford Derbys 63 B7
Twyford Hants 15 B5
Twyford Leics 64 C4
Twyford Lincs 65 B6
Twyford Norf 81 E6
Twyford Wokingham 27 B5
Twyford Common Hereford 49 F7
Twyn-y-Sheriff Mon 35 D8
Twynholm Dumfries 106 D3
Twyning Glos 50 F3
Twyning Green Glos 50 F4
Twynllanan Carms 34 B1
Twynmynydd Carms 33 C7
Twywell Northants 53 B7
Ty-draw Conwy 83 F8
Ty-hen Carms 32 B4
Ty-hen Gwyn 70 D2
Ty-mawr Anglesey 82 C4
Ty Mawr Carms 46 E4
Ty Mawr Cwm Conwy 72 E3
Ty-nant Conwy 72 E3
Ty-nant Gwyn 59 B6
Ty-uchaf Powys 59 B7
Tyberton Hereford 49 F5
Tyburn W Mid 62 E5
Tycroes Carms 33 C7
Tycrwyn Powys 59 C8
Tydd Gote Lincs 66 C4
Tydd St Giles Cambs 66 C4
Tydd St Mary Lincs 66 C4
Tyddewi = St David's Pembs 44 C2
Tyddyn-mawr Gwyn 71 C6
Tye Green Essex 41 D7
Tye Green Essex 42 B3
Tye Green Essex 55 F6
Tyldesley Gtr Man 86 D4
Tyler Hill Kent 30 C5
Tylers Green Bucks 40 E2
Tylorstown Rhondda 34 E4
Tylwch Powys 59 F6
Tyn-y-celyn Wrex 73 F5
Tyn-y-coed Shrops 60 B2
Tyn-y-fedwen Powys 72 F5
Tyn-y-ffridd Powys 72 F5
Tyn-y-graig Powys 48 D2
Ty'n-y-groes Conwy 83 D7
Ty'n-y-maes Gwyn 83 E6
Tyn-y-pwll Anglesey 82 C4
Ty'n-yr-eithin Ceredig 47 C5
Tyncelyn Ceredig 46 C5
Tyndrum Stirling 131 F7
Tyne Tunnel T&W 111 C6
Tyneham Dorset 13 F6
Tynehead Midloth 121 D6
Tynemouth T&W 111 C6
Tynewydd Rhondda 34 E3
Tyninghame E Loth 122 B2
Tynron Dumfries 113 E8
Tynygongl Anglesey 82 C5
Tynygraig Ceredig 47 C5
Tŷ'r-felin-isaf Conwy 83 E8
Tyrie Aberds 153 B9
Tyringham M Keynes 53 E6
Tythecott Devon 9 C6
Tythegston Bridgend 21 B7
Tytherington Ches E 75 B6
Tytherington S Glos 36 F3
Tytherington Som 24 E2
Tytherington Wilts 24 E4
Tytherleigh Devon 11 D8
Tywardreath Corn 5 D5
Tywyn Conwy 83 D7
Tywyn Gwyn 58 D2

U

Uachdar W Isles 148 C2
Uags Highld 149 E12
Ubbeston Green Suff 57 B7
Ubley Bath 23 D7
Uckerby N Yorks 101 D7
Uckfield E Sus 17 B8
Uckington Glos 37 B6
Uddingston S Lanark 119 C6
Uddington S Lanark 119 F8
Udimore E Sus 19 D5
Udny Green Aberds 141 B7
Udny Station Aberds 141 B8
Udston S Lanark 119 D6
Udstonhead S Lanark 119 E7
Uffcott Wilts 25 B6
Uffculme Devon 11 C5
Uffington Lincs 65 D7
Uffington Oxon 38 F3
Uffington Shrops 60 C5
Ufford Pboro 65 D7
Ufford Suff 57 D6
Ufton Warks 51 C8
Ufton Nervet W Berks 26 C4
Ugadale Argyll 143 F8
Ugborough Devon 6 D4
Uggeshall Suff 69 F7
Ugglebarnby N Yorks 103 D6
Ughill S Yorks 88 E3
Ugley Essex 41 B8
Ugley Green Essex 41 B8
Ugthorpe N Yorks 103 C5
Uidh W Isles 148 J1
Uig Argyll 145 E10
Uig Highld 148 C6
Uig Highld 149 B8
Uigen W Isles 154 D5
Uigshader Highld 149 D9
Uisken Argyll 146 K6
Ulbster Highld 158 F5
Ulceby Lincs 79 B7
Ulceby N Lincs 90 C5
Ulceby Skitter N Lincs 90 C5
Ulcombe Kent 30 E2
Uldale Cumb 108 F2
Uley Glos 36 E4
Ulgham Northumb 117 E8
Ullapool Highld 150 B4
Ullenhall Warks 51 C6
Ullenwood Glos 37 C6
Ulleskelf N Yorks 95 E8
Ullesthorpe Leics 64 F2
Ulley S Yorks 89 F5
Ullingswick Hereford 49 E7
Ullinish Highld 149 E8
Ullock Cumb 98 B2
Ulnes Walton Lancs 86 C3
Ulpha Cumb 98 E3
Ulrome E Yorks 97 D7
Ulsta Shetland 160 E6
Ulva House Argyll 146 H7
Ulverston Cumb 92 B2
Ulwell Dorset 13 F8
Umberleigh Devon 9 B8
Unapool Highld 156 F5
Unasary W Isles 148 F2
Underbarrow Cumb 99 E6
Undercliffe W Yorks 94 F4
Underhoull Shetland 160 C7
Underriver Kent 29 D6
Underwood Notts 76 D4
Undy Mon 35 F8
Unifirth Shetland 160 H4
Union Cottage Aberds 141 E7
Union Mills IoM 84 E3
Union Street E Sus 18 B4
Unstone Derbys 76 B3
Unstone Green Derbys 76 B3
Unthank Cumb 108 F4
Unthank Cumb 109 E6
Unthank End Cumb 108 F4
Up Cerne Dorset 12 D4
Up Exe Devon 10 D4
Up Hatherley Glos 37 B6
Up Holland Lancs 86 D3
Up Marden W Sus 15 C8
Up Nately Hants 26 D4
Up Somborne Hants 25 F8
Up Sydling Dorset 12 D4
Upavon Wilts 25 D6
Upchurch Kent 30 C2
Upcott Hereford 48 D5
Upend Cambs 55 D7
Upgate Norf 68 C4
Uphall W Loth 120 B3
Uphall Station W Loth 120 B3
Upham Devon 10 D3
Upham Hants 15 B6
Uphampton Worcs 50 C3
Uphill N Som 22 D5
Uplawmoor E Renf 118 D4
Upleadon Glos 36 B4
Upleatham Redcar 102 C4
Uplees Kent 30 C3
Uploders Dorset 12 E3
Uplowman Devon 10 C5
Uplyme Devon 11 E8
Upminster London 42 F1
Upnor Medway 29 B8
Upottery Devon 11 D7
Upper Affcot Shrops 60 F4
Upper Ardchronie Highld 151 C9
Upper Arley Worcs 61 F7
Upper Arncott Oxon 39 C6
Upper Astrop Northants 52 F3
Upper Badcall Highld 156 E4
Upper Basildon W Berks 26 B3
Upper Beeding W Sus 17 C5
Upper Benefield Northants 65 F6
Upper Bighouse Highld 157 D11
Upper Boddington Northants 52 D2
Upper Borth Ceredig 58 F3
Upper Boyndlie Aberds 153 B9
Upper Brailes Warks 51 F8
Upper Breakish Highld 149 F11
Upper Breinton Hereford 49 E6
Upper Broadheath Worcs 50 D3
Upper Broughton Notts 64 B3
Upper Bucklebury W Berks 26 C3
Upper Burnhaugh Aberds 141 E7
Upper Caldecote C Beds 54 E2
Upper Catesby Northants 52 D3
Upper Chapel Powys 48 E2
Upper Church Village Rhondda 34 F4
Upper Chute Wilts 25 D7
Upper Clatford Hants 25 E8
Upper Clynnog Gwyn 71 C5
Upper Cumberworth W Yorks 88 D3
Upper Cwm-twrch Powys 34 C1
Upper Cwmbran Torf 35 E6
Upper Dallachy Moray 152 B3
Upper Dean Bedford 53 C8
Upper Denby W Yorks 88 D3
Upper Denton Cumb 109 C6
Upper Derraid Highld 151 H13
Upper Dicker E Sus 18 E2
Upper Dovercourt Essex 57 F6
Upper Druimfin Argyll 147 F8
Upper Dunsforth N Yorks 95 C7
Upper Eathie Highld 151 E10
Upper Elkstone Staffs 75 D7
Upper End Derbys 75 B7
Upper Farringdon Hants 26 F5
Upper Framilode Glos 36 C4
Upper Glenfintaig Highld 137 F5
Upper Gornal W Mid 62 E3
Upper Gravenhurst C Beds 54 F2
Upper Green Mon 35 C7
Upper Green W Berks 25 C8
Upper Grove Common Hereford 36 B2
Upper Hackney Derbys 76 C2
Upper Hale Sur 27 E6
Upper Halistra Highld 148 C7
Upper Halling Medway 29 C7
Upper Hambleton Rutland 65 D6
Upper Hardres Court Kent 31 D5
Upper Hartfield E Sus 29 F5
Upper Haugh S Yorks 88 E5
Upper Heath Shrops 61 F5
Upper Hellesdon Norf 68 C5
Upper Helmsley N Yorks 96 D2
Upper Hergest Hereford 48 D4
Upper Heyford Northants 52 D4
Upper Heyford Oxon 38 B4
Upper Hill Hereford 49 D6
Upper Hopton W Yorks 88 C2
Upper Horsebridge E Sus 18 D2
Upper Hulme Staffs 75 C7
Upper Inglesham Swindon 38 E2
Upper Inverbrough Highld 151 H11
Upper Killay Swansea 33 E6
Upper Knockando Moray 152 D1
Upper Lambourn W Berks 38 F3
Upper Leigh Staffs 75 F7
Upper Lenie Highld 137 B8
Upper Lochton Aberds 141 E5
Upper Longdon Staffs 62 C4
Upper Lybster Highld 158 G4
Upper Lydbrook Glos 36 C3
Upper Maes-coed Hereford 48 F5
Upper Midway Derbys 63 B6
Upper Milovaig Highld 148 D6
Upper Minety Wilts 37 E7
Upper Mitton Worcs 50 B3
Upper North Dean Bucks 39 E8
Upper Obney Perth 133 F7
Upper Ollach Highld 149 E10
Upper Padley Derbys 76 B2
Upper Pollicott Bucks 39 C7
Upper Poppleton York 95 D8
Upper Quinton Warks 51 E6
Upper Ratley Hants 14 B4
Upper Rissington Glos 38 C2
Upper Rochford Worcs 49 C8
Upper Sandaig Highld 149 G12
Upper Sanday Orkney 159 H6
Upper Sapey Hereford 49 C8
Upper Saxondale Notts 77 F6
Upper Seagry Wilts 37 F6
Upper Shelton C Beds 53 E7
Upper Sheringham Norf 81 C7
Upper Skelmorlie N Ayrs 118 C2
Upper Slaughter Glos 38 B1
Upper Soudley Glos 36 C3
Upper Stondon C Beds 54 F2
Upper Stowe Northants 52 D4
Upper Stratton Swindon 38 F1
Upper Street Hants 14 C2
Upper Street Norf 69 C6
Upper Street Norf 69 C6
Upper Street Suff 56 F5
Upper Strensham Worcs 50 F4
Upper Sundon C Beds 40 B3
Upper Swell Glos 38 B1
Upper Tean Staffs 75 F7
Upper Tillyrie Perth 128 D3
Upper Tooting London 28 B3
Upper Tote Highld 149 C10
Upper Town N Som 23 C7
Upper Treverward Shrops 48 B4
Upper Tysoe Warks 51 E8
Upper Upham Wilts 25 B7
Upper Wardington Oxon 52 E2
Upper Weald M Keynes 53 F5
Upper Weedon Northants 52 D4
Upper Wield Hants 26 F4
Upper Winchendon Bucks 39 C7
Upper Witton W Mid 62 E4
Upper Woodend Aberds 141 C5
Upper Woodford Wilts 25 F6
Upper Wootton Hants 26 D3
Upper Wyche Hereford 50 E2
Upperby Cumb 108 D4
Uppermill Gtr Man 87 D7
Uppersound Shetland 160 J6
Upperthong W Yorks 88 D2
Upperthorpe N Lincs 89 D8
Upperton W Sus 16 B3
Uppertown Derbys 76 C3
Uppertown Highld 158 C5
Uppertown Orkney 159 J5
Uppingham Rutland 65 E5
Uppington Shrops 61 D6
Upsall N Yorks 102 F2
Upshire Essex 41 D7
Upstreet Kent 31 C6
Upthorpe Suff 56 B3
Upton Cambs 54 B2
Upton Ches W 73 C8
Upton Corn 8 D4
Upton Dorset 12 F5
Upton Dorset 13 E7
Upton Hants 14 C4
Upton Hants 25 D8
Upton Leics 63 E7
Upton Lincs 90 F2
Upton Mers 85 F3
Upton Norf 69 C6
Upton Northants 52 C5
Upton Notts 77 B7
Upton Notts 77 D7
Upton Oxon 39 F5
Upton Pboro 65 D8
Upton Slough 27 B7
Upton Som 10 B4
Upton W Yorks 89 C5
Upton Bishop Hereford 36 B3
Upton Cheyney S Glos 23 C8
Upton Cressett Shrops 61 E6
Upton Cross Corn 5 B7
Upton Grey Hants 26 E4
Upton Hellions Devon 10 D3
Upton Lovell Wilts 24 E4
Upton Magna Shrops 61 C5
Upton Noble Som 24 F2
Upton Pyne Devon 10 E4
Upton Scudamore Wilts 24 E3
Upton St Leonard's Glos 37 C5
Upton Snodsbury Worcs 50 C
Upton upon Severn Worcs 50 E
Upton Warren Worcs 50 C
Upwaltham W Sus 16 C
Upware Cambs 55 B
Upwell Norf 66 D
Upwey Dorset 12 F
Upwood Cambs 66 F
Uradale Shetland 160 K
Urafirth Shetland 160 F
Urchfont Wilts 24 D
Urdimarsh Hereford 49 E
Ure Shetland 160 F
Ure Bank N Yorks 95 B
Urgha W Isles 154 H
Urishay Common Hereford 48 F
Urlay Nook Stockton 102 C
Urmston Gtr Man 87 E
Urpeth Durham 110 D
Urquhart Highld 151 F
Urquhart Moray 152 B
Urra N Yorks 102 D
Urray Highld 151 F
Ushaw Moor Durham 110 E
Usk = Brynbuga Mon 35 D
Usselby Lincs 90 E
Usworth T&W 111 D
Utkinton Ches W 74 C
Utley W Yorks 94 E
Uton Devon 10 E
Utterby Lincs 91 E
Uttoxeter Staffs 75 F
Uwchmynydd Gwyn 70 E
Uxbridge London 40 F
Uyeasound Shetland 160 C
Uzmaston Pembs 44 D

V

Valley Anglesey 82 D
Valley Truckle Corn 8 F
Valleyfield Dumfries 106 D
Valsgarth Shetland 160 B
Valtos Highld 149 B
Van Powys 59 F
Vange Essex 42 F
Varteg Torf 35 D
Vatten Highld 149 D
Vaul Argyll 146 G
Vaynor M Tydf 34 C
Veensgarth Shetland 160 J
Velindre Powys 48 F
Vellow Som 22 F
Veness Orkney 159 F
Venn Green Devon 9 C
Venn Ottery Devon 11 E
Vennington Shrops 60 D
Venny Tedburn Devon 10 E
Ventnor IoW 15 G
Vernham Dean Hants 25 D
Vernham Street Hants 25 D
Vernolds Common Shrops 60 F
Verwood Dorset 13 D
Veryan Corn 3 C
Vicarage Devon 11 F
Vickerstown Cumb 92 C
Victoria Corn 4 C
Victoria S Yorks 88 D
Vidlin Shetland 160 G
Viewpark N Lanark 119 C
Vigo Village Kent 29 C
Vinehall Street E Sus 18 C
Vine's Cross E Sus 18 D
Viney Hill Glos 36 D
Virginia Water Sur 27 C
Virginstow Devon 9 E
Vobster Som 24 E
Voe Shetland 160 E
Voe Shetland 160 G
Vowchurch Hereford 49 F
Voxter Shetland 160 F
Voy Orkney 159 G

W

Wackerfield Durham 101 B
Wacton Norf 68 E
Wadbister Shetland 160 J
Wadborough Worcs 50 E
Waddesdon Bucks 39 C
Waddingham Lincs 90 E
Waddington Lancs 93 E
Waddington Lincs 78 C
Wadebridge Corn 4 B
Wadeford Som 11 C
Wadenhoe Northants 65 F
Wadesmill Herts 41 C
Wadhurst E Sus 18 B
Wadshelf Derbys 76 B
Wadsley S Yorks 88 E
Wadsley Bridge S Yorks 88 E
Wadworth S Yorks 89 E
Waen Denb 72 C
Waen Denb 72 C
Waen Fach Powys 60 C
Waen Goleugoed Denb 72 B
Wag Highld 157 G1
Wainfleet All Saints Lincs 79 D
Wainfleet Bank Lincs 79 D
Wainfleet St Mary Lincs 79 D
Wainfleet Tofts Lincs 79 D
Wainhouse Corner Corn 8 E
Wainscott Medway 29 B
Wainstalls W Yorks 87 B
Waitby Cumb 100 D
Waithe Lincs 91 D
Wake Lady Green N Yorks 102 E
Wakefield W Yorks 88 B
Wakerley Northants 65 E
Wakes Colne Essex 42 B
Walberswick Suff 57 B
Walberton W Sus 16 D
Walbottle T&W 110 C
Walcot Lincs 78 F
Walcot N Lincs 90 B
Walcot Shrops 60 F
Walcot Swindon 38 F
Walcot Telford 61 C
Walcot Green Norf 68 F
Walcote Leics 64 F
Walcote Warks 51 D
Walcott Lincs 78 D
Walcott Norf 69 A
Walden N Yorks 101 F
Walden Head N Yorks 100 F
Walden Stubbs N Yorks 89 C
Waldersey Cambs 66 D
Walderslade Medway 29 C
Walderton W Sus 15 C
Walditch Dorset 12 E
Waldley Derbys 75 F
Waldridge Durham 111 D
Waldringfield Suff 57 E
Waldringfield Heath Suff 57 E
Waldron E Sus 18 D
Wales S Yorks 89 F
Walesby Lincs 90 E
Walesby Notts 77 B
Walford Hereford 36 B
Walford Hereford 49 B
Walford Shrops 60 B

Place	County	Ref
Whitwell	Rutland	65 D6
Whitwell-on-the-Hill	N Yorks	96 C3
Whitwell Street	Norf	81 E7
Whitwick	Leics	63 C8
Whitwood	W Yorks	88 B5
Whitworth	Lancs	87 C6
Whixall	Shrops	74 F2
Whixley	N Yorks	95 D7
Whorlton	Durham	101 C6
Whorlton	N Yorks	102 D2
Whygate	Northumb	109 B7
Whyle	Hereford	49 C7
Whyteleafe	Sur	28 D4
Wibdon	Glos	36 E2
Wibsey	W Yorks	88 A2
Wibtoft	Leics	63 F8
Wichenford	Worcs	50 C2
Wichling	Kent	30 D3
Wick	Bmouth	14 E2
Wick	Devon	11 D6
Wick	S Glos	24 B2
Wick	Highld	158 E5
Wick	V Glam	21 B8
Wick	W Sus	16 D4
Wick	Wilts	14 B2
Wick	Worcs	50 E4
Wick Hill	Wokingham	27 C5
Wick St Lawrence	N Som	23 C5
Wicken	Cambs	55 B6
Wicken	Northants	53 F5
Wicken Bonhunt	Essex	55 F5
Wicken Green Village	Norf	80 D4
Wickenby	Lincs	90 F4
Wickersley	S Yorks	89 E5
Wickford	Essex	42 E3
Wickham	Hants	15 C6
Wickham	W Berks	25 B8
Wickham Bishops	Essex	42 C4
Wickham Market	Suff	57 D7
Wickham Skeith	Suff	56 C4
Wickham St Paul	Essex	56 F2
Wickham Street	Suff	55 D8
Wickham Street	Suff	56 C4
Wickhambreaux	Kent	31 D6
Wickhambrook	Suff	55 D8
Wickhamford	Worcs	51 E5
Wickhampton	Norf	69 D7
Wicklewood	Norf	68 D3
Wickmere	Norf	81 D7
Wickwar	S Glos	36 F4
Widdington	Essex	55 F6
Widdrington	Northumb	117 E8
Widdrington Station	Northumb	117 E8
Wide Open	T&W	110 B5
Widecombe in the Moor	Devon	6 B5
Widegates	Corn	5 D7
Widemouth Bay	Corn	8 D4
Widewall	Orkney	159 J5
Widford	Essex	42 D3
Widford	Herts	41 C7
Widham	Wilts	37 F7
Widmer End	Bucks	40 E1
Widmerpool	Notts	64 B3
Widnes	Halton	86 F3
Wigan	Gtr Man	86 D3
Wiggaton	Devon	11 E6
Wiggenhall St Germans	Norf	67 C5
Wiggenhall St Mary Magdalen	Norf	67 C5
Wiggenhall St Mary the Virgin	Norf	67 C5
Wigginton	Herts	40 C2
Wigginton	Oxon	52 F2
Wigginton	Staffs	63 D6
Wigginton	York	95 D8
Wigglesworth	N Yorks	93 D8
Wiggonby	Cumb	108 D2
Wiggonholt	W Sus	16 C4
Wighill	N Yorks	95 E7
Wighton	Norf	80 D5
Wigley	Hants	14 C4
Wigmore	Hereford	49 C6
Wigmore	Medway	30 C2
Wigsley	Notts	77 B8
Wigsthorpe	Northants	65 F7
Wigston	Leics	64 E3
Wigthorpe	Notts	89 F6
Wigtoft	Lincs	79 F5
Wigton	Cumb	108 E2
Wigtown	Dumfries	105 D8
Wike	W Yorks	95 E6
Wike Well End	S Yorks	89 C7
Wilbarston	Northants	64 F5
Wilberfoss	E Yorks	96 D3
Wilberlee	W Yorks	87 C8
Wilburton	Cambs	55 B5
Wilby	Norf	68 F3
Wilby	Northants	53 C6
Wilby	Suff	57 B6
Wilcot	Wilts	25 C6
Wilcott	Shrops	60 C3
Wilcrick	Newport	35 F8
Wilday Green	Derbys	76 B3
Wildboarclough	Ches E	75 C6
Wilden	Bedford	53 D8
Wilden	Worcs	50 B3
Wildhern	Hants	25 D8
Wildmoor	Worcs	50 B4
Wildsworth	Lincs	90 E2
Wilford	Nottingham	77 F5
Wilkesley	Ches E	74 E3
Wilkhaven	Highld	151 C12
Wilkieston	W Loth	120 C4
Willand	Devon	10 C5
Willaston	Ches E	74 D3
Willaston	Ches W	73 B7
Willen	M Keynes	53 E6
Willenhall	W Mid	51 B8
Willenhall	W Mid	62 E3
Willerby	E Yorks	97 F6
Willerby	N Yorks	97 B6
Willersey	Glos	51 F6
Willersley	Hereford	48 E5
Willesborough	Kent	30 E4
Willesborough Lees	Kent	30 E4
Willesden	London	41 F5
Willett	Som	22 F3
Willey	Shrops	61 E6
Willey	Warks	63 F8
Willey Green	Sur	27 D7
Willian	Herts	54 F3
Willingale	Essex	42 D1
Willingdon	E Sus	18 E2
Willingham	Cambs	54 B5
Willingham by Stow	Lincs	90 F2
Willington	Bedford	54 E2
Willington	Derbys	63 B6
Willington	Durham	110 F4
Willington	T&W	111 C6
Willington	Warks	51 F7
Willington Corner	Ches W	74 C2
Willisham Tye	Suff	56 D4
Willitoft	E Yorks	96 F3
Williton	Som	22 E2
Willoughbridge	Staffs	74 E4
Willoughby	Lincs	79 B7
Willoughby	Warks	52 C3
Willoughby-on-the-Wolds	Notts	64 B3
Willoughby Waterleys	Leics	64 E2
Willoughton	Lincs	90 E3
Willows Green	Essex	42 C3
Willsbridge	S Glos	23 B8
Willsworthy	Devon	9 F7
Wilmcote	Warks	51 D6
Wilmington	Devon	11 E7
Wilmington	E Sus	18 E2
Wilmington	Kent	29 B6
Wilminstone	Devon	6 B2
Wilmslow	Ches E	87 F6
Wilnecote	Staffs	63 D6
Wilpshire	Lancs	93 F6
Wilsden	W Yorks	94 F3
Wilsford	Lincs	78 E3
Wilsford	Wilts	25 D6
Wilsford	Wilts	25 F6
Wilsill	N Yorks	94 C4
Wilsley Pound	Kent	18 B4
Wilsom	Hants	26 F5
Wilson	Leics	63 B8
Wilstead	Bedford	53 E8
Wilsthorpe	Lincs	65 C7
Wilstone	Herts	40 C2
Wilton	Borders	115 C7
Wilton	Cumb	98 C2
Wilton	N Yorks	103 F6
Wilton	Redcar	102 C3
Wilton	Wilts	25 C5
Wilton	Wilts	25 F5
Wimbish	Essex	55 F6
Wimbish Green	Essex	55 F7
Wimblebury	Staffs	62 C4
Wimbledon	London	28 B3
Wimblington	Cambs	66 E4
Wimborne Minster	Dorset	13 E8
Wimborne St Giles	Dorset	13 C8
Wimbotsham	Norf	67 D6
Wimpson	Soton	14 C4
Wimpstone	Warks	51 E7
Wincanton	Som	12 B5
Wincham	Ches W	74 B3
Winchburgh	W Loth	120 B3
Winchcombe	Glos	37 B7
Winchelsea	E Sus	19 D6
Winchelsea Beach	E Sus	19 D6
Winchester	Hants	15 B5
Winchet Hill	Kent	29 E8
Winchfield	Hants	27 D5
Winchmore Hill	Bucks	40 E2
Winchmore Hill	London	41 E6
Wincle	Ches E	75 C6
Wincobank	S Yorks	88 E4
Windermere	Cumb	99 E6
Winderton	Warks	51 E8
Windhill	Highld	151 G8
Windhouse	Shetland	160 D6
Windlehurst	Gtr Man	87 F7
Windlesham	Sur	27 C7
Windley	Derbys	76 E3
Windmill Hill	E Sus	18 D3
Windmill Hill	Som	11 C8
Windrush	Glos	38 C1
Windsor	N Lincs	89 C8
Windsor	Windsor	27 B7
Windsoredge	Glos	37 D5
Windygates	Fife	128 D5
Windywalls	Borders	122 F3
Windywwe	N Lanark	120 C2
Wineham	W Sus	17 C6
Winestead	E Yorks	91 B6
Winewall	Lancs	94 E2
Winfarthing	Norf	68 F4
Winford	IoW	15 F6
Winford	N Som	23 C7
Winforton	Hereford	48 E4
Winfrith Newburgh	Dorset	13 F6
Wing	Bucks	40 B1
Wing	Rutland	65 D5
Wingate	Durham	111 F7
Wingates	Gtr Man	86 D4
Wingates	Northumb	117 E7
Wingerworth	Derbys	76 C3
Wingfield	C Beds	40 B2
Wingfield	Suff	57 B6
Wingfield	Wilts	24 D3
Wingham	Kent	31 D6
Wingmore	Kent	31 E5
Wingrave	Bucks	40 C1
Winkburn	Notts	77 D7
Winkfield	Brack	27 B7
Winkfield Row	Brack	27 B6
Winkhill	Staffs	75 D7
Winklebury	Hants	26 D4
Winkleigh	Devon	9 D8
Winksley	N Yorks	95 B5
Winkton	Dorset	14 E2
Winlaton	T&W	110 C4
Winless	Highld	158 E5
Winmarleigh	Lancs	92 E4
Winnal	Hereford	49 F6
Winnall	Hants	15 B5
Winnersh	Wokingham	27 B5
Winscales	Cumb	98 B2
Winscombe	N Som	23 D6
Winsford	Ches W	74 C3
Winsford	Som	21 F8
Winsham	Som	11 D8
Winshill	Staffs	63 B6
Winskill	Cumb	109 F5
Winslade	Hants	26 E4
Winsley	Wilts	24 C3
Winslow	Bucks	39 B7
Winson	Glos	37 D7
Winsor	Hants	14 C4
Winster	Cumb	99 E6
Winster	Derbys	76 C2
Winston	Durham	101 C6
Winston	Suff	57 C5
Winston Green	Suff	57 C5
Winstone	Glos	37 D6
Winswell	Devon	9 C6
Winter Gardens	Essex	42 F3
Winterborne Clenston	Dorset	13 D6
Winterborne Herringston	Dorset	12 F4
Winterborne Houghton	Dorset	13 D6
Winterborne Kingston	Dorset	13 E6
Winterborne Monkton	Dorset	12 F4
Winterborne Stickland	Dorset	13 D6
Winterborne Whitechurch	Dorset	13 D6
Winterborne Zelston	Dorset	13 E6
Winterbourne	S Glos	36 F3
Winterbourne	W Berks	26 B2
Winterbourne Abbas	Dorset	12 E4
Winterbourne Bassett	Wilts	25 B6
Winterbourne Dauntsey	Wilts	25 F6
Winterbourne Down	S Glos	23 B8
Winterbourne Earls	Wilts	25 F6
Winterbourne Gunner	Wilts	25 F6
Winterbourne Monkton	Wilts	25 B6
Winterbourne Steepleton	Dorset	12 F4
Winterbourne Stoke	Wilts	25 E5
Winterburn	N Yorks	94 D2
Winteringham	N Lincs	90 B3
Winterley	Ches E	74 D4
Wintersett	W Yorks	88 C4
Wintershill	Hants	15 C6
Winterton	N Lincs	90 C3
Winterton-on-Sea	Norf	69 C7
Winthorpe	Lincs	79 C8
Winthorpe	Notts	77 D8
Winton	Bmouth	13 E8
Winton	Cumb	100 C2
Winton	N Yorks	102 E2
Wintringham	N Yorks	96 B5
Winwick	Cambs	65 F8
Winwick	Northants	52 B4
Winwick	Warr	86 E4
Wirksworth	Derbys	76 D2
Wirksworth Moor	Derbys	76 D3
Wirswall	Ches E	74 E2
Wisbech	Cambs	66 D4
Wisbech St Mary	Cambs	66 D4
Wisborough Green	W Sus	16 B4
Wiseton	Notts	89 F8
Wishaw	N Lanark	119 D7
Wishaw	Warks	63 E5
Wisley	Sur	27 D8
Wispington	Lincs	78 B5
Wissenden	Kent	30 E3
Wissett	Suff	57 B7
Wistanstow	Shrops	60 F4
Wistanswick	Shrops	61 B6
Wistaston	Ches E	74 D3
Wistaston Green	Ches E	74 D3
Wiston	Pembs	32 C1
Wiston	S Lanark	120 F2
Wiston	W Sus	16 C5
Wistow	Cambs	66 F2
Wistow	N Yorks	95 F8
Wiswell	Lancs	93 F7
Witcham	Cambs	66 F4
Witchampton	Dorset	13 D7
Witchford	Cambs	55 B6
Witham	Essex	42 C4
Witham Friary	Som	24 E2
Witham on the Hill	Lincs	65 C7
Withcall	Lincs	91 F6
Withdean	Brighton	17 D7
Witherenden Hill	E Sus	18 C3
Witheridge	Devon	10 C3
Witherley	Leics	63 E7
Withern	Lincs	91 F8
Withernsea	E Yorks	91 B7
Withernwick	E Yorks	97 E7
Withersdale Street	Suff	69 F5
Withersfield	Suff	55 E7
Witherslack	Cumb	99 F6
Withiel	Corn	4 C4
Withiel Florey	Som	21 F8
Withington	Glos	37 C7
Withington	Gtr Man	87 E6
Withington	Hereford	49 E7
Withington	Shrops	61 C5
Withington	Staffs	75 F7
Withington Green	Ches E	74 B5
Withleigh	Devon	10 C4
Withnell	Lancs	86 B4
Withybrook	Warks	63 F8
Withycombe	Som	22 E2
Withycombe Raleigh	Devon	10 F5
Witham	E Sus	29 F5
Withypool	Som	21 F7
Witley	Sur	27 F7
Witnesham	Suff	57 D5
Witney	Oxon	38 C3
Wittering	Pboro	65 D7
Wittersham	Kent	19 C5
Witton	Angus	135 B5
Witton	Worcs	50 C3
Witton Bridge	Norf	69 A6
Witton Gilbert	Durham	110 E5
Witton-le-Wear	Durham	110 F4
Witton Park	Durham	110 F4
Wiveliscombe	Som	11 B5
Wivelrod	Hants	26 F4
Wivelsfield	E Sus	17 B7
Wivelsfield Green	E Sus	17 B7
Wivenhoe	Essex	43 B6
Wivenhoe Cross	Essex	43 B6
Wiveton	Norf	81 C6
Wix	Essex	43 B7
Wixford	Warks	51 D5
Wixhill	Shrops	61 B5
Wixoe	Suff	55 E8
Woburn	C Beds	53 F7
Woburn Sands	M Keynes	53 F7
Wokefield Park	W Berks	26 C4
Woking	Sur	27 D8
Wokingham	Wokingham	27 C6
Wolborough	Devon	7 B6
Wold Newton	E Yorks	97 B6
Wold Newton	NE Lincs	91 E6
Woldingham	Sur	28 D4
Wolfclyde	S Lanark	120 F3
Wolferton	Norf	67 B6
Wolfhill	Perth	134 F1
Wolf's Castle	Pembs	44 C4
Wolfsdale	Pembs	44 C4
Woll	Borders	115 B7
Wollaston	Northants	53 C7
Wollaston	Shrops	60 C3
Wollaton	Nottingham	76 F5
Wollerton	Shrops	74 F3
Wollescote	W Mid	62 F3
Wolsingham	Durham	110 F3
Wolstanton	Staffs	75 E5
Wolston	Warks	52 B2
Wolvercote	Oxon	38 D4
Wolverhampton	W Mid	62 E3
Wolverley	Shrops	73 F8
Wolverley	Worcs	50 B3
Wolverton	Hants	26 D3
Wolverton	M Keynes	53 E6
Wolverton	Warks	51 C7
Wolverton Common	Hants	26 D3
Wolvesnewton	Mon	36 E1
Wolvey	Warks	63 F8
Wolviston	Stockton	102 B2
Wombleton	N Yorks	102 F4
Wombourne	Staffs	62 E2
Wombwell	S Yorks	88 D4
Womenswold	Kent	31 D6
Womersley	N Yorks	89 C6
Wonastow	Mon	36 C1
Wonersh	Sur	27 E8
Wonson	Devon	9 F8
Wonston	Hants	26 F2
Wooburn	Bucks	40 F2
Wooburn Green	Bucks	40 F2
Wood Dalling	Norf	81 E6
Wood End	Herts	41 B6
Wood End	Warks	51 B6
Wood End	Warks	63 E6
Wood Field	Sur	28 D2
Wood Green	London	41 E6
Wood Hayes	W Mid	62 D3
Wood Norton	Norf	81 E6
Wood Street	Norf	69 B6
Wood Street	Sur	27 D7
Wood Walton	Cambs	66 F2
Woodacott	Devon	9 D5
Woodale	N Yorks	94 B3
Woodbank	Argyll	143 G7
Woodbastwick	Norf	69 C6
Woodbeck	Notts	77 B7
Woodborough	Notts	77 E6
Woodborough	Wilts	25 D6
Woodbridge	Suff	57 E6
Woodbury	Devon	10 F5
Woodbury Salterton	Devon	10 F5
Woodchester	Glos	37 D5
Woodchurch	Kent	19 B6
Woodchurch	Mers	85 F3
Woodcombe	Som	21 E8
Woodcote	Oxon	39 F6
Woodcott	Hants	26 D2
Woodcroft	Glos	36 E2
Woodcutts	Dorset	13 C7
Woodditton	Cambs	55 D7
Woodeaton	Oxon	39 C5
Woodend	Cumb	98 E3
Woodend	Northants	52 E4
Woodend	W Sus	16 D2
Woodend Green	Northants	52 E4
Woodfalls	Wilts	14 B2
Woodfield	Oxon	39 B5
Woodfield	S Ayrs	112 B3
Woodford	Corn	8 C4
Woodford	Devon	7 D5
Woodford	Glos	36 E3
Woodford	Gtr Man	87 F6
Woodford	London	41 E7
Woodford	Northants	53 B7
Woodford Bridge	London	41 E7
Woodford Halse	Northants	52 D3
Woodgate	Norf	68 C3
Woodgate	W Mid	62 F3
Woodgate	W Sus	16 D3
Woodgate	Worcs	50 C4
Woodgreen	Hants	14 C2
Woodhall	Herts	41 C5
Woodhall	Invclyd	118 B3
Woodhall	N Yorks	100 E4
Woodham	Sur	27 C8
Woodham Ferrers	Essex	42 E3
Woodham Mortimer	Essex	42 D4
Woodham Walter	Essex	42 D4
Woodhaven	Fife	129 B6
Woodhead	Aberds	153 E7
Woodhey	Gtr Man	87 C5
Woodhill	Shrops	61 F7
Woodhorn	Northumb	117 F8
Woodhouse	Leics	64 C2
Woodhouse	N Yorks	88 B5
Woodhouse	S Yorks	88 F5
Woodhouse	W Yorks	88 B4
Woodhouse	W Yorks	95 F5
Woodhouse Eaves	Leics	64 C2
Woodhouse Park	Gtr Man	87 F6
Woodhouselee	Midloth	120 C5
Woodhouselees	Dumfries	108 B3
Woodhouses	Staffs	63 C5
Woodhurst	Cambs	54 B4
Woodingdean	Brighton	17 D7
Woodkirk	W Yorks	88 B3
Woodland	Devon	7 C5
Woodland	Durham	101 B5
Woodlands	Aberds	141 E6
Woodlands	Dorset	13 D8
Woodlands	Hants	14 C4
Woodlands	Highld	151 E8
Woodlands	N Yorks	95 D6
Woodlands	S Yorks	89 D6
Woodlands Park	Windsor	27 B6
Woodlands St Mary	W Berks	25 B8
Woodlane	Staffs	62 B5
Woodleigh	Devon	6 E5
Woodlesford	W Yorks	88 B4
Woodley	Gtr Man	87 E7
Woodley	Wokingham	27 B5
Woodmancote	Glos	36 E4
Woodmancote	Glos	37 B6
Woodmancote	Glos	37 D7
Woodmancote	W Sus	15 D8
Woodmancote	W Sus	17 C6
Woodmancott	Hants	26 E3
Woodmansey	E Yorks	97 F6
Woodmansterne	Sur	28 D3
Woodminton	Wilts	13 B8
Woodnesborough	Kent	31 D7
Woodnewton	Northants	65 E7
Woodplumpton	Lancs	92 F5
Woodrising	Norf	68 D2
Wood's Green	E Sus	18 B3
Woodseaves	Shrops	61 B6
Woodseaves	Staffs	61 B7
Woodsetts	S Yorks	89 F6
Woodsford	Dorset	13 E5
Woodside	Aberds	141 D8
Woodside	Aberds	153 D10
Woodside	Brack	27 B7
Woodside	Fife	129 D6
Woodside	Hants	14 E4
Woodside	Herts	41 D5
Woodside	Perth	134 F2
Woodside of Arbeadie	Aberds	141 E6
Woodstock	Oxon	38 C4
Woodstock	Pembs	32 B1
Woodthorpe	Derbys	76 B4
Woodthorpe	Leics	64 C2
Woodthorpe	Lincs	91 F8
Woodthorpe	York	95 E8
Woodtown	Devon	9 B6
Woodvale	Mers	85 C4
Woodville	Derbys	63 C7
Woodyates	Dorset	13 C8
Woofferton	Shrops	49 C7
Wookey	Som	23 E7
Wookey Hole	Som	23 E7
Wool	Dorset	13 F6
Woolacombe	Devon	20 E3
Woolage Green	Kent	31 E6
Woolaston	Glos	36 E2
Woolavington	Som	22 E5
Woolbeding	W Sus	16 B2
Wooldale	W Yorks	88 D2
Wooler	Northumb	117 B5
Woolfardisworthy	Devon	8 B5
Woolfardisworthy	Devon	10 D3
Woolfords Cottages	S Lanark	120 D3
Woolhampton	W Berks	26 C3
Woolhope	Hereford	49 F8
Woolhope Cockshoot	Hereford	49 F8
Woolland	Dorset	13 D5
Woollaton	Devon	9 C6
Woolley	Bath	24 C2
Woolley	Cambs	54 B2
Woolley	Corn	8 C4
Woolley	Derbys	76 C3
Woolley	W Yorks	88 C4
Woolley Green	Wilts	24 C3
Woolmere Green	Worcs	50 C4
Woolpit	Suff	56 C3
Woolscott	Warks	52 C2
Woolsington	T&W	110 C4
Woolstanwood	Ches E	74 D3
Woolstaston	Shrops	60 E4
Woolsthorpe	Lincs	65 B6
Woolsthorpe	Lincs	77 F8
Woolston	Devon	6 E5
Woolston	Shrops	60 B3
Woolston	Shrops	60 F4
Woolston	Soton	14 C5
Woolston	Warr	86 F4
Woolstone	M Keynes	53 F6
Woolstone	Oxon	38 F2
Woolton	Mers	86 F2
Woolton Hill	Hants	26 C2
Woolverstone	Suff	57 F5
Woolverton	Som	24 D2
Woolwich	London	28 B5
Woolwich Ferry	London	28 B5
Woonton	Hereford	49 D5
Wooperton	Northumb	117 B6
Woore	Shrops	74 E4
Wootten Green	Suff	57 B6
Wootton	Bedford	53 E8
Wootton	Hants	14 E3
Wootton	Hereford	48 D5
Wootton	Kent	31 E6
Wootton	N Lincs	90 C4
Wootton	Northants	53 D5
Wootton	Oxon	38 C4
Wootton	Oxon	38 D4
Wootton	Shrops	49 B6
Wootton	Shrops	60 B3
Wootton	Staffs	62 B2
Wootton	Staffs	75 E8
Wootton Bridge	IoW	15 E6
Wootton Common	IoW	15 E6
Wootton Courtenay	Som	21 E8
Wootton Fitzpaine	Dorset	11 E8
Wootton Rivers	Wilts	25 C6
Wootton St Lawrence	Hants	26 D3
Wootton Wawen	Warks	51 C6
Worcester	Worcs	50 D3
Worcester Park	London	28 C3
Wordsley	W Mid	62 F2
Worfield	Shrops	61 E7
Work	Orkney	159 G5
Workington	Cumb	98 B1
Worksop	Notts	77 B5
Worlaby	N Lincs	90 C4
World's End	W Berks	26 B2
Worle	N Som	23 C5
Worleston	Ches E	74 D3
Worlingham	Suff	69 F7
Worlington	Suff	55 B7
Worlingworth	Suff	57 C6
Wormald Green	N Yorks	95 C6
Wormbridge	Hereford	49 F6
Wormegay	Norf	67 C6
Wormelow Tump	Hereford	49 F6
Wormhill	Derbys	75 B8
Wormingford	Essex	56 F3
Worminghall	Bucks	39 D6
Wormington	Glos	50 F5
Worminster	Som	23 E7
Wormit	Fife	129 B5
Wormleighton	Warks	52 D2
Wormley	Herts	41 D6
Wormley	Sur	27 F7
Wormley West End	Herts	41 D6
Wormshill	Kent	30 D2
Wormsley	Hereford	49 E6
Worplesdon	Sur	27 D7
Worrall	S Yorks	88 E4
Worsbrough	S Yorks	88 D4
Worsbrough Common	S Yorks	88 D4
Worsley	Gtr Man	86 D5
Worstead	Norf	69 B6
Worsthorne	Lancs	93 F8
Worston	Lancs	93 E7
Worswell	Devon	6 E3
Worth	Kent	31 D7
Worth	W Sus	28 F4
Worth Matravers	Dorset	13 G7
Wortham	Suff	56 B4
Worthen	Shrops	60 D3
Worthenbury	Wrex	73 E8
Worthing	Norf	68 C2
Worthing	W Sus	16 D5
Worthington	Leics	63 B8
Worting	Hants	26 D4
Wortley	S Yorks	88 E4
Wortley	W Yorks	95 F5
Worton	N Yorks	100 E4
Worton	Wilts	24 D4
Wortwell	Norf	69 F5
Wotherton	Shrops	60 D2
Wotton	Sur	28 E2
Wotton-under-Edge	Glos	36 E4
Wotton Underwood	Bucks	39 C6
Woughton on the Green	M Keynes	53 F6
Wouldham	Kent	29 C8
Wrabness	Essex	57 F5
Wrafton	Devon	20 F3
Wragby	Lincs	78 B4
Wragby	W Yorks	88 C4
Wragholme	Lincs	91 E7
Wramplingham	Norf	68 D4
Wrangbrook	W Yorks	89 C5
Wrangham	Aberds	153 E6
Wrangle	Lincs	79 D7
Wrangle Bank	Lincs	79 D7
Wrangle Lowgate	Lincs	79 D7
Wrangway	Som	11 C6
Wrantage	Som	11 B8
Wrawby	N Lincs	90 D4
Wraxall	Dorset	12 D3
Wraxall	N Som	23 B6
Wraxall	Som	23 F8
Wray	Lancs	93 C6
Wraysbury	Windsor	27 B8
Wrayton	Lancs	93 B6
Wrea Green	Lancs	92 F3
Wreay	Cumb	99 B6
Wreay	Cumb	108 E4
Wrecclesham	Sur	27 E6
Wrecsam = Wrexham	Wrex	73 D7
Wrekenton	T&W	111 D5
Wrelton	N Yorks	103 F5
Wrenbury	Ches E	74 E2
Wrench Green	N Yorks	103 F7
Wreningham	Norf	68 E4
Wrentham	Suff	69 F7
Wrenthorpe	W Yorks	88 B4
Wrentnall	Shrops	60 D4
Wressle	E Yorks	96 F3
Wressle	N Lincs	90 D3
Wrestlingworth	C Beds	54 E3
Wretham	Norf	68 F2
Wretton	Norf	67 E6
Wrexham = Wrecsam	Wrex	73 D7
Wrexham Industrial Estate	Wrex	73 E7
Wribbenhall	Worcs	50 B2
Wrightington Bar	Lancs	86 C3
Wrinehill	Staffs	74 E4
Wrington	N Som	23 C6
Writhlington	Bath	24 D2
Writtle	Essex	42 D2
Wrockwardine	Telford	61 C6
Wroot	N Lincs	89 D8
Wrotham	Kent	29 D7
Wrotham Heath	Kent	29 D7
Wroughton	Swindon	37 F8
Wroxall	IoW	15 G6
Wroxall	Warks	51 B7
Wroxeter	Shrops	61 D5
Wroxham	Norf	69 C6
Wroxton	Oxon	52 E2
Wyaston	Derbys	75 E8
Wyberton	Lincs	79 E6
Wyboston	Bedford	54 D2
Wybunbury	Ches E	74 E4
Wych Cross	E Sus	28 F5
Wychbold	Worcs	50 C4
Wyck	Hants	27 F5
Wyck Rissington	Glos	38 B1
Wycoller	Lancs	94 F2
Wycomb	Leics	64 B4
Wycombe Marsh	Bucks	40 E1
Wyddial	Herts	54 F4
Wye	Kent	30 E4
Wyesham	Mon	36 C2
Wyfordby	Leics	64 C4
Wyke	Dorset	13 B5
Wyke	Shrops	61 D6
Wyke	Sur	27 D6
Wyke	W Yorks	88 B2
Wyke Regis	Dorset	12 G4
Wykeham	N Yorks	96 B4
Wykeham	N Yorks	103 F7
Wyken	W Mid	63 F7
Wyke	Shrops	61 D7
Wykey	Shrops	60 B3
Wylam	Northumb	110 C4
Wylde Green	W Mid	62 E5
Wyllie	Caerph	35 E5
Wylye	Wilts	24 F5
Wymering	Ptsmth	15 D7
Wymeswold	Leics	64 B3
Wymington	Bedford	53 C7
Wymondham	Leics	65 C5
Wymondham	Norf	68 D4
Wyndham	Bridgend	34 E3
Wynford Eagle	Dorset	12 E3
Wyng	Orkney	159 J4
Wynyard Village	Stockton	102 B2
Wyre Piddle	Worcs	50 E4
Wysall	Notts	64 B3
Wythall	Worcs	51 B5
Wytham	Oxon	38 D4
Wythburn	Cumb	99 C5
Wythenshawe	Gtr Man	87 F6
Wythop Mill	Cumb	98 B3
Wyton	Cambs	54 B3
Wyverstone	Suff	56 C4
Wyverstone Street	Suff	56 C4
Wyville	Lincs	65 B5
Wyvis Lodge	Highld	150 D7

Y

Place	County	Ref
Y Bala = Bala	Gwyn	72 F3
Y Barri = Barry	V Glam	22 C3
Y Bont-Faen = Cowbridge	V Glam	21 B8
Y Drenewydd = Newtown	Powys	59 E8
Y Felinheli	Gwyn	82 E5
Y Fenni = Abergavenny	Mon	35 C6
Y Fflor	Gwyn	70 D5
Y Fflint = Flint	Flint	73 B6
Y-Ffrith	Denb	72 A4
Y Gelli Gandryll = Hay-on-Wye	Powys	48 E4
Y Mwmbwls = The Mumbles	Swansea	33 F7
Y Pil = Pyle	Bridgend	34 F2
Y Rhws = Rhoose	V Glam	22 C2
Y Rhyl = Rhyl	Denb	72 A4
Y Trallwng = Welshpool	Powys	60 D2
Y Waun = Chirk	Wrex	73 F6
Yaddlethorpe	N Lincs	90 D2
Yafford	IoW	14 F5
Yafforth	N Yorks	101 E8
Yalding	Kent	29 D7
Yanworth	Glos	37 C7
Yapham	E Yorks	96 D3
Yapton	W Sus	16 D3
Yarburgh	Lincs	91 E7
Yarcombe	Devon	11 D7
Yard	Som	22 F2
Yardley	W Mid	62 F5
Yardley Gobion	Northants	53 E5
Yardley Hastings	Northants	53 D6
Yardro	Powys	48 D4
Yarkhill	Hereford	49 E8
Yarlet	Staffs	62 B3
Yarlington	Som	12 B4
Yarlside	Cumb	92 C2
Yarm	Stockton	102 C2
Yarmouth	IoW	14 F4
Yarnbrook	Wilts	24 D3
Yarnfield	Staffs	75 F5
Yarnscombe	Devon	9 B7
Yarnton	Oxon	38 C4
Yarpole	Hereford	49 C6
Yarrow	Borders	115 B6
Yarrow Feus	Borders	115 B6
Yarsop	Hereford	49 E6
Yarwell	Northants	65 E7
Yate	S Glos	36 F4
Yateley	Hants	27 C6
Yatesbury	Wilts	25 B5
Yattendon	W Berks	26 B3
Yatton	Hereford	49 C6
Yatton	N Som	23 C6
Yatton Keynell	Wilts	24 B3
Yaverland	IoW	15 F7
Yaxham	Norf	68 C3
Yaxley	Cambs	65 E8
Yaxley	Suff	56 B5
Yazor	Hereford	49 E6
Yeading	London	40 F4
Yeadon	W Yorks	94 E5
Yealand Conyers	Lancs	92 B5
Yealand Redmayne	Lancs	92 B5
Yealmpton	Devon	6 D3
Yearby	Redcar	102 B4
Yearsley	N Yorks	95 B8
Yeaton	Shrops	60 C4
Yeaveley	Derbys	75 E8
Yedingham	N Yorks	96 B4
Yeldon	Bedford	53 C8
Yelford	Oxon	38 D3
Yelland	Devon	20 F3
Yelling	Cambs	54 C3
Yelvertoft	Northants	52 B3
Yelverton	Devon	6 C3
Yelverton	Norf	69 D5
Yenston	Som	12 B5
Yeo Mill	Devon	10 B3
Yeoford	Devon	10 E2
Yeolmbridge	Corn	8 F5
Yeovil	Som	12 C3
Yeovil Marsh	Som	12 C3
Yeovilton	Som	12 B3
Yerbeston	Pembs	32 D1
Yesnaby	Orkney	159 G3
Yetlington	Northumb	117 D6
Yetminster	Dorset	12 C3
Yettington	Devon	11 F5
Yetts o'Muckhart	Clack	128 D2
Yieldshields	S Lanark	119 D8
Yiewsley	London	40 F3
Ynys-meudwy	Neath	33 D8
Ynysboeth	Rhondda	34 E4
Ynysddu	Caerph	35 E5
Ynysgyfflog	Gwyn	58 C3
Ynyshir	Rhondda	34 E4
Ynyslas	Ceredig	58 E3
Ynystawe	Swansea	33 D7
Ynysybwl	Rhondda	34 E4
Yockenthwaite	N Yorks	94 B2
Yockleton	Shrops	60 C3
Yokefleet	E Yorks	90 B2
Yoker	W Dunb	118 C5
Yonder Bognie	Aberds	152 D5
York	York	95 D8
York Town	Sur	27 C6
Yorkletts	Kent	30 C4
Yorkley	Glos	36 D3
Yorton	Shrops	60 B5
Youlgreave	Derbys	76 C2
Youlstone	Devon	8 C4
Youlthorpe	E Yorks	96 D3
Youlton	N Yorks	95 C7
Young Wood	Lincs	78 B4
Young's End	Essex	42 C3
Yoxall	Staffs	62 C5
Yoxford	Suff	57 C7
Yr Hôb = Hope	Flint	73 D7
Yr Wyddgrug = Mold	Flint	73 C6
Ysbyty-Cynfyn	Ceredig	47 B6
Ysbyty Ifan	Conwy	72 E2
Ysbyty Ystwyth	Ceredig	47 B6
Ysceifiog	Flint	73 B5
Yspitty	Carms	33 E6
Ystalyfera	Neath	34 D1
Ystrad	Rhondda	34 E3
Ystrad Aeron	Ceredig	46 D4
Ystrad-mynach	Caerph	35 E5
Ystradfellte	Powys	34 C3
Ystradffin	Carms	47 E6
Ystradgynlais	Powys	34 C1
Ystradmeurig	Ceredig	47 C6
Ystradowen	Carms	33 C8
Ystradowen	V Glam	22 B2
Ystumtuen	Ceredig	47 B6
Ythanbank	Aberds	153 E9
Ythanwells	Aberds	153 E6
Ythsie	Aberds	153 E8

Z

Place	County	Ref
Zeal Monachorum	Devon	10 D2
Zeals	Wilts	24 F2
Zelah	Corn	4 D3
Zennor	Corn	2 C3